Praise for *A Difficult Par*

"Magisterial. . . . Hansen not only delves deeply into Jones's Walter Mitty–like personality, he sets Jones's achievements into the context of America's reach as the world's leading economic and cultural power. *A Difficult Par* is a rich three-dimensional account of an extraordinary and uniquely American life."

—John Strawn, author of *Driving The Green* and the former CEO of Robert Trent Jones II

"A narrative rich in detail. . . . Hansen ably shows us a life filled with unrivaled success and deep end-of-life disappointment." —*Kirkus Reviews*

"By a long way the best golf biography I have ever read, the first time, to my knowledge, that a historian of such eminence has shone the light of his professional skills on one of the game's major figures." —Adam Lawrence, editor of *Golf Course Architecture*

"A memorable portrait of the life and works of the father of modern golf architecture and depicts his remarkable succession from immigrant to immortal. A must-read for students of the game and its most noble names."

—Warner Bott Berry, author of *Scotsman's Dream*

"Essential reading for all who love golf and golf courses. There is no book like it, answering far more questions about the leading personalities and practices of modern golf course design than any author has ever achieved."

—Dr. Michael J. Hurdzan, former president of the American Society of Golf Course Architects

Courtesy of the Author

James R. Hansen is professor of history at Auburn University. He is the author of *First Man*, the award-winning biography of Neil Armstrong, which spent three weeks on the *New York Times* bestseller list. Hansen has published ten other books, all of them devoted to aerospace history. *A Difficult Par* is his first book about golf, though he has published articles and given many talks over the past twenty years about the history of golf course architecture, not just around the United States, but in Canada, Northern Ireland, Scotland, and England. A Hoosier native, Jim has played golf avidly since he was nine years old. He was a cocaptain of the golf team at Indiana University–Purdue University Fort Wayne (IPFW), his undergraduate alma mater. Jim earned a PhD in history from the The Ohio State University. For the past twenty-eight years, his family has made its home in Alabama, the site of the Robert Trent Jones Golf Trail.

OTHER BOOKS BY JAMES R. HANSEN

FIRST MAN:
The Life of Neil A. Armstrong.
New York, London, Toronto, and Sydney:
Simon & Schuster, 2005, 2012.

FOREVER YOUNG:
A Life of Adventure in Air and Space.
University Press of Florida, 2012.
With John W. Young.

TRUTH, LIES, AND O-RINGS:
Inside the Space Shuttle Challenger Disaster.
University Press of Florida, 2009.
With Alan J. McDonald.

THE BIRD IS ON THE WING:
Aerodynamics and the Progress of the Airplane in America.
Texas A&M University Press:
Centennial of Flight Series, 2003.

SPACEFLIGHT REVOLUTION:
NASA Langley from Sputnik to Apollo.
Washington, D.C: NASA-SP 4308, 1995.

A DIFFICULT PAR

ROBERT TRENT JONES SR.
AND THE MAKING OF MODERN GOLF

JAMES R. HANSEN

GOTHAM BOOKS

GOTHAM BOOKS
An imprint of Penguin Random House
375 Hudson Street
New York, New York 10014

Previously published as a Gotham Books hardcover

Gotham Books and the skyscraper logo are trademarks of Penguin Group (USA) LLC

The Library of Congress has catalogued the hardcover edition of this book as follows:
Hansen, James R.
A difficult par : Robert Trent Jones Sr. and the making of modern golf / James R. Hansen.
pages cm
Includes index.
ISBN 978-1-59240-823-8 (hardcover)   978-1-59240-939-6 (paperback)
1. Jones, Robert Trent.   2. Golf course architect—England—Biography.   3. Golf courses—Design and construction.   4. Landscape architecture.   5. Golf—History.   I. Title.
GV964.J68H36   2014
796.352092—dc23 [B]   2014000209

Printed in the United States of America

First trade paperback printing, May 2015

1   3   5   7   9   10   8   6   4   2

Set in Minion Pro   ·   Designed by Elke Sigal

To all the golfers, kindred spirits, and loved ones who have blessedly passed my way on life's journey from tee to green.

Robert Trent Jones Sr. (1906–2000)

As skilled as young Robert Trent Jones was as a competitive golfer (shown here in 1929), his destiny was to reshape golf's landscape through his design or redesign of more than four hundred courses in forty-three states plus Puerto Rico, twenty-eight countries, and five continents.

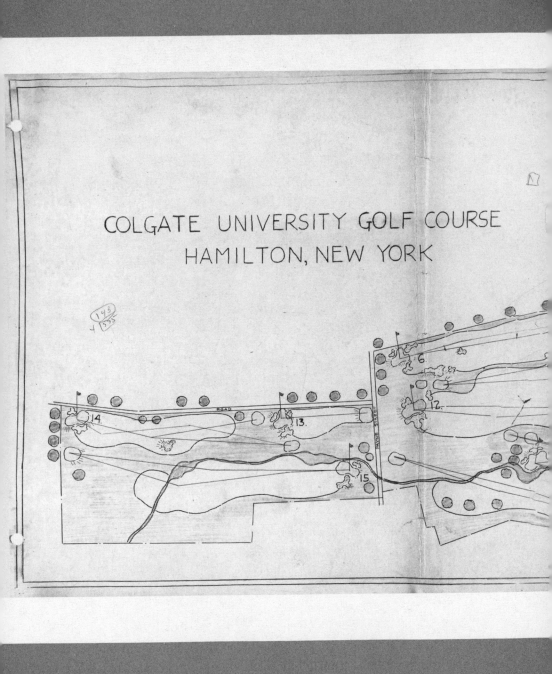

COLGATE UNIVERSITY GOLF COURSE
HAMILTON, NEW YORK

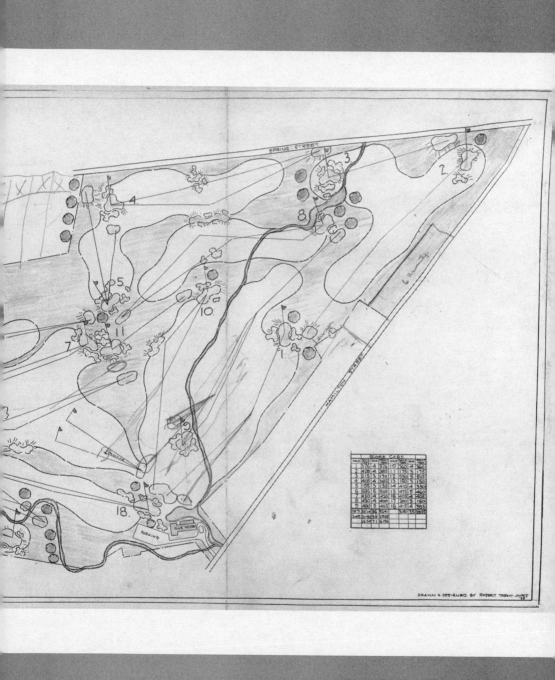

CONTENTS

CHAPTER ONE

FROM ELLIS ISLAND TO THE IVY LEAGUE

Six-year-old Robert Jones with his father, Rees, mother, Jane, and younger brother, Ernest, shortly after their immigration to America in 1912.

The small English boy, not quite yet six years old, desperately wanted to be the first person on the 1,550-passenger ocean liner to catch a glimpse of "Her." It was Monday, April 29, 1912, and dawn was about to break a few miles off the coast of New York. Nearly two weeks had passed since the big steamship, the *Caronia*, left Liverpool bound for New York Harbor. Young Robert Jones; his thirty-one-year-old mother, Jane; and his four-year-old brother, Ernest—three of some 13.5 million immigrants arriving in the United States between 1900 and 1920, nearly five million of them, as the Joneses were, from the British Isles—had spent virtually the entire Atlantic passage deep in the bowels of the ship. They and 897 other third-class passengers had battled seasickness, constant fear of storms, and, worse, the knowledge that the "unsinkable" RMS *Titanic*, on her maiden voyage, had sunk to the bottom of the ocean exactly two weeks earlier, the day before the *Caronia* had embarked.

When the announcement finally came that land had been sighted, they could stand the confinement no longer. In the pitch dark, with only dim oil lamps to guide them, the huddled mass in steerage quickly dressed, putting on clothes that had been saved for arrival in America. It wasn't easy for a small boy to get to a good vantage point, but, with his mother's reluctant permission, Robert raced far forward, dodging hundreds of fellow passengers blocking his way with their jittery bodies and messy arrays of trunks and travel bags. He just wanted to get to the front of the top deck, as fast as he could, so he would be the first to see the wonderful "lady" that his father, William Rees Jones, had written about to his family following his own arrival in America.

William had arrived a mere nine months earlier, in August 1911, but to the family, especially to Jane, their separation seemed far longer. A simple carpenter by trade ("like Jesus Christ," as son Robert would describe him decades later), William had been struggling in his native village of Ince-in-Makerfield, near to Wigan to the northwest of Manchester, to find profitable work. If not for occasional day jobs done for the railroads—two major lines traversed the township, one connecting to industrial Manchester twenty-two miles to the southeast and another to commercial Lancaster forty-one miles due north—William would have had no choice but to go into the coal mines like his father, grandfathers, and many generations of Jones men before them had done. But William wanted no part of the mines and the diseases of the lungs that came with them. So, in the summer of 1911, after celebrating his son Robert's fifth birthday, he sailed for New York via the cheapest route possible—by way of Rio de Janeiro— promising to send money for the family to join him as soon as he could manage it. The exhausting trip took seven weeks, with William entering the United States at Ellis Island on August 3, 1911. From there, he made his way up the Hudson River and along the Erie Canal to East Rochester, New York, adjacent to the booming Lake Ontario industrial city of Rochester, where he had heard the New York Central Railroad was hiring carpenters to build freight cars. By early 1912 he had scraped together enough money to send for his wife and children, who had moved in for the duration with Jane's parents in Wigan, a western borough of Manchester. The "place of residence" written on the ship's manifest for Jane and her sons was, in fact, Wigan, not Ince. Also, Robert's age was given as six, although he wouldn't turn so for a month and a half.

From his vantage point on the *Caronia* peering westward, the boy spotted what he first thought was a star in the sky. But as the ship sailed on, the star got bigger and bigger. Suddenly a hand appeared underneath, holding up the star. Then Robert saw an arm, a head, and finally the body of a woman. Even before he fully realized what he was seeing and could yell it out to the crowd, assorted groups of people began to cry with happiness and hug each other. A joyous bearded man in a tweed overcoat grabbed Robert and threw him up into the air. "We huv reached th' land o' oor dreams!" the man said, in what Robert would later come to know very well to be a strong Scottish brogue. "Whit dae ye think o' that, mae wee laddie?"

"Well . . . it's the Statue of Liberty, isn't it?" the boy ventured.

"Aye, t'is indeed, young Sur! See her thare wi' her yin arm raised heich, tae greet us n' welcome us a' tae America! Nay a finer sight in th' hail wide world, is thare now?!"

To the end of his life eighty-eight years later, the little boy who became the world-famous golf course architect Robert Trent Jones never forgot his moment of arrival in America. In fact, whenever he saw a picture of the Statue of Liberty on television or in the movies, he literally got chills and tears came to his eyes as he remembered what he felt the first time he saw Her. For him, the promise of America—of making a full, happy, and prosperous life for himself and his loved ones and, perhaps even more importantly, "making something big" out of himself—would always be palpable because it was so solidly grounded in the heartfelt and profoundly personal experience of immigrating to America as a child—and seeing the Statue of Liberty literally materialize out of what he thought was starlight.

The Jones family settled in a small home at 129 East Avenue in East Rochester. Until 1906, the town had been known as the Village of Despatch, incorporated in 1897 as a planned community designed around the New York Central Railroad tracks that ran through the center of the village. The name "Despatch" came from the Merchants Despatch Transportation Company (also known as the Merchants Despatch Refrigerator Line), a highly profitable company more than a half century old that manufactured freight cars—about half of them refrigerated—not just for the New York Central but also for the Cleveland, Columbus, Cincinnati and Indianapolis Railway and the Lake Shore & Michigan Southern Railway, all part of Cornelius Vanderbilt's railroad empire.

Employment at Merchants Despatch Transportation was reliable but hardly well paying. In 1914, the year Henry Ford startled the world by announcing that Ford Motor Company would pay $5 a day to its workers, William Jones started at $8 a week at MDT. Working fifty-two weeks a year gave him an annual wage of $416, which amounted to only about two-thirds of the national average. On other parcels of land that the company owned it built small, economical homes, like the one the Jones family occupied, for its labor force, much as American textile mills did for their workers. But East Rochester wasn't a single "company town"—it benefited from the presence of another major employer, the Aeolian Piano Corporation of New York City, a manufacturer of organs and pianos. Both companies employed a large number of immigrants, especially Italians. The "village of freight cars and pianos," in fact, came to be known as Rochester's "Little Italy," as more than half of the residents of East Rochester by 1930 boasted Italian ancestry.

It was not, however, a community known for its golf.

The game had already arrived in nearby Rochester, just a few miles to the northwest. In 1893, a group of five Rochesterians, led by tobacco magnate William

S. Kimball, set up a nine-hole course on a farm south of Genesee Valley Park (a Frederick Law Olmsted creation, from 1888), owned by Josiah Anstice. The course was so crude that it had no putting greens, only small flowerpots placed in holes that had been dug at various spots across a broad pasture by one of the Anstice farmhands. Nevertheless, enthusiastic about the sporting possibilities, the group got serious by 1895–96 and scouted out a new location in southeast Brighton (a few miles east of Genesee Valley Park), leased a nearby farmhouse to serve as a clubhouse, built one set of nine holes and then a second, and dubbed their society the "Country Club of Rochester."

Country clubs were sprouting up all across the United States at the turn of the century, with golf more and more the focal point of their activities. Rochester—one of America's first boomtowns thanks originally to its many flour mills located on the Genesee River, then to its position as a major manufacturing hub, and finally as a technological, medical, and educational center—was no exception. In 1901, a second group of Rochester men, "prosperous and of high repute," incorporated Oak Hill Country Club, building their preserve upon two farms along River Road near Mount Hope Cemetery, just above Genesee Valley Park. Though also begun with rough-hewn rural facilities—again a farmhouse for a clubhouse and lockers placed in a barn—the club quickly made major improvements, with a whopping 137 members paying full dues ($25 initiation and $20 per annum) by the second year. Such modest accommodations did not last long at either the Rochester or Oak Hill country clubs. In 1902, after a fire destroyed its farmhouse, the Country Club of Rochester built a handsome new clubhouse, designed with a classical but industrially progressive appearance by the notable local architect Claude Fayette Bragdon (1866–1946), who later went on to design the city's fine New York Central Railroad station and Chamber of Commerce Building.

Although membership in the private clubs was limited almost exclusively to Rochester's business and civic elite, interest in golf across America was also growing fast within the middle class, among both men and women. The game was also gaining some enthusiasm from immigrants, racial minorities, and others of more modest means. In 1899, a nine-hole public course opened in Genesee Valley Park itself; surrounded by the country clubs, public golfers here shared the fairways with a flock of eighty city sheep that grazed within the park grounds; they also had to play around the New York State Barge Canal—an operational leg of the Erie Canal—on three holes. But what they were doing was a sign of the American golf future: The course was only the fourth golf course in the country to be maintained at public expense, but its daily green fees more than paid for the cost of operations. In May 1917, a second nine holes opened at Genesee Valley Park, creating an eighteen-hole layout that measured 5,470 yards, extremely short by today's standards but a typical length for the era.

The first golf course designer to etch his name into Rochester golf was Donald Ross (1872–1948), the man who ultimately became the first full-time golf architect in the United States and who, with a local Rochester boy named Robert Trent Jones, would become a founding father of the American Society of Golf Course Architects (ASGCA) in 1947.

Donald Ross, from Dornoch in the far north of Scotland, came to America in 1899 at the urging of Harvard astronomer and golf lover Robert Willson. The son of a stonemason, Ross had apprenticed as a boy on the links at Dornoch, then moved on to Fife to learn club-making and greenkeeping from Old Tom Morris at St. Andrews. A fast learner with a brilliant mind for virtually everything related to golf (including the grasses on golf courses), Ross returned to Dornoch in 1893 and, at the ripe age of twenty, became the course's greenkeeper. It was on the Dornoch links that Willson would meet him and coax him into taking the job at the astronomy professor's home club outside Boston. Ross quickly put Oakley Country Club's original nine-hole course—which had just been laid out, rather roughly, by fellow Scotsman Willie Campbell (1862–1900)—through a complete redesign; essentially, Ross created a brand-new course. The members loved the club's new layout, among them James Tufts (inventor of the Arctic Soda Fountain and president of the American Soda Fountain Company), who persuaded young Donald to enjoy his winters more profitably by spending them as a golf professional at a resort his family was developing at Pinehurst, in the Sandhills region of North Carolina. Over the next dozen years, from 1900 to 1912, Ross designed four stellar courses at Pinehurst and earned himself a national reputation; by the mid-1920s, some three thousand men reportedly were building Ross golf courses each year in the United States, although not as Ross employees—they were laborers who were paid by the property owners through building contractors, not by Ross.

It was in 1912, the same year that Robert Jones came as a little boy to East Rochester, that the Country Club of Rochester engaged forty-year-old Donald Ross to improve its existing course enough to make it a candidate to serve as a venue for America's prime championship, the National Open, hosted by the

United States Golf Association. The club never did host a U.S. Open, but the major modifications made to it by Ross resulted in a marvelous new par-70 course with a beautiful yet challenging blend of natural and sculpted features, the aesthetic effect of which made club members puff up their chests with pride.

Robert Jones first stepped onto a golf course at the Country Club of Rochester in June 1917. He had just turned eleven. He had never seen anything resembling this broad expanse of rolling and neatly mown greensward, with its bountiful array of flowering bushes and trees, some quite large. Deep pockets of light brown sand in the course's many bunkers offset the verdant palette, and a beautiful stream meandered through much of the property. Jones knew nothing yet of golf itself, but the allure of the landscape overwhelmed him.

The cute pigtailed girl who sat in front of him in his sixth-grade class had told him that he could make money as a caddie if he went out to the country club. Her uncle had done it as a boy, and not only could a caddie make some nice money (at prosperous country clubs during the era, typically as much as seventy-five cents for eighteen holes), but on certain days when the course wasn't busy the pro sometimes gave the caddies a chance to play a round of golf themselves. The girl's last name was Hagen, and her uncle was none other than Walter Hagen (1892–1969), soon to become one of the world's most celebrated golfers. Walter had started shagging balls for members at the Country Club of Rochester at age seven. By nine he was spending his summers from dawn to dusk toting and cleaning clubs at CCR, becoming a favorite of many of the members. When Walter reached the age of fifteen, the club professional, Andrew Christy, made the prodigy his assistant, teaching him the art of club-making and the basics of greenkeeping. But it was playing the game that was to be Hagen's legacy.

In the same summer that Robert Jones moved to America, Hagen, nineteen, made his professional debut at the 1912 Canadian Open, held at Rosedale Golf Club in Toronto. He placed eleventh on the Tom Bendelow layout, which would be redesigned by Donald Ross in 1919. When Andrew Christy resigned his post as head pro at Rochester the following spring, Hagen was offered the job. That very summer of 1913, Walter played in his first U.S. Open, at Brookline, Massachusetts, finishing tied for fourth in a titanic contest won by lanky U.S. amateur Francis Ouimet, who defeated England's stalwart professionals Harry Vardon and "Big Ted" Ray in a playoff to become the first amateur to win the championship. The next year Hagen himself captured the event, at Chicago's Midlothian Country Club, shooting a dazzling score of 290 to tie the lowest total ever for a U.S. Open since it had gone to a seventy-two-hole event in 1898. Hagen's winning prize was $300. The victory launched him toward golf immortality, as he would win the U.S. Open once again (1919), four British Opens ('22, '24, '28, '29), five PGA Championships ('21, '24–'27), five Western Opens ('16, '21, '26, '27, '32), and one Canadian Open ('31). *The New York Times* wrote in 1924 that "The Haig" was "the greatest golfer who ever lived—bar none."

The first summer that young Robert Jones spent caddying at the Country Club of Rochester, Walter Hagen was still its professional, but by the boy's second summer of caddying, Hagen was gone. In 1918 he left Rochester for suburban Detroit, where he took the head pro position at Oakland Hills. Hagen visited his hometown of Rochester sometimes for exhibition matches, and young Jones would clearly remember one of those occasions for the rest of his life. Although he was able to pick up the trolley near his home in East Rochester, Jones still had to walk about a mile and a half to get to the club. One day as he was walking down the road, a white Packard roadster came streaking toward him, a bag of shiny new golf clubs sticking up out of the rumble seat. In the car was Hagen: well built, handsome, shiny jet-black hair, a flashy dresser, and exuding wall-to-wall charm. "As the car swept past carrying Walter Hagen in his usual grand style," Jones would recall for an interview late in his life, "I knew right then I had to somehow get involved with golf in some big way." With Jones, indeed, it was always to involve "some big way."

On a couple of occasions, young Jones got the chance to caddie for Hagen when the Haig returned to CCR. Jones also caddied for Harry Vardon in an exhibition match against Hagen and Ted Ray. "I was very much taken with Vardon's smooth swing," Jones later recalled, "and when I started playing, I tried to imitate his graceful and sweet swing." Emulating Hagen was an impossibility: "Nobody could imitate Hagen with that big sway of his body he had!"

For a while it looked like young Jones might become another Hagen—or at least another Bobby Jones. In 1916, when Robert was ten, fourteen-year-old golf prodigy Robert Tyre Jones, known as "Bobby," startled the sports world by winning his first two matches in the National Amateur Championship and giving the defending champion a tremendous battle before being defeated in his third-round match. "I was just plain overwhelmed by the fact that this sensational young golfer was named Bobby Jones," Robert recalled years later. "Boy, I began to work on my golf game after that. I felt that there was supposed to be an affinity between me and golf. I was the Bobby Jones expert in my neighborhood. All the rest of the kids were trying to copy Hagen, but I built my swing, my whole technique, on what I read about Bobby and the pictures I saw of him in the papers." (One version of how he became "Trent" Jones has Robert taking the middle name in his early teens after fellow caddies at the Country Club of Rochester teasingly compared him to the famous young Bobby Jones, choosing "Trent" because it was a family name derived from the River Trent in England. [It is not true that Jones's birthplace was a town on the River Trent, as the course of the river comes nowhere near Wigan or Ince-in-Makerfield or anywhere near the Welsh border.] Rather it is clear from his personal papers that Jones did not start *using* the middle name until 1930, following Bobby Jones's capture of the Grand Slam and Robert's entry into the golf design business.)

Although his caddying got him an occasional round at the country club, Robert really learned to play golf at a little course called Hillcrest, a makeshift nine-hole layout at the end of West Commercial Street in East Rochester, just a few blocks to the west of where Jones lived. Most of the golfers who played it—many of them raw beginners—called the course "Genundewah," the Native American name for the "Great Hill" situated at the head of Canandaigua Lake, one of New York's Finger Lakes; from Genundewah, according to legend, sprung all the Seneca peoples. Hardly a great hill, Hillcrest Golf Course was a sandy, sparsely grassy splice of ground, long and narrow, with a series of small ridges running through it.

Although not much to look at, Hillcrest Golf Course was enough to stimulate a love of golf, for Jones and for others of lesser means in East Rochester who wanted a taste of the new game. In fact, the tiny course amounted to more than that, as Jones looked back at it late in his life: "The course was built on a residue of Lake Ontario, on what we called a 'blow sand' area. It was really like playing on an undulating linksland. So it really trained me well for playing a wide variety of shots." At the start, Jones had only one club, a "mashie" (what today would be called a mid-iron) that he bought for fifty cents from a rack of old clubs in Walter Hagen's pro shop, and he learned how to hit it many different ways: as a "play club" (driver), as a "baffing spoon" (approach wood), as a mashie niblick (7-iron), as a niblick (9-iron), even as a putter. By the time he was fourteen, he was shooting par just with the one club. Eventually he got a second club by winning a caddie tournament at the course after shooting a 39.

The prize, put up by a doctor who was a member of the course, was a used mashie niblick. Jones thought the advertised prize had been a brand-new mashie niblick—designed with the new wide grooves that put a live backspin on the ball—that had just appeared on the market. Jones told the doctor he had been hoping for the new design. "So he got it for me," Jones recollected years later, "and when I hit the ball it would take the paint off, and the ball really backed up on the greens." Later that year the United States Golf Association outlawed irons with the unusually wide and deep grooves, just as it would do again in 1988.

The best thing for Jones was that he played Genundewah for free: "The greenkeeper was a German gardener who told me and a friend of mine that we could play on the course if we would cut the greens every day after school. So we did. One of us would steer the mower and the other pull with a rope, because it was too heavy for one kid to push. We would go fast, and when we finished, we played golf. I also was learning some things about golf courses, like how to grow grass on sand. There was no fairway irrigation on the course. They 'tied the sand down' by planting wheat. When it grew to a certain height they would cut it and throw down the grass seed, which would be held by the single stalks of the wheat."

By the time Jones was sixteen he was being called the most promising young golfer in Rochester. That year, 1922, he entered a 36-hole open tournament sponsored by the Rochester *Journal-American* at Genesee Valley Park. He had passed up a junior tournament the week before, thinking he could not enter both events. In the morning round he carried his own bag and shot 76; in the afternoon, with a friend for a caddie, he shot 69, a course record, and finished as the low amateur, one stroke behind the winning professional. The next day's headline on the local sports page read, ROCHESTER'S BOBBY JONES BREAKS COURSE RECORD.

"Right then I began to consider broader horizons as a player, but I had a stomach ailment that flared up. It turned out to be a serious duodenal ulcer, which landed me in the hospital for six months. I thought I was going to die. I played no competitive golf for the next two years. During that period I decided the life of a tournament golfer was not for me."

But what life was it going to be? His father had steady work in the railroad car shops, but he didn't make nearly enough money for college to be in Robert's future. In fact, Robert, known to most of his schoolmates as "a quiet kid," dropped out of East Rochester High School in 1922 after finishing the eleventh grade and went to work as a draftsman for Merchants Despatch Transportation, his father's employer. The job at Despatch was frustrating and unfulfilling, so much so that, over his dad's objections, he began looking for something else to do. Although he had given up the idea of being like Walter Hagen and earning a living as a touring professional, Jones's dream was still somehow to find a lucrative career in golf, and to "make it big."

If Hagen could not be his model, maybe Donald Ross could.

In the early 1920s, Ross had come back to Rochester for two major projects. First, he was turning 214 acres of farmland east of nearby Pittsford and five miles southeast of the Country Club of Rochester into a refined 18-hole course that became the Monroe Golf Club, which opened for play in 1924. Ross's compensation package included a $2,000 architect's fee and a construction fee of $54,000, based on an estimated cost of $3,000 per hole. The fee that Ross received for the second project—creating two new courses for a relocation of Oak Hill Country Club—was reported in the newspapers to be well more than double those figures. Jones had read about the projects in the Rochester papers; the Oak Hill deal in particular was making big news. In 1921 the burgeoning University of Rochester, with large endowments from Kodak's George Eastman, proposed a land swap with Oak Hill: The university would build its new River Campus on the banks of the Genesee, where the golf course was situated, and in exchange would give the club a 355-acre plot of farmland owned by the university just northwest of Pittsford. It was a sweet deal for the golf club, especially when its executive officers also managed to coax $360,000 in cash from the school. That was more than enough to pay for Donald Ross's fee, with several thousand dollars to spare—revenue that allowed for a stately Tudor-style clubhouse to be built with all the first-class amenities and accommodations needed for the new Oak Hill Country Club.

Eighteen-year-old Robert Jones may not have known exactly how much money Donald Ross was making on the Rochester golf course projects, but he understood that it was much more than any golf professional was making, even Walter Hagen. Furthermore, as an immigrant's son, a caddie, and a tournament golfer, he had seen in the case of Hagen—and directly experienced himself—the social prejudices and iniquities that faced a "lowly, uncouth" golf professional. Golf pros were not welcome to come through the august front doors of the Country Club of Rochester, Oak Hill Country Club, or any other private club in

America; they entered through the side or the back. But at CCR, Jones had seen with his own two eyes that Ross, America's most esteemed golf course architect, was welcome to stride right in through the club's front entrance. Ross's highly publicized new projects in the Rochester area coincided exactly with Jones's growing frustration with his drafting apprenticeship at Merchants Despatch. On weekends he even spent time watching Ross and his men building Oak Hill's spanking new courses. "I thought that maybe building courses might be the answer for me," Jones later recalled, "but I didn't know how to go about learning the business. There were no technical schools for it, and you couldn't go to a university and major in golf architecture, even if I had had the credentials to get in. I didn't know what to do."

He was smart enough, and desperate enough, to ask for help. One day at Merchants Despatch he walked into the office of Ray Humburg, the head of the engineering department, who, Jones had heard, was a golfer. A Cornell graduate, Humburg suggested that perhaps his alma mater in Ithaca could offer an answer. It had schools in the various disciplines, and golf course architecture really was a combination of professions. Without a high school diploma, however, how was Jones going to get into Cornell?

In 1925, at age nineteen, Jones's reputation as a player in the Rochester area got him a summer job as a golf instructor in Old Forge, New York, a hamlet in the Adirondacks a hundred miles northeast of Syracuse, where a nine-hole Donald Ross golf course had opened in 1921 (later named Thendara Golf Club.) There Jones became known not just as a very good player but as "a real instructor." On August 28, 1925, Jones was invited to play an exhibition match for the opening day of Sodus Bay Heights Golf Club, a small private club of sixty-four members that had just been established with a nine-hole course on the shore of Lake Ontario's Great Sodus Bay. Jones's opponent in the match was Wilbur Jack, the professional at nearby Newark Country Club. Jack was no slouch. In the 1923 PGA Championship at Pelham Country Club in Pelham, New York, Jack had come out of sectional qualifying to make match play. But in the exhibition round at Sodus Bay, Jones took him by two strokes.

The Sodus members liked Jones so much that they immediately offered him a job as their club professional, greenkeeper, and manager, all in one. The job didn't pay much, but the club was a gorgeous property for golf, with rolling hills and winds whipping off Lake Ontario. In early 1927 the club built a small golf shop with kitchen facilities and a small snack bar and a back room in which

Jones could sleep. (Most of his time at Sodus he stayed in a lakefront cottage owned by his cousin Lillie and her husband.) The workday started well before daybreak and usually didn't end until after dark, but Jones loved the place, built friendships with some of the members, and returned regularly to Sodus for short visits even after he moved out of the area. The golf season was short in northern New York, however, so Jones was employed only from late April into early October. The winters were long, with Jones trying his best to make his money last.

One of those early winters, with the help of a wealthy Sodus member by the name of James Bashford, Jones traveled south to Florida for a season of teaching golf at the Hollywood Beach Hotel Country Club. (Bashford owned a vinegar factory in Lyons, New York, and played a major part in the development of Sodus Bay Heights Golf Club.) A golf course had just opened at the resort, one designed by an English war hero named Captain Herbert Charles Coningsby Tippet (1892–1947), a friend of Carl Graham Fisher (1874–1939), the dynamic entrepreneur and real estate developer who almost single-handedly created the holiday resort of Miami Beach. Jones, in fact, gave Fisher some golf lessons; Captain Tippet, an outstanding golfer, needed none. But Jones and Tippet did spend time together discussing golf course architecture and contrasting British golf with American golf, and the conversations whetted Jones's appetite even more for getting involved in course design.

While wintering in Florida in 1927–28, Jones tried to make a little money playing competitive golf. In Miami Beach, the inaugural La Gorce Open was being held at La Gorce Country Club, owned by Carl Fisher. Tippet had designed the course, and both Fisher and Tippet encouraged Jones to enter the 1928 tournament. (The event was held from 1928 through 1931.) Among the top professionals playing were Johnny Farrell, Gene Sarazen, Macdonald Smith, Bobby Cruickshank, Al Watrous, and Tommy Armour. One of the few stars missing was Robert's namesake and early hero, Bobby Jones, the phenom from Atlanta, who was coming off championships in the '23 and '26 U.S. Opens, '26 and '27 British Opens, and the '24, '25, and '27 U.S. Amateurs. It was not an easy time for another young man named Robert Jones to be teeing it up in front of the gallery in a professional tournament, as the Jones from East Rochester later remembered: "I was nervous enough as it was, and when they called 'Robert Jones' to the first tee, the crowd pressed around, wondering if this was *the* Bobby Jones. It was not him, as my sudden attack of stage fright proved. Playing the first nine in a cold sweat, I was out in a seven-over 43, and it didn't get much better coming home. But I did finish the tournament, improving each round." It was an invaluable, if traumatic, experience, one that further convinced Jones that he, with his ulcer flare-ups, was not meant for a life of highly tense competitive golf—especially when further "Bobby Jones" mix-ups were inevitable.

Still, in the summers of 1928 and 1929, Jones played in the Canadian Open. In his autobiographical book *Golf's Magnificent Challenge* (1988), he remembered playing in the 1927 Canadian Open, held at the Toronto Golf Club and won by Tommy Armour. Jones recalled that he finished tenth. However, the official records of the Royal Canadian Golf Association clearly show no "Robert Jones" competing in the 1927 event. The records do show Jones playing in the 1928 and 1929 Canadian Opens. In 1928, when the championship was held at Rosedale Golf Club in Toronto, Jones shot rounds of 77-71-78-77. His 303 total, which was the same total he claims in *Golf's Magnificent Challenge* to have shot in 1927, put him in 37th place (not in 10th as he purported in his book). In 1929, when the championship was held at Kanawaki Golf Club near Montreal, Jones missed the cut, shooting rounds of 78 and 83. In both of his appearances in the Canadian Open, Jones's home was listed as Sodus Point, New York.

In truth Jones had already set out on a course that did not involve playing professional golf. In the spring of 1928 Jones had told James Bashford of his dream to become a golf course designer. Sympathetic, Bashford drove him to Cornell University, his alma mater, in his limousine and introduced him to the dean of the college of agriculture, Dr. Albert Russell Mann. It was a highly unusual request for a high-school dropout to want to enter Cornell for the purpose of learning how to design golf courses, but the agriculture dean, himself a golfer, listened carefully to the intent young man and offered him a chance: Jones could take classes in the college of agriculture as a non-degree "special student," but only after he went through tutoring in mathematics and chemistry. To take classes in any of Cornell's other colleges, Jones would also have to get permission directly from those deans as well, which Jones managed to do with Dean Mann's help, under the requirement that he take even more tutoring, including help with his drawing.

Jones started at Cornell in the fall of 1928. Bashford, his patron, gave him $1,000 to help him out. That generous allowance and the money Jones earned working summers at Sodus paid for his tuition, books, and living expenses. For the rest of his career, it seems that Jones was in constant search of other "Mr.

Bashfords," wealthy and influential men who could help him along his way in pursuit of the American Dream, and he was quite successful at finding them.

At Cornell from 1928 to 1930, Jones was virtually allowed to design his own curriculum, and he studied landscape architecture in the college of architecture, hydraulics and surveying in the college of engineering, and agronomy and horticulture in the college of agriculture. He also studied economics, chemistry, public speaking, journalism, and business law. Some of his grades were barely passing, and most of them were mediocre, but the effort was still admirable given that Jones had not graduated high school and was competing with students who had records that were good enough to allow them to enroll in an Ivy League school. He earned no better than a "C" grade in public speaking, which is surprising given how successfully he would verbally parley with many of his golf course clients in the coming decades. Though Jones was slightly older than his classmates, fellow students seem to have treated him just like one of them, perhaps not knowing that his admission into Cornell was a special case that would not lead to a degree. As with all students, college was not all work. In his second year he was asked to pledge a fraternity and was eventually elected president of the university chapter of Delta Kappa Epsilon. He very much enjoyed attending Cornell football games. In intramurals he showed off his basketball skills—he had been a very good player at East Rochester High and with an East Rochester semi-pro team known as the "O'Leary Perintons." Some weekends, when he didn't head back to work at Sodus, Jones attended parties and dances.

At a fraternity party in 1929, Jones met Ione Tefft Davis, a cultured and beautiful young lady from a prominent family in Montclair, New Jersey, who was a sophomore honors student—and eventual Phi Beta Kappa recipient—at Wells College in nearby Aurora, New York. The two started dating and exchanging romantic letters. As Jones would later extol many times, "That was the most important thing that happened to me at Cornell, or ever—meeting my future wife." Little did either Robert or Ione know that it would be five long years before Ione's imposing father—a cautious, rigorous professional engineer—would permit the pair to marry.

Jones may not have received a degree from Cornell, but he got what he went for—the advanced education and fundamental knowledge needed to design and build golf courses.

He was twenty-four when he left Cornell. After finishing up in Ithaca, Jones returned home, where he took an art course at a local technical institute. The class further developed his ability to sketch, which was to help him significantly throughout his career. "I became very good at it," Jones remembered years later. "For golf courses it meant I could visualize in my mind's eye what kind of hole should be created on any given piece of ground. I would sketch it and then work with the construction people to go and actually mold it."

The year was 1930, just months after the Wall Street Crash in October 1929, hardly the best time to be visualizing the start of any business, let alone the creation of golf courses.

CHAPTER TWO

BIG AMBITIONS IN DEPRESSED TIMES

It took extraordinary determination, persistence, and love of the game for Robert Trent Jones to stay on course for a career in golf architecture during the bleak economic times of the Great Depression.

The big dreams with which Robert Jones started his career were almost totally overshadowed by big black clouds. He left Cornell in the spring of 1930 with no degree in hand, no job, and virtually no money. The golf course design business he envisioned had no investors, no financial backing, neither an office nor a secretary, very few prospects, and certainly no construction crew. Although he had something of a local reputation as an excellent golfer, Jones had done no real golf course design—nothing except for some minor remodeling of tees and greens at Sodus Bay. From Cornell he had gained some important basic knowledge of the science of grasses and plants, how to give a public speech, how not to get cheated in a business contract, and how to handle some elemental landscaping and drainage problems, but his actual know-how when it came to designing courses was extremely limited—and his knowledge of the techniques for actually *building* a golf course was almost totally derived from what he had seen Donald Ross's men doing at Oak Hill. Most foreboding of all, in an already tight and quickly evaporating market for golf courses following the Wall Street Crash of October 1929, Jones faced competition from a number of well-established golf architects—notably Pinehurst-based Donald Ross; British-born Alister MacKenzie in California and his associate, Oklahoma's Perry Maxwell; Philadelphians A. W. Tillinghast and William S. Flynn; the British firm of Colt, Alison & Morrison Ltd.; and Chicago's Tom Bendelow, the former director of golf course development for Spalding sporting goods who was considered the "Johnny Appleseed of American Golf" for the hundreds of layouts he had produced in Canada (including Rosedale Golf Club in Toronto) and the United States. Each of those firms had proven records, a string of distinguished achievements, address books full of valuable business connections, at least meager bank accounts, and an arsenal of other resources to their names.

The most damnable black cloud vexing Jones personally in 1930 was the

stark difference in social status that was complicating his romance and proposed marital engagement with Ione Tefft Davis, the beautiful and brilliant
young lady, four years his junior, he had met at a Cornell fraternity party. At
Wells College, Ione learned to love Emily Dickinson poetry, majored in Philosophy, starred on the school's debate team, was perennially on the honor
roll, and graduated Phi Beta Kappa. (At Cornell, Jones had received average
to below-average grades and taken no humanities courses, and his writing—
as demonstrated in his many love letters to Ione—was very rough, full of
misspellings, and often ungrammatical, a sorry state of composition that Ione
continually worked to correct in her future husband.) If that wasn't intimidating
enough for the humble son of a blue-collar, immigrant family, Ione's blue-
blooded family traced its ancestry back to the *Mayflower*, enjoyed holidays in
France, and lived in a spacious, 4,000-square-foot patrician home in Montclair,
New Jersey, with views of the Manhattan skyline twelve miles away. Her father,
Howard Lee Davis, if not for an injury during training, would have run for the
United States in the Games of the First Olympiad in Athens in 1896; earned a
business degree at Yale; was active in Republican Party politics; and successfully climbed the corporate ladder to a vice presidency after serving as director
of technical employment and training for New York Bell Telephone. Worse yet
for Robert Jones, Howard Davis, in 1930, had just finished writing a manuscript
that would be published the following year in New York and London by John
Wiley & Sons under the title *The Young Man in Business*. In the textbook, Davis
not only highlighted his own successful rise from "apprentice, cadet engineer,
engineer, and superintendent of an electric light company" to corporate vice
president, he took it upon himself to diagnose and cure the typical mistakes
that young men made when starting out in business by replacing those common
errors with, in Davis's words, "the proper foundations" on which they might
build successful careers. As Jones quickly discovered, Howard Lee Davis was
not about to let his darling princess marry an uncultured young man who was
making many of those same mistakes and whose career goal (notwithstanding
his "special admission" into Cornell) was to do something as inconsequential
and non-lucrative as designing golf courses.

"I desperately want to do big things for you," one of Jones's early love letters
to Ione declared—notably by becoming, as he often wrote her, "the world's
greatest golf course architect." During what to Jones (but apparently less to
Ione) seemed an interminable four-and-a-half-year engagement, Jones sent her

well over four hundred letters—some of them while she was finishing school, some while she was touring with her mother and sister in Europe, many when she was back at home in comfortable Montclair, all of them by hand and almost all of them at least five or six pages long—trying, often in a dramatically earnest tone, to keep their love alive. Most of the time Jones was living at home with his parents or drifting around somewhere in upstate New York, staying either in the small office he had rented in downtown Rochester or with friends at Sodus Bay, but equally as often in some hotel room or another, where the letterhead was free. He wrote from the road, too, when he could afford to buy a few gallons of gas, motoring on patched tires along back roads with a map on the passenger seat, trying to get to a golf course job or, more likely, a prospective one. With very little money available for new golf courses or even course renovations in the first years of the Great Depression, Jones secured few jobs and, for those few he was rarely paid on time, if at all. He worked and lived alone, barely surviving materially and emotionally, living day-to-day and often hand-to-mouth on the hope of receiving his next letter from dearest Ione. Jones's letters are often excruciating to read, filled with depression, anxieties, fear of failure, and deep loneliness. At the same time his letters show a dogged determination to marry the woman he adored and to make a success of himself, to achieve a level of fame and fortune that would make Ione—and her father—proud. The letters are incredibly tender and moving and offer a wide-open window into Jones's psychological state as he started off on his career in golf course architecture.

The role of the golf architect in America meant something rather different than it did in the place where the game had evolved more naturally over a long period of time. American golf courses owed nothing to the shepherd and sheep whose grazing land at the water's edge provided the basic linksland forms in Scotland; they were more generally a thing created as much as a thing found, in keeping with the technological bent of the game's homeland. The American way of golf did not depend on eons of shifting tides and receding seas, and therefore it was reproducible and could be transported readily. Golf architecture thus was a part of "The American Century," an offshoot of the *American Genesis: A Century of Invention and Technological Enthusiasm, 1870–1970,* the title of technology historian Thomas P. Hughes's prizewinning book that explains how American inventiveness, systems building, and engineering led the United States to a position of global hegemony.

Even as the six-year-old boy who would become Robert Trent Jones stood on the deck of the *Caronia* drawing nearer to the Statue of Liberty, a uniquely American vision of a golf course had only recently taken shape on the north coast of Long Island's south fork. "The National Golf Links of America," the first true creation of American golf architecture, embodied Professor Hughes's "American Genesis" just as surely as the Wright Flyer represented it for aviation or Henry Ford's Model T automobile did for assembly-line mass production.

The designer of the golf course, Charles Blair Macdonald, was the son of an immigrant Scottish father and a Canadian mother. He grew up in Chicago, learned the game "knocking balls around a deserted Civil War training camp," and became such a good player that he won the first U.S. Amateur Championship in 1895. In the early 1870s, Macdonald attended the University of St. Andrews, where he studiously admired the Old Course and watched epic matches on the links involving Old and Young Tom Morris. Returning to Chicago, "C.B." made his living as a stockbroker, and a very successful one. He laid out the first nine holes of what became the Chicago Golf Club in 1892, added another nine a year later to make it America's first 18-hole course, and discovered a calling in golf architecture. He eventually created eighteen different courses in six states, the majority of them still considered absolute gems. He never accepted a fee; as quite a rich man, he didn't have to. For his unprecedented efforts, which included helping to establish the Amateur Golf Association of the United States, the body that would evolve into the United States Golf Association (USGA), Macdonald rightfully earned the title, "the Father of American Golf Course Architecture."

Macdonald was a great admirer of the old Scottish style of play, and his seminal idea behind The National was to reproduce a treasury of the best British architecture, thereby elevating the appreciation of the game in America. For The National, he created golf holes that were embellishments of some of the most famous holes in British golf: the "Redan," #15 on the West Links at North Berwick; the "Alps," #17 at Prestwick; the Road Hole and Eden Hole, #17 and #11 on the Old Course at St. Andrews; and the original "Sahara," #3 at Sandwich (Royal St. George's Golf Club) in England. Despite these influences, the golf course turned out to be distinctively "American" in many essential ways. First, it was massively expensive to construct—it cost roughly half a million dollars, the equivalent of $20 million today. Though Macdonald spoke with respect for the "naturalism" of the British links courses, his golf course was manufactured to be monumental in scale and grandeur. Macdonald found natural settings for some holes, but "where nature was deficient, it would have to be improved." No ordinary construction project could achieve his vision, so Macdonald engaged the services of thirty-seven-year-old Seth Raynor, a Princeton graduate in engineering who operated a surveying and landscaping business on Long Island. In what has been called "the most revolutionary action in course building of its time," Macdonald and Raynor arranged for ten thousand loads of topsoil to be hauled in, and they spread it around on what mostly amounted to wetlands. Where no natural settings for holes could be found—which was over most of the property—Macdonald and Raynor made them. Macdonald also established a turf nursery, the first of its kind, where he conducted experiments to discover the best grasses for The National's tees, greens, and fairways. The putting surfaces had to be watered artificially during dry seasons, so a complete irrigation system for the greens was installed. Decades before the "Green Section" of the United States Golf Association would develop specifications for constructing "USGA Greens," Macdonald made sure his greens were built "scientifically" to preserve moisture, with carefully measured strata of seaweed, loam, and topdressing. To assure that his turf was not only healthy but lush, Macdonald brought in the nation's foremost turfgrass specialist, Dr. C. V. Piper of the U.S. Department of Agriculture; a decade later, Piper would play an instrumental role in creating the USGA Green Section.

The National Golf Links of America embodied a uniquely American underlying approach not just to the game but also to landscape design, to architecture, to engineering, to nature itself. Historian David Nye has called the phenomenon "the American technological sublime," that bold dynamic ethos of transformation and reinvention accomplished "by large-scale applications of technological prowess." The name of the golf course itself—"The National"—conveyed the power, strength, and immodesty of Teddy Roosevelt's America. It was into that vibrant, entrepreneurial, and expansive America that the immigrant boy Robert Jones would arrive and create for himself a destiny.

After the inventor, as historian Hughes has explained, came the system. Following Macdonald came a host of different "American" architects (several of them immigrants—William C. Fownes Jr., George C. Thomas Jr., Donald Ross, Tom Bendelow, A. W. Tillinghast, Hugh Wilson, George Crump, and Seth Raynor, among others) who over the course of the next decades would give American golf an even more distinctive technological character, one that contrasted sharply with the naturalism of golf's British parent. Golf course designers in the United States began to eliminate many of the irregularities and random elements of the traditional Scottish links, with its mounds, craters, and tumbling, disorderly terrain. In its place, American golf architects cultivated, in the spirit of C. B. Macdonald, a scientifically managed landscape. Instead of routing a course over open, largely treeless terrain, which had allowed players on the old British courses to choose different strategic paths from tee to green, American architects recognized that the golfers who played their courses "[wanted] the ambiguity out of golf." American golfers wanted "perfectly maintained fairways from tee to green, mechanically groomed sand bunkers, and greens as smooth as the surface of a pool table, with the route of play set firmly within planted corridors." Americans came to embrace "unblemished lawns" and other artifice on their golf courses much more than the British, and with advancing technology the demands for this artifice redoubled. By the late 1940s, in place of the pans and slip-scrapers pulled by oxen or horses of the prewar generations, builders of U.S. golf courses had at their disposal bulldozers, steam shovels, and dump trucks with which they could move, or erect, small mountains of earth. By 1960, heavy earthmoving machinery had revolutionized golf course construction, turning fairways into highly engineered, sculpted, artificially contoured, and finely turfed designs.

Robert Trent Jones Sr. was not alone in bringing forth the archetypal American golf course or, for that matter, alone in creating everything that went into the paradigmatic modern championship golf course. But no architect singly did more to create those fundamental types of courses than Jones did— or once they were created, to bring them to the rest of the world.

Jones's first design job came very close to home, on a property within the town of Perinton, just east of Rochester, less than two miles distant from where he grew up. Jones's mother (interestingly, not his father) read in a local paper that a group of Rochester gentlemen had met on September 23, 1929, at the Blarney Stone Inn in nearby Webster, New York, a meeting that resulted in the incorporation of the "Midvale Golf and Country Club." Despite the stock market crash that occurred a month later (or perhaps *because* of it), the new Midvale club went on to buy up several farms on the Fairfield-Penfield line, forming a 144-acre tract of land on which they could build their golf course. Still taking classes at Cornell, Jones wrote a letter to Dr. Charles A. Lynch, Midvale's president, expressing interest in designing the golf course. Jones's reputation as a golfer was not unknown to Lynch or his fellow club members. But what really impressed the membership's executive committee was Jones's schooling at Cornell and the initiative he had shown by taking university courses that singly prepared him to design golf courses. So, in the early spring of 1930, Midvale decided to give the young man a chance, with the stipulation that a veteran golf course architect would oversee his work.

Midvale club president Lynch had asked Stanley Thompson, Canada's leading golf course architect, to come look things over at Midvale and see if he wanted to get involved. Most of Thompson's jobs were in Canada and his home office was in Toronto, but in 1930 a golf course architect was looking anywhere and everywhere to get work, and Thompson wanted to expand the business he was doing in the States anyway.

In early June Thompson visited the property and met with board members. He also met and talked with Jones and trekked around much of the property with him. As much as anything, Stanley wanted to get a feel for what Robert knew about designing a golf course. He asked the young American about the placement and contouring of the greens to see if he felt—as Thompson himself did—that they should blend harmoniously into the surrounding terrain. He asked about the placement of the par-3s and whether Jones had selected them first, as he himself would typically do, and then planned the rest of the other holes around them. Thompson asked if Jones thought the lines of the bunkers and greens should be sharp or easy and rolling, the latter being what Thompson preferred. He asked what plan Jones had in mind for clearing fairways, what trees should be left and why. He probed what Jones thought about the importance of the overall aesthetic effects of the golf landscape, not just the mechanics of the shotmaking but the beauty to be appreciated during the entire experience.

Jones initially feared that Thompson was competing for the job and would try to elbow him aside; in fact, that may have been the Canadian architect's plan at the beginning. But like the Midvale members, Thompson was "impressed that I'd done this Cornell work," Jones recalled. More importantly, the thirty-seven-year-old Thompson, from a close-knit family of nine siblings, very much liked Jones, and Jones liked him back. Though Stanley would stammer when flustered (a condition his family felt was brought on by his time in battle during the war), he had a gift for gab, and Robert also liked to talk, especially if it was about golf. The two men, thirteen years apart, hit it off well. Jones especially appreciated Thompson's *modus operandi* as an architect. In keeping with his convivial and relaxed personality, Thompson, in Jones's words, "would walk a property to get the feel of it, never taking a note, then sit back with a bottle of scotch and a good cigar and design the course." Before departing Midvale, Thompson told the club that he thought he could work with Jones. He told Jones to come up to Toronto when he could, at Thompson's expense, and play a round or two of golf with him so they could get to know one another better.

Jones jumped at the chance. But before he crossed the border at Niagara Falls and embarked on a train for Toronto, he tried to learn more about the man who would become his first boss and then his partner. As Jones would later declare, it was "a great stroke of good fortune" the day he met the "Toronto Terror," Stanley Thompson.

Jones knew about the "Amazing Thompsons." Born in Toronto in 1893, Stanley Thompson was one of five brothers and four sisters. All five boys had fallen in love with golf early as caddies at the Toronto Golf Club, the third oldest golf club in North America (founded in 1876), an exceptionally fine but tremendously difficult golf course built by Englishman Harry S. Colt. The club's Scottish golf professional, George Cumming (1879–1950), was a kind and generous teacher who taught all the Thompson boys to play the game with great skill, flair, and intelligence. (Cumming later become a partner in the Thompson golf construction and design business.) All five of the Thompson brothers— Nicol (b. 1880), Matt (b. 1885), Bill (b. 1889), Frank (b. 1897) and Stanley— performed so well in golf competitions in Canada and the United States that they came to be known collectively as the "Amazing Thompsons." Two of the brothers, Nicol and Matt, became professionals, while the others remained highly regarded amateurs. In what amounted to the Wild West days of professional golf in North America, the Thompsons, when challenged to a match, would drop everything, hop on a train to Cleveland or Chicago or wherever, and arrive with their clubs on the first tee just in time to take on the likes of Walter Hagen and Bobby Jones. Whichever pair of Thompson brothers teamed up for a four-ball match, they proved extremely hard to beat. As for Stanley, he won no elite championships, but the brothers regarded him as the most innately talented golfer of them all. A master at hitting low, hooking shots—and sometimes playing with only five clubs—Thompson liked to punch "run-up" shots onto putting surfaces, which was probably why he tended to design greens with generous front openings.

Jones knew much less about Thompson as a golf course architect, because most of Stanley's work had been done in Canada. Up to the time of their meeting in Toronto he had played only one of Thompson's courses: Lockport Country Club, in the town of Lockport, north of Buffalo, which Thompson had built in 1911. The only other New York course created by Thompson was Bartlett Country Club, opened in 1910 in the southwestern New York city of Olean, and Jones had never seen it. Most of the courses Stanley had designed in the States were located in northern Ohio or in Florida.

Robert knew even less about Thompson's solid technical education or his meritorious war record. After graduating from Malvern Collegiate Institute (until 1908 called "East Toronto High School"), Stanley had attended the Ontario Agricultural College (now part of the University of Guelph). During World War I, he served as a gunner on the Western Front, fighting in the Battle at Vimy Ridge and receiving a citation (signed by Winston Churchill) "for gallant and distinguished service in the Field." When the war ended, he took the opportunity to visit many of the top courses in England and Scotland. Upon his return to Canada, he decided to become a full-time golf course architect and got into the family landscaping and golf architecture business, which had been initially led by Nicol and George Cumming. When their father, James, died, Nicol called a meeting of all the brothers to decide their future. Since all but Stanley still had a passion for playing championship golf, the decision was made that Stanley should head the family business.

Thus was born Stanley Thompson & Company, Limited, formally incorporated in 1923, the same golden year that Bill won the Canadian Amateur Championship and the year after Nicol won the Canadian PGA. From its establishment until Stanley's meeting with Jones in 1930, Thompson's firm built no fewer than sixty-two courses: fifty-six in Canada (thirty-eight in Ontario, six in Alberta, five in Quebec, three each in Manitoba and Saskatchewan, and one in Nova Scotia) and six in the United States (three in Florida, two in Ohio, and one in Vermont). In 1929, the company completed ten new courses in Ontario alone. Only Donald Ross's portfolio outshone the Thompson résumé.

Jones traveled to Toronto on June 19, 1930 (the day before his twenty-fourth birthday), and stayed as a guest at the Royal York Hotel. His bill would be picked up by the Canadian Pacific Railway, which owned the hotel and for which Stanley Thompson had been building a series of golf courses, including the hotel's own Royal York Golf Club, which had just opened. Before enjoying any golf, Jones visited Thompson's office on the sixteenth floor of the Star Building, home of the *Toronto Daily Star* newspaper, in the city's main financial district. The next two days Jones played golf with Stanley, first at Mississaugua Golf and Country Club (a Donald Ross design that Stanley had modified and lengthened in 1927–28) and then at Royal York. On both courses Jones shot 71, which was even par in both places, "so I made a pretty good impression." (In 1946 Royal York changed its name to St. George's Golf & Country Club; Jones came to consider the course's dogleg-right par-4 17th hole as one of the finest holes in North America.) Both rounds were followed by glasses of Thompson's favorite scotch in the barrooms, which Jones very much enjoyed—along with Stanley's storytelling, much of it ribald (he was not known as "The Toronto Terror" for nothing)—because Prohibition was still in force in the United States (Thompson built a course in Richford, Vermont, in 1928 that purposely straddled the border, with two "international holes" and a "19th hole" in Quebec, which allowed American golfers to imbibe Canadian Club or another alcoholic beverage of their choice after their round before returning stateside.) One evening Stanley entertained Jones with dinner in the company of "some of the most prominent men of Toronto," if what Jones wrote later that evening to Ione is to be trusted; another evening he took Jones home for a dinner cooked by his wife, Ruth. For a young man with hardly any money in his pocket, Jones considered the Canadian's hospitality "royal, indeed!"

Back in his hotel room at the end of the day Jones felt elated and wrote a letter to "My Darling Ione"—not many evenings went by when he didn't—who was home in Montclair. Before leaving for Ontario, he had sent her a Western Union telegram in which he ventured, "MAY HAVE SOME WONDERFUL NEWS TO TELL YOU . . . LOVE, BOBBY." Now, writing from "a beautiful room with two beds!" on the seventh floor of the Royal York Hotel with a balcony overlooking the moonlit lake, an excited Jones was bursting at the seams to tell the woman he loved his big news. Not only would Stanley Thompson oversee the building of the Midvale golf course in just the manner that "Bobby" had hoped, but "Mr. Thompson offered me a proposition in an informal way to open an American office calling it the Thompson-Jones or vice versa to do business in a big way in the U.S. . . . . Stanley Thompson, Limited, are golf architects of national repute. They have done some wonderful work in Canada but not in the U.S. They want to break into American territory and that is why I am here. So he invited me to look over his organization, and here I am! They are doing now about a million dollars worth of work and with me in it why two million would be a cinch! One course they did at Jasper Park in the Canadian Rockies cost $500,000. Whoa! And they got 80% of that!! It really does look good and if they come through with anything worthwhile at all, we will be partners, with offices in Cleveland, possibly. Do you mind living in Cleveland, honey? I will know tomorrow just what it is all about and by tomorrow night so will you (by telephone)." Jones wrote more letters to Ione while in Toronto and in all of them visions of wedded bliss and a splendid career in golf architecture poured out of him, mixed with wild exaggerations of how much money Thompson's golf course projects were really worth. "Oh, darling, I think of you perpetually. . . . We shall be very happy, dearest. I have some grand plans. . . . If you were only with me it would be heaven itself . . . I could conquer the world."

Back across the border (with a bootlegged bottle or two in tow, one of them for Ione's father), Jones wasted no time getting things organized for Midvale. On June 30, 1930, he wired Thompson's general manager John Inwood—whom everyone called "Major" in honor of his service in the First World War—with a request for Thompson's general guidelines for "submitting proposals to Clubs for making a lay-out and looking after the supervision of construction" for a new golf course. Inwood reacted promptly, sending Jones a three-page letter spelling out the services normally provided by the architect ("preparing the layout"; "staking the location of tees and greens"; "preparing a plan showing greens, tees, fairways, and bunkers"; "supplying a plan of the water system, showing the size of the pipe and the location of the outlets"; and "preparing specifications for the construction of the course in detail") and the range of fees that could be charged for them. Inwood explained that the company's fees were "flexible" and "vary with the prosperity of the Club," and that "we have to size up the situation before we give any figures." Learning from Inwood's reply just how much money Thompson was charging for its current jobs was tremendously illuminating to Jones, as he had little notion of the going rates. When accepting a job on the basis of the total complete costs for building a course, including all construction and its labor and material, the upper range of what Thompson was receiving ran between $88,000 and $111,000 (the latter representing more than $1.5 million in 2012 dollars). For plans and specifications only, the charge could be as high as $4,500 for a prosperous club or client and as low as $1,500 for a course in a small town. For supervision of the construction, the average charge would be $5,000. Ideally, the Thompson firm also preferred to supply a club with three or four of its own men to act as general superintendents (at $350 a month) and foremen (at $235 a month), their salaries to be paid by the club and with Thompson "receiving our commission on their salaries as well as on labor and materials." In this way, Stanley Thompson & Company, Ltd., made much more money from every job but even more importantly had control of the quality of the course that was being built.

There was no single document more basic to Jones's budding understanding of the golf course business, and of the importance of controlling—and earning profits from—not just the design but also the construction of a golf course than Major Inwood's June 1930 letter. In the ensuing years, as soon as he was capable of it, and then for the rest of his long career in golf course architecture, Jones always sought to have his own construction companies build the golf courses he was designing—often without the client knowing that it was his own company that Jones was "recommending." It was in that legal—but perhaps deceptive—fashion that Jones would make a great deal of his fortune over a major part of his seventy-year-long career.

What most likely determined the precise details of the cooperation between Thompson and Jones on Midvale was the Canadian architect's very busy schedule. In the summer of 1930, Thompson had golf courses under construction in Ontario, Quebec, and Nova Scotia; he needed to pay visits to each of them during the summer months. In a letter dated July 10, 1930, Inwood informed Jones that Stanley planned to visit Rochester sometime the following week, "when he will complete the lay-out with you." But four days later Inwood wrote Jones again, telling him that Stanley would not be able to visit Midvale after all, as he had to attend to pressing matters involving his new golf courses in Montreal and at Digby on the western side of Nova Scotia. "He told me," Inwood related, "to request you to go ahead and complete the lay-out of the course, and specifications will have to be prepared. I shall be pleased to help you with the latter as far as possible, if you will give me the necessary data. I have sent you specimens of our specifications and estimates, so probably you can work it out yourself as well as I can; but if you are stuck, send us what data you can, and we will fix them up here."

Happy with the freedom that Thompson was giving him, Jones finalized a "blueprint" of the golf course and presented it to Midvale's executive board at its meeting on July 19; the board approved it. Jones informed the Toronto office, offering, "If this plan meets with the approval of Mr. Thompson, I plan to start work on construction the latter part of this week." (Inwood quickly answered, saying that Thompson was off at another course site and "has not had the time to check over your plan in detail, but thinks it's okay.") As for the contract, Jones sketched out what he thought was required in terms of material (grass seed, bent-grass stolons, fertilizer, sand) and equipment (notably a watering system) for thirty tees of 1,000 square feet each, eighteen fairways comprising 65 acres, eighteen greens averaging 7,000 square feet each (large even by today's standards), and ninety bunkers, along with how much each item would cost: a total of $49,100. Receiving Jones's estimate in Toronto, Inwood made only a few minor changes, retyped the contract and had the firm's solicitor approve it, and sent it back to Jones for signature by Midvale. Dated July 23, 1930 (the date that it was executed in Toronto), the document was signed only by Thompson, not Jones. For the plans and specifications of the golf course, "the Architect" was to receive $2,000, below the average fee that Thompson usually received. In addition, "the Architect" was to get "ten percent of the total cost expended by the Club in the construction of the course, for labor and materials and including the wages of any superintendent and foremen any remuneration of contractors, also including the cost of fertilizer, seed and bent grass." How exactly the money was to be split between Thompson and Jones was not a matter for the contract, nor do any other records make the division clear. It would hardly matter anyway, as Midvale Golf and Country Club could not—or at least did not—pay its bills. Neither Thompson nor Jones would make any money off the project.

As for the course design, Jones had already been well along with his routing of Midvale even before Thompson's visit to the property in early June. For young Robert, the task of "routing" the golf course seemed simple enough: to walk all over the property, comprehensively examining the ground in all of its diverse character and land forms; look for natural flats and ridges for landing areas and existing saddles and plateaus for greens; find knolls and shelves for tee boxes; survey natural drainage patterns so that rain-soaked soil would minimally inhibit play; and then sit down with his notes and a map of the property and arrange a nice circuit of golf holes starting from the best spot where the round of golf could begin (preferably near the proposed clubhouse) all the way around to the final, 18th green (also preferably near the clubhouse). Jones approached the routing of a golf course much more as an art than a science, using features of the land as elements in his design. After all, history's great courses—whether the Old Course at St. Andrews; the links at Dornoch Golf Club where Donald Ross learned his golf (it became "Royal" Dornoch in 1906, after Ross learned the game); Harry Colt's Toronto Golf Club; or even C. B. Macdonald's National Golf Links—all derived their virtuous character and nuances of strategy from the grounds on which they were situated. Even at this early stage of his career, Jones knew that fundamental truth: Above all, the character of the land *must* determine the style, location, and direction of every hole of a golf course.

But even in an era before bulldozers, most sites needed to be altered to accommodate golf. The Midvale site was hilly and interesting enough, but its soil was mostly covered with windblown sand. The sandy soil gave him the idea to give the golf course what he called a "links-land effect," with uphill, downhill, and sidehill lies created by the folds, swales, and tilts of the terrain; a hard and fast playing surface; bunkers in fairways that could not be seen from the tee; some blind shots into the greens; and green sites tucked into hollows or perched on plateaus. Of course, at this stage of his life, Jones had never seen a true links course. He had immigrated to America at age five and had not yet returned across the ocean to visit and play any of the great links of England, Scotland, or Ireland; he would not do so until the 1950s. He had seen pictures in books of the Old Course at St. Andrews and other British links courses, and he had grown up playing Genundewah, the sandy splice of undulating golf atop the hillcrest near his home that sharpened his golf acumen by requiring a wide variety of shotmaking abilities: low punch shots that would roll out many yards, curving shots to the right and to the left, deft blasts out of sand traps, precise little chips onto contoured greens. Jones wanted to incorporate those same qualities into Midvale. It was his first course—*only* his first course—but he wanted it to be great.

Although Jones was chiefly responsible for Midvale's design, the direct personal association he came to enjoy with Thompson helped to refine and sharpen his ideas about golf course design. "Naturalness" and "natural beauty" were hallmarks of Thompson's architecture, and Thompson himself was something of a "linksland-type architect," as Jones would later describe him. Well before the time of Midvale, Thompson had written: "Nature must always be the architect's model. . . . The development of the natural features and planning the artificial work to conform to them requires a great deal of care and forethought. In clearing fairways, it is good to have an eye to the beautiful. Often it is possible, by clearing away undesirable and unnecessary trees on the margins of fairways, to open up a view of some attractive picture and frame it with foliage . . . oftentimes the natural beauty of many a golf course, which the average player assumes was always present, has been created by the skill of the engineer who can see opportunities for beauty in the rough woods, swamps or fields that mean nothing to the unskilled eye. The absence or presence of the above features, among others, will decide whether continuous play on a course becomes monotonous or otherwise." This design philosophy of "natural artistry" appealed to Jones in some deeply felt and powerful ways. So, too, did Thompson's advice to Jones: "Make no little plans." Although Thompson in saying this was likely expressing a thought specifically about the plans for a golf course, Jones adopted the dictum as a guiding principle for his entire life.

In conjunction with the strong personal affinity between the two men, the key to their successful working association was their "creative resonance," a mutually strong and reinforcing intuitive understanding of each other's philosophies and approaches that led to an easy and free-flowing interplay of ideas, insights, and visions. Thompson and Jones were very open to one another, making it easy and natural for them to understand and appreciate what the other thought and felt. Virtually everything Thompson said to Jones, and vice versa, stimulated some sort of sympathetic response. Though each sometimes took, they almost always gave back.

If one had asked Jones in the early 1930s if *he* had designed Midvale, the young architect may well have deferred to Thompson—or at least asserted that he and Stanley had designed it together. But years later, when a far less magnanimous Jones was more interested in counting how many golf courses he had designed over the long span of his career than giving his mentor credit, he asserted to golf historians, "I created Midvale." Jones, not Thompson, certainly was the one who was on the property day-in and day-out, but he had plenty of help overseeing its construction. As John Inwood explained to Jones, "Mr. Thompson's policy on jobs of this kind is to use plenty of supervision as, with the work being scattered over the Course, it is vitally necessary." The Toronto office sent no fewer than three of its men to Rochester to serve as foremen to the local general contractor who was building Midvale.

Technically, the course was created by "Thompson & Jones, Inc." So nicely had the working relationship between Stanley and Robert become that a formal incorporation of their partnership was signed in Toronto and Rochester by the second week of September 1930. The two men would evenly share $2,000 in stock, with the Midvale contract being transferred over fully to the newly formed company.

The Midvale golf course was built using the typical construction practices of the day. "We formed the greens with slipscrapers and teams of horses," Jones later recalled. "It was virtually a hand operation, and it took seven days with four or five teams to shape a green. So I had a lot of time to think about what I wanted to do with them. I would make sketches then watch while the work was done." Having never been part of a golf construction project before, Jones regarded the work as "a very valuable experience." Because Jones believed that sandy soils couldn't grow grass well without fertilizer (it was one of the agronomic misunderstandings of the era; today's golf course designers specifically look for sandy soils), Jones went to the City of Rochester's sewage disposal plant: "We got their sludge and hauled it by the truckload over the eighteen miles to put on the golf course. And did it smell awful! People in the area hated it. We did not make a lot of friends during the construction. But when we worked the sludge into the soil it helped hold the moisture, so the grass grew very quickly and well." Only one matter of the course's construction approved by Jones was questioned by Thompson's men. When the Toronto office heard that Jones had approved some plowing of the fairways, Alan Bland, an Ontario Agricultural College graduate who had gone to work for Thompson in 1922, wrote to Jones to stop the plowing and only use a disk. Jones replied that he would stop, but justified his decision by saying that in one "anemic area" of the course "some shallow plowing might prove more efficient."

The course was completed and opened for play on the Fourth of July 1931. Measuring 6,468 yards (3,167 yards on the front nine, and 3,301 on the back), it played to a par 72. As was becoming the standard, there were two par-3s and two par-5s on each nine. The par-3s ranged in distance from 160 to 225 yards, the par-5s from 455 to 570 yards, and the par-4s from 315 to 440 yards. Five of the 18 holes had been routed through a large apple orchard, with the play weaving in, out, and between the trees. The rest of the course did play with a slight feel of a links, with the firm rolling terrain and lack of tree shelter promoting a game played more on the ground, with the ball rolling rather than lofted high in the air where the wind could alter its flight. Jones played the course on opening day with club board members and shot the low round of the day, a 74. He reported to Thompson that the greens had "developed a luxuriant growth but from lack of proper topdressing and treatment they are still a little rough as a putting surface." The Midvale greens were grown from a strain of Washington State creeping bent grass, an expensive species of turfgrass sent by Thompson's Golf Ltd. through customs at Niagara Falls, which meant more cost because of the import duty. The fairways were seeded with 4,500 pounds of Kentucky bluegrass and 2,000 pounds of Canadian bluegrass and the roughs with 4,500 pounds of Redtop fescue, 4,500 pounds of Chewings fescue, and 2,000 pounds of Sheep's fescue. Jones also arranged to buy a few acres of sod for the Midvale course (at $100 per acre) from the Cornell University Agricultural Experiment Station. McWane Cast Iron Pipe Company of Birmingham, Alabama, provided the piping for Midvale's watering system, which fed water from an artificial lake that was built near the middle of the property. None of these items came cheap. Fortunately, no underground drainage was required, which is often one of the most expensive aspects of modern golf course construction.

Unfortunately, the Depression hit Midvale very hard. Although 151 members had joined the club originally, the poor economy forced many of them to resign while the course was still under construction. The club could pay hardly any of its bills. What money it could raise went to Sweeney and Boland, the construction firm that built Midvale. By the time the course opened, Jones and Thompson were owed about $9,000, including the original $2,000 for the "Architect's fee." Several checks that Jones wrote off his Rochester account bounced. Thompson tried to help, but reported to Robert that "Collections are bad, and we have declared a private Moratorium with our Creditors." More than once Jones wired the Toronto office asking for as little as $50 to keep things going. He was getting neither his salary nor his travel expenses covered. In March 1931 he applied to the United States Golf Association for reinstatement of his amateur status (he had been a professional golfer since first taking the job at Sodus in 1926), chiefly because he could not afford to pay his PGA (Professional Golfers' Association of America) dues. By October 1931, Jones could no longer make his monthly car payment, and the finance company took his car (a 1928 Auburn 8-90 Speedster). Midvale tried various ways to come up with the money, but nothing worked out. Thompson's firm engaged a law firm to investigate the possibility of suing the club and taking over ownership of the entire property, but in the end the lawyers got next to nothing for the architects.

Thompson did his best to bolster Jones's spirits. On March 6, 1931, Thompson wrote to him: "Dear Bobbie: I would not be too disappointed . . . as often times these set-backs are a blessing in disguise. . . . We can start our New York business in a modest way, even if we do not get any Capital, we will be slowly arriving at the ultimate goal. . . . Cheerio, and do not be down-cast, for the Sun will be shining on the green sward before long."

But downcast Jones was, and growing more so with every passing month, as the laments he penned to Ione in the first six months of 1931 make abundantly clear: "Did quite a bit of work to-day, but have plenty to do to-morrow. Perhaps it will mean something"; "I just about wept on the shoulder of one of Midvale's members to-day, to show him how much I needed a check"; "I have been working rather strenuous myself but hell, I don't seem to accomplish much. That is a discouraging feeling to have but I can't get that way"; "I have been drinking during the past year but ever so modestly"; "I don't feel so happy to-day—money troubles. The future looks like it will be bright but the present is like a total eclipse. If I don't get a little money next week it is hard telling whether I shall be able to make the trip to visit you."

The fact that Ione forgot his birthday compounded his woes, but what really got him down was learning that she would be traveling with her family to Europe in a few months and staying for half a year: "A whole half year? 352/2=176 [sic] days. What a long time! Such a long time! Darling, have you really decided to leave me for all that time?" All Robert, the sad-eyed optimist, could do was keep declaring his love for her: "Some people think that they are in love but really they aren't. . . . But all of the world is insignificant compared to ours. . . . It makes me rather jealous to have all these people getting married. But for that little nest egg we must have we could too."

When his automobile wasn't in hock with the finance company Jones scouted for jobs as far as a tank of gas could take him. In late June 1931, Jones prepared a report for Thompson with a list of twenty-one clients, all but two of them in New York, and most of them concentrated in the central and western parts of the state: four of them in the Rochester area, seven in and around Syracuse (including Tuscarora Country Club, for which Jones would do some minor work), and the rest in and around the Finger Lakes region in the towns of Ithaca, Newark, and Geneva. Only a few of the prospective clients, such as the resort spa at Saratoga Springs, north of Albany, were looking to build a full 18-hole course, but the Saratoga course would not get built until 1936, and then not by Thompson & Jones. More were after nine-hole layouts to stand alone or add to an existing nine, but most were looking only for "3 new holes," "remodeling 3 greens," "adding one green and fairway trapping," and the like, and very few of them became jobs performed by Jones's company. The two out-of-state jobs that Jones was looking into involved the routing of prospective nine-hole courses in the Pennsylvania towns of Carbondale, north of Scranton, and Altoona, southwest of State College. Neither panned out.

Nor did Jones's visit the following year to Greensburg, east of Pittsburgh, where a "syndicate" of area businessmen headed by W. B. Craig had become interested in a public "pay-as-you-play" 18-hole golf course to supplement the area's nine-hole Greensburg Country Club.* Reflecting the high degree of stress that Jones was experiencing about every one of his golf course prospects during this early stretch of his career, he felt the Greensburg opportunity might very well prove to be the big break he needed both for launching his own career and for "getting ahead" with enough money to marry Ione. As he wrote Ione (then in France) on March 2, 1932, "We are just hanging our fate on it. It certainly is hard on one." His emotional investment in the "Pittsburgh job" was especially heavy because Stanley Thompson had not been involved in the sales pitch. "The syndicate haven't [sic] quite enough money yet," he wrote Ione in early June, "but hope to have more any day. [Mr. Craig] is trying to get enough that we can

---

* Jones apparently visited Greensburg in the fall of 1931 and played a complimentary round with W. B. Craig at the Greensburg Country Club, a nine-hole course that had been designed in 1904 by P. B. Graham of Carnoustie, Scotland. Asked to compare the Greensburg Club with the type of course Thompson & Jones would be building as the "pay-for-play," Jones sent back the following thoughts, which are highly illuminating of Jones's early approach to what he then considered to be "modern" architectural design: "The Greensburg course was built when American architecture was in its infancy. There are many courses a great deal worse but nevertheless Greensburg must be classed as 'antique.' It would be like comparing the modern car with that of 1910 to compare the two courses. As enumerating some of the outstanding flaws as I observed them in our round of golf, I hope that these suggestions will be considered as purely constructive. The greens are poorly located and of harsh design. The sequence of holes are [sic] monotonous in lengths 250 to 350 yards. The play of each hole is similar in strategy. The climbs are too severe in many holes which could have been eliminated by the changing of the location of the greens and varying the length of holes. The finishing holes are weak golf holes. Certain areas could be improved by planting, particularly the artificial lakes." Robert Trent Jones to W. B. Craig, 15 Oct. 1931, Jones Papers, Cornell University Archives. In the late 1930s, the Greensburg Country Club was expanded to 18 holes, but not by Jones. The plan for the expansion may have come from architect Tom Bendelow, who died in 1936.

build the course and seed this fall. In any event the job will be ours, if and when done. If that goes through I shall feel so proud in selling it completely, without Thompson's aid at all. . . . Everything will be all right, my sweet, and we shall be so happy." In late June, Jones assured Ione that "the Pittsburgh job is going through. I had a telephone call today. Isn't that the nuts? It looks like our break and dearest it's proven to me that I can sell a job without Thompson going near it, although his reputation did mean something. But look at the competition I beat out, even Dr. MacKenzie! . . . Oh dearest darling sweetheart, aren't you proud and confident of our future? They are only building nine holes but that's something. It ought to get us about $4000 of which I expect to get $2000 clear for us. Isn't it grand news!"

But as with so many of Jones's other prospects, when the word came that the job had fallen through—in the case of Greensburg with no golf holes at all being built—the young architect's sense of disappointment was acute. "I am getting down again, but not so deeply," he advised Ione, "and I am not going to let myself go. But I <u>must</u> see you before long. . . . Oh sweetheart, why must we be apart like this so often, so much? Somehow, someway we have got to get married in the fall, and in the meantime I have got to see you a lot. . . . We shall have all the money we need. It will be so much fun making it together, being responsible for each others [sic] success. We shall not make money our god. From what I have seen lately, money is one of those elusive articles. . . . I know that with all the different logs in the fire that we are bound to get a break soon. I want to get a nice break for us, dearest. . . . I am glad you have confidence in me. I'll prove to you that I'm worthy, too."

With the Depression worsening, very few prospective golf course projects were coming to life for anyone—and hardly any of them in the final form in which they had been conceived. In the summer of 1931, Thompson & Jones completed minor modifications on a Walter J. Travis design (from 1928) at Stafford Country Club in the town of Stafford, thirty miles southeast of Rochester, but it is not clear from the Jones Papers whether his company was ever paid for the work. A more substantive remodeling was supposed to be done by Thompson & Jones on Rochester's Locust Hill Country Club, a Seymour Dunn design from 1928, but it turned out to involve the building of just one new green, with a promise for a few more to be done when money was available.[†]

---

† In *The Architects of Golf* (p. 309), Cornish and Whitten indicate that Jones redesigned Locust Hill Country Club in 1931; no doubt based on this information, today's Wikipedia ar-

But it was not just the Great Depression that was plaguing Robert Jones, it was the onset of some serious depression. The stomach ulcer that had attacked him while he was a teenage golfer still vexed him, but his visits to the doctor in the early 1930s were frequent enough to suggest psychosomatic symptoms and hypochondria, though Jones's doctor was diplomatic enough not to call them that. "My nerves have been kicking up of late," he lamented in a March 1932 letter to Ione. "Saturday I went to the doctor. He said that I was allowing the bad times to take too deep a root in me. Perhaps I am. I am pretty melancholy today. I had better snap out of my morbid period of melancholy." A few weeks later he reported, "I had a chat with my doctor yesterday. He and I are pals. He said, 'Bobby, you make mountains out of mole hills, with your imagination at times.' I said, 'Yes, it's hell at times.' But he said it wasn't altogether bad, because that was the road of my ambition."

Unfortunately, very few of his ambitions were panning out, and those few design jobs that did either could not pay their bills or postponed the work indefinitely. Jones later remembered: "We had six or seven jobs, about $40,000–$50,000 worth of business, but I couldn't collect any money from them. I was getting a summons for a bill of only some $20–$30 owed to one of my suppliers, and here I had as much as $80,000 being owed me that I couldn't collect." Luckily, Stanley Thompson had become a good friend and still had some profitable business going up in Canada. Jones was able to keep his office and survive . . . barely. Thompson & Jones's corporation income tax form for fiscal year 1931 showed a gross income of $6,678, an indebtedness of $2,095.44, and a net worth of $26.24.

But Jones's greatest hope for profitable new work at the time took him back to Ithaca, home of his dear Cornell campus, where members of the Country Club of Ithaca were interested in adding a third nine to the 18-hole A. W. Tillinghast design that had opened in 1926. Comprising Cornell faculty, area business leaders, and many prominent alumni, the Country Club of Ithaca

---

ticle on Locust Hill Country Club asserts that Jones redesigned Locust Hill in 1931 when members expanded their course from a nine-hole course, which opened in 1925, to an 18-hole layout, when new acreage was purchased for the course. There is no information in the Jones Papers that Jones did anything at Locust Hill in 1931 (or before) besides build one new green. Substantiation for this lesser role can be found in a letter Jones wrote to Ione Tefft Davis on 26 May 1932, in which he wrote: "They are very pleased with [the new green I installed last year] and promise a complete re-modeling job as soon as things pick up." It seems correct then for Locust Hill Country Club to advertise its complete 18-hole course, which it does, as a Seymour Dunn design.

wanted a plan for a 27-hole layout, "saving as many of the existing holes as possible" from their established course. Jones's point of contact was Dr. Leonard Urquhart, a Cornell professor of civil engineering who had been one of Jones's teachers and happened to be chairman of the golf club's planning committee. Hearing about the country club's interest from a friend, Jones, in a letter dated January 26, 1931, told his former professor about his affiliation with the "famous International Golf Architect," Stanley Thompson, and how "the advertising possibilities that an architect would receive from a course that obtains players from every part of the United States such as your Club does" could enable Thompson & Jones to "charge less than our usual fee because of the possibilities of future benefits."

Receiving an interested reply from Urquhart, Jones drove to Cornell to see the property, bringing Thompson with him. Over the next several months, plans proceeded for building twenty-seven holes for the club at the Depression-era bargain price of $75,000. The price tag included a modest $2,250 architect's fee plus the standard 10 percent Thompson & Jones charged for supervising the construction. Doing what Ithaca wanted quickly became a highly complicated matter because not all of the land to be used for the course was owned by the club at the time Jones did the routing for the new course; some plots were leased from the university and a purchase of two new tracts amounting to 140 acres had not yet been finalized. Muddying the picture for Jones even more, some of the already existing golf holes involved land that the club had just sold. Jones was in the difficult position of trying to draw up a layout on a moving target. He couldn't even be sure of the site for the new clubhouse.

In good trust, Jones prepared an evolving set of plans and specifications to satisfy Ithaca; no course routing could be finalized and certainly no construction could start until details regarding the different tracts of land involved (owned, leased, just sold) had been settled. Jones did his best to stay on top of a complicated local situation. He even arranged with his Toronto office "to loan the Club the services of a competent superintendent at the time the Club decided to construct two new holes to replace the present eighth and ninth, without further cost to the Club other than the wages of the superintendent." Being "greatly in need of cash at this time to promote the coming season's work," Jones appealed to Urquhart on February 3, 1932, asking him to use his influence to bring about speedy action on the matter. In almost every letter written to Ione during this period, Jones mentioned the Ithaca money, saying the club was about to pay. In mid-May 1931, he wrote to his fiancée, "I suppose your [sic] interested in knowing the results of the trip to Ithaca. I can almost plan on the money the first of next week. The only reason I haven't it this minute is due to the fact the secretary and treasurer is [sic] out of town until Saturday. Can you beat that? One must have patience at times like these. The president told me that they had the money and he would get it. This was just a technical gesture on the part of the secretary that he didn't think necessary. I have been taxing my brain thinking of ideas for making some additional money. I feel optimistic that something will turn up."

Thanks to Urquhart's support, the club soon did write a check to Thompson & Jones in late May 1932, but only in the amount of $1,000. They would get nothing more. Jones wrote Ione again: "Ithaca hasn't paid us as yet. They have turned out to be a bunch of pikers. Claim they have to have a meeting of the whole board before our plan can be passed. What a life!"

Over the next two years Jones sent repeated letters, mostly to Urquhart, pleading for the full $2,250 architect's fee that had been enumerated in the contract. As for the proposal that Thompson & Jones had submitted "for a complete remodeling plan for eighteen holes," Robert emphasized how "it is necessary to bear in mind that the plans completed in 1931 cannot be used, for, basically, the entire set-up had changed," meaning that the exact pieces of property controlled by the Country Club of Ithaca for its new golf course had changed significantly since 1931. Unyielding, a special committee of the club's board of managers chaired by Dr. Cedric H. Guise, a Cornell professor of forest management, sent Jones a tart letter, dated November 22, 1934, declaring that "the Club did not enter into a definite contract with Thompson & Jones upon the terms claimed by you. . . . If a contract was a made . . . it included terms requiring competent supervision by the architect or his representatives throughout the performance of the work, weekly visits, and the loan by the architect of a competent superintendent. . . . Furthermore, it is clear that the architect was required to furnish working models or drawings of all greens, to stake out the ground for all tees and to blaze trees marked for removal. . . . Further the Special Committee thought it was most unusual and unprecedented for an architect to claim payment in full before furnishing all of the drawings, models and specifications, and before doing any of the work of superintendence and supervision. . . . The Board of Managers does not recognize any further liability or responsibility to Thompson & Jones, or to you individually, until such time as the Club may by mutual agreement go ahead with the construction of the new golf course."

Admittedly, there was no signed contract. Jones had trusted that Urquhart would take care of him, a native son of Cornell, and make sure that the Ithaca club membership appreciated the complexities of their golf course situation and the fragility of Jones's financial position.

But business was business, as Jones was quickly learning, and $2,250 was a lot of money in the depths of the Depression, even for those associated with an Ivy League school. Ithaca paid Jones nothing more and at the end of 1934 it suspended all further work on the golf course.‡ Interestingly, when Cornell in 1938 hired Jones to design and build nine holes, the university reclaimed the Country Club of Ithaca's eighth and ninth holes as the site for Clara Dickson Hall. Because it was going to lose two holes of its golf course, the country club decided also to give up an adjoining one, the seventh, to university control. Now needing three holes to make a complete golf course, the club hired Jones—who was

---

‡ In the official history of the Country Club of Ithaca, author Julian C. Smith summarizes the club's version of the story: "In June 1931 the Club retained the Buffalo firm of Thompson & Jones to plan a 27-hole layout, with the understanding that if the plans were accepted, the firm would be paid $2,250 for the final design. A set of plans was prepared and delivered and the Club paid the firm $1,000. For the next several years Thompson and Jones billed the club for the remaining $1,250, and each year the Club replied that the $1,000 already paid was plenty for the amount of work the firm had done, and that the matter was closed. The controversy was not resolved until 1939." *Breaking Ninety: A History of the Country Club of Ithaca, 1900–1989* (Ithaca, NY: The Country Club of Ithaca, Inc., 1990), pp. 45–47. This book seems not to have had access to the correspondence between Jones and the Country Club of Ithaca from the summer of 1939 over what he was owed. In a letter to Robert Hutchinson, the club secretary, on July 12, 1939, Jones wrote: "I did not mention the claim for $1,250.00 in my previous letter as I did not want anyone to think that I was in any way making any sort of veiled threat. However I am perfectly willing to waive any further claim to this money if I am retained as Architect for the Country Club for our regular fee of $1,500 for plans (not including supervision" (RTJ to Mr. Robert Hutchinson, County Courthouse, Ithaca, NY, 12 July 1939, Ithaca Country Club Files, JP, CUA). Though paid $7,248.00 for the three new holes, Jones asked for $8,500, to which Hutchinson replied: "The opinion of the members was that the sum of $8,500.00 plus the salary of a superintendent to supervise construction was very high for the building of only three holes. They asked me to inquire if you could not draft the new course in rough manner, not going into the details that you stated in your letter. . . . Perhaps, if this were done, your costs would not be so high and the Board could see its way clear to retaining your services for this three-hole project" (Hutchinson, The Country Club of Ithaca, to RTJ, 17 July 1939, Ithaca Country Club Files, JP, CUA). Jones accepted the compromise for $7,248, no doubt again with thoughts of how parsimonious the membership of the Country Club of Ithaca could be.

coming to Ithaca regularly anyway to build the Cornell nine—to create the holes. The three holes were completed by the end of October 1938, and Jones charged the club $7,248; wanting bygones to be bygones, he also agreed to consider the 1931 bill from Thompson & Jones to be paid in full. The Country Club of Ithaca played that new 18-hole layout until 1958, when it was supplanted by a completely new course designed on a different tract of ground by Canadian-born Geoffrey Cornish, an architect who also happened to start his career with Stanley Thompson. When that happened, the Tillinghast/Jones course was totally lost to Cornell's North Campus.

Thompson & Jones looked hard for alternative ways to stay in business. As Stanley himself had written Professor Urquhart in early March 1932 when pressing for payment of the full architect's fee from the Country Club of Ithaca, "We have been forced to take over some clubs in which we have an equity. This has embarrassed us temporarily, until such time as the golf season is under way and we can liquidate some of these assets." The company also promoted the construction of "short courses"—sometimes called "pitch and putt" or "Tom Thumb" courses—that wouldn't cost nearly as much to build or play, and could be played by every member of a family, including children; Jones himself was particularly enamored with the potential of such courses and had already built one at Sodus Bay. In addition, Thompson & Jones began advertising that it could save golf clubs money by taking over all of their course maintenance duties. "A vital problem facing Green Committees today," the firm's simple brochure declared, "is the efficient and economical maintenance of the course. Hit and miss methods of course maintenance are no longer good enough for the wide-awake Green Committee, and players are yearly becoming more critical of fairways, tees, greens, hazards and the up-to-datedness of the course in general." However, very few maintenance contracts were secured by Thompson & Jones, making them very little money.

With country clubs suffering so much financially, the company began to look more and more for clients like the "Pittsburgh syndicate" that had been interested in building more straightforward and less expensive "pay-as-you-play" courses. To make some money, Midvale Golf & Country Club opened their course in the summer of 1932 to such "greens fees," as Robert wrote with enthusiasm, to Ione: "This means that anyone with money (meaning $1.00 or $2.00) can play. Under this plan they should be able to pay us the $4,000 they owe us. They may be able to pay half of that before the season is over." Some money was indeed made, but Midvale was so far in debt and Thompson & Jones so far down the list of those who were owed money that the architects never saw any of the revenue from the open play. Anyway, in the spring of 1933 Michael E. Sweeney of Sweeney & Boland bought the course, free and clear of any debts, for $30,000 at a public auction.

Thompson's bread and butter still lay in Canada and, with so little work for Jones to do in the States in 1932, Stanley asked Robert to make a trip for him to Banff. Thompson had built the Banff Springs Hotel course at the popular mountain resort in Alberta's majestic Canadian Rockies in 1927. Chiseling a golf course out of rock in a valley formed by the convergence of the Bow and Spray Rivers, between towering 10,000-foot peaks, was totally unprecedented in the history of golf course construction. It was possible only through the largesse of the Canadian Pacific Railway, the developer of the resort, which spent a quarter of a million dollars just for the earthmoving project necessary to build the course. Hundreds of gondola cars filled with tons of soil were transported a thousand miles over the Rockies by the railway company to provide the fill that covered the entire golf course. In an age before sophisticated earthmoving equipment, the building of Banff, at a total cost of well more than a million dollars, was a monumental achievement.

As with the other golf courses that Thompson had built for the Canadian railway system, Thompson's company was expected to provide an annual written report to the railway on the condition of the course at Banff Springs as well as any potential for improving—and if possible reducing the cost of—the course's maintenance. This report had been made in the past by Alan Bland of Thompson's office. But Thompson wanted Jones to see his mountain gem, and he strongly encouraged Robert to make the 1932 trip, "all expenses paid."

Excited by the opportunity to make the longest and most adventurous trip since his boyhood immigration to America, Robert wrote Ione, "I am going away quite some distant [sic], to a place called Banff. My pass is R.C. 4716, almost sounds like if I were going to jail. The Canadian Pacific Railway is paying all the expenses, in addition a fee for my expert advice. Oh, sweet, I want to go and I don't. I hate to get all that distant [sic] between us again. If only this were our honeymoon. They say the place is wonderful. . . . When I get back from Banff, dearest, I am going to buy your ring. It may not be large but in keeping with good taste, which means with my present financial accumulations, later dearest, you will receive much more costly gifts but none that could express more love."

The trip was long, nearly 4,500 miles round-trip, but Jones was exhilarated by the experience. Besides staying three nights at the luxurious and majestic Banff Springs Hotel, "the Castle in the Rockies," Jones also stayed two nights at nearby Chateau Lake Louise with the stunning natural beauty of its emerald-green lake with Victoria Glacier rising above it. "This mountain country makes me feel very romantic, dearest. What a Don Juan I could be if you were here. . . . I am glad that I don't have to pay for this trip, everything cost a mint."

Jones got to play the golf course at Banff Springs and found it to be one of the most profound experiences he'd ever had playing the sport—truly "Golf on the roof of the world." By far the most memorable hole on the golf course for him was the 200-yard par-3 fourth hole, known as "Devil's Cauldron."

A great golf course must have great golf holes, with no poor or bad ones, and Banff Springs had several that were great, but none surpassed the breathtaking fourth. From an elevated tee 80 feet above the green, the golfer had to carry his shot over a small lake to a punchbowl putting surface that was steeply sloped from back to front. Framing it all were tall pine trees and the sheer wall of rock that was the 9,672-foot Mount Rundle. Although he made drawings around the entire golf course, Jones focused most of his sketches on the remarkable Cauldron hole. In what  turned out to be a nineteen-page written report for the railroad, Jones included a special section just on that hole, which he felt could be made even better. Jones ventured: "The 'Cauldron,' one of the finest holes that I have ever seen from the standpoint of a 'golf shot' and an unusual nature setting, would be greatly improved by the addition of shallow traps on the right and left walls of the green slopes." Attached to his report was his hand-drawn sketch, labeled "Proposed Flashing 'Cauldron'," that showed "the value of flashing and the use of bunkers as framework in artistic design." ("Flashing" referred to faces of sand that "flashed up" on a bunker slope for visibility, aesthetic effect, and, particularly, added drama.) On his sketch of the Cauldron, which showed five bunkers (today there are six), Jones also wrote "Note the large scale of the traps to harmonize with the mass of the surrounding mountains." Although the precise evolution of this now world-famous golf hole—*Golf Magazine* rates it as one of the world's four greatest par-3s—is not altogether clear, the photographic evidence suggests that Jones's concept for remodeling Devil's Cauldron was rather quickly accepted and put into effect. To this day, the greenside bunkering for the hole matches very closely the design that Jones put to paper during his visit to Banff in the summer of 1932. One of Jones's other sketches from Banff proposed a new position for the 18th green that would allow golfers to view the nearby waterfalls on the Bow River while putting out to conclude their round.[§]

But Stanley Thompson hadn't sent Jones to Banff to redesign his golf course. Most of Jones's lengthy report dealt with the condition of the turfgrass and other agronomic conditions that were so challenging in the cold mountain environment. The golf course's main problem was "winterkill" on the putting greens. Every winter the greens would die due to a combination of such winter season factors as low temperatures, ice sheets, and snow mold, and from problems known to botanists as crown hydration and desiccation. After talking over the problem with the greenkeeper (a man by the name of McCullough), Jones discovered that the grounds crew was putting the fungicide down too early, which allowed it to wash away and lose its effectiveness. What the greenkeeper needed to do, Jones advised, was simply put a dose of fungicide on early and another on later to protect the greens all winter long. Major improvements in the condition of the turfgrass over the next few seasons showed that Jones got it right. But it was a lesson that was later seemingly forgotten. Some fifty years later, when Jones was building two courses at Kananaskis, some twenty miles east of Banff in the Bow River Valley, the course superintendent from Banff—a young man who didn't know that Jones had played any part in growing grass at Banff Springs—came over one day and said to the distinguished architect, "You know, Mr. Jones, I'm just finding out that if I put fungicide down twice, I can keep the greens over the winter." Jones, then in his mid-70s, just smiled and told the young greenkeeper that he was glad to know that.

Jones benefited greatly from his Banff trip. To Ione he wrote: "Dearest, I am

---

§ The 18th hole at Banff in Stanley Thompson's routing now plays as the 447-yard dogleg-right 14th, and it's considered to be the toughest hole on the course, just as it was when it played as the closing hole. Over the years Banff has undergone several re-routings, primarily to better suit the location of the hotel.

so anxious to get back and hustle some new work so that we can get married. This trip has helped my confidence and I feel that I can get something in spite of the bad times. . . . I can hardly believe the transformation that has taken place within me. . . . I feel much for the better. . . . The trip has convinced me that my future in golf is assured. The whole thing gives me confidence. I certainly needed confidence a few months ago, but all is much better now, and I am much stronger. It takes real experience to make you that way. . . . I am going to work like hell to get some business even though it may not be large commissions. . . . I know that I have something special in the art of golf course design. With a well designed attack I can go places (that means us) and without a Dr. MacKenzie or Stanley Thompson behind me. When the new era in golf course construction is at its peak you will be the wife of the country's most famous golf architect."

The Banff trip kept Jones in a positive frame of mind for the rest of the summer, as did a stretch of some excellent golf in which he shot a number of par rounds or better, if his letters to Ione are to be trusted. But winters came early in upstate New York, and when the golf season and its business prospects frosted over, Jones's mood once again grew despondent. "It just takes one big job," he wrote Ione, "and that job is bound to come, darling. Certainly someone must balance the justice of the world and we are entitled to our happiness. . . . All my thoughts are about two things: you and ways to make enough money to get married. . . . Sometimes I feel so useless rather than progressing. I feel that I am standing still and I don't ever want to stand still."

Robert sought to make some money over the winter of 1932–33 by writing a few articles about golf; he shared the drafts of his compositions by mail with Ione and even got a young woman who had just graduated in English from the University of Rochester to help him improve his writings. Finally, Jones "crashed," as he described it to Ione, into the office of Fay Blanchard, the editor of the Rochester *Journal-American*, whom at the time he knew only slightly from playing golf at Midvale. Naturally skeptical, the editor took a quick look at the sample article that Jones had brought with him. Though he found it "a damn good article and mighty interesting," Jones told Ione that it was way too long for newspapers and had "too many ideas in it." The editor suggested that Jones try contacting a golf magazine, perhaps about writing a weekly series on golf. Jones took a small measure of satisfaction from the editor's encouragement, and went to work on such a proposal. But, as he wrote Ione, "These are really tough times to get any work done or accepted." Nothing he was trying seemed to be leading anywhere—and it definitely was not bringing in any money.

How desperate the straits had become is sadly illustrated by a communiqué from Stanley to Robert in the late summer of 1932: "If by any chance, you are able to lay your hands on the odd $50.00, it would be greatly appreciated. If you would put it in an envelope and mail it to me. . . . Last Thursday I drew a slight draft on the Company for $30.00, hoping that you would be able to get sufficient money to meet it. The draft is back to-day, and I am requesting them to put it through again. . . . Use every effort you can to pay the $30 draft. If you cannot raise money, hold the draft as long as possible, but let me know." Jones somehow managed to send Thompson the money. The following month Stanley asked for another $25, which Robert also scrounged up and mailed him. It couldn't have been easy for Jones. "I have sure been economizing on my meals lately," he told Ione. "Go into a coffee shop and look down the items to pick out the cheapest one. Oh, my dear, it is a sad state of affairs!"

When circumstances grew the most dismal, Jones reached deep for any optimism he could find. Throughout the fall and winter of 1932–33 his letters to Ione grew more numerous, often two and three times a day, one of them twenty-two pages long, and in each, while seemingly trying to lift Ione's spirits and keep up her confidence that everything would work out for the two of them, the spirits that really needed buoying were his own.

"I come down to the office each morning hoping to find some exciting mail that I can write you about but so far not much luck, but I think that I will be able to soon, and will I be happy! Won't you darling? There isn't a reason in the world, darling, as a wife of the leading golf architect we shouldn't be very happy. I'll soon be able to give you all the comforts of life that your [sic] used to and worthy of. We can take nice trips to Florida or California if we want in the winter or we can stay right home in Montclair. The few days at a time that I am away when business calls will only help to make our life a perpetual honeymoon. Don't you see, dearest, we have everything to look forward to and live for? You can be a big, big help to me, dearest, in my climbing the ladder of fame and whatever heights I scale will be equally due to you. . . . Spurred with my ambition we can't be kept down. 'Incentive is the drawing power of man,' and your [sic] the greatest ambition any man ever had. . . . Please don't think we won't be able to get married, we will."

Although he could not really afford it, while in Toronto on his way to Banff Jones purchased a diamond engagement ring for Ione; he used a big chunk of what was left of the $1,000 payment he had managed to get from Ithaca after he had paid all his most urgent debts. No man has ever been more excited about the ring he had found for his loved one than Jones. In letter after letter, the love-sick golf architect expressed the joy he found in the ring: "I am so keen and full of excitement about buying your ring. It's a beautiful cut. The color is 'blue-white.' It's supposed to be the finest. I want you to be so proud of this ring. . . . I wrote your daddy about my buying this ring and what I saved on it because of the rate of exchange. . . . I can't wait until I place it on your hand, dearest, with appropriate sentiments. . . . I had a real frank discussion with Thompson about my desire to get married, about moving my business to New York City, and about the additional salary I will need there in comparison to other cities. . . . Oh, dearest, I really do feel most optimistic about things. I know that they are going to break for us soon. They have got to and you mustn't be blue. We shall soon be very happy. . . . There are still times that I get a little blue, especially being away from you. I am really never quite as content as I am when I am with you, content in body and soul in an indescribable way. I'll also never be content in my pursuit of fame, and my effort to give something worthwhile to the world. Contentment there stunts all ambition and it dies. So we must continue to improve, and what a help mate you can be to me and I to you in our respective interests."

The next time he saw her, Jones gave Ione the diamond ring. She loved it, but perhaps not with as much excitement and adoration as he had hoped. That level of emotion would have been impossible to match.

One can only wonder how content Jones would have been if he had known that it would be two more years before they married—or understand how great a struggle it would continue to be to get his career as a golf course architect truly off the ground and making money.

CHAPTER THREE

A "NEW DEAL" FOR GOLF

Jones (middle) looks over the site for Durand Eastman municipal golf course in Rochester, New York, the first of several projects he did in association with the work relief programs of President Franklin D. Roosevelt's New Deal. To Jones's right in this picture (published in 1934 in the Rochester Journal-American) *is local sportswriter Dick Trabold. To Jones's left stands Patrick J. Slavin, the director of parks for the city of Rochester. The newspaper's caption to the photo reads: "The remodeled links will be one of the picturesque courses in America."*

The November 1932 election of Franklin D. Roosevelt as the 32nd president of the United States proved enormously helpful to the career of Robert Trent Jones. FDR's New Deal provided relief for the poor and unemployed and funded a great many public works projects, not just buildings, highways, bridges, and parks, but also public golf courses. Beginning in 1933, through the efforts of the Civil Works Administration, Civilian Conservation Corps, and Works Progress Administration, some six hundred golf courses were built or improved across the nation at a cost of more than $15 million (in WPA funding alone) and roughly another $3 million contributed by local governments. Most of the labor for the golf courses came from the relief rolls and was therefore done by hand with simple tools rather than with machinery driven by gasoline or steam. But "competent golf architects" were required to direct the construction work, some of which could be quite intricate.

No American golf course architect took advantage of these New Deal programs more than the young Robert Trent Jones, who hustled about various government offices at the state and local levels explaining just what a "competent" golf architect did and what expertise he uniquely had to offer. Jones sold those governments on the role that golf course development could play in the nation's economic recovery, and he took charge of a number of the projects while also volunteering his services as an adviser to the WPA itself. Without Jones's efforts, the New Deal would have still brought forth a major program of public golf course construction, but it is impossible to imagine Jones's career ever becoming as successful as it did—or perhaps even surviving the Depression—without New Deal assistance.

Even before Roosevelt's election, Jones was thinking about how politicians might "prime the pump" for some of his projects, pursuing "influential political contacts" who could help him get them off the ground. In the summer of 1932 he wrote a letter to the City of Rochester decrying the sorry state of the municipal golf course in Durand Eastman Park on the city's Lake Ontario waterfront. When after a few weeks he got no reply, Jones made an appointment with Patrick Slavin, Rochester's director of the bureau of parks. As Jones later told the story, he unadroitly got right to the point: The Durand Eastman golf course was an awful mess, he told Slavin, largely because it was designed by a greenkeeper and not an architect. "Your golf course is not very good, and I know what needs to be done to fix it." Slavin, who was riding a crest of civic good favor for leading a popular expansion of the city's zoo at Seneca Park (to include a Bengal tiger, a leopard, a jaguar, two kangaroos, and a white polar bear), was in no mood for such abrupt criticism, and he threw Jones out of his office.

Stung by the reproach, Jones related the story to his good friend, forty-year-old Harold Clapp, a wealthy local businessman whom Jones had gotten to know while building two new greens at Rochester's Locust Hill Country Club; Clapp was a member there, and also at the golf club at Sodus Bay where Jones had been pro. Back in 1921, Harold Clapp had launched what became a $300 million business selling baby food. His wife had become ill, and it fell to Harold to prepare a diet for his young son, who also happened to be sick. Mixing a formula from beef broth, vegetables, and cereal, Clapp created a "soup" on which the child did so well that Harold made it available to friends and then sold it through drug stores; the Clapp recipe became the first commercially prepared baby food in the United States. By the early 1930s, Clapp's Baby Foods were available nationwide and featured a line of nearly forty different food items. Well respected as the oldest name in baby food (five years older than Gerber), Clapp's in 1953 became part of Duffy-Mott, the leading U.S. manufacturer of commercially available apple-based products, particularly sauces and juices.

Fourteen years older than Jones, Clapp served as a kind of big brother to Robert, as well as a confidant and advisor. Robert made sure during one of Ione's rare visits to Rochester before they were married that the Clapp family all met her, and was "tickled" to report to Ione "how very much pleased and how much they liked" her.

Upon hearing about Jones's ill-fated meeting with the parks director, Harold Clapp suggested Robert try a different tack—emphasizing how the remodeling of Durand Eastman could give jobs to the city's unemployed. In late July 1932, the federal government would begin offering relief to the nation's jobless through the Emergency Relief and Construction Act (enabled by President Hoover and later adopted and expanded by FDR as part of his New Deal); the State of New York had already acted to create relief jobs months earlier. The unemployment problem in New York was as critical as in any state in the Union, with nearly every city reporting unprecedented numbers of able-bodied men without work. Governor Roosevelt had created the Temporary Emergency Relief Administration in October 1931, with an initial appropriation of $20 million in emergency relief for the unemployed. By tying the golf course work to a public works initiative, Clapp advised Jones, the golf architect could make a far more compelling case for remodeling Durand Eastman than by just calling it a bad layout.

The conversation with Clapp got Jones's mind churning. What he needed was to devise a comprehensive argument that did more than justify the remodeling of a single Rochester golf course; if he could provide a thorough and compelling rationale for building more municipal golf courses across America, he stood a reasonable chance of grabbing some of those design jobs for himself.

As election campaigning grew hot and heavy in the autumn of 1932, Jones got busy writing. He began his manifesto by explaining how golf in America was no longer just a rich man's sport but was becoming a game for the masses:

> The number of those playing the game of golf is growing by leaps and bounds, and will continue to grow. The inevitable shortening of the work week will increase the demand upon municipalities to construct public golf courses. In the past, the inadequacy of municipal golf facilities and the prohibitive cost of private clubs have limited the enjoyment of the game by the lower salaried and wage earning men and women. By the construction of municipal golf courses, the game is brought within the means of the average citizen.

Jones elaborated three main reasons why building a municipal golf course made for an "ideal project for work-for-relief labor":

1. It is self-supporting and quickly self-liquidating.
2. As much as 90% of the construction cost of an average golf course can be eliminated by using the labor of those whom the municipality must support in any case.
3. The permanence, the continuous tangible evidence of consideration for the taxpayers, and the fact that the course is

self-supporting and self-liquidating, give such a project genuine appeal to municipal governments.

In support of his reasons, Jones added that "several far-sighted municipalities," such as Philadelphia and New York City, were considering "taking advantage of the opportunity afforded by the present crisis to use work-for-relief labor for the construction of public golf courses." Knowing that politicians, commissioners, and other government officials would demand to see dollar figures for the cost of building a golf course, Jones offered:

The total cost of the construction of a first-class, eighteen hole golf course depends upon the contour of the land, the condition of the soil, such as hardpan, shale, or swamps, and obstructions, such as rock, trees, etc. Where machine methods are used as far as practicable, and labor is paid in cash, the average cost of the construction work varies between $50,000 and $90,000. If hand labor is used as far as practicable, this cost would be between $75,000 and $125,000. These figures do not include the cost of land. However, as about 90% of these latter costs are for direct labor, this amount would be saved by using the unemployed, who would otherwise receive equivalent relief without any return to the municipalities. By using this labor, the approximate cost for each eighteen hole golf course would be between $11,500 and $15,500, which would cover all material (grass seed, fertilizer, drainage tile, water pipes, etc.), architects' fees, and experienced construction supervision. Instead of using work-for-relief merely to beautify land generally by minor grubbing and trimming, this project produces a self-liquidating, park-like beauty of value to the life of the community, and a permanent monument to the far-sightedness of the municipal leaders.

Jones identified four ways by which municipalities could obtain the use of land suitable for a golf course:

1. Use of park land.
2. The interest of one or more public-minded persons may be enlisted to donate property or to give its use for this purpose.
3. Real estate developers may be glad to lease the land for a term of years at a nominal rental. Among the advantages thus gained by

them would be (a) a saving of taxes until a more promising time for development, and (b) the advantage that a golf course would afford in the development of nearby real estate owned by the same persons. In either case, nominal rental can be easily earned by the golf course. The development of adjacent property will increase the tax receipts of the municipality.

4. Long-term lease, with or without option of purchase.

The final section of the manifesto was critically important to Jones. It began: "The design and construction of a golf course is a highly specialized type of work to ensure that the course will have the popularity to make it a financial success." For the course to emerge as "a monument rather than a makeshift," it was essential that the course be designed and its construction supervised by an experienced golf architect. A layman, even if he was an experienced greenkeeper or golf professional, could not visualize "the latent possibilities of available land in its natural state." On the other hand, if a "proper golf architect" could be given his choice of 110 to 140 acres, he could "correlate the many possibilities of the land" and turn his creative vision into a golf course of "outstanding caliber— one which will give real and individual interest to the players."

Armed with his manifesto, Jones was ready to approach Rochester City Hall, overwrought though it was with the coming election. On October 13, 1932, Jones got a brief meeting with Charles S. Owen, the mayor of Rochester. Mayor Owen, a Republican stalwart who was running—as it turned out unsuccessfully—for state comptroller, only had a few minutes for Jones, but their meeting went well. "Oh, my darling," he told Ione, "I have just seen Mayor Owen. An East Rochester leader who is the commissioner of schools and a nice gentlemanly sort of man took me in and gave me a peach of an introduction. He said that I was an East Rochester boy that had made good (doesn't know I'm broke!), that I knew my business and that I was a good well liked boy. Then I discussed the proposition with Owen. He thought that it sounded feasible and should be done and that he would discuss it with Harry Bareham, the chairman of the Republican Party in Monroe County. He told me to come back in a couple weeks. The mayor had seen Banff. Oh dearest, pray for the week to bring success!" In a letter to Ione five days later, Jones added: "Darling, I do like the looks of the city proposition. Nothing, of course, is sure, but I couldn't have had much better luck up to this point. Now for the final closing. These are really awfully tough times to get any work done, but God is going to help us get this. I feel sure he will." When "a couple weeks" later came, Jones tried to see Owen a second time. "I tried to see the mayor," he wrote Ione, "but he was so busy he couldn't see me. He is worked to death and in a tough election battle himself. . . . Being political it's all long and drawn out, with much red tape, and the additional handicap of everyone being more interested in the election than golf courses. But it doesn't really look bad. If I were only able to get one job . . . I am trying so hard to get this work. Surely God will help us."

When the Democrats swept to victory in November, Jones told Ione, "I don't feel the election will effect [sic] my political ventures here, dearest. I intend going right back at them on Monday. It will be great if I can put it over." What Jones discovered, though, when he went "right back at them," was that "They are having an awful time in the city politics over the budget. So I can't approach them until after it blows over. It just seems to be one thing after another. I do wish that conditions would hurry and turn toward the bright side."

Having a lame-duck Republican mayor in your corner after an overwhelming Democratic victory hardly promised success, Jones realized, but he felt that any favorable view in City Hall about Durand Eastman would still be a big plus and make it that much harder for parks director Slavin to stonewall him. On November 25, Jones had a meeting in the office of C. Arthur Poole, Rochester's city manager. Backing him at the meeting were Harold Clapp and Samuel Clarence Steele, a fifty-eight-year-old Rochester investment broker who had also met Jones through golf. (Clapp, Steele, and Poole were close friends.) That evening Robert wrote Ione: "Mr. Steele and Mr. Clapp went with me to see the City Manager. He liked the idea and said he might go down with us to see the Mayor. . . . This job will become a reality sometime, I am sure. If it would only hurry up! Politics is a slow-moving vehicle."

With political support for his proposition seemingly well in the making, Jones felt it was time to bring his case to the public. On December 9, Jones went in for a talk with Fay Blanchard, the managing editor at the Rochester *Journal-American* whom Jones had approached about writing golf articles for the paper. (Earlier in 1932, Jones had actually started writing occasional stories on golf for the paper for a few dollars per article.) Jones told the editor how parks director Slavin had thrown him out of his office and how he had subsequently written out a rationale for why the city should use work-for-relief labor to remodel the golf course. Blanchard was more than sympathetic, because he had played Durand Eastman and also didn't like it. "If bison played golf that would be a grand course for them," Blanchard would later comment in a published editorial. "The hills are so sharp and steep that even the hardiest players become winded by the mountain climbing." Blanchard told Jones to give the *Journal-American's* sports editor his manifesto and any other material he had about his proposed golf course redesign.

A little over three weeks after Jones's visit to Blanchard, a letter to the editor ran in the *Journal-American* that was signed by a William R. Glavin of Rochester. Identifying himself only as "a frequent user of the Durand-Eastman Park golf course," Glavin urged "immediate action" in the matter of modifying the lakeside links:

> Rochester has a real opportunity to obtain a fair return on some of the money that is going for welfare work if it would put to work the men who would be willing to give their labor in return for the help they are receiving. There is work that can be done at Durand-Eastman Park. . . . Within its boundaries is an eighteen-hole golf course which with some modification could be made into one of the best courses in this part of the country. . . . [M]en who are receiving aid from the city could be put to work on the course at Durand-Eastman Park under the supervision of a competent architect and lengthen the course by using acreage that could be reclaimed with but little expense. The fees paid by the players make the course self sustaining and it is not a burden to the taxpayer. A project of this kind would give work to a number of men and would be of permanent value to the city. If the situation is carefully canvassed by the City Manager he will see the advantage of immediate action.

Who exactly the letter writer William R. Glavin was and what relationship, if any, he had with Jones, Fay Blanchard, Blanchard's sports editor, Harold Clapp, Samuel Steele, or anyone else friendly to Jones's proposition is unknown, but the contents of his letter were so close to what Jones presented in his manifesto— particularly the emphasis on the need for a "competent architect"—that Glavin's letter could not have materialized out of thin air. Seeing the letter published in the paper, a jubilant Jones wrote Ione: "I haven't told you of all the excitement that has been going on regarding the city work, because I am tired of building up your hopes and then letting them down. I wanted something concrete to tell you. I had wanted to say that I had put it over. People are doing so much for us: the papers with their campaign, Mr. Steele and Mr. Clapp seeing the big shots on my behalf and urging them as if it was their own deal. They are going back again the first part of the week if nothing happens. They want me to have good news for you, too."

The following week a second letter about Durand Eastman appeared in the *Journal-American*. This one was signed by a man named W. P. Gilbert, who also strongly advocated changes at the local golf course—and in doing so once again stressed the importance of putting the project "under competent supervision" and the "direction of a reliable architect." In his letter, Gilbert (whose precise identity, like Glavin's, is unknown), labeled several of the holes at Durand Eastman as dangerous in their present form (a few holes crisscrossed, and several landing areas for tee shots ran menacingly close to one another), a point that Jones himself made in his November 25 discussion with city manager Poole. In publishing Gilbert's letter, the sports editor added his own voice to the cause of the letter writer: "This department is heartily in favor of needed changes in the Durand-Eastman golf course, changes which could be made without incurring an expenditure not already planned. It has been suggested that unemployed men could be given work at the Durand links this winter and paid from the appropriation the city has made for relief projects."

Before the year 1932 ended, another long letter about Durand Eastman came in to the *Journal-American* and was published. It read:

> I have followed with interest the letters recently published in your column relative to modifying the golf course at Durand-Eastman Park and am surprised that this movement has not received greater support. For months the city employed a large force of men grading and re-grading the land occupied by a blast furnace at Charlotte [which had been operated by the Rochester Iron Manufacturing Co. in a northern part of the city, where the Genesee River flows into Lake Ontario]. This work has long since been completed. What are these men doing today in exchange for the relief they are receiving? Let us put them back on the job, this time on a project that will not only transform waste park land, adding materially to the beauty of Durand-Eastman Park, but which will also add sufficient yardage to the golf links to make it a championship course.... Money must be spent for relief, why not have something to show for it?"

This letter was unsigned and attributed by the editor only to "one of the regular patrons of the Durand-Eastman golf course." But one can infer from Jones's letters to Ione that he actually wrote the letter—and that he was not unacquainted either with William R. Glavin or W. P. Gilbert, the earlier letter writers. In one fashion or another, Jones, perhaps through the influence of Harold Clapp or Samuel Steele, was responsible directly or indirectly for all three letters.

The Rochester park director smelled a rat. As Jones recalled many years later, "Slavin called me into his office and said, 'You little son of a bitch, how do I get the newspapers off my back?'" Jones "quite innocently" replied, "Well, let's do it right this time. Let's get the ball rolling to get our golf course improved." Calming down, Slavin agreed. Besides the inflammatory newspaper stories, Slavin by this time had also heard from the mayor's office and from the city manager about Jones's proposition; he had also received a note favoring it from Harry Bareham, the Monroe County Republican leader. Now that relief work was an essential part of the proposal and now that the state and city were actively supporting public works, the parks director saw that the golf course project made good sense. Slavin warned Jones that he couldn't get more than $1,500 from the city council for an architect's fee, to which Jones replied that he "couldn't live on that for a year." Wasn't there some way to get more money? Slavin didn't think so, but he told Jones that he would look into it.

On February 8, 1933, Rochester's relief board passed the golf course project, which meant, as Jones told Ione, "that the labor is taken care of. Now we'll find a way to get mine. It will be much easier now."

But it wasn't that much easier—it actually took another five long and anxious months before the city deal came all the way through for Jones. One big concern for Jones was that Democrats were now in charge of the city, with Percival D. Oviatt replacing Owen as mayor and Theodore C. Briggs replacing city manager Poole. Ever the amphibian, Jones made sure that his "friends of influence" got him some "good Democratic introductions," but there were moments when he became "pessimistic for the prospects of the city. . . . This darn city job has me all on edge. It's so near and yet so far. I wish that it would get settled."

In June 1933 Jones submitted his prospectus for Durand Eastman's redesign. His plan, which was submitted officially on behalf of Thompson-Jones, Inc., Golf and Landscape Architects, 311-312 Wilder Building, Rochester, N.Y., read:

By lengthening the course from its present length of 4600 yards to a standard length of 6200, it will be possible to play 150 more people a day. The additional revenue from this increased play would self-liquidate the total job in approximately five years. The cost of future operation would be but little more than the present course, as there will be the same number of greens and tees, but with 20 additional acres of fairway to cut once a week, an additional half-day with a mower. The golf course being self-maintaining it would be no further burden to the City. It will beautify 20 additional acres of park land which is at present an eye sore. The present course is of a mountain-goat type, having many severe climbs which greatly tax the women and elderly men players. Nine of the eleven severe climbs will be eliminated and two decreased. . . . The course at present has nine short holes, holding up play and requiring 4 to 4½ hours to play a round. The lengthened course would cut the playing time to 3 to 3½ hours. The changes will not interfere with play or decrease the present revenue during the period of construction because the major changes are in the adjacent valley and those that are changed on the present course are not in the direct line of play. It will be merely a question of changing over when the new layout is ready for play.

Jones closed by repeating what had become his standard declaration of the need for a "competent architect": "The suggested changes will change the course from one of mediocre value to one of the finest public courses in the country, because the terrain at Durand-Eastman lends itself to interesting golf holes if designed under the direction of a competent architect."

For his architect's fee, Jones asked for $2,000.

The new Democratic regime knew that Jones had instigated the project, but Briggs, the city manager, wanted to know why, of all the golf architects who might be interested in remodeling Durand Eastman, Jones was the best for the job—and worth a fat $2,000. Briggs wanted to see Jones's credentials.

Given everything he had done to get the project off the ground, Robert was exasperated that he now had to prove his worth. In his answer to Briggs on July 10, 1933, he wrote, "The creation of a reputed architect is the very least of the project," Jones enjoined. "On rugged terrain such as Durand-Eastman twice the amount asked for could be spent in incompetent hands and still prove dissatisfactory." The $2,000 fee was "not extravagant. . . . Our figure during normal times would be three times the price asked. The services of any of the five of the countries [sic] leading architects, of which we are considered one, would greatly exceed this figure." (With the connection to Stanley Thompson, it was not an exaggeration for Jones to classify his business as one of the top five golf architect firms in the country; without the association with Thompson, it would have been a gross exaggeration.) In pressing his case for the need for a professional golf architect, Jones made some exaggerated claims about his own record as a golf course designer:

> Just as a carpenter without knowledge of seamanship would not be considered a designer of boats, an engineer, landscape architect or green layer cannot be expected to design a golf course. A competent golf architect should have a knowledge of the true profession mentioned above, also he must have a sound knowledge of the game of golf and understanding of the limitations of every type of golf. He must also have an endowed flair to create, and a knowledge of soils, furthermore a good deal of experience. I am certain that no one in the present employee [sic] of the city has this training. I have had this training and I have been associated with laying out many outstanding courses throughout the country, and have a reputation as being one of the leaders in this field.

He took five more paragraphs to describe the key elements of his design process: from the work needed to create a brand-new 18-hole routing through Durand Eastman's "rugged terrain," to the sketching of working drawings for all eighteen greens, to regular visits to the property for overseeing the construction and the growing in of all the new grass. "As a golf architect associated with a national reputation," Jones concluded, "I am naturally desirous of doing the work of my home city, being the only architect with the necessary training. I feel that I am justified in receiving this commission, especially since the fee is nominal. I can assure you that when the course is finished, no further attention will be necessary at a future date, and the course will be as fine as any municipal course in the country."

Briggs still had concerns. Above all, he worried that Jones, being such an outstanding golfer, would make the course "too difficult" for the average municipal hacker. Jones did his best to counter: "As you know, a municipal course must be designed quite differently from that of a private club. Practically all traps must be eliminated so that play will not be delayed, and maintenance will not run high. At Emerick Park, a municipal course near Fulton, New York, where I remodeled five greens, only one trap was used. This was used in a short hole which otherwise would have been uninteresting. If I am fortunate enough to obtain the commission for this work, it is not my intention to make the course hazardous."

During the first week of August, the Rochester city council authorized Briggs to give Jones the Durand Eastman job. As Slavin had warned, though, the councilmen would only allow $1,500 for Jones's fee. That was just not sufficient compensation for a "competent architect," Jones explained. Something had to be worked out.

Perhaps Jones got the idea from Harold Clapp, Samuel Steele, or one of his other savvy political friends: If the city council couldn't pay him the money he wanted as an architect's fee, perhaps the City of Rochester could pay him the equivalent by tapping into some of the emergency relief funding that was coming the city's way. The only real asset that had come out of all of his work at Midvale was ownership of a small turfgrass nursery lying on the periphery of the golf course. If the city council would only authorize a $1,500 commission, Jones asked Slavin if the parks director could buy grass for the city parks under the new federal relief program established by President Roosevelt. Slavin thought he probably could, to which Robert replied, "Then how about you buy $8,000 worth of grass?" Not spending $1,500 of city funds was an idea that Briggs liked, and so did the city council. So the deal was struck, one that worked out very nicely for all parties involved.

A jubilant Jones wrote to Ione, "It will be another fine course and a tribute to my architecture. Oh, it's really grand to be working again, doing something really creative and making money for our marriage. It's all I think of lately." In fact, he urged that they get married the following month, which was thinking far too optimistically for the sociable Miss Davis—and greatly rushing what would become eight months of wedding planning by the bride-to-be and her family. But Robert's enthusiasm could not be contained: "It won't be long before you're a mother, too. I'll be so nervous, we'll both be so proud and the baby will be the nicest ever."

Jones's remodeling of the golf course at Durand Eastman proved to be a great success but it hardly came off without a hitch. "The area in which I was to build the course was pretty bad," Robert would later recall, "virtually a swamp." No sooner had construction started than the seriousness of the drainage problem became known to parks director Slavin, who straightaway called Jones into his office. "This project is *your* doing," he charged, "and they're calling it 'Slavin's Folly'! The city engineers say there is no way on God's earth you can build a golf course on that property. It's quicksand."

Jones reassured Slavin that he could manage it. Just to be sure, though, he was calling in one of his professors at Cornell, B. B. Robb of the Department of Rural Engineering, who had taught Jones about drainage, to help him with the problem. Slavin came to the construction site on the day of Robb's visit expressly to hear the expert's verdict. The Cornell professor told Slavin, "Let the kid alone. He's doing all right." Essentially, Jones solved the problem by laying down some 6,000 feet of drainage tiles and making sure the landing areas for golf shots did not fall in the low areas.

The difficulty of the drainage solution at Durand Eastman was something Jones never forgot. "In more than a half century of building golf courses," the architect later remembered, "that was one of the hardest jobs I've had, at least until I encountered Mauna Kea thirty years later, on Hawaii's Big Island. But I built it, and the course drew raves from the local players and press. That gave me the experience, as well as the confidence, to build some pretty good golf courses on some ugly pieces of land throughout my career."

The new golf course at Durand Eastman did in fact receive "rave" reviews; better yet, those reviews brought out golfers: 6,970 of them in the thirty days following the course's opening in mid-September, some three thousand more golfers than had played the previous month. Several letters came in to city manager Briggs and parks director Slavin commending them on their roles in Jones's redesign. "The player always has the opportunity to shoot for the green," one of the letters applauded. "There are plenty of traps, but they are so placed as to catch the poor shot only. Moreover, the course is so laid out that the average player has equal opportunity with the advanced player. It is a wonderful improvement over the old course." Slavin was even more pleased by the compliments he got. "I write to congratulate you, Mr. Slavin," one letter offered, "upon the idea of utilizing the waste lands of this beautiful park and, what's more important, the work given to unemployed men." Years later, Jones reflected, "Slavin was impressed enough to offer me a job as assistant director of parks. 'You'll never make any money as a golf course architect,' he said. But I turned him down. I wanted to build golf courses."

It was not the Durand Eastman contract nor was it New Deal funding for any other of Jones's golf designs that finally persuaded Howard Davis to hand his daughter over to the young architect for a wedding ceremony that would take place at St. Luke's Episcopal Church in Montclair, New Jersey, on Friday, May 11, 1934. The use of public monies and welfare relief workers for the construction of a golf course was not something that Ione's staunchly Republican father endorsed. The clinching commission was Jones's getting the job to lay out an 18-hole course at Colgate University in Hamilton, New York; Ione's father considered that to be "dignified work." The university golf course was to be built entirely with private funds—and Howard Davis liked the sound of that. What impressed Ione's father even more was that his future son-in-law had managed to bring in one of the world's greatest golfers as co-designer for the proposed Colgate golf course.

In the early 1930s no golfer was winning more championships than the diminutive but powerful Gene Sarazen. In 1932 Sarazen won both the U.S. and British Opens. The following summer he won the PGA Championship, his third PGA win and his sixth major title overall. Honing his opportunism, Jones saw in Sarazen—whose nickname was "The Squire"—a tremendous opportunity to connect his own budding career in golf to one of the world's greatest, most respected, and best-liked golfers.

Prior to the Colgate project, Jones knew Sarazen casually from the tournament golf he himself had played back in the late '20s, and Robert always chatted with the genial golf champion from downstate New York whenever their paths crossed. In several respects, the two men were very similar. Born in 1902, Sarazen was only four years older than Jones. Both men came from working-class, immigrant families. Sarazen's given name was Eugenio Saraceni; his Italian father, who had emigrated from Rome, was a carpenter, just like Jones's. Both men grew up in the Empire State, Sarazen in Westchester County. Both came to golf through the caddie ranks. Both dropped out of high school. Both stood less than five feet seven inches tall. Neither wrote letters with correct spelling or punctuation, though, in Sarazen's case, deficiencies were more glaring. Both had well-educated wives who helped to teach their husbands the "better side of life." Both produced lasting, even epic, careers that landed them in the World Golf Hall of Fame. They died only a year apart: Sarazen in 1999 at age ninety-seven, Jones in 2000 at age ninety-three. For nearly seventy years, the two men remained good friends.

In the autumn of 1933, following Sarazen's PGA victory, Jones got the idea to partner with Sarazen on the design of the Colgate course. It was not a novel idea, as Alister MacKenzie was then partnering with Bobby Jones on the high-profile design of what became Augusta National. Architect Jones hoped that, just as the golden boy from Atlanta sought to build his ideal links in his home state, Sarazen, too, would delight in building his own ideal layout in New York. "I went to Gene and asked if he would like to help design his ideal golf course, just as Bobby was doing in Georgia," Robert later remembered. Always ready to match his golfing skills against Bobby Jones, Sarazen liked the idea of "matching up with Jones" again—this time with *two* of them—and agreed to come up and take a look at the Colgate property.

Jones wanted Sarazen to come to Colgate as soon as possible, as Dr. George Barton Cutten, the university president,* wanted to throw him a dinner. "Perhaps he may confer upon you a degree," Jones seriously teased. "Who knows? Maybe you'll be given the title 'Doctor of International Golf'!"

Before Robert could get everything ready for a Sarazen visit to Colgate, Gene left for Florida, where he would spend the winter of 1933–34 as the guest of the Miami-Biltmore Hotel in Coral Gables. It wasn't easy for Jones to get him to make the trek north. "I am sorry not to have been able to come up to Colgate," Sarazen wrote to Jones on November 26. "You know its [sic] a long trip coming up their [sic]. The expenses will be pretty high. I'd rather have you write me and tell me more about everything. The weather down here is perfect." To which Robert replied:

> I will endeavor to explain the whole thing in a nutshell. Colgate is ready to sign. . . . I know that a satisfactory understanding can be reached for all concerned. Offhand (and the thought is all mine) I feel that it would be worth about $5,000.00 to you in actual cash. Many thousand more from the proposition indirectly. . . . You ought to realize that the publicity from this venture will be primarily credited to you. It will start a ballyhoo during these dull winter months that will make your eight

---

* Naturally Jones became very interested in cultivating the support of Colgate University president George Barton Cutten (1874–1962), especially after he learned that Dr. Cutten was Canadian, born in Nova Scotia, and was a cousin of millionaire Canadian businessman Arthur W. Cutten, for whom Cutten Fields Golf Club in Guelph, Ontario, a Chick Evans layout that Stanley Thompson redesigned in the 1920s, had been named. In a letter to Jones dated January 18, 1934, Thompson responded to Jones's inquiry about the Cutten family: "In connection with Arthur Cutten, I met him in Guelph the year he let us look after his course when Chick Evans seemed to be falling down on the matter, and I know his brothers in Toronto and Guelph fairly well." Letter in Colgate Files, JP, CUA.

inch cup sensation of last winter seem minature [sic] and this dream will come true. Furthermore the association with a university of Colgate's standing will be elevating. It has dignity. Some of the wealthiest and most distinguished men in the country will be connected with this course. . . . Thousands of Colgate men will become your booster. You can't afford to pass it up. That is no bull.

Sarazen must have been convinced. The second week of January 1934 he took a train from Miami to New York City. As a big event had been planned for Sarazen on the Colgate campus, Jones was taking no chances. He met him in New York City and rode with him the rest of the way up to Hamilton. Suffering from an inflamed appendix, Robert put off his surgery until after he could get Sarazen to the university.

A visit by a U.S. Open, British Open, and PGA champion was a major event for the snug little campus in Hamilton, a village of less than three thousand souls and barely a thousand students deep in the Chenango Valley, halfway between Syracuse and Cooperstown. The university turned it into a gala event, highlighted by a speech by Sarazen in Memorial Chapel, the campus's largest auditorium.

Giving speeches was not a forte of the champion golfer. In front of a large crowd of college students—most of them from well-to-do families and almost none of them with swarthy complexions like his own—Gene Sarazen, national golf champion, for a moment reverted into Eugenio Saraceni, son of a poor Italian immigrant. On the ride to the campus, Jones could see Gene was getting very nervous. When they got to the hall, a standing-room-only crowd of about six hundred students was waiting for them. Bill Reid, the director of athletics, introduced Sarazen and the audience gave him a big hand. Shyly, Gene stood up but all he said was, "Fellows, I'm happy to be here," and then sat down. Jones rose quickly to help his friend: "Now, Gene, why don't you tell the audience about your match with Walter Hagen." As Jones later recalled the incident: "So Gene started telling the story, and soon he was at ease, strutting around like Hagen, mimicking him." Robert asked him another question, and another, until Sarazen "had the students sitting on the edge of their chairs for about an hour." When the two men got ready to leave, a beaming Sarazen whispered to Robert, "Listen, I'm going to do this at all the colleges." As it turned out, he ended up speaking to about twenty of them.

That evening, following a local VIP dinner hosted by President Cutten, Reid, who was also the town's mayor, told Sarazen and Jones they had the job if they wanted it. Soon an elated Jones was writing to Stanley Thompson: "It ought to be one of the biggest ventures we have had the good fortune to obtain. Working with the university gives the project dignity. Sarazen gives it color. Both will make it publicity of national scope. We will assure it is a good job." Thompson answered: "It sounds good. It will certainly be one of our best jobs." Showing his generous spirit, Thompson continued: "I realize that this should be an all American thing, and you will have the good opportunity of getting some favourable publicity for yourself out of this course. I will be glad to work behind the scenes with you, but your name should be brought to the front."

An article entitled "Sarazen Starts Drive for College Golf Courses" appeared in the next issue of *Golfdom* magazine, which was the golf industry's first (founded in 1927) and, in 1934, still only, business journal, based in Chicago. Unfortunately, the publicity was not exactly what Jones wanted, as it focused almost solely on Sarazen. Robert was especially concerned by *Golfdom* saying that Sarazen was not only committed to developing college golf across the country but "already has pending negotiations with other universities covering the construction of golf courses." That could be a major problem, Jones knew, because Colgate officials thought that what Jones and Sarazen were proposing was a one-of-a-kind links (like Bobby Jones's Augusta National), one that would become Sarazen's home course. Of greater concern to Robert personally was that Sarazen was being presented by the media as the chief designer of the Colgate golf course, and that Sarazen, too, would be supervising the course's construction.[†]

Annoyed by this overblown focus on Sarazen, Jones wrote a letter to Herb Graffis, *Golfdom*'s editor and founder, pointing out the need for a few corrections. "Sarazen is expressing his ideas in the Colgate course in the same manner that Bobby Jones did at Augusta," Jones explained to Graffis. "We [Thompson-

---

† The *Golfdom* article appeared in the February 1934 issue and was written by Leonard F. Wilbur. "Several unique features will be included in the new course," Wilbur's article stated. "Aside from the fact that the course will be the first one of its kind laid out by Sarazen, every one of the 18 holes will have a twin somewhere in the United States. In other words, Mr. Sarazen will choose his favorite 18 holes from different courses, and include them in the new course." Such a journalistic description clearly made the role of Robert Trent Jones in the course design secondary to Sarazen's.

Jones, Inc.] are commissioned in the same capacity that the late Doctor MacKenzie was occupied at the Augusta course."‡ Understanding Jones's concerns, Graffis answered sensitively:

> Thank you for giving me the dope on Sarazen's connection with the Colgate job. There has been quite a little speculation about this and I am very glad to learn exactly what the conditions are. I have a very strong admiration for Gene personally and for his knowledge of golf but I think he is a hell of a long way from being a golf architect. That line-up that is in effect ought to work out in great shape for all concerned. I think it's a tip-off for other pros who can move in on jobs, particularly CWA and PWA enterprises, to effect an arrangement with you so that a golf course of lasting substantial interest can be produced.

In truth, despite the publicity, no detailed contract for the Colgate course had yet been finalized. The university's financing of the course, which Bill Reid thought could be taken care of rather easily through donations from alumni, was not panning out. Meanwhile, Sarazen had flown down to South America to play a long series of golf matches. Upon his return, the golfer again made Colgate officials nervous by talking with the mayor of New York, Fiorello H. La Guardia (another son of Italian immigrant parents), and other city officials about how he wanted to help them build no less than a half dozen courses in the greater NYC metropolitan area.

Whether the blame falls on Sarazen for alarming Colgate alumni or just generally on the dark days of the Depression, the money needed to build the Colgate golf course did not materialize in 1934 or the first half of 1935. The last hope to get the course built was to acquire sufficient funds from the government through a proposal to the Works Progress Administration.

That proposal was sent to the WPA on August 15, 1935; significantly, it was submitted by Bill Reid in his capacity as Hamilton's mayor, with no indication at all that he was also Colgate's athletic director. Out of necessity, the golf course

---

‡ Dr. Alister MacKenzie (born 1870) died at his home in Santa Cruz, California, on January 6, 1934, less than four months before the inaugural Masters Tournament (then known as the Augusta National Invitational Tournament) on the Augusta National golf course he had co-designed with Bobby Jones. Details of Robert Trent Jones's associations with MacKenzie will be discussed in Chapter 4.

project had changed fundamentally from its original concept, from a golf course to be developed and owned by a private university and designed by golf champion Gene Sarazen as his ideal layout into a municipal golf course serving the Village of Hamilton. Sarazen's name was not mentioned in the proposal, not once, and Robert Trent Jones's appeared only once, in conjunction with the cost estimates built into the proposal. "If the project is approved," read the last item in the proposal, "a golf architect will be retained. . . . The enclosed cost estimates are based upon the figures of Robert Trent Jones, Golf Architect, who arrived at them from experience in building more than one hundred golf courses, five of which have been municipal courses with relief labor." (One imagines that Jones was responsible for the phrase "more than one hundred golf courses," which was a huge exaggeration, the kind that would become typical of Jones over his long career.) The exact details of the project's demise are not known, but the WPA, after awarding the Village of Hamilton its WPA project in November 1935, soon reversed its position and took the award away. The stated reason for the recall was that the village was already going to be receiving "a great amount of help in the building of the new State highway, the Federal Post Office and a sewer line." Jones's own explanation of the project's downfall (which was the same as Mayor Bill Reid's) was that "The Colgate golf course, which was to be built with WPA labor, was shot down because one of the professors complained to Washington, and there was no other money." That professor was J. Melbourne Shortliffe, a "free enterprise" and anti–New Deal stalwart in Colgate's economics department. FDR's New Deal had numerous strong critics on the political right like Shortliffe, and the WPA—nicknamed "We Piddle Around" by its opponents—drew much of the scorn.[§] Whoever the perpetrator was, the Colgate golf course was dead, at least for the time being. Between 1955 and 1958, a new nine-hole layout did get built for the campus, and Robert Trent Jones designed it, keeping the name of the campus's original course (Seven Oaks) and using some elements of the hole routings that he had drawn up in 1935 and filed away for safekeeping. Then, in 1964-65, Jones ex-

---

§ In the late 1930s and early 1940s J. Melbourne Shortliffe made a series of broadcast radio talks defending his version of "the American economic way" on a program sponsored by General Electric called the *Farm Forum*. One of his talks asked the question, "Will Democracy and Free Enterprise Survive?" (Aug. 22, 1941), another was entitled "Politics and Economic Freedom Must Not Be Taken for Granted" (Sept. 8, 1944). Professor Shortliffe would come to serve as the head of the Colgate economics department, and an undergraduate prize is still awarded annually by that department in his name. He retired from Colgate in 1947 and passed away in December 1954.

panded the course into a full eighteen. "Colgate University Seven Oaks Golf Club" turned out to be a wonderful links, and a very challenging one. In 1977 the national collegiate championship was conducted on the course, with the University of Houston winning the event (the team included future Masters champion Fred Couples) and Southern Cal's Scott Simpson (1987 U.S. Open champion) taking individual honors. Today, Colgate's golf course is ranked by different golf magazines on their lists of "best campus courses," "best public golf courses in New York," and "best courses you can play." Still, one wonders what the golf course would have been like if Jones had designed the course based on Sarazen's "ideal" eighteen holes, as originally planned.

It wasn't Colgate, but Jones did get started on a New Deal golf course in central New York in 1935—one that got built, flourished from the start, and, most important of all to Jones, made him a substantial amount of money. The location of the golf course was Green Lakes State Park, in Onondaga County near the town of Fayetteville, just east of Syracuse. It was a marvelous piece of ground for golf, with some beautiful land formations, set in a rolling and wooded terrain adjacent to one of the park's larger glacial lakes and its crystal-clear blue-green water.

A golf course already existed at Green Lakes, built right after World War I by Laurie Davidson Cox (1883–1968), a professor of landscape architecture in the New York State College of Forestry at Syracuse University. The problem with his golf course at Green Lakes wasn't that Cox was a poor landscape architect—in fact, he was one of the nation's finest—or that he didn't know or enjoy sports. To the contrary, Cox had played basketball, ice hockey, and lacrosse in college. The problem with Green Lakes was that Professor Cox wasn't a golfer and worse, in Jones's view, "knew nothing about golf." "Cox had built all the holes on a hill," Robert would explain, "and every time you hit a shot the ball would run all the way to the bottom." Having played the course, Jones felt he could improve it greatly just as he had done at Durand Eastman: "I figured I could route the holes around the back of the hill and end up with 18 holes on the flat without using the hill at all." The key to getting the commission this time lay not in politicking with a municipality, but in striking a bargain with the New York State park system—and in central New York that meant swinging a deal with James Evans.

In 1926, thirty-one-year old James Frederick Evans became director of state parks for the New York Central Region, based in Binghamton. Upon returning from service in the Marine Corps in World War I, Evans had graduated from Syracuse University in 1920 with a degree in civil engineering. He then began a career with the state doing highway work in the Department of Public Works. When the state park system was consolidated in 1924, Evans moved to the Long Island Park Commission, where he became a protégé of the highly influential technocrat Robert Moses, the trusted adviser of Governor Al Smith and a man whom historians have called the "best bill drafter in Albany" and the "master builder" of mid-twentieth century New York City. Evans came to serve Moses virtually as his personal aide and troubleshooter. According to Moses, Evans was a "born dyed-in-the-wool boulevardier, wheeler and dealer, especially in dealing with legislative leaders and heads of departments." In 1938, Evans would become director of the entire New York State park system. Evans was also an avid golfer.

Very early in his career Jones realized how important it would be to cultivate a friendship with James Evans, and he did exactly that. In September 1931, Robert wrote to Ione that Evans had written on his behalf to Robert Moses about the Durand Eastman remodeling ("I have had all sorts of letters in to Moses from the biggest people in the State, including Jim Evans. If we don't get this job I won't believe there is such a thing as influence.") By 1935, the two men were exchanging letters regularly, both official and personal, and addressing each other as "Jim" and "Bob."

Early in the spring of 1935, Jones and Evans together visited the Cox-designed golf course at Green Lakes State Park, no doubt at Robert's instigation. "It's a disaster," he told Evans, "but I can lay out a good golf course." Looking out over the site, the parks director asked, "How can you do it?" Walking the property, Robert showed him. "Okay, I can see what you are telling me. You can make some great holes by going back into the woods and avoiding the steep side slopes." I agree with you. But, you know, if I sent a bill for an architect to the

---

¶ Jones later described the construction of the Green Lakes State Park Golf Course as "a striking example of economy in green building, contrasting ideal conditions with those less desirable." This description comes from Jones's 1938 promotional booklet, *Golf Course Architecture* (p. 11): "The upper nine of the course made a loop around the base of a very high hill. The soil was so shallow and the slope such that it was more practical to fill for most of the green construction. A shovel [*author's note:* One assumes Jones meant more than one shovel] and sand trucks were used and finishing touches were applied by teams. The lower nine was on a large, natural shelf some forty feet below the upper nine. The terrain here was ideal, being gently rolling and abounding with natural green sites. In most cases but little work had to be done to make attractive greens, and those greens that needed molding could be done with soil from the immediate area of the green with slip-scrapers. So, on the same property, we had completely contrasting construction problems in creating two separate nines. The greens on the upper nine cost more than double the lower nine, and needed twice the time, yet in the quality of golf they are of equal caliber." No doubt, at the time of his discussion with James

State Board of Directors, they'd knock it out first thing; they'd cut out your fee." Left hand rubbing his chin, the savvy civil servant thought about it as they were walking back to their car. "Tell me, Bob, if I leased the golf course to you for a dollar a year, would you do it in lieu of a fee?" Now Jones had a hand to his chin. "Yes, I would if you do that, but on one condition: isn't there a Civilian Conservation Corps camp nearby? I'll agree to it but you need to get me CCC labor to rebuild the golf course the way I want it." Evans answered, "Okay, I'll do it, but we'll both probably go to jail for it."

Jones's redesigned Green Lakes State Park Golf Course opened in the summer of 1936—it played at par 71 and to a length of 6,212 yards—and was an immediate success. "We were charging green fees of a dollar on weekdays, two dollars on the weekends," Jones remembered. Evans arranged for his Central New York State Park Commission to give Robert "the concession management for the golf course and club house and all appurtenances thereto," which included "all articles sold through these units, including golf supplies and all food and beverages sold in the restaurant" as well as "the income from membership, green fees and locker fees." Jones made a lot of money from the sale of beer and liquor—at the end of the 1936 golf season at Green Lakes he reported to Evans that he had taken in $4,514.97 in alcohol sales and only slightly more than that, $4,578.75, in green fees; by 1940, those figures rose to $7,054.27 and $11,357.75, respectively. "Before long I was making about $10,000 to $12,000 a year out of it, which was a lot of money then." It was "a lot of money," indeed—the equivalent to roughly $160,000 to $190,000 a year in today's dollars; Robert had never made a tenth of that in any year.** With that sort of income, it wouldn't be long before Robert and Ione, now married, could move out of her parents' house in Montclair and buy a home of their own. (While the couple lived with Ione's parents, Jones worked out of their home, but the Davises divorced in 1936. As

---

Evans, Jones could not have been exactly sure how the reconstruction of the golf course would be done.

** It certainly appears from the Jones Papers at Cornell that James Evans in his capacity as "Engineer and Executive Secretary" of the Central New York State Park Commission had also arranged for Jones to hold the concession management for the golf course at Chenango Valley State Park near Binghamton; there is a contract indicating such, dated June 24, 1935, that is signed by Evans and Jones. There is also quite a bit of business correspondence between Evans and Jones about the operation of the golf course. It is curious that Jones never mentioned this apparent fact in any interview conducted with him. He was delighted to talk about the $1-per-year lease deal he made with Evans for the Green Lakes concession, so why not mention this second concession, which was also arranged for Jones at a cost of $1 per year?

Robert related in a March 1937 letter to Stanley Thompson, "the Davis home was broken up almost a year ago, and we had to find a place to live," which turned out to be an apartment at 92 Watchung Avenue in Upper Montclair. By this time Jones had rented a small office space at 6 East 45th Street in Manhattan, which he shared with *The Bermuda Magazine*; coincidentally, Robert and Ione had honeymooned in Bermuda. One advantage that he enjoyed in New York City was that he could visit his father-in-law, who was still an executive with the New York Bell Telephone Company, and "make calls to all my potential customers for free.")

An essential ingredient of Jones's success at Green Lakes was his ingenuity and entrepreneurship. For example, when he realized that golfers finishing their rounds were heading directly to their automobiles in the car park and not stopping in his clubhouse for refreshments, Robert reversed the front and back nines. Now when a foursome played out on what had been the ninth green, they had to walk right past the clubhouse before they could get to their cars and head home. Robert's till filled with cash.

His gumption and go-getter attitude can also be seen in how he promoted the "grand reopening" of Green Lakes in 1936. "I had to publicize the course," Robert later remembered. "So I wrote to the Spalding Company. At the time, Spalding was sending some great golfers—long-hitting Jimmy Thomson, Horton Smith (winner of the first Masters, in 1934), Lawson Little (winner of the 1934 and 1935 U.S. and British Amateurs) and Craig Wood (eventual winner of the 1941 Masters and U.S. Open)—around the country to play exhibitions and promote golf and, of course, sell Spalding golf equipment. I wrote to Spalding and they agreed to have one of the exhibitions at Green Lakes to open the course. I promoted it on area radio stations for a month and a half beforehand, and we got 8,000 to 9,000 people out there to watch. It was the biggest crowd that had ever been to a golf tournament in western or central New York."

The following year Jones decided he needed another exhibition to open the season, so he signed up Gene Sarazen and the young Sam Snead, only twenty-five years old but already making quite a name for himself, to come up to Green Lakes for $100 apiece and play against a couple of the local professionals. According to Jones, Snead and Sarazen "drove up in their own car, paid their own hotel bills, everything, so they didn't have much left at the end of it." When it was over, Robert asked Snead if he would do it again next year, and Sam said, "Okay, but not for what you paid us this time." Robert asked the long-hitting pro from western Virginia what he wanted and he said, "The gate." "You got it!"

Jones answered. Snead and Sarazen did come up the next year, and Jones gave them each $98, to which Snead, who had shot a 2-under-par 69, snorted, "Hey, there were a lot more people out there than that!" Jones replied, "I know, Sam, but we have no fences around the course and most of them were sneaking in without paying. I couldn't stop them."

Green Lakes was a godsend for Jones—it essentially got him through the Depression. (At the end of the decade, Gene Sarazen said to Jones in a letter: "I hope you are very busy. How is that gold mine of yours in Syracuse?")

It seems also to have helped him get through the Second World War. In his autobiographical 1988 book, *Golf's Magnificent Challenge*, Jones wrote: "When the war started, gasoline became so scarce that you couldn't drive anywhere, and golf was a low priority item. So our play dropped at Green Lakes and I decided to give it back to the state." But records in the Jones Papers clearly show that Robert continued to operate Green Lakes right through to the end of the war and beyond.†† Although receipts from the golf course did not earn him as much money directly, on the expense side of the ledger Robert continued to charge a great deal of his travel, hotel, and office expenses to the Green Lakes operation. In 1944, for example, he listed as expenses more than five thousand miles of automobile travel (at six cents a mile), forty days of hotel and meal expenses, and more than a dozen railroad fares. By this time he was living in Montclair, so frequent trips up to Green Lakes may explain the expenses. On the other hand, by the end of 1944, Carl Crandall, Jim Evans's successor as executive secretary of the Central New York State Park Commission, was writing letters to Jones questioning the expenses. The final year of Jones's operation of Green Lakes appears to have been April 1, 1945 through March 31, 1946. According to that last licensing agreement, Jones agreed to pay $600 to remain as the golf course operator, a far cry from the $1 per year that he had been paying annually since 1936. Robert did give up the concession, but he didn't do it until 1946, not 1941, and it wasn't because of gasoline prices or lack of golfers. He was moving on to more profitable ventures.

---

†† In early 1940 Jones also sought to acquire the concession management for the Valley View Golf Course in Utica, New York, which he had just finished remodeling with WPA funds. In a letter from March 1940, Utica's city engineer, Joseph B. Shaw, informed Jones that the municipality would itself manage the operation of its golf course. See RTJ to Joseph B. Shaw, City Engineer, City Hall, Utica, NY, 24 Feb. 1940, and Joseph B. Shaw to RTJ, 12 March 1940. Both letters are in the Utica Files, JP, CUA.

CHAPTER FOUR

PARTING COMPANY

Jones's business partnership with Stanley Thompson (1893–1953), Canada's leading golf architect, was essential to getting Jones's career off the ground, but by the mid-1930s Jones was getting enough work on his own that he no longer depended on Thompson.

On Wednesday, January 30, 1935, Jones received a cablegram from Rio de Janeiro. The message came from Stanley Thompson, who had been hard at work for three months in the clammy heat of summertime Brazil trying to get some business—any business—building golf courses in South America. Stanley's cable read: "GAVEA PASSED SAIL NINTH CALL PRINCE SIXTH PERSONAL ONEWAY FARE PREPARED STAY THREE MONTHS LEAST= THOMPSON." Thompson was telling Jones that the membership of the Gavea Golf and Country Club in Rio de Janeiro had just approved a deal for Thompson to remodel its 18-hole golf course; that Stanley had booked and paid for a one-way fare on the British liner *Western Prince*, which Robert should use to sail immediately for Rio; and that Robert should expect to stay in Brazil for no less than three months. From earlier wires and letters, Jones knew that Thompson had "several other leads in South America" and that Stanley believed that "this will be an outlet for our winter activities in the future."

Jones did not cable Thompson back a reply. Instead he sat down and wrote a long letter to his Canadian partner explaining why, as much as he wanted to make the trip, he just could *not* go. It was a difficult letter for Robert to write and, when he laid his pen down, Ione, his wife of seven months, wanted to look it over carefully. After all, she had a stake in the letter, too, as the paid trip to Rio was going to include her as well. Ione and Ruth Thompson, Stanley's wife of more than fifteen years, had, like their husbands, become friends. Ruth had written to Ione about her Rio adventures and told her American friend how anxious she and Stan were for the Joneses to join them in South America.

Ione didn't much like what Robert wrote to Stanley. It was not her husband's grammar or style that bothered her this time but rather the letter's underlying tone. Instead of emphasizing why it would be better for the future of Thompson & Jones, Inc., for Robert to remain in the States through the winter of '35, the letter dwelt far too much on how it would benefit Robert not to go.

Ione insisted that Robert write a completely new letter. It took two days to finish, and it is highly likely that Ione helped him with the version that was ultimately sent. Ione also wrote her own letter to Ruth Thompson, expressing how extremely sorry and deeply regretful she was that circumstances made it impossible for them to make the trip. When Ruth Thompson finally answered Ione's letter, it was nearly two and a half months later. Although still very friendly and sociable, Ruth told Ione how "awfully disappointed" they were when they learned that she and Robert would "not be coming South." It took Stanley even longer to answer Robert—and when he did, on April 19, it was just a curt note informing him that they were sailing home on May 2. The gist of Stanley's communiqué was to express his "great disappointment" that Robert had not come down to help him.

This incident was the beginning of the end of the partnership between Stanley Thompson and Robert Trent Jones and the start of Jones's own independent career. Although Thompson, Jones & Company was still advertising its services as late as 1940, the once dynamic working relationship between Stanley and Robert began to lose steam after Jones decided not to go to Brazil in 1935. In *Golf's Magnificent Challenge*, Jones asserted that his partnership with Thompson "remained strong until 1938" and that their "friendship lasted" until Stanley's death in 1953. More telling is Jones's answer to a question during a 1991 interview with a USGA historian: "Why was your partnership dissolved with Thompson?" Jones's reply: "It was dissolved because the WPA came along and I was going to work with the WPA in about four different areas." Jones no longer needed Thompson; his ability to make his own deals apart from Thompson, particularly those involving New Deal public works projects, would determine his future.

From the start of Thompson-Jones the working relationship between the two architects had been vague and imprecise. In March 1932, Stanley brought his brother Bill Thompson into the picture by making him a full partner in a new company, "Thompson, Jones & Thompson." Jones came to understand that he was still supposed to share with Stanley 50 percent of the profits made by Thompson & Jones, and he would henceforth also receive a third of the profits gained by Thompson, Jones & Thompson. The problem, as Jones well knew at the time the second company was formed, was that Stanley Thompson was in financial trouble. "Thompson is dead broke at present," Jones wrote. "He hasn't any money at all." And when Stanley made new deals for golf courses in Canada or abroad, which he managed to continue doing throughout the bad economic times of the early 1930s, there was nothing to stop him from making them through "Stanley Thompson & Company, Ltd.," his original incorporation and a business that Robert Trent Jones had no share in at all.

It is curious that Stanley Thompson amassed so little personal wealth while building so many golf courses over his forty-plus-year career. There's no question that the Canadian architect made a lot of money producing over one hundred golf courses in Canada, the United States, South America, and the West Indies from 1910 to 1952; it was just that Thompson managed to lose most of it through sloppy business practices, bad deals, and extravagant personal spending habits. As his biographer James Barclay has written, "If Stanley Thompson was a genius in the art and science of golf, he was an innocent in the fairways of money management—his own money, that is. Between spells of riches he had great bursts of near poverty. He is said to have made three fortunes and lost them. He died a pauper, much in debt, owing vast sums in taxes to the federal government." Thompson's "sanguine approach" to money "never stopped him from being generous, sometimes to a fault." Many times, he would send a case of whiskey to a contractor for work well done; or send money to a family with a sick child; or simply send a gift on a special occasion. But his generosity and financial frivolities could make it extremely hard on business partners and the people who worked for him; too often he could not come up with the cash he owed them.

Surely, part of the reason that Jones decided not to go to Brazil was that he had already done quite a bit of work for Thompson for which he got nary a taste of any of the money involved. When Robert visited Banff in the summer of 1932 and prepared the annual report required by the Canadian Pacific Railway, his expenses were covered but he received none of the consulting fee that went to Thompson. As part of that summer 1932 trip out to Banff, Robert went on to British Columbia and surveyed a property owned by the British Pacific Properties Company in West Vancouver; four years later, in 1936, it opened as "The Highlands" and was later renamed the Capilano Golf & Country Club, universally considered to be one of Thompson's masterpieces. But it was Robert who actually did the course routing for Capilano, based on his site visit and maps and photographs provided to him, with refinements then being made to Jones's routing by Thompson. The ingenious par-72, 6,578-yard layout on a steep hillside features hole-corridors with breathtaking views of the beautiful city of Vancouver. Jones also provided sketches for some of Capilano's green complexes that included not just the shape and contours of the putting surfaces but also the bunkering, again with the "flashing" that Jones so much loved.* Working from his New York City office, Robert formulated the plan for Capilano's watering system, and he worked closely with the Buckner Company, whose sprinklers he considered to be the best in the market, to see that the irrigation plan was properly installed. For the project Jones also interacted with James F. Dawson of Olmsted Brothers of Brookline, Massachusetts, which had been hired to work with Thompson on the overall landscaping plan for British Properties.

For all of his work involving Capilano, it appears that Jones was never paid a cent.

On the other hand, Jones appears not to have been always directly forthcoming with money rightfully due his senior partner, either. When it looked in the spring of 1934 like the Colgate job was going through, Thompson wrote a short letter to Jones about how the Colgate fees would be split and the need to clarify the revenue situation between the two of them. Stanley would again ask Robert for meetings to discuss their financial relationship no fewer than ten times in the next six years, but Robert never asked for one meeting about it with Thompson. This certainly seems to indicate that Thompson was more concerned than Jones was about how the money was being shared, or not shared.

Jones had to be questioning the value of the partnership in general and the Brazil trip in particular. Thompson was only certain of remodeling one existing golf course (Gavea Golf and Country Club) and hoped to land another remodeling job (Sao Paulo Country Club) and perhaps provide preliminary plans for up to two more. The reward surely looked meager to Jones for the required investment of at least three months of his time. He was moving forward with more WPA proposals as well as other projects of his own, all of which would

---

* Many golf historians and students of golf course architecture have credited Thompson with Capilano's course routing. For example, on page 230 of his 1996 book, *The Confidential Guide to Golf Courses*, Tom Doak writes: "Stanley Thompson did a shrewd job of routing the course on its steep sloping site, so that even the first six holes play downhill toward the Lion's [sic] Gate Bridge and the next nine tack up the hill, there aren't any holes (other than perhaps the downhill 6th) that are just goat-hill by nature." Even Canadian golf historian James Barclay conceded that "Jones did the course routing for Stanley Thompson's classic layout at Capilano" (*The Toronto Terror*, p. 80). And Robert Trent Jones asserted, "I routed the holes for Thompson at Capilano." (*Golf's Magnificent Challenge*, p. 80.)

keep him close to home, likely make him more money, and help to build his own independent reputation.

If Robert was to become "the world's greatest golf course architect," as he often told Ione he would, it was his own ship that needed to steam away.

One of the other factors that Jones cited for not being able to go to Brazil—in fact, what Jones called the "main complication"—was a newspaper contract he had just signed with King Features Syndicate (the premier distributor of comics, columns, editorial cartoons, and puzzles to newspapers across the United States) for a series of articles featuring a description of some of the world's most famous golf holes. The articles would be done in two parts: Jones would write about the architecture of each of the famous holes selected, while some of America's greatest golf champions—namely Walter Hagen, Tommy Armour, Gene Sarazen, Paul Runyan, Johnny Farrell, Leo Diegel, Olin Dutra, and Jess Sweetser[†]—would discuss the drama of how they played that hole on the way to winning one of their championships. In between the two columns would be a sketch of the hole to be hand-drawn by Jones. (Jones had written—actually, Ione had ghostwritten—a similar series of articles, without the involvement of professional players, under the title "Unusual Golf Holes," which appeared during 1933 and 1934 in the Rochester *Journal-American*. That series mostly featured courses in the Rochester area, including some holes at Midvale and Locust Hill that were the result of Jones's own work.) "It is hoped the articles will be published in about fifty papers all over the world," Jones told Thompson, "and it is expected that they will also be sold in South America, Australia and England." The articles "should prove wonderful publicity for us," Robert emphasized, making sure to tell his partner that some of the holes would come from Royal York, Banff, and Jasper Park, three of Stanley's best courses. "I could finish my end of these holes in a few weeks," he explained to Thompson, "but it is my re-

---

† The championship careers of Hagen, Armour, and Sarazen have already been mentioned in the text. Paul Runyan won the 1934 and 1938 PGA Championships. Johnny Farrell won the 1928 U.S. Open played at Olympia Fields Country Club in Chicago. Leo Diegel earned PGA Championship victories in 1928 at Baltimore Country Club (designed by A. W. Tillinghast) and in 1929 at Hillcrest Country Club (Willie Watson) in Los Angeles. Olin Dutra won the 1932 PGA Championship at Keller Golf Course (Paul Coates) in St. Paul, Minnesota, and the 1934 U.S. Open at Merion Golf Club's East Course (Hugh Wilson) in Ardmore, Pennsylvania. At The Country Club (Willie Campbell) in Brookline, Massachusetts, Jess Sweetser won the U.S. Amateur in 1922, and in 1926 at Muirfield (Old Tom Morris) in East Lothian, Scotland, he became the first American to win the British Amateur.

sponsibility to get the stories from the stars tied to the holes, which is difficult since they are playing golf all over the country."

Under the headline FAMOUS HOLES IN GOLF, Jones's articles were published as a King Feature in a number of national and a few international newspapers during 1935 and 1936. (A sampling of the stories includes "Tricky No. 11 at Merion Helps Dutra, Ruins Gene," referring to Olin Dutra's victory over Gene Sarazen in the 1934 U.S. Open; "No. 14 at Olympia Fields Intrigues 1928 Champ," involving Johnny Farrell's victory in the 1928 U.S. Open; and "No. 13 at Baltusrol Knows 'Downfall of Jones'," referring to George Von Elm's unexpected victory over Robert Tyre Jones in the 1926 U.S. Amateur.) What money Jones made for his writing is not clear from his records. Some part of the fees went to the pro golfers who did take part—but not all of the pros mentioned in Jones's letter to Thompson did, especially not some of the bigger names. Whether the writing assignment really stood in the way of his going to Brazil is questionable. And contrary to what Robert suggested to Stanley in his letter, none of Thompson's courses were featured because Stanley's best golf courses were all located in Canada, so no American championship had been played on them.

Jones gave Thompson one additional reason why he needed to stay in the States: The widow of the late Alister MacKenzie, Hilda MacKenzie, had recently written to him about a book manuscript on golf architecture that her husband had left unpublished. She was asking Jones to collaborate on the book, as her husband regarded the architectural principles of Thompson-Jones as quite similar to his own. "I am expecting her official approval in a week or two," Robert told Stanley, "and would go to work on it at once."

Once again, the truth was a little different than what Jones had related to Thompson. Jones had learned about the MacKenzie manuscript a full ten months earlier, upon reading Herb Graffis's mention of it in *Golfdom*'s February 1934 tribute to MacKenzie on his passing. Robert had never spent a great deal of time with MacKenzie, nor personally seen any of his other courses, but in early May 1932 he enjoyed a round of golf with him on the day prior to the official opening of MacKenzie's new Bayside course, on the northwestern end of Long Island.[‡] Along with MacKenzie, Jones had played that day with Innis Brown,

---

‡ The Bayside course no longer exists. It was sold in 1956 and turned into a residential development. The property that was the golf course is located today along 28th Avenue in the New York City borough of Queens, just north of Bayside High School. The original developer of the golf course was the Cord Meyer Development Company, a real estate giant that played a sig-

who with Grantland Rice was co-editor of *The American Golfer*, the leading golf magazine of its time.

Robert quickly made it known to Graffis that he was interested in taking charge of the MacKenzie manuscript and also in being the chief writer for *Golfdom*'s new architectural department—a spot that Graffis had discussed with MacKenzie. Making inquiries around New York City, Jones found that Scribner's, the publisher initially interested in the doctor's book, had decided that the market for the book was too small to merit publication. That discovery prompted Jones, in mid-October 1934, to write again to Graffis:

> The thought came to me that perhaps by combining the Doctor's ideas
> and our own the book might still be published. If so, it could be a fine
> and fitting tribute to the late Doctor and his work. If the idea were fea-
> sible, Mrs. MacKenzie's consent would be needed. Any material that the
> Doctor had written, and photographs of his work, could be sent to me.
> If the book were published and any remuneration were forthcoming,
> I would be willing that Mrs. MacKenzie receive the lion's share.

Graffis informed Jones that Hilda MacKenzie had returned to England with her son Tony Haddock but could be reached in care of Leeds College of Music, Cavendish Road, in Leeds, where Tony taught. Jones initiated a correspondence with Mrs. MacKenzie, asking if she would consent to allow him to get her husband's book published. Though no letter from Hilda MacKenzie seems to exist in Jones's papers, she apparently gave him the go-ahead, because Jones, after getting a copy of the manuscript from Graffis (and apparently later another one from Hilda), began to shop it around. Robert kept Graffis updated on his efforts. (Upon receipt of the manuscript from Graffis, Jones had replied: "I have just gleaned over it and received the same kick that I always do when I glimpse the doctor's art. He certainly was a genius.") An editor at McGraw-Hill showed interest, but the publisher wanted the help of a large subsidy or a guaranteed advance sale of books, neither of which Jones could arrange, although he tried. In late November 1936 he wrote to Dixwell Davenport, a member of the USGA Green Section and chairman of the greens committee at San Francisco Golf Club (a Tillinghast design from circa 1921):

---

nificant role in the overall development of Queens during the first half of the twentieth century.

I plan to bring out a new book in the Spring through the McGraw Hill Publishing Company, which will discuss the modern theories on trapping and green design. Part of this volume is an unfinished manuscript by the late Dr. MacKenzie. His widow sent it on to me for completion, stating that her late husband considered our work most similar to his in strategy and beauty.

Not long after that, McGraw-Hill told Robert there was no deal. Preoccupied with a number of new design jobs, he stowed away his copy of the MacKenzie manuscript in his files, where it remains to this day in the Jones Papers at Cornell.

Dr. MacKenzie's book, entitled *The Spirit of St. Andrews,* was eventually published, but not until 1995, after a copy of the manuscript was reportedly found by Raymond M. Haddock among the papers of his late father, Tony Haddock, MacKenzie's stepson. Believing there was no other copy, Sleeping Bear Press, the publisher, stamped the book with the label "The Lost Manuscript" and advertised it as "golf's equivalent to the Dead Sea Scrolls." The book became an instant classic and a must-have for every golf library. The book's acknowledgments made no mention of Robert Trent Jones's recognition of the book's worth back in 1935 and his efforts to get it published sixty years earlier. (Robert Trent Jones Jr. believes that it was his father's copy of the MacKenzie manuscript, which had been marked as "typed by Ione"—typed by her back in the mid-1930s from MacKenzie's handwritten manuscript—that somehow found its way from his father's office papers into the hands of Haddock and from there to Sleeping Bear Press.)

Jones did not go south in the mid-1930s, but his partnership with Stanley Thompson soon did. Thanks to the WPA and other New Deal programs, Jones's own golf course business had picked up so considerably from the down-at-the-heel years of the early 1930s that he no longer needed the collaborative work that Stanley Thompson could give him. Nor did he need Thompson's reputation to secure his own jobs; at least in the state of New York, Robert had begun to build a respectable résumé of his own.

Whether it was out of loyalty to his young protégé or due to the actual need for Robert's architectural or general business help, Thompson did not give up on Jones as quickly as Jones gave up on him. In virtually every letter that he sent to Robert from 1935 up to the start of World War II, Thompson asked if they could meet to talk over the future of their partnership. "By the infrequency of our letters," he wrote in January 1938, "one might think that we are not interested in each other now that times look better. I think that we should get together more frequently and exchange ideas." Three months later, Thompson repeated the message in even stronger terms: "I think it is imperative that we get together at an early date and formulate a definite working plan. . . . Let us get together soon." Two years passed and no such meeting happened. "I have been thinking for some time that you and I should get together and spend a few days so that we could renew our understanding and plan for the future," Thompson wrote in April 1940. "New business is showing up and expansion is necessary. I had hoped that my connection with you in the States would be more productive and profitable but I am not unmindful of the trying times that we have all been passing through the last few years. If you could arrange to come up to Toronto sometime within the next two or three weeks before I get on the road, I could explain to you what is on my mind and we could arrive at a mutually satisfactory arrangement for future operations." When another month passed, Thompson wrote again: "I have not heard from you in reply to my letter of April 19th. I presume you have been away. I am most anxious that we get together at the earliest convenience." Jones's reply was that, yes, he had been out of town. "I shall try to get up to see you within the next two weeks," Jones offered, but that visit also did not happen.

After this last exchange of letters in May 1940, not just regular business dealings but all routine correspondence between the two men came abruptly to an end. However, it does not seem that Thompson harbored any bad feelings against Jones. According to Jones's eldest son, Robert Trent Jones Jr., who was born in 1939, Thompson occasionally came to Montclair for friendly visits with his father and mother in the years after the war, and the Joneses' only concern about the visits was whether there was enough scotch in the house. In 1946 the former partners became two of the original thirteen members of the American Society of Golf Course Architects, an organization for which Robert served as the first secretary; Jones had lobbied hard for Thompson to be admitted even though he was Canadian. Together at the ASGCA's first annual meeting in December 1947, the two pioneering golf course architects posed for the group picture in front of the clubhouse at Pinehurst in North Carolina, apparently happy to be in each other's company again. But they did not stand right at each other's side.

Perhaps as partnerships go—in golf architecture or any other field—one should not expect more from the relationship than what Thompson and Jones gave to one another. Undoubtedly Thompson took great pride in Robert's accomplishments, which at the time of Thompson's death in 1953 had reached a major professional climax with his dramatic redesign of Oakland Hills Country Club for the 1951 U.S. Open.

Still, Thompson might have wondered—as we might today—what more could have been done to build great golf courses throughout the Western Hemisphere if the two men, once so creatively in sync, had not parted company.

CHAPTER FIVE

"A MODERN THEORY OF GOLF ARCHITECTURE"

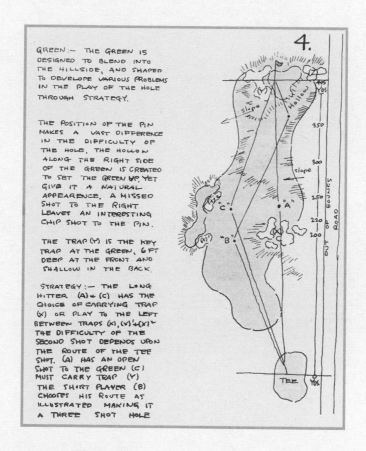

Jones designed the Seven Oaks golf course at Colgate University in 1935, but because of the Great Depression, the plans sat idle in a drawer until the late 1950s. This sketch of what was originally planned to be the long par-4 fourth hole is an excellent example of Jones's approach to strategic design.

In the four years following Jones's decision not to go to Brazil, New Deal funding helped him build four public courses in addition to his highly profitable work at Green Lakes. Three of the courses were located in New York: the 18-hole Amsterdam Municipal Golf Course, just northwest of Schenectady, finished in 1938; a nine-hole layout for his beloved Cornell University, ready for play in 1939; and a remodeled Valley View Golf Course for the city of Utica, opened in 1940. An additional Jones-designed WPA course, Pottawatomie Park Golf Course, came to life in St. Charles, Illinois, forty miles west of Chicago.

None of the courses that Jones designed in the late 1930s are today considered among his very finest, but they were very well done for their time and circumstances. He was developing his skill and philosophy, as well as honing his instincts for attracting and pleasing clients and making friends with rich and powerful people. And after a half decade of personal loneliness and emotional insecurity during the worst years of the Depression, Robert now had his devoted wife Ione, a very intelligent and discerning woman, at his side at home and at work. When it came to managing the quotidian business affairs of Robert Trent Jones's growing golf enterprise, Ione was the real brain and steady hand of the outfit.

Jones was one of the era's keenest observers of how technology was changing the game through much improved golf balls, golf clubs, turfgrasses, irrigation systems, and mowers. Improvements were also coming, he realized, as a result of heightened professional golf instruction, the wider publication of information in golf magazines, and even motion-picture and freeze-frame-camera analysis of the golf swing.* Robert embraced these innovations, envisioning a

---

* In early 1926 the United States Golf Association took slow-motion movies of Bobby Jones hitting golf balls; subsequently, in April 1926, The *American Golfer* magazine published a story (p. 14) about the USGA film, accompanied by photographs, entitled "Bobby Jones Under Slow Motion; Unorthodox Features of Amateur Champion's Style Revealed by Camera Analysis." Four years later, in 1930, the PGA of America made another film study of Bobby

bright, boundless future for golf both in the United States and abroad. He saw great potential in the dynamics of modern industrial society for fundamental improvements in the design and construction of golf courses and in how the modern golf designer could enrich the challenges of the traditional game with new strategic features. Well before he formally dissolved his union with Stanley Thompson, it was clear that Jones's driving ambition was to become *the* pioneering golf course architect who would define what "the modern golf course" could, and should, become.

In its first crystallized forms, Jones's philosophy of golf design and construction can be found in a number of his writings from the mid- and late 1930s, notably in a thirty-seven-page booklet entitled *Golf Course Architecture,* published in New York City in early 1938, which Jones wrote and apparently paid for on his own and which promoted his own reputation as a golf architect.

Jones felt—and rightfully so—that his career had begun at a decisive moment in the history of golf, on the cusp of a new era whose primary delivery agent was the professional golf architect. The opening section of his 1938 brochure began with an admonition: "For every dollar wisely spent on golf course construction there have been two dollars wasted." In the early growth of American golf, there had been some justification for this waste, "as there were no trained and talented architects." The first builders of American links "had to depend largely upon the advice of Scotch and English professionals." While many of the imports were "admirable players," only a few had "the technical knowledge or experience to construct an intriguing golf course." Progress was slow to come in the States until a crop of "truly American" talents—notably Charles B. Macdonald, who grew up in Chicago; Walter Travis, who moved to

---

Jones's swing, for the purpose of "simplifying the teachings of golf." In the PGA's publicity of its film, taken by C. Francis Jenkins of Washington, D.C., the organization asserted that this was "the first time all the movements of the golf swing are actually made clearly visible." In 1931–32 Bobby Jones himself made what is now a famous series of short movies graphically showing his golf swing in slow motion. These movies were shown commercially under the title *How to Break 90.* Robert Trent Jones was very aware of all of these film studies of the golf swing, and in 1934–35 he made proposals to Gene Sarazen for such motion-picture studies of his swing to be made. Such analytic studies of the golf swing derived from time-and-motion studies of factory labor pioneered by the likes of Frederick W. Taylor, the father of "scientific management," who himself was a very avid golfer and student of the game. On Taylorism and golf, see James R. Hansen, "Scientific Management Goes Golfing," *American Heritage of Invention and Technology* 14 (Nov./Dec. 1999): 20–27, and Shannon G. Taylor and Arthur G. Bedeian, "From Boardroom to Bunker: How Fred Taylor Changed the Game of Golf Forever," *Management & Organizational History* 2 (Sept. 2007): 195–218.

the United States from Australia at age twenty-three in 1885; George Crump, a Philadelphian; and Herbert C. Leeds of Boston—arose to create the first good courses that were distinctly American in character.

It was Jones's view that golf in North America, from its beginnings, was unique, because "we had to work with difficulties not facing our British cousins." Whereas the original British courses developed naturally on the linksland bordering the sea, where "wind-made bunkers and exquisite contours for natural green sites adapted themselves to grand golf courses," U.S. courses had to be "hand-made on meadowland." When the British brought the game inland during the Victorian era, instead of preserving "the charming, natural features" of the old links, they turned out many "ill-made and hard-featured golf courses . . . of hideous construction"; this was bewildering to Jones because "perfect examples" of what a great golf course should be, like St. Andrews, were "so near at hand." The earliest builders of golf courses in America, a great many of whom were British-born, committed "the same mistakes," producing golf courses of "hideous" military-like construction, exemplified at their worst by "traps resembling trenches with their systematically-dug holes and straight-faced, tomb-like mounds." But, "happily, such atrocities are now a thing of the past," Jones declared, thanks to the rediscovery of the "subtle features of strategic architecture" by the modern golf course architect.

This rediscovery was being made principally in America, Jones believed, because the unique difficulties of the American landscape challenged the country's architects to respond with creativity and imagination to the great environmental diversity facing them. Jones then named the "now-famous" American courses that "closed the gap" between the naturalistic virtues of the traditional seaside architecture and the artificially created monstrosities of the worst inland courses: "the spectacular courses along the blue Pacific at Pebble Beach and Cypress Point;" "the thrilling Rocky Mountain courses of Banff and Jasper Park;" and "Bobby Jones' Augusta National." For the first two illustrations in his booklet, he chose photographs of golf holes (what were then the third and 17th) at Banff Springs, a layout whose handiwork he could advertise as a production of Thompson & Jones.

The essence of Jones's booklet lay in the section labeled "The Modern Theory of Golf Course Architecture." According to Robert, this modern approach was "to create a balanced hole for the various classes of golfers." In the past, Jones wrote, "the majority of players who may have been termed average golfers were punished far out of proportion to their playing skill." Sand traps and bunkers were "placed in all areas of the fairway so as to catch a shot only slightly in error." Because "the technique of the average golfer's swing is subject to flaws more often than the good or expert golfer's, he was constantly in trouble." As a result, "the game of golf lost its thrill for him."

Later in his career, Jones would go to great pains to analyze the distance that touring pros were hitting the golf ball, in order to place fairway bunkers where they would challenge the best golfers to think more strategically about their tee shots. This wasn't an idea that only came to Jones in the 1950s. Already in his 1938 brochure, Jones referred to "an analysis of the situation" that he had been making at U.S. Opens, Canadian Opens, and the "Augusta National Invitational" (as The Masters was known from its inception in 1934 up until the 1939 tournament). His data about driving distances disclosed "that as far as the crack golfer was concerned, traps under 200 yards offered little or no hazard usually, whereas those same traps were constantly punishing the average golfer." (In 1938 Jones and everyone else in golf would have been astounded to know that seventy-five years later, traps not much shorter than 300 yards from the tee would offer little or no hazard to most pro golfers.) Moving fairway traps, in Jones's view, would "make the play for the average golfer less punishing without spoiling the character of the course or the playing value for the expert."

Even more than fairway bunkering, Jones's focus was on what today would be called "the green complex," involving not only the putting surface ("the green") but also the "collar" (the first cut of grass around the perimeter of the green), the "approach" (the cut of grass defined as a type of entryway into the green), the surrounding rough areas, and any greenside sand traps or bunkers. He paid special attention to the relationship between the green and any surrounding traps. This relationship needed to be designed, according to Robert, "so the hole could be tightened or eased by the extent that the pin was placed behind a diagonal trap." By doing so, modern golf architecture was departing significantly from the "old penal style of architecture, where the greens were flat and surrounded by a maze of clam-shell traps with a bottle-neck entrance" and "where only one problem was involved—the golfer had no choice other than to hit a perfectly executed shot to the green." Sadly, because the shot required was "often not in the average golfer's repertoire," the average golfer "realized he was doomed before he started." Jones had the answers—both psychological and physical—to the dilemma: "With the diagonal trapping, tongue greens [i.e., greens that incorporate tongue-like shapes, sometimes long and narrow] and alternate routing to the green, he can play a shot which he feels is within his range. This involves mental keenness as well as playing skill, as one must vary the manner in which one plays the hole on any particular day according to how well one is playing or, in the case of tournament play, according to the circumstances of the match."

Furthermore, Jones's style of modern architecture would correct an especially unfair aspect of the penal type of design: that a player could hit a shot only slightly off center and catch "a deep, ugly trap," whereas a shot badly missed "would avoid this trouble, enabling one to pitch the approach in close to the pin and get a par, thus equaling the golfer who had played the hole perfectly." It was not that Jones believed that everything about the playing of the game of golf could be rationalized and made fair; he knew that that was impossible and not even desirable, because it would take away much of the charm and fascination from an inherently enigmatic game. But he did believe that designers of golf courses needed to do everything they could do to make the game popular and enjoyable for all, no matter what level of skill the player possessed. Jones recommended framing the green "with long, well-formed mounds, placed strategically, thus presenting a definite problem to the hole." In this case, if a shot into the green was missed badly, the next shot facing the golfer would be "that much more difficult in proportion to the error." The golfer would then be "forced to play a hazardous shot over a mound and trap and is less likely to be putting for a par." On the other hand, the player who has made only a slight error, being closer to the green, will "not have to make a shot that requires the finesse of one badly missed."†

Continuing his emphasis on the critical importance of green design, Jones strongly advocated what he called a "dune type of green molding." By this, he meant the building of discernible slopes and contours into the putting surfaces in the form of mounds or ridges, like drifted sand, which gave contrast and definition to a green's internal shape and a ball's final landing area. Through the incorporation of "dune type green molding," the green surface itself was "given

---

† This design principle sets Jones at odds with many of his predecessors from the "Golden Age" of golf architecture. Harry S. Colt (1869–1951) believed that the purpose of a bunker was not to catch the bad shot but rather the shot that was not quite good enough. Colt's friend John L. Low (1869–1929) defined the purpose of hazards as being to tempt. In other words, these earlier golfing experts felt that a bad miss was, in general, its own punishment, and that in any case, golfers who miss shots badly are probably not good and thus don't need worse punishment. In this light, Jones's view is much more in sympathy with the views of such earlier golf course critics as J. H. Taylor (1871–1963) or Joshua Crane (1869–1964), who are associated with the *penal* theories of design.

The author would like to thank Adam Lawrence, the editor of *Golf Course Architecture*, for sharing this caveat about Jones's concept of strategic golf design.

a receptivity that inspires a confidence as one plays to the green, for one feels that a bold shot will not overrun the green too easily and, therefore, hits a crisp, sure shot to the pin rather than a doubtful, faltering shot." This type of design also created "a feature terminating each hole." It gave the hole "a feeling of isolation from any adjacent holes since the construction of the mounds build up a third dimension, blocking off part of the view beyond the green." He put two of his sketches of green-complex designs in the brochure. The first shows the green complex and environs of the dogleg par-4 third hole over an inlet of the Fox River on the Pottawatomie Park Golf Course in St. Charles, Illinois ("Although the site is attractive, the flashing of sod and sand is really what makes this a spectacular hole"). The second sketch shows the green complex for the 401-yard par-4 fourth hole that Jones planned for the Colgate University Golf Club ("This is designed to blend into the hillside, and shaped to develop various problems in the play of the hole through strategy"). Nowhere was his artistry as a golf architect more apparent than in this artwork.

No one can play a Robert Trent Jones golf course anywhere in the world today without being impressed by his fearsome use of sand. This constant element of Jones's architecture was a matter of fundamental consideration in his 1938 brochure. In relation to the greens, he wrote, "Sand can be oriented effectively in the face of any mounds so that they stand out from a distance, creating a fearful aspect." Throughout his career, Jones loved to employ this manner of bunker "flashing," for both strategic and aesthetic reasons. "The orientation of sand and sod, when effectively done," Jones knew, "makes an extremely attractive appearance." But his concept of the value of flashed sand bunkers was more advanced in its subtleties than mere appearance: "It is the modern theory that certain traps should have real penal value while others only a psychological effect so that a hole often plays more easily than it would seem at first glance."

Nor can anyone play a Robert Trent Jones course today without high regard for the contours of his putting surfaces. Here, again, Robert's sense of golf's aesthetic values was wonderfully strong. The surface of a green "must be of an undulating character rather than flat, as in the penal type of architecture; otherwise, there would not be a harmony of lines between the framework of the green and the green surface itself." Some of the undulations should be gentle, some bold, depending on the requirements of the various types of shots, but always the contours of a green and its environs should have "a natural, rather than an artificial appearance." Depicting this principle in his brochure was a photograph of what was then the par-4 16th hole at Green Lakes State Park Golf Course, in which "It should be hard to tell where the natural ends and the artificial begins," even though its character, accomplished on "what was originally a listless green site," was "dependent upon the artificially created features."

Later in his career, Jones would become well known for his long "runway" tees, but his basic concept for such tees was already apparent in 1938, with his statement that "double sets of tees" are "part of the modern scheme." By adding a second set of tees, a hole can be played shorter or longer depending on a golfer's skill level, age, or gender. Two sets of tees also mean that "a hole can be lengthened for championship play to make it a more trying test of golf." They further add "a constant variety of interest to the course as a whole" because it is then "possible to alter the yardage of the course." The tees can set at a different angle from one another, giving a hole "an entirely different playing quality," which is like having a brand-new hole. For variety, Jones also advised using different combinations of pin positions on the putting surfaces, with not all of the holes on a course being cut for any given day's round in the same general location, e.g., center, back, front right. This approach, too, he saw as a contribution from modern golf architecture, which encouraged designers to create the types of greens that made such "infinite variety" possible.

Finally, Jones turned his attention to the shapes of the fairways, which were not in the least incidental to the modern theory of golf course architecture. "Since it is the desire of the modern architect not to punish the average golfer too severely," he explained, "the fairways are shaped so as to give their narrowest areas where the crack golfers should land." This approach gave the average golfer "ample latitude" while tightening the hole to "punish the error of the expert," but did so "without necessitating the development of any greater fairway area than in the penal school where the fairway was the same width all the way from tee to green." Once more, beautiful form followed from function: "In appearance, the symmetry of curving lines is much more attractive than the long, ribbon-like fairways of the past; but, in addition, the bays and narrow necks created act as a yardstick for the player to judge his distance from tee to green."

Although Jones in his brochure began with a definition of "modern golf architecture" that centered on creating "a balanced hole for the various classes of golfers," the real essence of his architectural philosophy clearly rested in his championing of strategic design. To delineate this philosophy for his booklet, he made a schematic overhead drawing of the 527-yard, par-5 14th hole at St. Andrews, the Old Course's famous "Long Hole," which Jones tabbed as "the prize example of the strategic school of golf architecture." Despite the fact that the hole was more than a century old, Jones recognized that "it has stood up as an acid test of golf against the improvements of modern equipment." The "Long" was still a great hole, "for the traps are placed so adroitly that they challenge all classes of golfers seeking the shortest route to the hole." At the 200-yard mark out from the tee lay "a dangerous nest of traps" called the "Beardies," which short hitters could avoid by laying up short or playing out to their right or left, and that long hitters could try to carry. At 400 yards out, smack-dab in the middle of the fairway, lay "the famous and maliciously named 'Hell' bunker." Short hitters could intelligently lay up in front of "Hell" or play out to its left, leaving only a mid- to short iron to be hit diagonally into the green, while long hitters could risk carrying the deep and deadly bunker, maybe reaching the green in two shots and putting for an eagle, or also play out to its left. Neither the short nor the long hitter wanted to hit their drives or second shots to the right side of the 14th hole's fairway, Jones explained, because "a threatening boundary wall" came in close all along the right side; in addition, "a greedy pot trap" was located in front of the "boldly, sharply sloped green" to catch any who tugged their shot in from the right. Although he had not yet played at St. Andrews, or even yet returned to the British Isles where he had been born, Jones had discussed the hole with Stanley Thompson, who had played it, and also read all about the hole, particularly in Alister MacKenzie's manuscript for *The Spirit of St. Andrews.*

Interestingly, in the brochure Jones did not yet give expression to what he would later call the "heroic school" of golf course design, an offshoot of the strategic school, which he would feature on many of the golf courses he designed from the late 1940s on. In Jones's mind, the heroic design style emerged as a highly adventurous middle ground between the harsh old penal style and the modern strategic style that he helped to pioneer in the 1930s. Often incorporating water hazards, the heroic style confronted the golfer with a punishing hazard—one from which the player could not escape without some form of penalty but one that could be avoided if the player chose to take a safe but longer route around the hazard. The bolder player could "bite off" as much as he dared, as in the case of an intervening or diagonal hazard. Jones came to like these sorts of golf holes very much because they looked spectacular and stimulated an ambition for quick, fabulous, and highly memorable success by the golfer in the form of eagles or birdies. Ultimately, much of Jones's architecture would come to epitomize the "risk/reward" factor inherent in heroic golf (the higher the risk, the higher the reward), but in his 1938 brochure Robert did not give a single mention to what he would later call heroic design.

He also made no specific mention of Stanley Thompson. The name Thompson appears only on the brochure's last page, where Jones gave the contact information for his own office: Thompson & Jones, 45 West 45th Street, New York City. In contrast, Robert loudly tooted his own horn, especially in the last section of the booklet, entitled "Comment," wherein a number of leading names in golf were quoted with lavish praise for Jones. "Of the courses I have played designed by Robert Trent Jones," Gene Sarazen commented, "I have yet to find one that is not outstanding. He is the modern Number 1 Architect." "Robert Trent Jones is one of the most noted architects," the *National Golf Review* was quoted as saying, "his firm having built many famous courses throughout North and South America." (Of course, Jones had not gone to South America.) From an issue of *Town & Country* magazine came the statement: "The diagrams are by Robert Trent Jones, most brilliant of the young course designers." Noted golf professional Craig Wood said about Jones: "The architect of Green Lakes did an amazing job on an exceptionally rugged piece of terrain. It took a terrific imagination and a real knowledge of the value of golf shots." Lawson Little, winner of the 1934 and 1935 U.S. and British Amateurs (who would also win the 1940 U.S. Open), congratulated Jones "on your fine course, Green Lakes, one of the finest I have seen." Perhaps the most duplicitous quote of the bunch was the one attributed to "Mrs. Alistair [sic] MacKenzie." In his letter to Thompson of February 1, 1935, Robert had mentioned that Hilda MacKenzie felt that her husband regarded the architectural principles of both Thompson and Jones as quite similar to his own. In the brochure, Jones quoted from the letter MacKenzie's widow had sent him: "My late husband had the greatest admiration for your work, its strategy and beauty. He considered you among the world's finest." Mrs. MacKenzie might have been using the plural "you," as in Thompson and Jones, or even the singular "you," as in the firm of Thompson & Jones; in Jones's brochure it could only be interpreted to mean Robert Trent Jones alone.

More egregiously, Jones also included quotes about courses designed solely by Thompson long before his partnership with Jones began. "The Royal York is one of the best tests of high class golf in America," commented Horton Smith, two-time Masters winner. "A round of golf at Banff is the engraving of a life-time impression on any golfer," lauded the magazine *Canadian Golfer*. "The Constant

Spring Golf Course at Kingston, Jamaica, is the finest golf course in the British West Indies," was the comment from *The Illustrated London News*. Jones did not explicitly refer to these courses as his own, but by not mentioning Thompson, the brochure led unknowing readers to think that Jones was responsible for all the golf courses cited. Jones also included Thompson's solo courses on the firm's list of "more than one hundred golf courses covering both American continents, scattered from Vancouver to Nova Scotia, from northern Ontario to Brazil."

This may be why Jones didn't send any copies of the brochure to Stanley, despite repeated requests. "Our associate Geoffrey Cornish tells me you have produced a nice brochure," Thompson wrote to Jones on March 18, 1938. "Please send me a few copies." Robert drafted a short reply, which he seems not to have sent: "As a matter of fact, I had just a limited number of them made up, as that was all I could afford, and due to the demand for them after a review in a golf magazine, I find myself unable to supply you with any." Through his secretary, Thompson soon asked again. This time Jones definitely answered, saying he couldn't send any without paying for another printing. Anyway, "I think the booklet should be made to read a trifle differently for the Canadian run. In other words, I think the Canadian courses and your name should be featured more prominently." In subsequent correspondence between the two men, of which there was little, no more was said about the brochure. But it is interesting that in Jones's autobiographical retrospective, *Golf's Magnificent Challenge*, he stated that his partnership with Thompson "remained strong until 1938." The self-serving character of Jones's brochure that year—once Thompson somehow got a copy—may have been the final affront that undermined the relationship.

Robert Trent Jones's theory of modern golf course architecture consisted of more than just flashing up sand bunkers and narrowing fairways in landing areas. For him, being a modern golf architect also meant taking a highly entrepreneurial approach to the design and construction business. His brochure of 1938 was meant to drum up clients, rather than waiting for new jobs to come to him.

But there was another purpose for his booklet, a purpose that would take another two decades and more to reach fruition. That was to transform Jones from being merely a respected, up-and-coming golf architect into an internationally known "brand name," as famous as any of the biggest names in golf. Today, in 2014, golfers around the world are well aware of the big names in contemporary golf course architecture—Dye, Fazio, Nicklaus, Doak, Coore, Hanse, Kidd, and, yes, Jones (Robert Trent Jr. and Rees). The status enjoyed by "name" golf architects, today and for at least the past fifty years, rests in essential ways upon the highly entrepreneurial, fame-seeking ambitions of Robert Trent Jones as he first advanced them in the late 1930s.

What the young Robert Trent Jones lacked in business acumen in terms of handling accounting, knowing numbers, caring for details, assessing practicalities, weighing pros and cons and the like, he quickly learned to make up for—and then some—in salesmanship. "My dad always emphasized that business was the highest form of social status in America," explains his eldest son, Robert Trent Jones Jr. "He wanted to be a businessman. But he wasn't, not really. My mother used to say, 'He's not really a businessman, because to be a CEO or some other company executive, one really has to knuckle down, pore over figures, and make hard decisions.' Dad was much more the creative person who could foresee opportunities, and seize them, before all the others could or sometimes even knew what was happening. When he saw a chance to make something big, even out of nothing, he wasn't afraid to take it."

Having orchestrated a highly successful opening for Green Lakes State Park that featured a golf exhibition by Gene Sarazen and Sam Snead and that resulted in crowds of green-fee-paying customers coming to play his new golf course, Jones stepped up the strategy for his next municipal golf project, a WPA course that debuted in the summer of 1938 in Amsterdam, New York, a town near the Erie Canal just northwest of Schenectady.

Robert started working on "Amsterdam Muni" in the spring of 1936 and had its first nine ready for play by May 1937.[‡] Besides planning another gala golf exhibition, Jones worked hard with city officials to create new golfers well in advance of the opening of the course so it would be self-supporting immediately. As he explained to Golfdom's Herb Graffis:

---

‡ There is a remarkable photographic record of the construction of Amsterdam Municipal Golf Course now preserved by the USGA Museum and Arnold Palmer Center for Golf History at USGA headquarters in Far Hills, New Jersey. Taken by a WPA photographer (named "Kirk") throughout all phases of the layout's construction from 1936 to 1938, the images show everything that was done to build the course, including the installation of the irrigation system, preparation and seeding of fairways, erection of rustic wooden bridges to help players move through and across sensitive wildlife areas, and even the construction of the parking lot for the patrons. As USGA golf historian Rand Jerris has said about this rare photographic collection: "Together, they are a remarkable portrait of an important period in American golf course architecture that is poorly documented and largely underappreciated" ("A New Deal for Amsterdam's Golfers," 18 Dec. 2009, accessed on 1 Aug. 2012 at http://www.usga.org/news/2009/December/New-Deal-For-Golfers/).

[P]art of the fairways on the course have developed sufficiently so that there is a large area of fairway that will make an excellent practise [sic] plot. I have sold the Mayor [Arthur Carter, a Democrat] on the idea of retaining and paying for a professional to spend two days a week at the course giving group lessons free to various clubs such as the Rotary, Gyro, Y.M.C.A., etc., and in the case of individuals who do not belong to any clubs like these, the newspaper is running a coupon to be filled out and sent in so that groups can be made up of these.

The group lessons resulted in dozens of new golfers for the Amsterdam course when it opened. Herb Graffis loved Jones's ingenious approach to building a public golf clientele, and called Jones's strategy of bringing in a pro well in advance "the best damn thing I have seen lately and should be a feature of all WPA courses."

Jones delayed the grand opening of Amsterdam Municipal until July 19, 1938, by which time all the grass had grown in and was flourishing on the completed eighteen. He made sure the day was festive and brought in a Scottish band with bagpipers to play. The highlight for the huge gallery he attracted was an exciting match pitting Gene Sarazen and Frank Hartig, the first pro at the "Muni," against Tom Creavy, winner of the 1931 PGA Championship (and a Westchester resident), and another local golf pro, John Lord. The day was such a brilliant success that the crowd was "not too disappointed" when their favorites, Sarazen and Hartig, lost in a close match.

Jones had plenty of work to keep himself busy through the end of the 1930s. Several of his jobs involved remodeling assignments, some quite limited, at New York country clubs. Some of these tasks proved rather tricky, as the renovations involved established golf courses that had been designed by respected architects, with proud memberships wary of, or downright hostile to, any changes proposed for their courses.§ Although Jones was delighted by what he called "the revival of

---

§ Among those country clubs for which Jones did remodeling work in the 1930s were: Locust Hill Country Club in Rochester, a Seymour Dunn design from 1928; Stafford Country Club in Stafford, NY, designed by Walter Travis, also in 1928; Garden City Golf Club, originally designed by Devereux Emmet (as his first course, then named Island Golf Links) in 1899 and later redone by Walter Travis in 1916; Bonnie Briar Country Club, a course originally designed by Scotsman Archie Capper which then underwent a major reworking by A. W. Tillinghast in 1921 with further remodeling by Devereux Emmet in 1928; Niagara Falls Country Club, a Tillinghast design from 1919; and Vestal Hills Country Club, whose original designer is unprivate clubs throughout the country" (his brochure of 1938 highlighted his re-modeling work at Garden City Golf Club), he had come to prefer public projects very strongly over private ones. Considering some of his experiences with country clubs, one shouldn't be surprised. He and Thompson had never gotten their due at Midvale; and the members of the Country Club of Ithaca turned out to be, in Robert's words, "a bunch of pikers." Thankfully, for his biggest jobs, he didn't have to assuage "greens committees," the small groups of usually seven to eleven men—large enough to promote discussion but small enough to reach timely decisions—that comprised the ruling bodies for golf at most country clubs.

In his wariness about greens committees, Jones was not alone. Every golf architect since the advent of the country club in America had faced the thorny problems of dealing with them. In his manuscript for *The Spirit of St. Andrews*, Alister MacKenzie lamented: "The history of most golf clubs is that a committee is appointed, they make mistakes, and just as they are beginning to learn from their mistakes, they resign office or are replaced by others who make still greater mistakes, and so it goes on." Jones could not have agreed more. The ideal member of a greens committee, in Jones's view, was one with patience, practicality, an open mind, an even temper, a thick skin, a sense of humor, good listening abil-ities, and the wisdom to differentiate between valid criticism and unreasonable member expectations. But he knew from experience that too many greens com-mittees were populated by arrogant hotheads, loudmouths, ambitious egoma-niacs, frustrated semi-professionals, amateur architects, backseat drivers, golfers who placed personal agendas above the common interests of the membership, and micromanagers who interfered with their superintendents and made un-realistic demands on the turfgrass and the overall course condition. Working with such committees made the task of getting an architectural job particularly difficult and unpleasant, and it made the many months of actual labor on the golf course—and getting paid for it promptly—a real chore.

Jones devoted the last two pages of his 1938 brochure to the problems of dealing with fussy greens committees. The section began with a long quote from "Adventures with an Architect," a story written by Bernard Darwin, the golf editor of the London *Times* and once a captain of the Royal and Ancient Golf Club of St. Andrews. In his story, Darwin puts his golf architect in the role of Scottish author Sir Arthur Conan Doyle's brilliant sleuth, Sherlock Holmes:

---

known. (The original Vestal Hills course no longer exists; in 1957, it was replaced by a new Vestal Hills Country Club at a different location, which was designed by Geoffrey Cornish.)

I had no keener pleasure than in following Holmes in his professional investigations, and in admiring the rapid deductions, as swift as intuitions, and yet always founded on a logical basis, with which he unraveled the problems which were submitted to him. This was in effect, what I said, in the manner of Dr. Watson, as I bade goodbye to an eminent golf architect after spending two days in his company. It was, in some ways, a rather humbling experience, though I am really very humble, anyhow, as regards my architectural qualities; but the feeling of being a foil to Holmes's brilliance was by no means disagreeable. If the architect could see some things more quickly than I could, and other things which I should never have seen at all, I could console myself with the reflection that it was his job. It was only natural that he should be good at it, and that seems a point worth emphasizing, because there are sometimes members of greens committees who think that they can do this job by the light of nature, and they generally make the saddest mess of it.

No doubt Jones took delight in Darwin's likening the golf architect to Sherlock Holmes and would have loved to have had Darwin on any of the greens committees with which he had found himself working. Robert was certain that the progress of modern golf rested mainly on the professional golf course designer. "A golf course can be at once challenging and fair to the duffer," Jones declared. "The differences between a poor and a good course are obvious, but the differences between a good and an outstanding course are subtle." Only the "competent architect" who made golf course architecture "his life's work" could be trusted to be in complete command of those subtleties.

It was not Jones's brochure but his friendly business relationship with Chicago's Herb and Joe Graffis that got Robert his first job outside the state of New York. Since making each other's acquaintance, Jones and the Graffis brothers had regularly exchanged information that could be beneficial to one another: Robert shared various golf and golf course stories for possible publication in *Golfdom*, and the Graffis brothers passed on names of potential clients for new or remodeled golf courses. In this case, a man by the name of Lester J. Norris had contacted the magazine editors for the name of an architect to build a new course in his hometown of St. Charles, Illinois, forty miles west of Chicago. Herb wrote a letter back recommending an "up and coming" young architect from the state of New York, "a pretty regular fellow," and "a member of the best firm of golf architects in the world," by the name of Robert Trent Jones. Norris had never heard of him.

When Jones got a phone call from Lester Norris in early 1936 asking him to come meet him in Chicago so Norris could talk to him about designing a golf course, Robert had no idea who the man was. "He told me he was chairman of the park board in the town of St. Charles roughly forty miles west of Chicago," Robert recalled years later, "and wanted to build a course on some land adjacent to the Fox River. I thought he had just some kind of secretarial job." Because Robert at the time was planning to go west for some other prospects anyway, he agreed to travel to Chicago to learn firsthand what Norris had in mind. Arriving at Chicago's LaSalle Street Station on the 20th Century Limited, Jones was met by Norris for the drive to St. Charles. As soon as he saw Norris's "big new Buick," Robert knew he was not someone's secretary. But it wasn't until he agreed to do the job that he found out that Norris was on the board of directors at Texaco and one of the company's biggest shareholders, and that his wife, Dellora Angell, was the heiress to both the Texaco and Gates barbed-wire fortunes (she was the niece of John "Bet-a-Million" Gates), and "happened to be a multimillionaire in her own right." Norris was also quite well known in his own right, having previously worked as a cartoonist for the *Chicago Tribune*.

Not only did Robert and Ione end up becoming friends with Lester and Dellora Norris, but Robert's visit to St. Charles resulted in three different golf course projects. The one Norris initially had in mind was to be built on a mere forty-two acres along the Fox River that had been given by the Norris family to St. Charles's Pottawatomie Park District (the first public park established in the state of Illinois under the Illinois Park Act of 1911). The land allotted was too small for anything more than a nine-hole golf course, the construction of which began in the summer of 1936 and took three years to finish. When the course opened for play on Saturday, July 1, 1939, the green fee was 25 cents for the first nine holes and 15 cents for each additional nine, a bargain price that was below the cost of most public golf in the United States at the time.

Although it was only nine holes, Jones came to consider Pottawatomie Park Golf Course to be one of his "exceptionally fine" layouts. He turned a property with some beautiful stands of oak and hickory trees into a wonderfully scenic golf course that was 3,150 yards long and played to a par 35. He was particularly proud of the 330-yard par-4 fourth hole, which he described as "a drive and pitch." A hole featured a sharp dogleg left, and the short second shot was played to what was virtually an island green situated on a peninsula formed by the Fox

River to its rear and an inlet to its left and front. If the watery surroundings weren't enough, three large sand traps also protected the sides and back of the green, as did a half dozen elm trees.⁵ Jones later called the hole his first island green.** In 1980, when Pete Dye's now world-famous island green premiered as the par-3 17th hole at TPC Sawgrass in Ponte Vedra Beach, Florida, Jones declared to some golf writers and fellow architects that he had "designed a better island green more than forty years earlier, before World War II." That boast may be highly arguable, but there is no question that Jones produced a very special

---

¶ Built on a low-lying peninsular in the Fox River, the green for Pottawatomie's par-4 island hole (#4) was the last green finished on the course, largely because it required more than 5,000 cubic yards of fill to be hauled in by trucks. The third, fourth, and sixth holes played either along or over the river and its inlet, requiring a great deal of fill generally, and a couple of bridges, one spanning a lagoon roughly 80 feet wide, had to be built. A great deal of the final construction work waited upon the funding enabled by the passage of a park bond issue on March 14, 1939. An item in the local paper about the bond issue read: "It will be gratifying to see the varied activities at Pottawatomie Park finished up, as it has been a long drawn out job, and much money expended by the WPA, as well as private funds which have been so generously given. It will be a playground which few townships in the state can match" ("Park Bond Issue Gets Voter's OK; Carried by Vote of 555 to 331, for Park Improvements," *Kane County Chronicle*, Mar. 15, 1939). On-site construction of the golf course was managed by two local men: Al Swanson and Norman Wilson; Wilson, in particular, sent regular written progress reports to Jones, and asked Robert to keep him in mind for other construction jobs around the country. In one report, Wilson wrote: "As to my understanding of golf course construction, particularly your style of design, I believe that it is good—a more practical knowledge, now, I might say—and that I can 'feel' what is good from the standpoint of balance, variety, and contrast in green moulding" (Norman Wilson, 228 W. Fourth St., Geneva, IL, to RTJ, 45 W. 45th St., New York City, 18 June 1938). Jones seems to have visited St. Charles for a few days each year between 1936 and 1939 to ensure that his plans were being carried out faithfully. At one point in early 1939, Wilson did advise Jones, "Personally, I don't think the job here is as good from the standpoint of quality of workmanship, but I suppose that's because of the poor starts, frequent interruptions, and then finishing up in a big hurry" (Norman Wilson, 1015 Second St. S., St Charles, IL, to RTJ, 20 Mar. 1939). All of the reports on the construction of the Pottawatomie golf course are in the St. Charles Files, JP, CUA.

** Just which golf course possessed America's first island green is uncertain, but it seems clear that it was not Jones's fourth hole at Pottawatomie Park Golf Course in Illinois. The original course at Baltusrol Golf Club in Springfield, New Jersey, built by Louis Keller in the late 1890s, some twenty years before A. W. Tillinghast designed the Upper and Lower courses at Baltusrol, had a hole—the par-4 10th—nicknamed "Island," whose green was totally surrounded by water. As golf writer Dan Jenkins wrote about the hole: "Once, during an exhibition match, Walter Hagen drove into the water. But in those days the balls floated. Hagen took off his shoes and socks, walked into the pond, hit the ball off the top of the water and made a birdie." Jenkins, "Baltusrol Golf Club, Springfield, New Jersey," in *Sports Illustrated*'s *The Best 18 Golf Holes in America* (New York: Delacorte Press, 1966), p. 45.

nine-hole public course for the citizens of St. Charles. *Golf Digest* placed Pottawatomie in fifteenth place on its 2010 list of the best nine-hole courses in America. (In 1928 architect Herbert Strong had designed an island green for his 144-yard 9th hole at the Ponte Vedra Club at Florida's Ponte Vedra Beach, a course that Jones redesigned in 1948 and to which Jones added a third nine in 1962. Pete Dye and his wife, Alice, knew all about the much earlier island green at Ponte Vedra when they built the 17th at nearby Sawgrass in 1980.)

In addition to that little gem, Jones was asked by St. Charles Country Club to do some minor remodeling of a few of its greens and bunkers, which he did. Also, Lester Norris, who was an avid golfer (and a member at St. Charles CC), hired Robert to design a private course on his estate a short distance east of Pottawatomie. On subsequent visits to Illinois, Jones not only watched over the construction of the parks district golf course and directed the renovations at the country club, he also built an eight-hole golf course (curiously, with nine greens) on 23 acres of the Norris Estate. Some of the holes crisscrossed, and some wrapped around one another. The golfer also had to play over and around five large ponds. It was a totally private course used only by the Norris family and their friends.

Fittingly, Jones ended the 1930s by building a golf course for Cornell University, the school that at the end of the previous decade had given a young man without a high school diploma the chance to follow his dream and become a golf architect.

Jones's aspirations for the Cornell course could not have been higher. His intent was to design "the finest golf course that it is possible to construct on this excellent terrain, with large greens and tees, bold green contours, and impressive, attractive traps"—in sum, a golf course that embodied every significant element of his theory of strategic golf architecture. For the architect-as-artist, the canvas couldn't have been better: "The property has an ideal terrain for the development of a golf course of outstanding caliber. Gently rolling land, replete with natural green and tee sites, it is extremely well adapted for an infinite variety of golf holes—holes that will call for every variety of golf shot."

Jones laid out a complete 18-hole course, with a county road separating the two nines. From the championship tees, his conception played to a par 72 at a distance of 6,711 yards (3,505 on the front, 3,206 on the back). Half of the par-4s were longer than 400 yards, which was quite long for par-4 holes during that era. (Actually, 400-yard par-4s were long holes for most of the rest of the twentieth century, even for professionals. With today's golf balls and clubs, they no longer are, not even for many amateurs.) The par-3s were also highly challenging, at distances (in sequence) of 220, 170, 170, and 186 yards. All but one of the par-5s played longer than 500 yards, which was not always the case in pre–World War II golf course design. From the "regular" men's tees, the length of Jones's layout was a manageable 6,329 yards (3,272 on the front and 3,057 on the back).

Unfortunately, not enough money came through for Jones's full concept to be built. Cornell's president, Livingston Farrand, felt it was unlikely that the WPA would give money to a university for something like a golf course when the school was primarily a private corporation; its only state institution was its College of Agriculture (Farrand may very well have had the public controversy over Colgate's proposed WPA golf course in mind). In the end, only one of Jones's nine-hole circuits could be built: the shorter back nine lying west of Warren Road, where more of the designated property was already owned by Cornell. The course officially opened on April 15, 1941; a month later, the Cornell golf team played its first intercollegiate match on the course, against Syracuse University. Jones attended both events and was very proud of all the compliments he got about the course, crowing "Wait till we get my other nine built! It's even better!"

That "front nine" would not come about for another thirteen years. Once it did open, it became the site of several prestigious college and junior tournaments; in September 1991, the university renamed the facility "The Robert Trent Jones Golf Course at Cornell University." *Golfweek* magazine ranked it in 2011 as the twenty-sixth best college golf course in America.

Robert Trent Jones ended the decade of the Great Depression in a far different situation and frame of mind than he had begun it. He was an established golf course architect with a burgeoning reputation. Though technically still in partnership with Stanley Thompson, for all practical purposes he was working independently. He was successfully getting his own jobs and employing his own construction foremen to ensure that whoever built the golf course would follow his specifications. By the late '30s he was making a very good living, annually earning the equivalent in today's dollars of roughly $200,000; at the start of the decade he often didn't have a dollar in his pocket he could call his own. His contacts in the world of golf were extensive and growing. He had befriended a number of championship golfers, golf magazine and newspaper editors, sports-writers, golf course owners, officers of the New York State and United States Golf Association, not to mention dozens of club professionals and greenkeepers. Also among his friends and associates were several influential business owners, elected officials, city engineers, state parks commissioners, and federal bureau-crats and administrators. His list of clients was moving away from total reliance on public projects to include a number of country clubs and private courses for individuals of considerable wealth. True, most of his connections were concen-trated in the environs of New York, but Jones's horizons were beginning to broaden as he looked to expand his business across many states of the union—and, someday, beyond them.

Personally, his life had changed even more fundamentally. Gone were the loneliness, the depression, the chronic concerns about his health, and the emo-tional insecurities of living life mostly alone. And Robert finally was married to his dearest Ione. As he knew she would, Ione became more than just his wife: She was his rock, helper, right hand, confidence-builder, ego-booster, teacher and editor, financial adviser, secretary, administrative assistant and file clerk, travel agent, moral compass, and his closest confidant and best friend. She was the perfect counterpart to an ambitious and driven husband—a sensitive and loving partner who would always listen to him talk about his schemes and his big dreams, however wild or far-fetched some may have sounded. He could be away from home for days or weeks, and he would know that Ione would be at home, devotedly taking care of anything important that came up and waiting for his return. She was a lovely and gracious person, a charming and sociable lady who knew how to act and what to say in every social or business situation. As Robert himself later said, Ione was "the foundation of my career." Herb Graffis, who became a friend of the family, called her "the best public relations man in America."

As the decade ended and the chaos and destruction of another global con-flagration descended, Ione would also become the mother of his children, two sons who chose to follow in their father's footsteps, thereby creating what would be, arguably, the most extraordinary—and certainly, the most factious and petulant—dynasty in the history of American golf course architecture.

CHAPTER SIX

ON THE HOME FRONT

Himself an avid golfer, James F. Evans (1895–1972), the director of parks for the State of New York, played a leading role in securing funding for the construction of New Deal golf courses throughout the Empire State, a half dozen of them designed by Robert Trent Jones (to Evans's right). PGA star Gene Sarazen (to Evans's left, 1902–1999) helped boost Jones's projects by offering some design ideas and by playing exhibitions at the gala opening of Jones's publicly funded golf courses.

On January 7, 1941, exactly eleven months before the Japanese attack on Pearl Harbor, Herb and Joe Graffis mailed out a letter to all of their prospective *Golfdom* advertisers declaring that "a boom year is beginning for the golf business" in America—as the brothers trumpeted it, it would be the "BIGGEST BUSINESS AND GOLF PLAY SINCE 1928!" The editors were not exaggerating. As historian George B. Kirsch has explained: "In 1941 prospects for golf in the United States on both private and public golf courses seemed promising, even as war raged in Europe and Asia and the nation moved closer to direct involvement in the conflagration. Most of the country clubs that had survived the ravages of the Depression were in sound condition, and municipal links had benefitted enormously from the assistance provided by New Deal programs. Business at winter golf resorts was booming." The statistics for 1940 showed that 2,351,000 golfers played 63,406,000 rounds of golf on 5,209 golf courses (27 rounds per golfer/12,172 rounds per course)—all of those numbers setting U.S. records. Although 3,288 (or more than 61 percent) of the total number of golf courses were private, only 650,000 (27 percent) of the golfers were country club members; both of those percentages were the lowest in the history of American golf, reflecting the democratization of the sport. Golf play among both women and juniors was growing markedly, up more than 75 percent at many courses around the country. Sales figures from Spalding, Wilson, and other U.S. golf equipment manufacturers indicated that roughly a half million new sets of golf clubs had been bought by Americans in 1939–40.

The year 1939 had started out in an awful way for Robert Trent Jones and the entire Jones family. In the frigid early-morning hours of January 3, Robert's younger brother Ernest, thirty-one years old, was found dead in his automobile, a victim of carbon monoxide poisoning. Ernest's car was parked in the driveway outside the East Rochester home of twenty-three-year-old Emily Wojeck, "his young woman companion," who told police that "she and Jones had driven in about 1:00 A.M. and had sat in the car talking." The next thing she remembered was feeling ill and dizzy, opening the door, and falling to the ground. Partially recovering, she "looked into the car and discovered Jones was dead." The headline about the incident in the next evening's Rochester *Democrat and Chronicle* read, GAS KILLS MAN; GIRL ESCAPES. Curiously, Robert would make nary a reference to his brother's death—or, for that matter, to anything at all about his brother—in any of his writings from that era or later. Over the ensuing decades he would also make hardly any references to Ernest in any of his autobiographical writings or any of the interviews conducted with him about his life history. According to son Bobby, "To outsiders, my father never talked about serious emotional or family matters, because he felt it would reveal weakness. As for my grandmother Jones, she never really recovered from Ernest's death."

For Robert, there was not much time for grieving. Shortly before his brother's death, Ione had become pregnant. On July 24, 1939, the child was born, a beautiful tow-headed son. The adoring parents christened him Robert Trent Jones Jr., a natural appellation for a first-born (although technically, the boy was the first Robert Trent Jones, because his father's given name was simply "Robert Jones" and he only added "Trent" to distinguish himself from the golf champion).

As proud as he was to have a son and a namesake, Robert, like the majority of American fathers of that generation, spent little time helping Ione at home with the baby. Indeed, Jones was busier than he had ever been. "I have been swamped all summer doing about ten courses," he wrote Herb Graffis in early October 1939.

Three of the golf courses that occupied a lot of Robert's time in the autumn of 1939 were new WPA projects. One of them involved a major remodeling of the 18-hole Valley View Golf Course for the Municipal Golf Association of Utica. The ceremonial opening for Valley View came on July 15, 1941; the course got very positive reviews, especially from the city golf association: "Now that we have one of the very finest golf courses that I have ever seen, with our large grass tees, sporty undulating greens, good fairways, and water on all tees and greens, the only thing remaining is that the course be kept in proper condition." Robert took care of that matter for Utica by taking over all the course maintenance duties for an annual fee, a deal similar to what Thompson & Jones had been offering to clubs back during the worst of the Depression.

Jones's second new WPA project was a nine-hole course to be built for the town of Hancock, New York, just east of Binghamton. Construction got started in the summer of 1939, but WPA funding dried up well before the course was finished, and it was abandoned until after the war. (With the help of postwar reconstruction funding arranged by New York's formidable public servant Robert Moses, Jones returned to Hancock to finish the course, which opened for play in the summer of 1947.)

The third of Jones's WPA projects did not get very far before being terminated for lack of funding. It was to be another New York State Park golf course, near the village of Speculator, a resort in the Adirondacks known not just for its skiing but also for being the favorite training site for heavyweight boxing champions Gene Tunney, Max Baer, and Max Schmeling. As late as September 1942, ten months after Pearl Harbor, Robert was still making occasional visits to Speculator for work on the course, but it seems not to have been finished, or at least was never made operational, and plans for the course were not revived after the war.

Throughout the 1930s Jones's career as a golf course architect unquestionably depended upon government money being available for public golf course projects. By the end of the decade, however, that well was running dry, and Jones knew it.* Fortunately, his reputation had grown to the point that

---

* In the late 1930s Jones helped two other New York towns go after WPA funding for public golf course construction, both of them in Franklin County, which lies along the Canadian border in the northeastern part of the state. The first of these WPA proposals was for the construction of a nine-hole golf course for the town of Malone, the county seat. Submitted for consideration by the WPA on October 6, 1937, the Malone proposal asked for a total of $63,382.70 to create a variety of recreational facilities, including a swimming pool, tennis and shuffleboard courts, and the golf course, the last of which accounted for the lion's share of the budget: $38,850. There are no records known to the author to indicate that Malone received any help from the WPA in the form of funding or labor. However, an 18-hole golf course known as the Malone Golf Club, which was designed by English immigrant Willard G. Wilkinson, was built in Malone in 1939. Perhaps WPA support was involved, but we know definitively that Jones was not. Five decades later, however, in 1987, Jones did finally build a course in Malone, for the Malone Golf Club. Jones's course, which plays at 6,592 yards and a par of 71, was dubbed the "West Course," while the original Wilkinson layout became the "East Course."

The second WPA proposal involving Jones, which was submitted to the WPA on May 8, 1938, came from the town of Altamont, some thirty miles west of Lake Placid. (This town of Altamont should not be confused with the town of Altamont in Albany County; properly identifying the correct "Altamont" is even more difficult because the town changed its name in 2004 to Tupper Lake.) From the WPA, the town board of Altamont requested $57,109.00, all

private clients were seeking him out to design courses for them. Not all of these contacts led to jobs, and some that did lead to jobs were stopped in their tracks when the United States entered World War II in late 1941. One that did proceed led to the design and construction of a course for Fairfax Country Club in Fairfax, Virginia, a facility which later became known as the Army Navy Country Club Fairfax. In March 1940, Jones got an assignment to design his first golf course in the mid-Atlantic region, a nine-hole layout for John S. Connolly, owner of J. S. Connolly, Inc., based in Bethesda, Maryland, one of the country's leading distributors for "Grass Cutting Equipment & Supplies for Parks, Cemeteries, Schools, Estates, Golf Courses." Not only was Jones "impressed with this land you have purchased and the fine possibilities you have for an outstanding course," he was, as he wrote Connolly, "anxious to have a course of my design in the Washington, D.C. area." By the fall of 1940, Jones had finished nine holes, and Connolly wrote to Jones, "If we have any growing weather at all, it should be in good shape by spring. . . . I think it is going to be a very pleasant and attractive course." Work on a second name started in the spring of 1941, then came Pearl Harbor, stopping further work on the course. Connolly served in the war as a U.S. Army major. In June 1945 Jones wrote to him, successfully getting the project going again and finishing the second nine holes of the course in 1946. (In 1952 Jones built a second nine for the Country Club of Fairfax [originally known as Court House Country Club], a completely different

---

of which was to be used for the expansion of an existing course in the hamlet of Moody from nine holes to a full eighteen. The identity of that existing nine-hole course in the Moody neighborhood of Altamont is uncertain; it must have been the original nine holes of Tupper Lake Country Club; either that, or the Moody course no longer exists. What is known is that a second nine was added to Tupper Lake Country Club in 1941; perhaps this was the additional nine-hole layout that Jones had helped the Altamont town board propose to the WPA in May 1938. It is not known whether Altamont received any WPA assistance and, if it did, why Jones did not get to do the course design. The "genealogy" of Tupper Lake Country Club, a highly scenic course with panoramic views of surrounding mountains and lakes, is perplexing. Author Bradley S. Klein indicates in his *Discovering Donald Ross: The Architect and His Golf Courses* (Chelsea, MI: Sleeping Bear Press, 2001), p. 346, that the original Tupper Lake Country Club was a Ross design from the year 1915. The website for Tupper Lake Golf Club, as the club is known today, advertises that the 6,003-yard, par-71 course is, in fact, a Ross design, but from 1932. Curiously, authors Cornish and Whitten in *The Architects of Golf* (New York: HarperCollins, 1981), p. 434, show English-born Willard G. Wilkinson as the architect who created the first nine holes of the Tupper Lake Country Club in 1932. Their book also has Wilkinson designing the second nine that was added at Tupper Lake in 1941.

Copies of both of the towns' WPA proposals are extant in the Jones Papers at Cornell.

facility, in Fairfax County, whose front nine had been designed by William F. Gordon.)

The private clients that worked out best for Jones in the war years were those who possessed so much money or exerted so much influence that U.S. entry into the war did not upset their personal ambitions for building private golf courses. Robert was fortunate to tap into a couple of these lucrative situations, making enough money from them to build a little "war chest" to help carry him and his family through the near total stoppage of any golf course work until after the war. (Jones purchased an upper-middle-class home at 114 Montclair Avenue in Upper Montclair just before the war started for $15,000, the equivalent of roughly $250,000 in 2014 dollars.)

The enriching experience of getting to know Lester Norris in Illinois showed Robert just how much he relished rubbing elbows with captains of industry and other men of great talent or wealth. "My father was always fascinated by the idea of being socially respectable," relates his son, Robert Trent Jones Jr. "Coming from the state of New York, and moving to New York City in particular, which was the commercial capital of our nation, he felt that the highest order was the commercial giants of New York City in various forms. In addition, the people who could afford to build golf courses were giants in their own communities." The ambitious immigrant son of a father who built railroad cars with his hands in East Rochester wanted to climb to the top rung of the American social ladder. He wanted to make deals with the giants, build golf courses for them, and socialize with them. More than that, he wanted to *be* one of them.

In 1937, Jones got the first of what would turn out to be many opportunities over the subsequent course of his career to become associated with "the rich and famous." The chance came thanks to his friendship with golf champion Gene Sarazen.

In 1933 Sarazen had bought a parcel in rural Brookfield, Connecticut, called Valley Ridge Farm, where the "Squire," as Gene came to be called, raised chickens and ran a herd of a half dozen Guernsey cattle. Not far to the northwest of the Sarazen farm, across the state line in Pawling, New York, lived the adventurer, world traveler, and CBS radio personality Lowell Thomas. If Sarazen was that area's country squire, Thomas was its feudal baron. Thanks to the generosity of his popular radio program's chief sponsor, Sun Oil, Thomas and his wife, Frances, had purchased a vast 2,000-acre estate at the north end of Quaker

Hill, a hamlet a mere hour's commute by train to Thomas's office at the RCA Building in Manhattan. Purchased in 1936, the Thomas estate was an absolutely stunning property, much of it majestically situated atop a plateau in fertile Dutchess County, with a scenic lake, beautiful rolling farmland, and miles of wooded acreage. When Sarazen first visited the estate, he told Thomas that it was the closest thing to Shangri-La he had ever seen—the only thing was, it didn't have a golf course on it. "I have just the guy to design it for you," Sarazen offered. "His name is Robert Trent Jones, and he's a good friend of mine." Before long, Thomas phoned Jones and the two men met for lunch in a New York City restaurant. Hearing about Thomas's Quaker Hill demesne, Robert couldn't wait to get up and see it. Marveling at a panoramic view that stretched for forty miles in every direction, he told Thomas that he had never in his life seen a better tract of land for a golf course (Jones would make this inflated comment about his golf course sites many times during his career), that it was "a natural meadowland that could be converted into fairways with a minimum of disking and harrowing." Thomas told him to get working on it. Later, in a letter to Jones, Thomas extolled: "I am delighted you are so enthusiastic and I hope it turns out to be one of the most satisfactory courses anywhere on earth!"

Shortly after making his preliminary routing plan for the Quaker Hill golf course, which was to be only nine holes, Jones asked Sarazen to meet him at the Thomas estate so he could show him his plans for the golf course. While Sarazen and Jones walked the grounds together, a man on horseback rode up. It was a local resident who just happened to be Thomas E. Dewey, the prominent district attorney for New York County (Manhattan) who would be elected the governor of New York in 1942, lose the presidential election to Roosevelt in 1944, and almost defeat Harry S. Truman in 1948. "How are you going to lay out the course?" the mustachioed Dewey boomed in his gruff, deep voice. Jones explained his plan, to which Dewey replied, "Well, I guess that looks all right," then curtly rode away. "What a nice guy," Jones remarked, impressed as he always was with men of power and influence. Sarazen expressed a different opinion: "He's an asshole."

When completed in 1941, the golf course became the home of the Quaker Hill Country Club. With two distinct teeing areas for each hole, which enabled an 18-hole round, the Quaker Hill course played to a distance of 6,110 yards and a par of 70. Although very playable, it was a challenging and never-boring golf course, whose contoured greens required a lot of local knowledge. (In 2010, *Golf Digest* ranked Quaker Hill as the twentieth-best nine-hole golf course in

America.) Its membership was kept deliberately small and highly select. Among those paying annual dues were the president of Dow Jones, the editor of *The Wall Street Journal*, a number of leading corporate lawyers, a few heads of New York City advertising agencies, the aforementioned Thomas Dewey, and other notable full-time or part-time residents of the Quaker Hill area. The club's first president was the noted American writer and poet Archibald MacLeish; when MacLeish was not making golf wagers with his good friend Lowell Thomas, he served as FDR's appointee as the Librarian of Congress.

One of the most remarkable features of the Quaker Hill Country Club—a feature that Jones enjoyed but for which he was not responsible—was the club-house, a converted nineteenth-century barn. Upstairs in the loft of "The Recreation Barn" was a mammoth fireplace 30 feet high and 20 feet wide with embedded mementos from Thomas's worldwide travels, including a 4000 B.C. stone from the ancient kingdom of Ur in Mesopotamia as well as stones from St. Peter's in Rome, an ancient Mayan ruin, a Buddhist shrine, and a Hindu temple; also a stone from the Robert Peary monument at the western tip of Greenland, a block from the Empire State Building, a piece from the head of George Washington on Mt. Rushmore, as well as stones from Thomas Edison's home, the Grand Coulee Dam, and the Golden Gate Bridge—gifts from Thomas's many influential friends around the world. Saturday night dances were held at "The Barn," lively and privileged social events that Robert and Ione were delighted to sometimes attend. At one of the parties Robert and Ione met former President Herbert Hoover, IBM president Thomas J. Watson, and Will H. Hays, the former chair of the Republican National Committee and former U.S. Postmaster General who was president of the Hollywood-based Motion Picture Producers and Distributors of America (and the namesake of the infamous "Hays Code" for censorship of American films). At another one of the Barn shindigs, the Joneses met singer-actor Bing Crosby, who was also a very avid golfer and someone that Robert would get to know very well after the war. (In October 1940, Robert and Bing played their first round of golf together at Pine Valley Golf Club in New Jersey, followed by dinner; Jones called Crosby "a swell guy.")

At some point during the construction of the Quaker Hill golf course the idea came to Jones—or to Thomas, or to both of them—that a second, smaller golf course should be built on Thomas's land, on some nice acreage less than a mile from the country club. This links would become Thomas's personal playground. Lowell called it simply his "Hammersley Hill course," which was the original name for the lake on his property before he changed its name to "Quaker Lake." (Hammersley Hill was also the name of the handsome red-brick Georgian mansion in which the Thomases lived on Quaker Hill. In 1935, before Thomas bought the property, the total value of the estate was estimated to be $1.5 million, equivalent today to more than $25 million.)

The Hammersley Hill golf course was not completed until 1947. For Thomas's private enjoyment, Jones made it a sporty four-hole routing that could be played from different tees so that the golfer had various ways to play a full eighteen. It was a highly unusual course, with excellent greens and one extraordinarily long hole measuring 870 yards that played to a par of 7.5. (According to one of the rules that Thomas apparently made up for the course, any ball hit to within a club-length of the hole was a "gimme" and counted as only a half-stroke.) There were two holes that played to pars of 3.5 and 4.5. One of the "nines" that could be played from a certain combination of tees had a cumulative par of 37.5. Unfortunately, the golf course no longer exists. A few of the greens are still puttable, and the realtor in charge of the property (the asking price in 2009 for just this portion of the former Thomas estate was $15 million) asserts that the course could be easily resurrected.

On the eve of World War II, Jones had one final brush—for the time being—with millionaires wanting their own golf courses. James H. R. Cromwell, husband of the immensely rich tobacco heiress Doris Duke, wanted a private 18-hole layout built at Duke Farms, the glorious 2,740-acre estate near Somerville in Hillsborough Township, New Jersey, some fifty miles southwest of New York City. "This estate is one of the most beautiful, horticulturally, that I have ever seen," Jones wrote to Herb Graffis in October 1939, in the midst of building the golf course at Duke Farms. Cromwell wanted it finished as quickly as possible, and it was ready for play in the spring of 1940. Very little is known about the layout, other than it was a full eighteen holes and took beautiful advantage of some of the property's nine little lakes. In one of the lakes, Jones built an island green par-3, 110 yards from the shore and reachable only by a rowboat. "You'll be surprised how difficult it will be to hit that green," Jones warned Cromwell and his friends. "You'd think anyone would be able to hit a green area of 6,300 square feet with a niblick pitch, but when you stand on that tee on the edge of the lake and see all that water that you can also hit—why, I'm telling you, the psychological pressure is terrific. It makes the hole almost as rugged a par-3 as the sixteenth at Cypress Point or the ninth at Yale." It seems certain that the course never saw much play before Cromwell was appointed ambassador to Canada in 1940; with Doris and Cromwell divorcing in 1943 (their union was considered the veritable "marriage from hell"), the golf course did not survive much past the war. Perhaps the links reminded her too much of her ex-husband, whom she came to despise. But she always loved Duke Farms, and she later became devoted to a number of horticultural and ecological projects on the property, which remained her chief residence.

For Robert Trent Jones, as for millions of other Americans, the news of the Japanese attack on Pearl Harbor came as an interruption to a radio program on an otherwise tranquil Sunday afternoon. Robert's family had grown—on September 16, 1941, Ione had given birth to a second son, Rees Lee, named after his paternal grandfather. It was 2:30 P.M. and baby Rees and his brother Bobby Jr., a toddler of two and a half, were taking their afternoon naps. Robert and Ione were in their easy chairs listening to the start of CBS Radio's regular broadcast of *The World Today* when the program was interrupted: "*The Japanese have attacked Pearl Harbor, Hawaii, by air, President Roosevelt has just announced. The attack was made on all naval and military activities on the principal island of Oahu.*" Immediately, the Joneses knew it was no hoax. A real war had come to the United States—a war into which the country would pour everything it had until it won. Instantaneously, Jones knew, "golf architecture is dead for the duration."

Robert couldn't be sure he wouldn't be drafted. He was thirty-six years old and with a wife and two infant children, but the needs of the U.S. military in wartime would prove to be gargantuan. The goal of FDR's administration was to have nine million men in the armed forces by the end of 1943. Every man between twenty-one and forty-eight (changed in December 1942 to between eighteen and thirty-eight) was eligible for selection by the lottery system being used by the country's four thousand local draft boards. In April 1942, the Selective Service System even held a special registration for the draft targeting men between forty-five and sixty-four years of age—not for active military service but for help on the home front.

Jones was a highly patriotic American and highly pro-British, but he definitely did not want to be drafted. Back in January 1941, just weeks after the Selective Service System had been established for the possibility of the first

peacetime conscription in American history, Robert wrote a rare letter to his
father instructing him about the affidavit that he should sign to inform Selective
Service that Robert was contributing significantly in a financial way to his
parents' care and well-being. "It is quite unlikely that I should be called in this
draft," Robert told his dad, "but if it came to a knock down and drag out fight,
your signing this affidavit might make the difference of my going to war or not."
In October 1942 Jones notified the Upper Montclair draft board that his home
address had changed from 92 Watchung Avenue, Upper Montclair, to 217
Orange Road, Montclair, New Jersey. Even as late as 1943 Robert was soliciting
letters to be sent to his draft board from three different doctors who could
certify to problems with his health: first, from the doctor in Rochester who had
treated his peptic ulcer back in the early 1930s; second, from a Manhattan physician who certified that he was currently suffering from "persistent" prostate
and bladder infections that will "continue to require urologic treatment for
some time"; and third, from an ocular specialist in Montclair who informed the
draft board that he had been treating Jones for "a chronic ethmoiditis" that was
limiting his eyesight in both eyes. To some readers, it may seem that Robert was
overdoing it, but his concerns about being drafted were not ill-founded. Many
married men of his age or older with children were getting drafted or at least
being tagged for special war work on the home front.

Although the Jones family of four would not experience the war as personally, or as tragically, as a great many American families would, their experience of the war had a great deal in common with the experience on the home
front of all American families during the emergency. The rationing of food and
gasoline became a way of life, with Robert scrounging every last ration coupon
he could to purchase the necessary gasoline for his automobile trips out to his
jobs around New York and New Jersey. When he could manage it, he would buy
a new pair of silk stockings for Ione, a luxury in short supply because silk was
needed to manufacture parachutes for the military. But Ione did not always
wear them. Although she was a woman accustomed to dressing well and fash-
ionably, she considered it patriotic to wear her old silk stockings even if they had
holes and runs in them.

Robert was away just about as much during the war as before it, going by
train into his small New York City office or driving out to one of his courses
under construction. Most nights he would make it home for homemade meals
that Ione prepared using whatever her ration coupons could get her. Unlike tens

of thousands of women who were hired to replace men in the factories or take other jobs, Ione had two little boys to take care of, so she worked at home, doing what she could to help the war effort by salvaging her tin cans, bottles, paper, and even fats left over from cooking. Sometimes she would have a neighbor lady babysit Bobby and Rees while she walked to the local Red Cross to help with one of the many thousands of blood drives held around the nation to aid America's fighting forces. Rees was too young to remember anything from the war years (he was born four months before Pearl Harbor and turned four years old the month of the Japanese surrender), and Bobby, who started the first grade right after the war ended, today can remember only a little: "I remember we'd close our dark 'blackout' curtains, turn off the lights, and go downstairs and hide under the tables during air-raid drills. My mother would tell stories to keep us entertained, which she was very good at, as she had graduated first in her class at Wells College, minoring in English literature." As terrible as the times were in many essential respects, there was a heightened sense of excitement during the war that almost all Americans felt at one level or another.

It is fortunate for those who are interested in Jones's complete life story that Robert was so concerned about getting drafted into the military, because the best summaries of what work he was doing during the Second World War, on and off golf courses, can be found in letters he sent on his own behalf to his draft board.

"Wars just aren't any good for people in our business," Jones wrote to Joe Graffis in February 1942. As much as possible, Robert kept himself busy "cleaning up some of the courses that were started prior to Pearl Harbor," but it wasn't easy to do when both the money and the labor for course construction were vanishing into the war machine. Some of Jones's most talented and experienced superintendents of construction—men like Willis Garrett, Alfred Ulrich, and William Baldwin—volunteered for military service or were drafted. Of the three, Baldwin deserves special mention, because Jones valued him highly, treated him generously, and kept Bill working with him as his chief construction superintendent for the next forty years.

During the war Jones "spent a little time working as a turf consultant for the government, which was trying to figure out why airport runways were breaking down." Jones's records show that he consulted on the grass runways for an air base in the army's Second Corps Area, whose headquarters was at Fort Jay on

Governors Island in Upper New York Bay. He also "worked with the Air Base in Syracuse in a condemnation job"—an army project north of the city involving the building of three 5,500-foot runways that were displacing several inhabited farms. In addition, as he related to Joe Graffis on January 7, 1942, just a month after Pearl Harbor, Robert got a government contract "working on a recreational center for a machine gun plant, which came along at a most welcome time in the low ebb of the golf business." But in his letters to the draft board, the principal war work that he emphasized was his work for "Plant No. 4" of the International Business Machines Corporation in Poughkeepsie: "This is part of a large contract and at the present time involves the completion of a pump house, water system, and dam." As Robert explained to Selective Service in December 1943, "This plant is engaged solely in the manufacture of guns for the Army."

Although he put his work for IBM at the top of the list of the "war work," what he emphasized most of all to his local draft board was the growing importance of his associations with the New York State Postwar Planning Commission. Long before it was certain the United States and its allies would defeat Germany and Japan, various government bodies at the federal, state, and local levels around the country were already starting to plan ahead, not just to retool into a peacetime economy but also to stimulate a better national well-being as a whole, with fuller employment, improved public services, and, if possible, the resolution of many of the nation's most critical social issues. Thanks to his close friendship with the state parks commissioner in Albany, James Evans, who in turn was the right-hand man for Robert Moses, Jones had all the political connections he needed to participate actively in New York's planning for its postwar public works projects. For Robert, it was as if the New Deal would be happening all over again, with nice chunks of public money potentially being available for future golf courses and other recreational building projects. To Selective Service, Robert summarized his involvement with the city and state in the following way:

New York City: Department of Parks. This is an important post-war plan for which I have been retained as a specialist since they have no one in either the engineering or architectural developments who could prepare these plans.

New York State: Department of Parks, Albany, New York: Preparation of post-war plans; operation of a golf course under lease [a reference to the management concession he held for Green Lakes State Park Golf Course].

As a final item, Jones told the draft board that he had just been commissioned by the city of New Canaan, Connecticut, to start working on their postwar plans.

If New York City's Robert Moses wasn't the person most responsible for keeping Jones busy and making money during World War II, then it was Thomas J. Watson, the head of IBM. As mentioned earlier, Jones got a contract in early 1942 to build a pump house, dam, and watering system for IBM Plant No. 4 in Poughkeepsie, a large facility that was manufacturing guns—specifically, aircraft cannon—for the U.S. military. Tom Watson, it turns out, was also a golfer. He had met Jones at the Lowell Thomas estate (Poughkeepsie was the seat of Dutchess County) and had played golf at Quaker Hill on its festive opening day. Watson thought that since Jones was going to be spending time in Poughkeepsie anyway, why not have him build a golf course that could be part of "a complete recreational center" for his IBM employees?

An anecdote from the IBM golf course project illuminates how Jones interacted with a powerful client and found a way to persuade that client that the golf architect really knows best when it comes to building a golf course. Early on, while Jones, Watson, and ten of Watson's minions were walking the property, the IBM president pointed at a large hill and suggested that Jones "put a tee up there" to take advantage of the beautiful view. Jones replied that it was "a pretty steep climb to the top," but Watson rebutted, "Well, they're out here for the exercise, aren't they?" "Well, yes," Jones admitted. "Why don't we all climb up there and take a look?" By the time the group made it to the top, everyone in the party was totally winded. "Well, I think we can forget about *this* hill," Watson conceded. "Go ahead and build the course the way you want." When Jones finished the course in 1945, Watson urged him to take his fee—some $13,000—in IBM stock. "But I had a family to feed," Jones remembered many years later, "and I refused. I've occasionally wondered what that stock would be worth now." (In 2000, the year Jones died, the stock would have been worth approximately $15 million.)

Dedicated with patriotic pomp and circumstance on July 15, 1944, just five weeks after D-Day, the course was called the IBM Country Club. Initially it had only nine holes, although three months prior to the opening, Jones was already telling friends that the course "probably will be lengthened to eighteen holes before too long, and should prove to be a very profitable job." The original nine holes played to a par 35 and a distance of 3,265 yards. Never lacking for words to praise his layouts, Jones told reporters on opening day that "One could travel throughout the whole East without finding a more thrilling, beautiful and interesting nine-hole course." It was, indeed, a beautiful golf course, built from some fine farmland and wooded acreage that IBM had purchased soon after the war started, with majestic oaks framing a number of holes and views of the surrounding mountains in three directions. From the first tee on a clear day, golfers could see Newburgh Bay, a wide section of the Hudson River just upriver from the Hudson Highlands. Meandering through the grounds was Casperkill Creek as well as a section of Revolutionary Lane, a narrow road dating back to the Revolutionary War. To the gala opening, Robert brought Ione and their two little boys; they joined the IBM employees and their families for a picnic in a wooded area that was part of Plant No. 4's new recreation center, which also featured three tennis courts and several horseshoe pitching areas. IBM president Watson hit the ceremonial first tee shot (but not without first addressing the audience about what it meant to be an IBM employee), with other officers of the corporation then trying out their driving abilities. Jones was introduced to an appreciative crowd and he smacked the longest drive right down the middle of the fairway. The month of the course's opening, the IBM employee magazine, *Activity,* carried an article by Jones in which he explained his "theory of modern architecture" and exactly how all of its principles were embodied in the new course that he had built for them. It was hardly an easy golf course. Four of its six par-4s played longer than 400 yards, including one that was 440. The two par-3s played 190 and 200 yards.

A second nine did get built by Jones at the IBM Country Club; it opened shortly after war's end. It was enjoyed by generations of IBM employees in the Hudson Valley, who just by being IBM workers received automatic membership privileges.† Eventually the family-oriented club got Jones to reconfigure the

---

† Not all IBM employees looked upon the new recreation center with total favor. Some felt that IBM president Thomas Watson used the country club to keep out labor unions. As soon as any employees started to talk about unionizing, IBM corporate leadership would say, "OK, you want a union? Then we're going to close the Country Club." Whether it was due to the country club or not, the fact is that IBM employees never unionized. One man who worked for IBM from 1951 to 1989 who was interviewed about the history of the country club said that

routing of the two nines, and this created a completely different layout, one that had both nines playing to a par of 36. When that happened, the course from the back tees stretched out to 6,690 yards. When IBM scaled back its operations in Poughkeepsie in the late 1980s, the company sold the golf course to a real estate development company, which turned it into Casperkill Golf Club, with a private membership, which later became a public course. In 1988 New York–based golf architect Stephen Kay did some remodeling of the Casperkill course. Even today, the golf course is considered one of the best in the Hudson Valley and is advertised appropriately as a Robert Trent Jones design.

In his later years Jones would describe his World War II golf design business as "catch-as-catch-can." The phrase belies how much drive, initiative, and behind-the-scenes salesmanship it took on his part to get the few jobs that he did. In addition to his many rich and powerful friends, he had excellent connections inside the major golf organizations, including the USGA, PGA of America, National Association of Greenkeepers of America (founded in Toledo in 1926), state golf associations of New York and New Jersey, Metropolitan Golf Association of New York City, as well as the golf associations of a number of other towns and cities, not just in his home state of New York. As a result, he was strategically positioned to tap into information networks that could show him where and when real opportunities for building golf courses would come to light.

It is not precisely clear how Jones got the assignment late in the war to design golf courses for two military hospitals, Halloran General Hospital on Staten Island and the Lyons General Hospital in New Jersey, thirty-six miles west of New York City. He was certainly well aware that the U.S. Army, besides keeping many of its on-base golf courses open for play by officers and enlisted men as well as by soldiers recuperating from battle injuries, had also taken over a number of large existing facilities of different kinds and purposes and converted them into military hospitals. Some of these places already had golf courses on or around their grounds—the most notable being Ashford General

he "did not necessarily see it as a negative thing that IBM has never had a union," but he definitely felt that the company had "used the aesthetic and recreational resource to manipulate its employees." See Eli Jones, "The IBM Country Club and Golf Course," July 26, 2010, accessed on August 19, 2012 at http://blogs.vassar.edu/casperkill/the-ibm-country-club-and-golf-course/. This July 2010 article was a result of the Casperkill Watershed Oral History Project carried out by the Environmental Research Institute and Environmental Studies Program at Vassar College.

Hospital in White Sulphur Springs, West Virginia, home to the Greenbrier Hotel, where convalescing veterans could enjoy, with clubs and balls donated to the hospital, two complete 18-hole courses and one nine-hole course. "The importance of golf in the physical reconditioning of patients cannot be overemphasized," proclaimed Colonel Clyde M. Beck, Medical Corps, U.S. Army, the commanding officer of the installation. "Muscles are exercised that have long been dormant. Eyes are strengthened and coordination of mind and muscles is re-developed. Not only does golf do this for our patients, but this sport permits the men to get out into the fresh air and sunshine."

The USGA, PGA of America, and other golf organizations had launched patriotic campaigns to help with the war effort. By the end of 1942 the USGA had sold more than $3.7 million worth of war bonds and stamps (Ione bought hundreds of dollars' worth for her family), primarily through contributions by member clubs and the staging of charity events around the country known as "Hale America" tournaments, held on Memorial Day, the Fourth of July, and Labor Day. For its part, the PGA (with more than 2,000 members in 1941) offered several programs to support the troops. The Metropolitan section of the PGA, the largest in the country, raised some $21,000 to help build a golf course at Halloran General Hospital, an institution originally built by the New York State Department of Mental Hygiene for the care of "mentally disabled children" but one that the Army took over as soon as it was finished in 1942. When the Army moved ahead with the idea of building a small golf course on the grounds, the job of designing it went, without much fuss, to Jones, who by the middle of the war was quite well known in the New York City area as one of the country's leading golf architects.

With only 23 acres to work with, Robert could only squeeze in nine holes, all of them par-3s and a few of them not much more than "pitch-and-putt[s]." "The thrill holes of golf are most often the little ones," he told the newspapers and golf magazines. "It is in the short hole category that we find the greatest number of golf's famous holes. Therefore, when I was asked to design the PGA golf course at Halloran General Hospital, I thought that it would make a unique and interesting course if we adapted in principle and designed to the site some of the world's greatest short holes." The holes that the little course emulated were, in order of play: #15 Redan hole at North Berwick in Scotland; #10 Gibraltar hole at Moortown Golf Club in Leeds, England; #15 at Cypress Point on California's Monterey Peninsula; #10 at Winged Foot in Mamaroneck, New

York; #11 at the Old Course at St. Andrews; #9 at Pinehurst No. 2 in North Carolina; #16 at Augusta National in Georgia; #18 at Garden City Golf Club on Long Island; and #3 at Philadelphia Country Club's Spring Mill course.‡ "These holes are not copies," explained Jones, "as copies always fall short of the original in that they do not fit the site. But the principle of the trapping and some of the features that made the original holes great have been adapted in principle."

The ingenious little golf course at Halloran General Hospital opened for play in May 1945. After looking over a print of the course layout that a friend sent him, Herb Graffis wrote to Jones to tell him: "This is one of the swellest things I've seen. The idea of getting the best short holes of the world together is really a knock-out."

It did not remain a golf course for long. In 1947 the New York State Department of Mental Hygiene took the hospital and its grounds back and converted them to their original purpose as the Willowbrook State School, a state-supported institution "for children with intellectual disabilities." Today, the land that had been the golf course is part of the campus of the College of Staten Island.

Happily, the golf course that Jones built at the army hospital in Lyons, New Jersey, still exists. Dedicated on Memorial Day 1947 to all New Jersey golfers who died in the Second World War, the course was named the Coakley-Russo Memorial Golf Course in honor of two New Jersey professional golfers, Lt. Francis X. Coakley and Sgt. Nick Russo, who were killed serving their country. Once again, there was only enough land for Jones to make it a nine-hole layout but, unlike the Halloran hospital course, not all the holes were par-3s. At a length of 3,300 yards from the back tees, the course played to a par of 34.

Jones started building one more military course before the war ended, and it was a prestigious one, for the United States Military Academy at West Point. The key to Robert's getting this job was impressing Colonel Lawrence M. "Biff"

---

‡ Given the significant remodeling work that Jones would do for Robert Tyre Jones on the par-3 16th hole at Augusta National in the late 1940s (covered in the next chapter), it is interesting to read Robert's description of what that now world-famous hole at Augusta had been, and Halloran's replica of it: "The seventh hole at Halloran is patterned after the sixteenth at Augusta National, which has a creek cutting across the green at a diagonal and the slope of the green is quite sharp toward the creek. As there was no water at Halloran, a trap has taken the place of the creek in the original hole. The contours of the green and the trap behind the green are of the same principle." RTJ quoted in "Halloran Course is Exhibit of Famous Short Holes," *Golfdom* (Fall 1945): 36, 40.

Jones, West Point's athletic director (a position then called the "Graduate Manager of Athletics"). The architect pulled in the big guns to impress Colonel Jones, who had coached the Army football team from 1926 to 1929, when Jones was attending Cornell. Three men that we know wrote letters to West Point on Robert's behalf were James Evans, Robert Moses, and Lowell Thomas. In his letter, Moses told the athletic director that "Jones has the reputation of being one of the outstanding golf architects of the country. He is now preparing some plans for the State Postwar Public Works Planning Commission and has acted as a golf course consultant for the County of Nassau and other municipalities. I am familiar with his work and I am sure he would do a good job for you."

Whatever it was that most impressed Colonel Biff Jones, he gave Robert Trent Jones the assignment. This time, instead of WPA relief workers, the architect had the free use of German POWs to do the labor. The work was strenuous and included blasting the corridors for some of the golf holes out of solid rock. One day during construction Jones took Gene Sarazen to see the course work getting under way. Robert asked Gene if he wanted to go down into a small group of trees and watch the prisoners at work cutting some of the trees down with chain saws. A proud American and the son of an Italian immigrant, Gene shot back, "Mussolini and the Italians surrendered yesterday, and there's no way I'm going to get close to a bunch of Germans!"

At war's end, only twelve of the holes at West Point were done, and the Army could provide no more money at that time to complete it. As it turns out, the course wasn't finished until well into the 1950s. Playing to a par of 70, the layout was barely 6,000 yards long, but because it was very hilly, with lots of elevation changes that created uphill, sidehill, and downhill lies, it played more like a 6,500-yard golf course. In the ensuing decades, the Army's golf teams would play their home matches on the course, and Patriot League Golf Championships would be held on it no less than four times. As challenging as Jones's creation proved to be, for many golfers it was the property's great scenic beauty that left the deepest impressions. Jones himself would always consider the course at the U.S. Military Academy to be one of the very prettiest, and trickiest, that he ever built. Up to that point in time, it also proved to be the most expensive that Robert had ever built.[§] Financed by the Army Athletic Association,

---

§ At West Point, Jones saved some money by getting the sand for the traps from Army cargo ships anchored in the Hudson River. As Jones explained: "The way it worked, those transports

"principally out of its profits on football," the cost topped $350,000 for just those first twelve holes that required much dynamite blasting through solid rock.

The first decade and a half of Robert Trent Jones's remarkable career coincided with "fifteen years of sustained crises both for the United States and its golfing community." By 1946, having weathered both depression and war, Jones was, like America itself, ready to put all the troubles and cares aside, flex his muscles, and expand his golf course business to a position that surpassed even his grand ambitions when he started out. Just as the United States would become the globe's most dominant power after 1945—and just as he had told Ione repeatedly back when he was proposing their marriage—Robert sought to become nothing less than "the world's greatest golf architect."

Over the next few decades, starting with the very first major golf course that he would build in postwar America—Peachtree Golf Club, for legendary Bobby Jones, in Atlanta—Robert Trent Jones would arguably become just that. Along the way he would not only create dozens of outstanding new golf courses for American golfers from coast to coast, but he would also export his theory of modern architecture to faraway parts of the world. In doing so, Jones's designs would establish many of the defining forms, shapes, and challenges of the modern golf course and forever alter the essential character of the layouts—and thus the character of the golf—on which major championships would be played.

---

would sail in convoy for Europe loaded down with war supplies. After dumping their cargoes, they'd pull in near any convenient beach and take on sand for ballast. Well, one of these convoys was routed to Scotland, and I like to think that some of the bunkers at the Point are filled with the authentic stuff, scraped right off the dunes of the linksland." Normally, Jones had been getting the sand for his courses around New York from such nearby locales as Northport, Port Washington, and Port Jefferson—all on the North Shore of Long Island. The sand he got from Port Jefferson, which was dredged from the bottom of Long Island Sound, was "whiter than the Northport and Port Washington varieties and therefore preferable" to Jones. The architect experimented with Jones Beach sand, but "it was so fine that the wind quickly whipped it out of the traps." Early in his career Jones was not finicky about the sand for his traps: "Any reasonably white sand will do, and almost invariably a beach or a quarry fairly near the course can provide it." RTJ quoted in Herbert Warren Wind, "Profiles," *The New Yorker* (4 Aug. 1951): 41.

CHAPTER SEVEN

FROM PEACHTREE TO THE DUNES

Walking the property in 1946 that was to become Atlanta's Peachtree Golf Club were Robert Tyre "Bobby" Jones (far left) and Robert Trent Jones Sr. (far right). With them (from Trent's right) were club founders Charles Currie, Doc Irvin, Dick Garlington, Charlie Black, and John O. Chiles.

Robert Trent Jones's professional association with Bobby Jones, founded on their collaboration in the creation of Peachtree Golf Club outside Atlanta in the years immediately following World War II, led to an enduring friendship. Sharing the same name was a curiosity, but Trent Jones's shrewdness in linking himself to the great golfer worked greatly to his professional advantage as well as to the advantage of his heirs. Even now, fifty years into the golf course design career of Robert Trent Jones Jr., people still ask Trent's eldest son if he is the son of the famous golfer. And like his father, Bob Jr. was not beyond allowing the confusion to go without comment rather than correcting it.

Peachtree took its energy from a constellation of social, economic, and business forces that were invigorating golf in post–World War II America. Some golf historians even refer to the years from 1946 to 1960 as the "second golden age" of American golf (the first golden age was in the Roaring Twenties, when Bobby Jones captured the nation's imagination with his brilliant championship play). Among the most influential factors driving golf ahead following World War II, as historian George Kirsch has pointed out, were "a rising standard of living for blue- and white-collar workers, new rounds of suburbanization and the extension of resort and retirement communities, the promotion of golf by media celebrities (especially Bing Crosby and Bob Hope), the advent of golf cars (today called 'carts'), popular heroes (especially Ben Hogan and Arnold Palmer), and the rise of television." Even before President Dwight D. Eisenhower, elected in 1952, showed his passion—some contemporaries even said obsession—for the little white dimpled ball, a golf boom had hit America. From Maine to California, memberships at private clubs rose dramatically while lines of golfers waiting to get to the first tee on public courses grew longer and longer. This created an explosive demand for new golf facilities of every kind: 18-hole layouts, nine-hole designs, par-3 courses, pitch-and-putt courses, and driving ranges, the latter often with "putt-putt" (or miniature) golf courses alongside them. The post–World War II boom was a bonanza for the golf course design and construction industries, and no one feasted on this cornucopia more than Robert Trent Jones.

The drive to create Peachtree Golf Club started even before the war ended. It was the brainchild of T. R. Garlington, a member of the USGA Green Section Committee who was then president of the Atlanta Athletic Club, a sporting association founded in 1898 that had quickly sprouted after the turn of the century to more than seven hundred members. As he looked ahead to postwar Atlanta, Dick Garlington knew that although the AAC's only golf course—the 18-hole layout at East Lake, some four and a half miles east of downtown—was splendid, it would hardly be sufficient to satisfy the postwar demand for golf likely to come from AAC members. (Originally designed by Tom Bendelow between 1904 and 1907, the East Lake golf course was totally redone by Donald Ross in 1913; it was on this course that the young Bobby Jones cut his teeth as a golfer.) But Garlington didn't want to build just any old golf course. Consulting on the matter with his good friend Robert Tyre Jones Jr., the two men agreed, in Bobby Jones's words, that "we should try to build a course as near like the Augusta National as possible, and better, if possible."

Although Robert Trent Jones was a well-known golf course architect along the central Eastern Seaboard by 1945, he was not well known in Georgia—and he was not really even that well known to Bobby Jones. Robert first heard about the opportunity to design a course for the Atlanta Athletic Club from Ed Dudley, a five-time winner on the PGA circuit who had been Augusta National's club professional since 1932. As Trent Jones would later tell it, "Bobby Jones asked Dudley 'who's the best architect' to build a new course and Dudley said, 'it's Robert Trent Jones.'" According to Robert, "Bobby already knew a little about my work and knew that I had worked early in my career with Stanley Thompson, whose courses Bobby greatly admired." According to Bobby's explanation at the time of the course's opening, "Our choice was Robert Trent Jones of Montclair, New Jersey, on the basis of courses of his that we had seen, his training, and most important the fact that his conception of golf course architecture so perfectly agreed with our own."

Before talking to Bobby Jones about the job, Robert followed Dudley's instructions and in late April 1945 wrote a letter to Dick Garlington stating his strong interest in the job and summarizing his architectural credentials. (Bobby

Jones was not mentioned in Robert's letter.) Under separate cover, the course designer sent to Atlanta "some renderings of some of our post war planning work"; in that packet Robert included a copy of his brochure from 1938 that laid out his views. Garlington responded quickly:

> I was pleased to hear from you this morning with regard to the Golf Course we are figuring on building. . . . I don't know anything about your fees and before we make any definite arrangements about you coming down here to look at the site, I would appreciate your writing me and letting me know what sort of proposal you have in mind. . . . We wouldn't want to go to our associates in this situation without being able to tell them just what the detailed cost of the complete job would be.

To which Jones answered:

> With regard to the fee, the yardstick which we normally use is ten per cent of the cost of construction. If you and your associates on the other hand wanted a flat figure rather than a cost-plus proposal, I could work that out after seeing the site and finding out how often you would want me to supervise the construction. As for the initial trip, I should be glad to come to Atlanta just for my expenses, and such a trip of course would obligate you no further in any way unless we came to an agreement for the design and supervision of the course.

Robert concluded his letter with an offer to "exchange ideas, after which if you desired to retain me, I could then proceed with the development of the route plans, and give you some idea of possible routings while still in Atlanta." In the meantime, Robert got a long-distance phone call from Bobby Jones telling him that when he did make his way down to Georgia to stop in and see him first, as Bobby would show him the land that the AAC had in mind for the golf course.

As soon as he could manage it, Robert boarded a train for Dixie. Arriving in Atlanta, he took a taxi straight to "Jones, Williams & Dorsey, Counselors at Law," Bobby Jones's law office located in Suite 1425 of the Citizens & Southern National Bank Building on Broad Street in downtown Atlanta, a building that was the city's first steel-framed skyscraper. According to Robert:

After a lunch Bobby said, you know, "it's a pretty day. There's still time to play nine holes. Let's go out to East Lake, where I'm a member, and we'll play nine holes." Bob Jones the architect played with borrowed clubs and shot 36 for the nine holes. Bob Jones the player shot 29, as I recall, knocking down the flag with every shot. He had just returned from the army,[*] was in his early forties, and had not yet come down with the debilitating illness [syringomyelia, a disorder in which a fluid-filled cavity formed within his spinal cord, crippling him and restricting him to a wheelchair] that eventually was to take his life.

Early in the round, on the 210-yard par-3 second hole, Robert struck his tee shot a mere three feet from the hole. Bobby Jones turned to a group of East Lake members who had caught up with them to watch and said, "Gentlemen, *this* is Bobby Jones." On their trip back into town, Jones said to Robert, "What are we going to call you?" Robert replied, "There can be only one Bobby Jones in Atlanta, and that's you. From now on, I'll be Trent Jones. It's a family name that comes from the River Trent in England." In interviews conducted with him later in life, Robert would declare, "I've been Trent Jones ever since, both north and south of the Mason-Dixon line." (In truth, Jones had been using the name "Trent" and the initial "T" long before his 1946 round of golf at East Lake; he had employed the name professionally since at least the summer of 1930 to distinguish himself from Tyre Jones, but at the same time to be known by an autonym strikingly similar to golf's most famous name so that people around the golf world would naturally confuse the two names, to Trent Jones's advantage.)[†]

---

[*] During the Second World War, Bobby Jones served as an officer in the U.S. Army Air Forces, reaching the rank of lieutenant colonel. Some Army leaders wanted Jones to play exhibition golf in the United States, but Bobby insisted on serving overseas, eventually serving in England as an intelligence officer with the 84th Fighter Wing of the Ninth Air Force. While stationed in England, he made the acquaintance of General Dwight D. Eisenhower. With Ike's troops, Jones landed in Normandy on June 7, 1944. He then spent two months with a front-line division interrogating POWs. Another one of Jones's contributions to the war effort came when he allowed the United States to graze cattle on the grounds at Augusta National from 1942 to 1945. For a biography of Jones, see Sidney L. Matthew, *Bobby: Life and Times of Bobby Jones* (Sleeping Bear Press, 1995).

[†] Interestingly, Bobby Jones told his friends and associates in Atlanta to refer to Robert Trent Jones as "Bob": "I might caution you on one other thing—that Robert Trent Jones, though known as 'Trent' in Atlanta, is everywhere else known as 'Bob,' so that where you mention his name I think you should probably use the complete form." By "the complete form," Bobby

Early the next morning Bobby drove Trent out to show him the parcel of land that the AAC had in mind for its golf course. Trekking over the property, the two men visualized tee shots and approaches into green sites, and Trent made a rough layout of a possible series of holes. Walking back to the car, Trent made it clear he was not happy with what he saw: "Bob, it's not good enough for you. I don't think it's going to be a great enough golf course for your reputation and name." "Trent, I am glad you feel that way about it," Bobby answered, "because so do I, and so does Dick Garlington. We just wanted to know your opinion before we ruled it out." It dawned on Trent that he may have just passed a test, one proving to the legendary golfer that the architect from New York knew a great piece of ground for golf when he saw one, and that this property they had visited was not that.

Three weeks later Trent got a call to come back to Atlanta. With the help of a man by the name of John O. Chiles, an officer of the Atlanta Athletic Club who was a leading real estate developer and "an important guy in Atlanta," Bobby and Dick Garlington had been "combing North Fulton County on topographical maps" and had "inspected several pieces." It was quite a job to find a piece of ground that was large enough, did not have intersecting roads, and offered the gently rolling terrain necessary for a great course. Ultimately, Chiles found a property that looked quite promising. Located out near Oglethorpe University, it was a tract of 240 acres at the intersection of Peachtree and Ashford Dunwoody Roads in DeKalb County, twelve miles northeast of downtown (close to what is today the fashionable Buckhead area of North Atlanta). The site was gently rolling, nicely wooded, and gorgeous, part of a handsome antebellum estate on which General William Tecumseh Sherman during the Civil War had set up his headquarters while setting fire to much of Atlanta. As the story goes, Sherman was so taken with the beauty of the estate's Cobb Caldwell mansion that he ordered it spared from destruction—ultimately, the mansion became the site of the Peachtree clubhouse.

It did not take them many steps onto this second property before both Joneses knew they had a great piece of ground. In his first written analysis of the layout he envisioned for the property, the architect stressed for Bobby some of

seems to have meant "Robert Trent Jones" and perhaps not to refer to Trent as "Bobby." Letter from Robert Tyre Jones, Jones, Williams, Dorsey & Hill, Suite 1425, Citizens & Southern National Bank Building, Atlanta, GA, to Mrs. Green W. "Irene" Warren, Atlanta, GA, 27 Feb. 1948, Peachtree Files, JP, CUA.

the striking similarities that he saw between what would become the Peachtree golf course and Augusta National: "I should like to have you note more particularly that by the use of the natural ravines, depressions and hilltops, fourteen of the eighteen greens are slightly elevated, such as the fourth, tenth, thirteenth and fifteenth at Augusta, and the other four greens which are uphill could be made elevated such as the eighteenth green at Augusta." According to Trent, when Bobby joined him at the site so that the architect could show him for the first time the corridors for the eighteen holes he had picked out, "We went through the property and it was very wooded. We went nine holes and it was rough going and Bobby said to me, 'Look, I'm not going to go anymore; I've had enough. Everything you are doing is all right with me.'"

"Many golf courses are built on much less land," Bobby Jones later explained, "but we considered it important that we have ample room between fairways and ample opportunity to lengthen the holes should there be any great change in the driving power of the ball." None of the land came cheap, but Bobby had enough clout in his home city to pull the money together. At a luncheon with twenty of his friends, which Trent Jones also attended, Bobby said, "Fellows, it's taking me five or six hours to play a round at East Lake, and if I have to do that I'm going to give up golf. Some of us think there should be a new course in town. We have picked out the land, Trent here has made a layout, and we want to buy it. I would like your support, so I'll need a big check from each one of you by next Monday morning." Jones got the money—roughly $3,000 from each of them, though years later Robert would claim the demand was for $100,000 apiece. Each of the twenty wealthy Atlantans got a share of the new course. Soon after that, fifty more shares were sold. "That taught me," Trent recalled years later, "that when I got into big ventures, I wanted a partner with muscle." Buying more land than was needed for the golf course also turned out to be an excellent business decision, for the AAC soon sold off the excess land for enough cash to pay for the entire course, the total cost of which proved to be roughly half a million dollars.

The planning of the golf course began in May 1945. Construction started in February 1946. The first nine holes were opened for play in October 1947, with the second nine ready for golfers in July 1948.[‡]

---

‡ When speaking of Peachtree, Bobby Jones always emphasized that "we would never have undertaken this course unless we had been able to count on the active supervision of Dick Garlington." According to Bobby, Garlington had "a knowledge of golf course construction and maintenance which I consider to be superior to that of anybody in this section [of the

Peachtree Golf Club brought Robert Trent Jones his first significant national publicity, with *Life* magazine running a feature story on the challenges of the new course, entitled "Par-Buster's Nightmare," in its March 1951 issue. Under a picture of Trent sitting at his drafting table ran the caption: "Architect Jones, who regularly shoots in the 70s, has designed 75 courses, redesigned 80 others, and considers the Peachtree course his best effort to date." Though Trent was exaggerating the number of courses with which he had been involved, his pride in Peachtree was authentic. He believed that Peachtree would set a standard for modern golf course architecture, and nothing in golf design that came after Peachtree would change his mind. Many of its features were incorporated into countless courses, both Jones's and others.

Situated as it was on a fabulous piece of gently rolling terrain, Peachtree introduced several design elements that came to define a Robert Trent Jones golf course, while at the same time reflecting some of the classic strengths that Bobby Jones and Alister MacKenzie had built into Augusta National a decade and a half earlier.§ A broad and expansive layout, the course as routed by the

---

country]. I consulted, of course, with Trent Jones on the design and O.K.'d everything he did and I think he did an excellent job, but if the golf course measures up completely to our expectations, it will be due mainly to the efforts and ability of Dick." Robert Tyre Jones to Mrs. Green W. "Irene" Warren, Atlanta, GA, 27 Feb. 1948, Peachtree Files, JP, CUA.

§ In February 1948, after Peachtree's first nine holes opened for play, Bobby Jones prepared an "AUTHORIZED STATEMENT OF ROBERT TRENT JONES" that he sent to Trent, asking for him to sign and return it, so Bobby could make it available to Mrs. Irene Warren, who was preparing an article on Peachtree for an Atlanta newspaper. In its entirety, the statement read:

> In designing the golf course for the Peachtree Golf Club, I was guided by the conception of golf course architecture pioneered at the Augusta National. To meet this meant achieving a course testing for the expert and pleasurable and not too difficult for the average player. Also, it meant developing a course featuring broad park-like vistas and panoramas which so enhance the enjoyment of the game by providing beautiful surroundings in which to play. The site selected for the golf course was ideally suited to this sort of treatment, being ample in size, with a nice balance of wooded area and open land and featuring broad rather than abrupt slopes. I have attempted to carry this bold treatment throughout in the construction of large greens and bold contours, with bunkers in some cases of almost awesome proportions. It is not for me to say that I think the finished course will be the best or one of the best in this country, but I can, with all justification, say that I am immeasurably pleased with the result as I see it today. [Signed] Robert Trent Jones, per RTJ, Jr.

Trent Jones responded with the following note: "Dear Bob, I have your letter, and happy to hear that Irene Warren is writing an article about Peachtree. I have no objection to your putting words in my mouth, for you do it so well. I am enclosing the statement signed, and I see no need to change it. . . . Sincerely, Trent." RTJ to Robert Tyre Jones Jr., Jones, Williams,

Joneses had no parallel or shared fairways, so that each hole could offer a theatrical drama all its own. Rather than requiring golfers to play across Peachtree's many hills, they designed the course so the play went up and down the valleys, minimizing the burden of climbing for older club members. As Trent knew, while the creation of individual holes was vital, the routing of the overall course was the most important element of design. "The good and great architects accomplish this difficult task," Trent explained, "all the while creating the illusion that these were holes built on ground just lying there, waiting to be grassed over."

The layout Jones perceived as he contemplated the site placed great emphasis on strategic play. He imagined a course that would demand even more cerebral dexterity than physical skill by presenting shot options for the player to ponder. It would reward patience and cunning for players capable of hitting a wide variety of shots, while still giving an advantage for the occasional daring play by a golfer who could carry out crucial shots with great skill. In all these ways collectively, the Peachtree design epitomized Trent Jones's philosophy that every hole should be "a difficult par but an easy bogey."

The design of the teeing areas was vitally important to Trent Jones's strategic design. He gave more thought to the design of tee boxes at Peachtree than he had ever done previously, later saying that throughout the history of golf course architecture "one of the most overlooked elements of the golf course has been the tee." Early during his design of the Peachtree course, Trent said to Bobby, "Bob, I know you want this to be a championship course, but most of your members are well over sixty. They want a course on which they can have fun. The only way you can have a championship course and a course that is still comfortable for the membership is to create flexibility in the tees. That way the average golfer will arrive in the same target area as the better player or even ahead of him. He may still have to use a longer club than the better player, but at least he now has a chance to reach the green with his second shot. From the championship tee, he wouldn't have a prayer." For Peachtree, Trent built tees that averaged nearly 90 yards in length and gave each one of the teeing areas four sets of markers placed at different distances. A few of these "runway tees," as they came to be called, reached more than 100 yards. The tee for the par-3

Dorsey and Hill, Suite 1425, Citizens & Southern National Bank Building, Atlanta, GA, 3 Mar. 1948, Peachtree Files, JP, CUA.

11th ran for 80 yards. Trent dubbed it the "longest tee for a par-3 in the U.S.," which, in fact, it may have been.

Tees with such versatile lengths allowed Peachtree to be played from under 5,500 yards for the "Short Course" to over 7,200 yards for the "Long Course," depending upon a player's choice or ability. (The par-3 11th played as short as 150 yards and as long as 230 yards.) Shortly after the course opened, a Peachtree member by the name of Bob Woodruff, who was the president of Coca-Cola, approached the architect in the locker room and asked, "Trent, how many more shots would I take if I played one day from the front of the tees and the next day from the back?" Jones knew that Woodruff normally shot between 95 and 100, and that the difference between the forward tees and the back tees was close to 1,700 yards. He told Woodruff that his score would go up by twenty-five shots, a prediction at which Woodruff scoffed. When Jones returned to Peachtree three weeks later, a contrite Woodruff came up to him and said, "You were right. I took twenty-six more shots from the back of the tees than I did from the front." Trent replied, "You've just seen a great example of how tee placement can change the playability of a golf course." Another rationale for the long tee boxes, Jones told Woodruff, was that they could be cut very easily by one man with a single pass of a wide gangmower, reducing the time and cost of course maintenance, which saved money for the Coca-Cola president's club.

In the late 1940s anything over 7,000 yards was gargantuan length for a golf course, and Peachtree's club members, all 155 of them by 1950, enjoyed bragging that their par-72 course was the longest in the United States: The front nine measured 3,549 yards and the back nine 3,670, adding up to a total of 7,219 yards. Part of the reason for the extremely long yardage was Trent's belief—one that proved to be correct—that livelier balls and clubs would soon be improving play and also that golfers were becoming stronger, more athletic, and more schooled in the proper mechanics of the golf swing.

Over the next twenty years, Jones would build extremely long tees for a number of his golf courses, including those at Coral Ridge Country Club in Fort Lauderdale, Florida, a course built in 1956, which Trent would also come to own, and at the Dorado Beach Hotel Golf Course, built in Puerto Rico in 1958 for Laurance Rockefeller. Although the runway tees made sense from a maintenance standpoint and for greater flexibility of play, they could also do some damage to a player's psyche. "I was playing one day at Dorado Beach with Rockefeller," Jones recalled later in his career. "Laurance went to the front of a tee, put his ball on a peg, and said to me, 'Trent, why do you make these tees so long? I get up here at the front and feel like a sissy.'"

Jones knew immediately that he had to do something to resolve the problem, so at most of his courses after Dorado Beach, instead of having one long tee, the architect broke up the teeing area into four or five separate tees. That way the player who wanted to play from the front or middle tee did not necessarily even know that the "tiger tee" (a term used in golf long before Tiger Woods) was back there. Breaking up a tee into individual areas also had "the added advantage of increasing both the flexibility of a hole and the beauty of a teeing ground." The flexibility was not just in terms of length; by positioning tees from side to side, the architect could also change the angle of the hole and the way it played. For example, as Jones explained to his clients, by moving a tee just 10 or 15 yards to one side or the other, the layout of a hole could be changed from a straightaway to a dogleg. A fairway bunker could be brought into play more directly for the better player using the back tee, or it could be taken more out of line for the higher-handicapper playing from the shorter tees. If there were trees in or near the teeing area, the designer could also take advantage of them to change the playability of the hole even further. More and more after the 1950s, Jones would design free-form rather than square or rectangle tees for his courses. He felt that this added to the interest and beauty of the teeing area and increased the flexibility of the hole from any given tee. Free-form tees also avoided "the problem of square or rectangular tees that are built askew to the line of play, a common occurrence in the past," which often resulted in players lining up their shots incorrectly, not realizing that the tee actually was pointing them into the woods. "A free-form tee seldom provides an alignment aid," Jones told clients, "but its very nature makes the thoughtful player aware that he must be more careful with his aim and be sure not to use the tee markers for that same purpose." He also gave careful thought to the size of tees: "forward tees, because they get so much use, must be made bigger, especially wider, so they can be maintained properly, [whereas] the back tees, used by only the better players who are fewer in number, can be smaller." But not even the back tees should be so small as to be uninteresting or to inhibit the hole's flexibility. Jones also loved it when he could elevate his tees above the level of his fairways. "Especially on rugged terrain," he felt, "the more elevated the tee the more beautiful the hole becomes." Differences in elevation were also "critical to the play of a hole." As he would explain to many of his clients, "Playing a 140-yard shot from

120 feet up is a lot different than playing it from green level, especially if you are seeing the hole for the first time. Firing the ball into the air and waiting to see where it will come down is . . . well, interesting." After several trips around the course, a golfer would learn what club to hit to reach the green, but the breeze from that height would likely be changeable enough to affect the shot, sometimes quite dramatically.

Another of Peachtree's principal features was its large putting surfaces. One of Jones's core beliefs, going back to his days with Stanley Thompson, was that the sternest defense any golf course could muster lay in the design of its greens. As early as the end of the 1940s, Jones felt that improved strains of turfgrass were making putting surfaces smoother and more consistent than ever before. It seemed inevitable to him that this tendency toward smoother, quicker greens would accelerate as agronomists and seed companies developed new grass strains. So Trent, in league with Bobby Jones, put a great deal of thought into the design of Peachtree's greens, ultimately building putting surfaces that were extraordinarily large for their time, averaging some 8,000 square feet in size; in fact, the two Joneses believed that at 14,500 square feet, their green on the par-4 10th hole was the "largest green in the U.S." (C. B. Macdonald's original greens at the National Golf Links of America averaged some 12,500 square feet; Jones actually shrank them when he redesigned the course in 1948. Also, the ninth green at Yale University Golf Club was more than 15,000 square feet.) Starting with Peachtree, Trent also began to give some of his greens three or four distinct decks, each deck separated by a long, sweeping slope. His goal was to present rather large targets for average golfers, but much smaller targets for skilled players.

Although Peachtree was much like Augusta National in many landscape and architectural respects, the basic difference between the two courses lay, in Trent's view, in the design of their greens. Although the greens on each course had five or six prime pin positions, of which at least four were ideal for tournament play, the greens at Peachtree, although undulating, were not nearly as severe, the slopes were not as continuous and tilted, and the crowns were not as prominent as those on the greens at Augusta. As Jones explained:

The undulations at Peachtree are folds between the various pin positions, and the greens there are larger in keeping with this principle. The greens on both courses are of the plateau type for the most part. But the greens at Augusta generally fall from back to front, while the various pin areas at Peachtree fall in no general direction but take the nearest obvious outlet to all sides of the green. This plenitude of possible locations for the cup, coupled with the extreme length of the tees, gives Peachtree its tremendous flexibility and the possibility for infinite variety.

According to Trent, this flexibility and variety was "the mark of a course that can be great for players at all levels of skill and strength." All of America's greatest courses—Augusta, Cypress Point, Pine Valley, and now Peachtree—had greens that varied from hole to hole, much more so than many of the great British links courses like Carnoustie, Troon, Muirfield, and St. George's, all of which had relatively flat greens. "Variety is important not only within an individual green," Jones believed, "but among all the greens on a course." The way he preferred to design them was to give each green "a slightly different mold," by varying the slope in individual portions of the green, the tilt of the whole green, or the pockets and swales that he built into his greens. "The general concept might be the same," he knew, "but the look should vary, one sweeping one way, one another, the contours subtly or sharply different, each blending in the most natural way into the site chosen for the green."

Here again variety was the key. "The variety of green design is infinite," Jones would assert. "There are elevated greens, greens at fairway level, terraced greens, greens tilted toward or away from the player, dished-in greens that collect the ball, mounded greens that reject all but the most precise shots, greens protected by trapping on the sides or by trapping in front, greens guarded by creeks or ponds that demand the ball be carried to the proper position . . . or various combinations of all these characteristics." In Jones's view, "all these various and varied designs contribute to the joy of playing a golf course . . . or to the frustration of golf when the player fails to meet their demands." In all of these respects of variety, Peachtree set a very high standard.

Borrowing from the style of his architectural mentor Stanley Thompson, Jones created at Peachtree what many came to regard as his trademark style of bunkering, with "flashes" of sand protruding up and around a green and set off with jagged edges, giving golfers a "natural" look reminiscent of the precipices of a windblown dune like those found at the primordial links courses, which was quite a trick to create in Atlanta. At Peachtree, treacherous traps blocked the very large 10th green in particular, with high lips on a trio of expansive bunkers in front and to the side of the green that made it nearly impossible for a golfer to bounce his ball out of a bunker, as he could on many poorer courses.

To offset the paucity of bunkers at Augusta, Bobby Jones and Alister MacKenzie had introduced elevated and highly contoured greens, which Trent Jones considered a stroke of genius. "Not only did it make it more difficult for the professional who has more trouble with greens than sand," as Trent understood, "it made it easier for the average golfer, whose problems are the opposite." At Peachtree, the handful of fairway bunkers built for the course were carefully placed by the Joneses so that a long hitter's stray shot could end up buried or otherwise precariously settled in the sand. Generally speaking, Jones followed what MacKenzie said about bunkers: "Ordinary bunkers are, as a rule, made in quite the wrong way. The face is usually too upright and the ball gets into an unplayable position under the face. The bottom of the bank of a bunker should have a considerable slope, so that a ball always rolls to the middle."

Another feature of the modern golf course that Robert Trent Jones loved and put to superb use at Peachtree was the water hazard. No architect would ever incorporate water hazards—often in the form of small lakes, natural or man-made—as boldly, extensively, or effectively as Trent Jones. "When we were designing Peachtree, Bobby said to me one evening, 'You know, Trent, getting in a water hazard is like being in a plane crash—the result is final. Landing in a bunker is similar to an automobile accident—there is a chance for recovery.'" Trent could not have agreed more. While bunkers were certainly the most common hazard on a golf course, water was by far the most feared, for good reason. As the architect would later write, "Too many golfers just get up and wail [sic] away, seldom considering the consequences. The best advice I can give is this: When confronted with multiple hazards, steer away from the most dangerous. You can play out of sand. You can play out of trees and rough. Seldom can you play out of water. Other than the out-of-bound stakes, water is the ultimate penalty."

At Peachtree, Jones put bodies of water directly into play on no fewer than four holes, most spectacularly on the par-5 second hole (which played from 513 to 555 yards), where the green was virtually an island. Here the golfer had the option of playing the hole "strategically" or "heroically." A birdie golfer who pounded his drive 275 yards down the fairway was faced with the chance of making a daring downhill shot of more than 200 yards across a pond and onto the green lying just on the other side; the ordinary golfer, who was lucky to drive his golf ball 200 yards, could play his second shot up near a group of trees to the right of the pond, then hit a pitching wedge into the green and have a good chance to make a par or perhaps even a birdie. In its heroic character the second at Peachtree was somewhat similar to the par-5 15th hole at Augusta.⁵

Heroic golf holes emerged in Jones's mind as a highly adventurous middle ground between the severe penal style that had dominated golf architecture into the early 1900s and the strategic style that he and Thompson helped define in the 1930s. Often incorporating ponds, lakes, or streams, the heroic style confronted the player with a punishing hazard but one that did not have to be crossed for better or worse, as would have been the case in the old days of penal design; rather, it tempted the better player to gamble on a heroic carry to get into position for a birdie or an eagle, while "always leaving an option for the lesser player to take the safer route." In Trent's view, there "must be a just reward for those attempting the heroic carry, and there must be a way around for those unwilling to take the risk." Without the alternate route, heroic carries would be unfair; without the reward, they would be meaningless. He knew that heroic design would provoke the better players especially—and not just those playing championship golf—to go for the reward of a sensational shot rather than "play safe" and avoid the risk of bad fortune.

During the construction of Peachtree, the two Joneses spent quite a bit of time together. "We did a little traveling together," Trent remembered. "He needed to go down to Augusta. We went from his house. He took with him the clubs that

---

⁵ Actually, Trent Jones considered number 15 at Augusta more penal than strategic. A straightaway hole that back in the late 1940s barely played 500 yards, the 15th at Augusta was "marvelous," Jones explained, because it offered the opportunity to gamble, but it was a highly dangerous gamble: "A second shot to the green almost always has to be played with a fairway wood or long iron, and it has to be a near-perfect effort. Slightly short and the ball is likely to roll back into the water. Slightly long and it will bound over the green up into rough beyond, from which recovery is difficult because the crowned green at that point falls away from the player. If the player chooses to lay up short of the pond on his second shot, he still must carry the water with a difficult pitch that usually must be struck from a downhill lie. There really is no alternate route to the putting surface. All of this makes it a hole on which thinking is extremely important and shot execution even more so." It was this sort of challenge—but one less penal—that Jones had in mind when he designed Peachtree's par-5 second. RTJ, *Golf's Magnificent Challenge*, p. 237.

he had used to win the four majors (including 'Calamity Jane,' his famous putter) and they're still in the Augusta clubhouse on the wall." Four decades later, in a television special on the 1989 Walker Cup being held at Peachtree, Bobby (who died in 1971) was quoted as saying, "I played golf with Trent Jones a lot during that period." Trent Jones, then in his eighties, got a kick out of hearing Bobby's compliment on the show that "Trent is a very good amateur golfer." As for Trent's opinion of Bobby: "He was terrific. He and I became good friends, and I came to admire the man greatly. We all knew what a great player he was, but he was much more than that—a lawyer, a marvelous writer and student of words, a sportsman, and, most of all, a gracious gentleman." As for Trent's evaluation of Bobby's greatness as a golfer: "One night we were having dinner at a restaurant and some oaf came up to Bobby and said, 'Bob, don't you think Ben Hogan is the greatest player there's ever been?' Jones's neck reddened perceptibly but, ever courteous, he replied, 'You know, the only thing you can hope to be is the best in your time.' He was that, and he was one of the best of all time in many ways."

Because Trent had done such a good job in Atlanta with Peachtree, Bobby wanted him to do some renovation work at Augusta National. This Trent carried out between 1946 and 1950.

In Trent's view, the golf course that Bobby Jones and Alister MacKenzie had laid out in the early 1930s was a "premier example of beauty, strategic design and playability, an enjoyable challenge for the amateur of every skill level, and a demanding test for the tournament players." Moreover, there was no designer of any era that he admired more than Dr. MacKenzie. But MacKenzie was not a perfect designer, nor Augusta a perfect golf course; there was room for improvement. For one thing, in Trent Jones's view, MacKenzie was often "guilty of exaggeration, especially with his greens." At Augusta, the green at the 180-yard par-3 sixth hole had a very pronounced mound at the top right of the putting surface that Trent felt was too extreme. "MacKenzie would do this occasionally on his courses," Jones critiqued, "and this is my only objection to his approach." He even admitted that the slower green speeds of the earlier era invited more extreme contouring.

With more than a decade of play at Augusta by 1946, including nine Masters Tournaments (the event was not held from 1943 through 1945 due to the war), Bobby Jones himself realized that several improvements could be made at his beloved Augusta golf course. (Some had already been made, including repositioning the 7th and 10th greens by 1939.) Together the two Joneses, during their collaboration on Peachtree, began to share ideas about how to make Augusta even better. It wasn't long before Bobby made sure that he and Trent got the chance to implement some of them.

The first of Trent's projects at Augusta involved the course's 18th green. "In 1946 I was watching the finish of the Masters with Bob Jones," Trent later recalled. "Ben Hogan came to the final hole needing par to tie Herman Keiser, and he put his second shot on the plateau at the back of the green. The hole was cut on the lower level. Hogan was only about twelve feet away, but I said, 'Bob, he can't stop the ball within ten feet of the cup because the slope is sharply downward, and he'll probably miss the putt coming back.' That's what happened." Shaking his head, Bobby said, "Trent, that's not fair. We've got to change that." So, a few weeks after the tournament, Trent returned to Augusta and worked with Bobby, "taking some dirt off the top shelf and padding the bottom of the green until we thought it was fair." The following year, a golfer faced with the same putt that killed Hogan's chances in 1946 had an excellent chance of rolling his ball quite close to the hole. And the putting surface was only part of the remodeling job; Augusta's 18th green also needed to be a dramatic stage upon which the final scene of the Masters Tournament would be enacted year in and year out. To give a clear view to the maximum number of spectators, Trent reworked all of the terrain surrounding the green on the back and to both sides.

The directing officers of Augusta National appreciated Trent's redesign of the 18th green complex so much that the following year, in 1947, he began to rework a number of other greens on the course, including on the par-5 eighth, par-3 12th, and par-5 13th.** Most significantly, the architect began a major re-

---

** Trent Jones considered the 13th hole at Augusta National "one of the world's classic par-5 holes, perhaps the best par-5 ever built" and "the perfect model of the risk-versus-reward philosophy." Though measuring just 485 yards (until lengthened to 510 yards within the past decade), and in fact the same length as Augusta's par-4 10th hole, the 13th can be reached easily in two shots by most professionals, yet as Trent liked to warn, "danger lurks with every swing." In his view, the hole was "a superb example of a strategic hole that does not require great length to be intimidating, penal, and rewarding at the same time." *Golf's Magnificent Challenge*, p. 236. There is some very interesting correspondence between Trent Jones and Bobby Jones about Trent's redesign of the 13th green. In late April 1954, Trent mailed to Bobby three alternative models for a redesign of the green: "One indicates the slope of the green from the high side to the low side, with one continuous tilt, with a trap on the front forefront of the green and a trap on the back of the green. If you will set the flags as indicated for pin positions

shaping of the entirety of the par-3 16th, turning an average hole into one of the world's most beautiful and dramatic.

As originally designed by MacKenzie and Bobby Jones, the tee for the 16th hole was situated directly beyond and to the right of the par-5 15th green. Players hit across a narrow tributary of Rae's Creek to a small, poorly bunkered green at the base of the slope below the sixth tee; the distance of the hole was only 145 yards. For years Bobby's mind had been churning over different ideas about what to do to strengthen the hole, as both club members and pros playing in the Masters considered the 16th a feeble imitation of the incomparable par-3 12th, which at the time the 16th superficially resembled. Visiting the 16th hole together, the two Joneses decided that, instead of a short par-3 over a creek, the hole could be greatly improved by damming the creek, rotating the direction of the hole by 90 degrees, and creating a mid-to-long-iron tee shot over a relatively large pond.

From the new tee, the hole played about 190 yards. Completely abandoning the old green, they built a new one shaped like a bean, terraced at the back and right and sloping from right to left toward the water. Protecting the green were two bunkers snug to the right of the green. In 1948 the Joneses added a left-side

---

you will see that by playing above the hole the play can come [in] the birdie putting area on all shots. Actually it would not be necessary for the player to take the risk of going too near the creek if the pin were on the lower side, as he could play above it and carom in. Perhaps the most difficult shot would be required when the pin is placed in the upper left forefront of the green, near the trap. The second model has two valleys going through it, as we last discussed. The valleys should not be too sharp, otherwise anyone hitting the valley will almost invariably be putting for a birdie. The third model indicates several pin positions, all protected, and the outlets running in different directions. *It is my feeling that this model is best for the purpose for which you are making this change, namely, not making birdies too cheap* [author's emphasis]. . . . If you want to go to Augusta, I think the surface could be changed (in any of these ways) in one day, provided the bulldozer was on hand and available when we arrive. P.S. The two traps indicated on the left side are in the hillside of the existing slope, and comparable to your present trapping there. . . . In other words, these are not proposed new traps." (RTJ to Robert Tyre Jones Jr., 1425 Citizens & Southern Bank Building, Atlanta, GA, 23 Apr. 1954, in Augusta National Files, JP, CUA.) In early May 1954 Bobby Jones responded: "I sent the models on to Augusta, and Cliff Roberts and Ed[Dudley] like the one with the two levels. They are going to have this roughed in and I expect to go down and have a look at it one day during the last week of this month. I do not see any need for you to make a special trip unless I call on you at the time." (Robert T. Jones Jr., Jones, Williams, Dorsey & Kane, Counselors at Law, Citizens & Southern Bank Building, Atlanta, GA, 5 May 1954, in Augusta National Files, JP, CUA.) One might guess that the models of the 13th green that Trent Jones sent to Bobby Jones in the spring of 1954 are preserved by the Augusta National Golf Club.

bunker as well and expanded the putting surface directly behind that bunker to provide for yet another very challenging pin position. In the coming years, the combination of the water and the green contours on Augusta's spectacular par-3 16th provided the Masters with some of its most thrilling moments. More than that, Jones's redesign transformed the 16th into an extraordinarily beautiful hole that quickly became, once television coverage of the Masters started in 1956, one of the world's most beloved and famous par-3s.

After the hole was finished, Clifford Roberts told the press that Bobby Jones, not Trent, had done the remodeling and, in fact, that Trent had nothing to do with it—for whatever reason, Roberts apparently wanted Bobby to have all the credit. Trent's reaction? "Well, Bob certainly had input," he said, "but the design was mine." Not until Roberts wrote his 1976 book, *The Story of the Augusta National Golf Club*, did he concede that Trent had made the major contribution.

Trent's redesign work at Augusta did not stop there. In 1950 he turned another one of its more ordinary holes into a truly great one. This time the focus was on the par-4 11th, which had been playing to a maximum of 375 yards. As Jones remembered the project:

At the time, it was a drive-and-pitch hole. The tee was just above the 10th green and the hole doglegged to the right. A big hitter could slice the ball around the corner and almost get to the green. It was really an inadequate hole for the length the professionals were driving the ball. So I went down into the woods on the other side of the 10th green and immediately saw how I could make the hole better. Set the tee back 40 or 50 yards into the woods and make the player drive uphill through a chute of trees. Then dam the creek that ran by the left side of the green to make a small lake. Then it would be a great hole. So that's what we did, and we came up with a hole that scares the hell out of the pros during the Masters. It now plays to 445 yards [by 2012 it was playing to 505 yards] and usually requires a medium-to-long-iron second to the green. When the pin is set on the left side, nobody goes for it. Ben Hogan once remarked that if you ever saw him any place other than the right side, you'd know he missed the shot. The remodeling job wasn't without problems, incidentally. Bob Jones didn't want to do it. But Clifford Roberts did, not only because it would dramatically improve the hole but also because it would relieve the gallery congestion around

the 10th green and old 11th tee. And Roberts won out. Then he and I
got into a brouhaha, because I wanted to take out a big tree about
30 yards in front of the new tee and he didn't want to. He was madder
than hell, but I won that one.

In Trent's view, there was "no better example of how an ordinary par-4 can be
made into a great one" than the work he did at Augusta to remodel the 11th so
that it presented the golfer with a perilous second shot into a green seriously
threatened to the left by water. For the hole, he also reshaped the green (based
on a plasticine model he had shown Bobby Jones and Clifford Roberts) by
putting a short neck extension onto the back left part of the putting surface.
Jones felt, as MacKenzie had, that plasticine models were "useful to teach the
greenkeeper points in construction he would not otherwise understand."

In the late spring of 1950 Trent Jones also made a few changes to the first
hole at Augusta, adding a fairway bunker to "make a better looking as well as a
better playing hole." At the request of Clifford Roberts, Trent also sketched out
a new footbridge to take golfers across Rae's Creek to the green of the par-3
12th hole, the foundation of which was also a dam (as at the 11th green), this one
raising the water level in the creek by about a foot. It was this bridge, with modifications, which was later named in honor of Ben Hogan, who won the 1951 and
1953 Masters, the latter with a then record score of 274 (or 14 under par).

Many changes have been made to Augusta National since 1950, but it can
be argued that none have proven more essential to improving the course than
those made by Robert Trent Jones.

One of the most important pioneering developments in American golf during
the immediate post–World War II era was the establishment in 1947 of the
ASGCA, the first professional organization of "golf course architects" anywhere
in the world. Not surprisingly, Jones was not merely one of the ASGCA's
fourteen founding members; he was also one of the major driving forces behind
the society's creation.

In July 1937, English-born Alfred H. Tull of the firm Emmet, Emmet &
Tull, Golf Course Architects based in New York City (Tull took over the practice
after the death of Devereux Emmet in 1934), wrote a letter to Jones stating that
"it is about time golf course architects got together to protect their interests."
Such a society should "be formed by a few active golf course architects in the

East, and then extended to take in all properly qualified applicants." The organization's setup should be "as simple as possible, with by-laws modeled after those of the American Society of Landscape Architects." Tull laid out three basic objectives of his proposed society: first, "a minimum scale of fees" and an agreement upon "a maximum amount of service we shall render gratis"; second, "a code of ethics" that "protected one another from undue competition once we have been retained by a client"; and third, "group advertising of the society," which Tull called "the only ethical way to make golfers conscious of the fact that there is available, a group of qualified, responsible golf course designers, and that good courses do not just happen, or come from the efforts of the nearest 'pro' or chairman of green committee." Tull sent his letter to Jones and six other East Coast golf architects: Wayne E. Stiles, based in Boston; John R. Van Kleek, a former partner with Stiles who would work on the design of golf courses for Robert Moses and the New York City Parks Department during the war; Walter B. Hatch, a Donald Ross associate whose office was in North Amherst, Massachusetts; J. B. McGovern, who ran an office for Ross in Wynnewood, Pennsylvania; Herbert Strong, a British-born professional golfer turned golf architect who had built some two dozen courses in the United States and Canada from a business based in New York; and Philadelphia's William S. Flynn, a trained civil engineer who had helped architect Hugh Wilson complete the East Course at Merion Golf Club in 1925, redesigned Shinnecock Hills on Long Island in 1931, and partnered with Howard Toomey to operate one of the busiest golf construction firms in America. (Curiously, Tull did not send the letter to Ross, Maxwell, or Tillinghast.) Of these seven men, only three of them, ten years later, would become founding members of the ASGCA: McGovern, Stiles, and Jones. In the interim Strong and Flynn died, in 1944 and 1945, respectively. After the war, Van Kleek did most of his work in South America, and Hatch left the golf business to become a tax collector. Why Tull, who initiated the idea, was not a charter member of the ASGCA is unclear. He was not even admitted into the society until 1963.

The ASGCA's stated purpose was, according to Jones, "to protect and upgrade the profession and to advance concepts and techniques of design consistent with the spirit of the game by collective thought." But even Paul Fullmer, the society's longtime executive secretary and historian, admitted that there was more behind the establishment of the society than the recognition that "there would be a boom in golf because people were looking for recreational opportunities after five long years of war." Clearly, the "names" in the business "wanted to establish higher fees, keep newcomers out of the business and retain the majority of work in their hands." Such self-interest—as in the formation of guilds since the Middle Ages—was the rationale for the creation of nearly all professional associations in modern America.

At forty years old, Jones was the youngest charter member by eleven years (Robert Bruce Harris was second youngest, at fifty-one); his youthfulness was most likely part of the reason he was chosen at the first meeting to serve as secretary-treasurer, which meant he took the minutes for all meetings and collected from each member a $10 annual due (which went up to $25 the following year). The average age of the fourteen founders was sixty, with two of the architects older than seventy (Robert White was seventy-three, Donald Ross, seventy-four).

Significantly, the ASGCA accepted Stanley Thompson into the organization, recognizing that an architect of Thompson's stature deserved to be a charter member even though he lived and worked in Canada. (In 1969, the society accepted an architect based in Mexico City, Percy Clifford, evidence that ASGCA membership was open to anyone practicing anywhere in North America.) Not only did the group admit Thompson, they asked him to serve as its first vice president, which he did. Robert Bruce Harris was elected president. According to Fullmer, the founders had "implored Donald Ross to be the first president, but the legendary architect didn't believe he was physically up to taking on any additional responsibilities." So Ross, whose health was in serious decline (he would die the following year), was elected honorary president by acclamation.

Jones had a major hand in writing the organization's constitution, bylaws, and code of ethics, which were formally presented for adoption at a special meeting held in Chicago on December 10, 1948. The original Articles of Confederation, also approved in Chicago, formulated the purpose of the society:

> To organize and to promote good fellowship among golf course architects, to extend the traditionally high standards of golf for sportsmanship and fair play to the professional practice of golf course architecture; to improve the scientific and practical efficiency of the profession and to provide training for new members, to foster the game of golf and to assist the United States Golf Association and other orga-

nizations and individuals working for its advancement; and to cooperate constructively with members of overlapping professions. No part
of the net earnings of the corporation shall inure to the benefit of any
private shareholder or individual.

Jones also was very involved in defining a schedule of fees that would be used by
ASGCA members as "a general yardstick" for what they charged clients: (1)
Minimum Fee Per Day: $50 and expenses; (2) Minimum Fee for 9-Hole Pre-
liminary Plan: $350 and expenses; (3) Minimum Fee for 18-Hole Preliminary
Plan: $700 and expenses; (4) Minimum Fee, New Course, for Plans: 5 percent;
(5) Minimum Fee, New Course, for Supervision: 5 percent; (6) Minimum Fee
for Complete Plan, Nine Holes: $2,000; (7) Minimum Fee for Complete Plans,
Eighteen Holes: $4,000. All of these dollar figures represented a nice increase in
the architect's typical fees from before the war.

In 1949 Jones became the ASGCA vice president as well as the society's
"publicity chairman." At the annual meeting held at Montego Bay in Jamaica in
January 1950, Jones was elected ASGCA president. His term in the office followed a year in which Stanley Thompson had presided. (Robert Bruce Harris
served as the president for the first three years.) For the next five decades, everyone in the ASGCA acknowledged Trent as "the Main Man within the Society." He and his wife Ione were fixtures at ASGCA meetings, with Mrs. Jones
taking over the leadership of "the ladies group" to keep the wives busy while
their husbands conducted their business or played golf.†† "All the younger wives
looked up to Ione," Paul Fullmer wrote in his history of the ASGCA, "who was
a sophisticated, well-educated lady, yet very down-to-earth when it came to
dealing with people." In 1976 Trent was the recipient of the society's first Donald
Ross Award, since given annually to a member of the golf industry who has
made a significant contribution to golf in general and golf course architecture
specifically. By that time, the American Society of Golf Course Architects' influence in advancing standards for the design, construction, and maintenance

---

†† The first woman course designer to become a member of the ASGCA was Alice Dye, wife
of golf architect Pete Dye. She became an associate member in 1983 and a regular member
three years later. Through 2013 only three other women had been admitted to the ASGCA: Jan
Beljan (Associate Member, 1990; Regular Member, 1996), Vicki Martz (Associate Member,
2000; Regular Member, 2003), and Cynthia Dye McGarey (Associate Member, 2011). The
latter is the niece of Pete and Alice Dye.

of golf courses, with all the attendant ramifications, was evident throughout the world of golf.

Besides Peachtree and his work at Augusta, Trent built a number of other courses from 1946 to 1950, including five nine-hole layouts and eight full 18-hole courses. Additionally, he managed to add six holes to the twelve he had finished before war's end at West Point for the U.S. Military Academy. Many of Jones's endeavors kept him relatively close to home, but his business was quickly becoming more national. Five of his projects were in Georgia. He also built or renovated courses in Virginia, South Carolina, Tennessee, Alabama, Ohio, Michigan, and even out on the West Coast, in Oregon. Business was booming for Jones, with eighteen courses being worked on in one way or another at virtually the same time during the last two years of the decade.

Some of his renovation work—ten projects in all—during this period was especially noteworthy. In 1946 Jones was brought back (he had done renovation work there in the late 1930s) to blue-blooded Tuxedo Club, located in Orange County amid the Ramapo Mountains some forty miles northwest of New York City, for some further refinements to its sixty-year-old golf course. (In the mid-1950s, Trent would build a brand-new and very challenging eighteen for Tuxedo Park after its existing course was overtaken by the construction of the New York State Thruway.) In 1948 he reconditioned a few of the bunkers and greens at the National Golf Links of America, Charles Blair Macdonald's 1911 seaside masterpiece on Long Island, and he made similar improvements at the West Course at Winged Foot Golf Club in Mamaroneck, New York, a classic A. W. Tillinghast design from 1923 on which Bobby Jones had won the 1929 U.S. Open but that hadn't hosted the championship since. (Winged Foot's next Open came in 1959.)

One of the most interesting 18-hole projects that Jones undertook in the late 1940s was the construction of the Hampstead Golf Course in Long Beach, New York, across the street from where C. B. Macdonald had created—with herculean effort and the engineering assistance of Seth Raynor—his phenomenal Lido Golf Club between 1914 and 1917. This links-style course was built on a thin strand of barrier beach between the Atlantic Ocean and Reynolds Channel—it was basically a marsh with a lake some four to six feet deep covering 10 to 15 acres—that Macdonald called the "most unpromising territory" ever chosen for a golf course. Macdonald and Raynor filled the site with valleys, hills, bunkers, and water hazards, all at a cost of some $750,000 (more than $17 million in today's dollars). Sadly, the amazing golf course lasted only fifteen years before it was sold to real estate developers during the Depression.

But in the postwar economic boom, the construction of new golf courses was again ascendant and memories of the epic challenges of Macdonald's Lido course, which many golfers considered at least on par with the National Golf Links of America (famed golf writer Bernard Darwin called the Lido the "finest golf course in the world"), led to another Long Island developer bringing in Robert Trent Jones to build a comparable course over virtually the same demanding terrain. Completed in 1949 and originally named the Hampstead Golf Course at the Lido (changed to the Lido Golf Club in the 1990s), the picturesque and challenging links featured windswept holes echoing the old Macdonald design. Eleven of the holes had water in play, and they were no easy task even when the wind was not gusting, which was rare. The 487-yard par-5 16th hole ranks as one of the greatest heroic or "risk-reward" holes ever designed by Jones (even if it was pretty much a copy of Lido's old 4th or "Channel" hole). A relatively short par-5, the 16th forced the golfer to decide off the tee whether to play aggressively or lay back while looking at a Y-shaped fairway surrounded by water on all sides; even down the center of the fairway, at the branch of the "Y," lay the risk of hitting one's second shot from a shallow bunker. Playing up the right side of the "Y" was the shortest route to the green, but it also meant a tougher approach into the putting surface, which was long and narrow and angled away from the fairway from left to right. As Jones and other architects in the 1950s came to talk more and more about their "signature" holes, there was no question in anyone's mind that the par-5 16th at Lido was Jones's signature hole and one of his most exacting and memorable. For a number of years, the Hampstead Golf Course was rated among the top courses in the New York metropolitan area. Unfortunately, by the 1990s, it had devolved into a poorly run "muni."

More and more in the years after building Peachtree, Jones's designs came to feature heroic golf holes. What many came to regard as the quintessential expression of an heroic hole was the 576-yard par-5 13th hole at the Dunes Golf and Beach Club in Myrtle Beach, South Carolina. Doglegging sharply—almost at a right angle—around a lake, the 13th at the Dunes was a bold and historically significant component of the new 18-hole golf course that Jones completed in 1949.

———

In key respects the Dunes Golf and Beach Club, his first resort course, represents a turning point in Jones's career, not only because it was the first of what would turn out to be his many "resort courses," but also because it helped to set the stage for the evolution of Myrtle Beach as a vacation destination. Trent Jones understood the benefits both to himself and his clients of demonstrating a golf course's ability to contribute to a region's economic development. With more than 120 golf courses there by the end of the twentieth century, South Carolina's "Grand Strand" was crucial to this evolution. Only the second course at Myrtle Beach, The Dunes showed the early way forward to a golf tourism industry that was just learning to adjust to the opportunities created by postwar prosperity.

Trent Jones's entrée into the Myrtle Beach scene came from his longtime friendship with a golf professional by the name of Jimmy D'Angelo. Jones had first met D'Angelo, who was four years younger than Trent, in the mid-1930s when Jimmy worked as head pro at Baederwood Golf Club north of Philadelphia. Throughout the late '30s, D'Angelo wintered in Myrtle Beach, giving lessons at the Ocean Forest Club, the only golf course in the area. After the war, he returned to South Carolina looking for permanent employment. "When I came down here, everybody thought I was out of my mind," he said in a 1998 interview. "Nobody had ever heard of Myrtle Beach." Friendly with many of the local notables, including George W. "Buster" Bryan, an enthusiastic golfer, D'Angelo eagerly recommended his friend Trent Jones when he heard about the possibility of a new golf course being built on 270 acres of land donated by the local lumber, farming, and real estate giant Myrtle Beach Farms in exchange for $5,000 in club stock. D'Angelo assured Bryan that he would find no one better to design the golf course than Jones. On the promise that he would become the new course's head pro if the project was completed, D'Angelo agreed to sell both memberships and stock in the club.

When Jones first toured the proposed site, he saw "a lovely piece of land" studded with live oaks where the Singleton Swash, a creek that cut through a sandbank at Myrtle Beach, emptied into the Atlantic Ocean. Although it was not a true seaside course, it did lie in tidal lowlands and was as close as Jones had come to a seaside course to that point in his career. The result, he knew, could be a stunning course, one that would make quite an impression once golfers—and golf writers—discovered the warm ocean-side pleasures of Myrtle Beach.

Jones later described himself as "a father who plays no favorites" in terms of his golf courses, but his fascination with the potential of the Dunes led him to make more frequent visits to its construction site than he had made, or would subsequently make, to most of his other projects. "You've got to see Myrtle Beach," Jones told a friend in 1951. "I've been able to work the water into six holes, and you've never seen a more excited group of members. At lunchtime they drive out from their offices and wander over the nine holes we finished in '49 and the new nine we've just opened." He loved the way the Swash brought out the character of the holes, and he was enchanted by the sense of movement brought on by the tides and how the water, "in and out, always moving," changed the strategy of the holes as it welled up in the channels and then receded.

Whenever he had the chance, Jones expressed great enthusiasm for the Dunes, an enthusiasm based not only on his genuine love for the piece of ground on which he was building the golf course but also for the handsome architectural fee he received for his design: $8,000, or twice the figure that the ASGCA had established as the minimum fee for the complete plans of an 18-hole course. Add to that the fact that Jones also got the lion's share of the $20,500 construction contract to build the course. Technically, William Baldwin, who had been building golf courses for Jones since the original nine at Cornell in the late 1930s, was the building contractor, but in truth Baldwin's company, whose business address was 114 Montclair Avenue, Montclair, New Jersey—the same as Jones's home-office address—was owned by Jones, with Baldwin a paid employee. (In 1951, Jones created the Contour Construction Company with Baldwin as its titular head, in a small office at 40 Church Street, Montclair, New Jersey, less than five minutes from the Jones residence. A second company, William Baldwin Golf Construction, was created about the same time and ultimately housed next door to Contour Construction.) It was a ruse that Jones would employ over and over again throughout his long career, sometimes with his clients totally aware of the situation and other times not. In the case of the men in charge of the Dunes, they seemed to recognize what was going on and accepted it not only as ethical but as the very best way to get the greatest golf possible out of their architect.‡‡

‡‡ In all fairness, it should be pointed out that not until the 1960s were there any construction companies that specialized in the building of golf courses. That doesn't mean that more generic builders didn't submit bids for golf course construction contracts, but typically they did not have the expertise or experience to compare with what Jones's own companies could achieve, particularly in the shaping of greens. The first specialized golf-course construction

With Myrtle Beach offering only two golf courses, making any sort of major national impression took a while. It also took artful salesmanship and some shrewd talent for generating good publicity—things that both Jimmy D'Angelo and Trent Jones possessed in spades. Every year after construction of the Dunes course began in 1948, Jones himself, sometimes with his family in tow, would stop off in Myrtle Beach on his way to Augusta to watch the Masters. This gave him an idea, which he passed on to D'Angelo as well as to his good friend at *Golfdom*, Herb Graffis: Why not make a pitch to all the journalists who would be covering the Masters for their newspapers and magazines, inviting them to stop off in Myrtle Beach for some golf at the Dunes Golf and Beach Club? D'Angelo loved the idea as a way of getting publicity not only for the Dunes but for Myrtle Beach in general; Graffis loved the idea as a great way to get the Golf Writers Association of America together in one place for an annual business meeting and to enjoy some golf. In 1954 D'Angelo formalized the invitation and organized a testimonial dinner in honor of none other than Robert Trent Jones, and, with the help of Graffis, asked some eight dozen golf writers to stop by for the Myrtle Beach event on their way to Augusta. The writers "all came by and felt sorry for me," D'Angelo remembered. "They went back and wrote articles about Myrtle Beach. That's just what we wanted." The annual pilgrimage to Augusta via Myrtle Beach ensured that "any golf writer worth his salt was going to know about the city, and be reminded of it year after year."

Without question, the reputation of Myrtle Beach was greatly enhanced by one of the most memorably heroic holes that Trent ever designed: the Dunes' 576-yard par-5 13th hole. Here's how Jones described the spectacular hole:

> The 13th hole at the Dunes in Myrtle Beach, 576 yards from the back, 522 yards from the regular tees and angling sharply to the right around a large lake, is an archetypical heroic dogleg. The tee shot is straightaway, and the player has the option of hitting anything from a driver to an iron. The iron is the safer play, but it leaves a longer carry across the lake on the second shot. On the second shot the player can bite off as

---

company to come to life in the United States was Wadsworth Golf Construction, based in Plainfield, Illinois. The company began operations in 1958. There is no history of Wadsworth, but there should be. The best discussion of Wadsworth's operation, its history, and its significance lies in John Strawn's marvelous book *Driving the Green: The Making of a Golf Course* (New York: HarperCollins, 1991).

much as he wants—the more he bites off, the closer he is to the green for his third shot, providing he clears the water. The second shot has to be with a fairway wood or a long iron for the bigger hitter if he wants to get within short-iron range of the green. If the golfer chooses to play safe with an iron and carry just the corner of the lake, he usually is unable to get home with his third shot.

For some three decades following the opening of the Dunes course in 1949, no golfer reportedly ever managed to hit the 13th green in two shots, so demanding was the length and shape of the hole and the water and bunkering to the front and sides of the green. Following Jones's examples at Peachtree and the Dunes, a great number of new courses built in the 1950s and 1960s would feature at least two or three holes of this sort of heroic character. Whether they scored birdies or double-bogeys on them, most golfers came to love the formidable challenge—and often majestic appearance—of such heroic golf holes.

The par-5 13th served not only as the signature hole of the Dunes Golf and Beach Club but also as a type of signature for the entire Myrtle Beach golf boom. Today, six and a half decades after opening, the Dunes is still rated as one of the top ten courses one can play in the state of South Carolina and one of the top thirty resort courses in America. To the extent that one golf hole can ever bring the reputation of a city or region to golf greatness, it can be said that Jones's 13th at the Dunes did just that for Myrtle Beach.

By the end of Robert Trent Jones's second full decade in the golf course design business, only one credential was missing from his burgeoning résumé, and it was literally a "major" one: He had not been involved in the design of a single golf course chosen to host the U.S. Open or any other major national championship, either at the professional or amateur level.

But that was about to change.

In the spring of 1949 the Oakland Hills Country Club in Birmingham, Michigan, retained Jones to revise its Donald Ross layout for the 1951 U.S. Open. Perhaps even more than had been the case with Peachtree, this important new opportunity elevated his career to a paramount level and, by masterfully taking full advantage of it, he earned the reputation as the world's number-one designer of supremely difficult golf courses. In turn, this embroiled him in some serious and highly publicized controversies about his golf course designs for the first time in his career, controversies that ended up helping his career much more than hurting it. As the architect to whom the United States Golf Association most regularly turned to toughen its courses for the national championship, Jones forged a new, more challenging character for modern championship golf—thereby changing the nature of all golf, in America and worldwide—that lasts until this day.

CHAPTER EIGHT

THE ADVENT OF THE "OPEN DOCTOR"

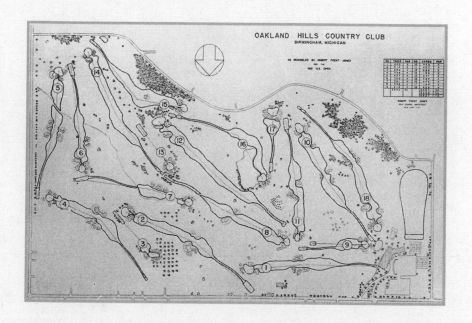

The layout of Oakland Hills Country Club, Birmingham, Michigan, as re-designed by Robert Trent Jones Sr. for the 1951 U.S. Open.

Robert Trent Jones's transformation into a celebrated national figure began in 1949 when the leadership of Oakland Hills Country Club, in conjunction with the USGA, hired him to remodel their South Course for the 1951 U.S. Open. Recognized since its opening in 1917 as one of America's finest layouts, the South Course had hosted Opens in 1924 and 1937; by 1947, however, the "grand lady of Midwestern golf" was showing her age, and even Donald Ross had acknowledged the need to lengthen the course and modify many of its features. Ross died in April 1948, however, before any renovation could begin.

Trent Jones was not solely responsible for the course's cunning redesign. Two influential collaborators were as much to blame for the extraordinary toughness of the revised layout as Jones. The first was Joseph C. "Joe" Dey Jr., a skilled amateur golfer and talented Philadelphia sportswriter who in 1934, at age twenty-seven, became the executive director of the USGA, a post he held for thirty-four years, until he became the first commissioner of the PGA's Tournament Players Division, later to become the PGA Tour, in 1968. Jones remained his very good friend for all that time, right up to Dey's death at age eighty-three on March 3, 1991. They were like-minded about preserving the dignity of par, as well as the dignity of the overall game. Jones and Dye both believed that Oakland Hills absolutely had to be made a much sterner test of golf.

Jones's second collaborator was John Oswald, whose name is rarely mentioned in any history of golf, but who in 1949 was serving as chair of Oakland Hills's greens committee. As knowledgeable about golf and as dynamic in personality as either Trent Jones or Joe Dey, Oswald actually pushed the hardest to turn Oakland Hills into "a rugged, if not impossible, course" for the 1951 U.S. Open. Nicknamed "Big John" as much for his strong views as for his body type, Oswald evoked the personality and style of Clifford Roberts, the autocratic chairman of Augusta National. Like Roberts, Oswald was "a proponent of the theory that a greens committee should have an odd number of members, and three were too many."

Not surprisingly, given the proximity of Oakland Hills to Detroit, Oswald was a top executive in the U.S. automobile industry. An engineering graduate of the University of Michigan, Oswald had gone to work in 1925 for Errett Lobban Cord, the boldly innovative entrepreneur who by the end of the 1930s was in control of the manufacturing of Cord, Auburn, and Duesenberg automobiles. As the chief body designer for both Cord and Auburn, Oswald was responsible for the styling of a number of remarkable motor cars, most notably the 1929 Cord L-29 model, considered by many of today's antique car buffs to be one of the most beautiful automobiles ever built. When Auburn ceased production in 1936, followed the next year by the demise of Cord and Duesenberg, Oswald moved to General Motors where he became the chief body engineer for Oldsmobile. Following World War II, Oswald left GM to head up body styling and engineering for Ford, where he played a major role in the design of the company's automobiles through the 1950s, including the Crestliner, Victoria, Mainline, Fairlane, and Thunderbird.

For Oswald, as for many Detroit automobile executives, membership in a prestigious suburban golf and country club served both social and business purposes. Competition among the suburban golf clubs—the Country Club of Detroit, Bloomfield Hills Country Club, Plum Hollow Country Club in Southfield, Birmingham Country Club, and Oakland Hills—was fierce, with members at each club taking justifiable and sometimes inordinate pride in the quality and difficulty of their home course. But among all of the fine Detroit-area country clubs, OHCC—the only one to have ever held the U.S. Open—boasted the highest pedigree. (Plum Hollow did stage the PGA Championship in 1947, and Birmingham Country Club and Meadowbrook Country Club would do the same in 1953 and 1955, respectively.)

No member of a Detroit golf club held stronger views about enhancing the reputation of his home course than did John Oswald. Furthermore, no American *engineer* of the era applied his engineering aptitude and approach to golf course design more thoroughly than he did. Even golf authorities as experienced and as knowledgeable as Joe Dey and Trent Jones, both devout believers by 1949 that the only way to preserve the sanctity of par in modern championship golf was to stiffen the tournament layouts, had a hard time matching Oswald's intense commitment to fortifying the challenges of "his" Oakland Hills for the '51 Open.

Oswald was determined to make Oakland Hills so tough that it would punish a player's tiniest mistake. At his course, only the greatest shotmaker in the world could emerge a winner. What he demanded, in sum, was a layout that would suit an engineer's demand for machinelike precision and perfect execution. The U.S. Open was "the greatest title there is," he said. "The course should be so hard, nobody can win it." Oswald came to the course for an hour or two almost every day during the reconstruction to assess the work. He wanted to ensure that Jones was turning Oakland Hills into the most difficult course on which any golf championship had ever been played, anywhere.

Oswald's advocacy of an engineering approach to course design and to the playing of the game provided Jones and Dey with a more defined conceptual framework from which to guide this transformation—an American technological paradigm aimed at producing a tightly managed, carefully engineered, less casual, and more orderly playing field, intended to foster a new style of golf: the "power game." Power golf would be played more through the air, requiring shots executed with greater exactitude, rather than on the ground, with all its inadvertent and unpredictable turns and bounces, as had been the case with the classic courses.† Power golf required a more manufactured landscape, brought forth with the help of additional technologies, notably advanced irrigation systems and much higher quality turf.

---

* John Oswald was not the first American engineer to make a strong connection between the methods of engineering and the game of golf. Some fifty years earlier, at the turn of the century, Frederick Winslow Taylor (1856–1915), the pioneer of time-and-motion study and scientific management (Taylorism), systematically applied his ideas for greater efficiency in factories and other industrial settings to the game of golf, ultimately spending more time and energy growing grass for putting greens and experimenting with swing mechanics and innovative club designs than he did maximizing the efficiency of such industrial labors as loading pig iron onto railroad cars. (See James R. Hansen, "Scientific Management Goes Golfing," *American Heritage of Invention & Technology*, Spring 1999, 14 (4): 20–27.) Though F. W. Taylor did not apply his ideas specifically to the design of golf courses, there is no question that, in line with Taylor's type of industrial thinking, American golf developed a distinctive technological character in contrast to its more naturalistic British parent. For more on F. W. Taylor's engineering approach and its significance for American golf, see also Shannon G. Taylor and Arthur G. Bedeian, "From Boardroom to Bunker: How Fred Taylor Changed the Game of Golf Forever," *Management and Organizational History*, 2007, 2 (3): 195–218.

† In considering the redesign of Oakland Hills for the 1951 U.S. Open for his biography of Donald Ross, Bradley Klein wrote: "Following World War II . . . came the era of modern golf—and with it, a vision of power jointly championed by the USGA (and its Executive Director Joe Dey) and the man who would quickly become its architectural poster boy, Robert Trent Jones Sr." Klein, *Rediscovering Donald Ross*, pp. 288–89.

The trio transforming Oakland Hills for the '51 Open deplored the tendency over the previous twenty years for par to lose its significance, particularly in championship play. "Before 1930, the golfer who equaled par for eighteen holes had to hit his shots like a champion," Jones said. "Seventy-two was a score that a Bobby Jones or a Walter Hagen was proud of." The average winning score at the U.S. Open in the 1910s had been 297.125 shots for the four rounds (an average per round of 74.3) and in the 1920s had only gone down slightly to 293.8 (73.45 per round), all of which were well over par. But the decade of the '30s saw a major improvement in the winning scores, down to an average of 287.5 for the four rounds (or 71.875 per round), which was under par for the first time. For the five Opens played in the 1940s prior to the start of the remaking of Oakland Hills (the Open was not played from 1942 through 1945 due to the war), the average winning score fell another five shots, to 282.6 (or 70.65 per round). When Trent Jones and Joe Dey looked at the winning scores from just the three postwar Opens of 1946–48, they saw the winning score fall even farther, to a 280.66 total (or 70.165 per round). Thus, in the thirty years since Donald Ross had designed Oakland Hills, the average score it took to win the Open had fallen by a total of nearly 16.5 shots, more than four shots per round. To Jones and Dey, these were seriously worrisome numbers—they indicated that championship golf was no longer the defining test of excellence. It was time to reverse the trend and restore the principle of the "difficult par."

Jones contemplated the conditions and attributes of a course that would allow even an ordinary level of play to produce an even-par or below-par round. Though fully aware of the impact of new technologies on golf—notably, the change from the wooden to the steel-shafted club; the smaller golf ball that was easier to control yet still flew farther (what Jones called "the hopped up ball"); and the invention of the modern sand wedge (by his buddy Gene Sarazen, who had unveiled his creation while winning the 1932 British Open)—Trent Jones felt that it was not merely new technology that was bringing down the scores in championship golf. Just as much to blame was "the way tournament promoters, catering to our national infatuation with record breaking" had been "softening up the courses when they should have been stiffening them to keep pace with the improved equipment." By "softening," Jones meant something both figurative, in the overall sense of setting up a golf course to play relatively easy for the pros, and literal, in the way that they were watered to such a degree that "even a rotten approach shot" would stay nicely on the green. Furthermore, instead of letting the rough grow, tournament directors in league with club officials were taking "all the terror out" of missing the fairways by cutting the grass short throughout the course, making a lie in what should have been penal rough play nearly as easily as a shot from the middle of the fairway. Worse, when the agronomic conditions of a golf course were even a little suspect, it was not at all unusual for the officials in charge to allow the golfers to take "preferred lies" on the fairway, which meant that they could pick their balls up, clean them, and then either drop them or place them back on the fairway grass. Under such forgiving conditions, it wasn't surprising to Jones that "the big boys" were shooting in the middle 60s, making the guys who scored only 72 "inconsolable for days."

For the previous fifteen years, Jones had compiled information that no one else in the golf industry had. Starting in the mid-1930s, Jones attended every U.S. Open that he could; the only three he missed were the '37 Open at Oakland Hills, the '38 Open at Cherry Hills Country Club in Denver, and the '41 Open at Colonial Golf Club (which was renamed "Colonial Country Club" the following year) in Fort Worth.

On his own initiative and with the approval and cooperation of Dey, Trent Jones began making a series of tests starting at Oakmont in 1935 to chart just how far the golf ball was traveling—both in the air and with all of its "rollout"—as hit by every player in the tournament field. In later decades, of course, the PGA and USGA would keep such driving statistics, as well as comprehensive data on other significant performance categories. What Trent Jones started doing at Oakmont in '35—systematically collecting data on driving distances for an entire tournament field—was unprecedented.

In selecting the hole for any year's test, he chose the hole most likely to bring out "the true character of the normal hitting of the country's finest golfers." The hole needed to be more or less flat, with little or no slope to distort the results. It couldn't be so tight or narrow that players would tend to "steer" the ball. He wanted the outcome based on a full typical drive. Jones also considered the prevailing wind when choosing the hole to monitor, hoping to eliminate weather effects. Jones typically chose a long hole—a par-5 or a very long par-4—where players needed length and were not afraid to "cut one loose." In the early years, he paid a couple of young caddies a penny a ball each to assist him in collecting his data. In the early morning prior to the round, Jones walked off 200 yards from the tee and then, again pacing off the yardage, made short chalk lines at the edge of the fairway indicating every ten yards from 200 to 300 yards. As play began, Jones collected his two young caddies, walked with them out to the test hole, and positioned them on the edge of the test fairway—the first boy at some 225 yards to watch and then race into the fairway to mark where the tee balls would land, the second boy at between 250 and 260 yards to chase down the ball to the point where it stopped rolling. Moving up and down along the edge of the fairway, Jones would quickly stand even with the position of the first boy, noting on a clipboard the yardage the ball had flown, before moving farther down the fairway to get level with the second boy so he could write down the total driving distance.

Year after year, Jones would spend one day at the U.S. Open charting driving distances. In 1954 at Baltusrol, Jones brought along his own teenage boys, Bob Jr. and Rees, for the first time to start running down the golf balls for his tests. From his years of distance testing, Jones knew when he began remodeling Oakland Hills exactly how far the pros were driving the golf ball. He had proof that they were hitting it a lot farther than they had been in the late 1930s. The data showed him that, with very few exceptions (notably Paul Runyan, the shortest-hitting member of the PGA Tour), virtually all entrants in the '51 Open could be expected to drive the golf ball at least 236 yards in the air. They would be flying their tee shots right over Donald Ross's original fairway bunkers, which had been deployed between 200 to 220 yards from the tees; the professional golfers were also getting rolls of 35 yards and more, meaning that the total length of their tee shots was some 275 yards.

"To my knowledge, I was the first to really measure how far the tournament professionals drove the ball," Jones later claimed. In his view, his tests proved that "if architecture is to keep pace with the play of modern golf . . . the strategy and hazards of the holes must be conceived in such a manner that there will be a problem, and that those shots that are missed in the light of modern play will be punished accordingly." His motives, Trent admitted, were "selfish," as "I wanted to see how far they really hit the golf ball so I could design my courses accordingly."

At Oakland Hills, what he saw was "a great course that now lay virtually defenseless." It was his task—with the full support of Joe Dey and John Oswald— to put the teeth back into Ross's golf course.

Jones's first move was to "fill in all the obsolete traps situated at the right and left sides of the fairways." Bunkers lying 200 to 220 yards from the tee were "useless hazards," Jones observed, and "no obstacles to the professional golfer."

Jones's crew replaced these traps—sometimes regardless of terrain—with new ones situated at distances ranging from 230 yards to 270 yards from the tee, which put them smack-dab in the normal target area of most professional golfers.[‡] As Jones's younger son Rees would later explain, "Dad wanted the penalty for a bad drive to be the same for Sam Snead, who drove it in the third bunker, as it was for Jerry Barber, who hit it in the first." In all, Jones built sixty-six new bunkers, creating strategic obstacles in the form of sinister clusters of sand with steep faces that pinched into the fairways from both sides, thereby guarding what became hourglass-shaped fairways so zealously that many golfers would choose to hit short of them rather than risk a run through the narrow alleyways.[§] Jones's new bunkering style demanded accuracy off the tee and imposed stiff consequences for failure. Making it worse, the construction crews laid sod and overseeded rye grass all around the edge of Jones's new sand

---

[‡] In 1948 Jones had raised the hackles of members of Winged Foot Golf Club near Mamaroneck, New York, when he added a new trap to the first hole of the East Course, placing it close to the middle of the fairway. "It's the worst trap I've ever seen—the lousiest, stupidest, goddam silliest trap that anyone ever built," snapped one of Winged Foot's scratch golfers. "Who ever heard of sticking a trap in the middle of a fairway to catch a perfect drive." Hearing of the complaint, the next time he visited Winged Foot he took a pad and paper, found the disgruntled member, and instructively sketched out the first hole. "Look," he said, "you've got a longish par 4 just about 420 yards long, comparatively straight and flat, no undulation to the green. As it stands, this hole is no test for your gang of low-handicap golfers. They could drive all over the lot and still come up with their par." Then adding his trap into the little sketch, Jones continued: "Now, what I did was tighten up the hole by forcing you low-handicaps, the fellows who can drive over 200 yards, to place your tee shot within a more limited area. That trap isn't in the middle of the fairway. It crooks into the fairway about 15 yards from the rough on the left, 210 yards or so from the back tee-markers, and follows the edge of the fairway for 20 or 25 yards. We widened the fairway on the right some 15 yards so the long hitter has a 50-yard width of fairway to shoot at. That's certainly sufficient." Quotes taken from Herbert Warren Wind, "Profiles," *The New Yorker*, 4 Aug. 1951: 39. Clearly, Jones had been applying his principles of modernization to several championship golf courses prior to making the comprehensive changes he carried out at Oakland Hills.

[§] In his autobiographical *Golf's Magnificent Challenge* (1988), Jones wrote (pp. 212–13): "I don't usually like to see trapping down both sides of the fairway. I have done it at certain times, usually to force the professional to make a decision on whether he should drive the ball long and super-straight or lay up short of trouble, as I did at Oakland Hills. And it can be done for variety or special purposes. But it should not be a routine practice, because it gives the player no options. It says to him, 'You have to hit the ball right here, right between the bunkers. There is no other place to go.' It's better to tighten the hole by placing a bunker at the dogleg, for example. That makes it effective for the entire hole. Move the hole around the trap, so you put a premium on driving as close to the bunker as possible. But if you don't [drive it there], your penalty is simply a longer next shot."

traps, preventing erosion and sometimes stopping a ball from rolling in. This rye grass "grew more luxuriantly than the surrounding grass," making it extremely hard to hit out of the deep rough. As one golf historian has noted, "Thus Jones's tremendous bunkers became an even bigger hazard." Because of the deep rye grass, sometimes playing a ball from just outside of a bunker was harder than playing one that lay within.

The changes in the bunkering, in Jones's view, were "not unfair." What they did was present the top tournament players of the early 1950s with the "same sort of task—no harder and no easier—that the top players of the earlier generations had experienced, giving par some meaning again." The pros had to "hit a straight tee shot or risk trouble." If they wanted to "gamble on muscle," they could try to shoot over the bunkers. The choice was left up to the golfer, depending on his daring and his confidence in his driving abilities. From the start of his redesign, Jones adamantly denied that he was "tricking up" the golf course: "My changes simply forced the professional to make decisions. If he used the driver off the tee, thus gaining a shorter and easier shot to the green, he had to hit it straight. If he laid up short of the bunkers, he was faced with a longer, much more difficult shot into a tough target area."

On many of the holes, Jones extended the teeing areas or built new tees. This technique converted the course's two easy par-5s—the eighth and the 18th—into long and difficult par-4s. The changes resulted in only a slight increase in the course's overall championship yardage, from 6,850 to 6,927 yards, but the conversion of the two par-5s gave Oakland Hills a new par standard of 70, a number that Jones considered to be a "realistic par."

Jones made several other changes to Oakland Hills—he later claimed that he "changed every hole," doing "extensive work" on the golf course. Some golf historians have written that Jones did little or nothing to Oakland Hills's greens for the '51 Open, but Jones always claimed that he had done highly significant work on the green complexes without altering the basic design of Ross's greens: "We redesigned, enlarged, and re-contoured greens. Fortunately, Ross's great greens, with their crowns, swales, terraces and slopes, were large enough and needed only a little revamping, except for the installation of a tongue area here and there. On a few of the greens we actually softened the contours which we thought might be too harsh or too tricky. I also increased the number of greenside bunkers to restrict unprotected entrance areas and to provide a variety of hole-locations that would pose a true championship examination."

Club members at Oakland Hills who expected Trent Jones to simply re-affirm the renovation plan that Ross had devised for their course before his death were badly mistaken.[5] But Jones assured them that his remodeling plans were very much in the spirit of Ross's design. "Ross certainly was of the strategic school," explained Jones, aligning the old master with his own approach. "Ross believed that golf should be a pleasure, not a penance, and that a beautiful, natural course would be far better received by the majority of players than an artificial layout that demanded too much of most. Ross was a master at de-signing courses that would test all the shots, particularly the long irons and the approach to the green." Where Jones seemed most to differ from Ross, at least in terms of his remodeling of Oakland Hills, was that Ross believed that the "tee shot, the longest shot, should be allowed the most room for error, and often his fairways seem inordinately wide." But, as Jones tried to explain to the OHCC membership and to others who were alarmed by the changes, "Almost always the drive [on a Ross course] has to be played into a specific area of the fairway to afford the ideal shot into the hole." Therefore, Jones felt, to restore those super-lative shot values that Ross's designs typically demanded, Jones had to repo-sition the fairway bunkers and tighten the approaches to the greens. The purpose was not to change the essential character or put his own stamp on Ross's "very fine" design, but "to restore the playing values that had been lost because of the advances in technology and the abilities of the golfer."

Not everyone, then or now, was convinced by Trent Jones's insistence that Donald Ross would have approved. Today's foremost expert on Ross and his golf courses, Bradley S. Klein, rejects Jones's now six-decades-old assertion. "The original design by Ross offered diagonal bunkering throughout the golf course, which at least afforded optional angles of play," Klein contended. "Trent Jones, by contrast, removed all the strategy when he placed sand on both sides of the targets. You either hit it straight or you suffered." When golf course archi-tects use the word "strategy" they mean players must make a choice about how

---

¶ An important factor in reassuring OHCC members about Jones's redesign of their golf course was Al Watrous, head professional at Oakland Hills. Watrous was a fine player who would not only play in the '51 Open but also make the cut, finishing in a tie for 45th with a score of 303 (77-75-77-74). Watrous walked faithfully at Jones's side through much of the re-modeling, hitting thousands of shots at the request of the architect so that he could better evaluate the shot values on every hole. See John Garrity, "Making the Monster," *Sports Illus-trated*, June 10, 1996, available in the SI Vault at http://sportsillustrated.cnn.com/vault/article/magazine/MAG1008246/index.htm.

they intend to play a hole, and there are risky routes and safe passages from tee to green. Jones's Oakland Hills, Klein concludes, eliminated strategy by demanding a single, do-or-die route. Jones's fairway bunkers created "miniscule targets off the tees," and Jones similarly "shrink-wrapped" the greens. In Klein's assessment, this meant "Goodbye ground game, hello aerial golf." What Jones did to the bunkers and to the target areas, according to Klein, "helped brutalize" not only the competitors at the 1951 Open, but "two generations of Motown golfers as well."

Another expert on modern golf architecture who does not accept Jones's claim is Tom Doak, one of today's most accomplished American golf course designers. "Jones's redesign of 1950," Doak has written, "turned the South course into one of the world's most severe tests of driving, with wasp-waisted landing areas hemmed in by fairway bunkers on both flanks on most of the longer holes. For a short hitter confined to the back tees, many of the long holes [at Oakland Hills] reverted to driver-spoon-wedge affairs, with none of the bunkers coming into play. This is not my favorite concept."

Doak's criticism is one that Trent Jones would have rejected. From the start of his redesign, and for the rest of his years, Jones asserted that Oakland Hills, as he remade it, "worked just as well" for the average club member as it did for the top pro. "I have never built golf courses just for the pros. I always have worried more about the duffer. I've never built a course on which a professional couldn't score 65 if he's playing well. Sometimes I got the idea that they wanted me to build courses on which the pros could score in the 60s even when they were playing badly. But I'm not a fiend. I don't hate golfers. I love golfers. That's why I have built them such good courses to play." In Jones's view, Oakland Hills could be both a superb course for members and also a supreme test for a modern Open championship. What it took to serve as the latter were the special added ingredients of fast greens, tight fairways, deep and challenging rough, and tough pin positions. There is no question but that this recipe, ladled up in big doses for the 1951 U.S. Open, would make for one of the most difficult, most controversial, most memorable, and most fundamentally transformational championships in the history of golf.

Serious concerns about what Trent Jones was doing to Oakland Hills began to surface months before the tournament began. Invoking "baleful tones," sportswriter Marshall Dann in the November 15, 1950, issue of the *Detroit Free Press*, warned that "Winter snows are about to hide some fearful things which are taking place at Oakland Hills CC"—"things" embodying a "madness" that shall "give nightmares" to the golfers who will be stepping up to the first tee at the U.S. Open in June. To quell the rumors, the USGA went so far as to briefly suspend the construction taking place on the course, although Joe Dey had not only known about but had sanctioned what Jones was doing to toughen the layout. The USGA executive director reported to the golfing public that his people had made a "close inspection" of the remodeling and were satisfied that all the work was going "according to plan."

But the spark turned into flame when the first pros came to Detroit in the spring following the Masters to play an early practice round or two. After their initial look at what Trent Jones had done to the Donald Ross beauty, some of the pros offered high praise and benediction. Gene Sarazen did not disappoint his old friend Robert Jones, saying about the new Oakland Hills: "It's the greatest test of a golf course I've seen in a long time." Another of the venerated stars of the game, Byron Nelson Jr., visited Detroit in the spring of 1951 for the express purpose of looking at the golf course, in anticipation of trying to qualify for the Open field. Nelson, who played in occasional select events like the Masters and U.S. Open following his retirement from the pro golf circuit in 1946 at age thirty-four, told a reporter at the conclusion of his practice round, "There's nothing unfair or tricky about the new traps."

But Sarazen and Nelson were in the minority. Most players who came to Detroit considered what Jones had done to the golf course "unfair" at best and at worst a "calamity." With very few exceptions, the courses where the pros were used to competing had been laid out in the 1920s or even earlier and were thus suited more for the amateur competitors, primitive golf equipment, and casual playing conditions of that time. Confronted with a new style of championship golf course purposefully designed for the "new breed" of professional golfer "using steel-shafted clubs, balls that took off like rockets, and swing patterns that added greater length to every drive," many of the professionals resisted. They were used to dominating courses, not finding ways to simply make par. Accustomed to courses where a missed or misjudged shot rarely led to a bogey, let alone something worse, players arriving for the '51 Open experienced what Trent Jones called a "psychological shock" when confronted with the rigors of the new Oakland Hills.

One of the pros who sternly criticized the course was Dr. Cary Middlecoff, the champion of the '49 Open at Medinah. "The fairways are so narrow," scowled Middlecoff, "that you have to walk single file, Indian style." More howling came from "Slammin' Sammy" Snead. In 1949 Snead had enjoyed one of the greatest years ever in professional golf, winning the Masters and the PGA Championship and finishing second at the U.S. Open behind Middlecoff. After shooting a 3-over-par 73 in his first time around the remodeled Oakland Hills, where in 1937 he had finished second in the Open behind Ralph Guldahl, Snead hooted: "I thought I was going to a golf tournament, not on a safari. It's a nightmare. Just awful. We've got to play it, but we don't have to like it." Picking up on the nasty remarks being made by the pros, local reporters invented even more colorful terms of disparagement, such as "hellish," "the Oakland Ogre" and "a golfing rattlesnake."

Never before in the history of any U.S. Open—or the history of any other golf tournament, for that matter—did the competitors complain so loudly about the architectural character of the host golf course. As John Garrity later wrote in *Sports Illustrated,* neither Snead nor any of the other pros, nor any of the golf writers of the day, realized that in criticizing the redesigned golf course, they were "voicing one side of an argument that would rage for the rest of the century." Oakland Hills in June 1951—"long, tight and overgrown with dense rough"—marked "the USGA's first effort to contrive a U.S. Open course of unsurpassed difficulty." With Joe Dey's blessing, John Oswald had hired Trent Jones to toughen the South Course at Oakland Hills to such a degree that his redesign would "separate the skilled players" from those who "crashed their way around easy layouts," posting scores that "made them look like great players but who really were not."

Oakland Hills proved, indeed, to be the most rugged course on which the Open championship had ever been played. The golf course defeated everybody in the field, not just on the first day but for the entire tournament. In a field of 162 players, not a single competitor matched par on either of the first two days. The best score in the opening round came from Sam Snead, one of the tour's longest hitters. Despite his complaints about Jones's redesign, Snead managed to get around the South Course in a 1-over-par 71. Only two competitors were within a stroke of Snead. One was Clayton Heafner, a thirty-seven-year-old veteran professional from Charlotte, North Carolina, and free-swinging twenty-nine-year-old Al Besselink, an NCAA champion while at the University of Miami who had just started playing the tour but who had managed a 12th-

As a twenty-year-old, Robert Jones (back row, middle) played semiprofessional basketball with an East Rochester team, the O'Leary Perintons.

Though Jones was admitted to Cornell as a special student who could not earn a degree, his fellow students held Robert in such respect that he was asked to pledge Delta Kappa Epsilon, one of North America's oldest fraternities. He is sitting in the center of the first row in this picture, because his fellow Dekes had elected him their president for 1929–30.

By the time he was fourteen, Jones was shooting par playing with just one club. In 1928, at age twenty-two, he finished thirty-seventh in the Canadian Open.

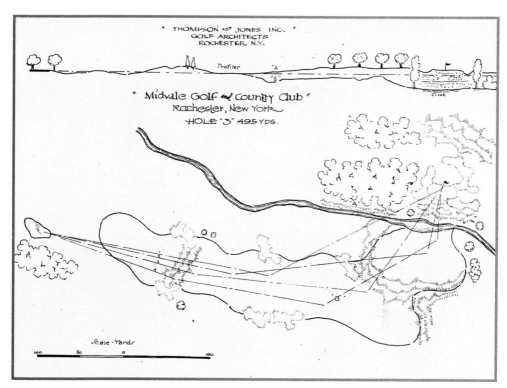

THOMPSON AND JONES INC.
GOLF ARCHITECTS
ROCHESTER N.Y.

Profiler "A"
"B"
Creek

"Midvale Golf and Country Club"
Rochester, New York
HOLE "3" 495 YDS.

Scale Yards
100   50   0   100

Map of what was originally the 495-yard par-5 third hole at Midvale Golf and Country Club, designed by Thompson & Jones, Inc., in 1930. A "heroic" second shot might reach the green in two but be at risk of falling short into a stream. Today, the hole, playing as number eight, can be stretched to 535 yards. It is Midvale's number one handicap hole and should be considered as one of Trent Jones's greatest early golf holes.

Jones could not marry his sweetheart, Ione Tefft Davis, until he could prove to Ione's father that he could make a living designing golf courses.

This series of three photos from 1934 shows the construction of the challenging 440-yard dogleg-left par-4 hole at the Durand Eastman golf course in Rochester. It ranks as one of the greatest par-4s that Jones ever built. Still considered to be Durand's most difficult hole to par, it requires a long tee shot that has to be drawn around a heavily wooded corner to have any chance of getting home in two.

Following their wedding at St. Luke's Episcopal Church in Montclair, New Jersey, on May 11, 1934, Ione's mother and father, themselves soon to be divorced, hosted a small reception at their suburban home. Ione sits in the rear, still in her wedding dress, with Robert to her left and her three sisters to her right. Standing behind Robert is his twenty-six-year-old brother Ernest, who will die tragically five years later from carbon monoxide poisoning. The older couple sitting center-left is Ione's mother and Trent's father. Trent's mother is sitting two people to Trent's left. Ione's father was apparently the photographer for the picture.

NINTH HOLE

GOLF COURSE for
LOWELL THOMAS
PAWLING, N.Y.

Jones's sketch of the closing hole on the nine-hole course he built for Lowell Thomas on his farm in Pawling, New York, from circa 1938. Note the nineteenth-century barn in the background, which was used as the clubhouse for what became Quaker Ridge Country Club.

CORNELL UNIVERSITY
GOLF COURSE
ITHACA, NEW YORK

ROBERT TRENT JONES
GOLF ARCHITECT
NEW YORK, N.Y.

SCALE

Map of Jones's preliminary design of the first nine holes at Cornell University, finished in 1937. After Jones completed a second nine at Cornell in 1953, the original nine-hole layout became the back nine.

William Rees Jones sits with his grandsons, Bobby (to his right) and namesake, Rees, in 1946.

The founding fathers of the American Society of Golf Course Architects met in 1947 at Pinehurst, North Carolina. Left to right: William Bell, Robert White, W. B. Langford, Donald Ross, Robert Bruce Harris, Stanley Thompson, William Gordon, Robert Trent Jones Sr., William Diddel, and J. B. McGovern.

Rees (left) and Bobby give their mother, Ione, a golf lesson while on vacation in Florida in 1952.

In 1954 Jones designed a three-hole golf course for President Dwight D. Eisenhower at the Camp David retreat in the wooded area of Maryland, northwest of Washington, D.C.

place finish at his first Open in 1950 at Merion. The average score the first day for the field was a fraction under 78, 8 over par. As Jones remembered the hubbub surrounding the opening round, "The cries that went up from the touring pros, accustomed to easy courses, split the heavens! Instead of the usual cluster of sub-par rounds, they struggled in with scores in the middle 70s and even in the 80s. 'Foul!' and 'Unfair!' they screamed. Instead of being able to approach with a wedge and putt for a birdie on almost every hole, they found instead that a missed shot cost them a stroke." But this, in Jones's view, was "the purpose of a truly championship course." At Oakland Hills, the pros were on a "real course" where one will get "mighty few scores below par" and where "par will mean something" because the golf was being played on a course with "true character."

No player was more disgusted with his first-day performance than Ben Hogan, the defending champion. The brilliant thirty-eight-year-old ballstriker from Stephenville, Texas, winner of an amazing thirty-seven tournaments in the three and a half years since he had come out of the Army Air Corps at the end of World War II, opened the tournament with a dismal 76, which put him in a tie for 41st place. The tough Texan's sour golf made the biggest news of the day—as it should have. Hogan was not just the defending champion, he had come out on top in three of the past five Opens—really three of his past four, as Ben had spent most of 1949 recuperating from a devastating head-on collision with a ten-ton Greyhound bus on a foggy west Texas morning. Throwing himself across his wife, Valerie, and likely saving her life, Ben suffered a double-fracture of his pelvis, a fractured collarbone, a broken left ankle, a chipped rib, and several life-threatening blood clots in his legs.

For months after the accident, it seemed unlikely that Hogan could ever return to professional golf, at least not to anything like his top form. But in 1950 Ben astounded the golf world by winning the Open at Merion, then started the 1951 season with a victory at Augusta. Going into the Oakland Hills championship, Hogan was doggedly confident, shooting for his third Open, his ultimate goal being to surpass the four Open crowns won each by Willie Anderson and Bobby Jones.

Hogan played a couple of early practice rounds on the course, then in five straight days of practice leading up to the start of the championship took the time to "mentally photograph" the course. He determined just where "the slits" between the new bunkers were and thus where each of his tee shots needed to go. He knew the best angles into the greens and where he wanted to leave his approach shots to have the easiest putts on the sloped and terraced greens. Ben felt sure that Jones's redesigned layout, because it was so strategic in character, suited his game perfectly, giving him a distinct advantage over his competitors."

There is a story that has been told over the years at Oakland Hills that suggests that Hogan may have played a small part in Jones's course redesign. According to the story, Hogan visited the course during its reconstruction and was doing some putting on the practice green when Trent Jones spotted him and walked over. Pointing out toward the tenth hole, Jones asked Hogan, "What do you think about the new fairway bunkers we've built out there?" "Too close," muttered Hogan. Jones asked Hogan to grab his driver and try to hit one over what was then the solitary right-side bunker, whose far edge ran out to some 235 yards from the tee. Hogan promptly, and easily, knocked a ball well over the bunker. According to the story, by the next afternoon Jones had installed a new trap "precisely where Hogan's drive had landed," at a distance stretching from approximately 250 to 265 yards. When Jones was asked about this story many years later, he answered, "I don't remember that. But I can tell you Hogan would have had an opinion." Hogan may have been partly responsible for the new fairway bunker on the 10th hole, but the Oakland Hills membership on the eve of the '51 Open laid the onus for the hole on Jones. "Just received a letter from a friend of mine at Oakland Hills," wrote fifty-eight-year-old Francis Ouimet, the legendary winner (at twenty years old) of the 1913 Open at The Country Club in Brookline, Massachusetts, in a June 6, 1951, letter to Jones, "who thinks that trap you placed on number ten (I have not seen it, of course) requires a 'rifle' and not a golf shot."

On the first day of the '51 Open, instead of his normally sharp and intelligent game, Hogan played the "stupidest round of golf I ever played," he told reporters. His "stupidity" started with an error in judgment on the very first hole: From the middle of the fairway, he chose a 2-iron rather than a 3-iron for his second shot, only to drill the approach 10 yards over the green, leading to a

---

** Hogan once said about strategic golf design, "A good golf hole should have both character and appeal. It shouldn't ask a golfer to play shots that are beyond his ability, but it should present him with an interesting challenge when he hits the shots that are called for. Golf is a game in which you play your first shot on a hole in order to play your second from the best position, and so on. It's a thinking game, a game of controlling the ball." Hogan quoted in RTJ, *Golf's Magnificent Challenge*, p. 40.

bogey. "Bad thinking," he muttered. By Ben's count he made five more errors that day, producing his worst first round in an Open since 1939. Normally razor-sharp, Hogan was much more disgusted with himself than he was with the golf course. That night he sighed to his wife, "I made six mistakes and shot 6 over. You can't steal anything out there."

Day two proved only slightly easier for the field—and easier for Hogan, who also improved, but only by three shots, down to a 73. (The cut to reduce the field to fifty-five for Saturday's two rounds came at 152, 12 over, a higher cut line than at any major championship since the mid-1930s.) The big news on day two was the collapse of Sam Snead, who soared to a 78. It was not the first time that Snead had fallen so precipitously in a major tournament, and it would not be the last. One player, thirty-three-year-old Dave Douglas, a long and lanky former club pro from Newark (Del.) Country Club, managed to shoot a 70. Together with his first day score of 75, the even-par round put Douglas into second spot, one stroke behind thirty-four-year-old South African Bobby Locke, whose rounds of 73 and 71 put him on top of the leaderboard at four over par.

Just eight strokes separated the field from top to bottom at the start of play on Saturday, and virtually everyone left in the field had a chance to win. Trent Jones thought Locke, a two-time British Open champion and one of the finest putters who ever lived, was likely to hold on, and Jones wasn't beyond betting a few dollars that the South African would emerge victorious.[††] Even Hogan, just five

---

†† There is evidence in the Jones Papers that Jones occasionally made a friendly bet on the outcome of golf tournaments. It is certain that he entered an annual Calcutta at the Masters. A Calcutta is a form of betting pool that became common for various types of golf tournaments (also auto races) in which the "gamblers" bid in an auction for the "ownership" of a particular competitor, say Ben Hogan, the proceeds from which are then put into a pool for a "payout" that has been prearranged in terms of a scale of percentages going to the gambler who "owns," say, the first-, second-, or third-place finishers. At the 1951 Masters, which Hogan did win, Jones won $948 in the Calcutta pool. He got the money for having "bought" Lew Worsham and Dave Douglas as his competitors and for their finishing in a tie for third and fifth place, respectively. He shared the pool winnings with John B. Morse of Pebble Beach, California; Bob Woodruff, a member of Atlanta's Peachtree Golf Club who was the president of Coca-Cola; T. R. Garlington; and John O. Chiles. He also shared the winnings with his own son, Robert Trent Jones Jr., who got his own $948 share, no doubt thanks to his father putting in the Calcutta money for his eldest son. On May 1, 1951, Morse wrote to Jones about his winnings: "The secret of our success lies in the fact that we associated ourselves with Brother Woodruff, who has never been known to lose a pool of any kind. It was grand seeing you and obviously a good and profitable time was had by all." (Morse to Jones. 20 Vesey St., NY, 1 May 1951, Augusta

strokes back, doubted he could catch up. "A couple of 69s might take it to-morrow," a friend encouraged Hogan on Friday evening. "I'm afraid it's out of reach," Ben replied. "Even two subpar rounds might not be good enough. I'd have to be Houdini to win now."

But even while shooting 9-over par for the first two days, Ben's extraor-dinary ball-striking abilities were evident. One of his playing partners for the first 36 holes, thirty-nine-year-old Al "Red" Brosch, said, "The first day I thought Hogan was the luckiest man I'd ever seen. I'm playing uphill, downhill and sidehill shots all day, and every one of his second shots is from a level lie. On the second day, I realized he was playing his shots from exactly the same spots as the day before." Though Brosch's story might be exaggerated, Trent Jones accepted it as "indicative of Hogan's ability to map out a course and then apply his skill to make the necessary shots." The story also led Trent Jones to issue one of his most arresting insights into his lifelong appreciation for great shotmaking: "It is dif-ficult for the architect to defend against that kind of ability, nor should he want to. That's what the game is all about."

Indeed, Hogan's brilliant performance on Saturday would stand as one of the great defining moments in modern championship golf. In those days, the men who made the cut played 36 holes on "Open Saturday," as it was known. Playing two rounds in championship conditions was a grueling experience for many of the players, but especially so for Hogan, whose injuries in the car ac-cident had left his legs and lower back significantly weakened.

In the morning round, Hogan came out and whipped the course for fourteen holes, getting his round to 3 under par. But he floundered on the last four holes, finishing with a double-bogey and two bogeys for a score of 71. He had improved his score every round, from 76 to 73 to 71, but coming off the 18th green that late morning, where Trent Jones was standing as one of the thou-sands of spectators, Ben was hot; his anger was directed at himself for letting the course once again force him into critical mistakes.

Still, Hogan had crept up the leaderboard. He was now within two strokes of the lead, held jointly at 218 (8 over) by Locke and forty-one-year-old Jimmy Demaret, the latter shooting the morning's best round, an even-par 70. (The

---

Files, JP, CUA.) With the three men splitting the pool equally, the total amount of money that went to those who "bought" Worsham and Douglas was $5,690.25. In today's dollars, that amounts to over $51,000. It is not known whether Jones ever participated in a Calcutta for a U.S. Open or even if there was one.

average score of the field for the third round was 75.98. There were four scores in the 80s.)

Hogan ate his lunch between rounds in complete silence. But behind the grim mask, his mind was churning. He was picturing every tee shot that he would have to pull off that afternoon. Amidst those images, a compelling insight flashed to the fore: Playing it safe had not proven successful, neither for Hogan nor anyone else. Sitting two behind Demaret and Locke with eighteen left to play, Hogan understood that it was time to attack. No more clubbing down off the tee to stay behind the flanking bunkers. That had only made for long second shots into the greens and less chance for precise direction and distance. Hogan decided to abandon his cautious approach for a frontal attack on the heavily fortified Oakland Hills. He would use his driver on par-4s and par-5s whenever he could. Instead of playing for the fat part of the greens, he would take dead aim on the pins. If he lost the tournament and failed to defend his Open titles, he would at least go down fighting rather than surrender to the bullying schemes of Jones's redesigned golf course. Hogan was confident that he could "go low," he told USGA official Ike Grainger, the blue-blazered referee for Hogan's group that Saturday afternoon, as they walked to the first tee. "I'm going to burn it up."

Hogan played the front nine flawlessly, but his birdie putts just wouldn't drop. He shot 35, even par. It was good enough to sail past Demaret, who would succumb to a final-round 78, but Jimmy was just starting his round as Hogan made the turn. Ben started the back nine not knowing how well the leaders were going to play, but he felt sure that he would need to play at least two strokes under par if he was going to catch the tenacious Locke. Clayton Heafner, tied with Hogan after three rounds with a score of 220, was threatening to post a nice below-par round as well. If Hogan was to win, he knew he needed to play a great back nine over a superb stretch of diverse and exacting holes.

At the 448-yard par-4 10th, Ben split the center of the extremely narrow fairway—on the very hole where Jones had added a distant bunker after Hogan met the architect's dare to carry the forward sand trap some 215 to 230 yards out on the right edge of the fairway. (During round three, according to a hole-by-hole "Location of Tee Shots" chart that Jones prepared after the tournament, one-third of the field had missed the 10th fairway; with the wind against them, none of the players during the morning round had carried a tee shot over either the left-side or the Hogan-inspired far-right-side bunker.) From the middle of the fairway, Ben then hit what he would later call a "career" 3-iron from 200 yards away to within five feet of the cup. Making the putt for a rare birdie on the 10th, he started the back nine with a flourish. Pars followed at the 407-yard par-4 11th and the 566-yard par-5 12th but, on the 169-yard par-3 13th hole, a beautifully struck 6-iron left him a difficult 15-foot putt that he managed to make, taking him to 2-under for the round.

The next hole—a 447-yard straightaway par-4—was a bruiser, as difficult to birdie as any hole in championship golf had ever been. Hogan had bogeyed it in the morning round and on Thursday. What made the 14th hole such a major test wasn't a narrow landing area; the 14th had no fairway bunkers on it at all.‡‡ Rather, what faced them on this long par-4 was a second shot into a capricious wind. The breeze forced them to hit at best a 2- and 3-iron, if not a fairway wood, onto a green that was guarded by three disconcerting sand traps and that

---

‡‡ Trent Jones selected the long par-4 14th hole as the hole on which he would track the driving distance of the golfers playing in the '51 Open. Because of its length and because it had no fairway bunkers, it was a hole on which the pros would let loose with their drivers in an effort to get down the fairway as far as possible. Jones also selected the hole because on Thursday, June 14, 1951, the wind was negligible on the hole, neither favoring or hurting the distance of the tee shot. His statistics for the entire field of 163 players showed an average "carry" in the air of 236.055 yards; for the total field, the average driving distance for the carry plus the rollout was 265.742 yards. For the pros whose balls landed and rolled in the fairway (eighty-one, or almost exactly half the field) the average carry-plus-roll was 276.740 yards. The course's agronomic conditions, firm and fast, were obviously conducive to roll. The average number of yards of roll for the entire field on the 14th hole during the first round was 29.687 yards; for the eighty-one pros who hit the fairway, the roll average was 40.685 yards. Jones's statistics showed that seventeen golfers flew the ball more than 260 yards in the air, and twenty-three golfers, with carry and roll, hit their balls farther than 290 yards. Thirteen of these hit their balls more than 300 yards. The longest carry—276 yards—was hit by an amateur, J. Lutz Jr., who ultimately missed the cut; the second-longest carry belonged to another golfer who missed the cut, professional Arthur Anderson, at 270 yards. Hogan's teeshot on the hole carried 264 yards with only four yards of rollout. Bobby Locke's drive carried only 225 yards but had 45 yards of carry, taking his ball to 270 yards off the tee. The longest drive with carry and roll was hit by Arthur Anderson, at a total length of 335 yards. Jones's charts of driving distances, which he had been doing for several years and would continue to do for several years into the future, make for some very interesting reflections on the state of the game at the time and how the changing technologies of the golf ball and the golf club, as well as the evolving athleticism and fitness of the professional golfers, have affected championship play over the decades. Some but not all of his driving distance charts are archived at Cornell University in the Jones Papers. The title of this specific chart is "Drive Chart, 51st Open Championship, United States Golf Association, 1st Round—14th Hole, Oakland Hills Country Club, Birmingham, MI." Jones prepared most of his charts, including this one, on drafting paper that was 25 inches wide and 42 inches long.

fell away on the backside, making it almost impossible to hold the ball on the putting surface. In an extreme rarity for a professional event, not a single birdie was recorded on the vexatious hole over the entire four rounds of the '51 Open. Hogan again could not make par: Unable to get his ball up into the hole in two after missing the green long, Hogan recorded the single blemish on his otherwise fabulous back nine.

His bogey on number 14 made recovery on the next hole critically important. In the morning round, Ben had made double-bogey on the 392-yard, dogleg-left par-4 after driving into the ugly bunker at the corner of the dogleg. This time Hogan left his driver in the bag and hit a "spoon" (three-wood) into a comfortable spot short of the bunker. From there he struck an exquisite 6-iron to within five feet and drained the putt. He was back to 2-under for the round.

By the time he arrived on the 16th tee, Hogan had heard that Bobby Locke was running into trouble. In both rounds on Saturday, Locke had hooked his ball on the 437-yard fifth hole into one of Jones's new bunkers that lay hidden over the crest of a hill. From that bunker Locke had made a bogey in the morning and would make a double-bogey in the afternoon. After the tournament, the South African star blamed his ruin on that blasted sand trap. Jones defended the positioning of the offending bunker: "Normally I don't like to hide bunkers, although I have on occasion. . . . [S]ince this was the final day after a week of practicing and competition, Locke surely knew the bunker was there."

As Hogan reached number 16, Locke was in the midst of three consecutive bogeys. Hogan was in the lead. The real threat to Ben was Heafner, who was 1-under for the afternoon round. Still, the championship would likely be Hogan's if he could continue his sharp play for three more holes.

The 16th wasn't just the golf hole that Robert Trent Jones had changed the most from its original Ross design, it was also considered by many as Jones's masterpiece of redesign at Oakland Hills.§§ The hole had been a straightaway

---

§§ In 1965 *Sports Illustrated* and its chief golf writer, Dan Jenkins, selected the 16th hole at Oakland Hills as one of the best eighteen holes in America. In 1972 the hole was the scene of Gary Player's "miracle" second shot from the rough, over trees to within three feet of the hole. Player made the putt for birdie and won the PGA Championship. See Dan Jenkins, with Foreword by Ben Hogan, *Sports Illustrated's The Best 18 Golf Holes in America* (New York: Delacorte Press, 1966), 128–35. As Trent Jones said of Gary Player's shot, "It was an historic shot, fittingly made on a great hole" (RTJ, *Golf's Magnificent Challenge*, p.180).

Not all experts on golf course design agree that the 16th at Oakland Hills is a great hole. "As for the sixteenth hole," writes golf architect Tom Doak, "the sharp dogleg to the right around a

350-yard par-4 where the second shot had to carry only about 75 yards over a small lake. Subtly changing the fairway routing, Jones sharpened the turn to a dogleg-right; he also reshaped the green. This transformed the hole into a 409-yard test of nerves, one typically requiring a second-shot carry of some 160 to 190 yards over the pond to what was now virtually a peninsula green, the right half of which jutted nearly to water's edge. Thanks to Jones, the 16th had become a supremely challenging hole whose mid-to-long-iron tee shot into the green threatened doom from every angle.⁵⁵

The gallery was huge for the last day of the tournament, nearly eighteen thousand people, and by the time Hogan came to the 16th tee a horde of spectators had galloped over in his direction to see him play the rest of the way in. Staying with his aggressive approach, Hogan took a driver and rifled it some 290 yards. From there it was just a 9-iron over the lake to the pin, which was set on the right side in the new wing of the green created by Jones to allow for a hole location that was dangerously close to the water.*** Ben's short iron floated gently down and spun to a quick stop on the firm surface just four feet from the cup. The crowd roared its approval, only to issue a large groan when Ben's putt slipped past the hole. Still, it was a par on a very difficult hole. On 17, a tough,

---

willow-lined pond, which is the standard choice for golf writers' lists of great holes, I don't understand all the fuss; it's a good hole, but it's just a water hole" (Doak, *Confidential Guide to Golf Courses*, p. 158).

⁵⁵ Interestingly, in his biography of Ross, Bradley Klein asserts that the 16th at Oakland Hills today "plays very much as Ross had intended. Jones sharpened the turn on this dogleg-right but most of the hole was created by Ross, including the forced-carry approach over what was then a former farm pond." Klein also states that "In redoing the course for the 1951 U.S. Open, Trent Jones touched neither the routing nor the green sites" (Klein, *Discovering Donald Ross*, pp. 288–89). To say that Jones didn't touch the green sites is not to say that Jones did nothing to change the greens. As already indicated in this chapter, Jones redesigned, enlarged, and re-contoured several greens at Oakland Hills, which included the addition of a few tongue areas. There is no question that Jones's reshaping of the right side of the 16th green, which made it jut right into the water, was a significant change from the old Ross green that made the hole more difficult. It also seems debatable whether playing Jones's hole, at 409 yards, can be said to be playing the same hole that Ross intended, at 359 yards. The *USGA Golf Journal* featured "A Great Golf Hole: The 16th at Oakland Hills" in its September 1963 issue.

*** Tom Doak calls the greens at Oakland Hills "among the most severe throughout 18 holes that I have seen." The most severe pin placements, Doak explains, "are at the wings of the greens, which are folded up like gull-wing doors, while the center section of many greens is a deep hollow that tends to gather balls. Of course, if your ball doesn't gather, you're left with a breakneck downhill putt." Doak, *Confidential Guide to Golf Courses*, p. 158.

194-yard par-3 where he had made a bogey in the morning, Hogan hit a solid 2-iron to the middle of the green; two putts kept him at 2-under for the round with just one hole to play.

The closing hole at Oakland Hills offered what Jones thought a finishing hole to a major championship should offer and then some: a difficult and exacting test of nerve and ability. It was a long par-4, 459 yards, with a pronounced right-hand dogleg. There was a wicked panoply of a dozen bunkers: six flanking the tee shot's landing area, three to the right, and three to the left; two bunkers, left and right, located some 20 to 30 yards in front of the green, which played almost like cross-bunkers and whose appearance from beyond 150 yards made the golfer think that the putting surface started sooner than it did; plus four meandering sand traps that surrounded the front third of the putting surface. Undeniably, Oakland Hills's 18th hole lived up to Jones's concept of a "difficult par."

A favorable wind had the 18th playing much easier on Saturday than it had during the first two rounds. On Saturday morning, according to Jones's "Location of Tee Shots" chart, more than a dozen players hit their tee balls well past 300 yards on the closing hole, easily carrying their drives past the flanking bunkers; Hogan had been one of them. With a nice breeze still behind him, Ben pounded another drive that flew well over the trio of bunkers on the ridge to the right side of the fairway, leaving him roughly 160 yards to the hole. With a 6-iron in hand, Ben smoothed his approach safely to the center of the green, leaving his ball fourteen feet above the flag.

By the time he made his way to the putting surface, the final green was "completely ringed by the gallery, with only the front entrance clear, and fans standing twenty and thirty deep, craning to see the finish." Hogan's putt was downhill and very fast, and the defending champion hit it ever so gently. The ball crept down the slope, trying to snuggle up to the hole for an easy tap-in par. Trickling on and on, the ball found the front of the cup and dropped in. The huge throng of spectators roared its delight; Hogan had made an unlikely closing birdie. Bobby Locke heard the mammoth cheer and understood that the roar could only be for Hogan. The championship belonged again to the talented Texan.

Hogan finished with a 67, 3 under par. It was the best round of the tournament by two strokes, and nearly nine strokes better than the 75.98 that had been the average for the field during the Saturday morning round. The only other sub-70 score of the completed championship was the 1-under-par 69 that Clayton Heafner shot in the final round. Hogan's total of 287, 7 over par, and runner-up Heafner's 289 tally, 9 over par, more than testified to the extreme difficulty of the new Oakland Hills course. Locke, who finished his round an hour and a half after Hogan, came in with a disappointing 73, winding up four strokes in arrears. To Robert Trent Jones, "the most satisfying feature" of the 1951 Open was that "at the end of the tournament the names of the top players were at the top." (Finishing right behind third-place Locke were several of the era's best players: Julius Boros and Lloyd Mangrum at 293; Al Besselink and Paul Runyan at 294; Sam Snead at 295; and Jimmy Demaret and Lew Worsham at 296.) When a major tournament was played on a true championship golf course, Jones boasted, "You rarely get an outsider as the winner." In the architect's view, "this is as it should be."

In later years Hogan would call his 67 the best round he ever played.[†††] Some golf historians have called it "the greatest round ever played by anyone"— and one "played in cold anger inspired by the challenge of the golf course."

Hogan's remarks during the trophy presentation on the lawn of the Oakland Hills clubhouse forever marked the '51 Open and Robert Trent Jones's course redesign as a decisive launching point for the advent of modern championship golf. Speaking with what one reporter called "the grim satisfaction of a conqueror," Hogan declared, "I'm glad that I brought this course, this monster, to its knees. If I had to play this golf course every week, I'd go into some other business."

Trent Jones received a much more personal version of Ben's gruff upbraiding, which Jones recounted in *Golf's Magnificent Challenge*:

His quote, as Ben received the trophy, was, "I finally brought this monster to its knees." But, in fact, because Ben was a little miffed at the fact that the sweeping changes and extensive remodeling I did made the course so much tougher than it had been, he commented later to my wife Ione, "Mrs. Jones, if your husband had to play on the courses he designs, your family would be on a bread line." My response to that

---

[†††] As for Trent Jones's opinion, he felt that Hogan's 67 was "a great round" but, in the long view, "not any greater, or one iota less great" than, for instance, the 67 shot by Walter Hagen at Muirfield in the 1929 British Open.

when I heard about his comment was "only a great golfer could win on my courses." . . . Well, I haven't yet had to resort to the bread line, and Hogan never did concede that it was a good course, but he later admitted that he might have won more Opens had he been able to play them on more Trent Jones courses.

Shortly after the '51 Open was over, golf writer Herbert Warren Wind penned a highly complimentary and widely read article for *The New Yorker*, which appeared in the magazine's August 4, 1951, issue. Fifteen pages long, "It was a very flattering article," Jones was happy to say. "Many of my friends and associates read it and told me they thought it was great." More than a mere feature story, Wind's essay amounted to a short, heroic biography of forty-five-year-old Jones's already remarkable Walter Mitty–type life. In the article, Wind—Jones quickly came to know him as "Herb"—laid out several of the key aspects of Jones's story that made him uniquely qualified to become mid-century America's preeminent golf architect. As Wind stated early in his article, "Nearly all the men who built the country's thousands of courses have been either golfers who branched out as designers or landscape architects who branched out into golf." But most of these men had "one shortcoming or another." If the fellow knew his golf, he didn't know the first thing about drainage and irrigation. If he were solidly grounded in the fundamentals of engineering, then he didn't have a real feeling for the game of golf. Jones's preeminence as an architect, Wind explained, was "an inevitable result of his being both a real golfer and a far-sighted planner; he is the first and so far the only member of his profession who decided upon his career at an early age and educated himself for it."

No golf architect—not even Ross or MacKenzie—had ever been so gloriously featured and aggrandized in print nationally. But Wind's article was a landmark not just because of its tributes, but also because Wind was explaining to American golfers why golf course architecture should be vitally important to their understanding of the game. It made the country's golfers aware of the importance of not just appreciating golf course architecture but of studying the strategies built into course design so they can become better players. As Wind wrote early in his article, "The extensive ignorance about golf architecture that most non-golfers and some golf authorities reveal is a source of perpetual amazement." Quoting Jones:

They seem to have picked up the idea that on the seventh day the Lord rested and created the fairways and the hazards—you know, checked all the pin areas on the Old Course at St. Andrews. . . . I can understand how a carload of non-golfers out for a Sunday drive will pass a golf course and take it for granted, the way I take the automobile and the automobile's radio for granted. But what beats me is the people who have been close to golf all their lives and still think that the only thing the golf architect has to do is carve out the traps and toss some grass seed around.

In a nutshell, this was the thesis of Wind's article: that instead of looking at golf courses with a blank attitude of neutrality, or simply with a mixture of pleasure and nervous anticipation, the golfer should see a golf course as strategic design and as a purposeful work of art. The architecture of a golf course should be important to golfers, not only so they can better appreciate the inherent beauty and aesthetic character of the design, but also so they can play the game in a more confident and effective way. Paying attention to the architecture will put the golfer more in concert with the essential principles of the game. Doing so will enhance the golfer's appreciation of a golf course both for its natural and manufactured features; better yet, paying attention to the architecture can actually improve the golfer's performance and result in a better score.‡‡‡

Following Jones's work for the 1951 Open, Oakland Hills would forevermore remain "The Monster." It became an appellation that, in Jones's view, "may or may not be justified" but that nonetheless stuck and became legendary. Today, after subsequent redesigns, Trent's son Rees expresses the opinion that

---

‡‡‡ Herbert Warren Wind continued to write about the history of golf architecture for the rest of his long and distinguished career. In 1966 *Golf Digest* published a lengthy two-part series written by Wind about the history of golf course architecture, which was as significant as his 1951 piece in *The New Yorker* in terms of stimulating American golfers to pay more attention to the design of the courses they were playing. More than that, it inspired some to pursue golf architecture, or the study of golf architecture, as a profession. For example, Bradley S. Klein, *Golfweek*'s current editor for golf course architecture, wrote in a 1997 essay: "I stumbled upon [Wind] by chance in 1966, when as a twelve-year-old I read his two-part series in *Golf Digest* about the history of golf course architecture. New York-based course architect Stephen Kay later told me that reading those two articles changed his life and made him determined to go into course design. The effect on me was similar." Klein, "A Thousand Words to Clear His Throat: Herbert Warren Wind," in *Rough Meditations* (Chelsea, MI: Sleeping Bear Press, 1997), p. 43.

Oakland Hills is "not a monster anymore, just a great test of golf." Members of OHCC and their guests may disagree, so proud have they become of their precious monster. As golf writer John Garrity would later write, "The Oakland Hills of June 1951 proved too difficult for member play. [John] Oswald had several of the Jones bunkers removed, and subsequent years have seen greenside traps and other features reappear and vanish in harmony with various national championships."

Trent Jones's 1951 redesign of Oakland Hills is historically significant for becoming what Jones himself came to call the archetypal "twentieth-century test for twentieth-century conditions." It was the project that created an entirely new position in the architectural hierarchy, a coveted one, of being the person entrusted by the USGA to alter a golf course for its ultimate championship. The moniker of "Open Doctor" wouldn't be coined until the early 1960s, but after Oakland Hills there could be no question as to whom it described. Years later, his oldest son, Robert Trent Jones Jr., asserted, "That tournament *made* my father. In those days, golf architecture was like stagecraft. Nobody cared who designed the sets." Jones's redesign of Oakland Hills, as immortalized in prose by Herbert Warren Wind's essay, changed that attitude forever.

CHAPTER NINE

THE TRENT JONES ERA

Until Jones's modernizing of championship golf courses for U.S. Opens, people talked about golf courses but not about the people who designed them. Suddenly, with the rise of Robert Trent Jones signature courses in the 1950s and 1960s, golfers began talking about the course architect—and most of the time they talked about Jones.

On January 4, 1953, Jones's former mentor and business partner Stanley Thompson died suddenly and unexpectedly from a brain aneurism, at fifty-eight. Thompson and his second wife, Helen, were staying at the Royal York Hotel in Toronto preparing for a trip to Bogotá, Colombia, where Thompson had contracted to build several courses, when the fatal seizure occurred. (His first wife, Ruth, had died in her sleep from a heart ailment in September 1944, while she was still in her early forties. Three years later, in 1947, Stanley married Helen Turnbull Duthie, a divorcée with two children whom Stanley and Ruth had known for many years.)

Helen Thompson had called Ione at the Jones home in Montclair to tell her of Stanley's death. Trent was away in Miami working on the remodeling of the La Gorce Country Club. After a consoling conversation with Helen, Ione called Trent and gave him the bad news. Trent tried to put a call through to Helen at the Thompson home in Guelph, but he could not reach her until the following day.

Learning of Thompson's death, Jones sent notes to fellow ASGCA members to inform them of the "very sad news." To ASGCA officer William H. Diddel, Jones wrote, "I can't express the personal loss I feel." Since the breakup of their company, the two men had stayed in touch and remained friendly, and Stanley dropped in to the Jones home in Montclair from time to time for brief visits and a glass or two (or three) of scotch. As with most of Thompson's friends, Jones worried about Stanley's health and well-being, especially after Ruth's death and before Stan remarried. Jones knew that the convivial Canadian, with "his hearty manner and roast-beef complexion," was far too fond of his whiskey—and, in combination with his overly generous ways and sloppy business habits, Thompson over the course of his career had frittered away several small fortunes. Jones knew Stanley could squander money but he did not know just how bad things had gotten financially for Stanley until after his death. When the executor of Thompson's will assembled his creditors, it was to inform them that

Canada's greatest golf architect had died not merely penniless but more than $500,000 in debt, the equivalent in today's dollars of more than $4 million. No one was happy that Thompson had died a pauper's death. After some difficult discussions, all the creditors agreed to forgive Stanley's debts—a display of the love and respect that they had for him. One of the men to whom Thompson owed the most money declared at this meeting, "Stanley did more for us individually than we did for him."

Thompson was buried in Mount Hope Cemetery in Kitchener, Ontario. The cemetery was some eighteen miles west of his home in Guelph, where Stanley lived and had gone to college. According to his biographer, James A. Barclay, Thompson had gone to Mount Hope just a few weeks before his death for the burial of a friend, George Lang, a former president of the Royal Canadian Golf Association. At Lang's gravesite, Stanley was "so impressed by the quiet serenity of the cemetery" that he came back home vowing to be buried there rather than in Guelph or in Toronto at St. John the Baptist Norway, in the cemetery where his parents had been laid to rest. An obituary in the *Canadian Sport Monthly* read:

> Scion of the greatest golfing family in Canadian history, Stan was un-challenged for a number of years as the finest golf architect in the world. His courses, 200 of them, stand as living memorials to his ability. Stanley was a debonair gentleman in good times and bad . . . an exponent of the grand manner in life, capable of recouping lost fortunes with the magnificent flourish of a fictional character. Yet there was a shyness about him that was in marked contrast to his great zeal for his work and his mode of living. He bore the mark of genius and gave much to life and left us, who remember and loved him, the lifelong thrill of taking mashie in hand and dueling with his unmistakable artistry for the rest of our days.

Thompson's golf courses, said the obituary, "like his friendship, only become more intriguing and mellower, with the passing of time, yet his twinkle and spark will be missed as long as a single golfer who knew him continues to play the game."

More than a hundred people attended Thompson's funeral. Several mourners were members of the Cutten Club, the golf course in Guelph where the Thompsons lived. Friends came from golf courses that he had built over his forty-year career, a few traveling great distances across Canada. The Royal Canadian Golf Association sent representatives to pay their respects. Also at the gravesite on that cold winter morning was a small group of men whom Stanley had taken under his wing, brought to work at his Toronto and Guelph design studios, and mentored into talented golf course architects in their own right: forty-five-year-old Howard Watson, whom Thompson had sent to Rochester in 1930 to help young Jones begin his work at Midvale; Clinton E. "Robbie" Robinson, another apprentice dispatched to New York from time to time by Thompson in the early 1930s to help Jones undertake various projects; thirty-eight-year-old Geoffrey S. Cornish, who had initially come to work for Thompson in 1935 to evaluate soils for the new Capilano Golf Club in West Vancouver but who stayed with Stanley for four years before becoming greenkeeper at St. Charles Country Club in his hometown of Winnipeg. Robert Trent Jones did not attend the ceremony. He was in Florida, where, in addition to remodeling the old La Gorce Country Club in Miami, he was preparing for a presentation to the Jacksonville Beach city council on plans for a new public golf course. Given how close Jones and Thompson once were and how crucial Thompson's support had been to launching Jones's career, his decision not to travel north can at least be described as consistent with his pattern of always putting his work first. Ione sent flowers and sympathy cards to Helen Thompson and members of the Thompson family, but Jones stayed in Florida. The protégés of the great Canadian golf architect—Watson, Cornish, and Robinson—made note of their former colleague's absence.

Nineteen fifty-three was undeniably a busy year for Trent Jones. Business was booming as never before. Five million Americans were playing golf, with the value in land, clubhouses, and golf course construction estimated at $2 billion. The United States had five thousand golf courses, but four thousand—80 percent of them—were considered, at least by Jones, to be "out of date." National business magazines were projecting that "Eventually, America will probably well support 15,000 golf courses," with the average cost for the construction of a new course projected to be, according to Trent Jones himself, from $175,000 to $225,000. On a suitable site, a single job "should take from one and a half to two years" to complete. The "great potential reservoir" for new golf courses in America was not in major metropolitan areas but in cities of from 25,000 to 100,000 people.

"In America golf is being forced out of metropolitan areas by the growth of the urban area and by real estate development," explained Jones. Optimistically, the architect felt that the travel problems for city-dwellers "will be solved in time by helicopters." That utopian vision may have proved true in the coming years for ultra-rich corporate executives working in downtown office buildings, but hardly for anyone else.

In the four years following the end of World War II, Jones's firm had completed a total of twenty-two projects, one more than Jones had finished over his entire career up to that point. In 1949 alone, his company completed what was for it a record number of projects: twelve. By the end of the decade, the Jones company's tally for the period 1949 to 1959 stood at eighty-four golf courses, or nearly eight course completions per year. Jones's business had expanded far beyond his core base in the Mid-Atlantic region. Although twenty-five of the eighty-four courses were in New York, New Jersey, Connecticut, and Pennsylvania, the other fifty-nine golf course projects ranged from Maine to California, twenty-four states in all. During the 1950s Trent's company also moved outside the continental United States for the first time, building golf courses in the Bahamas, Bermuda, and Puerto Rico. How much money Jones made from his seven dozen golf projects between 1949 and 1959 cannot be ascertained precisely, in part because Jones, besides charging his architectural design fees, made considerably more money through his shadow construction companies, for which there was separate billing and accounting. From the assorted bills, receipts, and other accounting documents in the Jones Papers at Cornell, a rough calculation can be made of Jones's total business income from 1949 to 1959. At a minimum, the total came to $850,000 (or an average of $10,119 per project), the equivalent today of $7.2 million (or $85,714 per project). Trent Jones was not just the world's best-known golf course architect; he was likely also the world's wealthiest.

The most visible sign of his growing prosperity was the family's new home at 173 Gates Avenue in Montclair. Designed by noted architect Clifford Charles Wendehack, who in 1923 had built the stylish clubhouse at Winged Foot Golf Club, the Joneses' new house was built in the Tudor style with brick facings and a slate roof; it was not quite a mansion, but it was certainly a beautiful three-story home located on one of Montclair's loveliest tree-lined avenues. Jones was not a man for showing off what he owned or what he had. He drove around in old cars, because he didn't like to worry about making a show of himself to other people with his wealth or position. But Trent was extremely proud of his

Gates Avenue home. It was one of the few possessions that he was very fond of. Ione felt the same way about the house, although she also cared for her jewelry and the fur coat she wore at very special events. In 1987 Mrs. Jones would die in that house. What happened to ownership of the Gates Avenue house after her death would turn into one of the most distressing family matters that Trent and his sons would have to face.

To keep up with his booming business, Jones expanded his office operations and supporting staff. In the years before the end of World War II, Jones's entire operation consisted of three people: himself; William Baldwin, who headed the construction work; and Ione. All three were indispensable and overworked. That was certainly true for Ione, who, along with caring for two precocious boys about to enter their teenage years, managed the books, did all the billing, handled the correspondence, created and maintained the filing system, and kept track of all the money and bank accounts. As oldest son Bob Jr., who turned fourteen in 1953, recalls, "Mother was in charge of the domestic scene and also ran the business bookkeeping, and did so according to the business principles that her father, Howard Davis, had taught her, not really by what Dad taught her. Truth was, she taught Dad." Without Ione's skills for organization, her intelligence and cleverness about all types of business matters, her highly developed skills in communication (both written and over the telephone), her meticulousness in keeping records, and her sensible approach to taking in and spending money, Trent's operation could not have prospered as it did. Again, Bob Jr. remembers: "Dad always wanted to be a businessman, but he wasn't really. Mother used to say, 'He's really not a businessman,' because directing a business is really fairly boring: laborious accounting, running numbers, negotiating contracts, talking tough, making hard decisions. My father was much more the creative person who could foresee where good opportunities were developing and then move to take advantage of them quickly. But those instincts of Dad's, when un-tempered, as they often were, could also get him into trouble. It was Mother who truly had the head for business and who made everything work. Without her business savvy, Dad would have found himself lost . . . or worse."

Ione faced another serious challenge when her youngest son, nine-year-old Rees, contracted poliomyelitis in the late summer of 1950. The boy nearly died. The polio that afflicted him was not the paralytic type that could cripple its victims, but rather the strain that attacked the central nervous system, causing severe pain in the head, neck, back, abdomen, and extremities, along with fever, vomiting, lethargy, and irritability. Worse in many ways than the paralytic form of polio, the virus Rees contracted could also lead to meningitis and/or encephalitis.

There was no cure for polio (this is still the case today), but there was also no vaccine that could prevent someone from contracting the disease; the Salk vaccine did not become available in the United States until the spring of 1955. Young Rees received the standard protocol: He was hospitalized, placed in an isolation ward, put on a ventilator to support his breathing, and given analgesics for pain and antibiotics to prevent secondary infections. When Rees recovered sufficiently to return home, he still needed around-the-clock nursing, provided almost exclusively by his mother, who hardly left her son's side for several weeks. Mother and son grew extraordinarily close during his recovery. Their warm and loving relationship would persist right up to Ione's death four decades later, and this special allegiance would come to define the emotional geography of the Jones family: Ione's and Rees's profound lifelong attachment set against the bond between the two Roberts, father and first-born son. Robert Jr., not just the eldest son but the namesake, and his father bonded in an altogether different way than Rees aligned with his mom, relating to one another "man to man," as Dad would have it, though their activities together were greatly limited by the fact that Bobby himself was quarantined for many weeks. It should not be surprising, then, that Rees in later years would come to feel that "Dad always liked Bob better" and that Bob Jr. thought that "Mother favored Rees because of his polio and because she felt that Dad gave me more time than he gave Rees and she needed to even things out."

With Ione spending so much of her time nursing Rees back to health, she had much less time to handle the affairs of her husband's office. So for the first time the Joneses required a secretarial assistant, a role held for several years by two young women before Eileen Vennell, who would stay with the company for three decades, was hired. To help with the care of the household, Ione also hired her first maid, an African-American woman by the name of Clara Williams, who came from Atlanta, where she had worked for a family residing adjacent to the East Lake course where Bobby Jones was a member; it's likely, in fact, that Bobby Jones or his wife, Mary, made the referral.

But it was not only Ione who needed help. With a dozen burgeoning prospects at hand and more on the horizon, Trent took on his first design associate, Francis J. Duane, a young landscape architect who had graduated from the State

University of New York in 1944. Duane worked for Jones for seventeen years, until 1963, when he ventured out on his own to design golf courses. During his time with Jones, Duane assisted with the design or remodeling of approximately fifty golf courses in eighteen U.S. states plus Puerto Rico, along with three foreign countries (Canada, Colombia, and Jamaica). As Trent Jones later reflected back on the need for Duane and the fruits of his employment, "These were rich years, about to become better."

Duane was by far the most important addition to Jones's operation, but other hires proved their value as well. Into the Vesey Street office—Jones had moved the company from Midtown to Lower Manhattan in 1944—to assist Duane with the drafting work came a young man by the name of Thomas Palazzotto. A professional illustrator, Julian Michele, was employed on a piecework basis to elaborate on Jones's sketches, taking them, as much as possible, to the point where they acquired the explicitness of a photograph. A final addition to Jones's staff was George Kingdom Troensegaard, a turfgrass specialist. Jones himself knew quite a bit about grasses, especially those suitable for use on golf courses in the Northeast and Mid-Atlantic: the bluegrasses, fescues, and bents. But as Jones expanded his business to other parts of the country and overseas in the 1950s, his company had to become familiar with several other species of turf-forming grasses: Bermuda, carpetgrass, centipede grass, and zoysia (itself comprised of three principal species) in the South and the Caribbean, and buffalo, blue grama, and the Fairway strain of crested wheatgrass in the Great Plains region. Jones and his crew also had to become more knowledgeable about the so-called "temporary grasses." In the North the temporary grasses included Redtop as well as domestic and perennial rye, which were being used seasonally to a greater and greater extent to furnish a grass cover until the slower-growing "permanent grasses" could become established. In southern climes, temporary grasses were getting "overseeded" in the fall more and more in order to provide green turf on greens and fairways over the winter months when the southern grasses, notably Bermuda, were dormant. In the 1950s, a considerable amount of turfgrass research was being done at federal and state agricultural experimental stations as well as by state college and university agriculture departments—more and more of it in association with programs of the USGA's Green Section and of the Golf Course Superintendents Association of America (GCSAA). This research led to a host of advances in agronomic theory and practice that Jones felt his company needed to comprehend, if not master.

The company workload made it impossible for Bill Baldwin to personally oversee all of the construction work underway. Baldwin was Jones's captain in the field who knew exactly what "the general" wanted, especially in his putting surfaces, with all their contours, slopes, multiple spots for pin positions, and surrounding bunkers and mounds. Bill could also get on a bulldozer and shape every feature of a golf course himself. But with so many construction jobs under contract to Jones's firm, Baldwin needed to show the foremen of local construction crews how to build a golf course according to Jones's exact specifications. Baldwin also recruited the local talent needed to do all the work, which could range from civil engineers to day laborers with shovels. In the mid-1950s, Jones hired John Schmeisser to serve as the company's second supervisor of construction.

Not that "General Jones" didn't occasionally go out to command the troops. By the early 1950s Trent typically devoted at least three days a week to inspection trips, working the other days in his Lower Manhattan office. But rarely did a five-day, forty-hour work-week suffice, given the demands for the company's services. Jones spent many evening and weekend hours at home sketching holes and taking care of business. Two rooms of his Montclair home were set aside for business: a small workroom in the attic and the entire sun parlor at the back of the house. In the evenings he tended to work in the attic, but during daylight hours he much preferred the sun parlor, with its natural light and serene view out onto a well-kept backyard lawn. Inside the parlor, he arranged two massive desks and a row of metal file cabinets. It was in this sunny home office that Ione also did most of her work for the company.

In 1944 Jones had moved his Manhattan office out of its fifth-floor room at 45 West 45th Street in order to get more space for his design firm. The 20 Vesey Street building, which offered him a larger office at a similar price, was located just above the business district halfway between Broadway and Church Street (in the early 1970s the World Trade Center would be built just around the corner). The gray, stone commercial building faced the picturesque yard at St. Paul's Church but, being only ten floors high, offered no scenic view in any direction. Jones usually met his clients uptown, at a nice pub or restaurant, or at the Yale Club, an impressive twenty-two-story neoclassical building near Grand Central Station. In such a sociable environment, over cocktails and a nice lunch, Jones spun his magic as a pitchman. Trent excelled at these hearty man-to-man dealings, whose goal was to excite clients to spend lots of money on golf course projects. As he later explained, "You have to create the money. I have created money from nowhere. That takes imagination and determination. I had to be a good salesman. Usually if you're a good salesman, you don't have any problem. If I'm convinced, they're convinced—at that, I am the best. And when you are the best, they give you a free hand."

Initial meetings with a client usually happened before Jones saw the client's property and were preparatory to a site visit. Not every tract of land that clients aspired to turn into a golf course was actually suitable for golf and, when a tract absolutely wasn't, Jones let the client know it but not before exploring what other properties the client might have that could work out better. By the 1950s, with the availability of big bulldozers, other heavy earthmoving equipment, improved turfgrasses, and advanced drainage and irrigation systems, there weren't many properties that couldn't be *made* suitable for golf. Jones had a talent—or, perhaps, an inclination—to see those possibilities; in his mind's eye, he could see a golf hole just about anywhere. And in those rich three-dimensional visions of a golf landscape, and in his talent for floridly communicating his grand sporting visions to clients, lay one of the main ingredients in the formula of Robert Trent Jones's extraordinary success in the golf course design business.

As he was moving into the third—and by far the busiest so far—decade of his career, Jones was refining and systematizing the process by which he designed golf courses. After inspecting and approving a client's site, he typically returned to his desk at Vesey Street to draw up preliminary plans. Step one was to get both an aerial photograph and a topographical map of the land. From those two different but precisely informative views of the property, Jones turned to his new illustrator, Julian Michele, to prepare a master drawing of the photograph and map combined. In this master drawing would be all of the property's notable features: its lakes and ponds, its streams, its roads and boundary lines, along with all the contours of the terrain. Michele would make three or four copies of the master drawing and then turn them over to Jones or Duane so that the designers could plot routings for the golf course. On these masters, the architects, using thin strips of gummed tape, would indicate the shape, position, and direction of each hole in relationship to all the others. Then draftsman Thomas Palazzotto took over, tracing his bosses' rudimentary layouts onto final copies of the master drawing, modifying them as Jones or Duane directed, to eliminate such "undesirable elements" as steep climbs (which would require grading), long walks between greens and tees, blind approaches, and fairways whose landing zones were too close together. At this stage of the process, Jones would often make another site inspection to check, point by point, the desirability of the tentative course. Returning to Vesey Street, Jones would work alone, or with Duane's input, to make the needed changes.

Then it was time for Jones to show his client the plans that his staff had developed. This meeting to close the deal could take place at the client's office, the proposed golf property, or again at a Manhattan restaurant. Jones usually showed the client two or three possible course routings, with a summary of estimated costs for each. In Trent's leather briefcase would be contracts prepared back at Vesey Street for each of the alternative golf courses; but the architect always made it abundantly clear which design, in his expert opinion, would produce the best golf course. If the client was happy, Jones would bring out for signature the specific contract for the agreed-upon course. If the client was not happy, Jones had no choice but to return to his office and come up with new routing plans.

Sometimes lack of closure sent Jones back to eyeball the property again, looking for a layout that had been missed. But very few clients doubted Trent's judgment. As Wind explained, "The Jones his clients know is the golf aficionado whose veneration for the game matches their own and who has the knack of designing courses that look natural, are fun to play, judiciously punish bad shots and reward good shots, and, while providing a stiff test for the expert, do not break the back or the spirit of the average golfer." Most clients felt fortunate that Robert Trent Jones, the world's greatest golf architect, had agreed to not just design but to judiciously oversee the building of a golf course for them. Jones stressed to his clients that the best person by far to build the new golf course was "William D. Baldwin, president of Contour Construction Company," a "talented contractor" with whom Jones had worked many times over many years and who in all cases had "produced golf courses of the highest type and quality." By the end of the 1950s, Jones used two main construction companies that he owned himself, Baldwin's and another called Florida Golf Corporation, headed by John Schmeisser, his other principal construction foreman. More than once, Jones would have Baldwin and Schmeisser go to a client for whom Jones was designing a golf course and submit bids for shaper work that were supposedly competitive and seemingly coming from two independent companies, when both actually belonged to Jones. Such backdoor games were common and unquestionably a conflict of interest. Some clients knew the truth, and some didn't. To those who knew, it seemed mostly not to matter. What they wanted was the best Robert Trent Jones golf course they could get. Who better than Jones himself to oversee the construction?

With signed contracts for design and construction in hand, Jones was ready to start building the golf course. Working with a local construction crew from the detailed plans Jones's office had provided, Baldwin (or his local foreman) oversaw the clearing of trees and brush. This began with a single swath made by a bulldozer down what was to be the centerline of each fairway. This center-cut literally gave the architect and his construction superintendent a path from which to work—a rough but manageable dirt walkway. Taking that walk, they could confirm the width of the corridor that was to become the golf hole. They could also determine which trees, plants, and other vegetation should be kept, which should be cut down, and which specimens should be carefully uprooted and removed to a temporary nursery on the property for possible replanting behind greens, around the clubhouse, or at some other "beautifying" location. Usually all the trees and brush that stood left and right of the centerline out to what was to be the edge-lines of the fairways were knocked down by the bulldozer, dragged away, and burned in a big trench. Any trees that Jones wanted to keep—precious species like oaks were almost always kept until the architect decided what to do with them—were tagged with surveyor's tape, typically red or yellow, which indicated to the construction crew to leave those trees alone. Out beyond the fairway edge-lines, in what was to be the rough, just the opposite was true: Any trees that Jones wanted cut down were tagged with the colored tape for elimination.

Every construction project had its pitfalls, problems, and mistakes. Jones's hackles were raised when a construction crew didn't adhere to his directions. This was especially true if it involved the construction of a green. Like any golf architect worth his salt, Jones was very finicky about his putting surfaces and "surrounds." Besides taking the time and care to draw pencil sketches of each one of his green complexes, he used ordinary modeling clay, colored green, to sculpt a model of each green, one that was scaled twenty feet to the inch. If a water hazard surrounded a green, Jones depicted its shape and size with blue clay. He painted sand traps onto the green clay with white enamel. Trent had very specific ideas about how his green complexes were to be built, and he did his best to make sure they got built just that way. Though he himself never operated a bulldozer, Jones often stood in his shirtsleeves directing his "shapers," as they came to be called, "with hand signals and vocal exhortations," until the machine operators scooped and buffeted the earthwork into the precise shapes he had defined. (His eldest son, Bob Jr., believes that "Dad never worked on a bulldozer because he never lost his awareness of the social distinction, perceived or real, between working-class people and professional people." He lived his entire life "insecure about his immigrant British working-class beginnings and aspired to move up in the world through success in a sport that was still mainly upper class.")

It is clear from his travel and billing records that he took more visits to the golf courses that he found the most fascinating or in his opinion had the most potential for becoming a great golf course. "By this time," Jones later recalled, "I began to feel that my career was so well established, and that from now on I would design and build only the best courses and solidify my position as the best known architect in the world of golf. Even after expanding my offices and my staff, I personally still had so much work that I didn't have time to think of anything else. Building sensational golf courses became my goal, and I made every effort to reach that goal. I used to take the boys on my business trips to look at property or supervise courses I was building. Some of our family vacations were spent at places where I was building courses." In *The New Yorker* profile, Wind mentioned that Jones, in the last six months of 1951 and first six months of 1952, had been "unable to stay away for more than three weeks at a time from the eighteen holes he built for the Dunes Golf and Beach Club at Myrtle Beach." During the rest of that decade, the same would be true for a number of other projects that he favored because he felt they added the most to his esteemed reputation—and thereby most affected the dollar figure he could charge for his work.

Jones was an ambitious man whose achievements fueled ever-grander aspirations. In December 1951, five months after the Open at Oakland Hills, he entered into an agreement with PGA star Sam Snead for the most mammoth golf construction project in the history of the game.

Trent's association with Sam Snead went back to the exhibitions of the mid-1930s that Sam had played for Jones at Green Lakes State Park—events for which Snead did not think that Jones had paid him enough of the gate. But over the years Jones and Snead had remained friends, and by the early 1950s both men saw an opportunity to make a boatload of money together. Both men were at the top of their game. Even more so than Byron Nelson or Ben Hogan, Snead was American golf's most popular "superstar" by the early 1950s. Snead was dominating the professional circuit, with eleven tournament wins in 1950 alone, PGA Championships in 1949 and 1951, and a Masters title in 1949 (with subsequent victories at Augusta in 1952 and 1954). "Slammin' Sammy" was also arguably the truest American golf icon, the Daniel Boone or Davy Crockett of the links. From humble origins in the mountains of western Virginia, Snead had "learned his sweet swing practicing barefoot in a cow pasture, using limbs or sticks as makeshift clubs." The entire golfing nation saw Snead as a "hillbilly," one whose "folksy, homespun humor and early success made him a darling of the media" and the most democratic of all American golfers, one who never felt totally comfortable setting foot inside a snooty private club. But Jones knew that Snead also "knew the basic ploys of how to make money."

The idea behind the joint business venture—which Trent Jones came up with and took to Snead—was to develop a national chain of "Sam Snead Country Clubs," multipurpose golf facilities not for the elite but for the average American golfer. According to the agreement between the two men, first signed on December 3, 1951, each Sam Snead Country Club was to be "a compact layout [of 30–40 acres] for the development of modern golf course play and instruction with a sheltered driving range, a short-hole [par-3] golf course of eighteen holes, an enormous putting green with thirty-six holes, a Tom Thumb golf course [a putt-putt or miniature golf course], an attractive club house for the complete selling facilities of clubs and golf clothing, an outdoor vending service, an outdoor movie theatre for instruction by slow-motion pictures by Sam Snead and illustrating and narrating the swings of all the great golfers, past and present, in such detail and with such simplicity that the instruction is good for new golfers and experienced golfers as well." The design of the Sam Snead Country Clubs, according to the agreement, "will be done in such a manner as to make them eye-appealing in their beauty without the unattractive look of most present driving ranges that are lacking an aesthetic appeal." A Sam Snead Country Club "will appear from the highway to be a small country club, with grass, flowers and shrubbery making it attractive and beautiful to the eye."

Snead signed on to the project, but no Sam Snead golf complex of such magnitude was ever built. The two men renewed their agreement in 1954, but the scope of each project was scaled down from the original concept. The idea that Jones and Snead pioneered was an "executive" course, designed with shorter yardages for a faster pace of play to suit the needs of corporate executives and other businessmen who did not have time on weekdays (or weekdays after work but before sunset) to complete an 18-hole round on a standard-length golf course. The total par for such a course would typically be less than the standard 72, but more than a course of all par-3s.

In the late 1950s and early 1960s, Jones built his first two "executive" golf courses in association with Snead, both of them in Florida. The first, the American Golfers Club in Fort Lauderdale, opened in 1958; six years later, Jones built the All American Golf Course in Titusville, near Cape Canaveral. In the next ten years, eleven more executive courses were laid out and constructed by Jones, Inc., four more in Florida, four in California, and one each in Virginia, Minnesota, and Nevada. For a while, the executive course concept was quite popular. The trend was short-lived, however: Full 18-hole courses allowed for executives and other golfers to play only the "front" or "back" nine of a golf course, so executive-style courses were not truly needed. It is not clear how many of Jones's later executive courses—those not known as "All-American"— were done in league with Snead, if any.

Trent Jones was so busy with highly visible, well-paying jobs that not having the grandiose plans for Sam Snead Country Clubs materialize barely produced a blip on his radar screen. What was much more important to the architect through the 1950s was to keep being asked to remodel venues for the U.S. Open.

In the spring of 1948, well before anyone knew how the redesign of Oakland Hills would turn out, Baltusrol Golf Club in Springfield, New Jersey, had contracted with Jones to modernize its golf course in the hope of attracting the U.S. Open. Serving in an advisory capacity for the project was fifty-five-year-old Francis Ouimet, who in 1913 as a twenty-year-old had shocked the golf world by winning the Open at The Country Club in Brookline, Massachusetts.

Even more so than Oakland Hills, Baltusrol boasted a proud history and an esteemed lineage. Founded in October 1895 on a property owned by Louis Keller, the publisher of the *New York Social Register,* the club was named for the original owner of the land, a man named Baltus Roll who was murdered at his home on February 22, 1831. The original course was the site of the 1903 and 1915 U.S. Opens, as well as four other national championships, before the club engaged A. W. Tillinghast to build a second course; "Tilly" convinced the membership to let him tear up the existing course and replace it with two 18-hole circuits that he completed in 1922, known as the Upper and Lower courses. The next U.S. Open at Baltusrol was held on the Upper Course in 1936.

When World War II ended and the USGA resumed its national champion-ships, Baltusrol was eager to host another Open, but the USGA had reserva-tions. The winning score in 1936—by an obscure New York–area pro named Tony Manero—was 282, breaking the existing record by four strokes; the total was seventeen shots lower than Sam Parks Jr.'s first-place performance the pre-vious year at Oakmont. The club recognized that it would need to lengthen and modernize if it wanted to be considered. In 1948, at roughly the same time that Oakland Hills was contracting with Trent Jones, the Baltusrol board of gov-ernors turned to Jones for its own remodeling. Jones, whose home in Montclair was only twelve miles from Baltusrol via the Garden State Parkway, was well known to club officials, and Jones was already quite familiar with the Till-inghast designs. Still, he came to visit the club several times in the late 1940s to take a fresh look.

From his inspections, Trent told the board at Baltusrol that, as great a course as the Upper was, the higher-lying layout just did not have the space for the new teeing areas needed to lengthen the course to modern championship standards. The layout that could best be transformed into a U.S. Open venue, in Jones's view, was the Lower.

Baltusrol's board appreciated the enthusiasm with which Jones explained how much he loved Tilly's designs. Like Tillinghast, Jones generally "hated blind shots and hidden hazards," but the partially blind shots at Baltusrol, where the golfer could see the pin but not the surface of the green, were of excep-tionally high playing value. Truth be known, Jones had his issues with some of Tillinghast's philosophies as an architect; in particular, he felt that Tilly's greens tended to be too small, too tightly bunkered, and too dished in, and that his green slopes were sometimes too extreme for reasonable putting. Fortunately, the greens on Baltusrol's Lower Course were atypically quite large—and, as Jones described them at the time, the putting surfaces on Baltusrol Lower were "filled with soft hollows and imperceptible crowns which make the simplest putt require keen concentration and a delicate touch."

Over the years Jones would relate very different versions of how much work he did to alter Baltusrol. In a 1991 interview with the USGA, Jones stated, "I re-modeled Baltusrol slightly." But in an autobiographical recording from 1996 that was transcribed by his secretary, Marge Darwell, Jones claimed, "This was an extensive remodeling job, and everyone was pleased with the results. Bal-tusrol was considered a championship course, so it was a great honor for me to remodel it, and I received many compliments for the work I did." What can be said with certainty is that "Jones's strengthening efforts brought the Lower course up to modern championship length without infringing upon the subtle character of the original Tillinghast design." Adding length was definitely the biggest reform—Jones tacked on some 400 yards and got the Lower up to a length of 7,027 yards for championship play. Played at par 70, that made Baltusrol Lower one of the country's longest golf courses in the 1950s.

At Baltusrol the changes that Jones made to the par-3 fourth hole on the Lower Course led to one of the most incredible anecdotes in the entire career of Robert Trent Jones—for that matter, in all of golf history. Over the years Jones repeated the story many times, almost always with variant colorful wording and often with a slightly different punch line, but always to the same jaw-dropping effect:

> It was at Baltusrol that I struck one of history's famous golf shots, perhaps the best-known shot ever hit outside of tournament competition. Certainly it was the ultimate squelch. Shortly after the remodeling of the Lower Course was finished in 1952, I was challenged by a critic who contended that I had made the fourth hole too difficult. Suggesting that the hole, which I had lengthened to play at 194 yards over water, be tested to determine what needed to be done, I led my critic, along with tournament chairman C. P. Burgess and Baltusrol club professional Johnny Farrell, to the tee. Each of those three put his tee shot on the green. Then I struck a mashie shot that landed six feet in front of the hole and went into the cup on the first hop. "Gentlemen," I said, "I think the hole is eminently fair."

In another version of the story, Jones explained:

> During the remodeling, the President of the Club told me that a lot of the members were complaining about the fourth hole which I had touched up into what was later called "one of the greatest par threes in American golf." The first shot has to carry over a large pond to an island green. The members claimed it was too difficult and they wanted me to change it. I suggested that some of the members come down with me to take a few shots at the hole. They didn't do badly, but when it was my

turn, I made a hole-in-one. I turned to the members and said, "Case closed—nothing needs to be changed." [*author's note*: Jones exaggerated in calling the fourth an "island" green. The putting surface was on a plateau that had three sand traps to the rear and one trap on the front left at the edge of the water, but it was not an island green in the pure sense of being encircled by water. What Jones did at the fourth was reshape the green, reshape the rear sand traps, and lengthen the tee to the point where the hole required, even for the pros, anything from a 5-iron to a 4-wood, depending on the wind. Jones also added a distinctive rock wall at the water's edge to guard the front of the green; the original facade was made of logs and compacted earth.]

Sports Illustrated golf writer Dan Jenkins called the hole "one of the most striking par 3s in the world," a magnificent hole that summed up "all that is good about Baltusrol in terms of beauty and challenge." In his 1966 book *Sports Illustrated's The Best 18 Golf Holes in America*, Jenkins chose Jones's redesigned par-3 as the best fourth hole in the country and added to the legend of Robert Trent Jones:

> Members of Baltusrol immediately protested that Jones had made the hole too difficult. Hearing of their complaints, Jones went out to the 4th hole one afternoon with Baltusrol's pro, Johnny Farrell, the club president and head of the club's Open committee. "I had been so sure that the new tee would make the hole that I had offered to bear the expense of building it myself," Jones later recalled. The foursome played from the new tee, and after the three others had shot, Jones hit his iron into the cup. It was a hole-in-one, the ultimate in one-upmanship. "As you can see, gentlemen," Jones remembers saying, with considerable satisfaction, "this hole is not too tough."

The Baltusrol Golf Club tells its own version of the "miracle at the fourth":

> Jones was criticized by members for making their fourth hole too difficult. "Let's go play the hole and see if there is anything that needs to be done," Jones suggested as he led the principal critic along with head pro Johnny Farrell and C. P. Burgess, General Chairman of the 1954 Open

Championship, to the fourth tee. They all struck shots. After Farrell and the two members hit the green, Jones struck his shot and sank it for a hole-in-one! "Gentlemen, I think the hole is eminently fair."

Whatever the precise facts, the iconic significance of the oft-told tale was clear to his clients, present and future: Do not challenge the architectural genius who can prove his points by making holes-in-one. If the miracle shot at Baltusrol was not enough to quiet them, he could—and did—tell them that he "had almost done the same thing a few years earlier." At the Rockrimmon Country Club near Stamford, Connecticut, for which Jones completed the first nine holes in 1949, he had designed a 170-yard par-3 that the club's green committee thought "looked longer and would demand some kind of wood shot." Trent sent Frank Duane back to the car to get his 4-iron and a couple of balls. "I needed just one," Jones would brag, "striking a shot that landed three feet short of the pin and stayed there. That ended the argument."

One wonders how many other times Jones pressed his luck by hitting such chancy, off-the-cuff, "prove it" tee shots. Armed with the bravado tales of Baltusrol and Rockrimmon, he may not have pressed his luck. Better just to tell the stories and let the legendary prowess of Robert Trent Jones win the day.

At the 1954 U.S. Open, Jones's redesigned fourth hole held up well. The eventual winner, Ed Furgol, a thirty-seven-year-old pro from St. Louis whose 4-over-par total of 284 nosed out a young rising star by the name of Gene Littler by one shot, helped himself immensely by playing Baltusrol's fourth in even par. Ben Hogan, in his quest for an unprecedented fifth Open title, managed to do the same. Not so lucky was virtually all of the rest of the field, as competitors played the hole with as many bogeys (or worse) as pars over the four days.

To Jones's credit, Baltusrol Lower is considered to this day to be one of the very best examples of an outstanding golf course *redesign*, the major criterion for which is that the redesign is able to keep almost all the essential features, and certainly the inherent flavor and high quality, of the original golf course. Following right on the heels of Jones's more radical—and thereby more controversial—remodeling of Oakland Hills for the '51 Open, a lighter touch in the reworking of Baltusrol was just what the doctor ordered. After every revolution there comes a period when change "normalizes" and gains are consolidated. Thus began a relatively more placid manner of redesign following the "rising" of the '51 Open.

Trent Jones was definitely on a roll. Between 1950 and the end of 1953, his company finished twenty-five projects. Along with the highly publicized remodeling projects at Oakland Hills, Baltusrol, and Augusta, "Robert Trent Jones," a sole proprietorship until 1958 when Jones incorporated his business as "Robert Trent Jones, Inc.," completed five new 18-hole layouts during that four-year span.

Two of those courses were built in Eisenhower Park, located on Long Island in East Meadow, New York. In the first third of the twentieth century, the property that ultimately became Eisenhower Park belonged to the exclusive Salisbury Country Club. This conclave, the centerpiece in the social life of wealthy families along the North Shore, featured five 18-hole golf courses, which made Salisbury Country Club the largest golf complex not just in the United States but in the world. The crown jewel of the club was the "Links" course laid out in 1914 by Devereux Emmet. The course played host to the 1926 PGA Championship, an event won by Walter Hagen; in the gallery of spectators on one tournament day was a young Robert Jones.

All of the golf courses, save Emmet's Links, disappeared during the Depression when the estate owners were unable to pay their taxes and the county assumed control of the property. For Jones, getting the opportunity to build golf courses in Eisenhower Park, formally dedicated as such by Nassau County in October 1949, was no small honor. He crafted two solid public golf courses—the "White" and the "Blue," which opened in 1950 and 1951, respectively; Emmet's course became the "Red." Both of Jones's courses featured elevated greens and well-placed bunkers. The White could be stretched to 6,932 yards, whereas the Blue played no longer than 6,049. Jones's idea was to build highly playable courses that complemented the grand old Links. For both of the new courses he built identical, side-by-side par-3s, the idea being that if a foursome of daily-fee golfers got stacked up due to slow play, instead of waiting for the green to clear, they could play the "open" par-3, thereby keeping the flow of play around the course moving. "This was never done before," Jones later recalled, "and everyone loved the idea."

A truly original concept, he used the "twin-hole "approach on several other golf courses, including Raymond Memorial Golf Course, an 18-hole layout in the western suburbs of Columbus, Ohio.

Remodeling jobs dominated the Jones portfolio in the early 1950s. From 1950 to 1954 Jones remodeled twenty-one courses. "Remodeling had become a necessity in the golf world," recollected Jones years later, "because of the improvement of the ball and the more sophisticated design of clubs, which allowed the players to hit the ball farther." Besides the redesigns he did for U.S. Opens, one of the most distinguished courses that Jones touched up during this period was Belle Meade Country Club, a beloved Donald Ross design (from 1921) in Nashville, Tennessee. On his itinerary of redesigns, in fact, were a handful of courses that had been designed originally by Ross: Portland Country Club in Falmouth, Maine; Detroit Golf Club's North Course; Siwanoy Country Club in Bronxville, New York; and the Country Club of Buffalo in Williamsville, New York. On most of the others Jones was also working to modernize courses laid out by some of the early greats in golf course design, including Willie Park Jr. (Pittsburgh Field Club in Pennsylvania), Charles Blair Macdonald (St. Louis Country Club in Clayton, Missouri, and the Mid Ocean Club in Tucker's Town, Bermuda), H. S. Colt (the Country Club of Detroit in Grosse Pointe Farms), Walter J. Travis (Round Hill Club in Greenwich, Connecticut), Devereux Emmet (Powelton Club in Newburgh, New York), and Herbert Strong (Ponte Vedra Inn & Club [Ocean Course] in Florida, just south of Jacksonville).

Personal recommendations from club members at Baltusrol to club members at the Olympic Club in San Francisco were an important factor in Trent Jones landing his third U.S. Open course redesign, for the 1955 Open at Olympic. "Baltusrol is in marvelous shape and as tough a golf course as I have ever played, although I have not played Oakmont," wrote Baltusrol member J. Edwin Carter to Olympic member Robert A. Roos Jr. on May 1, 1954, six weeks before the '54 Open at Baltusrol began. "Robert Trent Jones has done a terrific job, it seems to me, along with our Greens Keeper Edward Casey, and it would certainly behoove you to try to engage his services for the Lakeside Course if you have not already hired an architect." Making an impression on Roos was essential, as Edwin Carter knew, not just because Roos was an Olympic Club member, but because he was serving as general chairman of the USGA 1955 Open Championship.

Jones was well known to the Olympic Club by reputation but not personal familiarity, as the Atlantic Coast–based architect had done no work to this point anywhere in California, nor even spent much time in the Golden State. His very first trip to California was in January 1953 when he attended the seventh annual ASGCA meeting at the Ojai Valley Inn in Ojai, just northwest of Los Angeles. It was during this trip that Jones made his first visit to the Monterey Peninsula, where he played Pebble Beach and Cypress Point. Whether Jones visited any San Francisco Bay–area golf courses before flying home to New York after this first California visit is uncertain. There is nothing in the Jones Papers to indicate that he stopped off at Olympic.

The Olympic Club sent a special committee to New Jersey to scout out what Jones had done to modernize and toughen Baltusrol for the '54 championship. After taking a close look at the Lower Course and watching the four days of the tournament, the committee quickly came to the conclusion that it wanted Jones to redesign its course for the major championship. Naturally, Jones accepted the offer. Olympic officials then gave Jones a written list of the club's preliminary thoughts about what needed to be done to remake their golf course for the championship, hopefully turning it into a golf course that would not just stand up to the pros' onslaught but actually fight back vigorously to the point of knocking those pros down.

Although Olympic had never before been the site of a national competition, it had hosted the San Francisco Open, the last time in 1946 when Byron Nelson shot 283 and won by nine strokes. The membership at Olympic felt that its golf course needed to be refortified to stand up better to the test. They worried about their short 6,430-yard course, which was built in the early 1920s and on which even a number of Olympic's better players regularly busted par. The land for the original Lakeside course had been a treeless expanse of sand dunes situated between the Pacific Ocean and Lake Merced. In 1924, when the course was completely redone by architect Willie Watson and greenkeeper Sam Whiting, more than forty thousand eucalyptus, pine, and cypress trees were planted on the new Lake Course (and another thirteen thousand were planted on the Ocean Course). By the time the USGA selected Olympic for the '55 national championship, the trees on the Lake Course had risen to an average height of sixty feet, and a few of them soared to a hundred feet. Evergreen giants lined every fairway, leaving narrow avenues 75 to 80 yards wide. The visual effect of this deeply forested landscape was striking, with deep lines of tall trees forming funnels to direct tee shots and abruptly swat down errant shots. Never in his career had Trent Jones faced such a challenge of tight tree-lined corridors determining the shape of holes and restricting lines of play.

According to Jones's proposed plan, work was to be done on every hole of the golf course except for the stretch from #11 to #17. The most expensive hole in the remodeling was #7, whose cost alone tallied $11,750. Included in that price was $400 for tree removal, $4,000 for constructing and grading a new tee, and $4,600 for construction and care of a new green.

It was not surprising that the seventh hole at Olympic needed so much attention. A weak, 266-yard par-4, its green was "open and vulnerable, and even though the ground ran uphill, the green could be driven." Jones constructed a thin bunker that stretched all the way across the front of the green, so a tee shot could no longer roll onto the putting surface. He also shaped a new green that was contoured quite severely with three decks rising from front to back. As for the fairway on what was now a devilish "short four," it was practically eliminated. A good drive had to be hit to what Jones called a "dewdrop fairway," a mere 25 yards wide, which began at 210 yards from the tee and ran up the 25 yards to the new cross-bunker defending the path to the green. Some called it a radical solution, but it was definitely effective. In the 1955 Open, "the seventh still wasn't the strongest hole at Olympic, [but] it no longer gave up birdies quite so easily."

Another hole at Olympic that Jones altered dramatically was the 14th, a 410-yard par-4 with a broad fairway that swept to the right and a bunker at the left front of the green. A big hitter would fly his tee shot to where the fairway pitched rather sharply sideways, sending the ball so far that only a pitch was left into the green. Here Jones pulled in the rough line from the right, forcing the drive farther to the left. He filled in the left greenside bunker and swung another bunker diagonally across the right front of the green so that the only opening for the approach shot was from the left. These changes totally changed the strategy of the hole: The tee shot now needed to be played down the left side, which meant it would be closer to the tree line and nearer greater danger.

Overall, Jones increased the length of Olympic from 6,430 to more than 6,700 yards. New tees made it harder for golfers to use their drivers on some of the par-4s and even on a couple of the par-5s. Narrowing the fairways as the USGA wanted, he brought in the rough lines from 25 to as much as 40 yards. For the Open, the rough was allowed to grow in some places to eight inches, again according to USGA specifications. It was no ordinary rough, either, but rather "a perennial ryegrass that the players had not encountered before, and that turned out to be far tougher and more punishing than anyone expected." Imported from Italy years before, the grass grew tall and tangled, with blades up to three-eighths of an inch wide. That jungle grew not only in the rough, but also around the fringes of the greens. Chipping a ball close to the hole from the nasty elephant grass into tight positions on very fast and highly contoured greens was, for many players, asking too much.

With all the narrowness to both sides caused by the heavy tree lines and the deep, tangled rough, there was no need for fairway bunkers; but Jones (some say perversely) created one solitary bunker—the only one on the entire golf course—and strategically placed it on the long par-4 sixth so it would catch drives hit to the left. (The bunker on #6 fairway must have been an afterthought for Jones, because its creation was not on the final cost-estimate document that he submitted to the Olympic Club's Properties Committee.) When the pros arrived for their practice rounds, they instantly realized that there was going to be only one way to play Olympic: by hitting fairways and greens.

And those small greens! Jones built six new greens, adding some treacherous slopes and contours that made it necessary for the pros to negotiate their approach carefully. The greens became the predominant factor in protecting par at Olympic, and they did so extraordinarily well. "The fairways are wide," wrote *Sports Illustrated* writer Dan Jenkins, "but the greens are not—twelve steps will get you from one side of the 18th green to the other. Once reached, they are deceptive, full of hidden breaks that make three-footers seem like thirty." Jones, however, made no changes to the closing green. Protected by bunkers front, left, and rear, the green, from a shallow shelf at the rear, sloped sharply toward the front. If the hole was cut on the front portion and an approach shot wound up on the back plateau, getting down in two putts, in Trent's words, "definitely requires God to be on your side."

In a manner quite different from Oakland Hills or Baltusrol, Jones turned Olympic into yet another image of the modern championship golf course. It had no water hazards. It had only one fairway trap. But it had new length, new strategies, and some new greens and greenside traps that added a great deal of treachery. Although not a radical redesign, Jones's alterations brought about "a remarkable change" in the course. As one sportswriter described the design for the 1955 championship, "It was brutally hard—not as punishing as Oakland Hills, but rugged nonetheless. Complaints from the players were still common. Nearly everyone claimed Olympic was unplayable and that the rough that crowded practically to the edge of the green prevented recovery for a shot that ran just a little off the putting surface. . . . Furthermore, the rough was allowed to grow too long. The targets seemed unusually small, and the players were asked to hit them from too great a distance."

Trent Jones attended the '55 Open and, like the many thousands of spectators who walked amidst the big trees lining Olympic's fairways, he was confident that Hogan would take the crown. So, too, with only a couple of holes to play, was Hogan himself. Walking off the monster par-4 17th with a par (it was the first time he had parred the hole in the tournament), Hogan told his caddie, Andy Zitelli, "We got this thing by three shots." Hogan was so sure that a par would win him the tournament that he didn't try hard to make the uphill seven-foot putt he faced on the final green; instead, he cozied his ball up close to the hole for a sure tap-in. His even-par 70 round and 287 total would certainly be good for the victory—about that Hogan and everyone else was quite sure. Limping off the 18th green, Hogan saw the USGA's Joe Dey, tossed him his golf ball, and said, "Here you go, Joe, this is for Golf House," meaning the small museum at USGA headquarters (which at the time was still located in New York City). Trent Jones was standing right next to Dey when Hogan made the remark, and he was within earshot when, seconds later, Gene Sarazen, color commentator for NBC television's coverage, congratulated Ben for winning his fifth Open title.

But naming Hogan the winner proved embarrassingly premature. As Jones recalled years later, "Everyone thought Hogan was the winner. This would have been his fifth Open championship, so everyone was excited. Well, the tournament was on national TV for only the second time, and after Hogan had finished and been announced the winner, the network went off the air. No one suspected that a fellow still on the golf course two hours behind Hogan was about to turn everything topsy-turvy." That player was Jack Fleck, an obscure driving-range pro from Davenport, Iowa, a man who so idolized Hogan that he wore the same type of white "flat-cap" (sometimes called an "Ivy cap" or, in Scotland, a "bunnet") that Ben wore. Fleck also played irons from Hogan's company; he even used a new putter just off the Ben Hogan golf club company's assembly line. (When Fleck arrived at Olympic for the tournament, he came without any wedges; he had ordered two new ones from Hogan's company, and Ben hand-delivered them before the championship started.) While Hogan was being announced the winner on national television, Fleck was standing on the 10th tee, having shot a 2-under-par 33 on the front nine; he needed to pick up one more stroke to par in order to force a playoff, but when he made a bogey on the par-4 14th to fall two strokes back, Hogan's lead looked safe. But Fleck birdied the short 15th and followed with a par on the par-5 16th. A birdie on the uphill 461-yard 17th, which had been turned into a par-4 for the Open, seemed to be out of the question, but Fleck almost did it: A big drive followed by a powerful brassie (2-wood) left him a 40-foot downhill birdie putt that just barely slipped past the hole. But the par still gave him a chance. In the clubhouse an attendant quietly passed the word to Hogan that Fleck needed a birdie on #18 to tie him. "Good luck to him," Ben answered thinly, then adding under his breath before he went off to take his shower, "I hope he makes 2 or 4." Hogan's legs had struggled through 36 holes on Olympic's hills; he wanted no part of another round on Sunday.

But Fleck made birdie on his final hole, using his Hogan-brand putter to curl a tricky seven-foot, sidehill, right-to-left breaker into the center of the hole. His round was a 67 for a total of 287, same as Hogan's. Fleck's amazing final round of 3-under, coupled with a second round 1-under 69, meant that the driving range pro had shot two of the only six sub-par rounds of the tournament. The next day in the playoff against his golf hero, Fleck shot his third sub-par round, a 69, to beat Hogan by three shots. (Hogan showed great sportsmanship and even a little humor in the loss, at one point waving a towel in front of Fleck's putter as if to cool it down. And it was true—for the entire tournament, Fleck's Hogan-brand putter had been on fire.)

Trent Jones didn't stay for the playoff; on Sunday morning he took his scheduled flight from San Francisco to Portland, Oregon, where he was doing some touch-up work on the Portland Golf Club. To Jones, Fleck's win at Olympic was a wonderful rare instance in which a very good player elevated his performance—through dedication, intelligence, sound strategy, and a lot of luck—to an extraordinary level of play.

Host clubs hired Robert Trent Jones to remodel their golf courses for two of the next three U.S. Opens. In 1956 his extensive remodeling on Donald Ross's East Course at Oak Hill Country Club in Pittsford, New York, added substantial length and twenty-seven new bunkers to catch the errant drives of the modern professional golfer. He left his imprint in one fashion or another on seventeen of the eighteen holes. Golf architecture expert and Donald Ross specialist Bradley Klein has called Jones's remodeling of Oak Hill for the 1956 Open "a typical modernization of the mid-1950s." But in Jones's view, what he did at Oak Hill was take an up-to-date look at what Ross's thirty-year-old course had to offer and customize it to meet modern championship standards.

However, there can be no question that Trent Jones, in his process of modernizing Oak Hill, destroyed some of the "compositional unity" of the original Ross layout, which included such features as "lightly mounded greens that tipped forward about three feet from back to front" and putting surfaces that "rolled continuously and were not composed of distinct sections."

"By everyone's reckoning," Klein acknowledges, "these changes enabled Oak Hill to return to major championship status," which is exactly what the club wanted. "But in the process," adds Klein, "the gentle integration of bunker forms and hole styles" that were so superbly characteristic of Oak Hill and other great Ross designs was "sacrificed." Jones's "dramatic modernization . . . eliminated much of the old ground-game character" that had been available to golfers at Oak Hill and other classic American courses. After Jones's redesign, golfers were forced to play aerial games similar to lobbing darts onto small targets that were so stoutly defended by bunkers that it was no longer possible to run the ball onto a putting surface from anywhere out in the fairway.

Interestingly, Herbert Warren Wind, in his preview of the '56 Open published in *Sports Illustrated*, called Jones's work at Oak Hill "minor remodeling." The only major change that Wind mentioned was 100 yards of added overall length compared to what the course had played at for the 1949 U.S. Amateur at Oak Hill. Curiously, Oak Hill's own records indicate that the East Course played at its original Ross-given 6,538-yard distance for the 1949 event, which would mean that Trent Jones had added 364 yards; it played to 6,902 yards for the '56 Open. The course, a par 70, offered only two par-5s for championship play: the 571-yard fourth and the 602-yard 13th. The three finishing holes were potent on their own but brutal in succession; carved through a forest, the two-shotters played to distances of 441, 463, and 449. The formidable 18th not only played uphill but was frequently buffeted by winds off nearby Lake Ontario. A solid tee shot on the mild dogleg to the right required an extremely demanding second shot that was all carry to a green set on a ledge. In other words, Oak Hill challenged players with an incredibly hard finish. If a player managed to get through this "terrible trio" of holes sixteen through eighteen and shoot even par, he had definitely played a great round.

A highly deserving Dr. Cary Middlecoff won the championship trophy without ever breaking par. After opening with a 1-over 71, Middlecoff shot three straight rounds of even-par 70. His 281 total won the crown for "The Golf

Doctor," as he came to be known, by a single stroke over Julius Boros and Ben Hogan; together, the top three finishers certainly rated as three of the greatest players of the era. The East Course played with enormous difficulty for all four days. There were only seven sub-par rounds total, and none of the players who achieved that once did it twice. The two lowest scores of the championship were Bob Rosburg's 68 on opening day and Hogan's 68 on day two. The cut came at 149, or plus-7.

Jones brought all of the paradigmatic elements of his modernization scheme to his final U.S. Open redesign of the 1950s: the 1958 Open at Southern Hills Country Club in Tulsa, Oklahoma. Laid out in 1933–34 by Perry Duke Maxwell, a retired Oklahoma banker of Scottish descent who had served for a couple of years as Alister MacKenzie's assistant, Southern Hills had hosted the 1946 U.S. Women's Amateur and the 1953 U.S. Junior but no major professional championships. To get the premier event in all of golf, the U.S. Open, club officials knew they had to upgrade and toughen their course. Maxwell had died in 1952; his son Press had inherited his practice, but club officials did not feel that Press Maxwell would carry much weight with a United States Golf Association still dominated by the East Coast golf-club establishment. But Robert Trent Jones, a proven commodity, would likely do the trick for them. With Jones on board, club officials felt that their chances of getting an Open were excellent even though the weather in eastern Oklahoma during the early summer was likely to be stormy, sweltering, or both.

Jones was happy to help out, and happy to be renovating a Perry Maxwell course. It was his first time doing so, and what he found when he first surveyed Southern Hills was, in his opinion, not just one of Maxwell's best, but one of the country's best layouts. (Jones had not yet seen Prairie Dunes Country Club in Hutchinson, Kansas, which Perry Maxwell designed in 1937, perhaps in part because the course remained a nine-hole layout until Press Maxwell finished a second nine in 1957 based on his father's original routing.) Trent Jones and Perry Maxwell were not close friends, though both were charter ASGCA members. Jones knew Maxwell for some of his own noteworthy remodeling work, notably his redesign of some greens at Augusta National (including the first, 10th, and 14th), Pine Valley, and the National Golf Links. Jones also appreciated Maxwell for the three new holes he had remodeled in 1940 (the third, fourth, and fifth) at the Colonial Club in Ft. Worth for the 1941 U.S. Open, which Trent considered "the three best holes on the course." Maxwell's redesign work was distinctive, frequently adding what came to be known as "Maxwell Rolls," the uniquely severe contours and undulations characteristic of a Maxwell-designed putting surface.

For the '58 Open, Jones put Southern Hills through what had become his typically dramatic—some called it "brazen"—redesign. The facelift included new back tees for a number of short holes. As a result, no fewer than five of the par-4s on the course would measure 450 yards or more. The shortest par-5 on the course, #13, was transformed into a 469-yard par-4. What made the remodeled hole especially brutal, besides its length, were the two ponds in front of the green and the five sand traps completely surrounding it. New tees also gave the par-3s added length, with two of them now playing longer than 200 yards (the 218-yard eighth and 210-yard 14th). As he had done with all of the other U.S. Open courses he had redesigned, Jones filled in redundant fairway bunkers that the pros would have no trouble carrying, cut new flanking traps some 20 to 30 yards farther down the fairway, and sculpted fairway bunkers to lay tighter to the edge of Southern Hills's many doglegs. He revised several greenside bunkers, extending existing traps and introducing a few new traps to fortify what the USGA was likely to make into the championship's pin positions. Jones made almost all of the traps steeper and deeper and gave them the characteristic "flashing" of sand—in this case, white sand—that Jones admired and adopted from Stanley Thompson's architectural style. Trent totally rebuilt the green for the par-4 seventh. Judging that the Maxwell Rolls were just too severe on the existing green for modern green speeds, Jones came up with an entirely new design that was larger and flatter and that, although still replete with tilts and turns, gave the golfer a more realistic chance to make putts. Some critics did not like the new green (or the containment mounds that Jones built around it), feeling that they were out of character with the green complexes on the rest of the course.

To get Southern Hills into mint U.S. Open condition, Jones also supervised a second type of course preparation. Along with the USGA, he worked with the superintendent to make sure that the fairway widths were narrowed so that tee shots would have to be accurate or end up either in Jones's new flanking bunkers or nestled into the lush rough that had been allowed to grow tall and thick—and at Southern Hills it was Bermuda grass, which made the nastiest type of rough of all. Jones also made sure that the grass around the greens for the championship was allowed to grow much higher than normal. He also wanted the maintenance crew to prepare the fringes of the putting surfaces so that there was only a narrow strip of "apron" (or "collar") the width of the green's mower (about a yard). Everywhere outside this small perimeter of apron Jones wanted "fringe rough." All of this greenkeeping, in Jones's design, was meant to put a premium on hitting greens and to make chipping for pars from nestled lies in gnarly Bermuda rough a dicey proposition. The greens were watered only moderately, which wasn't expected to be an issue for the Oklahoma golf course in June, where the weather could be both windy and dry. Because the paradigm of modern championship play now insisted on very fast putting surfaces, greens mowers were set to a height of three-sixteenths of an inch, or 0.1875 inches. On greens like those at Southern Hills, with their "Maxwell Rolls," the combination—some said mismatch—of fast greens, severe undulations, and mischievous cup positions was sure to make three-putting commonplace. When temperatures sizzled into the 90s at the '58 Open, with high humidity to match, the greens turned bone hard and lightning fast and were nearly impossible to hold. In the first round, not a single player matched par 70. Jones's old friend, Gene Sarazen, still trying to compete at age fifty-six, shot an 84 and called the course's condition "ridiculous," not so much for its design as for its setup. Ben Hogan shot 75 and never got into contention; Sam Snead also had a 75 on day one and followed with an 80, missing the cut in an Open for the first time in eighteen years. Although what Trent Jones and the USGA wanted for a U.S. Open was not souped-up and hardpan conditions, the arduous challenge that resulted at Southern Hills did not run contrary to the philosophy of modern championship golf that they'd been developing since Oakland Hills—although, as many came to feel, perhaps it should have.

Forty-two-year-old Tommy Bolt, a native Oklahoman and great ballstriker who had won six PGA events and finished third at the '55 Open behind Fleck and Hogan, captured the crown, shooting 3-over 283. "Terrible Tommy," a nickname he earned early in his career for throwing clubs, tantrums, and even the occasional right hook in a fistfight, managed to break par for only one of his rounds, a 69 on Saturday morning. Young Gene Littler shot 67 that same round but collapsed in the afternoon with a 76.

Before the tournament, Jones had predicted for his friend Herbert Warren Wind's U.S. Open preview in *Sports Illustrated* that the winner at Southern Hills "will not shoot lower than 283 or higher than 287." Jones, in a sense, was exactly right: Tommy Bolt's winning score was 283; Gary Player finished second with 287.

No one was involved in golf course projects during the last six years of the Eisenhower presidency more than Robert Trent Jones. From January 1955 until John F. Kennedy came into the White House in January 1961, he built twenty-three new 18-hole golf courses, seven nine-hole golf courses, one 27-hole complex (for Upper Montclair Country Club in New Jersey), and one two-hole "pitch and putt" course for the estate of multimillionaire William B. MacDonald Jr. in Bal Harbour, Florida. He also carried out the remodeling of twenty-seven golf courses, bringing him in close touch with many original designs from the 1910s and 1920s by such talented earlier architects as Willie Park Jr., Donald Ross, C. H. Alison and Harry S. Colt, Alex Findlay, Herbert H. Barker, Tom Bendelow, John Bredemus, Devereux Emmet, Bert Way, and A. W. Tillinghast. But he also modified recent layouts and altered the results of previous redesigns by his contemporaries, notably Dick Wilson. All told, Jones finished fifty-nine jobs during the six-year period.

Besides his U.S. Open redesigns, one of the biggest projects undertaken by Jones in the Eisenhower decade was the creation of 36 holes of championship golf at the Broadmoor Golf Club in Colorado Springs, started in 1954 but not completed until 1965. The instant Jones saw The Broadmoor (known back in the age of the railroads as the "Grand Dame of the Rockies"), he flashed back to Banff and memories of his inspection visit in 1932 to Stanley Thompson's great mountain valley golf course. Arriving at the Colorado resort, gorgeously situated in the foothills of the Front Range and with splendid vistas of Pikes Peak, Jones could see another extraordinary mountain golf course, an 18-hole layout designed by Donald Ross in 1918 with a routing so ingenious that all its tees and greens were visible from the main hotel building. Jones's assignment in 1954 was to build an additional nine holes, thereby easing the demand for play on Ross's thirty-six-year-old beauty.

Jones performed his task well, finishing a fine nine-hole layout in a timely manner—and, in the process, refreshing his knowledge of the special requirements of creating a good mountain golf course. "Elevation and the density of the air are factors to be accounted for," Jones would emphasize. "The ball goes farther in Chicago than it does at sea level, and it goes even further in the Rocky Mountains. The typical firmness and dryness of the indigenous turf also is a factor, as are the prevailing winds. It makes it tricky for the architect." Jones discovered that, at lofty altitudes like those found in Colorado, "a 7,400-yard course will play like one of 6,700 or 6,800 at sea level." He also learned that "the architect also must consider the effect of the thin air on the player. . . . [Y]ou have to remember not to make any long, steep climbs [for your golfers] in the rarefied mountain atmosphere."

Jones was building the new nine holes at The Broadmoor at a very opportune moment. On April 1, 1954, President Eisenhower signed a law authorizing the construction of the U.S. Air Force Academy in the razorback foothills of the Rampart Range just north of Colorado Springs. The Academy was a major development for both southern Colorado and for the Air Force, which had only been an independent arm of the U.S. military since 1947. Air-power advocates had been pushing for a separate air force academy for decades. Several of Eisenhower's wealthy admirers raised funds to build an 18-hole golf course at the U.S. Air Force Academy, which they intended to name for Ike. Jones himself loved Eisenhower, a member at Augusta National, and he had been introduced to him by none other than Bobby Jones. The president was also a client: At Eisenhower's Camp David retreat, Trent had designed a golf hole with a green surrounded by three different tees, so that the president "could hit from different perspectives."

At the new Air Force Academy, Jones created an 18-hole championship golf course with all of the characteristic features of a Robert Trent Jones course: large greens, long teeing grounds, and fairway bunkers that required 250-yard carries. (Jones's firm was also hired to do the engineering design for the golf course's irrigation.) Because it was situated at an altitude of seven thousand feet, those carries were the sea level equivalent of 225 yards. Laid out over a unique landscape that Jones described as an "alpine desert," the Blue Course at the Academy played to 7,301 yards from the back tees, 6,515 from the middle, and 5,559 from the forward tees. The formal dedication of the course took place in the spring of 1959, coordinated with the graduation ceremonies of the first class of Air Force cadets. The difficulties of the long and mostly flat layout were subtle and disguised, lying primarily in the fast and tricky greens whose dominant break flowed away from the mountain. For many years, *Golf Digest* ranked Jones's layout the third-best course in Colorado.

That same year, 1959, Jones went to work on a much bigger project at The Broadmoor. The resort initially wanted Jones to build a fourth nine to add to his earlier layout, thus creating a second complete eighteen. But while looking at the property that was available for golf at The Broadmoor as a whole, Jones came up with a better idea: He would create two championship 18-hole courses, borrowing holes from the Ross original to blend into new routings that would incorporate some of Jones's previously designed holes and some new holes. There were risks in this approach; by divvying up an honored and venerated Ross course, Jones could be seen as destroying a masterpiece. When it was completed in 1918, Ross's layout had been the highest golf course in the United States, at 6,400 feet, and Ross had declared it his "best work." Jones regarded his combined design not only as an innovative solution to the challenge of creating two courses—the East and West courses—but as an overall improvement to Ross's original.

Jones's plans married nine slightly modified holes from the Ross course as the first six holes (#1–#6) and the last three holes (#16–#18) of the blended East Course, coupling them with nine new holes (#7–#15) of his design. He took a similar approach to the West Course: Holes #1 through #6 were Ross holes, as were #15 through #18; #7 through #14 would be Jones's. The East Course from the back tees played 7,355 yards at par 72; and the West Course played 7,016 yards at par 71. The two courses offered quite different playing conditions apart from the difference in length. The East Course was more heavily tree-lined and offered an array of spectacular approach shots. The West Course had more doglegs and steeply angled greens.

The result for The Broadmoor was just what the client wanted. In the 1960s, Broadmoor was renowned as an American golf mecca. Its international reputation as an outstanding luxury hotel and spa gave instant credibility to the new golf courses, and the quality of the golf courses also enhanced the appeal of the resort. The East Course would host a number of national and international events, including the 1962 Curtis Cup Match between the U.S. team and Great Britain and Ireland, which took place the same year the East Course opened. It also hosted two U.S. Women's Amateurs (1982 and 1984), one U.S. Men's Amateur (1967), two U.S. Women's Opens (1995 and 2011), and one U.S. Senior Open (2008). Jack Nicklaus won the U.S. Men's Amateur at Broadmoor in 1959 while it was still the Ross original. The East and West courses completed by Trent Jones did not open for play until 1965. Twenty-year-old Robert Trent Jones Jr. played in the 1960 NCAA Championships at The Broadmoor as part of the Yale University team. (Bob Jr. arrived in Colorado Springs for the NCAAs after attending the 1960 U.S. Open at Cherry Hills in Denver with his father. Sadly, Trent's father, William Rees Jones, passed away the last day of the Cherry Hills Open, at age seventy-nine. Trent flew back to New York to help Ione make the arrangements; Bob Jr. returned for the funeral after the Yale team missed the cut in the NCAAs. In 1968, shortly after joining Robert Trent Jones, Inc., Bob assisted his father in a highly unique remodeling of The Broadmoor's East Course, one that reversed its routing.)

Trent Jones believed he learned something new from every golf course project, and among the lessons he acquired in Colorado was an understanding of the design solutions that would work best for creating a good golf hole on a mountainous site. Jones had limited experience on steep sites prior to the Broadmoor job. "In general, holes that play uphill should be held to a minimum in mountainous terrain," Jones later wrote. "That's another reason, other than construction considerations, to build mountain courses in valleys wherever possible. Steep slopes and large rock formations are less of a factor there." As his work at The Broadmoor made clear, ingenuity was a major requirement when building courses in the mountains: "This is where the inept architect is found out. The architect's plan must suggest the ruggedness of the setting, but in a passive rather than an active sense. Blind holes should be avoided." One bonus of building courses in the mountains was the ready availability of water, usually in the form of rushing streams. "These give the architect a natural hazard, beautiful, interesting and a challenge to the player that can be incorporated into the design." But as with all golf courses, wherever they're built, "The ultimate test of a mountain course should be its shot-making requirements, not the physical demands it imposes on a player, no matter how hard the architect has had to work" to build the course. (The arrival of the institution of the golf cart in American golf would add a great deal of flexibility into the design of mountain golf courses. Bob Jr. would end up designing seven courses in Colorado.)

Incidentally, while working on the Broadmoor courses, Jones was out inspecting a green early one morning with Bill Baldwin when out of the woods about a hundred feet away from them came a mountain lion. "I didn't think he was interested in us joining him for a round of golf," reflected Jones, thinking back to the frightening incident. But at the time he yelled to Baldwin, "Bill, let's get the hell out of here!" Starting back to their jeep, Bill, who was a big, tall fellow, started running and got way ahead of Jones. "Bill, don't run," Trent shouted. "They chase you if you run." "Okay, I won't run," Bill replied, "but I'm going to walk damned fast." Jones encountered plenty of exotic wildlife while building golf courses—not just the occasional mountain lion but coyotes, fox, cougars, wolves, bears, poisonous snakes, and scorpions.

Many students of golf course architecture and its history believe that Robert Trent Jones produced his finest courses from 1955 to 1960. In interviews and autobiographical writings done late in his life, Jones seemed to concur, although he never disparaged any of the work he did before or after this peak period of creative achievement. Unfortunately, no one ever asked him, nor did he ever volunteer, what distinguished his portfolio of "big strong courses" from this period. Why do such courses as Old Warson Country Club (1955) and Bellerive Country Club (1960) in St. Louis; Coral Ridge in Fort Lauderdale (1956); Shady Oaks in Fort Worth (1956); and Point O' Woods Golf & Country Club (1958) in Benton Harbor, Michigan—among possible select others from the same time period, including Duke University Golf Course (1957) in Durham, North Carolina; Houston Country Club (1957) in Texas; Tanglewood Park Golf Club (West Course, 1957) in Clemmons, North Carolina; Otter Creek Golf Club (1959) in Columbus, Indiana; along with the aforementioned Eisenhower Blue Course (1959) and Broadmoor East Course (begun in 1959) in Colorado Springs—endure among Robert Trent Jones's greatest all-time golf courses?

Had he been asked, Jones could have mentioned how, by 1955, his work was benefiting from his twenty-five-plus years of experience designing and building golf courses. He had accrued considerable wisdom while facing the challenges of building courses not only in the United States but soon also abroad, already having finished two courses overseas that could arguably be added to the list of Jones's finest: Dorado Beach Hotel Golf Course (1958) in Puerto Rico and the Cotton Bay Club (1959) in Eleuthera in the Bahamas. Through his remodeling efforts on courses laid out by golf's greatest architects, Jones had spent considerable time pondering and learning from a series of tutors that included not just Thompson but also MacKenzie, Ross, Maxwell, and Tillinghast. Through his U.S. Open redesigns he had learned how to deal with cry-baby pros, tournament and greens committees, media relations people, tight schedules, and much more. Jones had built a talented staff; by the mid-'50s he was no longer working alone but benefiting from the help of assistant designer Frank Duane, and soon from the help of other assistants who were equally if not more talented. Then there was Bill Baldwin, who had been his chief construction superintendent since the late 1930s; Baldwin had grown immensely in his engineering abilities, his technical and aesthetic sense of green design, and his ability to contour and shape landscapes to add beauty and interest to a golf course while still harmonizing with what the boss dictated. Finally, Trent also had the benefit of new technologies that were being brought to bear on golf course design and construction by the mid-1950s: bulldozers and other earthmovers, electronically automated irrigation and sprinkler systems, and a range of hardier and more manageable turfgrasses.

Put all of these elements together and you have the foundation for the outstanding Robert Trent Jones courses of the late 1950s. "It has been said that I ushered in a new era in golf architecture during this period," Jones would later reflect. "I'll leave that for others to decide. Certainly many of the design factors that went into my layouts had appeared in courses over the centuries. But I do feel that the introduction of the heroic concept, skillfully mixed with the strategic and, occasionally, the penal, set new standards for the modern golf course. I followed the same strategy in my many remodeling jobs. I did not want stretches of rough from the tee to the fairway or hazards in spots that would penalize and paralyze the higher-handicappers. I spent a lot of time taking out cross-bunkering and other penal attributes of the older courses and putting in options that would help those players. In effect, I was cleaning up architecture."

Not everyone in golf liked the way Trent Jones scrubbed the classic courses—nor was his innocuous description of his approach plausible to his critics. Many thought that Jones, in creating his version of the modern golf course, was aggressively obliterating classic elements of their beloved game. His critics felt that making a par on a Robert Trent Jones golf course was not just "difficult," it was *too* difficult—and they rejected the corollary, too: bogeys were *not* "easy." To the detractors, Jones's designs demanded too much of the golfer— or at least posed a different test from their predecessors. Jones's courses demanded power more than finesse. They required aerial prowess rather than a combination of controlled ball flight and mastery of the ground game. Jones's courses necessitated forced carries to snug and narrow targets rather than providing golfers with the freedom and latitude to create inventive shot angles or diagonal approaches larded with erratic bounces and rolls. In other words, the Jones paradigm of the modern golf course required a new brand of "power" shotmaking that severely tested the abilities of the finest golfers to shoot under par while condemning most golfers—not just the below-average—to higher scores and a more frustrating experience, no matter which set of tees he or she played from.

What by the end of the 1950s might have seemed like a general acceptance of the Robert Trent Jones model of modern golf was, for most golfers, a grudging acceptance. In the 1960s, as nationally televised golf entered millions of American homes and the nation's champion golfers, notably Arnold Palmer and Jack Nicklaus, became "superstars" and celebrities in their own right, Robert Trent Jones, the country's most eminent designer of golf courses, claimed the spotlight as well, actually coming to relish the nicknames that the media gave him: not just "The Open Doctor" but "The Golf Architect the Pros Love to Hate."

Trent Jones would not back off—far from it. Rather, he would give the anti-Jones forces even more ammunition during the 1960s by designing a second generation of modern golf courses—Firestone, Bellerive, Congressional, Spyglass, and Hazeltine—that were even "bigger and stronger." Even more than Oakland Hills and his other U.S. Open redesigns of the 1950s, these new courses of the 1960s would provoke the greatest architectural controversies of his career.

And from those controversies, Jones's business and reputation as the world's greatest golf architect would only continue to grow and prosper.

CHAPTER TEN

"THE ARCHITECT THE PROS
LOVED TO HATE"

No architect in history exerted more influence on the game of golf—particularly championship golf—than did Robert Trent Jones Sr. in the 1950s and 1960s. In those two decades, Jones designed or remodeled such outstanding courses as Oakland Hills, Baltusrol, the Olympic Club, Firestone, Spyglass Hill, and Hazeltine, all of which were courses that many stars of the game criticized because of their high level of difficulty and immunity to low scoring.

As the 1950s dwindled and the '60s dawned, a subtle shift took place in Jones's status within the golf establishment. In a very real sense, he became a significant part of The Establishment, with all the power and influence that such a position entailed.

In the previous decade, he had worked at the behest of the United States Golf Association and clubs selected to host major championships, modernizing classic courses to keep them challenging for the era's professionals. Now, however, he was sought out by clubs interested in attracting such championships with the kind of big, strong courses that were his signature. The name Robert Trent Jones was enough to bring a golf course to the attention of the USGA and PGA Tour—and if it wasn't, the man himself was liable to drop a few hints in the appropriate ear.

Firestone Country Club in Akron, Ohio, was a pleasant enough course, home to the Rubber City Open on the PGA tour, created as an amenity for the Firestone Tire and Rubber Company's executives and employees. But Harvey Firestone Jr. and his brother Raymond—sons of the company founder— imagined something bigger, taking note of the rising popularity of television in general and televised golf in particular. They recognized that a revamped golf course, stern enough to host a major event, could serve their corporate interests by bringing national attention to the Firestone name, enhancing the reputation of their company and the city of Akron as well.

The Firestones hired Trent Jones to redesign their course, and this action was enough for the PGA in early 1958 to grant its 1960 Championship to the as-yet-unseen reworking of Firestone Country Club. With the power of his reputation thus demonstrated, Jones could name his fee; he asked Harvey Firestone for $200,000 and got it. That sum (roughly $1.6 million in today's dollars) was likely the largest single fee ever paid to a golf architect for a course remodeling.

"I remodeled it totally," Jones would later say. "Drastic changes were made. I added over fifty bunkers and two ponds. I built two brand new greens and completely remodeled the other sixteen, enlarging them to two and three times their original size and building in the contours that would provide adequate pin positions for tournament play." All that was left of the course as originally designed were the fairway routings, which Jones had kept for economic reasons. The redesigned course came out to 7,180 yards, more than 400 yards longer than the old one; par nonetheless dropped from 72 to 70.

One of the first pros to play the new Firestone was Bob Rosburg, winner of the 1959 PGA Championship, in a promotional round with Billy Casper, the 1959 U.S. Open champ. Rosburg shot an even-par 70, and after the round he told reporters, "It used to be a fun course. Now it's at least five or six shots harder. The greens are much different, and the course is much longer. I don't think it will fit my game." Other professionals arriving for the '60 PGA Championship echoed these impressions. "It's so tough that even my clubs got tired," Al Brosch told sportswriters after a practice round.

Stories about the remodeled course were part of the reason Ben Hogan chose to enter the PGA for the first time since his auto accident in 1949. (To satisfy the demands of broadcast television, the PGA changed its championship format from match play to medal, or stroke, play in 1958. That change made it possible for Hogan to play the event again; his legs would not have to bear up under the rigors of two rounds a day for four days, which is what winning in the match-play format required.) "I want to find out for myself if everything they say about that Firestone course up there is true," he declared.

By the time the PGA was over, there was little question that Jones had created yet another "monster." In the opening round, thirty-six of the 184 starters failed to break 80. There were just six rounds under par the first two days, six more on Saturday, and one on Sunday; in the end it was won by Jay Hebert with a 281 score, 1 over par for the tournament. Hogan shot 74-75-77 and missed the 54-hole cut; Rosburg was similarly eliminated after rounds of 74-75-77.

Arnold Palmer was a 3-to-1 favorite in the PGA after winning the Masters and U.S. Open and falling one stroke short in his first British Open. Palmer held the first-round lead at Firestone with a 67, but got derailed by a triple-bogey eight on the par-5 16th hole in Saturday's third round, ultimately finishing in a tie for seventh. He kept his thoughts about Firestone mostly to himself, but it was evident to everyone attending the tournament or reading the papers that he did not much like Jones's redesign. Calling the whole golf course "a little gruesome," he pointed directly at the 16th as "the worst," and a hole he "frankly hated." "Those bunkers and that water—ugh!" Thirteen years after the tournament, in his 1973 book *Go For Broke!*, Palmer was still complaining about the hole:

> The fact is, I feel this is a terribly unfair hole, not only for professionals but particularly for the everyday kind of golfer who must endure it. . . . You are not rewarded for overcoming difficulty. You are simply faced with yet another difficulty, and another and another. Holes that have such constant and unremitting difficulties . . . cannot fit into a strategy of bold enterprise, but only into a strategy of determined defense.

Trent Jones was well aware of Palmer's criticism of the hole, and of the entire Firestone course. His response was that not every hole called for the attacking, aggressive approach that was Arnold's forte. Sometimes a great hole, even a long par-5, called for a more judicious strategy. Jones's message to the world's greatest (and most popular) golfer was simple: Going for broke on a great hole can sometimes break you. The triple-bogey was not the architect's fault, it was Palmer's.

The Firestone course continued to come under fire, with some of the attack aimed directly at the essential nature of Jones's architectural approach. Critics among the pros and sportswriters described the layout as "charmless" and "monotonous" for its endless parallel fairways, calling it "a typical Jones course: long, hard and boring."

Jones defended his approach staunchly: "Well, the course is certainly long and difficult, but it is hardly boring. Despite the parallel fairways—and there I had no choice, because I was expected to keep the original routing—there is a diversity of water, sand, fairway and green designs that provide a different challenge on almost every hole." Firestone, in Jones's view, was a great test of golf. "It's penal where it has to be penal and it's strategic where strategy is called for. There is a diversity that provides a different challenge on almost every hole."

In time, Firestone Country Club became one of the most highly regarded and best-tested venues in golf. It hosted two more PGA Championships (1966 and 1975) and a regular tour event, the American Golf Classic, from 1961 to 1976. (The last of these was played over a new second course that Jones built for Firestone, called the North Course, completed in 1969.) The World Series of Golf was played on Jones's original Firestone creation (now called the South Course) from its inception in 1962, for thirteen years matching the four major winners over 36 holes, later becoming a fuller-field event. Today it is one of the World Golf Championship tournaments, the WGC-Bridgestone Invitational. In the end, Trent considered Firestone South one of his five best all-time courses and the very best remodeling job of his career. As he noted, it proved neither too long nor too hard for touring pros. "I prefer to think of it as a course on which par is the standard," he explained, "although that standard usually is beaten by today's great players. But when they do, they have played extremely well."

Congressional Country Club wasn't thinking of national championships when it first approached Jones in 1954. The club—established in 1924 with a founding membership that included Secretary of State (and soon President) Herbert Hoover, John D. Rockefeller (Sr. and Jr.), Vincent Astor, a handful of DuPonts, and Charlie Chaplin—had outgrown its initial eighteen holes and contracted with Jones to create a new nine. It soon became apparent that the addition was no mere relief nine but superior to either of the originals: the "Gold" nine laid out by Devereux Emmet in 1924, or the "Blue" designed at the same time by Emmet but improved by Tom Winton in 1927, Donald Ross in 1930, and Alfred H. Tull in 1951.

The new nine officially opened for play on August 3, 1957, with Vice-President Richard M. Nixon slicing a ball off the first tee. Jones's creation played 3,329 yards (from the back tees it was a full 3,600), with two par-5s of greater than 550 yards and all five par-4s longer than 400. The average size of Jones's new greens was 7,343 square feet, about 65 percent larger than the greens on the old eighteen.

Even before the opening, Jones concluded that Congressional should turn the new nine into the back nine of the main course, retain the Blue as the front nine, and make the Gold the "extra" nine. A key element of Jones's plan was to undertake a major remodeling of the Blue Course, upgrading it to harmonize with the new nine, giving Congressional a fully modernized golf course deserving of a major championship. The board of governors quickly agreed, giving Jones the approval for the redesign.

Even before the work on the Blue Course was finished, Jones got in touch with the USGA and PGA to solicit their interest in staging a major championship at Congressional. The USGA had staged its Women's Amateur Championship there in 1959, over the existing Blue and New nines, but Jones dreamed of a U.S. Open at a golf course that was *his*, far more than any of his Open re-designs, with nine holes that were wholly his and nine so significantly reworked that they might as well have been. And where better to stage such an event than in the U.S. capital, within shouting distance of the White House?

The USGA considered the '59 Women's Amateur a "rousing success," a "paragon" for all of its tournaments. Congressional boasted an enormous club-house, ample parking, an eager membership, a large urban population—and most of all, a big, scenic Robert Trent Jones golf course. The association granted the 1964 Open to Congressional, pending resolution of a few issues.

One such vital matter was the problem of the 18th hole. The last hole on Jones's "Blue back nine" was a 170-yard par-3. In and of itself, having a par-3 finishing hole should not be a problem; several great courses have had par-3 finishes, including the Devereux Emmet/Walter Travis Garden City Golf Club, Alister MacKenzie's Pasatiempo Golf Club, and Bobby Jones's beloved boyhood course in Atlanta, East Lake. But the last time the U.S. Open had concluded on a par-3 was back in 1909 at Englewood Golf Club in New Jersey; it had not hap-pened in any major since the PGA at Hershey Country Club in 1940.

Jones found a practical solution that satisfied both the USGA and most of Congressional's members: He took two holes from the old "Gold" course, re-modeled them significantly, inserted them into the routing of his new nine at the 16th and 17th, and converted what he had designed as the par-4 17th into the new 18th. This proved to be an inspired decision. The new finishing hole played through a narrow chute of trees to a peninsula green that jutted into a lake some 445 yards away, and surrounding the now-18th green were great "hillside vantage points for thousands of birdie-watchers," a virtual Olympic amphi-theater. Jones estimated that some thirty-five thousand people could watch the closing drama at the final hole—and the drama would be heightened if the cup was cut in the very back left corner of the right-to-left diagonal green, putting it tremendously close to the water's edge.

As usual, the golf course generated complaints that Jones had created an-other "monster"; at 7,059 yards and par 70, it was the longest course yet for the Open. Jones himself described his back nine as "a big, rough monster," in con-trast to the front side, his remodeling of the Blue, which was "a subtle stretch of holes which golfers will have to pamper and cajole." The finishing nine required players to "grab it by the throat and wrestle with it."

Due to a combined heat wave and drought, Congressional in 1964 did not have the thick, choking rough considered standard for a U.S. Open setup; according to Robert Sommers's history, *The U.S. Open: Golf's Ultimate Challenge* (1989), "the irrigation system had kept the fairways lush and green, but the water didn't reach the rough," which "withered and died." Low rounds were possible; Palmer opened with 68-69, and twenty-nine-year-old Tommy Jacobs matched the Open's 18-hole record with a 64—and still called Congressional "the toughest course I've ever played."

In the end, no one was talking about the course's difficulty—despite just nine sub-par rounds in four days—but rather the blistering temperatures and the courageous performance by Ken Venturi in battling heat exhaustion over 36 holes on Saturday to win with a 2-under total of 278 (72-70-66-70). The temperature was well over 100 on the final day, and a USGA official reported seeing a thermometer register 112 degrees near the 14th green. Years later Jones commented, "Ken Venturi had a tough time, though. The weather was withering. It attacked Venturi so badly that the presiding doctor advised him to withdraw. But he was determined to finish, and after a great struggle he won. This was his first victory in four years, and he never won another major tournament after this one. But Ken will be remembered for his courage and fortitude to face the great odds that were against him."

Venturi's harrowing experience—by the end his playing partner was picking his ball out of the hole for him, and he could barely focus enough to sign his scorecard—led the USGA to eliminate Open Saturday and instead schedule four rounds over four days, much to the delight of television networks and audiences.

The Open at Congressional enhanced Jones's already formidable reputation. USGA executive director Joe Dey particularly praised the 18th hole: "It's the only true stage ever seen in golf," Dey told the press after the tournament. "It was set out in the lake with nobody crowding it"—yet thousands of spectators could watch the action from the neighboring hillsides. For that, he singled out Trent Jones for an ingenious design.

Jones was now at the apex of his career. The next year's U.S. Open would be held at Bellerive Country Club, an original Trent Jones design that was only five years old. His new course in Chaska, Minnesota, Hazeltine National Golf Club, opened in 1962 and had already been chosen for a U.S. Open in 1970. Having two designs hosting Opens in a decade would be an accomplishment for any architect; the fact that they were new, truly still raw, and as yet untested at the championship level was great testimony to Jones's status as America's ranking figure in course design. He was not merely the "Open Doctor" who modernized and otherwise prepared other designers' grand old courses for national contests, but had earned the title of "Master Architect" of modern golf.

Bellerive was not a popular choice among the PGA players. The majority of players coming to Missouri for the '65 Open focused on its gargantuan length— nearly 7,200 yards for a par-70 course. As they had at Congressional, the experts predicted that only long hitters like Palmer or Nicklaus could possibly win the tournament. Nicklaus fed that perception with his pre-Open comment, "I think Bellerive puts too much premium on power."

But Jones insisted that the course would favor not the longest players but rather those who best kept the ball in play, avoided hazards, chipped and putted extremely well, stayed patient, played intelligently and strategically, and kept their cool for 72 holes.

Bellerive was a brand-new golf course, but an old club. It was originally established in 1897 in north St. Louis as the St. Louis Field Club, and moved to the lightly populated suburb of Normandy in 1910. The name Bellerive was an homage to Louis St. Ange de Bellerive (1700–1774), the last French governor of the Illinois Country and last French commander in all of North America. It also translates as "beautiful riverbank," an apt name for a course five miles from the Mississippi.

With postwar urban growth pushing golf clubs farther and farther out into the suburbs, Bellerive put its 125-acre site on the market in 1957 and purchased a prime piece of farmland lying west of the suburb of Creve Coeur, twelve miles from downtown St. Louis. The driving forces behind the move were club members Clark Gamble, descendant of one of the founders of Procter & Gamble, and Hord Hardin, a prominent attorney and twenty-two-time Bellerive club championship winner. Trent knew Hardin from Augusta National, where Hardin was a member and later club chairman; he also served as USGA president in 1968–69.

The property in Creve Coeur—selected with Jones's input—had rolling hills, a meandering creek, and many wooded slopes. Jones built a course that the members nicknamed "the Green Monster of Ladue Road," with six par-4s longer than 450 yards and par-5s measuring 580 and 606, and he built it with a potential U.S. Open in mind. He knew it would be the "youngest"—and again the longest—course ever to host an Open, and that's exactly what it became: The USGA awarded Bellerive a U.S. Open before it was even a year old.

To achieve such a distinction, Jones and Hardin knew, the golf course had to display a combination of "great shot value" and "playing value." Bellerive demanded that tee shots be straight as well as long; approach shots into the greens had to take into account the shapes and contours of the green surfaces. The greens themselves were big and easy to hit, but Jones built them with undulations that varied from "subtle to bold in character," so that their dramatic contours and shapes made them play much smaller than their actual size. As he explained in a June 1965 article for the *USGA Golf Journal*, "the areas in which the hole will be cut in the four days of the Open are necessarily quite confining. Because of the putting problems, the remaining areas of the green are just as much a part of the hazards of the hole as are the traps, the rough, and the water."

Even at the end of his career, Jones considered Bellerive to be one of his best layouts, and he was especially pleased with the routing. He planned the holes around the winding creek, using it to strategic effect on half the holes. With two additional small ponds built near the greens, there was water in play on eleven of eighteen holes.

The architect's prediction about the golf course not particularly favoring long hitters proved accurate. In the opening round, Nicklaus shot an 8-over 78; Palmer had 76s on the first two days to miss a cut for the first time in four years. "This course baffles me," he said after the second round. Many others thought that Bellerive, in terms of course condition and maturation, wasn't ready for the Open. Some areas in the rough and around the greens were still pretty raw, and at least one fairway "rippled like a washboard with grass that had not yet knitted closely."

The championship was won by twenty-nine-year-old South African Gary Player in a playoff over Kel Nagle, an outstanding forty-four-year-old Australian who won at least one tournament every year from 1949 to 1975. Player was not a short hitter, but he was hardly among the tour's longest, and Nagle was even shorter. Bellerive surrendered only eight rounds below par—none of them by Player in any of his five efforts—and no score lower than 68. Again, par was the gold standard that the United States Golf Association and Robert Trent Jones felt it should be.

Bellerive has since hosted many national and world championship events, including the PGA Championship in 1992 and the U.S. Senior Open in 2004. In

2008, it welcomed the BMW Championship as part of the FedEx Cup Playoffs; prior to that event, the golf course underwent a year-long renovation by Rees Jones, Trent's son. Rees significantly rebuilt his father's design while maintaining much of his style, making even more small targets within the large green contours than his father had done. In May 2013, Bellerive hosted the Senior PGA Championship, becoming only the third club to stage all four of the rotating men's championships. In 2018 it will be the site of the 100th PGA Championship; Rees Jones, Inc., has continued to do work on the course.

Robert Trent Jones himself called the property that became the golf course at Spyglass Hill his "dream" golf course and "the greatest challenge of my life." It was located on the breathtaking Monterey Peninsula, some ninety miles south of San Francisco and one of the most beautiful spots in all of America. In his rare visits there, Trent Jones had watched blue-green waves from the Pacific crash against copper-brown rocks where colonies of seals alternately frolicked and dozed; seen beachcombers picking up shells or straining to hear the call of whales; pondered the hills and craggy bluffs that tumbled into the sea, and surveyed the uneven, snow-white sand dunes, twisted wintergreen cypress trees, and towering virgin pine. A California poet once described the Monterey Peninsula area as "the finest meeting of land and water in existence." Jones wholeheartedly agreed, even more so when the word "turf" was added to the mix. This little nose of land already featured two of America's greatest links, Pebble Beach and Cypress Point; if the Monterey Peninsula was not "the golf capital of the world," as Del Monte Properties, Inc., its corporate owner and developer since the 1910s, touted, then it was undeniably "the golf showplace of the world." It was only natural for Jones to want to design a golf course for Del Monte that would be as good, if not better, than Pebble or Cypress. If Jones could accomplish that, he knew the golf course would be "destined to become one of the greatest 18 holes of golf in the game."

Spyglass Hill brought him into contact with one of California's richest and most influential entrepreneurs, Samuel Finley Brown Morse, the so-called "Duke of Del Monte." Over the course of his long life (1885–1969), he accumulated more wealth than even his distant cousin, Samuel Finley Breese Morse (1791–1872), the painter and inventor who contributed to the development of both the telegraph and Morse code. The wealth of the younger Samuel F. B. Morse came from decades of land and real estate development. Leaving the East

Coast for California in 1916, Morse became manager of the Pacific Improvement Company, a corporation in charge of liquidating the assets of the "Big Four"—C. P. Huntington, Leland Stanford, Mark Hopkins, and Charles Crocker—builders of the Central Pacific Railroad. In 1919 Morse formed his own company, Del Monte Properties, and bought up many of the assets for himself. This enabled him to buy 7,000 acres on the Monterey coast, land that included Hotel Del Monte, Pacific Grove, Pebble Beach, Rancho Los Laureles (now the village of Carmel Valley), and the Monterey County Water Works. Morse acquired all this for $1.34 million. With this land, his goal was to develop "one of the greatest private parks in existence"—one that not only conserved forest, wildlife, coastline, and oceanfront but promoted the controlled growth of an elite residential community within it. For the enjoyment and recreation of those privileged to live in the Del Monte Forest, Morse in the 1920s built three majestically scenic golf courses on what would evolve into the most valuable golf properties in the world: Pebble Beach Golf Links, in 1919 (laid out by Jack Neville and Douglas Grant); Monterey Peninsula Country Club (designed by Robert Hunter, Seth Raynor and Charles Banks), in 1926; and Cypress Point Club (Alister MacKenzie, architect) in 1928. In association with these golf courses, Morse built the exclusive Del Monte Hotel and The Lodge at Pebble Beach. Morse's control over the development of the Monterey Peninsula was so strong that it was said not a single tree in Del Monte Forest could be removed without his personal approval.

Sam Morse had always envisioned a string of golf courses around Del Monte Forest's shoreline, and in the late 1950s he authorized the construction of a second golf course at the Monterey Peninsula Country Club, one ultimately designed by Californian Bob Baldock and former ASGCA president Robert Bruce Harris. Called the "Shore" course, it opened in 1961, with the original golf course on the site then becoming known as the "Dunes" course. By the early 1960s, given golf's boom in the Eisenhower/Arnold Palmer/TV era and additional residential development in the Del Monte area, the demand for tee times on the fabulous golf courses of the Monterey Peninsula began to exceed supply. This was especially true at Pebble Beach Golf Links, the only course on the peninsula open to the public. The executive director of the Northern California Golf Association, Robert B. Hanna, proposed to Sam Morse that the NCGA fund the building of another course, with the Pebble Beach Company (which Morse headed) putting up the land, as long as thirty days a year were reserved on the course for NCGA tournaments. Morse accepted. There was a perfect lo-cation for the course, to be open to the public like Pebble Beach, on a 200-acre tract of land along 17-Mile Drive situated almost exactly between Cypress Point and the Monterey Peninsula Country Club. From its sand dunes down by the coast to the dense pine forest up above, the site offered a broad sweep of pictur-esque Monterey Bay, with the city of Santa Cruz to the north and Point Lobos to the south. There seems to have been little doubt in Morse's mind who should design the new golf course; he wanted the best architect in the world to build it, and almost everyone in 1960 believed that to be Robert Trent Jones.

The original name for the golf course was "Pebble Pines." Jones loved the name and was dismayed when Morse changed it to Spyglass Hill in September 1964. He learned about the change of name informally one day while working out on the course. Writing to Richard Osborne, who was running Del Monte Properties for Morse, Jones stated his feelings without trying to push his case too hard:

> I can understand . . . why you feel "Pebble Pines" might not be appro-priate in view of the local context and while I like the name personally and feel it has some benefit because of its associations with this area, I now consider it a thing of the past. I do, however, want to tell you of the reaction of others as well as myself to the name "Spyglass Hill." It is my personal feeling that a name is what you make it and it is really the character of the course, the character of the club and the character of the people that make a club great or not. At any rate, as you undoubtedly know, names are cut short and this would indicate that the course could be called Spyglass or the Hill course. It is my own personal feeling that Spyglass Hill doesn't adapt itself well to the golfing ver-nacular; building a yacht club, I could see where it would fit appropri-ately and might be terrific. The reaction I get in discussing this with others, the reaction of the other founder members I hear indirectly, is that the name is being held up to ridicule, and the feeling is developing that it is being forced on the founder members. This is the thing that bothers me; and I don't think anything as wonderful as this should have any animosity attached to it. This is the reason I am writing to you and wonder if you will reconsider the possibility of other names in order to make the name completely acceptable to all concerned.

If "Pebble Pines" was unacceptable, Jones asked, why not then please consider the following alternatives: The Forest Club, Del Monte Forest Club, Sandhill Golf Club, Sand Forest Golf Club? "If, after reading this letter you still feel that you want to stick to your name . . . there will be nothing further said or mentioned on my part."

In no other instance during his career was Jones so badly mistaken about how well a name would ultimately work out: "Spyglass Hill" has stood now for nearly fifty years as one of the best, most memorable, and most evocative names ever conceived for a golf course. Jones did not sufficiently value Sam Morse's passion for local history: According to legend, Scottish novelist Robert Louis Stevenson had taken inspiration for his 1883 classic, *Treasure Island*, while staying in the Monterey area, occasionally roaming the hills and sandy dunes of Pebble Beach and environs. Early in his novel, Stevenson described a seaside vista of bays, inlets, and sand dunes as seen from a nearby hill that was marked on a treasure map as "The Spy-glass." From his visits to the property, Morse got the idea that golfers from the clubhouse and first tee would see something very close to Stevenson's description, thereby providing "a wonderful visual introduction" to the golf course.

On September 23, 1964, Francis A. Watson, the club president, sent a letter to all the founding members elaborating the reasons for the change from Pebble Pines to Spyglass Hill:

> Perhaps the overriding factor was the conviction [of the board of directors] that we are bringing into being a golf course that will be one of the truly great and beautiful courses in the world. Such a course not only deserves but requires an independent, distinctive identification of its own. Additionally, it seemed important that the name should be related to the area where the course is located. Pebble Pines or any combination involving those words would be construed by many to identify this course as the No. 2 course at Pebble Beach. This we want to avoid. Additionally, the word "pines" is the part of the name of many courses throughout the country.

As one of the founding members, Trent Jones received Watson's letter. Knowing the architect's discontent, Richard Osborne sent him a second letter, explaining,

"The name was suggested by S.F.B., who has, I think, a great feel for these matters. It is the name of the hill on which the club house is located. Most important of all, it isn't a name that will be confused with any other golf course in the area. When people see it, they will identify the course immediately." Once aware that Sam Morse himself was behind the name change, Jones relented, although "Pebble Pines" continued to show up in Jones's correspondence for several more weeks.*

Building Spyglass turned out to be one of the most challenging projects, in a technical sense, of his career. "When I first walked through the site," Jones later recollected, "I saw that the view was spectacular but the terrain was neglected and overrun by weeds, trees, and bushes. It was a mess. We had our work cut out for us." The first task was to clear the ground. Basically that meant everything that could ruin a good fairway or interfere with a golf shot—all the trees, stumps, roots, limbs, brush, and other debris—had to be removed from the specified areas. "As of this writing," wrote one onlooker from Del Monte Properties in September 1964, "bulldozers are operating like 'Arnie's Army' in eliminating pine trees by the hundreds." In conjunction with the heavy earth-moving equipment came tractors of various sizes, wood chippers, chain saws, whatever it took to clear the land for the playing corridors. Along with the massive tree and stump removal, some sophisticated engineering procedures were required for dealing with a deep ravine that cut across the property. At Spyglass, as elsewhere, the operation was done in three phases, giving Jones and his construction crew a chance to make adjustments to his plans after each phase. The hundreds of trees and thousands of bushes cut down or ripped up were moved to a low spot or trench to be set on fire and burned to ashes. This

---

* To help encourage the sale of founding memberships at Spyglass Hill, Robert Trent Jones, Inc., bought four of the memberships—one for Trent and one for each of his two sons. The fourth went to Harvey Raynor, a former tournament supervisor with the PGA whom Jones had taken on as a part-time employee because Raynor had connections in California that could potentially help drum up new business for Trent's company. Raynor worked out of a new office of RTJ, Inc., set up in Palo Alto, headed by Robert Trent Jones Jr. (The organizational history of RTJ, Inc., and its addition of a West Coast office, will be covered in Chapter Eleven. As for Raynor's effectiveness in attracting business for Jones, his one success seems to have been Laguna Seca Golf Ranch, an 18-hole course in Monterey, California, that Jones, Inc., completed in 1970.) The cost of each of the four founding memberships at Spyglass Hill was $2,500. Jones's company deducted this $10,000 as a business expense in their 1964–65 federal tax return, a deduction that ultimately was questioned by the IRS and reduced to an allowable deduction in the amount of a single membership.

had to be done very carefully, of course, and the procedure had to comply as closely as possible with local ordinances (the Environmental Protection Agency, established in 1970, would impose even stricter regulations). As Jones well knew from experience, burning could be risky, especially in a wooded area near expensive houses. When he and his crew were first clearing the land at Spyglass, they were burning huge piles of material in what was to become the par-4 13th fairway one day when the fire flared out of control. For a while things looked so bad, according to Jones, that "I thought we were going to burn down the whole Del Monte Forest. . . . There is much more to the transformation from raw land to finished course than the layman realizes."

Trent absolutely loved the way his design of Spyglass Hill turned out—all 6,972 yards and par 72 of it. As he later explained: "Spyglass contains an unusual mixture of seaside, links-type holes and parkland atmosphere. The first five holes, starting from deep in the woods and heading immediately to the sea, demand target golf through sandy wastes, deliberately reminiscent of Pine Valley but with the water in the background and buffeted by the ocean winds. The rest of the course winds through towering Monterey Pines and cypress in the Del Monte Forest, and is deliberately reminiscent of Augusta National." He loved the course's dramatic change of pace; if some saw the mixture of woods and open sand as "severe," so be it, but for most golfers, Jones felt, the combination was highly original and extraordinarily rare in its beauty. For Jones, Spyglass Hill would always be "a very special course" and one that he believed was "unique as well as great" because there was "such a variety in the character of the holes." Especially on the opening five holes played in the dunescape down by the ocean, the wind played havoc, disguising its direction and velocity and "making great shots land in such unanticipated locations" that the golfer could "become really confused and lose patience." Late in life, Jones gave a lengthy interview for the USGA's Pamela Fox Emory Oral History Collection, and Spyglass Hill was the only one of his courses for which he provided a detailed hole-by-hole description. In that interview, Jones also emphasized that Samuel Morse liked it very much and said everything from the design of the tees to the undulations of the greens constituted a "work of art."[†]

---

† Enhancing the artistic quality of Jones's design was the literary connection to Robert Louis Stevenson. Every hole on the Spyglass Hill golf course was given a name in accordance with the story of *Treasure Island*. For example, hole #2, a 395-yard par-4, was "Billy Bones." Like the character in the book, "he appears early, doesn't stay long, but is long remembered." Hole #12, a 178-yard par-3 was "Skeleton Island," because "The shape of the green and lake guarding it

Jones was especially partial to the par-4 fourth hole, which even from the back tees played only 376 yards. In some respects this is a surprising choice because it seems, even to his son Bob Jr., "the antithesis of his basic design principles" (i.e., long runway tees, fairways that extend from tee to green framed with large bunkers, and expansive, contoured elevated greens).[‡] Totally treeless but bordered with forbidding sand dunes crowned with stands of ice plant—an invasive succulent from South Africa originally introduced to hold the shapes of the dunes—the fourth plays roughly parallel to the coastline with a fairway that slides gently from an elevation of ninety feet at the start of the fairway to an elevation of seventy-nine at fairway's end. Off the tee (at an elevation of ninety-seven feet), the golfer could opt to keep his driver in the bag and hit a 3-wood or long iron, thereby playing for proper ball placement on the correct side of the fairway, usually to the right. But with the tee being so close to the ocean and the sea breezes often lashing fiercely, many golfers chose to hit a full driver to get as near to the end of the dogleg as possible, at which point the hole turns sharply to the left. "When you reached the end of the full drive," Trent explained, "you rested on a relatively level fairway." From there a golfer played a mid- to short iron over a large waste of dune at the corner of the dogleg into a small "punchbowl," a wonderfully natural green site that made for a long and very narrow putting surface that canted from right to left and was mostly hidden from the golfer's view when making his second shot. Over the green and to the right sat more dunes to catch any ball that traveled long. What made the hole so unique, in Trent Jones's estimation, was how he was able to design the hole using the land's natural contours to create three distinct zones. The hole was designed to lead the golfer "downhill in steps." According to Trent, "That turned out to be quite different and unique, and everybody loved it." The fourth hole at Spyglass, nicknamed the "Blind Pew," is a rebuttal to the contention that all of Trent Jones's golf course designs are homogeneous and unvarying. It demonstrates the great architect's ability to adapt his design to the natural setting.

Spyglass Hill got a great deal of media attention even before it opened for

---

lead the way to the treasure. Hole #14, a 560-yard par-5 was "Long John Silver," for being a "double dog leg . . . that will dominate the whole card." Trent Jones did not choose any of the names for the holes (it is likely he had never read the book), but he was delighted by them.

‡ Robert Trent Jones Jr., *Golf by Design: How to Lower Your Score by Reading the Features of a Course* (Boston and New York: Little, Brown and Co., 1993), p. 254. Spyglass Hill was one of the first projects on which Bob assisted his father after joining the business. The entry of the two brothers into their father's profession will be discussed fully in Chapter Eleven.

play. Jones could always count on Herb Graffis for some strong favorable advance publicity. The construction of Spyglass Hill was the cover story in *Golfdom* in September 1965. In the photo on the cover, a tractor was shown mowing rough to the side of the par-3 11th, whose green, like all the rest at Spyglass in the fall of 1965, was not yet grown in—certainly not well enough for a course opening planned for the following spring. The caption that Graffis wrote for the photo read, "Turf at the moment is only struggling to be seen on California's Monterey Peninsula, but already they are saying that nobody is going to take any liberties with this formidable seaside links." On March 11, 1966, when the golf course first opened (for members only), the *Monterey Peninsula News* ran a story about it at the top of its front page. MORSE OPENS NEWEST COURSE, the headline read, accompanied with a large picture of S.F.B. himself, in a three-piece suit, hitting the ceremonial first shot off the opening tee. The next day, in a lengthy article in the *San Francisco Examiner* titled, SPYGLASS COURSE A DAZZLER, sportswriter Nelson Cullenward wrote, "All of the superlatives in the English language weren't enough to describe the beauty and toughness of the new Spyglass Hill golf course. . . . It has everything—the testing links of Pebble Beach and the beauty of Cypress Point wrapped up into one. . . . There isn't a commonplace hole in the entire 18. Each has character of its own and makes heavy demands on the golfer." Nationally, news of Spyglass's opening came to many through James C. Anderson's story for United Press International, SPYGLASS HILL COURSE RATED WITH WORLD'S BEST, distributed to more than 1,200 newspapers and hundreds of radio and TV stations. One of the more interesting items reported by Anderson in his UPI story was that Trent Jones himself, "a pretty fair golfer with a ten handicap, came a cropper when he played it for the first time—starting out with a triple bogey eight on the first hole." Though it was indeed "a difficult par," Jones proved that *not* every hole he designed was an "easy bogey."

The Bing Crosby Pro-Am, informally known as Bing's "clambake," had been an annual event on the Monterey Peninsula since 1947. Played in mid- to late January over four days with a field of top PGA pros and celebrity amateurs, the Crosby took place on the Peninsula's three golf courses: Pebble Beach, Cypress Point, and the Monterey Country Club. In June 1966, the Crosby tournament announced that Spyglass would replace the Monterey Peninsula Country Club as one of the three courses for the 1967 National Pro-Am. The decision was potentially great news for the Spyglass members as well as for

Jones, but it also carried great risk. Spyglass Hill, as Trent would later acknowledge, was simply not ready for championship play. "One full season is not enough to grow grass, especially on the greens," Jones observed. It would have been prudent to wait another year at least before making Spyglass part of the Crosby lineup, but because everyone involved was so anxious to bring the nationally televised event to Spyglass, Jones's golf course would be exposed to some of the strongest criticism that any of his golf courses would ever receive.

The PGA of America tried to convince Bing Crosby not to use Spyglass Hill until it was a more mature golf course. After making an inspection tour of the layout in mid-September 1966, Jack Tuthill, the PGA's supervisor of tournaments, advised Robert T. Creasey, the PGA's executive director, that "it will require two years to prepare it properly for tournament play. Certainly it cannot be wisely considered for the 1967 tournament." No one associated with the Crosby or with Spyglass Hill—and certainly not Robert Trent Jones—was amenable to reconsidering the decision, especially with the tournament only four months away. A. G. Michaud, president of Del Monte Properties, wrote back to Creasey: "As long ago as March of this year, the architect for our Spyglass Hill Golf Course, Mr. Robert Trent Jones, reported that the course could be properly prepared for the 1967 Crosby Tournament. Mr. Jones and his staff have repeated their conclusion upon continued inspection of the course many times, the last occasion being approximately a month and a half ago. Our Manager of golf, Mr. Roger Larson, is also confident that the course can be properly prepared for the Crosby Tournament in 1967."

Trent was in Spain, overseeing the Sotogrande Golf Club project in Cádiz, and he directed Bob Jr. to investigate. Bobby reported back that Del Monte would speed up its efforts to remove trees and clear up rough areas, and the PGA agreed to revisit in two weeks' time. Before the matter got resolved, however, it erupted into newspaper headlines. On November 3, 1966, the controversy was laid bare in a story in the *Los Angeles Times* by columnist Bill Shirley, indicating that the use of Spyglass in the next Crosby was still up in the air. *Golf World* repeated the rumor in its November 18 issue. Columnist Dave Lewis of the *Long Beach Independent* wrote that there was "a sharp clash" between Bing Crosby and the PGA over whether the course should be used.

Bing Crosby more than hinted to the PGA brass that he would withdraw sponsorship if Spyglass wasn't part of his 1967 tournament. Crosby had the backing of Samuel Morse, who wrote a succinct letter to Bing and his brother

Larry, the tournament chair, saying that the PGA's executive director "quite frankly, gives me a pain in the neck."

"I have had more experience in tournament play and the conditioning of golf courses than Mr. Creasey, or probably anybody else in the country, putting it modestly," Morse observed in his letter to the Crosbys, "and the Spyglass Hill Course is in perfect condition. If there are any complaints, it won't be the fault of the course."

So "Pretty But Deadly Spyglass Hill" became part of the Crosby.[§] As anxious as competitors were to play the course for the first time (pro Billy Casper was quoted as saying "That's all we talked about at the San Diego Open last week"), as soon as they arrived on the Monterey Peninsula for the 1967 Invitational, complaints about the course—another Robert Trent Jones "monster"—began in earnest. Several of the pros openly stated their dislike of the golf course's length. Arnold Palmer was polite but, for him, outspokenly critical: "It really makes no difference to me whether they lengthen or shorten a course, but it does seem a little ridiculous to build a course which is not playable for the majority of golfers." Veteran pro Doug Ford summed up his initial feelings about Spyglass: "It's very tough and I'm not kidding! I could barely find the tee on the next hole after putting out each time." One of the amateurs in the Crosby event, Los Angeles Dodgers ace pitcher Sandy Koufax, quipped after playing his first round at Spyglass: "It is a great place. I hope they build a golf course here some day." In one stretch of seven holes, Koufax lost seven balls. Lee Trevino

---

§ It is interesting to note that future USGA president Frank D. "Sandy" Tatum Jr., then a prominent San Francisco attorney, wrote to his friend at Del Monte Properties, Roger Larson, just a few weeks before the 1967 Crosby National Pro-Am Invitational was played at Spyglass Hill: "I played Spyglass Hill over the weekend. It was very impressive. The job you have done in getting it into shape borders on the miraculous. Every pin placement was fair (I do not mean that in the moderate but rather in the just sense). The course looked and played as if it were much older and more seasoned than it is." Frank D. Tatum, Law Offices of Cooley, Crowley, Gaither, Codward, Castro & Huddleston, Montgomery St., San Francisco, CA, to Mr. Roger Larson, c/o Del Monte Properties Co., Pebble Beach, CA, 5 Jan. 1967. The next day, A. G. Michaud, Del Monte's president, forwarded a copy of Tatum's letter to Robert Trent Jones Sr. Copies of both letters are in the Spyglass Hill Golf Club Files, JP, CUA. It should be said that Sandy Tatum (born in 1920) was a great amateur golfer. He was a member of the Stanford University team that won back-to-back NCAA Championships in 1941 and 1942; more than that, Tatum captured the NCAA individual title. He served on the USGA Executive Committee from 1972 to 1980, the last three years of which he headed the USGA. Tatum and Trent Jones became good friends, as did Tatum and Jones's two sons, especially Bob Jr., who, like Tatum, lived on the West Coast.

would later say about the course: "They just ought to hang the man who designed it. Ray Charles could have done a better job."

Many of the critical comments, not unexpectedly, focused on the mediocre conditioning of the course. Dutch Harrison, who had been playing pro golf for forty years, moaned: "The first five holes will kill you! They are playing real rough. . . . The course isn't ready. They should give it time to grow up. Some of us may never get through putting." Frank "Bud" Hoelscher, a Santa Monica native and two-time winner of the California State Open, groaned, "The greens are terrible. There's no grass on them." Jack Tuthill told reporters, "I can't think of any course we've played on the Tour during the last couple years that is in such bad condition. Several of the holes are unfair, and the contour of the greens is too severe." Billy Casper, golf's leading money winner in 1966, agreed: "Some day it will be a good course, but right now it is anything but good. The course needs a lot of work. The greens are difficult to putt as the undulations make the ball do strange things. To a point, it's unfair, because only one per cent of the golfers can play greens such as this. . . . If we get one of those rough, blowy days, when the wind is really blowing off the ocean, nobody will make a putt."

Bing Crosby stubbornly persisted in defending the use of the golf course for his Invitational, but at the same time he advised the amateurs entered in the tournament about the extraordinary difficulty of Spyglass: "Because we're playing the lengthy Spyglass Hill this year, saving time in the course of play is going to be imperative. For this reason I must request, even implore, amateur players to pick up their ball on any hole where it appears [their] score on that hole is irrelevant and of no value to his team." To the pros, Crosby warned that Spyglass would play at least six shots harder than the Monterey Peninsula Country Club. Before Jack Nicklaus teed off for his first practice round at Spyglass, Bing bet him "that he can't break 72 from the tiger tees at Spyglass." Nicklaus didn't manage that the first time around the links, shooting 76, but won the bet in his second practice round with a 2-under 70.

Perhaps Nicklaus should have saved the 70 for the actual tournament, as Jack could do no better than 74 at Spyglass in the real competition. (Nicklaus played Spyglass on Sunday, which was only round three of the tournament because mile-a-minute winds had canceled Saturday's play, extending the event to a Monday finish.) Early in the week of the tournament, Crosby officials announced that the course was playing so tough that the back tees would not be used; rather, all the golfers, including the pros, would move up to the middle tees, which at 6,600 yards played about 400 yards shorter than the "tiger tees." Because of the spotty condition of the grass in many of the fairways, the PGA agreed that "winter rules" should be in effect at Spyglass but not at the other two courses. This meant that the golfers could, without penalty, improve the lie of their golf ball when the ball came to rest in the fairway. A ball hit into the rough would have to be played "as it lies."

Although it produced the highest scores of the three courses by a rather significant margin, how good or bad the scores were at Spyglass Hill during the 1967 Crosby International was largely determined by the weather. The golfers who played Spyglass on Thursday, the opening day of the tournament, had the best of it with partly cloudy weather, light breezes, and temperatures in the 60s. Four pros shot 2-under par 70s at Spyglass that day: New Zealand's southpaw Bob Charles, winner of the 1963 British Open; Jack Burke Jr., holder of the 1956 Masters and PGA Championship titles; Oklahoma journeyman pro Jerry Pittman; and twenty-five-year old Jim Colbert of Kansas City, Kansas.

On day two, as the skies turned dark and brought rain, persistent fog, and colder temperatures, Spyglass transmogrified into the course everyone had feared. Scores on all three courses ballooned in the inclement weather, but at Spyglass the scores of some of the best pros soared into the high 70s and even into the 80s: Gene Littler and Doug Sanders (78), Tommy Aaron (80), Babe Hiskey and Billy Farrell (81), and Tom Weiskopf (88). The course also ate the lunch of first-round leader Joe Carr, who followed up his 68 at Cypress Point with a gruesome 82. Don Massengale, the defending champion, went down to disaster with an 80, thanks to horrid play around the greens. As the newspapers reported, Massengale was "unimpressed by the course and doubted it had much future." Dave Hill stumbled in from rain-soaked Spyglass Hill with an 80; his other three rounds at the Crosby were all very good—73, 70, and 71—leaving him with a tie for seventh place and a bad taste in his mouth for Robert Trent Jones's designs. As for the amateurs who teamed up with the pros, who knew what scores they actually shot? One reporter suggested that their average score back on day one, when the weather was good, was 88 to 90, but with the host encouraging his fellow amateurs to pocket their balls once their score no longer mattered on a hole, the real average was impossible to determine. If all of them had "played everything out" on every hole, it might well have approached 100.

Crosby hoped Robert Trent Jones Sr. would play in the event, but he gave his spot to son Bobby, because, as Bobby today relates, "Dad didn't want to look bad on his own course." Paired with pro Larry Ziegler, who shot 80 on Spyglass Hill, the Ziegler-Jones team missed the Sunday cut. Trent walked in the galley and did interviews. In front of reporters Jones conceded that the greens were bumpy and a few of the greens needed some adjustment, mostly enlargement for more pin positions. But generally Jones disagreed with critics of the course, saying "This course isn't in any worse condition than some the pros play on the tour." Jack Tuthill disagreed. "That's not so," he said. "I wish Mr. Jones would name one."

Friday's weather on the Monterey Peninsula was cloudy, windy, and getting colder, but Saturday's heavy rains and sixty-mile-per-hour winds ruined Spyglass Hill's chances of showing itself in a good light. Tournament officials canceled the day's play, washing out the entire round. Those who had made the cut would come back for round three on Sunday and finish the tournament on Monday. Contrary to what Sam Morse, the Crosbys, and the Joneses had said about how well Spyglass would drain and hold up to bad weather, when play resumed on Sunday morning the golf course was very soggy, and drying out took much more time than it did on the other two courses. Jack Nicklaus, who had been one of the few complimenting the golf course earlier in the week, experienced the muddy mess that was Spyglass that Sunday on the very first hole. Nicknamed "Treasure Island" for its green, which seemed from the fairway to float in a sea of sand, the opening hole's natural wasteland was filled with what seemed like quicksand. Nicklaus's approach shot on the par-5 604-yard hole buried itself in the greenside quagmire, which required him to fudge a wedge out as best he could. After three-putting for a double-bogey seven, Jack rallied back strongly, finishing with a round of 74, one of the best rounds at Spyglass that day. He lost his one-shot lead to Billy Casper, who got around a much less messy Pebble Beach that Sunday in 3-under 69. The next day, Nicklaus, happily back on Pebble Beach, birdied five of the last seven holes, shooting 31 on the back side en route to a 4-under 68. Casper's last-round 74 earned him second place, five shots behind Jack. Arnold Palmer was third, seven strokes back.

The best one-liner of the entire tournament came from an anonymous amateur after his round at Spyglass Hill: "We played the course under some unfortunate conditions: It was open."

Jack Tuthill had been right: Spyglass was not ready for tournament play. Many years later, Robert Trent Jones Sr. would acknowledge as much. More than one of the five lakes on the back nine, he knew, had been suffering seepage. Some holes had problems, as Jones would explain, "due primarily to the fact that the construction budget had not provided for enough money to guarantee effective overall drainage." ("Let's not worry right now about drainage," Trent had told son Bobby, "we will do that later.") Unfortunately, when the course got a lot of rain—and everyone associated with Spyglass and the Crosby had to know that heavy rain was likely in January—the immature turf was bound to get boggy and saturated. The subsurface of the soil on holes #6 through #18 was mostly clay, not sand.

Without sufficient "grow-in" of the bent grass on the putting surfaces and fringes, a design feature that Jones had built into the course—tilting the aprons of the greens to give golfers a better look for their approach shots—would turn menacing. That's exactly what happened when the tournament committee cut the holes for the championship too close to the aprons. Chips and putts with any speed at all heading toward those pin positions wouldn't stop until the ball had trickled off the green. Not even in U.S. Open conditions did the pros have to put up with such treachery. All of these factors contributed to the nasty complaints about Spyglass, and perhaps only its architect retained the conviction that it was a golf course for the ages.

In the weeks following the '67 Crosby, the controversy over Spyglass Hill continued to bubble and boil, with sports columnists debating the question of whether Jones's new golf course was a "'Tricky Monstrosity' Or A Competitive Gem?" Even Bing Crosby expressed reservations about returning to Spyglass the following year. "They did not live up to the commitments they made to us last year about conditions at Spyglass," he said in a statement to the press. "Unless they are improved, I seriously doubt the course will be approved for the tournament in January."

No column about the Spyglass controversy got more attention than the one written by nationally syndicated *Los Angeles Times* sportswriter Jim Murray. One of the country's most talented sports columnists, Murray had a great flair for sarcasm and he knew a great quote when he heard one. The weekend of the clambake, Murray collected the juiciest jabs taken at Spyglass Hill's expense and was happy to share them with his millions of readers across the country:

- "I wouldn't play it again for $5,000 in unmarked bills and a letter from the internal revenue saying it was untaxable. Robert Trent Jones should be made to play it at gun point twice a day. The fairways are harder than Wall Street."—PGA veteran pro Claude Harmon.

- "It's the first course I ever saw that was longer from green-to-tee than from tee-to-green. In New York I'll call a cab to go that far."
  —PGA pro Doug Ford
- "It's an 18-hole marooning. You come off it emaciated and waving your shirt aloft for help from passing ships."—Anonymous pro
- "Why couldn't it go the other way around? Uphill for one hole and downhill for 17? The Red Cross should insist on it."—PGA pro Dave Marr

Murray had fun with the wisecracks, but his column actually sided with the defenders of Spyglass Hill and Robert Trent Jones. A high-handicap golfer himself, Murray brilliantly evoked the feelings of millions of "hackers" around the country by making fun of pros who complained that golf on Jones's courses had become too hard for them. Golf on *any* golf course was brutally hard for most people:

> The pros could not be expected to hail [the golf course]. Dempsey didn't care for Tunney, either. Batters kept hoping it wasn't Koufax's turn when they got in the lineup. Did Samson say "Take back this little lion and bring me a bigger one with rabies"? . . . The pros see it as a business rival with sharp practices. It has things like marked traps, so you can see where Trent Jones puts sand and where God did. In God's sand, you can sole your club. In Trent Jones' it's vice versa. I love every unplayable inch of it. Every golf course in the world is Spyglass Hill to me. I can take an 11 on a hole putting on the living room rug. I ALWAYS end up a round of golf having walked more than three times the regular yardage. That's because I played a zig-zag route. My feet, back, ears, and teeth always hurt after 18 holes.

Murray took delight in the way the holes at Spyglass were named after Robert Louis Stevenson characters, and he likewise turned that against the pros who complained about Jones's course:

> No. 12 is "Skeleton Island" from the rotting bones of birdies lying there. No. 4 is "Blind Pew." There is "Black Dog" and "Long John Silver." (560 uphill yards into the wind—yo, ho, ho and a bottle of rum!) I'm sick of

holes that should be named the "Even Baby Makes Three" holes—or where they should be named "Blind Drunk" holes because a guy can make a birdie even if he sees two flags and has hiccups. No, Spyglass! Run up the black flag with the skull and white bones on it! Ready, you 18 black-legged scoundrels, here comes those swabbies in alpaca and alligator sailing along on a sea of birdies and eagles. Avast ye 18 sea dogs, prepare to board, delay the birdies, and clobber them with bogeys, or else string every man-jack of you lubbers from the highest yardarm in the Dry Tortugas!

One can only imagine the twinkle in his eye and wide grin on his face when Trent Jones realized that despite the title placed on the column (SPYGLASS: AN AMBUSH), Murray was on his side.⁵

In his first opportunity to speak to an audience following the '67 Crosby, Jones made his feelings known loud and clear. At a black-tie banquet in Philadelphia on February 20, 1967, about a month after the tournament, Jones was honored with an award from the Sales and Marketing Executives of Philadelphia. As he had throughout his career, Jones sought to control the perception of himself and his work: "Tournament winners always say something nice about the course. Those who shoot under 75 rarely say anything about it. Those who shoot over 75 . . . well, each of them will have something different to complain about. It seems that most of the players figure the architect is their natural enemy. But, really, the caliber of a course is determined by the public, not by the pros." About Spyglass specifically, all Jones said was, "I know of no course in the world that isn't better five years after it is opened. Like fine wine, a golf course gets better with age." But the city reporter who attended and wrote about the event focused, as Jones should have expected, on his blast at the pros. With the headline GOLFERS MY BIGGEST CRITICS, the story of Jones's speech made it into papers all across the country.

---

⁵ Trent Jones received a mix of letters from friends and acquaintances about the Jim Murray column, some thinking that it was negative to the architect. One who did not and wrote to him happy about Murray's message was a prominent Los Angeles attorney by the name of John Thomas, who had done some work for Samuel F. B. Morse and Del Monte Properties. Congratulating Trent for "the Spyglass Hill masterpiece," Thomas enclosed a copy of the Murray article from the *Los Angeles Times*, saying "Jim Murray is usually very tight with his praise," so Jones should be very happy. John M. Thomas, Attorney at Law, Security Federal Bldg., Wilshire Blvd, Los Angeles, CA, to RTJ, 7 Church St., Montclair, NJ, 8 Feb. 1967, Spyglass Hill Golf Club Files, JP, CUA.

The controversy over Spyglass Hill only energized Jones to keep building the type of golf courses he had been building and, rather than staying quiet when the pros publicly criticized his layouts, to give it right back to them in spades. As son Rees would later say, "Dad stirred up a lot of the controversy himself, to gain publicity." Although he had done some of that "stirring up" long before the '67 Crosby, the deluge of criticism directed Spyglass's way marked a turning point in Jones's response to criticism of his courses. Not that he hadn't "taken on" the pros many times before; he had, almost regularly, ever since Oakland Hills. But the strenuous and well-publicized complaining about Spyglass, a golf course that he loved perhaps above all his other original designs up to that point in his career, stirred Trent to mount a vigorous defense of his golf design principles and his reputation. It wasn't all about his ego; it was also a calculated business strategy to not simply roll with the punches but to incite controversy, to add fuel to the fire and thrive on the flames. He approached all publicity, even harsh criticism, as positive overall, in that it kept the brand name "Robert Trent Jones" before the public as the one golf architect whose work was worthy of debate, the one designer whose name everyone knew.

So when the Crosby did, in fact, bring its Invitational back to Spyglass in January 1968, Trent Jones thought he was ready for his critics—but they too had refined their arguments, and new voices had joined the chorus. Young Texas pro Dudley Wysong, just off victories in the '66 Phoenix Open and '67 Hawaiian Open, called Spyglass Hill "an abortion." Dean Martin, a decent amateur golfer, joked, "They ought to give everybody a two-club-lengths drop—off the course." This time even Nicklaus was on the side of what Jones publicly called "the crybaby touring pros." Jack called the contours on some greens "ridiculous," referred to the course as "a monstrosity," and joked that the "humpy greens" looked like "dinosaur graves." The fact that he finished eighth this time around rather than winning the event—and shot 75 with five three-putt greens (with two misses from 18 inches) at Spyglass—might have had something to do with his negative frame of mind. "It's impossible," the Golden Bear said after his round. "You can't putt those greens." Even Johnny Potts, the winner of the tournament who carded a nice 71 at Spyglass Hill on Friday, when asked his opinion of the golf course, simply said, "You couldn't print it."

The fact that it was Nicklaus who was criticizing Spyglass Hill stung Jones more than the barbs that came from lesser players—particularly now that Nicklaus had announced that he himself was going into the golf course design business. "The modern tournament pro is becoming soft," Jones told journalists.

"He pretends he's playing heavyweight courses of more than 7,000 yards, but they are usually reduced to around 6,600. The pro doesn't want any bad rough. He wants fairway traps from which he can reach the green. He complains if the greens have any rolls or contours at all. It's getting so—because they demand it—every hole is a drive and a wedge. This makes the entire game dependent on an eight or 10-foot putt. It's very boring." Jones repeated an argument that he had expressed several times before, which was that the tournament pros were laboring under the misconception that the public wanted to see scores in the mid-60s. "On great courses, yes," Jones said. "Like Nicklaus's 65 at the Masters, Palmer's 65 at Cherry Hill in Denver in 1960 and Ben Hogan's 67 at Oakland Hills in 1951." But the spectators also felt that "a golfer should be justly rewarded for a good shot and penalized for a bad one." That was "not the case today," charged Jones. "The pros feel they must be able to hit the green from the rough, they must play the par fives with a drive and five-iron and have no problems on the greens. . . . They criticize the greens because they three-putt them. . . . I think the 72s that were shot by men like Bobby Jones, Walter Hagen and Tommy Armour in the old days were greater than the 66s and 68s we're seeing under conditions today."

Some pros struck back. "The trouble with Robert Trent Jones is he doesn't play his own courses," snorted Al Geiberger—who, coincidentally, played especially well on Trent Jones's Firestone course, winning the 1965 American Golf Classic and the 1966 PGA Championship there.

One veteran professional who preferred to remain anonymous responded by saying that Spyglass was "the biggest place of butchering of a piece of ground since Sherman marched through Georgia." Some sportswriters took issue with Jones's counterattack, singling out his comment that today's low scores were "like somebody breaking Babe Ruth's home run record on a softball diamond." To that, the editor of *Golf World* wrote: "In all due respect to Mr. Jones' sentimentality toward a past era, his premise is ill-conceived in this age of super athletes and super equipment. Pardon the cliché, but records are made to be broken and spectators want to see them broken."

Immediately after the conclusion of the 1967 Crosby, Jones began working with the club to fix what they mutually acknowledged were real problems. One of the biggest changes came in redesigning the green at the par-3 fifth, which was increased in size by 40 percent to help golfers hit a green that sits "in a Sahara of sand a few yards away from the Pacific." He also eliminated a small sand trap on the left front and brought the putting surface into that area. In a private letter to Del Monte Properties president Aime Michaud, Jones wrote, "The good press on this change will certainly strengthen our case with the PGA."

Jones also enlarged the two back tees on #3, rebuilt the 12th and 13th tees, and thinned some of the trees around the 14th green, which he rebuilt and enlarged to the right side by about a third. He attacked the drainage issues, in many places replacing French drains that had not functioned well at Spyglass because of its various soil types. Jones wanted Spyglass to clear the underbrush from the forest edge along the fairways, but the golf club did not have sufficient funds to carry this out as quickly or as thoroughly as he wished. This issue affected play on all the holes from #6 through #18. "The holes in the forest at Cypress Point are much cleaner," Jones pointed out. If Spyglass were improved in this way, "it will not only improve the golf course and speed up play, but will give us the final ammunition to assure the PGA will be reasonable at the Crosby."

By the time the '68 Crosby was played, the underbrush situation at Spyglass had gotten better but the general condition of the course had not improved nearly enough to satisfy the pros, PGA officials, Crosbys, Northern California Golf Association, Spyglass membership, or even Robert Trent Jones. Elements of the course's drainage and irrigation systems were flawed, with some areas of the fairways remaining wet and others always dry. Jones's construction company had designed and installed them, so it fell to Trent to defend and eventually to fix. "The big problem with Spyglass," Bob Jr. told the press, "is that it is not in its best shape in the winter. And that's when the Crosby is played." Many trees still needed to be thinned to allow more sunlight to reach the greens. Jones Sr., with Bobby's help, went on to remodel the sixth, eighth, and fourteenth greens, lessening the severity of breaks for most putts. Interestingly, according to PGA statistics, the sixth and the eighth (along with the sixteenth) over the many years of the Crosby and subsequent AT&T National Pro-Am would play among the toughest on the entire PGA tour, despite the fact that Jones made the greens on those holes slightly easier.

Slowly but surely, the controversy over Spyglass evaporated. (In 1976, the only year Spyglass wasn't used for the Crosby, the tournament avoided it because of a drought and improper pesticide application that made seven greens on the densely wooded back nine unplayable; Jones endorsed the decision not to play Spyglass that year.) In the coming years the world of golf came to recognize it as an excellent golf course, with some golfers liking it better than even Pebble Beach, for the very reason that early critics panned the course: the deliberate transition from the Pine Valley–like dunescape of the first five holes to the elevated Augusta-like woodlands of the rest of the course. By the late 1970s and 1980s, most of the touring pros came to like it a great deal and said so. As the golf course aged and matured, it remained a stern test of golf, certainly one of the toughest in the world from the championship tees. For several years after its opening, the official course record at Spyglass—with the ball played "as it lies" and hit from the back tees—stood at only 2-under-par 70; this was carded in the California Amateur by Forrest Fezler, who would later win one Tour event and finish second in the 1974 U.S. Open at Winged Foot. Today the course record at Spyglass is 62, held jointly by Phil Mickelson and Luke Donald, both shot during the AT&T National Pro-Am. *Golf Digest* has ranked Spyglass as high as fifth on its list of America's greatest public golf courses, and *Golfweek* today places it quite high on several of its "best" listings: the twenty-first-best modern course; eighth-best resort course; sixth-best Tour course; and second-best course you can play in California (behind only Pebble Beach). Not bad for a golf course that was so viciously assailed when it first opened five decades earlier.[**]

[**] Spyglass Hill was not the last controversy for the Jones family on the Monterey Peninsula. In 1986 a new Jones course opened at Pebble Beach. Known as Poppy Hills Golf Course, its designer was Robert Trent Jones Jr. Beginning in 1991, Poppy Hills replaced the Monterey Peninsula Golf Club as part of the AT&T Pebble Beach National Pro-Am. (Monterey Peninsula had come back into the rotation after the highly exclusive Cypress Point Club decided in 1991 to bow out of the tournament.) The owner and developer of Poppy Hills (6,861 yards, par 72) was also the Northern California Golf Association, and the NCGA moved its headquarters from Spyglass to Poppy Hills during Poppy's construction. The pros quickly discovered that they weren't very fond of it. They found it to be a "fairly good routing over difficult terrain" (Doak, *Confidential Guide to Golf Courses*, p. 215) but complained that the heavily wooded Del Monte Forest layout had too many doglegs. The result was some extremely pretty holes but holes that didn't have much of a landing area. They also condemned the course's huge greens, which "Robert Trent Jones II" (the name of Bob Jr.'s firm) specifically designed that way to spread out the traffic for what was expected—and turned out to be—heavy public and resort play, but that critics said "presented more 4-putt opportunities than any other course in the world." Oversized greens such as this slowed down play to a crawl, "since golfers take way more time to read a putt than hit a chip." Like Spyglass Hill, Poppy Hills also experienced some problems with its irrigation and drainage systems. Poppy Hills fell into such disfavor that, in 2010, it was replaced in the Pebble Beach National Pro-Am by a remodeled Shores Course at the Monterey Peninsula Country Club. Still, that meant that from 1991 to 2010, the Joneses had designed two of the three courses played in the AT&T Pro-Am. Beginning in the spring of 2013, Robert Trent Jones II began a major renovation to "naturalize" the course and improve its drainage and irrigation. In the first years of its operation, while it

The last golf course controversy of the "Robert Trent Jones Era" was in many ways the worst, bookending the Jones era as lasting from the afterglow of Oakland Hills in 1951 to the fire in the haystack that was the 1970 U.S. Open at Hazeltine.

Hazeltine National Golf Club—which declared its ambitions with the second word of its name—had its origins at one of the grand old clubs in the Twin Cities of Minneapolis/St. Paul. The Minikahda Club dated back to 1898, when its nine original holes were laid out by Robert Foulis and Willie Watson (the club's first pro, who also designed the nearby Interlachen Country Club). It expanded to 18 holes in 1907, hosted the 1916 U.S. Open won by Chick Evans, and was remodeled shortly thereafter by Donald Ross.

In 1960, Minikahda was becoming increasingly hemmed in near downtown Minneapolis and faced the possibility of losing several holes to freeway development. Totton P. Heffelfinger—Minikahda member, former president of the USGA, and part of one of the richest and most influential Republican Party families in Minnesota—went looking for a parcel of land with the thought of either relocating the club or creating an "out-of-town" companion to it. He found what he thought was an ideal site with a nice large lake some twenty miles to the southwest of the cities. His fellow Minikahda members preferred not to move from their historic course—it was the site of the 1927 U.S. Amateur won by Bobby Jones as well as the 1957 Walker Cup, and it remains in that location today—and so "Tot" Heffelfinger decided to proceed with plans for a new club of his own.

---

was still being used to play the AT&T Pebble Beach National Pro-Am, the national golf magazines all listed Poppy Hills in one of its "Best" or "Top" categories. After it became clear that the course was being strongly criticized and would no longer be part of the AT&T National Pro-Am, Poppy Hills disappeared from almost all of the listings. There is reason to think that the golf course will return to the lists as soon as its remodeling is finished. After the renovation work done in 2005 by the late Michael Strantz, the Shores Course at the Monterey Peninsula Country Club (originally designed by Bob E. Baldock and Jack Neville in 1959) resurfaced on the lists, in 2013 occupying #43 on *Golfweek*'s list of "Best Modern Courses." Interestingly, Robert Trent Jones Sr. commented on his son's design of Poppy Hills in his 1987 autobiographical book, *Golf's Magnificent Challenge*. Trent wrote (p. 95) that Bobby's course "was criticized because of the contours of the greens and the molding. On some of his holes I think there was justification. And we'll soften it. Bobby has asked me to soften it. But basically it is a good course." It is not clear to the author whether Trent, eighty-one years old at the time he wrote this, actually ever helped his son in any remodeling of the golf course. Trent also discussed Poppy Hills in his 1991 USGA interview with Alice Kendrick, p. 44.

He turned to Trent Jones, whom Tot knew well from his terms as USGA president in 1952 and '53, the years between the Opens at Oakland Hills and Baltusrol. Trent, a fan of college football from his days at Cornell, also knew Heffelfinger as a star player for Yale (as was his grandfather, William Walter "Pudge" Heffelfinger, Class of 1891, who was inducted into the College Football Hall of Fame in 1951). Heffelfinger took Jones out into the countryside near what was then the quaint little town of Chaska. Well-kept farms full of corn dotted the landscape, and virtually all the roads were made of gravel. Jones was still hoping to develop a nationwide chain of "executive" golf courses, as he had since his dealings with Sam Snead in the 1950s. Heffelfinger liked the idea, and hired Jones to design what opened as the "Executive Golf Club of Minnesota" in 1962.

Neither the name nor the concept flourished. When other "executive clubs" did not materialize for Jones around the nation and few members were attracted to the Chaska club, Heffelfinger renamed the golf course "Hazeltine National Golf Club" in honor of the adjoining Lake Hazeltine.

Both Heffelfinger and Jones felt that they had created a golf course with the potential to attract major tournaments, something that was becoming harder for the old classic clubs of Minnesota—Minikahda, Interlachen, Minneapolis Golf Club, and Keller Golf Course in St. Paul[††]—because they played too short for national championships. Both men decided they wanted to bring a U.S. Open to their new course.

[††] The Twin Cities area had four grand old golf clubs that over the years had hosted a number of major championships. The Minikahda Club itself, besides hosting the 1916 U.S. Open, also hosted the 1957 Walker Cup. But at 6,760 yards and par 72, the course was a little too short to be considered for a U.S. Open. The closing four holes were all par-4s under 400 yards, giving the course a weak finish. Interlachen Country Club, a layout in the suburb of Edina that Ross redid in 1919, had hosted the 1930 U.S. Open (that Bobby Jones won on the way to his Grand Slam) and the 1935 U.S. Women's Amateur, but it, too, was no longer being considered for any of the men's majors. Interlachen (6,900 yards, par 72) did host the 2002 Solheim Cup and 2008 U.S. Women's Open, however. Finally, there was the Minneapolis Golf Club in St. Louis Park, site of the 1940 Western Amateur, 1950 U.S. Amateur, and 1959 PGA Championship. Playing to par 72 at only 6,798 yards, it, too, was considered too short for the U.S. Open. In winning the 1959 PGA Championship at Minneapolis Golf Club, Bob Rosburg had fired closing rounds of 68 and 66. The Keller Golf Course in St. Paul, designed in 1929 by Ramsey County engineer Paul N. Coates Jr. as a public facility, hosted the National Amateur Public Links Championship in 1931, PGA Championship in 1932 and 1954, Western Open in 1949, as well as the Saint Paul Open, a regular stop on the PGA tour from 1930 to 1968. At 6,566 yards and par 72, it, too, played too short by the 1960s to host either the PGA Championship or U.S. Open. From 1973 to 1980, Keller Golf Course was the venue for the LPGA Tour's Patty Berg Classic.

If the golf course had not been designed by Trent Jones, if Heffelfinger had not been a past USGA president, if USGA executive director Joe Dey did not like Trent Jones's golf courses and count him as a good friend, if the USGA had not been interested in moving its national championship to all regions of the United States—including a place in the Upper Midwest other than Chicago—Hazeltine National Golf Club, young and unproven, would not have gotten more than a passing glance as a possible U.S. Open site. But it was, and he was, and he did, and it was, and so the USGA decided to give Hazeltine a look-see by awarding it the 1966 U.S. Women's Open. Patty Berg, the legendary Minnesota golfer, would serve as both the honorary chair of the event and a competitor. The USGA would have this opportunity to see how the golf course played under championship conditions, how well the club's maintenance crew handled course conditioning, and how effectively the club and community volunteers planned and administered the heavy load of logistics that went into staging a major national championship.

Hazeltine more than lived up to everyone's expectations—particularly the golf course, which devoured most of the players. Sandra Spuzich won the event with a score of 297, 9 over par. The course setup played to 6,305 yards, long for a women's tournament at the time. In the entire field, there was only one round under par the first day, a 71 by legendary Mickey Wright. Susie Maxwell Berning finished the tournament in a tie for ninth place and never shot a round better than 75. The ten *top* finishers cumulatively shot ten rounds of 80 or worse in the tournament. Although the competitors surely had complaints about Robert Trent Jones's golf course, they were not voiced to the press. Unlike the PGA tour, the LPGA was still building its place in the world of golf and trying to build its audience (the USGA gave women's golf a boost with its sponsorship of the national telecast of the Women's Open), and LPGA leadership made it clear to its players that making negative comments about the golf courses they played would not do their tour any good.

Early in 1967 the USGA announced that the men's Open would come to Hazeltine three years hence, in June 1970. In retrospect, the Hazeltine layout seemed destined for controversy, especially among the pros whose memories of Spyglass Hill were still fresh. The course stretched to 7,410 yards, which was an extraordinary length even for a Trent Jones course. All four of the par-5s exceeded 600 yards. The golf course had an unusually high number of doglegs, a few of them quite sharp, for which Jones was not entirely to blame: As Jones later recalled, Tot Heffelfinger "had insisted that a children's course be built alongside the regular course." Needing to keep the kids close to the clubhouse, Jones placed the short course between the first and ninth holes. Although the idea of teaching kids to play golf and giving them a nice place to do it was certainly to Heffelfinger's credit, the result for Jones was a property constrained in some key regards. In Jones's words, "This required land we would have preferred to use for the regular course, adversely affecting four holes on the front nine."

A preview of the idiosyncratic challenges of the golf course came in the Minnesota Golf Classic, a regular tour event played at Hazeltine for the one and only time in the summer of 1967. Lou Graham won the event (played from 1930 to 1956 as the Saint Paul Open) with the highest winning score relative to par on the tour that year, even though PGA officials had reduced the length of the course to "only" 7,234 yards. A number of the pros were highly critical of the Hazeltine golf course. One of them was Ken Venturi, who was playing in one of his last tournaments before retiring from competitive golf to become a television golf commentator. Venturi told golf writers, "I like to play a course to a pattern. But you cannot play to any pattern at Hazeltine. You just have to drive the ball off the tee and hope you wind up in a reasonably good position. I don't think the terrain was sufficiently exploited." Apparently unaware of Trent's early career as a golf club professional and the fact that he competed in the Canadian Open and a few other tournaments, Venturi speculated that "The main problem about Hazeltine is that the course was designed by a man who does not, and never did, play championship golf." Fortunately, Venturi, as lead analyst for CBS's golf coverage, would learn more about the subjects he discussed than when he made his public comments about Trent Jones during the Minnesota classic.

Recognizing the great difficulty of Hazeltine, the USGA shortened the golf course even more for the '70 Open, down to 7,151 yards, and kept par at 72. But as soon as the practice rounds started, criticism of the golf course grew hot and heavy. A regular critic of Jones's courses, Bob Rosburg, quipped that there were so many doglegs that Jones "must have laid it out in a kennel." Billy Casper remarked that on many approach shots he "needed radar to spot the flagsticks." Lee Trevino said, "If anyone shoots 280 on this course, the Pope is a possum." Those comments were bad enough, but Jack Nicklaus's published comments about Hazeltine did bother Trent Jones, despite his pragmatic acceptance of the benefits of any publicity. In a June 1970 issue of *Sports Illustrated* that pre-viewed the Open at Hazeltine, Nicklaus declared that most if not all the holes were blind—meaning that golfers could not see their landing areas from the tee. The course "lacked definition." On the very first tee, the golfer "could see neither the green nor the fairway." On another hole, he "had to aim at a chimney on Tot Heffelfinger's roof."

Jones disagreed strongly, and he was not about to let Nicklaus's remarks pass unchallenged. As soon as he arrived at Hazeltine before the Open, Trent conducted a press conference and went over every hole, pointing out that "just because a green cannot be seen from the tee does not make it a blind hole." "Maybe Jack Nicklaus is blind," Jones offered. He told the sportswriters that Nicklaus had not yet even seen the course when he "dictated" the story to *Sports Illustrated*. "Nicklaus wants to be an architect himself," Jones charged. "He picks on our courses even though most of the world likes them. He announced before playing it that he was under contract to write a story about it, and that he was going to write a 'bad' story." Trent advised Jack that for his play in the upcoming British Open the following month at the Old Course, he had better get used to aiming at buildings on his tee shots, because on several incoming holes at St. Andrews those were the best targets he would have. (Apparently Jack did just that, because he won his second British Open title in July 1970, shooting 5-under and defeating Doug Sanders in a playoff.)

The complaints at Hazeltine might not have gotten so nasty if the weather hadn't been so miserable. As one reporter who was there later recalled: "No one could remember wind of such velocity during an Open. It swept out of the northwest at thirty-five miles per hour at its weakest and gusted over forty, nearly uprooting a huge scoreboard anchored in place by six-by-six pilings driven four feet into the ground, ripped tents covering television towers and left their tattered shreds snapping in the gale like whips, and churned the waters of Lake Hazeltine to froth, littering the 10th green with foam. A glob landed on Gene Littler's [putting] line, and he had to wait for it to blow away." Littler struggled home with a 77, which was better than about half the field was able to manage. Twenty players shot 83 or worse. Arnold Palmer, Bob Rosburg, and young Johnny Miller shot 79; Gary Player succumbed to an 80, Bert Yancey to 81, and Dave Marr to 82. And they all *made* the 36-hole cut. So, too, did Nicklaus, who opened with an 81, including a 43 on the front nine. He finished at 304, plus-16. Short of missed cuts, it was his worst performance in a major to that point in his career; he eventually finished tied for 49th. "I could not stop myself from disliking the course," Nicklaus wrote later in his autobiography, "and played it accordingly."

Then there was the case of Sam Snead. USGA official Frank Hannigan recalled years later that Snead tried to get disqualified after shooting 79 the first day. When Snead started to leave without signing his scorecard, playing partner Lee Trevino, who shot 77, called back to Snead: "If I've gotta come back here tomorrow, you're coming back, too!" Snead shot 79 again the second day, signed that card, and then packed up and went home.

On Friday, the winds fell and so did the scores, but not by much, and the complaints about the course got crustier. In what one reporter called a "bizarre exchange" in the press tent after round two, Dave Hill, an eight-time winner on the tour, including a victory just two weeks earlier at the Danny Thomas Memphis Classic, said if he had to play Hazeltine every day he would find another game. "What does it lack?" a writer asked. "Eighty acres of corn and a few cows," Hill replied. "They ruined a good farm when they built this course." A writer followed up, "What do you recommend they do with it?" "Plow it up and start over," Hill snorted. "Understandably," as Trent Jones remembered, Hill's bum comments "did not sit well with the USGA or the good folks at Hazeltine," nor with the PGA tour, which slapped him with a $150 fine. The cocksure Hill paid the fine "practically on the spot," and then "let everyone know" he was "tempted to pay double the amount of the fine" just for the privilege of voicing his opinions about the course again. All this came from a player who ultimately finished *second*; after an opening-round 75, Hill came back with scores of 69, 71, and 73—a total of 288, even par.

Twenty-five-year-old Englishman Tony Jacklin, the defending British Open champion, was the winner at Hazeltine. The first Briton to win a U.S. Open since Ted Ray in 1920, Jacklin finished at 7-under 281, the only golfer in the field under par. He led the championship from wire to wire with rounds of 71, 70, 70, and 70. "I felt good about playing Hazeltine," Jacklin would later write in his autobiography, "though it wouldn't be accurate to say I fell in love with it. More than anything it was the conditions that suited me. Good strong breezes on a difficult golf course with lots of blind shots. Not that different from links golf when you think about it, although of course it was not linksy at all in terms of its soil and grasses." Another contributing factor to his victory, Jacklin felt, was how all of Dave Hill's complaining, and the reaction of the media and the galleries at Hazeltine to it, "took a lot of the attention and heat off me." Jacklin remembers "telling somebody at the time that I was going to let him do all the talking and I was going to do all the playing." Tony played the third round with Hill, and "up and down the fairways he went with the sound of the crowd mooing after him. . . . I went about my business as the crowd mooed him mercilessly. In different circumstances, I might have even tossed in a 'Moo' of my own here and there to stick the needle in him, but I was far too involved in my own game to pay much attention."

In at least a couple of important ways, the 1970 U.S. Open at Hazeltine proved to be a watershed. Dave Hill's highly publicized censure of the golf course seemed petty, the sort of childish whining that a golf professional should avoid. Hill's cranky candor made fussing about golf courses by PGA pros unacceptable—at least temporarily. Complaints about golf courses had been on the rise ever since Jones's redesign of Oakland Hills in 1951. Strong opinions about championship venues, in particular, had received close media attention. Until Hill's notorious mockery of Hazeltine, much of the media coverage of the pros' criticism was neutral if not tending toward approval. But the gratuitous cruelty of Hill's wisecrack about "eighty acres of corn and some cows" changed that sentiment substantially. The members of Hazeltine and the officials of the USGA were truly offended, and Hill's fellow pros learned to button their lips. It would be years before a new generation of golfers, sportswriters, and architecture critics would take up the cudgel.

A column written by veteran sportswriter Dan Jenkins the week after the Open embodied and reflected the shift in attitude, not least because golfers struggling to pay dues and green fees had trouble summoning much sympathy for golfers "forced" to make a living playing a game. "The touring pros have been making it increasingly plain in recent years," Jenkins scoffed, "that they object to any track with a tree, a pond or a par five that can't be reached with a drive and a swizzle stick." Tony Jacklin's civility and good manners in winning the Open also quietly drove home the point. "I personally didn't see the problem with Hazeltine," Jacklin would remark. "Why was everybody complaining? We were all playing the same course."

To be fair to Dave Hill, he had no idea how golf fans would react to his Hazeltine comments. For a *Golf Digest* story many years later, Hill repeated what he had tried to tell people in the months after the tournament—that his comments during the Open were "tongue in cheek" and that the writers had egged him on by "laughing their tails off" and "rolling on the floor" in the pressroom. He thought everyone was having fun with what he was saying. "But, man, when they wrote it up!" Hill's quick wit and biting sarcasm quickly turned him into some sort of unruly villain, more notorious for his acrimony and anti-establishment appeal than for his golf game—which, in fact, was very good. Of course, it didn't help that after the '70 Open, Hill claimed in front of reporters that he had paid a local Chaska farmer so he could borrow his tractor; if Hill had won the championship, he was going to drive the tractor out onto the golf course while hoisting the trophy.

For Trent Jones, the 1970 U.S. Open had a mixed legacy. As much disdain as there was for Dave Hill's comments, the controversy over the fairness and overall quality of Trent's design did some damage to the club's reputation, threatening to hurt Hazeltine's chances to host future championships. As for Jones's own reputation, he still seemed to thrive on controversy and getting his name in the papers, no matter whether good things were being said about him or bad. He realized that Hazeltine had problems; even before Jacklin hoisted the trophy sans tractor, Jones had been working on ideas to improve the course. Tot Heffelfinger and the Hazeltine board wanted him to get right to work, fixing the problem holes and doing further needed remodeling. Heffelfinger also brought Jones back to add a nine-hole "executive" course at Hazeltine, which Trent completed in 1974.

Satisfied with the changes, the USGA returned to Chaska for the 1977 Women's Open. The revised course played a little easier, with Hollis Stacy winning the title at 292, 4 over par. In the spring of 1978, Jones diplomatically asked Dave Hill for some help: "I wanted to get Dave's ideas on the plans we have for Hazeltine. He is a man of definite ideas and a player who has viewpoints that are worth considering." Hill returned the compliments: "I am glad Mr. Jones invited me to come here. He does me a great honor by outlining the proposals for the course. What he has shown me here, and what has been done, has convinced me that it will be a much better golf course than it was. There is no doubt it will be a great championship test. Play a tournament on it? You could play the U.S. Open on it—and if they do, I'd play in it. You can quote me on it."

Six years later, in 1983, the U.S. Senior Open came to Hazeltine. Some of the pros who had played in the '70 Open were now old enough (fifty years or over) to compete. One of them, fifty-two-year-old Billy Casper, won the event with a 288, which was only 4 over par (the course played at par 71 for the seniors). Criticism of the golf course was minor, and scores, though quite high overall (the 36-hole cut came at 155, or 13-over), included twelve sub-par rounds.

The regular men's championship returned to Hazeltine in 1991, but not until after Trent's architect son, Rees, had overseen a major remodeling of his father's golf course. Starting in 1988, Rees's company straightened out many of the bothersome doglegs, particularly on what had always been a highly problematic hole, #7, a long par-5 that involved an almost 90-degree turn to the right. Prior to Rees's remodeling, Trent changed the 16th hole from a par-3 to a par-4 and the 17th hole from a par-4 to a par-3. The upland for the new 16th fairway, which was originally thought to be part of an unusable wooded, swampy area bordering Lake Hazeltine, was discovered by Hazeltine members Reed MacKenzie and Warren Rebholz. Having this new parcel enabled Trent to make these changes. The revised 16th—a gorgeous, "shortish" (404-yard) par-4—now stood ready to become one of the great par-4s in championship golf. So confident was the USGA about the changes at Hazeltine that it invited Dave Hill back to play the course prior to that championship. "I like it," the man who will forever be known for being Hazeltine's arch-critic offered. "Part of it is maturity, of course. When we played in 1970 the greens were new and the trees were about as big around as my wrist. It's all very mature now. When you stand at the first tee the first thing that catches your eye isn't a silo, but a nicely bunkered green at the end of the fairway. The new 16th and 17th holes are gorgeous. It's a lovely, fun course, yet demanding." In his golden years, it gave Trent Jones great pleasure to point out that "even Dave Hill now says he likes the course."

In their classic encyclopedic history, *The Architects of Golf*, Geoffrey S. Cornish and Ronald E. Whitten labeled the 1950s and 1960s the "Robert Trent Jones Era." Cornish had known Trent since the mid-1930s, and kept plasticine models of greens molded by Trent in his office throughout his long career as New England's leading course designer. For the chapter following the one on the Trent Jones Era, Cornish and Whitten used the title, "The New Breed." "Although the fame of Robert Trent Jones had not abated nationally or internationally," the co-authors noted, "other architects began to influence the field of course design. They were Desmond Muirhead, George Fazio, and Pete Dye." All three of these new-breed architects began designing courses in the 1960s, and each in the beginning was undeniably influenced by the Jones paradigm. "My first golf courses were copying Mr. Jones," Dye has recalled. One example of that came at Radrick Farms Golf Course on the campus of the University of Michigan, which Dye designed in 1965. But soon thereafter, Dye got to thinking to himself (and saying to his wife and design partner, Alice), "Well, I can't just go around copying Jones. I better do the dead opposite." That light bulb of unconventional creativity first went on over his head when Dye was designing Crooked Stick, outside his hometown of Indianapolis. Inspired by Scottish courses with their smallish greens, undulating fairways, pot bunkers, and bulk heading with railroad ties, Dye, in Crooked Stick, produced his first major work. Three years later he would build, with some ideas from Jack Nicklaus, the Harbour Town Golf Links on Hilton Head Island in South Carolina. "Mr. Jones had just built Palmetto Dunes at Hilton Head and I admired it, but I thought if I do something, I need to do something just the opposite." Harbour Town became a highly unique layout: It was a short course, unlike Trent's behemoths, with very small greens and fairways carved out of the pines and cypress, but despite all this, it was still a course spiced with a linksland flavor. It might be going too far to say that Pete Dye's architecture represented the "anti-Jones," but it certainly evolved—and evolved very quickly in the late 1960s—into something much like a deliberate repudiation of the main elements of Jones's designs.

The 1970 U.S. Open at Hazeltine may not have put a period on the Trent Jones Era, but it did insert a comma—or better yet, a caesura, a "sense pause"—in the flow of his career within the broader evolution of American golf course architecture. It wasn't that Jones's business went into any sort of decline after Hazeltine, far from it. In the decade of the 1970s, Robert Trent Jones, Inc., would continue to dominate the golf course design business not just in the United States but worldwide—from 1970 to 1979 the company finished a total of 111 projects in twenty-nine states and nineteen foreign countries, a total of 1,395 holes. More major tournaments would still be played on courses that he designed or remodeled—or kept refining—than those of any other architect: U.S. Opens at his new Highlands course at the Atlanta Athletic Club in 1976 and at Baltusrol Lower in 1980; PGA Championships at Oakland Hills in 1972, his new East Course at Tanglewood Park Golf Club in North Carolina in 1974, Firestone in 1975, Congressional Country Club in the bicentennial year of 1976, and Oakland Hills again in 1979. But his dominance from 1970 on would be less complete, less of a total hold on the psyche of the PGA pros, or for that matter on the taste of golf courses favored by the average American golfer. No one who dominated the golf scene the way Trent Jones did could be universally liked, and Jones wasn't. A growing number of people in American golf—mostly some golf professionals (Jack Nicklaus and Tom Weiskopf, to name two) and fellow golf architects—simply didn't care for the "round-faced, puckish-looking little man," now pushing seventy years old. "Anti-Jones forces," as Trent called them, definitely existed by 1970, and their legions were growing.

Besides Desmond Muirhead, George Fazio, and Pete Dye, there were other "New Breed" architects who appeared on the scene in the 1960s, some of them professionally trained course designers with backgrounds mostly in landscape architecture but a few in civil engineering, others touring pros eager to exploit the opportunity to put their own player brands on the exploding number of golf courses going up worldwide.

But the two talented and ambitious young architects who would most affect Jones's life and career, without question, were his own two sons, Robert Trent Jones Jr. and his younger brother, Rees. "Bobby," as his dad called him, joined his father's firm in 1962, establishing a West Coast office in Palo Alto. Rees came on board in 1965, soon taking over supervision of the East Coast office in Montclair. Trent could spend most of his time down in sunny Fort Lauderdale, where he and Ione enjoyed an apartment in a waterside high-rise and worked out of an office at Coral Ridge Country Club, a place he built in 1956 and came to own, a place he loved as his "family's golf course." Without the brains and energy of the "Jones boys," their father's business could never have attracted, taken on, and finished all of the work that came to Robert Trent Jones, Inc., in the 1960s and 1970s.

Building the world's golf courses became quite the family affair.

CHAPTER ELEVEN

A FAMILY AFFAIR

After graduating from Yale in the early 1960s, both of Trent's sons spent more than a decade doing substantial design work as part of their father's company before leaving to pursue successful careers. In this photo taken on the third green at Spyglass Hill in 1967, Trent is flanked (to his right) by eldest son Robert Trent Jones Jr. and (to his left) by son Rees.

Golf was never far from the center of attention in the New Jersey home of Robert Trent Jones. Trent did not push his boys to follow his path as a golf course architect, but the game itself enveloped his sons, Bobby and Rees, both at home and play, from infancy. Golf was the family's lifeblood, as Herbert Warren Wind discovered when he visited with the Jones family at its Montclair home while preparing his 1951 *New Yorker* profile:

When Jones is at home in Montclair, he makes a commendable effort to segregate his professional interests in the sun-parlor office and the attic work-room. Neighbors who call on Sundays find, at first, no indication that the household deviates in the slightest from the standards of respectable, commutable New Jersey. The LP recording of "The King and I" whirs softly in the background while Jones pours bourbon for his friends, listens to the plans his two young sons have concocted for winning a community scrap-collecting contest, and putters around with smoked-trout spread and crackers. This illusion of conformity is seldom maintained for more than an hour. A friend who spent a Sunday there this summer gave, upon returning to the calm of New York, a résumé of dinner with the family. "During the soup course," he said, "there was nothing unusual except that Jones got a call from the head of the construction committee at Colorado Springs, asking him when he would be sending along a copy of the new plans for the sixteenth green. After that, there wasn't a mention of golf until Mrs. Jones apologized for the spinach, saying it was as sandy as Pine Valley. Halfway through the dessert, Bob Jr. and Rees left the table and in a few minutes appeared swinging their golf clubs and asking their father to correct their form. When the maid came in with the coffee, Jones told me how lucky they were to get her. After all, she came from Atlanta, and worked for a family that had a home on the East Lake course, the very course where Bobby Jones learned the game. Then we got away from it all. We went out and played eighteen holes."

It was not just Dad who was consumed with his golf design work: Mother, too, was deeply involved in managing the family business. When Trent was out on the road building golf courses, Ione would sit vigilantly at a desk in an office of her own, directing a volume of work that was enough to keep two personal secretaries busy, as well as paying the bills, keeping track of Trent's schedule, typing letters, and talking to clients on the telephone. Ione was so concerned that she might miss an important call—an opportunity from some new prospect or a message from Trent—that she regularly took a phone to bed with her under the covers. Still taking advantage of her father's high-level post with New York Bell, Ione had a telephone installed in virtually every room of her house, nearly a dozen in all.

On the rare days when Trent was home and free to spend time with the boys, he usually took them with him to the golf course or, if it was evening, to a nearby driving range to hit a bucket of balls. Trent gave them mini-lessons on how to swing the club or play specific shots. He was not overbearing about it, but some of his instructions were more ardent and time-consuming than either boy cared to receive. For "vacations" Trent and Ione loaded the boys into the backseat of the car and drove them to places like Myrtle Beach, Pinehurst, and Fort Lauderdale—where Trent was almost always overseeing projects. By the time they were high-school age, Bobby and Rees had seen firsthand on several occasions just how a golf course gets built.

Rees recalls traveling with his dad as a thirteen-year-old to the '55 Open at the Olympic Club in San Francisco, while Bobby stayed at home so he could play one of his summer golf tournaments. "We flew across the country in a Douglas DC-3," Rees remembers. "On the way back we stopped in Houston, where Dad was doing the Houston Country Club. I'll never forget it. It was one of the few times I was on a trip alone with Dad. Also, I'll never forget how hot it was in Texas. I'd never experienced that kind of heat and humidity before in my life."

Rees and Bob also remember the many occasions when their peripatetic father was absent from an event that was important to them. One such memory for Rees came in the ninth grade when he received the Sons of the American

Revolution Award for "the best all-round person." Neither father nor mother was able to attend the ceremony because they were in Rochester attending the 1956 U.S. Open. Rees didn't even realize that they would not be able to come until Grandfather Davis showed up at the door that morning to drive him to school.

Bobby spent time in his father's company the following year during the construction of the South Course at Wilmington Country Club in Delaware. "The deal had been worked out by my mother," Bobby relates. "I had gotten interested in aviation, and I wanted to take flying lessons. Dad didn't want me to fly. He would lead me toward those things that interested him. He would be more oppressive to me, whereas Mom's attitude was positive: 'You can make it. I'm here to help you, but you figure it out.' My mother always encouraged me to do anything I wanted, as long as I did it well. She would negotiate with him deals to let me do what I wanted, but I had to earn the money: 'If you earn the money, then you can have flying lessons.' Well, how do I earn the money—I'm only sixteen? 'I'll make a deal with your father to teach you how to run a bulldozer.'"

Trent drove his son to Wilmington and put him under the direction of John Schmeisser, Jones's construction superintendent at the site. "I learned how to run a bulldozer and use its blade to move the earth around," Bob remembers. "My job was to work on one of the greenside bunkers and to shape it into the green." Trent left him with Schmeisser for the next two weeks, missing what could have been a bad accident one day when the bulldozer Bobby was operating flipped forward and threw him off the front end. "The bulldozer was still moving," Bob remembers, "so I had to get out of there real quick, which I did, or I would have been badly mangled. It might have even killed me."

When Trent returned a fortnight later to Wilmington, he was distressed not so much by word of Bobby's mishap but by how little progress his son had made with his assigned task of shaping that single bunker. "You're never going to be any good to me unless you can work faster," he told his son. "What else have you done?" "Nothing," Bobby answered. "That's it." "Well, I have a design-and-build contract here," stressed Trent, using a term whose meaning was lost on Bobby at the time. "If you work that slowly, I'm going to go broke. I think you should go back to playing golf. We'll figure out how to pay for your flying lessons some other way."

"Dad was very polite about it, really," Bob remembers. "He was very complimentary. He didn't abuse me in any way. But time meant money, and he didn't want me wasting his time, or mine." Bobby got the money he needed for flying lessons. Schmeisser confirmed that Bobby had been working ten-hour days. "Dad paid me 'union scale.' I used the money for flying lessons and got a federal pilot's license while I was still sixteen, a year before I could even get a driver's license in New Jersey." I didn't mind going back to playing competitive golf; I preferred doing that."

Of Trent's two sons, Bobby was the more avid golfer and the superior player. In the summers of his teenage years, he played in tournaments sponsored by the New Jersey State Golf Association and the Metropolitan Golf Association of New York, placing high in a number of them. He was on the Montclair High School golf team that in his senior year won the state championship. He was also a member of the U.S. junior team that played the United Kingdom's junior team at Winged Foot in 1956. In his mid-teens Bobby started taking lessons from Tommy Armour, the "Silver Scot," ten years Trent's senior and the winner of the '27 U.S. Open, '30 PGA Championship, and '31 British Open. He also took lessons while he was in high school from Claude Harmon Sr., Winged Foot's head pro, who in 1948 became the last club professional to win a major championship, the Masters. Enrolling at Yale in 1957, Bobby made the university golf team, but it was not easy; four other players on the team were their state junior champions. Bobby made the team by winning his qualifying match, playing the last three holes in a March snowstorm. As good a player as he was, Bobby never seriously contemplated playing professionally, nor did his father or mother project that ambition onto him. "My mother would say, lightheartedly, 'Your father's a genius, a dreamer, and there's only room for one pro in the family.'"

While Rees could be competitive—mostly with his older brother—Bobby was competitive with everyone. "If I went after something, I was really going to go after it," Bob today recalls. "If I was going to be a Boy Scout, I had to be an Eagle Scout. If I was going to be an Eagle Scout, I was going to be the leader of the patrol."

---

* A few years later as a college student at Yale University, Bob and three of his friends from Beta Theta Pi fraternity started an informal flying club. Using a rented Piper Tri-Pacer (a four-seat light aircraft with fixed landing gear), Bob and his friends flew excursions that took them as far away as Sandusky, Ohio, a distance of 509 miles from their home airport in New Haven, Connecticut. He discontinued his piloting after his college years.

As for Rees, in Bob's view, "he wanted to do what I did. I became an Eagle Scout so he became an Eagle Scout. I get into Yale, so he has to go to Yale. I pledge Beta Theta Pi, he becomes a Beta." Rees sees his path differently. "I played basketball and baseball in high school over golf, unlike Bobby. He got a pilot's license, I didn't. Sure, I went to Yale, but that's where my mother wanted me to go. She encouraged me to go there because that's where her father went and she had already befriended people in the administration at Yale. Our family had a relationship there." The competitive nature of the Jones boys arose naturally from living with and observing the driving ambitions of their parents. "Our father was highly ambitious," Bob says with emphasis. "Our mother was very ambitious, too, more in a social sense. The whole ethos of our family was, if you're going to do something, be the best at it."

Rees did not share Bobby's personality; he also sought excellence in everything but he wasn't as compulsive about it. "Rees was always a good tournament player as a youngster," Trent recalled. "He could have been as good as Bobby, but he was into baseball and basketball and never worked as hard at golf as he might have. He was proud of the fact that he was as good as he was without having taken lessons from anybody but me." At Yale, he failed to qualify for the freshman team by one stroke, but the benefits of the vast Jones family social network continued to work on his behalf. "Because Bobby had been on the team, I knew Coach Al Wilson. As soon as I became a sophomore, he wanted me to be the manager of the freshman team."

Rees moved up to manager of the varsity in his junior year, practicing with the team, and that year he played with the Yale team that traveled to the NCAA Championships at Duke. Trent Jones had laid out the Duke University course in 1957; in 1994 Rees redesigned it, making it, in his words, "stronger and longer and with re-contoured greens." Rees also sent his daughter, Amy, to school at Duke.

Playing their college golf on the classic C. B. Macdonald golf course at Yale was undoubtedly valuable for their later careers as golf architects. Like their father, both Bobby and Rees became great admirers of the work of Macdonald, who designed the Yale course with his assistants Seth Raynor and Charles Banks. Yale was a memorable layout, built in the mid-1920s over incredibly rugged and rocky land, almost entirely wooded, and with a diverse range of golf holes that reflected the boldness and complexity of Macdonald's approach to golf architecture. The course—whose deliciously devilish combination of severe bunkering and treacherous greens Bobby and Rees had played hundreds of times over their college careers—had to have made a strong impression on the two young men.

Rees entered Yale already enamored with the idea of being a golf course architect. In an application he submitted for admission to Cornell, the seventeen-year-old Rees wrote: "Cornell is one of the few places where I can take courses that will give me a broad cultural background and at the same time take advantage of courses offered in other departments of the university to secure special knowledge and training towards going into golf course architecture, my father's profession." Cornell accepted Rees, but so did Yale. Bobby was already on the New Haven campus, and Ione wanted her sons to have a broad liberal arts education similar to what Wells College had provided her. She appreciated her husband's technical abilities, but she also knew her husband's intellectual limitations and wanted her sons to acquire a broader liberal arts education. Cornell might be able to train Rees (and Bobby, who had also applied to Cornell) better in the particulars of a given career, but she wanted her sons during their college days to cultivate a broadly informed intellect without specifying in advance how that intellect would be used, which was exactly what a Yale undergraduate education in the postwar decades was designed to achieve.

At Yale both Bobby and Rees followed an innovative new degree program known as "American Studies," a broad-ranging curriculum that emphasized the interdisciplinary study of literature, history, the arts, and the social sciences. Bobby's goal was to go to law school, but perhaps not to become a lawyer. "I was interested in government," Bob relates today. "It wasn't politics, it was public service. I was looking at public service as a career because Yale was inculcating me with that civic spirit." For ten weeks in the summer of 1959 he worked as an intern in the office of U.S. Senator Stuart Symington, Democrat from Missouri and a 1923 Yale graduate. It was a plum assignment for any college student, and golf had a lot to do with Bobby getting it. "I ranked in the middle of my class at Yale. Even my advisers wondered how I was selected. Two factors explained it. One, Senator Symington played golf, avidly. Two, my father bumped into him one day when he was in the company of Laurance Rockefeller, who my father knew well from building Rockefeller's Dorado Beach Golf Hotel Golf Course in Puerto Rico in 1958. To Senator Symington, Rockefeller said, 'You know, his son is interested in what you do.' 'Really?' Symington answered. 'Does he play golf as good as you, Trent?' Dad said, 'Oh, he's better.'" Bobby was in the group of Yale students that was submitted to Congress, and his selection reflected the power of the golf connections that ultimately flowed from Trent's business fame. The first time Symington spoke to Bobby after his internship started was to ask him to line up a game. "Oh, you're Trent's son," Symington said. "I can't play with you this week, but would you like to play at Chevy Chase [Country Club] next weekend?" From then on, almost every weekend, Bobby played golf with the senator. At the time Bobby was playing to a one- or two-handicap, and his job was "to stay quiet and make five-foot putts so Senator Symington could win his bets."

Bobby returned to Washington the following summer, traveling to the Democratic Convention in Los Angeles as director of "Youth for Symington." It was an exciting summer, with Symington a serious contender, though the nomination ultimately went to Senator John F. Kennedy from Massachusetts. Though Bobby went into his internship thinking primarily about public service, the electricity surrounding the presidential campaign pitting Kennedy against Vice President Richard M. Nixon attracted Bobby to partisan politics. Unlike Trent, who had adapted his political views to what was best for his golf design business and embraced a Republican view of the world, Bobby became a Kennedy supporter and an active, lifelong Democrat.

After graduating in 1961, and "feeling a yen to break away from family traditions," Bobby went west, where he entered Stanford University Law School. (Apparently Trent had been planning for Bob to join the family business, and later recalled that he was "dismayed" when Bob decided to go to law school.) In his second semester, however, Bob found the study of law "less to his liking than I expected" and quit school. He would, after all, rather design golf courses like his dad. But he didn't want to return to the East Coast and work directly with his parents. He loved the San Francisco Bay area and felt that his politics and social sensibilities were much more in tune with a California lifestyle. He convinced them both that the family business could expand into new markets, not just in California but throughout the Pacific Northwest, desert Southwest, and across the Pacific to Hawaii and even to Japan—but to do so, Robert Trent Jones, Inc., would need a West Coast office. He told his mom and dad that where he was already living, Palo Alto, would be the perfect spot for launching that new business hub.

On November 7, 1962, the West Coast office of Jones, Inc., opened for business at 374 Waverley Street in a small storefront in a shopping plaza not far from downtown Palo Alto. According to the story in the *Palo Alto Times*, the office would be headed by twenty-three-year-old Robert Trent Jones Jr., "former Stanford graduate student," with the assistance of Harvey Raynor, "ex-tournament supervisor for the PGA."

The creation of the West Coast office took place while Rees was in his senior year at Yale. To get the technical background he would need to design golf courses, he entered the landscape architecture program at the Harvard Graduate School of Design. There he met a recent graduate in history from Princeton University, Cabell B. Robinson, and the two became close friends. After a year together studying at Harvard, Cabell convinced Rees to leave Harvard, move out to California, and enter an undergraduate degree program in landscape architecture offered at the University of California at Berkeley. Rees agreed and the two young men gained admittance into Berkeley. After the first year, however, Rees lost his draft deferment and was about to be drafted into the Army, choosing instead to go into the Army Reserves. In 1965, following a year of military training, Rees returned home, where he joined his dad's firm, soon taking over supervision of the East Coast office in Montclair. When Cabell Robinson graduated from the Berkeley program in June 1967, Rees persuaded him to come to work with him in New Jersey. In 1970, with prospects for a number of Jones golf courses in Europe, Trent sent Cabell to Spain to organize a European office. Over the next seventeen years, Robinson handled most of the Jones projects done in Britain, Europe, and North Africa.

Trent could not have been more delighted. He was the progenitor of a true family business, and proud that both of his boys were following in his footsteps. "That helped not only in the design of courses," Jones later recalled, "but also in the business end of the operation. I was spending more and more time in the air, and poor Ione was struggling with the details at home. When Bobby and Rees arrived, it took a lot of pressure off her. . . . Although neither Bobby nor Rees decided to become golf course architects until they were adults, I suppose it was inevitable that they did. They literally grew up in the business."

The biggest assist to Ione over the coming years, and to Trent as well, would come not from their sons but from Roger G. Rulewich, a civil engineer—and another Yale graduate (Class of '58)—who joined the firm at age twenty-five in 1961, before either Bobby or Rees had come on board. For the next thirty-two years, Rulewich toiled in loyal obscurity for Trent and Ione, helping to build and carry out the business behind the scenes. While both Bobby and Rees would leave their dad's employ to establish firms of their own, Rulewich stayed on as

Trent's chief associate and, although receiving almost no national attention or acclaim of his own, developed into "a major force in the profession of golf architecture" and "among the most active course architects in the world." Without the talents, hard work, and loyalty of Roger Rulewich over all those decades, the trajectory of Robert Trent Jones Sr.'s career could not have reached the summit and scope that it did in the last three decades of his life. Ultimately Trent Jones would acknowledge Rulewich's indispensable contributions. "There are many talented and technically competent architects working today," Jones stated in the late 1980s, "some of whom perhaps don't get the recognition they deserve because they don't have their own firms and are tied in with the so-called bigger names. Roger Rulewich, my chief designer, is one of these. Roger is one of the best in the business and has a wonderful feeling for routing a golf course." From the start, Rulewich was not just "a wonderful employee," but Trent's "most valued employee." And not just an employee for Jones, either, but "my best friend," more like a third son, but one with a laid-back and easygoing personality quite different from either Bobby's or Rees's. "I don't know what I would have done without him for all these years."

Their meeting was providential for both Trent and Roger. "At Yale I took a degree in civil engineering," Rulewich explains. "I had very little touch with golf other than Yale having its own golf course. I had not played golf before coming to college. I had roommates who played, though not very well, so I started playing a little at Yale, an intimidating course. I didn't really know at the time how extraordinary that golf course was; I just thought that was what golf courses were like. I also didn't know what a golf course architect did, and didn't know much about the background of the game at all."

After graduation, Rulewich went to work for a big landscape architecture firm in New York City by the name of Clarke & Rapuano. Dr. Gilmore Clarke, who had been the head of Cornell's department of architecture, was the head of the firm, which was doing a lot of work on parkways and other public projects around metropolitan New York. When it became clear that the tedious engineering work required at Clarke & Rapuano wasn't for him, Rulewich put out his résumé to some architectural firms to see what he could find, using a placement service for alumni administered by the Yale Club in New York City. The job service responded with a lead to "Robert Trent Jones, Golf Architect." Rulewich didn't know who Jones was, so he assumed Jones was an architect who built golf clubhouses. They met at the Yale Club. "Mr. Jones told me what he did, and I couldn't believe that he didn't do any building architectural work but instead designed golf courses; that was how little I knew. He said he needed someone with an engineering background and offered me a little more money than I was making. 'Just give your company the appropriate amount of time for you to leave,' Jones told me, 'and then head down to my office in New York.' Well, I really disliked what I had been doing, so I ran right back to the company and told my boss, who was one of the partners, that I was leaving.

"The next day when I walked into Jones's office on Vesey Street and told them I was their new employee, nobody knew what I was talking about. Mr. Jones wasn't there and he hadn't told any of them he had offered me a job. So it was an interesting walk-in, 'who are you?' kind of thing. No one seemed to be doing much. There was a secretary [Mary Psihas] sitting there smoking cigarettes and reading the newspaper, a financial business partner and accountant [Richard M. Sargent] at a desk who I learned came into the office only now and then to do the books, and a draftsman [John Benedetto] in the back room, but he wasn't doing any work because he was going to night school and studying during the day." The other key person in the office, Frank Duane, wasn't around, either. "Duane was pretty responsible for a lot of Jones's work on projects in the region, so I didn't meet him for several days." Left almost entirely on his own, Rulewich looked around the office and did what he could to assist with some of the drafting of projects that were already underway. It wasn't long before Frank Duane left the Jones business and went out on his own. "I think Frank thought that my being there was going to take some of the work away from him," Roger speculates.

One of Rulewich's chief early accomplishments was moving Jones's operation from the office in Lower Manhattan to Jones's home in Montclair. "I suggested to Jones that maybe there wasn't a point to having the office in New York City. I guess at one time he must have thought a New York address was important, on his stationery, if nothing else." The key to what became a successful move was organizing the many dozens of golf course blueprints that lay in disarray in a dusty closet of the Vesey Street office. "All of Jones's course plans had been wrapped up in brown butcher's paper, a number or name scribbled on them, and thrown into the closet," Rulewich remembers. "It was murder to go back there to find anything. Many of the labels had been torn off so I had to go through every single one. I spent months and months unwrapping and going through them, afraid to throw anything away, creating a better system for all these plans.

"The Montclair home was a big house. They had some extra rooms in the back of the house that we turned into office space. Jones would spend time there when he was at home; so that was his office. Before that, the rooms would have been servants' quarters or something. That became Jones's office, his operation.

"I wasn't given a lot of direction. I was always trying to find out what the heck this golf course architecture was all about. I started reading about Jones; in terms of finding out about architecture, I didn't know where to start other than Jones himself. I found Herbert Warren Wind's article in *The New Yorker*. I also saw a *Sports Illustrated* article ("Golf's Battling Architects," July 2, 1962) about how Trent Jones and Dick Wilson were the two premier architects at the time and something of rivals. I learned by osmosis. There was no 'Robert Trent Jones 101'."

As it would be for Rees when he joined the business in 1965, on the occasions when Rulewich first got out on projects, it was Bill Baldwin who taught him what building a golf course was really all about. "Bill was a great guy. We learned an awful lot through Bill. He was always involved in shaping and breaking down the parts of the golf course." After Frank Duane left, Rulewich spent more time in the field, sometimes alone and sometimes in the company of Jones, gradually learning more and more about both the design process and dealing with clients. One thing Roger learned quickly by being with Jones out on business was that "I think the force of his personality was what caused him to succeed with a lot of people. He was great at meeting people. He somehow met people at the right time in the right place. His ears were always cupped for anyone who was talking about golf. So much of the business he was able to generate was based on personal contact and his salesmanship, and the public speaking aspect."

Rulewich didn't play golf very well, which Trent felt could be a great disadvantage when dealing with certain clients. "Roger was not a good golfer. He couldn't drive the ball more than 200 yards. So I said to him, 'I've got to teach you. You've got to play better golf. You can't judge anything as a golf course designer unless you know the shot values.' I taught him how to swing better and he got so he became a pretty big hitter. He developed a good feel for championship courses."

Roger always listened. He took to being tutored willingly, carefully, and with an open mind. Rulewich was not lugging the personal and emotional baggage that Rees and Bobby carried. They had to deal with the psychological effects of descending from, and ultimately competing with, their famous father, but they also had to contend with the implications of their increasingly fraught fraternal rivalry.

In June 1965, Robert Trent Jones turned fifty-nine. In the thirty-five years since he had launched his architectural career at Midvale, he had finished 175 projects, including fifty-nine 18-hole courses, three 27-hole layouts, one three-hole and one two-hole project, and eighty-four different remodeling jobs. In just the previous five years his company had completed seventy-four jobs in twenty-six states and five foreign countries. More than three-quarters of the U.S. projects were east of the Mississippi River.

Having Bob Jr. on the West Coast was a definite boon to the Jones business. As Bobby had said to his father before opening the office in Palo Alto, "We're missing a lot of business in the West." The biggest bonanza came in California, from San Diego County (where Pauma Valley Country Club, a top 100 course, had been designed by Trent Jones and built by Bill Baldwin in 1960) all the way north to the Oregon border. The projects included Mission Viejo Country Club in San Juan Capistrano; Valencia Country Club near Santa Clarita; several executive courses, both with and without the partnership of Sam Snead; redesigns of San Gabriel Country Club, Bel-Air Country Club, the California Golf Club of San Francisco, and the Stanford University Golf Club in Palo Alto. The Palo Alto office also administered Robert Trent Jones projects in Arizona, Nevada, Oregon, Idaho, North Dakota, Nebraska, Kansas, Texas, and Alaska.

Eugene Country Club in Oregon is one course from this period that boasted a top-100 listing in the rankings of virtually all the golf course magazines after Trent (with some assistance from Bobby) reworked it in 1965–66. As Trent later remembered the process, "It began as remodeling and finished as one of the most startling reversals, literally, that I have ever heard of. It was a nice course that wound through beautiful trees a hundred feet or more high. But somehow it seemed all wrong. We tramped the property and studied it. I wanted to reroute some holes, but that would have meant removing some of those magnificent trees. Bobby kept saying, 'Dad, you can't do that.'" Bobby had played Eugene Country Club in the 1959 NCAA Men's Golf Championships, and he had a feel for what the course had been, especially as play related to the layout's massive stands of evergreens, maples, oaks, and ornamentals—some sixty varieties of trees in all. "Large trees frequently induce you to hit short on your approach shot when they're positioned just off the back of the green," Bobby reminded his dad. "From a psychological point of view, players often become preoccupied with the prospect of playing out of trees, which causes them to under-club. In addition, if the trees are larger than the course's other trees or the trees you're used to seeing, they make you think the green is considerably closer than it is."

But the key to the redesign wasn't the trees as much as it was the water hazards on the golf course. "I finally figured out what was wrong," explained Trent. "Wherever the water came into play it was in front of the tee instead of the green. So Bobby and I discussed reversing a few of the holes. Then I suggested we reverse the entire course. I took the idea to the board of directors, and it was so shocking that they bought it. The membership had to vote on it, and it was a year before we got approval, by one vote. A lot of folks don't want to give up their favorite holes, you understand. So we reversed the course, building championship greens in place of the tiny ones there and adding a few other embellishments. When it was finished, most of the members who had been against it came to us and told us how glad they were we had done it."

In the opinion of both Trent and Bobby, their redesigned Eugene Country Club became one of the great unknown courses in the country. It was the site of the 1978 NCAA Championships, won by Scott Simpson, a future U.S. Open winner. In 1987 Eugene Country Club was selected in a survey conducted by the American Society of Golf Course Architects (and run for the ASGCA by Bobby) as one of the best 100 courses in the United States.

It didn't take long for Bobby the apprentice to start moving away from his father to his own design philosophies and approaches. This movement toward independence can be seen in the design of the two 18-hole layouts at Silverado Country Club in the Napa Valley in 1966–67.

The original Silverado Country Club opened for play in 1955. In 1966, a wealthy Stockton farmer-turned-real-estate-developer, Ed Westgate, purchased the Silverado property for $3 million. Aspiring to turn Silverado into a "destination resort," Westgate's company built California's first condominiums on the property and turned to RTJ, Inc., to add a second golf course. It was an ambitious project, one worth a great deal of money. Most importantly, due to Silverado's location only eighty miles from Palo Alto, Silverado provided Bobby with an opportunity to put his personal stamp on a prominent project.

In retrospect, Bobby would view the Silverado project as the moment when he moved from being his father's apprentice to designing golf courses of his own making. "The young must eventually 'fly on their own,'" Bobby would say, and Silverado was his "time of parting" from his father's dominant influence. People had said that "Dad's courses were getting too tough," and Bobby "wanted to ease the pressure by offering more play options than my father was wont to do." He agreed with Westgate that for the golfers who came to enjoy themselves at a luxury resort like Silverado, the golf courses shouldn't be too demanding or hard to play. Bobby and his dad had some heated discussions about what to do with the golf courses, and Trent disagreed with many of Bob's choices, but Ed Westgate said he liked the character of the layouts that Bobby was proposing. Besides going with a shorter overall length for each of the two golf courses, Westgate also liked how Bobby wanted to incorporate "many of the already existing natural and cultural features of the site into the course design for enhanced dramatic effect." While designing Silverado, Bobby told his father, "You can come by and criticize it, but I want this to be mine. And I may not accept your criticism."

Yet Dad nonetheless influenced Bobby's design work at Silverado. As Trent Sr. had done at The Broadmoor, Bobby didn't just build a second golf course at Silverado; he transformed elements of the existing 18 into essential components of two new challenging courses. From the regulation tees, Bobby set up the North to play to 6,351 yards and the South to play 6,213 yards. Women played the courses at 5,757 and 5,719 yards, respectively, which actually were not short measurements for the games of most women. Although Silverado possessed many characteristics in common with the golf courses of Trent Jones Sr., some of its architecture did communicate a noticeably "gentler feel," especially on the South Course, which golfers found a pleasure to play, with straightforward fairways, benign bunkerings, and flatter, easier-to-putt greens.

For the most part, Trent welcomed the divergent perspective Bobby was developing. For example, when Jones, Inc., got the job in 1968 to build the West Delta Park Golf Course in Portland, Oregon, Trent assumed that Bobby would create a course that was in some basic ways quite different from his father's work. Located in the Columbia River floodplain near its confluence with the Willamette, West Delta was a dead-flat site just minutes from downtown Portland whose main attribute was its incredible views of Mount Hood and Mount St. Helens. Rather than demanding a championship golf course un-suitable for the needs of beginning golfers, seniors, and most amateurs, Bobby conceived of a municipal golf course with "a generally easygoing demeanor" that could become "the flagship of public golf in Portland." Though the length of the par-72 layout could be stretched to 6,608 yards, Bobby's design made the greens large and welcoming, the bunkering only moderately difficult, and the teeing areas of appropriately flexible distances for golfers of all skill levels.[†] When the course opened for play in 1971, Trent came to take a look at West Delta Park Golf Course and was happy to add it to the list of courses his company had designed. He took special pride in it being a public course, a genre for which "I have received many compliments over the years."

Once Bobby began to break from apprenticeship under his father at Silverado and West Delta Park to a more independent approach to design, it was not likely that he would accede ever again to his father's dominant architectural style, even when the work was being done under the imprimatur of his father's company. In the chapter on Silverado in the 1988 book *The Golf Courses of Robert Trent Jones, Jr*, the editors assert that after the completion of Silverado, "[i]t was now time for him and his father to part ways professionally. Bobby started his own company." That company was not Robert Trent Jones II, however, which was not established—for domestic work—until 1976. Bobby's first company, begun in 1972, was Pacific Planners International, Ltd., based in New Caledonia, an island off the northeastern coast of Australia. Pacific Planners was a company exclusively for non-U.S. projects. Within the United States, from the time of Silverado's completion in 1967 until the creation of RTJ II nine years later, Bobby continued to do his work for Jones, Inc., the parent company, or under the name of the corporation he created in 1965, Robert Trent Jones of California, Inc.[‡]

---

† West Delta Park Golf Course eventually got so much play that the city called Bob Jr. back to expand the facility to 36 holes. The new course, called "Great Blue" after the great blue heron rookery inside the park, opened one nine at a time in 1988 and 1992. At 6,916 yards, it was more challenging to golfers than the original course, which became known as the "Greenback Course." Both were fine public courses and were ranked among the best in the Pacific Northwest. When construction started on the second 18 in 1988, an ordinance of the Portland city council changed the name of the overall facility to Heron Lakes Golf Club. In 2000, Heron Lakes hosted the U.S. Amateur Public Links. See Brandon Tucker, "Portland, Oregon's local favorite, Heron Lakes Golf Club, gives muni courses a good name," *WorldGolf,* 8 Apr. 2010, accessed on 7 Aug. 2013, at http://www.worldgolf.com/course-reviews/heron-lakes-golf-club-portland-oregon-11210.htm.

‡ Some accounts of Bobby's leaving his dad's company and starting his own business assert that the date for these events was 1972; other accounts place them in 1974. However, the establishment of Robert Trent Jones II did not take place until 1976. One source for this latter date

That doesn't mean that Bobby wasn't the primary architect on many of these jobs. In its portfolio of completed golf course designs, the website of Robert Trent Jones II today includes all of the following: Birnam Wood Golf Course in Santa Barbara (1968); the two eighteens of Crestview Country Club (1969); the redesign of Glendora Country Club (1969–70); Laguna Seca Golf Ranch in Monterey (1970); Incline Green Golf Course at Lake Tahoe and Lakeridge Country Club in Reno (1971); Rio Rico Golf Course in Arizona (1971–72); Spring Valley Lake Golf Course in California's Apple Valley (1971); Eagleglen Golf Course in Alaska (1972); Lake Shastina's regulation and par-3 courses (1972); the Slick Rock Course at Horseshoe Bay in Texas (1972–73); Bodega Harbour (1974–76); the executive course at Forest Meadows Golf Course and Resort in Calaveras County (1974); the Elkhorn Course in Idaho's Sun Valley (1974–75); and Oxbow Country Club in North Dakota (1975). All of the above courses are also listed in the official portfolio of Robert Trent Jones Sr.; all were built under contract to RTJ, Inc. Bobby continued to direct a number of projects both for Jones, Inc., on the West Coast and under contract to Robert Trent Jones of California, Inc., which was established in 1965 but understood by all parties involved to be a subsidiary of RTJ, Inc. In other words, for this period of between five and nine years, the operation Bobby ran was organizationally ambiguous; he was designing golf courses both for himself and for his father, often without any clear distinction even in the mind of the client as to what was going on behind the scenes at RTJ, Inc., Robert Trent Jones of California, Inc., and RTJ II.

Though Bobby saw Silverado as the "parting place" where he began to take over the design of Robert Trent Jones, Inc., golf courses, travel records and other documents in the Jones Papers at Cornell indicate that his dad visited nearly all of Bobby's projects at least once or twice—and some of them more than that. Also, Trent usually provided his son with a number of hand-drawn sketches of

---

is a letter from Richard M. Spray of Bobby's Palo Alto office to Editor, Golf Market Report, National Golf Foundation, Inc., 200 Castlewood Dr., North Palm Beach, Fla., June 1, 1979. Under a letterhead reading "Robert Trent Jones II, Golf Course Design and Recreational Planning," Spray wrote: "As noted on the attached copy of your May 1979 GMR [Golf Management Report], you have Robert Trent Jones, Inc., credited as GCA. This is incorrect: the firm name should read Robert Trent Jones II. We are making a point of calling this to your attention by letter inasmuch as you may not be aware that we are now (and, in fact, have been since 1976), a completely separate company from Robert Trent Jones, Inc." This letter was made available to the author from the files of Robert Trent Jones II, Palo Alto, CA.

green complexes that he asked Bobby to incorporate into the golf courses. About the golf course at Laguna Seca Ranch, for example, which was finished in Monterey County in 1970, the editors of the 1988 book on Bobby's courses explained: "Laguna Seca is a rugged 18 holes of golf. Robert Trent Jones Sr. began work on this course, and then gave the work over into the capable hands of his then-assistant, Robert Trent Jones Jr. This course is said to play like a mellow yet exciting combination of both the master architects' styles. As he loves to do when it is possible, Robert Trent Jones Jr. melded his course into its countryside: he has designed a course that weaves through copses of oaks, winding uphill and down." About Lakeridge Country Club, finished in 1971, the editors of the book concluded: "This course is a symphony in green, created by that maestro among golf course designers, Robert Trent Jones Jr." About Bodega Harbour's nine holes along the Pacific Ocean, completed in 1974, the editors simply and directly called it a "Robert Trent Jones Jr course."

Some might wonder how Bobby could have moved from apprentice to the status of master architect in the less than ten-year time frame in which he had been working with and for his father. But Trent himself had come just as far as a designer from 1930 to 1940, had boldly promoted himself as one of America's greatest architects by the end of the 1930s, and had even stretched, for promotional purposes, to take credit for the design of some of Stanley Thompson's golf courses. Bobby's growth seems consistent with the ambitious example set by his father, and with the traits of the personality that Bobby, the namesake, seems both to have inherited and learned.

Besides being a great asset for business up and down the West Coast, Bobby's Palo Alto office provided a convenient jumping-off point for the expansion of RTJ, Inc.'s business into Hawaii and beyond. This business blossomed in the Aloha State very quickly after Hawaii joined the Union in August 1959 as the 50th state. In the Hawaiian Islands, Trent took on the design of some of the most challenging, profitable, and noteworthy golf courses of his entire career. Bobby's assistance and outright direction in some of these Hawaiian projects proved highly formative to his own career as a golf architect, enabling him in the end to build many more golf courses in Hawaii and throughout the Pacific than even his father had.

Hawaii has been one of the world's most popular travel destinations for more than half a century. We are accustomed to seeing a couple million tourists a year traveling to the Islands for vacations, romantic getaways, golf holidays, and honeymoons. But that wasn't the case before 1960. Until Hawaii was granted U.S. statehood, tourism to the territory amounted to fewer than ten thousand visitors a year. Along with the advantages that came with statehood, there were several other factors that quickly changed Hawaii's tourist economy. In March 1960 the DC-8 and other commercial jet airliners began to fly to Honolulu from the West Coast, which cut the flying time by three hours. With United Airlines, Eastern Airlines, and other major companies promoting travel to Hawaii, millions of dollars poured into Madison Avenue to create alluring TV and magazine advertising campaigns. In 1961 the hugely popular Elvis Presley movie *Blue Hawaii* made millions of dollars and stimulated millions of Americans, young and old, to dream about hula dancers. Two more Elvis-in-Hawaii films came to the big screen by 1965. Add in the popularity of such regular TV programs as *Hawaiian Eye,* which aired on the American Broadcasting Corporation television network from October 1959 to September 1963, and it's easy to understand why, by 1967, the number of tourists to Hawaii had jumped from fewer than ten thousand in 1960 to more than a million.

In the early 1960s, Jones built three new golf courses in the Aloha State. Two were created in league with large hotel and resort developments, while the other came to life in association with one of Hawaii's largest-ever planned residential communities. The projects took him to each of the three major islands: Oahu, Maui, and Hawaii, better known as the "Big Island." Then in 1969, along with adding a course on the northwest coast of Hawaii, he sent Bobby to Kauai, where they built 27 holes for a major new resort on the north shore of the "Garden Isle." And that was only the beginning of the Jones brand in the Hawaiian Islands: In the following decades, Bobby would himself build ten original resort and subdivision golf courses on Maui, Hawaii, and Kauai.

The $40-million American Factors/Pioneer Mill Company resort development at Ka'anapali Beach on the western shore of Maui first brought Trent Jones to Hawaii. Originally founded in 1849 as a retail and sugar business, American Factors was the dominant sugar company in Hawaii, the founder of one of its best-known department stores (Liberty House), and at its peak the owner of more than 60,000 acres of land, five thousand of which was in Ka'anapali on Maui, one of the most lush and beautiful of the Hawaiian Islands. It was land that had a special place in the heart of native Hawaiians because Ka'anapali lay just north of Lahaina, which, besides once serving as the seat of royal government in the Kingdom of Hawaii, had been the center of the global whaling industry, with sailing ships moored at its waterfront even into the twentieth century. But as with many native historical sites in the Hawaiian Islands, business, real estate, and industrial "progress" overwhelmed much of Ka'anapali's heritage. In the early 1960s, American Factors, in association with the Pioneer Mill Company (Hawaii's largest sugar processor), began to develop 800 acres of thickets and cane fields on a two-and-a-half-mile-long, crescent-shaped Maui beachfront into the Ka'anapali Beach Resort. Waiting for the very first guests to arrive at the Maui resort would be an 18-hole, championship-caliber golf course designed by Robert Trent Jones.

For the Royal Ka'anapali Golf Course, Jones took advantage of a rolling landscape to create gently sloping fairways, many with tight approaches to large, contoured greens. In his original routing Jones had the golf course begin along the sea, then hug the shoreline before winding its way into the rolling foothills of the West Maui Mountains, then finally turning downward toward a long lagoon where the "lower nine" finished near the clubhouse. The "upper nine" (later called the "Mountain nine") began by immediately moving into the more severely contoured land of the foothills; the holes were shorter and had no water hazards, but the greens were much more severely contoured to "capture the flavor of the mountainous terrain on which they were built." Altogether, Royal Ka'anapali was a "big course," as Jones described it, stretching to 7,215 yards at par 72 from the back tees. For tournaments, he felt it would be "a course from which only true champions will emerge, since they will have to play all the shots in their repertoire to score well here."

It did not take long for Trent to be proven right. In 1964 the Canada Cup was held on the golf course, barely two years after it had opened. Prior to the tournament, the two nines were reversed so that the closing nine played closest to the shoreline; Jones also made some other refinements to toughen up the course a bit more for the event, including lengthening some of the holes on the Mountain nine. The competition was 72 holes of cumulative medal play, with two-man teams representing some twenty nations. The home state of Hawaii was honored with an invitation to enter a team of its own. The United States team of Jack Nicklaus and Arnold Palmer won the Cup, going away with a record total for the event of 554, an average of 69.2 per round. Nicklaus and Palmer finished first and second in the contest for the individual title, with twenty-four-year-old Jack edging thirty-five-year-old Arnie by two shots, 276 to

278. Ted Makalena thrilled his fellow Hawaiians by tying Gary Player of South Africa for third place at 279. After the event, Palmer praised the 18th hole as one of the best and most challenging par-4 finishing holes he had ever played. At 449 yards, the hole played longer than it looked, hugging the lagoon the entire length of the fairway all the way to the green. There was universal agreement that the tournament was "one of the most successful in the world-wide series that began in 1953" and that Jones's first golf course in Hawaii, located in not just a picturesque but a "breathtaking" setting, had turned out to be a real gem.

At Royal Ka'anapali, Trent invested more than his time, talent, and energies as a golf architect; he also invested some of his money. More and more often from the 1950s on, Jones had begun to settle less and less for just being the golf architect; he wanted a piece of the action in the overall real estate development. At Ka'anapali, American Factors paid him a $200,000 architect's fee, a quarter of which he took in the form of a minority ownership in the golf course and related cottage hotel.

Over the course of his career, once word got out that Jones was building a golf course in a certain part of the country, other potential clients who lived or worked in that area quickly popped up to offer him additional work. In the case of Hawaii, once American Factors brought Jones to Maui to build Royal Ka'anapali, it didn't take long for another Hawaii resident to contact Jones about building a golf course for a major new resort that he was building on the island of Oahu. That man was Henry J. Kaiser of Kaiser Aluminum.

Henry Kaiser (1882–1967) was himself a relative newcomer to the Islands. In 1954 the industrialist—who became known as the father of modern American shipbuilding for constructing the World War II fleet of Liberty ships—came to Hawaii on a vacation with his second wife. Finding no satisfactory hotel accommodations on Honolulu's Waikiki Beach, he rented a house near Diamond Head, then sat back and wondered who would "house the hordes of mainlanders" that he felt sure would someday soon discover the natural beauty and balmy climate not just of Oahu but of all the Hawaiian Islands. Kaiser was not the sort of man to sit on his ideas. In 1914 he had founded a paving company that was one of the first to use heavy construction machinery. In the early 1930s his firm was one of the prime contractors in building the Hoover, Bonneville, and Grand Coulee dams. During World War II he mass-produced the Liberty ships. In 1945 he established a company that built automobiles. The following year, he founded Kaiser Aluminum, which came to dominate the aluminum industry worldwide. In the early 1950s, he created the Kaiser Permanente medical care program for his many thousand employees, the forerunner of modern HMOs; he also established Kaiser Federal Bank.

It is hard to say whether Kaiser fell more in love with the beauty and climate of Hawaii or with the potential of turning Hawaii into a hugely profitable tropical paradise and a wonderful place for affluent people like Kaiser himself to live, spend money, and cultivate the tropical good life. In 1960 Kaiser brought Trent Jones to Hawaii to build what was initially planned as a complex of three courses to go along with a mammoth residential development that Kaiser was building less than fifteen miles around the coastline east of Honolulu, amidst some of the most breathtaking sightseeing points and attractions in all of Oahu. Kaiser dubbed his development "Hawaii Kai," borrowing the native Hawaiian word "kai," meaning "seaside," which was also the first syllable of his own surname. Although Hawaii Kai was largely a residential development, it was to include, besides the three golf courses, a marina, plus channels for boats separated by fingers of land (or by islands) upon which home lots and commercial properties were laid out for sale.

The first plot of land that Kaiser assigned to Trent Jones for a golf course lay at the base of Makapuu Cliffs and was to be an executive 18-hole layout; the other two courses, of regulation length, were to be constructed later after the Hawaii Kai development had grown sufficiently in size—at least, that was the original concept. On that snug piece of land, Jones created a wonderful 2,223-yard, par-54 golf course on a site where the trade winds were always blowing and golfers enjoyed stunning views of the extinct Koko Head Volcano from every hole. On a clear day, golfers could see across the water to Maui and Molokai; in the winter months, players could catch a glimpse of whales spouting water. It was not an easy golf course, even though the average distance per hole was less than 125 yards. Jones made the greens small, and the terrain for the putting surfaces was naturally sloping and undulating. When Hawaii Kai opened in 1962, it proved to be a great test of a golfer's short-iron, chipping, and putting skills, and a very enjoyable course to play.

In the end, only one other golf course got built at Hawaii Kai, and Trent Jones didn't build it. In August 1967, Henry Kaiser died at age eighty-five. All planning for the other two courses temporarily came to a halt. By the time the project was revived in the early 1970s, Jones, Inc., was too busy building other courses, not just across the United States but also in England, Morocco, Italy,

Switzerland, and Brazil. (In this period Bobby was growing the Jones name by building courses as far away as Japan and Thailand.)

The third and largest Hawaiian project for Trent Jones in the early 1960s was the creation of Mauna Kea Beach Resort Golf Course. Completed in 1966 at a cost of $2 million for just the 18-hole golf course alone, the entire resort project (the hotel cost $15 million) was financed by venture capitalist Laurance Rockefeller, the fourth child of John D. Rockefeller and the brother to David Rockefeller, CEO of the Chase Manhattan Bank, and prominent New York politician Nelson A. Rockefeller, the governor of New York and later U.S. vice president under Gerald R. Ford.

In the 1950s, Rockefeller had begun to build high-priced resorts in purposefully remote and unlikely places—difficult-to-get-to locations where he could combine his principal interest of making money with conservation of the natural environment, not for the future but for the here and now, when people living now could enjoy it. His initial such venture had been Jackson Lake Lodge in the Wyoming wilderness of Grand Teton National Park. That was followed by Caneel Bay Plantation on the distant island of St. John in the U.S. Virgin Islands. Then came Little Dix Bay on the mountainous island of Virgin Gorda in the British Virgin Islands, a secluded resort requiring a small plane, boat, and jeep trip to get there. Dorado Beach, where Jones built his first golf course for Rockefeller, was as convenient as any of his resorts to get to, and it was located twenty miles down the coast from San Juan with a connecting route "more byway than freeway." Hawaii definitely interested Rockefeller, who, in the early 1960s, incorporated his collection of resort properties into Rockresorts, Inc. ("Rock," of course, short for "Rockefeller"). Later in the decade, besides going ahead with and finishing Mauna Kea, Rockresorts built the Woodstock Inn in Vermont and The Boulders in Carefree, Arizona.

A pioneer in every sense, "with a big name, a big bankroll, and the nerve to risk millions of dollars in some of the world's littlest places," Rockefeller was more than willing to build a resort in Hawaii. His method of doing business was highly professional and totally thorough—he left no stone unturned. He would build a paradise resort in Hawaii, but not without feasibility studies and a personal inspection of possible sites.

Trent Jones was an instrumental part of Rockefeller's Hawaiian search. Rockefeller invited Trent to Hawaii not long after he had completed his work at Dorado Beach. "As we were flying over the Big Island, he suddenly pointed out and said to me, 'Trent, that's exactly the kind of beach I'm looking for.'" Rockefeller was looking at Kaunaoa Bay, a half-mile-long, crescent-shaped cove protected by rock outcroppings and ringed by sand and scrub. As he and Jones soon discovered, it was part of the Parker Ranch, a tract of nearly a quarter million acres along the Kawaihae coast on the northwest shoulder of the island. (Besides being one of the largest cattle ranches in America, Parker Ranch was also one of the oldest, founded in 1841.) Towering above it some twenty-eight miles to the southeast was majestic Mauna Kea, nearly fourteen thousand feet high at its peak, the highest point in all of Hawaii, and its neighbor Mauna Loa, still an active volcano, almost as high as Mauna Kea and a great deal more massive, twelve miles farther away to the south. From the air, the landscape looked spectacular for Rockefeller's first Hawaiian resort: snowcapped mountains on one side and the rolling, furiously beautiful Pacific on the other.

On the ground, however, the site did not look nearly as inviting. As Trent recalled, "The land was hostile, almost like a moonscape. What we were considering for the golf course was a lava wasteland, over 230 acres of lava hills. The site was so dry, located as it was on the leeward side of the island with scant rainfall, that only scattered cactus plants were growing there. It was the most challenging terrain I had ever faced. But the potential certainly was there."

Only on the rarest occasion had Trent Jones been forced to tell a developer or club builder that the land that the client had chosen was not suitable for a golf course; almost never in his career had there been a place where he felt a golf course just could not be built. Rockefeller's site on the Big Island's lava-covered northwestern coast came as close to being an impossible property to work with as anything Trent had ever come across. But it was also one with the most sensational potential.

"We took a walking tour of the property, and I was excited," Jones remembered. "The terrain was undulating, almost like linksland. There were elevations for the tees, nice pockets for the greens, everything you would want for a great golf course. But the land was desolate, covered with brown volcanic rock, cinder, large boulders and scrub-like vegetation in the higher areas, impenetrable jungle in the valleys that was fed by moisture from the ocean. The average rainfall was only eight inches."

"Trent, how are you going to grow grass on this place?" Rockefeller asked him. "It depends on whether we can work with the lava rock," Jones replied. "If it can be crushed, maybe it can be used as a soil base. If it can, and if there is enough water, I think we can build a golf course." Jones picked up two rocks and hit them together. They shattered. He picked up two other rocks and they didn't shatter. "We have two kinds of lava here," he told Rockefeller. "One of these lava types will crush, so we have a chance of making a soil out of it. The other, the 'blue rock,' doesn't crush, so we'll have to find some other way to handle it."

Jones brought his West Coast construction superintendents John Dellis and Homer Flint to the Mauna Kea property; the duo had been the contractors who had just built Spyglass Hill. Their construction crews crushed sand, used rollers with spikes on them, dug out a well to get the water, and spread the crushed lava, rust-red in color, over the soil. About two months later Rockefeller and his wife paid a visit. They saw 15 acres of grass where only rugged lava rock had been. As Jones remembered, "the two of them were like kids!" They were so surprised and happy to see all the green grass. "Okay, let's go ahead now," Rockefeller exclaimed.

It was an arduous process, hacking fairway corridors and green sites out of the lava flow that had covered the area eons before, and then preparing a soil from the lava in which turfgrass would grow lush and green. Using heavy machinery fitted with a specially ribbed roller that Jones and Homer Flint themselves invented, they crushed the lava into a red dust the consistency of talcum powder and spread almost a foot of it over the entire course. The wind blew the dust around something awful, forcing the construction crew to wear face masks. Many pairs of pants were ruined because the red dust wouldn't come out. It took repeated gradings and rollings by the bulldozer with the special spikes to crush all the brittle lava down to the powdery consistency that was needed. To stabilize the crushed lava, Jones mixed it with lime from piles of coral sand that had been dredged from nearby Kawaihae Bay to create a harbor for local fishing boats and the occasional yacht. Pulverized in the same way as the volcanic rock, this material was then spread liberally over the lava soil to a thickness of three inches. All of this artifice required a great deal of water to stabilize the shapes and allow the grass to flourish. Two wells, each some four hundred feet deep, were dug, and an elaborate automatic underground watering system was designed and installed to pump a million gallons of water onto the seeded fairways and greens, a volume of water that later proved sufficient to keep the Mauna Kea course in prime condition all year round. The watering system was one of the first fully automatic underground irrigation systems installed on a golf course anywhere, and at Mauna Kea it created a virtual oasis in the desert.

"When the seed sprouted," Jones recalled with pride, "we got the cleanest grass you've ever seen. There were no weeds, because nothing had ever grown in the material before." All 130 acres of the golf course grew a thick carpet of a new variety of hybrid Bermuda grass, a strain so well suited to Hawaii's tropical climate that the grass emerged with all the fine qualities of mainland bent grass. As for the course's sand traps and bunkers, numbering 120 in all, the coral sand from the harbor dredging was so bountiful that Jones and Flint used it to fill all of them. To beautify the landscaping, Jones brought in hundreds of coconut palms and indigenous Hawaiian flowering trees and plants, including rainbow shower, the bright red wiliwili flower, monkeypod, and Chinese Banyan. Besides accenting the landscape, these plantings helped anchor the topsoil to the lava base.

Through it all there was still the problem of the blue rock lava that wouldn't crush. As it turned out, "blue rock" was the bane of local contractors in Hawaii, especially road builders and pipeline installers, because it was so difficult to break up. The largest bulldozers and backhoes were regularly humbled by the dense rock, which forced contractors to revert to expensive drilling and blasting techniques. A great deal of such excavating was also needed at Mauna Kea. As Jones later described it, "It was totally unworkable, and the larger portions had to be blasted, buried, or bulldozed. Those portions we could handle we used as coarse foundation for the tees and greens or to fill in fissures and crevices."

In more than a half century of creating golf courses, building the golf course at Mauna Kea was, by Jones's own estimation, the hardest job he had ever encountered, the most difficult site since the Durand Eastman Park Golf Course in Rochester, which he had built with WPA labor—and no heavy machinery— in the early 1930s. Mauna Kea was also by far the most expensive course he had built, costing some $2 million, the equivalent of more than $15 million in today's money. It may very well have been the most expensive golf course ever built up to that time, by anyone. But its construction methods made it easier, and cheaper, for subsequent golf courses to be built in Hawaii on similar lava-covered properties. By the mid-1980s there were five or six courses along the coastline of the Big Island, including some built by son Bobby (Waikoloa Village Golf Course and the Beach Course at Waikoloa Beach Golf Club) that "might never have been built without using those procedures."

Mauna Kea turned out to be exactly the jewel of a golf course that Rockefeller wanted for his latest and most lavish resort: a golf course that—like the ultra-modern, $15 million, open-air Mauna Kea Beach Hotel (*Esquire* magazine once named it one of the three greatest hotels in the world) that went with it—made an instant and lifelong impression on visitors.[§] Driving the twenty miles from the Big Island's Kona airport to Mauna Kea, all one saw was barren lava fields. Then, all of a sudden, a verdant haven appeared, like a mirage. The visual effect was spectacular. When golfers played the links, they were even more surprised to find that Mauna Kea wasn't just an extraordinarily beautiful golf course with panoramic views of sea and land, but an often seriously challenging par-72 layout—yes, some in the golf media again labeled it a "monster"—if played at its full length of 7,144 yards (today, after a complete tee-to-green "restoration" by Rees Jones finished in 2008, it can be stretched to 7,370 yards). Trent, as was his wont, also built tees that permitted golfers to choose a much shorter yardage—6,593 yards from the regular tees and 5,644 yards from the women's teeing areas.

Jones's layout on the Big Island met, and exceeded, all of the essential criteria required of an outstanding golf course: shot values, balance of design, aesthetics, course conditioning, memorability, resistance to scoring. For the first twenty-five years after its opening in 1966, Mauna Kea was voted the best golf

---

§ Trent Jones and Laurance Rockefeller became good friends during the times they spent together building Dorado Beach and Mauna Kea. Trent later remodeled a private course on the Rockefeller Estate on the Hudson River in New York, a layout that the Rockefeller family and their guests played for many years. The two men kept in touch with one another, with Jones always considering it "a privilege to be his friend" (RTJ, "Just Me, Trent Jones," p. 51). For Rockefeller, he also built the course at Carambola Golf Club on St. Croix in the Virgin Islands. Part of another famous resort, Carambola (6,843 yards, par 72) opened for play in 1967. That same year Jones remodeled the course at Jackson Hole Golf & Country Club in Wyoming, which Rockefeller had just bought. Six years later, in 1973, Robert Trent Jones, Inc., put Rockefeller's Jackson Hole course (an original Bob Baldock design) through another redesign, this time with Bobby doing the work. In 2007 Bobby's company, Robert Trent Jones II, finished a major renovation of what from the start has been considered one of Wyoming's top golf courses. Another Rockefeller course on which Trent Jones had done a great deal of work was Woodstock Country Club in Woodstock, Vermont, site of another one of Laurance Rockefeller's elegant inns just a mile away. Jones built the original 18 holes at Woodstock in 1963 and refurbished it in 1969. While working at Woodstock, Jones stayed either at the inn or in the guest quarters of the Rockefellers' summer home there. Over the course of his career, Trent Jones Sr. designed or remodeled some ten golf courses for Laurance Rockefeller. Besides being one of his biggest clients, Rockefeller was also, in Jones's words, "my entrée into the world of high finance" (RTJ, *Golf's Magnificent Challenge*, p. 101). Exactly what matters of high finance this involved for Jones other than some investments in Rockefeller's resort golf courses is not clear.

course in the Hawaiian Islands. For many years it was also the only golf course in Hawaii rated among the top 100 in America by *Golf Digest*. Today, *Golfweek* rates it as the fifth-best course in the state and the thirty-first-best resort course in America.

The pièce de résistance at Mauna Kea was its third hole. Although Trent never put the story into his own writings or told it in a published interview, legend has it that when visiting the property for the first time with Laurance Rockefeller and seeing the cove of Kaunaoa Bay—over which he could imagine hitting a shot from a cliff-side tee to a well-protected green on a tiny spit of land 200 yards away—he said, "Larry, if you allow me to build a golf course here, this'll be the most beautiful hole in the world." Although prone to hyperbole in his praise for almost every site on which he ever built a golf course, this time Trent Jones was not exaggerating. The par-3 third at Mauna Kea, where an inlet of the mighty Pacific forms the water hazard, turned out spectacularly well, ranked over the years by different golf magazines as one of the best holes not just in America but in the entire world of golf.

"Without question, the third at Mauna Kea is one of my greatest creations," Jones would assert during the last years of his life. In his view, the only par-3 that compared in terms of being both sensationally beautiful and extraordinarily difficult was the par-3 16th at Cypress Point on the Monterey Peninsula. Alister MacKenzie's creation required a carry of 218 yards to reach the green. Daunting even from the front of the tee, Jones's played at 178 yards to the front of the green, 210 to the middle, and had three other tees that reduced the shot's demands to 167, 158, and 113 yards. "There is no more glorious challenge than to stand on the 16th tee at Cypress Point or on the third tee at Mauna Kea and be faced with a full carry over the surf pounding below, the ocean breezes whipping around you. Nor are there any more beautiful sights than standing looking at those two tee shots."

There is no question that pictures of this single hole at Mauna Kea promoted golf tourism to Hawaii more than any two dozen photos of any other golf course in the Islands. "Is Mauna Kea's third hole the world's most spectacular? You decide." That caption—set under the picture of Jack Nicklaus hitting his tee shot on the third at Mauna Kea with the blue Pacific over his left shoulder, an image captured during a "Big Three" golf match between Nicklaus, Palmer, and Player in early December 1964—was not only featured over and over again in Mauna Kea's early advertising campaigns, but the photo virtually became the iconographic image of the special experiences that Hawaii had to offer golfers.[5] (For the "Big Three" match, the PGA stars did not play the third hole from the back tee that Jones had built, which stretched the hole to 270 yards, because Gary Player could not carry his tee shot all the way across the deep blue Pacific in a facing wind. All three parred the hole, playing it from 210 yards.)

Bobby assisted his father a great deal in Hawaii, especially at Mauna Kea. But by the early 1970s he was doing more than assisting, primarily because his dad was busy designing golf courses very far away from Hawaii—in southern Europe and even in North Africa for such potentates as the Aga Khan and the king of Morocco. Dad's absence freed Bobby to take charge of the entire 27-hole project (a regulation 18 and a nine-hole par-3) at Princeville (named for Prince Albert, son of Hawaii's King Kamehameha IV and Queen Emma), near Hanalei on the north shore of Kauai. "If there's a finer place to build a golf course," Bobby exclaimed at the time, "I haven't seen it." Magnificent coastal scenery, a mélange of raw ocean cliffs, unspoiled beaches, verdant rain forests, and waterfalls tumbling down mountains into the sea placed every enchanting attribute Princeville had to offer into Bobby's lap. In 1961, Bobby and his wife, Claiborne, had honeymooned at nearby Hanalei Plantation, and Princeville gave him the chance to return to the paradise that was Kauai, to a plateau between the beautiful Hanalei Valley and the sea on the north end of Hawaii's northernmost island, where he hoped to build "27 holes of unparalleled scenic beauty and marvelous playability."

The developer for the 11,000-acre Princeville Ranch, Eagle County Development Corporation of Denver, Colorado, wanted to take no chances when it

---

[5] The taped and then nationally televised "Big Three" golf match between Palmer, Nicklaus, and Player, which was played on December 8, 1964, was the christening event for the Mauna Kea golf course. Not always a big fan of Trent Jones's course designs, Nicklaus won the match and lauded the layout, declaring it "more fun to play than any course I know." The official opening of the golf course, as well as the hotel, came on July 15, 1965. Another early event that promoted visits to Mauna Kea was *Shell's Wonderful World of Golf*, a taped weekly series sponsored by the Shell Oil Company that ran on NBC over the winter months and that featured the world's outstanding golf courses. In 1968 the producers filmed a segment at Mauna Kea involving a match between Peter Alliss from England and Americans Al Geiberger and Dan Sikes. Sikes won the exhibition with an even-par 72. Trent Jones's old friend, Gene Sarazen, was the on-course expert commentator for the entire *Wonderful World of Golf* series, which aired from 1961 to 1970. Interestingly, the only other time that the popular TV series came to Hawaii was in 1964 and featured Trent's then recently opened Royal Ka'anapali Golf Course. The match was between Floridian Dave Ragan and New Zealander Bob Charles, winner of the 1963 British Open.

came to choosing the designer and builder of the golf course for its new resort community. In announcing that Robert Trent Jones would be designing and building the Princeville golf course, ECDC president L. Douglas Hoyt stated, "Our survey conclusively indicated that we would best be assured protection of our capital investment through retaining Robert Trent Jones." Golfers "having no other knowledge of the course," said Hoyt, would be "willing to travel to Hawaii to play if it was a Jones course."

Apparently it did not matter to ECDC which Robert Trent Jones actually produced the course. Working in the library of the original plantation house overlooking Hanalei Bay, Bobby laid out the holes for the three nines like the spokes of a wheel, reaching out to the ocean and coming back. He made the greens on each nine rather large, in his dad's style, but he contoured them more lightly, keeping their profiles low and opening the approaches into them in a manner quite unlike his dad's characteristic greens. "I softened the course a bit for the resort player," said Bobby, thereby distinguishing his design from the "monster" reputation of even his dad's resort courses like Mauna Kea.

As soon as Trent had a chance, he went to take a look at his son's work. Bobby was especially anxious to show him the seventh hole on the Ocean Course, which played across the ocean similar to the third at Mauna Kea, though less dramatically. He made a point to tell his dad that the hole sat atop its cliff quite a few feet higher above the foaming sea than either the third at Mauna Kea or the 16th at Cypress Point. "Dad can be a very accurate critic," Bobby later told the press. "When he told me, 'good job,' it was a supreme compliment. I felt I had earned his respect."

Although Princeville (which opened in 1971) rightfully credits Robert Trent Jones Jr. as the original designer of its golf course, it sits to this day on the official list of courses designed by Robert Trent Jones Sr. as well. But today it is even more a product of Bobby's firm, thanks to the addition of a magnificent, multimillion-dollar golf course, "The Prince" (par 72, 7,378 yards), which opened at the Kauai resort in 1991. For many years, Golf Digest ranked The Prince the number-one golf course in Hawaii and one of America's top 100 courses. Today, Golfweek lists it as the second-best course in Hawaii (behind only the Plantation Course at Kapalua, on Maui) and the twentieth-best resort course in America. (Upon the opening of The Prince, the original 27 at Princeville came to be known as Princeville Makai.)

Princeville was not the only Jones Inc. course in Hawaii principally created by Bobby. At Kamuela on the Big Island, Bobby also produced the first 18 of what would turn out to be 36 holes at Waikoloa Village. Just down the coastline, fewer than ten miles from Mauna Kea, play began at Waikoloa Village in 1972. Once again, this golf course was under contract to Jones, Inc., which places it on Trent's official list of designs even though Bobby had by this time taken charge of all the Jones work in Hawaii and beyond, into the Pacific Basin. In 1974, also for Jones, Inc., Bobby produced the 18-hole Pacific Harbour Golf Course on the island of Fiji. In his autobiographical *Golf's Magnificent Challenge*, Trent praised both courses: "Bobby did 27 magnificent holes *for us* [author's emphasis] at Princeville on Kauai, and Pacific Harbour in Fiji. Those were, respectively, the sites of the 1978 World Cup and World Amateur Championships. It was the first time the two events have been played in the same year on courses designed *by the same architect* [author's emphasis]." The words that Trent used to praise Bobby's work on these two golf courses are illuminating. The prepositional phrase, "for us," seems intentional, perhaps to remind the world—if not Bobby—that whether Bobby did the golf architecture and built the courses in the Pacific or not, the achievement properly belonged to Jones, Inc. The phrase "the same architect" at the end of the second sentence reinforces this perspective.

In a similar fashion, Trent and Bobby collaborated on a big project in Japan in 1972. One of the country's most powerful business leaders, Yoshiaki Tsutsumi, the heir to the reins of the Seibu Corporation, selected Jones for a 36-hole project in Nagano at a place called Karuizawa, a popular highland resort for visitors from Tokyo. On this occasion, Rees made a rare trip with Bobby to "present our services"; their dad did not go. Bobby recalls: "We offered a price for the 36 holes on the way to Haneda airport as Rees and I were leaving Japan. But a 'negotiation' took place after our trip when the man representing Mr. Tsutsumi, a Mr. Sawai, called me when I was with Dad in Acapulco and wanted us to lower our price. Dad agreed to it because Tsutsumi's people were going to design and install the irrigation system themselves. Dad then traveled with me on my second trip to Karuizawa, upon which we did the design work" on what was a difficult site, with "precipitous slopes and deep valleys in the mountains." One of the nights there, Trent had the pleasure of experiencing his first earthquake, something Bobby was familiar with as a resident of the San Francisco Bay area. A few years later, Bobby returned to the complex to do another course followed by yet another eighteen. Trent never returned to Japan after the initial 36 holes were completed. After the completion of the fourth course, the Seibu Corporation renamed the facility "Golf 72," which Bobby was told by Tsutsumi had "as much to do with the Asian philosophy of numerology" as it did with the number of holes or pars of each course. During that period Bobby flew to Japan on a near-monthly basis. In 1993 Bobby completed an additional course at Karuizawa. Today there are six courses there. In September 2014 the World Amateur Team Championship will be played at Karuizawa 72 Golf, on its East Oshitate and East Iriyama courses.

It did not take Bobby long after setting up shop in Palo Alto to begin establishing the foundations for his own golf design business. Back in 1957, his dad had set up the original Robert Trent Jones, Inc., primarily for tax purposes, with all four members of the family sharing equally in the company's fortune. In California, Bobby, the former Stanford law student, soon found what he felt were legitimate and even necessary reasons to create an additional corporate entity, which he called "Robert Trent Jones of California, Inc." Whether the "Robert Trent Jones" in the corporate name referred to Senior or Junior was purposefully not stipulated.

The formal incorporation, registered in Santa Clara County on December 6, 1965, was intended to solve two problems, as Bobby explained to his dad, mother, and brother: The first was that Robert Trent Jones, Inc., being a New Jersey corporation, had never been authorized to do business in the state of California and thus could be charged with operating illegally in the state. Creating the new corporation fixed that problem by "permitting us to do California work legally for the first time, and also to enter into contracts with public agencies in California." Apparently, it was also important for the officers of Bobby's corporation to be California residents, as the three "incorporates" of Robert Trent Jones of California, Inc., were Bobby, his wife, Claiborne, and a secretary in Bobby's Palo Alto office, Theresa Johnson.

None of the other members of the Jones family, including Trent Sr., saw the need for Bobby's corporation. Since 1960 the parent company had undertaken half a dozen projects in California without any legal issues being raised. No problem had arisen in any of the other western states—or in any other state, for that matter. Everything Trent had designed had been done through Robert Trent Jones, Inc. To the family, Bobby's new company only seemed necessary if Bobby was going out after his own work, which by the mid-1960s seemed to be exactly what he was starting to do.

It frustrated Bobby that he could not make his family understand what the situation was like for him out in California and how he was only following the legal advice he was getting from well-informed lawyers in the Bay area. As

Bobby explains today, "RTJ, Inc., had never qualified to do business in California. It had never paid any California tax. The state's Franchise Tax Board, which is like our California IRS, started honing in on the company. I kept getting these threatening notes from the FTB and I didn't know what to do. It's pretty uncomfortable when you keep getting these really nasty notices from the Franchise Tax Board. Sometimes these taxing authorities like to make an example out of somebody with a big name. I tried to get Dad to agree to let me get RTJ, Inc., qualified to do business in California and start paying taxes in the state, but Dad just flat-out refused. He had always been pretty lucky up to this point when it came to tax matters,** and he just refused. Dad just wouldn't buy into it. I would go to him and approach him and talk about it, and he'd go, 'No, I'm not going to do that.'" Bobby felt that he had no choice but to do what needed to be done on his own.

In 1968 Bobby built his first golf course that wasn't directly aligned with his father's company but rather with Robert Trent Jones of California. Notwithstanding the stated reason for creating this corporation in the first place, the golf course was located in Arizona. Nestled among the red rocks of Sedona, 115 miles north of Phoenix, Oakcreek Country Club was designed to be "player friendly,"

** In the period 1963–64, the Internal Revenue Service went after Trent Jones, claiming that Jones, through the creation of two foreign corporations in the Bahamas for golf course work in the Caribbean region, was illegally keeping money outside the United States that was then not taxed. Jones owned both of the Nassau corporations and when one of the companies needed money Jones would arrange to transfer it from one to the other and vice versa, with none of the money transactions being very well documented by Jones's accountants. The IRS claimed that Jones had to pay taxes on all this money as an individual, because what Jones was doing was giving a dividend out of the one corporation to the other corporation and then turning around and making a capital contribution to the other. In the IRS's view, Jones owed tax on the dividends. After several months of investigation, the IRS dropped the case, not able to prove its claim. What made Jones lucky in this case was that the IRS based its suit against Jones on the charge that he was benefiting from a "triple dividend" scheme, which was what could not be proved. But, in reality, all of the people and all of the real business activities of the two Bahamian corporations resided in Montclair, New Jersey, not in the Bahamas. The IRS didn't really need any proof of triple dividends. Jones's two companies were corporations completely engaged in trade and business in the United States, which meant they were supposed to pay U.S. tax. It didn't matter where they were incorporated. If a company was engaged in U.S. trade and business, it had to pay tax in the U.S. If the IRS had made those charges against Jones rather than trying to prove he was involved in triple dividends, it would have been a slam-dunk case. It was exactly such luck in his dealings with the IRS that led Trent Jones to think that he wouldn't need to pay any taxes in California, either.

All of the documents related to this IRS suit against Jones from 1963–64 can be found in Jones's IRS files within his papers at Cornell.

allowing "plenty of room for error" and always giving the golfer "an opportunity to recover and get errant shots back into play." Curiously, the membership of Oakcreek, from the club's inception to the present day, has erroneously believed (and advertised) that its golf course was "designed by the famous father and son team of Robert Trent Jones, Sr. and Robert Trent Jones, Jr."[††] Indeed, the course did possess several noteworthy features "in the usual Trent Jones manner"— meaning in the manner of Trent Sr. Many of the fairways were tree-lined doglegs. Many holes had fairway bunkers strategically placed in the landing areas. Most of the greens were at least slightly elevated and were surrounded by large swirling bunkers. But Bobby had designed the golf course in its entirety. If his father came out even once to consult on the golf course, there is no record of it in the Jones Papers at Cornell.

That same year, 1968, Trent decided to "consolidate in himself ownership of all the European and Caribbean design and construction operations." In response to his father's action, Bobby wanted the same deal for himself for all of the western and Pacific business. To Bobby's satisfaction, at least, he felt that his

---

[††] It would have been very easy for uninitiated clients and those not knowledgeable about the golf design business in America at the time not to know the difference between Robert Trent Jones Sr. and Robert Trent Jones Jr.; that is still the case today for many people. (Also, there is the persistent confusion between Robert Trent Jones—either one of them—and Robert Tyre "Bobby" Jones Jr.) Prior to Robert Trent Jones Jr. starting his own independent business, it still would have appeared to many people that the Palo Alto office was the *headquarters* of Robert Trent Jones, Inc., and the business home of Robert Trent Jones *Sr.* All anyone had to do was to look at the letterhead on the stationery coming out of Palo Alto. At the top in the center of the letterhead were the three lines: "Robert Trent Jones, Inc.—360 Bryant Street—Palo Alto, California 94301." To the left side of the letterhead it read: "P.O. Box 301—Montclair, New Jersey 07042." To the right the letterhead read: "P.O. Box 4121—Fort Lauderdale, Florida 33304." Anyone who didn't know the actual circumstances of Jones's company would think that the "Robert Trent Jones" that was the head of Robert Trent Jones, Inc., worked out of the Palo Alto office and that Montclair and Fort Lauderdale were the branch offices, not Palo Alto. The same thing is true when it came to the contracts that put Bobby and the Palo Alto office to work— contracts that were issued to Robert Trent Jones, Inc., at its Palo Alto address and that were signed by Bobby in a handwriting that looked strikingly like his father's, and that sometimes typically ended entirely without the complete suffix "Jr." but only with the letter "J" written smaller than the rest of the letters. Upon reading this footnote, Bob Jr. has commented: "Almost every client who invests millions of dollars in their valuable land does 'due diligence' first, including contacting former clients to see how we work. My father was aware of, and insisted on, this form of letterhead and had similar stationery printed in Fort Lauderdale with Fort Lauderdale as the central office. He was trying to create the sense of perspective in the marketplace for a personal business service." Robert Trent Jones Jr. comments on draft of Chapter 11, communicated to author by e-mail, 28 Jan. 2014.

father agreed in 1968 to the arrangement. Unfortunately, the agreement between father and eldest son—dividing the Jones golf empire from east to west, just as the Treaty of Tordesillas in 1494 divided the New World between Portugal and Spain—was "not reduced to writing," and subsequently became a central bone of contention between Bobby and Rees, especially when Trent could not remember later whether he had agreed to the arrangement with Bobby or not. After Bobby went his own way from 1972 on while continuing to direct and profit from the West Coast business of RTJ, Inc., Rees grew increasingly upset over what he felt was the impropriety of Bobby's "dual operation." Ione, a loving mother toward both her sons, could not help but sympathize with Rees, feeling that he was getting the short end of the stick. Troubling questions and hurtful suspicions bubbled and boiled within the Jones family all through the early 1970s, until the distress got to the point that the brothers could no longer work together.

If Bobby was Portugal and Trent was Spain in the family business scenario, Rees was England, France, or Holland—take your pick. He was a third party for whom any treaty that divided the world east from west, and that kept him out of the mix, was patently unfair and wrong. But where the other European nations in the sixteenth and seventeenth centuries simply ignored the "Tordesillas meridian" and went sailing off wherever their fighting and cargo ships could take them, Rees was in no position to do much other than complain to his father and mother about what he felt was "my brother's double-dealing."

Rees, too, had worked hard for his father, helping Robert Trent Jones, Inc., design and build twenty-six golf courses in ten different states, without blurring the line about who was actually doing the designing and whether Rees personally deserved or desired any credit or publicity for it. There was never a question—not to this day—that the courses were done by, and should be attributed to, his father's firm.

It is ironic, then, that Rees seemed to his father a less devoted student of his parental mentoring than Bobby. As Trent recalled in his interview with the USGA in 1991, "The boys came into the business, and we taught them. Both of them learned their basics from me. Rees wouldn't listen to me so I sent Bill Baldwin, who had been with me all those years, to teach him the basics. Rees just wouldn't listen to me. He wouldn't do much that I wanted him to do. For example, if I wanted him to shape a green and mold a green, he would say, 'Your greens have too much contour; the green should be flatter.' Then he'd make a green and everybody hated it. Then I said to myself, 'Look, he's not listening to me. I'll let Bill Baldwin, who's been with me some forty years, teach *him* what I taught Baldwin. Rees learned my principles from Baldwin more than from me because he would listen to Baldwin. And Rees turned out to be a good architect. And so did Bobby. . . . But Bobby listened to me." Not that Bobby would always agree with his father; Bobby often defiantly stood up to him, sometimes at the top of his voice, sufficiently confident to resort to what brother Rees has referred to as "shouting matches." To Trent, though, it *seemed* that his eldest son was not as resistant to his ideas when actually he often was, and very strongly so.

For the first four years with his father, Rees was paired on virtually every one of his trips into the field with Roger Rulewich. Together, the duo learned what they needed to know about the practical side of golf course design and construction primarily from Bill Baldwin, whom Rees came to consider virtually a second father. Rees and Roger also got along very well. Both were Yale graduates, and they sometimes crooned the school's famous standard, "The Whiffenpoof Song," variously imitating Bing Crosby, Perry Como, and even Elvis Presley, so that the song's lyrics ("To the tables down at Mory's, To the place where Louis dwells . . .") could be heard all around the Montclair office. Roger was five years older than Rees, but Roger was himself not much more than an on-the-job trainee when it came to building golf courses. Neither Rees nor Roger felt superior to the other. That made for a very good working relationship.

The golf business was still booming in the late 1960s, despite the Vietnam War and associated upheaval, enough to keep RTJ, Inc., busy with jobs on both coasts. In 1969 Rees and Roger worked on four golf courses together, with two of them getting quite a bit of input from Trent. That was not so much the case, however, for The Springs Golf Course at the House on the Rock Resort in Spring Green, Wisconsin, located forty miles west of Madison. There, Trent left most of the design and all of the heavy lifting to his junior associates, who answered the call by creating a fine 6,562-yard, par-72 layout, one that for a period of time was on *Golf Digest's* list of best public courses. The same was true for Ferncroft Country Club in Danvers, Massachusetts, twenty miles north of Boston, where Rees and Roger were principally responsible for the 6,632-yard, par-72 golf course, which from 1980 to 1990 hosted the LPGA's Boston Five Classic.

Before handing the details over to Rees and Roger, Trent provided significant input on the design of Chanticleer Course, a new course at Greenville Country Club in South Carolina. Building Chanticleer was a profitable job for

Jones, nearly half a million dollars in revenue. (A "chanticleer" is a fictional rooster and a choice name for a club located in the same state as the University of South Carolina Gamecocks and the Coastal Carolina Chanticleers). Trent's construction company, Florida Golf, headed by John Schmeisser, did most of the construction, for which it was to be paid $158,190. The layout that RTJ, Inc., produced thrilled the membership at just the time that Trent's reputation was peaking—both in terms of national stature and national controversy—with the course's grand opening coming in September 1970, just a couple of months after the Open at Hazeltine. For Chanticleer's formal opening, sixty-eight-year-old Gene Sarazen came up from his home in Florida to play the course, in a foursome that included his old friend Jones. Sarazen told the local media, "It's a better course than Pinehurst No. 2. It has more character than the Country Club of North Carolina." Trent Jones himself spoke with particular pride about the 18th hole, declaring that it had "turned out to be a very special and challenging one because the second shot to the green has to be carried over a lake, and there are several difficult pin positions on the green." Trent went so far as to call it "one of the greatest finishing holes in golf history." In making that sort of remark about the hole, one can be sure that Trent played a principal part in designing it, although in *Golf's Magnificent Challenge* he credited Rees for being "primarily responsible for the Chanticleer Course." Rees Jones, Inc., would completely upgrade the layout in 2001. *Golf Digest* currently ranks it as the eleventh best course in South Carolina—five spots higher than Trent Sr.'s seminal creation in Myrtle Beach, the Dunes Club.

In the five years prior to Rees's leaving his dad's business in October 1974, Rees and Roger would continue to work most of their projects as a team. Together they would lead RTJ, Inc., through the design and construction of some outstanding golf courses, testimony to the growing experience and maturation of skills of both Rees and Roger as designers.

Crag Burn Club, one of RTJ, Inc.'s most innovative designs of the era, was built on polo grounds belonging to the Knox/Goodyear family at their summer home just southeast of Buffalo, New York. Fittingly, the name of the estate was Crag Burn, built from two Scottish words meaning "top of the bluff" and "small stream." It was an extraordinarily beautiful property, although it had gotten a little shabby from disuse by the mid-1960s. The driving force behind the golf course was Buffalo-born and raised Robert Millard "Bobby" Goodyear (1925–2011), grandson to Frank H. Goodyear II and his wife, Dorothy Knox, daughter of Seymour Knox, one of the founders of the Woolworth Corporation. In 1952, Bobby, an accomplished sportsman and low-handicap golfer who was by that time living in Aiken, South Carolina, won the Palmetto Golf Club's Eighth Annual Pro-Am with Ben Hogan as his partner, shooting a best-ball 61. Sometime in the mid-1960s, still living in Aiken, Bobby got the idea to take his family's polo ground, which had become overgrown with weeds and brush, and make it into a world-class golf course.

Trent spent a great deal of time on Crag Burn, though he left many of the details to Rees and, in this case, Cabell Robinson, who both got along very well with Goodyear. Unlike many of RTJ, Inc.'s clients, Bobby Goodyear insisted on participating actively in the design of his golf course. He didn't want a paradigmatic Jones course; in fact, he was "adamant" that Crag Burn "be kept small and manageable." The property featured a mix of heavily wooded sections and open fields, and Trent, in consultation with Rees, Cabell, and Bobby Goodyear, decided to capitalize on the differentiated terrain by designing the front nine as a parks-style course running through the woods and giving the back nine a links-like feel as it moved through the open spaces. Trent came to consider Crag Burn, which opened for play in 1972, "one of our most innovative designs." He credited Rees and Cabell for their input in creating "a forerunner to the return to natural golf courses," a trend that would blossom in the 1980s. He also considered his company's Crag Burn experience as "an example of how a knowledgeable client [Bobby Goodyear] can contribute to the making of a great course."

The upscale Turnberry Isle Yacht & Country Club was part of a master-planned high-rise residential development in North Miami known as Aventura. Jones, Inc., built two courses there in the early 1970s. Rees and Roger had a big hand in creating the layouts, but Trent always took credit for the club's most unique feature, a huge "triple green" with 49,936 square feet—more than an acre—of putting surface. "I was asked to give the club 'something special,'" Trent would recall, "so I built the biggest green in the world." The green served three different holes: the ninth of the North Course and the sixth and ninth of the South Course. The back of the triple green at Turnberry was so wide—491 feet—that Trent's good friend Julius Boros, the Hall of Fame player who represented the North Miami club on the Tour, once tried to hit a 6-iron across it, repeatedly failing by three to five yards.

As Rees took more and more responsibility for designing and building his father's golf courses, he, as brother Bobby had done, was developing his own architectural ideas while still working to satisfy clients that they were receiving a "signature" Robert Trent Jones golf course.‡‡ And as he did with Bobby, Trent eventually came to appreciate the unique style of his younger son's golf course designs. Looking back at Rees's architecture from the vantage point of the late 1980s, Trent remarked: "Rees does not believe so much in length as I do but in smaller, well-fortified targets surrounded by varied features. He leaves a lot of his greens open in front, believing that hazards to the side penalize the good player more than the higher handicappers. He uses grassy hollows and swales around the green, trying to penalize the shot to the degree it is missed, retaining the ball closer to the putting surface if it is only slightly off-line. Many of the greens Rees builds sweep up in the front, like those at St. Andrews, a style I have always preferred. His greens are marked by more gentle transitions as opposed to abrupt terraces. Long putts will break, but putts from close around the hole will be relatively easy. Rees considers himself a multi-themed architect, which means that he is constantly seeking variety, trying to give the player a new experience on every hole, not just on every course. As a result, his later courses have become more visually exciting. He also classifies himself as an 'architect of definition' rather than one of deception. He wants the golfer to know what he has to contend with, and Rees works very hard at showing him the intended target, both off the tee and into the green. . . . Rees's courses can be demanding, but he strives always to make them playable for all. Like Bobby and me, he offers options to accommodate all skill levels."

"We design our courses generally for people who play golf, not only for

---

‡‡ Robert Trent Jones Sr. is generally credited for being "the first architect whose name was a selling point in the marketing of a course, a phenomenon that led to greater recognition and higher fees for those at the top of the profession" (Tom Doak, "The Course of Architecture," in *Golf in America: The First One Hundred Years* [New York: Abrams, 1988], ed. George Peper and the editors of *Golf Magazine*, p. 116). There is little question that Jones deserves this credit. More than that, Jones is often credited for inventing the term "signature design." That credit is given, for example, in *Grounds for Golf: The History and Fundamentals of Golf Course Design* (New York: St. Martin's, 2003), by noted golf writer and historian Geoff Shackelford in his chapter on "Schools of Design." Roger Rulewich recalls that he "first heard of this sort of hallmark label when we put out an ad for *Golf World*" in the mid-1960s, "Give your course a signature." According to Bob, Jr.: "The question of 'signature' golf courses definitely originated with my father. He and I were together with Baron Paul Rolin in a Brussels fine art museum during his work on the Bercuit golf course. Rolin noted that a signed painting by a master, such as Rubens, was much more valuable than unsigned copies made from the master's school. I was there and Dad immediately understood and created the slogan 'Give your course a signature, designed by *Robert Trent Jones*.' The first ad featured a picture of Spyglass Hill." Robert Trent Jones Jr. comments on draft of Chapter 11, communicated to author by e-mail, 28 Jan. 2014.

golfers," Rees would say a few years after he started his own design firm. "Why take this great form of recreation and turn it into torture? The battle should be fun and fair."

Working for their father was not always easy—perhaps even most of the time—for either Rees or Bobby. Sometimes, by leaving his projects almost entirely in their hands and not spending much time in the company of the client or at the course site, Trent put his sons in very uncomfortable positions. His absence angered some clients, who wanted to know why the great architect didn't have time to spend on the building of the course that it was so handsomely paying him for. Getting a Robert Trent Jones "signature" course was not enough; many of the clients of Jones, Inc., expected Senior Jones to be directing the work personally, or at least to show more interest than he was doing at many of the sites for his golf courses.

The most embarrassing incident for Rees took place at Fort Gordon in Augusta, Georgia, in 1975. "The formal opening of the golf course at Fort Gordon was going to be a big deal," Rees remembers. The place was the home for the headquarters of the Army Signal Corps, and it employed some thirty thousand military and civilian personnel. During the Vietnam War, it was the main training location for the Army Military Police Corps. "A number of Army generals were going to be there for the opening of the golf course," Rees recalls, "and everyone expected my father to show up there for the festivities, give a little talk, hobnob with the brass, hit a ball off the first tee, and so forth. Dad knew that everyone expected him to be there; I certainly did. I drove over to the Augusta airport to pick up Mom and Dad and into the terminal came Mom but no Dad. 'Where the heck is Dad?' I asked Mom. 'He's not coming. He didn't make it back from Europe.'" At Fort Gordon, Ione and Rees did what they could to excuse Trent's absence, but the Army officials would not have any of it. They were extremely upset. At the close of the event, the officer in charge of the base, Major General Charles R. Myer, came over to Rees and growled at him, "Tell your father that we never want him here *again*."

By the early 1970s, disputes between Trent and his sons and between the two brothers over how to run the family business were becoming commonplace and more and more serious. Looking back to that period in the history of the Jones family, it is perhaps surprising that Bobby and Rees didn't part ways with their father even sooner than they did. Trent's comments about his sons leaving the company included the following, from several different sources, published and not:

"Rees always contended I was too much of an optimist. He always urged that we take a more conservative business approach. But I'd been through hard times, a lot harder than we came to face in the economic downturn that came with the oil crisis of 1973 and the real estate collapse of 1974."

"More importantly, both of my sons had their own growing young families, and I think they both felt they simply had to get out on their own."

"Bobby had been working in the burgeoning Pacific Basin, while I had been spending a great deal of time in Europe. Rees was doing great work from Texas to Massachusetts. Each designed some magnificent courses with my firm, and each would get even better after they left. In retrospect, it was good they left. Otherwise they would have had to wait until I died to establish their reputations. That would have been too bad, because the reputations of both are growing bigger and bigger in the world of golf."

"Both of them learned a great deal from me, I like to think, but they really grew in their abilities after they went out on their own. I like to think their design principles are much like mine, but their expressions are different. I would come to learn a lot from them actually, and some of my own later courses came to reflect what I picked up from their ingenuity and innovative approaches."

"At times my sons and I have become disputants, sometimes combatants. I suppose that's true in all father-son relationships, and it becomes especially intense when all work in the same profession. I don't know how good a father I have been, nor do I know how good they consider me to have been. As much as I was gone, a great deal of their upbringing was left to their mother, and thank God she was so good and strong."

"I do know that I love them, and I am proud of them, as individuals and masters of their profession. If this is indeed the legacy Ione and I have left, it is the greatest contribution we could have made."

Perhaps the story of Bobby and Rees leaving their dad's company should be left right there, with what Trent had to say about it when looking back some fifteen years later, with a more objective perspective, with pride in both of his sons, and with the forlorn hope that Bobby and Rees could someday overcome their differences and forgive each other for all the hurts and jealousies they felt, and, if not truly embrace each other, at least get along civilly, without the disdain, enmity, and feuding that came to dominate everything about their bitterly sour sibling relationship. After all, both of them benefited enormously from being the sons of Robert Trent Jones, whether they wanted to admit it or not. Both of them got jobs to design golf courses from major clients that they surely would never have gotten, at least not as early in their careers as they did, if they hadn't enjoyed the contacts and entrée that came to them only as part of the legacy of a self-made man for whom nothing had ever been given freely. It was easiest for Bobby to take advantage of the legacy, because he was the namesake; Rees certainly came to believe that was the case. But Rees, too, was the offspring of the world's best-known golf course architect, and that positioned him to take advantage of opportunities that did not come so naturally to other talented, hardworking architects who lacked such a pedigree.

But our understanding of the life story of Robert Trent Jones Sr. cannot be considered complete without examining what caused the lasting rift between his two sons. After all, the feud between his two sons endures as an unwanted but major part of Jones's legacy.

By the early 1970s Bobby had put together quite an operation on the West Coast. To prospective clients, the Palo Alto office was submitting a polished, twenty-page package of material demonstrating "our qualifications to conceive, design, finance, construct, and operate" not just golf courses but other types of recreational facilities as well. In these proposals, Bobby was not shy about presenting his credentials:

- Vice President, Robert Trent Jones, Inc., and founder/director of West Coast office in Palo Alto, 1962 to date. President, Robert Trent Jones of California.
- Widely acquainted throughout golfing world with various clubs, their operations and management personnel; industry associations; tournament directors and site selection committees; playing professionals; golf course superintendents; related professionals in architecture, engineering, and planning; etc.
- Contributed significantly to building a firm that preserves green spaces and recreation in urban growth areas through master planning.
- Personal experience on some 50 golf course projects throughout the world, mainly in the western United States and Far East, either in charge of design or as design coordinator.
- Member, American Society of Golf Course Architects [Associate

Member, 1964; Member, 1967]. Contributed articles to professional magazines.

- Golfing honors include: Member, U.S. Junior Golf Team to compete against Scotland; Member, Yale Golf Team; Member, Eastern Intercollegiate Championship Golf Team.
- B.A., Yale University; and post-graduate studies at Stanford University.
- President of Woodside [civic organization], and active in community and political affairs, both local and national.

After Bobby's résumé came the credentials of the two full-time employees who by 1970 were working for him in the Palo Alto office: Richard M. Spray, whom Bobby had hired in 1965, and Orris "Bud" Sexten. (Harvey Raynor, who had worked in the Palo Alto office at the time of its establishment in 1965, was no longer working for Bobby by 1970.) Spray held a degree in mechanical engineering from Purdue University and an MBA from Harvard, and he also had five years of experience with Stanford Research Institute in Menlo Park, where he specialized in "techno-economics." Sexten had been with Gulf Oil from 1945 to 1962 as a troubleshooter and sales representative. During his time with Gulf he gained a significant background in general construction and project administration. In 1962, Trent had hired him to head up one of his construction companies; in 1967, Sexten took charge of constructing the RTJ, Inc., course at Fountain Valley (later to be renamed the Carambola Golf Club) on St. Croix in the Virgin Islands, and after that he moved to California to work on projects for Bobby. From 1967 to 1971, Sexten directed the work of four field superintendents on some twenty different jobs, the great majority of them administered through the Palo Alto office.

By the early 1970s Bobby had also entered into partnerships with two local companies. One of them was Daniel, Mann, Johnson & Mendenhall, whose San Francisco division was located close to Palo Alto in nearby Redwood, California. A multidiscipline organization practicing in the fields of planning, engineering, architecture, and economics, DMJM–San Francisco Division had a resident staff of fifty-five professional and supporting personnel with the expertise needed to handle the wholesale creation of community park and waterfront recreational areas, which they did throughout the Greater San Francisco Bay area. DMJM played a big part in the development of Ka'anapali Resort on

Maui, where Jones, Inc., built the golf course. Just being able to advertise that Daniel, Mann, Johnson & Mendenhall was one of its associates added a great deal to what Jones, Inc., could offer from the Palo Alto office.

A second firm that Bobby had brought into partnership with his West Coast office was Metcalf & Eddy. Also conveniently located in Palo Alto, Metcalf & Eddy's western regional office was staffed with more than fifty engineers, technicians, and administrative personnel specializing in water-pollution control and environmental engineering. By 1970, concern for the environment had become an urgent national issue. Although golf courses were not yet a focus of primary concern (by the 1980s, they definitely would be), any business or industrial endeavor involving the environmental effects of landscaping and building was drawing increasing public and government scrutiny, especially in California. As a California resident and progressive Democrat, Bobby was very aware of the growing environmental movement, both in the United States and abroad. His feelings about ecology and preserving a healthy natural environment were among the factors that had motivated him to design courses that were different from his father's, who for forty years—like all other golf architects—had been building golf courses with little if any concern about their possible environmental impact. Bobby's pragmatism told him that environmentalism with careful attention paid to water, land, wildlife, and habitat would have to be part of the golf design and construction agenda; a partnership with Metcalf & Eddy, a recognized national leader in the field of water-pollution control, made great business sense.

By 1972 Bobby had set himself up nicely for a comprehensive golf architecture and construction business that was completely independent from his father's operation. In addition to Richard Spray managing operations and Bud Sexten serving as director of field operations for the Palo Alto office, Bobby had added thirty-one-year-old Gary R. Baird to his staff. Holder of a bachelor's degree in landscape architecture from California State Polytechnic University in Pomona, Baird would assist Trent in some projects, but mainly served as Bobby's senior designer.

In Bobby's view, everything he was doing out West he was doing to help his father, boost the business of RTJ, Inc., and thereby help the entire family, including his brother. At the same time, Bobby was preparing himself and his Palo Alto operation to cut the cord with the parent company, create a separate business, and grow that business to the point where it became a distinguished and profitable golf architecture practice of its own. In the eyes of other members of the family, especially Rees, Bob was "out too much for himself." While Rees was dutifully working for his father from the home office in Montclair, mostly on projects in the eastern half of the United States, there was Bobby, in Rees's mind's eye, "out in sunny California" (Bobby recounts that he was much more likely to be in an airplane seeking work in Fiji, Malaysia, or other parts of the Pacific), growing more and more independent in his operations as each month went by, making his own deals for jobs, building courses virtually on his own, taking charge of his dad's construction companies or creating such companies of his own, having his own bank accounts, generating his own publicity, increasingly taking credit as the primary designer of the resulting "Jones" golf courses, and taking advantage of the confusion between his father's name and his own.

Worse, in the eyes of the East Coast office, Bobby was putting himself in direct competition with the family firm, trying to divert business from RTJ, Inc., in New Jersey to RTJ of California, Inc., a company in which Trent, Ione, and Rees held no stock. In a summer 1974 meeting to discuss the situation, Rees asked his mother directly if this were "the type of thing that you, Mother and Dad, who've worked as you say all your life for this company—do you want to be fighting within the supposed framework of your corporation for jobs? . . . When we had a Phoenix lead and I went out on the lead at Dad's request, because no one was getting along with Bobby at the time, Bobby came and pilfered the files and took the information and the names." According to Rees, Bobby had approached other clients on developing projects to try to persuade them that he should design the course—which would allow him to give the construction work to one of his own shadow companies. And in an incident confirmed in the same meeting by Paul A. Colwell Jr., Trent and Ione's longtime business and legal advisor, Bobby contacted an Idaho golf course that was falsely claiming to be a Robert Trent Jones design, asking that it cease and desist—and demanded $5,000 compensation for damages, payable to Bobby's California corporation. (Colwell noted, "[W]hoever was at the other end of that thing certainly would have nothing kind to say of Robert Trent Jones, the individual, the firm or what have you.")

Whether all of this was actually happening or not, what mattered was Rees's firm conviction that it was. The younger brother grew more and more concerned by what he came to regard as Bob's expropriation of the family's assets, principally the good will residing in the brand name "Robert Trent Jones."

Nineteen hundred and seventy-three was not only a turbulent year for the

Jones family, it was a tragic one. In the Menlo Country Club swimming pool that spring, little David Brewster Jones, three years old, the second child of Bobby and Claiborne, drowned. It was a horrible loss for everybody in the Jones family. Bobby and Claiborne were deeply grieving for months, experiencing an agony from which parents never really recover. No loss is worse in this world than losing a child, particularly in an accident of this sort. Bobby remembers the aftermath of David's death not only because it plunged him and Claiborne into the depths of despair, but because coming out of it meant seeing the need for greater clarity and purpose in his life, personally and professionally. "The tragedy forced the whole issue of the business situation," Bobby remembers. "I realized I just had to cut the cord with Dad's company. Get everything straightened out. Get on with my own career. Working with my own company was the only way I could do it. Dad didn't bother with details. Somebody had to take care of them for him. Somebody had to clean things up. For a long time Mother and I made things happen. Rees and Roger were off doing their thing. Dad looked at everything before it went forward. He fiddled with everything. But he was busy elsewhere, always in Europe or somewhere you couldn't reach him. So I took charge of the situation and did what needed to be done."

For the time being, the only independent golf architecture firms that Bobby owned was Pacific Planners International, Ltd. in New Caledonia and Robert Trent Jones of California, Inc., the legal relationship of the latter to the parent company remaining quite unclear. In early 1975 Bobby tried to clarify it. In March he sent his dad a letter marked "Personal and Confidential." In it, Bobby outlined "our discussion relative to the continuation of our interfamily relationship," a discussion that occurred when Trent had visited Palo Alto earlier in the month. It was a conversation to which Rees had not been privy, and Bobby wanted to keep it that way. The letter laid out what Bobby asserted his father had agreed to in the Palo Alto meeting in terms of how Robert Trent Jones, Inc.—both the New Jersey and western states corporations—should operate together in the future. According to the plan that Bobby put to paper, Robert Trent Jones, Inc.:

1. Would remain the basic Western hemisphere architectural firm.
2. Two offices operating essentially autonomously, but cooperatively as independent project centers would be maintained at Montclair and Palo Alto.
3. Legal ownership and officers to remain the same.

4. A minimum of two regular meetings would be held each year in April and November to take up prepared agenda for goals, accountability, finance, and whatever other business policy matters needed to be brought up.

As for the ownership of the many different Jones corporations, most of them involved in golf course construction:

1. R.T.J. proposed a new construction company owned by R.T.J. and R.T.J. Jr. to continue ongoing Western operations with continuing management in R.T.J. Jr.
2. R.T.J. offered an interest in European companies corresponding to percentages of Western construction company.
3. R.T.J. offered to put the stock in trust or will it to R.T.J. Jr. or R.T.J. Jr.'s heirs.
4. Those corporations in which stock is issued are reaffirmed.

As for the Jones family's real estate, Bobby's letter stated that Trent had agreed that "Each family member can join or not in real estate developments as he chooses" and that "Repayment of loans and regularization of corporations will take place forthwith." The last statement in Bobby's letter read: "As part of the overall partition and resolution, dissolution and or merger of some existing corporations may take place, depending on tax planning. Monies received will first be used to regularize personal and inter-corporate debts before other purposes."

The meaning of this last statement in Bobby's letter is not altogether clear, but it seems to mean (at least in part) that Bobby's Palo Alto operation was to utilize some of the revenues of Jones, Inc.'s West Coast business, including money that was already in California bank accounts and/or receipts still to be paid to Jones, Inc., by West Coast or Pacific Basin clients. If that was, indeed, what that last statement meant, it is no surprise that Bobby did not want Rees to see the letter, because Rees would have definitely concluded that Bobby, in Rees's words, was "double-dipping"—that is, making money off his new ventures under the banner of Robert Trent Jones of California, while helping to fund it by utilizing money belonging to Robert Trent Jones, Inc., New Jersey.

In 1974 the real estate market collapsed and a lot of developers, not well financed to begin with, ran out of money. Lots of people, including course architects, were not getting paid. Bobby had very little cash; the same was true for his father. In early May 1974, Paul Colwell prepared a seven-page report that laid out the full financial situation of Robert Trent Jones, Inc. Its position was not good. Projections of East Coast operations showed "reduced income over the next 6–12 months as the company has not been engendering the volume of business equal to the past several years." The "limited profit picture" would not be serious if Jones, Inc., had some cash reserves, but it didn't. On the contrary, it was in a "severe borrowed money position." Complicating the financial situation was the fact that a significant amount of debt—more than $550,000—was due to be paid for different "inter-corporate loans" wherein, for example, one of Jones's shadow companies (say Federal Golf) owed money to another one of the shadow companies (say Baldwin Golf Construction). Some of Jones's companies—Newgolf, Contour, Baldwin, Puerto Rican Golf, Florida Golf, American Golf Course Construction, Commonwealth—were doing profitable business, but their bank accounts held little cash, as Colwell stated, because "the companies have been raided for borrowings for other ventures," including loans to Jones, Inc., or to Trent personally. Colwell warned Trent that these intercorporate and personal borrowings were "all fraught with disastrous tax consequences." Also troubling was the fact that Trent had made commitments to various European properties (to be covered in the next chapter) totaling some $3.5 million. And as for the personal finances of Trent and Ione, the couple had "almost no liquidity in the form of cash or securities." Their personal indebtedness came to almost half a million dollars. The short-term remedy of the cash flow problem, Colwell told Trent, was to sell a property of some significant value located in suburban St. Louis, a tract of land that Jones had purchased back in the early 1960s when he was working on Bellerive and that was worth enough to "provide RTJ, Inc., with a cash reserve conservatively estimated in excess of $300,000."

Jones, Inc., was so strapped for cash by the summer of 1974 that revenue from Bobby's projects on behalf of the parent company could not be overlooked. Bobby, it seemed to Montclair, wasn't sending on to the East Coast office all of the money it was due. In early July 1974, Bobby received a terse letter by registered mail that was signed by Trent, Ione, and Rees. The letter told him, in no uncertain terms, that all RTJ, Inc., funds "now on deposit in California be sent to Montclair" for deposit in the RTJ, Inc., bank account in New Jersey. The brusque communiqué did nothing to improve relations inside the family, suggesting as it did that Bobby was holding on to RTJ, Inc., money that he was not entitled to for his own purposes.

In October 1974 Rees left his father's company, establishing "Rees Jones, Inc., Golf Course Design," which is the same company from which he designs and builds his golf courses today. Even if the headquarters of the Jones brothers' firms were not a continent apart, theirs was hardly a relationship conducive to arriving at an agreement over who should possess what from the family's original company. At the time of Jones, Inc.'s incorporation in January 1957, a stock certificate was issued to each son for 151 shares, with 149 shares to Ione and another 149 to Trent, for a total of six hundred shares. (It was apparently for tax purposes that the boys, then only seventeen and fifteen years old, were given slightly more than half the shares.) In the years to follow, no additional stock was issued nor had there been any change in the stock ownership. Essentially, each member of the family owned 25 percent of the company. On April 30, 1973, the family entered into a "buy-sell agreement" in which all four of them agreed that "the stock of the company is worth $300,000" and that, upon the death of any of them, "the company must buy that person's stock for $75,000." (Interestingly, the buy-sell agreement was something that Trent initially refused to sign.) But the corporate situation had grown much more complicated than who owned what stock in Jones, Inc., and how much it was worth. There was a large and ungainly intercorporate structure to deal with, one that was stuffed full with shadow construction companies, some of them quite profitable. The value of just the California corporations totaled $679,500. Divvying up the spoils opened a Pandora's Box. According to Bobby, "Rees did *not* think that Dad's Eastern companies should be put into the equation of our settlement, just the West Coast companies. He felt that the Eastern companies should be divided between just Dad, Mom, and himself; I should be left out. At the same time Rees argued that all of the West Coast companies *should* be put into the pot, the companies that I had grown. His idea, as I saw it, was 'what's mine is mine, and what's yours is part-mine, too.'"

Bobby told Rees that, back in 1968, Dad had given Bobby ruling interest in all the West Coast companies.[§§] Rees didn't believe it. He had heard nothing

[§§] The California companies and their estimated valuations at the end of 1973 were: CalGolf ($121,000), John Dellis Golf Construction ($235,000), DenGolf ($38,500), Fairway Golf ($67,000), RTJ of California ("approximately $20,000"), Kansas Golf ($43,000), Northlake Construction ($100,000), Pacific Golf ($5,000), and Southwest Landscape ($50,000). Paul A. Colwell, Memorandum to File, "Conference of November 28, 1973, between Colwell, Fleder,

about it and wanted to see the agreement in writing, which Bobby couldn't show him because he and Dad had not put it down on paper. (Bobby asserts today that "there was a written agreement signed by my father and me in Sun Valley, Idaho, in the summer of 1974. My recollection is that Dad took his copy with him and mine remains in my archival files.") Rees asked his dad if he could remember agreeing to give Bobby controlling interest in the West Coast companies; Trent, now sixty-nine years old, couldn't remember for sure if he had or hadn't. Rees reminded his father that he had made some promises about the business to him, too, which needed to be kept. Trent replied, "Son, if I have to keep all the promises I have made, I would never make any."

Bobby defended his control of the West Coast companies. In a letter dated November 27, 1974, he told Rees: "I have owned the beneficial interest in the construction companies in the West, subject to Dad's discretion and advice as to the capital that had been accumulated prior to that time, both as to issued and unissued stock." Beyond that specific defense, however, Bobby told Rees that his brother's rancor and suspicions had gotten so bad that he just could not deal with him anymore. "In the last two years, I have been made increasingly aware of your dissatisfaction with the understandings which had been previously arrived at between Robert Trent Jones, Sr., and me. For the purpose of arriving at solutions to problems, you and I met on many occasions, and I have reluctantly come to the conclusion that you and I no longer function productively together. Indeed, within the last six months, in spite of many invitations and opportunities to meet and talk with me, you have consistently refused to do so. It is most unfortunate that you have taken the rigid position that the only thing to be done was for you to receive 'what you had rights to,' and you thereby disregarded the economic and functional realities of an ongoing business, and gave a weight and substance never intended to a tax planning decision made by Dad and me many years ago. . . . I sincerely and deeply regret the antagonistic polarization of our business and personal relationship. Rees, I can see how you have been somewhat handcuffed in your attempts to work out and manage the situation in Montclair. I think it is too bad the relationship can't be worked out. I'm sure you have done a splendid job under difficult conditions. I hope that the business problems can be resolved speedily so that each of us can spend

---

Cohn and Harrington," 28 Nov. 1973, Paul A. Colwell Jr. Files, JP, CUA. It is curious that the value of RTJ of California is given as "approximately $20,000" when none of the other figures are deemed approximate.

the energies which have occupied so much of our time in the last year and a half, doing constructive and productive work, and that the ground work may be finally laid for reestablishing a relationship of openness and respect between you and me. I wish you good luck and Godspeed."

Rees did not believe Bobby's message was sincere. Instead of an improvement in their relationship, the letter provoked more resentment, and Rees chose not to respond to it. A couple of incidents in 1975 made Rees even angrier with Bob. More of a problem for Bob than provoking Rees's anger was knowing that the incidents also seriously upset Trent.

An April 1975 press release announced that "Robert Trent Jones, Inc., California, USA," had been retained to build a golf course in Malaysia. (Ultimately called Bukit Jambul Country Club, the golf course was completed in 1992 under a contract to Bobby's company, Robert Trent Jones II.) The press release was doubly troubling to Trent and the folks in Montclair. First, the release didn't make it at all clear that "Robert Trent Jones Inc., California, USA" was *not* the same as the parent company of Robert Trent Jones Sr.—"Robert Trent Jones, Inc."—but instead relied on the misleading declaration that "Robert Trent Jones, Inc., will plan and supervise construction of the golf course." What made Trent even madder was that the release claimed the company that would be building the Malaysian course was a firm that had designed and supervised the construction of more than four hundred golf courses, *including Augusta National*. From this press release came a flurry of stories published all around the world saying, "Robert Trent Jones, Inc., designers of the Augusta National Golf Club, will plan and supervise construction at the Tanjong Penggerang Tourist Complex, Kuala Lumpur, Malaysia." One place where the story appeared was the *Augusta Chronicle-Herald* of Augusta, Georgia.

The Augusta National Golf Club was extraordinarily vigilant about defending the purity of its golf architecture and was not about to let the press release go unchallenged. Though Clifford Roberts and other leaders of the club knew that Trent had made some major changes to the course, they never regarded those changes as anywhere close to sufficient to qualify him as one of the course designers. That recognition belonged solely to Robert Tyre Jones and Dr. Alister MacKenzie. The manager of Augusta National, Philip R. Wahl, wrote Trent Jones a letter in May 1975 that was tough for Jones to read, and with the letter Wahl enclosed a copy of the *Augusta Chronicle-Herald* article. "It contains an untrue statement about Robert Trent Jones, Inc., being the designers of the

Augusta National Golf Club," Wahl wrote. "The above is by no means the only instance that has come to our attention where your company has apparently caused or permitted incorrect statements about your being the designer or builder of the Augusta National golf course. I have been asked to inform you that this Club must require a complete retraction in writing plus a promise to see to it that such incidents do not occur in the future."

Though privately fuming, Trent sent a politely worded but no-nonsense apology to the Augusta club manager. In his retort Jones explained that neither he nor his company were responsible for the publicity release—it had been pro- duced by the management services firm (Stanley Consultants, Inc., Muscatine, Iowa) that was providing the economic, marketing, and design engineering for the development of the new Malaysian tourist complex. Furthermore, as for the design of the Augusta National golf course, although he admitted taking great pride in having executed "certain modifications to the course including the design of a completely new 16th hole," Jones emphasized that he had always given "full credit to those responsible for a design concept which greatly has influenced golf course architecture." He had "the highest regard for the work done by Mr. Jones and Dr. MacKenzie and for the great contribution each made to the game." "I would not conceive attempting to plagiarize [sic] their efforts," he told the Augusta club manager.

Trent was embarrassed by the reprimand and, although he was speaking truthfully when he told Augusta's club manager that neither he nor his company were responsible for the incorrect statement, Trent wasn't so sure that Bobby, or Bobby's operation in Palo Alto, hadn't been involved to some degree in pro- moting the perception that there was a long-standing link between Robert Trent Jones, Inc., and the design of Augusta National. Earlier that spring, Bobby's office in California—specifically, Richard Spray—had taken the initiative to prepare a new brochure for *Robert Trent Jones, Inc.,* [author's emphasis] and, at the back of the brochure, had listed Augusta National at the top of the list of golf courses that Robert Trent Jones, Inc., had "Remodeled or Partly Remodeled." Although this was, in fact, the case—Trent did deserve more credit for remod- eling Augusta than Augusta National would ever give—the issue at hand for Jones and his Montclair office was why a brochure for *Robert Trent Jones, Inc.,* was being produced in California in the first place.

No one in Montclair questioned the need for a new company brochure, but everyone in the New Jersey office believed that the *headquarters* of Jones, Inc., needed to be in charge of creating it. Careful thought had to be put into a new brochure, based on a well-studied understanding of its content and emphasis, its budget, and its production. "A brochure is not intended for internal use," Paul Colwell pointed out in a memo meant more for Bobby's operation in California than for Trent. Rather, the purpose of a brochure is to "fill the needs of those to whom it is directed—to sell, to inform, to romance if you will. Other than the quality and attractiveness of the graphics it is critically important that an objective evaluation be made to determine what information should be included in the brochure."

Angry about the brochure's provenance, Trent quickly made it clear in writing to everyone associated with his business that all publicity that "involves reference to me or to Robert Trent Jones, Inc." from now on had to be "cleared" with Red Hoffman, his part-time publicity director and consultant in the Montclair office, whose other job was as a sportswriter for the Newark *Star-Ledger*. In a June 26, 1975, letter to Bobby, Trent expressed his unhappiness about the brochure and, more seriously, about Bobby's conflation of the multiple "Robert Trent Jones" identities. The letter has to rank as one of the frankest "lay it on the line" messages he ever sent his eldest son:

> Dear Bobby:
> I understand that you said you are going to make up the brochure and you are going to send me a letter to that effect.
> As president of Robert Trent Jones, Inc., I insist that you do not make the brochure and that even though you plan on paying for it I think you will pay out of Robert Trent Jones, Inc., funds.
> *Maybe it is time that we settle who is Robert Trent Jones, Inc.*, I am putting you on notice that I am ready to move unless you come to your senses.
> Sincerely,
> Robert Trent Jones

The letter was sternly formal, and not signed with the customary "Dad" or "Father."

There is no record of Bobby making any written reply to his father's rebuke. Confusion continued to reign for many more months over how Bobby was running his business, seemingly as a mix of his own RTJ of California, Inc., and the family's RTJ, Inc., based in New Jersey. It was becoming increasingly clear to all that a complete separation was the only workable solution. ("Maybe I could sleep again," Ione said to Rees and Colwell as they discussed the situation.) Paul Colwell wrote Bobby's lawyer Walter Harrington on September 24, 1976, "What decisions if any have been made as to the question of doing business in California by RTJ, Inc.?" Harrington responded the same day: "Please be advised that the California operations are being run as Robert Trent Jones of California, Inc., the California corporation, and not the New Jersey corporation. While there may be some continuing uncertainties about the status of the employees, particularly as to payroll and insurance [the Montclair office had already informed the Palo Alto office that it would no longer pay for its employees' Blue Cross/Blue Shield health insurance], it is our position that the payment by New Jersey, and the provision of other services, is purely nominal and as an accommodation to the corporation. . . . *It's messy, leaky, but the boat will probably still continue to float, until the entire matter is resolved* [author's emphasis]."

It did not take long for Colwell to reply on Trent's behalf: "Mr. Jones has been advised that business undertaken by the California office is in the name of and in fact performed by Robert Trent Jones of California, Inc., This effects a complete termination of those persons formally employed by Robert Trent Jones, Inc., notwithstanding the fiction of their still being on the payroll. *Mr. Jones requested that I advise you and Bob, Jr., that he does not accept the new arrangement and will not accept it unless the stock of Robert Trent Jones of California, Inc., is issued to Robert Trent Jones, Inc., or to the four Joneses in the same percentage as the stock of Robert Trent Jones, Inc., is held* [author's emphasis]." In sum, Jones Senior was calling for Bobby to either share the value of his California corporation with the rest of the family, or separate the operations of his California-based company totally from those of the parent company. After all, that was the way it was now working on the East Coast, with Rees's new company operating in a totally independent manner from the parent company. In this respect, it may have been easier for Rees than it was for Bobby because he didn't have the opportunity to confuse clients and the golf world by having the same name as his famous father.

Nor were the holes in the "messy, leaky" but still floating vessel plugged at the end of 1976 when Bobby proposed terms of an agreement over their corporate holdings and relationships. According to the proposal, Rees and Bobby would each now hold 45 percent of the assets of Robert Trent Jones, Inc., the parent company, while Ione would get the other 10 percent.⁵⁵ Bobby's California company, Robert Trent Jones of California, Inc., would be dissolved. In its place Bobby would establish "Robert Trent Jones II." With it Bobby could keep the Trent Jones brand name but now had to wield it with clearer—if not *much* clearer—differentiation from his dad's business. At the same time Bobby kept all of the California construction companies save one, CalGolf; valued at nearly $150,000 in 1976, CalGolf was bought by Rees, and he still owns it. Bobby states today that "Rees did not buy CalGolf. It and its assets were distributed to him. It is my recollection that Mom helped determine who got what of the Western assets." Rees asserts that Bobby's version is pure fiction. According to Rees, his dad never agreed to what Bobby's lawyers had proposed, leaving everything still up in the air, and contended over, between his two sons. Furthermore, there is clear documentary evidence that Rees did buy CalGolf. A letter from Walter H. Harrington Jr., Bobby's chief California lawyer at the time, to Paul Colwell, the chief counsel for Robert Trent Jones Inc. in New Jersey, dated October 25, 1979, spelled out the terms of Rees's acquisition of CalGolf. That letter stated that, following a meeting of RTJ Inc.'s board of directors on July 13, 1979, "payment in full was made to Robert Trent Jones Jr., of $51,037.79, which, with the cancellation of the existing indebtedness to him of $20,584, resulted in a net distribution of $71,621.79.

It would take a lengthy book of its own to thoroughly explore the personal and professional drama that characterizes the rivalry between Bobby and Rees Jones. Whether such a book about the intense and never-ending fraternal feud should be written is another matter. Would such a book offer any insights of real

---

⁵⁵ In 1979 the New Jersey accounting firm of Lerman & Greenberg set the total assets of Robert Trent Jones, Inc., at $564,000. Of this amount, $32,501 was in the form of cash. Current liabilities stood at $620,130. This meant a deficit of $56,130. However, much of the $482,320 in debt lay in intercorporate loans that Jones, Inc., owed to his own shadow companies. Another one of the loans was "Payable to Officer," meaning most likely to Trent Jones himself. Two "Officer Salaries" were given (likely paid to Trent and to Ione) in the amounts of $139,507 and $45,000, or a total of $184,507, equivalent to $593,665 in today's dollars. It is also interesting to see how much Jones was paying for business travel—for air travel ($35,725), for other travel ($28,064), for meals and lodging ($15,127), and for telephone and telegraph ($19,150); in all, those travel and travel-related expenses added up to $98,066, or $315,534 in today's dollars. Lerman & Greenberg, Certified Public Accountants, 99 Morris Ave., Springfield, NJ, Accountant's Report, "Robert Trent Jones, Inc.: Statement of Assets and Liabilities on a Cash Basis" and "Statement of Cash Receipts, Disbursements, and Retained Earnings," n.d. [ca. Feb. 1980], in Financial Records of Robert Trent Jones, Inc., JP, CUA.

historical significance to the history of golf course architecture? Would it shed more light than heat on the last decades of Robert Trent Jones's remarkable life in golf? As early as 1973, Trent said in confidence to his advisor Paul Colwell that he "lamented his relationship with his sons." It is hard to see, in light of what happened between the brothers after 1973, how they gave him anything less to lament.

Not that Trent wouldn't enjoy the future company of his two sons, or deeply appreciate the love and assistance that each one of them, if always separately, gave to their father and mother. Trent worked again with both Bobby and Rees, but never the two of them together, on different course projects. Over the coming years Rees would remodel many of his father's golf courses; they would even remodel some together, such as the Country Club of North Carolina, which they completed in 1980. RTJ golf courses that Rees Jones, Inc., would remodel completely included the Atlanta Athletic Club (Highlands Course: '94, '96, '06; Riverside Course: '03); Mauna Kea ('08); Congressional (Blue Course: '89, '10); Bellerive ('07, '11, '13); Duke University ('93); The Chanticleer at Greenville Country Club ('01); Golden Horseshoe in Williamsburg, Virginia ('98); and Playa Grande in the Dominican Republic (in progress). Golf courses for which Rees's company would do partial remodelings were Oakland Hills (South Course: '04, '06, '13), Hazeltine National ('88,'10); Baltusrol (Lower Course: '92, '96, '97, '99, '13; Upper Course: '92, '96, '97, '09, '13); Crag Burn ('98); Montauk Downs ('08); Quaker Ridge ('92–'95); Palmetto Golf Club ('89); and The Dunes Golf and Beach Club ('03).*** Beginning in 1988, Rees and his band of design associates were hired to remodel seven U.S. Open venues, eight PGA Championship courses, and the layouts for five Ryder Cups, two Walker Cups, and a Presidents Cup. Trent was not always 100 percent happy with what Rees did to change his golf courses, and he was not shy about telling him so when he felt that way, but Trent came to admire Rees's work. In *Golf's Magnificent Challenge*, Trent picked out the following layouts as his favorite Rees Jones golf courses, calling them "gems": Pinehurst No. 7; the new eighteen for Bryan Park in North

---

*** Over the years Rees Jones, Inc., benefited from the employment of a number of talented golf architects, including (in alphabetical order): Keith Evans, Greg Muirhead, Bryce Swanson, and Steve Weisser, as well as some excellent construction men, such as Clyde Hall. So, too, did Bobby's company, with such individuals as Gary Baird, Jerry Martin, Bruce Charlton, Donald Knott, Michael Poellot, Gary Linn, Kyle Phillips, Mark Rathert, Donald Boos, Ty Butler, Mark Voss, Michael Gorman, Dwain Steinke, and Jay Blasi.

Carolina; Stoney Creek in Virginia; Jones Creek in Georgia; Charleston National in South Carolina; Woodside Plantation and Haig Point in South Carolina. It tickled him to point out that Ron Whitten, the golf architecture writer for *Golf Digest*, called Haig Point, a private course on Daufuskie Island, "better than the neighboring Harbour Town," a Pete Dye design long considered among America's hundred best.

In his 1988 book, Trent also expressed sincere admiration for Rees's "restoration" of what was to be that year's U.S. Open Course, The Country Club, in Brookline, Massachusetts. Taking the nearly one-hundred-year-old golf course "back in style, not in design," Rees produced a course that the competitors in the '88 Open loved, proclaiming it "one of the best and fairest" they had ever played in the championship. "They all seemed to enjoy it, and fairness and the quality of enjoyment is one of the trademarks of a Rees Jones work," his father was proud to say. "It is an example of a remodeling, or restoration, if you will, that was done with integrity and without an architect's ego getting in the way." Golf historians consider Rees's work at Brookline to be his "first triumph" and the moment when he became "a leading figure in golf architecture." The acclaim that came to him with the restoration of The Country Club for the '88 Open paved the way for him to make modifications for the '91 Open at Hazeltine and to be brought in to Congressional in 1989 to modify the Blue Course in preparation for the '97 Open. The imprimatur of "The Open Doctor" had clearly passed from father to son.

Trent was also very impressed with Rees for authoring, along with illustrator Guy L. Rando, "a scholarly and influential book" for the Urban Land Institute entitled *Golf Course Developments* (1974), in which, among other things, he outlined five basic course layouts for real estate projects. Given his own interest and participation in real estate/golf developments over the years, Trent respected how his younger son had grown so successful not just in the golf design business, but in his overall business sense, too. It was not always an arena in which Trent excelled, and he valued his sons for being smarter about certain aspects of business.

Looking with admiration at his sons' talents and contributions as golf course designers, Trent could forgive—but likely never forget—the traumas associated with the eternal feuding between Rees and Bobby. Even more than with Rees, Trent continued to do projects with Bobby, a few in the United States but mostly overseas. Bobby, like his father—and unlike his brother—loved to travel and enjoyed accompanying his father to golf course destinations far and wide across the planet. In the end Bobby would build golf courses in thirty-five different countries, his father in twenty-seven.

Reviewing in 1988 his eldest son's first twenty years of designing golf courses on his own, Trent described Bobby's approach to golf architecture in the following way: "Bobby is the quintessential naturalist, letting the land dictate the design of his holes and courses. His creations are sometimes more flamboyant than mine, but he always does a wonderful job of blending his work with the surroundings. His holes and courses are in harmony with the environment. He considers golf an outdoor chess game and so puts emphasis on the mental aspects of the game. His courses tend to be more strategic, with some mixture of penal and heroic holes. He believes that all elements of the game—strength, accuracy, club selection and finesse—should be tested, that a Ben Crenshaw should not be allowed to win just because he's the best putter." Trent described his son's architectural style as "eclectic," with his golf courses impossible to stereotype, each one being different from the others. He credited Bobby for building a string of great courses around the world, notably Joondalup Resort Golf Course (1985, 27 holes) and The National Golf Club (1988) in Australia; Pondok Indah Country Club in Indonesia (1977); Pine Lake Golf Club (1984), Golden Valley Golf Club (1987) and Hokkaido Country Club (1981) in Japan; The Links at Spanish Bay (1987, co-designed with Tom Watson and Sandy Tatum) and Poppy Hills Golf Course (1987) on the Monterey Peninsula; Sugarloaf Golf Club (1986) in Maine; SentryWorld Golf Club (1982) in Wisconsin; and The Prince on Kauai (1991). He was delighted when *Golf Digest* named SentryWorld the best new course of 1984, and when the USGA chose it as the site of the 1986 U.S. Women's Public Links Championship.

As proud as he was of the independence of his sons' careers in golf architecture, he loved it when the boys came to him wanting help. When Poppy Hills became part of the AT&T Pebble Beach National Pro-Am in 1991 (five years after the course opened), it received a great deal of criticism, especially from the touring pros, for its difficult terrain crisscrossed by streams and even more for its huge undulating greens, which according to one critic presented "more four-putt opportunities than any other course in the world." According to Trent, "Bobby came to me and said, 'Dad, you've got to help me soften the contours.' So that's what I helped him to do. He's done a lot of good work around the world. Rees also has done some great work. So we've become a triumphant family." Bobby and Rees would both serve prominently in the American Society of Golf Course Architects, the prestigious professional organization that Trent had helped found in the late 1940s. In 1978, Rees, at age thirty-six, became the youngest president ever to serve the society. Eleven years later, in 1989, Bobby rose to the presidency.

In 1979 the Metropolitan Golf Writers Association, an organization founded by Trent's friend Fred Corcoran in 1952, presented its "Golf Family of the Year Award" to the Joneses. The award seems ironic when we look back, not because the Joneses didn't deserve to be honored for their contributions to the sport, but because of the deeply troubled relationships within the family. At the time, however, the feuding between Bobby and Rees was not known to the golf public. Sportswriters had written dozens of stories about the Jones family of golf architects, but none of them had investigated deeply enough to discover how troubled the family situation actually was under the surface. That changed rather dramatically with the publication in April 1982 of a long feature story in *Signature* magazine entitled "The Feud of the Fairways." Its author, Jolee Edmondson, told a story that was apparently too hot for *Golf Magazine*, where she worked as a contributing editor, so she sold it to *Signature*, an exclusive luxury travel magazine.

The slug for Edmondson's ten-page story read: "It may be tee time at the golf club, but Trent Jones and family are teed off at each other." If the golf public did not know about the trouble inside the Jones family before the publication of the Edmondson article, it certainly would after reading it. First off, she called the Joneses golf's version of the wealthy, scheming Ewing family of the hit TV series, *Dallas*. "The Ewings sit around over grits and smoked sausage at the Southfork every morning and argue about how they're going to drill well No. 28. Whereas Robert Trent Jones and his boys, Robert, Jr., and Rees, don't much discuss anything, least of all business." How Edmonson got her inside information about the Joneses, "a fragmented dynasty," is not known, but somehow she had come to understand a great deal about what had happened inside the family: "They all labored under the legendary banner of the senior member. Then love and loyalty got tangled with myriad other desires and emotions, and the familial trio scattered." All of the direct quotes in the story came from Bobby, and Edmondson lived in San Francisco, so it seemed that most of her information came from him. (Bobby does not remember talking to her; however, "a fact-checker for the magazine called me and the thrust and tone of Edmondson's story caught me by surprise. I even asked, 'Have you been talking to a former disgruntled employee?'") "Family businesses are not easy," she quotes

Bobby as saying, "but family creative businesses are impossible." "In a sport that prides itself for being supremely harmonious and serene," Edmondson's article continued, "three of its most respected figures, all in the family, no less, are caught up, not in combat or cold war, but in a sort of chill."

Edmondson gave each of the Jones men a chance to explain his position on what happened to the parent company when the real estate market collapsed in 1974, and for the brothers to explain why they went their own way:

Rees: Dad is a supreme optimist. Even if we had the crash of '29 again, he'd believe that 1930 was going to be the greatest. But I was responsible for 15 employees—had to do the hiring and firing and, in essence, run the East Coast operation. I had all the responsibility and none of the authority. Clients would scream and yell at me, but the moment Dad flew into town they'd bow and scrape—he was deified in their eyes. But I got the brunt end of it. As a result, I developed a rash and an ulcer. "Rees, someday you're going to have a nice small business and design a few courses a year the way you want to." Well, I was 33 and I thought, "Why someday?" So I quit.

Trent: There were very few people who didn't pay us. That's the gloom in Rees. He always thinks I'll go broke with my "wild" ventures. He thinks the whole world's going to hell and there'll be no more golf courses built.

Bobby: We had to get control of our own lives. As in any mentor relationship, there were a lot of emotions involved when the split came, but my dad and I are very strong-willed people and it was best that we worked out of our separate niches.

Bobby, much more than Rees, would claim that his father too often took credit for the golf courses that he, Bobby, had actually designed, literally saying things like "Well, I created you, you created it, therefore it's my work." To which Bobby replied, "Hey, wait a minute! Where does that leave my mother?" Trent, on the other hand, accused Bobby of "intentionally dropping the Jr. from his name, because he wants people to think he's *the* Robert Trent Jones."

Edmondson's sympathies rested squarely with Ione and Ione's understanding of what had happened to her two sons. "You know, it's pretty hard to be the 'children of,'" Ione was quoted as saying. "You look at your historical biographies and most of the male children of famous men either become wastrels or monks." . . . "I think it's wonderful that they did break away."

No subsequent published article has done a better job of providing important insights than Edmondson's piece from 1982. The closest was an article entitled "The Jones Boys," by John Garrity in the May 31, 1993, issue of *Sports Illustrated*. "It was a Freudian psychodrama," Garrity quoted an anonymous source in the golf industry. "You had these three very intelligent, very talented men acting like children."

Many more aggravating issues would come between them in the coming years—e.g., Bobby's concerns over Rees taking the title, "The Open Doctor," and Rees's irritation at his brother for taking all the profits from a clothing label named "Robert Trent Jones." Furthermore, the friction between the brothers made it difficult to get their father's papers to the Cornell University Archives. There still are issues to resolve concerning the ownership and ultimate disposition of all of Trent's memorabilia, which is extensive.

None of the later bitterness between Bobby and Rees could ever shatter the love that Trent felt for his two sons. Edmondson understood that about Trent, too, ending her article with affectionate remarks from Jones Sr. "You know, in spite of Bobby's aggressiveness, he has a deep regard for me. Whenever we say goodbye, he hugs me and says, 'I love you, Dad.'" To his dying day in June 2000, Trent would remain naïvely optimistic that his sons would return to him. As he told Edmondson in 1982, "Rees and Bobby will soon be coming back to my firm. It's good that they went out to prove themselves. But they'll come back. . . ."

CHAPTER TWELVE

THE SUN NEVER SETS . . .

Jones remodeled the Glyfada Golf Course in Athens, Greece, for the 1979 World Cup, won by the U.S. team of Hale Irwin and John Mahaffey. It was one of several courses Jones updated and toughened for international competition. From 1976 to 1991, Trent completed nearly as many projects internationally (forty-one) as he did in the United States (forty-seven).

By the 1960s Trent Jones was well under way to "branching out beyond the continental borders," with projects underway in Europe, the Caribbean, and in the Hawaiian Islands and the Pacific Basin, as well as his first work in Canada since leaving Stanley Thompson (London Hunt & Country Club, in London, Ontario, finished in 1962). By the early 1970s, he was flying three hundred thousand miles a year to visit his far-flung portfolio of projects. "My home is in a Boeing 747," he would joke.

Jones's success in the Caribbean was aided by his friendship with Juan Trippe, the president of Pan American World Airways. In 1958 Pan Am inaugurated its jet service, using both DC-8s and Boeing 707s, on daily flights from New York and Miami to Bermuda, Nassau, San Juan, Jamaica, Santo Domingo, Panama City, Caracas (Venezuela), Lima (Peru), Brasilia, Rio de Janeiro, and Buenos Aires. Expanded golf development meant more tourists, which meant more travelers, which meant more flights. With that formula in mind, Trippe made Trent Jones a paid employee of Pan Am, "to render advice and consultation with respect to golf and other recreational facilities needed to encourage travel over our world-wide air system." Pan Am paid Jones an annual salary of $10,000 for his services, and gave Jones a special passenger status on their flights, both domestic and foreign.

A year later, Trans World Airlines (TWA) gave Trent Jones free membership in its "TWA Ambassadors Club," naming him as one of the "outstanding men who believe in the future of air travel." The airline—which flew into most U.S. cities and was one of America's largest domestic carriers—gave Jones "full privileges" to this "world-famous club" whose membership was "by invitation only," including access to club facilities at all of the airports that TWA served. (TWA also had feeder operations from smaller cities in the American Midwest, and a large European and Middle Eastern network served from its main hub in New York City.) With such strong relationships with Pan Am and TWA—and others he soon cultivated with American, United, and Eastern—Trent Jones pretty much had his worldwide air travel covered.

Jones made his first visit to Puerto Rico at the invitation of Berwind Country Club, which was established in 1930 with a nine-hole golf course north of the town of Rio Grande, some twenty-three miles east of San Juan. The course had small tees and sand greens, and the club wanted Jones to add a second nine on some rolling meadowland. Jones was not terribly excited by the site or the existing nine holes. "If the new nine holes were built in the manner of the existing nine holes, it could be done very cheaply, in the neighborhood of $25,000," Jones told the club. For an additional $50,000 it would be possible to rework the entire course, grassed greens included.

Something that did excite Jones, however, was a property he had seen about forty miles to the west, on the coast near the town of Dorado, which he called "one of the most outstanding golf properties that I have had the opportunity of visiting anywhere." The land belonged to a family whose ownership of the property dated back to 1905, when Dr. Alfred Livingston, a physician from Jamestown, New York, bought 1,700 acres along the northern coast and developed it into a coconut plantation. In 1923, Livingston's daughter, Clara (1900–1992), inherited the land. After Hurricane San Felipe tore through Puerto Rico in 1928, destroying the Livingstons' original wooden home, Clara built a much more fortified home that she called simply "Su Casa." Designed to withstand the strongest storm, the Livingston hacienda, painted pink and designed in a colonial style, had thick concrete walls, long wooden eaves, and hardy Spanish clay tiles on the roof. (In 1937, the hacienda welcomed a famous visitor, Amelia Earhart, a friend of Clara's. Puerto Rico was Earhart's first stopover on her fateful attempt to fly around the world. Clara Livingston herself was the 200th licensed woman pilot in the world, and she served as a flight instructor in the War Training Service during World War II.)

"A course built on this land has the potential of becoming a world renowned golf course of the character of Pebble Beach in California and in the manner of some of the famous English seaside links," Jones wrote in a ten-page report on his Puerto Rico trip. "It would be a tremendous attraction and would inspire a pilgrimage of golfers from the United States." Jones was unaware that the property adjacent to the Livingston plantation was a large estate owned by Laurance Rockefeller, and that a part of it had served since the 1920s as a private beachfront compound for Rockefeller family winter vacations. Nor did Trent know that Laurance Rockefeller was a member at Berwind Country Club.

Eager to make the Dorado course a reality, Jones first raised the prospect to Berwind's board of directors, asking it to reconsider its plans for the second nine at its existing site and instead consider reestablishing the club at Dorado Beach, where Jones would build a totally new course far superior to anything possible at its Rio Grande location.

The club balked. The price tag for a new golf course was much higher even than the $75,000 figure that Jones had told them it would cost for a nine-hole addition combined with a remodeling of the original nine. The real price tag was closer to half a million dollars, money that Berwind was not prepared to spend. (Moving to new sites by old clubs was common in this era.)

Enter the forty-two-year-old Rockefeller, who heard about Trent Jones's proposal at a propitious time. Rockefeller was contemplating the development of a resort hotel—and possibly a housing subdivision for as many as a hundred families—on his family's beachfront property west of San Juan. Rockefeller and Jones met several times to talk about the "Dorado Beach Development," although he first offered to help finance the resort development in association with the Berwind board. When the club continued to drag its feet, Rockefeller decided to pursue it on his own. He bought the Livingston property and gave Jones the go-ahead in March 1955 to start clearing it for the Dorado golf course.

Jones stewed over his fee for several weeks in 1955 before advising Rockefeller. Never before had he designed a course for such a wealthy man—and never before had he built one outside the forty-eight states. He wasn't sure how much, if any, of the golf course's construction one of his shadow companies could do, or how much would have to be done by companies with contracts, permits, and equipment already operating in Puerto Rico.

"On countless occasions, both in writing and verbally, in the past few months, I have tried on Laurance's behalf to get you to send us an agreement outlining the financial terms under which you will undertake architectural work on the golf course at Dorado," wrote Allston Boyer, a contract lawyer who worked for Rockefeller. "These entreaties both to you and your office have been ignored. This matter has reached a stage where something definitely has to happen. I am off on Sunday for a week to the Virgin Islands and Dorado. If upon my return to the office we do not have this agreement, I will be forced to take up the matter with Mr. Rockefeller."

The letter prompted a quick reply from Jones. He wanted his standard fee, 10 percent of the total cost of the construction, which Jones estimated at a quarter of a million dollars (or $1.9 million in today's dollars) *exclusive* of his fee. Trent also wanted an amount equal to 10 percent of the salary of the engineer who would be in charge of supervising the building of the course, a requested amount that Trent ultimately did receive. Without question, Dorado turned out to be one of Jones's biggest paydays as an architect.*

"Dorado lay on one of the most spectacular pieces of ocean beach in the Caribbean," Jones later recalled. "But we had to chop our way through a tropical jungle that was so thick we could only clear a few feet at a time. What we left of the jungle of trees came to frame and define the fairways, making the course a natural arboretum. A natural lake and two artificially created lakes were interspersed throughout the play of the course." Jones summoned all the extravagant phrases he'd perfected in pitching his previous courses to describe Dorado, assigning adjectives to each hole. The third, for example, was a "cunningly subtle" hole, "a teaser where the shot is flanked by woods on the right and water on the left. The Sneads of the game, fearing the woods, will attempt a slight hook, but therein lies the subtlety, for the slightly controlled hook may become the uncontrolled pull." The fifth was a "treacherously fatal" hole, "edged by the ocean at the tee," "lake-flanked its full length on the left, tree-lined to the bend on the right, and with a treacherous trap at the 250-yard mark." It was a "birdie possibility with two good shots, and one can always hope to prove the magic formula '2 plus 1 makes 3,' a blessed formula for egos; but with a hooked tee shot, and a hooked second, disaster lurks on the shoreline. Players have played themselves out of tournaments by taking high scores of 9, 10, and 11 here." No one could hype a golf course design better than Trent Jones, and for Dorado he pulled out his grandest hyperbole.

If the notion of a "signature hole"—the hole on a golf course that was the most visually and emotionally pleasing, if not the most challenging—had been around in the 1950s (the appellation seems not to have been invented, by golf marketing people, until the early 1990s), the signature hole at Dorado Beach

---

* Laurance Rockefeller placed Henry O. Beebe, who was vice president and general manager of Caneel Bay Plantation, Inc., as his representative for the Dorado project. (Caneel Bay was one of Rockefeller's first RockResorts. It opened in 1956 on the northwest side of St. John, one of the U.S. Virgin Islands.) Beebe was a longtime associate of the Rockefeller family and headed up Laurance Rockefeller's very large construction project in Williamsburg, Virginia. He was an architect and an engineer by profession. Beebe was personally responsible for supervising the construction of the Dorado Beach Hotel and the letting of contracts. He also supervised the building of the golf course, working closely with Trent Jones. See Allston Boyer, 30 Rockefeller Plaza, New York, NY, to RTJ, 20 Vesey St., New York, NY, 27 June 1955.

would have been the 13th. Although a relatively short par-5 of around 500 yards, the hole featured a double-dogleg around two water hazards, confronting the golfer with the dilemma of whether he should chance two long shots over water or take the safe route and possibly be faced with a 150-yard third shot. After playing the hole for the first time, Jack Nicklaus called it one of the world's toughest holes, one of the few statements from Nicklaus that Trent Jones loved to quote. (Jones would hate the appellation "signature hole." It is ironic, then, that some golf historians have attributed the invention of the phrase, for marketing purposes, to Trent. Over the years Jones learned to be as good at marketing his golf courses as he was at designing them—in some cases, the marketing may have been even better than the golf course. But he didn't need the phrase "signature hole," which has since become a standard marketing term used by virtually every golf course, to do it. When asked about which hole was his signature hole on a golf course, he would reply, "I designed all 18, therefore, my signature is on all of them.")

Trent added 18 more holes to Dorado Beach Hotel Golf Course in the mid-1960s, at which time the original layout came to be known as the "East Course" and the new 18 as the "West Course." It is not an exaggeration to say that Dorado Beach turned out to be one of the greatest resort areas in the world. For at least two generations, the very words "Dorado Beach" recalled an era of glamorous travel, when jet-setters and Hollywood stars like Elizabeth Taylor and Ava Gardner, even the likes of President John F. Kennedy, buzzed down to Puerto Rico for some time in the sun. In an earlier era they might have gone to Havana, but the Castro revolution in Cuba eliminated that possibility; Puerto Rico and Dorado Beach—and Laurance Rockefeller—were the lucky beneficiaries. For a while, Dorado Beach was *the* place to go in the Caribbean, as much of a scene as St. Bart's is today, the *ne plus ultra* of Caribbean resorts. Having an outstanding Trent Jones golf course at Dorado Beach enhanced the place's reputation.

Jones himself came to Dorado Beach as often as he could, always as Laurance Rockefeller's special guest. During one of those visits, Ed Dudley, the pro at Dorado Beach (who was also president of the PGA of America at the time) told Trent that he had "a great kid in his caddie yard and suggested I play golf with him." The caddie was only seventeen, but as Jones saw for himself, he had a "terrific" golf game. His name was Juan Antonio Rodriguez, but he told "Mr. Jones" to call him "Chi-Chi." One of the most popular players on the PGA Tour, Chi-Chi Rodriguez would win thirty-eight professional tournaments (twenty-two on the Champions Tour) and become the first Hispanic golfer inducted into the World Golf Hall of Fame. "Rockefeller, Chi-Chi, and I were together often, and we became very good friends," Jones would remember. "Chi-Chi later married a Hawaiian girl, and they built a home on the Dorado Beach golf course property. It's beautiful and one of the largest homes on the course. He is a very generous guy and everyone loves him, and he became an important figure in the world of golf."

Before starting the design of Dorado Beach in 1955, Jones spent a considerable amount of time in Bermuda at the request of Juan Trippe, the president of Pan Am. Trippe and a small group of investors had purchased the Mid Ocean Club, a classic Charles Blair Macdonald design dating back to 1924; Jones had played the course in May 1934 while on his honeymoon with Ione in Bermuda. He made a number of recommendations for updating Mid Ocean, but the club—which made it clear to Jones that it did not want him to rework it much—carried out only a few of them. The club's official history notes that Jones's "touch at Mid Ocean was light, subtle and restrained. Respecting the design of Macdonald, [Jones] reworked a number of tees and bunkers, enhancing a slightly aging masterpiece rather than indulging in invasive surgery." Jones's own documents demonstrate that he was prepared to make much bolder changes, but the club gave him neither the go-ahead nor the money to do so.

Trent Jones spent significant parts of the next four decades building golf courses throughout the Caribbean, making a great deal of money along the way in association with the development of some of the region's most luxurious resorts. But what Jones truly wanted was not to work for wealthy developers but to *be* one. He had one such opportunity on the Bahamian island of Eleuthera—a skinny crescent 110 miles long that was less than an hour flying time from Miami—where he accepted an investment stake in lieu of his fee for his involvement in the Cotton Bay Club.

Jones did his best to get some of his friends to invest with him in the Cotton Bay Club, suggesting that they accept positions on the board of directors, or at least lend their names to the club by accepting honorary memberships. Gene Sarazen was asked by personal letter from Jones; so was Francis Ouimet. To persuade Ouimet to join the board, Jones listed some of the prominent figures who had already agreed to serve: Arthur Vining Davis of Alcoa Aluminum;

Lowell Thomas; James M. Cox Jr., president of Cox newspaper and television interests; William Danforth, the founder of Ralston-Purina; Jess Sweetser, an executive with the Curtiss-Wright Corporation, best known in golf for being the first American-born player to win the British Amateur (in 1926); and William Waldorf "Bill" Astor II, "Lord Astor," the 3rd Viscount Astor and a member of the British House of Lords. Trent sent a similar letter to Bobby Jones, again citing some of these illustrious names. "While I know that you probably won't be able to use it much," he wrote to his friend in Atlanta, alluding to the great golfer's declining health, "you would do us a great honor if you would accept an honorary membership in this club. We should also appreciate it if you would serve on our advisory board." Within a fortnight, Trent received a letter back accepting the honorary membership but not the post on the advisory board. Ouimet also quickly wrote to Trent, also accepting only the honorary membership. (In writing to other prospective members and investors, Trent said that Bobby Jones and Francis Ouimet had agreed to become "directors" of the club, a direct distortion.) Problems involving the construction and financing of the golf course and resort cottages at Cotton Bay Club delayed the full completion of the course until 1959. It was both a great golf course and the sort of exclusive club that Jones and the other founding members intended, with "some outstanding men in business life" anchoring a "very distinguished membership." In 1963, *Shell's Wonderful World of Golf* featured a match at Cotton Bay between Arnold Palmer and Julius Boros. Neither pro broke par 72.

The club, however, did not prosper as Jones expected, dashing his hopes for massive riches. Its revenues nose-dived after the Bahamas gained independence from Great Britain in 1973. Over the next ten years, most of the large resorts—not just on Eleuthera, but throughout the Bahamas—were abandoned by their owners or compelled to be sold to government-favored Bahamian interests. In 1994 it shut down completely.

Jones's travels for Pan Am took him to the Dominican Republic, where he eventually built two courses, and down to Brazil at last, accompanied by Ione, some twenty-five years after he was first supposed to join Stanley and Ruth Thompson there. He remodeled Thompson's Itanhangá Golf Club in Rio de Janeiro, and built a new course to coincide with the creation of the country's new capital, Brasilia, in 1960. He also designed a course in Colombia, on a property in Cajicá just north of Bogotá, that was more than 8,000 feet above sea level, some 2,000 feet higher than the Broadmoor. Known as the Club El Rincón de

Cajicá, Jones's course hosted the 1980 World Cup, in which the Canadian team of Dan Halldorson and Jim Nelford held off a strong challenge from the Scottish pairing of Sandy Lyle and Sam Torrance.

Years later, the perils of working in an unpredictable foreign environment were brought home for Jones at a course in a lush tropical valley on the northwest side of St. Croix in the U.S. Virgin Islands, a few miles in from the sea. When it opened to rave reviews in 1966, the 6,843-yard, par-72 layout was known as Fountain Valley Golf Course. The name was changed to Carambola Golf Club in the mid-1980s as a result of one of the most violent acts ever to occur on a golf course.

What came to be known as "The Massacre at Fountain Valley" took place on Wednesday, September 6, 1972—coincidentally, the same day that eleven members of the Israeli Olympic team were killed (along with a German police officer) at the Munich Olympics. It is not known whether the killings at Fountain Valley were a case of a robbery gone bad or, as was more likely, a political act expressing resistance to U.S. colonial rule; it resulted in the death of eight people inside the Fountain Valley clubhouse. The intruders came into the clubhouse wielding shotguns, handguns, and submachine guns; their victims included four golf tourists, three golf course staff members, and a greens superintendent whom Jones, Inc., had just sent down to St. Croix to work on the golf course. Eight more people, most of them employed by the golf course, were wounded by the five masked assailants, one of whom was a U.S. Army Vietnam veteran who had grown up on St. Croix; the others also came from the Caribbean and were later found to have had affiliations with the Puerto Rican separatist group FALN (Fuerzas Armadas de Liberación Nacional, or, in English, the Armed Forces of National Liberation) and with the American Black Panther movement.

The fact that Fountain Valley was built as the centerpiece of a luxury Caribbean resort complex owned by Laurance Rockefeller was neither unknown nor irrelevant to the "Virgin Island Five," as they came to be known during their highly publicized trials. The early '70s was a turbulent period, with supporters of the Virgin Island independence movement agitating for self-rule. News of their campaign was not widely reported by either local or regional media; the ruling powers were fearful that news of the conflict would damage the tourist industry on which the health of the Virgin Islands' economy depended.

Neither Trent Jones nor Roger Rulewich were at Fountain Valley that tragic afternoon, but they certainly knew about it, as Jones was spending a great deal of time during 1972 in Puerto Rico building the Cerromar Beach Hotel golf course at Dorado Beach and anticipating many more Caribbean projects. But the massacre had a devastating effect on tourism to St. Croix and the rest of the Virgin Islands. "Eastern, American and Pan Am flights from the Mainland became ghost ships in the sky," lamented one travel magazine writer in 1975, three years after the killings. "Hotels, restaurants and stores were virtually deserted. Shop owner Betty Sperber reported daily sales plummeting from 'around $400 to $7 and change."

St. Croix's campaign to resurrect its tourist economy included the First Annual St. Croix Pro-Am Invitational Tournament, held at Fountain Valley in November 1974. The event featured fifty professional golfers, including Don Bies, George Archer, and Mike Hill, playing with 150 amateurs, many of them "top executives of leading U.S. corporations." But the island's vigorous public relations campaign was not enough. The memory of Fountain Valley was too fresh, and news reports about the trials of the five perpetrators, who would be sentenced to life in prison, sustained the impression that the Virgin Islands were a dangerous destination. That fear was refreshed in 1982, when one of the five killers—the Vietnam veteran Ishmael Ali LaBeet, who had been taken back to St. Croix in connection with a civil suit he brought against the U.S. District Judge on the island—hijacked an American Airlines jet as he was being returned to the mainland under heavy security and forced it to take him to Cuba, where he was granted asylum. (LaBeet, who would now be sixty-six, is thought to be still living in Cuba.)

The name Fountain Valley remained so notorious that the course was renamed Carambola Golf Club in the mid-1980s, the name taken from a great eighteenth-century sugar plantation. The massacre also made Trent Jones a little jittery about the Caribbean. After finishing Cerromar on the north coast of Puerto Rico in 1972, he waited five years before undertaking another Caribbean golf course, on Martinique. In the aftermath of the assault on Fountain Valley, the demand for new Caribbean resorts all but evaporated, and with it any call for Jones's services. Later in the 1990s, his son Bobby picked up where he left off, designing five courses in the Bahamas, Puerto Rico, Nevis, Aruba, and Barbados, also renovating his father's East Course at Dorado Beach in 2011.

The life of a golf architect doesn't carry many obvious risks beyond the stress of constant travel. Golfers might be upset, and sometimes even get angry, when faced with the difficulty of Trent Jones's golf courses, but this is symbolic rather than genuine wrath. A year before the tragedy on St. Croix, Trent himself would narrowly escape danger while visiting one of his new golf courses across the Atlantic.

In 1969 King Hassan II of Morocco asked Jones to design a golf course for him near his summer palace in Rabat, the nation's capital. The king, to put it mildly, was a golf nut. He first became interested in the game in 1968, after his physician recommended that he give up tennis because of a cardiac condition. Plunging into the game, he brought Claude Harmon, who he was told was the world's greatest golf instructor, to Morocco for weeks of lessons. When he decided to build his own royal golf courses, he asked who was the world's greatest golf architect and was told it was Robert Trent Jones. So the monarch dispatched a messenger to bring Trent Jones to Rabat. Trent brought son Bobby with him, and when they first met the king they "found him inside the palace walls playing golf on a little course he had constructed there, pausing every once in a while to sign some papers."

During that first visit, the king told Jones he wanted him to build "the most magnificent" golf courses the world had ever seen. It came almost as a royal command, and for Jones it was another affirmation of his lofty place in the world: He had long ago promised his darling Ione that he would become "the world's greatest golf architect," and now his prominence was such that even an African potentate knew him by name.

Between 1969 and 1974, Jones built two 18-hole layouts plus an additional nine at Royal Dar Es Salaam, seven and a half miles southeast of Rabat in the Temara Forest. The courses were built by the Moroccan army. The Red Course, completed in 1970, was an extremely long course, 7,523 yards from the back tees, and played to an unusual par of 73. The Blue Course, finished in 1974, was not nearly as long, but hardly short at 6,785 yards. Both courses lay on undulating terrain covered by more than a thousand acres of cork oak forest. In 1974 Jones also finished the Green Course, a nine-holer suitable for a fast round during lunch, but also a good course for playing lessons and a less competitive environment for a more relaxed and friendly game. All three courses were lush and gorgeous, their oasis-like beauty enhanced by displays of hibiscus, hyacinths, and banana plants. Halfway around the Red Course, which was used for the king's tournaments, golfers found a magnificent lake whose shore was lined with begonias, camellias, and tropical grasses. Pink flamingos flocked in such abundance that they, too, seemed a pageant by nature for the pleasure of the king and his guests.

Trent developed a very friendly relationship with the king, and at one point Hassan invited the architect to his birthday celebration. It would take place at his palace, situated on the ocean between Rabat and Casablanca, and the festivities were to include a round of golf and prizes.

"Just before attending, I was in Paris, where I ran into John Laupheimer, then a Philadelphia businessman who was later to become a USGA executive committee member and then commissioner of the Ladies Professional Golf Association," Trent explained. "I told John where I was going and he asked to come along. He would come to regret that I said 'Yes, join me. I'm sure it'll be fine.'

"We flew from Paris to Casablanca, where we rented a car for about a thirty-mile drive to the north. When we drove into the palace grounds in my rental car, there were soldiers who wouldn't let us through. I told them I was a friend of the king and they finally let us go in, but when I got to the spot where I usually parked, I saw only one car there and figured something was wrong. I thought it might be better to go back to the area where everyone else was parked, which we did. Then we went off to attend the awards ceremony.

"John and I walked over to the first tee, where the prizes for the golf tournament were about to be awarded. All of a sudden a group of cadets in battle fatigues showed up and started firing at the palace. I asked somebody what was going on, and he said, 'It must be part of the entertainment.' I said, 'This is not entertainment, because chunks of the palace are coming off.'"

Two of the king's highest ranking military officers, General Mohamed Medbouh (a golfer whom Trent had previously entertained at the Bob Hope Classic in Palm Springs) and Colonel M'hamed Ababou, had organized a coup d'état to be carried out by their cadets during the party. "We started running to find a good place to hide," Trent recalls. "We found an old railroad car parked by the first tee and used it as shelter. No sooner had we gotten inside than a bomb exploded on the putting green. The cadets came after our group, which included members of the king's military staff. It was probably fortunate for them that they were all in golf clothes.

"We were forced out of our hiding place in the railroad car by soldiers and made to walk to a nearby corner of the golf course, where they lined us up. Anytime someone would try to sit down, they would nudge him with a bayonet. I had on a Dorado Beach cap, and one of the soldiers grabbed it, threw it on the ground, and stomped on it. I didn't know whether it was me he didn't like or the name or color of the golf club on my hat. (Yellow was the code for the coup conspirators.) All of us were very upset and wondered what was going to happen next.

"Eventually one of the soldiers came up to me and to Laupheimer shouting in French, 'Diplomatique?' I thought, This is it. I'm a diplomat. So I pulled out my passport and showed it to him. Laupheimer did the same. We were pulled away from the others and told we didn't have to stand up anymore, that we could go sit down. 'But don't sit too close to the bushes,' we were warned, 'because somebody might come through and shoot you.' At that point Laupheimer said, 'I wonder if I have double indemnity.'

"After about an hour and a half, with dusk falling, a man came out of the palace and said, 'The king is alive. Long live the king. You may go.'

"As we were walking back to our car, we passed the place where I had first intended to park. The lone car there had been blown to bits. I was thankful I didn't have to explain that to the rental car company."

Trent later learned that the king had been taken prisoner and put in a small pavilion on the palace grounds. Rabat's main radio station had been taken over by the conspirators, who announced that the king had been executed and a republic founded. In truth, the coup ended just a couple of hours after it started when troops loyal to the crown regained control of the palace in combat against the rebels.

The putsch, though it failed, made Trent wary of returning to Morocco. (That year, as a Christmas present, Bobby gave his dad a bulletproof vest. Trent was not amused. He never brought it out of the closet it was put in.) One 18-hole golf course had been finished, but King Hassan II wanted 27 more holes. Just as Jones started to feel it was safe to return to Rabat, a second coup was launched to unseat and kill the king. On August 16, 1972, four military jets from the Royal Moroccan Air Force fired upon the king's Boeing 727 while he was traveling back to Rabat from France. Jones saw the news on TV that evening. Several bullets had hit the fuselage of the king's jetliner but failed to bring the plane down. The rebellious fighter planes flew on to Rabat where they strafed an awaiting reception of dignitaries, killing eight. The man behind this second failed coup, General Mohamed Oufkir, Morocco's defense minister, committed suicide as soon as it became clear that the king had survived the air attack.

Jones's company would return to Morocco, not only to finish the second eighteen (Blue Course) and additional nine (Green Course) in 1974, but later to build the Royal Golf d'Agadir and Golf de la Palmeraie, both 18-hole layouts, in 1987 and 1991, respectively. But Jones himself did not go back, not even to please the golfaholic king.[†] The Agadir course, to be built within the heavily guarded ramparts of the royal palace, was laid out entirely by Cabell Robinson.

For a while, it seemed that the Moroccan king was stiffing Jones out of the half million dollars owed to Trent for the Agadir project. Cabell Robinson tells the story:

> The palace contacted Mr. Jones about doing a job there and I was sent to look into the matter. The land was beautiful dunes covered with eucalyptus and other scrub and lay between the new palace under construction and the sea. I was told that we had to have the course ready to play within six months! Obviously this was not going to work and I told the head of the palace project that we could probably have the course built and planted within six months but it would not be ready for play for several months thereafter. This was acceptable. I told the director that we did not have time to do formal plans for bidding, etc., and I was asked if we needed them. Knowing that we could lay out the course on the ground in such ideal and sandy topography, I told him no, we would do things as we went along. He was quite okay with this approach. We would supply on-site supervision and the palace would supply whatever machinery, materials, and labor were necessary to get the job done on time. An agreement was quickly signed and we started almost immediately. I laid out fourteen holes on my first visit, telling our site supervisor that the remaining four would be found on my next visit. Things progressed smoothly for several months but then payments ceased and at Mr. Jones's request we stopped all work and left

---

† In 1971, the same year that Royal Dar Es Salaam opened for play, King Hassan held the first annual Hassan II Golf Trophy, a tournament that brought together not only some of the world's best players but also celebrities from the business world, arts, and other fields. The king's novel idea was to pay homage to all men and women who, like him, were golf fanatics. The first winner of the Hassan II Trophy was U.S. PGA tour player Orville Moody, winner of the 1969 U.S. Open. The late Payne Stewart twice won the Trophy, in 1992–93. The event was held at Royal Dar Es Salaam in Rabat until 2011, when it moved to Agadir. The last American to win the Trophy was PGA professional Erik Compton, best known for undergoing two successful heart transplants, the first in 1992 when he was twelve.

the site. Several months later, in a thin airmail envelope with no return address or covering letter, we received a check for $500,000. Having now been paid the full amount, we returned to the site and finished the course albeit in a bit more than the six months originally discussed. We subsequently learned that the palace only paid its bills once a year regardless of the number of invoices and reminders sent.

So, in fact, the king did pay his bill. The result was an extremely private 18-hole golf club inside the walls of the palace, so private that it has never been listed in many golf course directories. In recent years, however, it has been used several times for the Moroccan Open. As Cabell Robinson remembers, "This was the first course during my nearly twenty years with Mr. Jones that he never saw the course, neither before nor during construction, nor once completed." Jones did not travel to Morocco for the opening of the La Palmeraie course in 1991, either. According to Robinson, "Two brothers from Casablanca, the promoters, drove to El Jadida to see me on a course I was doing there on the coast. The object of their visit was to ask me to convince Mr. Jones to make a final visit for the opening ceremony at La Palmeraie. According to them he was still owed $75,000, an amount which they said would be put in escrow for payment immediately on his arrival in Morocco for the opening. I passed the message on to New Jersey. Mr. Jones never really enjoyed his trips to Morocco and especially not after his experience at the birthday party. The result was that he never went to the opening and was never paid."

By 1970 Trent Jones had enough work in Europe to open a permanent office on the continent, and he persuaded Cabell Robinson to head up its operation. Robinson had assisted Trent with some of his preliminary work on the Cerromar Beach Hotel golf courses in Puerto Rico, on the redesign of the North Course at Oakland Hills, and on the layout of Crag Burn in upstate New York, and Jones found Cabell laid-back and pleasant, and he liked the way he assimilated what Trent tried to teach him. "He taught me the major lesson of my professional career," Cabell asserts, "that golf course architecture was more art than science." Nonetheless, Cabell did not care much for the urban sprawl of northern New Jersey, and he wanted to return to the West. "I gave Mr. Jones eighteen months' notice of resignation, which was pretty fair, but he took no notice of my notice." Instead of letting him go, Jones told Cabell he needed him in Europe. "I had no interest in Europe whatsoever at the time," Robinson recalls. "I had my heart set on going out West. I loved the Rocky Mountains. Mr. Jones put me on a trip to a course he was doing in France, and I eventually agreed that I would stay at least two years."

In 1970, Cabell moved to Spain, the site of most of Jones's European action at the time, where he set up a small makeshift office in an inexpensive rented room in Fuengirola, in the center of the Costa del Sol. He ended up staying in Europe, not just until 1987 when he left Trent Jones to set up his own practice, but to this very day. Over those seventeen years with Jones from 1970 to 1987, Robinson handled almost all of Jones's work in Europe, the British Isles, and North Africa. Into the European office also came architect Don Knott, who had been trained by Bobby in California, and later Les Furber, from Saskatchewan, Canada, who had been trained as a shaper in California. Both were involved in the Costa del Sol office that Robinson headed.

Jones first ventured into the European market with projects in Spain. The impetus behind the first project came from a wealthy and influential client, retired U.S. Army Colonel Joseph McMicking, a member of General Douglas MacArthur's staff throughout World War II. McMicking was married to a wealthy Filipino heiress named Mercedes Zobel de Ayala y Roxas. The Ayala Corporation was the country's oldest and largest business conglomerate, founded by a handful of German and Spanish families, including the Zobel and Ayala clans, back in the middle of the nineteenth century. McMicking had plenty of drive and ambition of his own. After WWII, he became a successful real estate developer who did business all over the world. In the United States, with the help of his brother and others, McMicking founded a venture capital firm in California that would be instrumental in funding the Ampex Corporation, a pioneer in audio and videotape technology. At the same time, while living and working mostly in his wife's home country of the Philippines, McMicking won international recognition—and made a great deal of money— for his "exclusive and sensitive land developments" in the Makati section of Manila. But these ventures weren't enough for Colonel McMicking. "When he first saw the Andalusian areas of southern Spain," Trent Jones remembered, "he thought it was such a beautiful site he bought a few of the old estates because he had an inspirational idea that building and selling condominiums around a golf course would be a very prosperous adventure." One day in 1961, after learning the identity of the world's greatest architect from business associates, McMicking walked into Jones's New York City office and told Trent (who knew nothing about McMicking at the time) that he "wanted to build a golf course in Spain and had heard that I was the man to do it."

McMicking had found a promising property right off the Costa del Sol, just west of the port city of Málaga. He knew that if the formula that had worked so well for his real estate developments in the Philippines were to work in Spain, he would need "beautiful countryside" and "enough land"—thousands of acres—"to ensure that the environment was protected." He would need an adequate water supply for irrigating the golf course in what was a very arid region, which he secured from the Guadalmedina River adjacent to the property by fiat from the Franco government.

The property consisted of three *fincas*, or country estates, in the province of Cádiz on the southwestern tip of the Iberian Peninsula that "met the requirements" and had "no development for many miles around." The three estates were called Sotogrande, Paniagua, and Valderrama. Within a few months, McMicking had acquired the Sotogrande and Paniagua *fincas* and started to service them with roads. It took a few more months before he could finalize his purchase of Valderrama.

Jones could not wait to see McMicking's property and to get to know the colonel better. "On my first trip to Cádiz," Jones remembered, "I asked Joe about a series of stone towers along the shoreline. He said they were used to watch for the coming of the Phoenicians. When they were spotted, fires would be lit along the coast to warn the populace. That was more than two thousand years ago, he pointed out, and I thought, 'We've been in existence in the United States for two hundred years and we think *we're* old!'" It was the first of many history and cultural lessons that high-school dropout Jones would get from McMicking and other European clients.

The property was extraordinarily beautiful. As Jones described it, it was "situated on exquisite natural terrain between the pure splendor of the Sierra Blanca Mountains, with glimpses of Gibraltar and North Africa in the distance from the more elevated areas of the land, and the surrounding beauty of old cork oak trees, olive trees, and millions of wildflowers." What McMicking was giving Jones to work with was "a gorgeous sight to behold." The property was also next to virtually the only river on the Costa that flowed in volume year round.

McMicking called his new development by the *finca*'s historic name, "Sotogrande." The golf course was the Club de Golf Sotogrande. All along, the idea was to finish the course—it opened for play in 1965—in order to generate premium prices for the adjoining residential real estate, whose first stage of development was to feature large plots for the building of individually designed custom homes.

Club de Golf Sotogrande (later *Real*—"Royal"—Club de Golf Sotogrande, a title bestowed by Spain's king) turned out to be one of Robert Trent Jones Sr.'s most outstanding designs, not just in Europe but anywhere. Today it remains one of the most significant golf courses in the history of golf course architecture, because it was here in Cádiz that an American-style golf course, with American turfgrasses, was first introduced to southern Europe. For the fairways, Jones put in Bermuda grass, smuggling in two suitcases a couple sacks of sprigs from his course in Fort Lauderdale to provide a nursery from which all the fairways were planted. He originally tried Bermuda on the greens, but he found that Penncross bent worked better. He couldn't find good local sand for the bunkers, so he used crushed marble from nearby Andalusian quarries, which worked "admirably, not only as a substance to play from but also for the white, gleaming accent points to surrounding environs" of verdant green. With the hot, dry climate of southern Spain, it was mandatory to install a fully automatic irrigation system. The system installed at Sotogrande was the first tee-to-green system in Europe.

But it was not just the U.S. turfgrasses that brought American golf to Spain, and thus to all of Europe. The golf course architecture was also distinctively Jonesian: Long runway tees. Flanking fairway bunkers. Water hazards in play on seven holes, five of them on the incoming nine. A stern 6,910 yards (par 72) from the back tees. "The course [Jones] has fashioned embodies the American concept of design probably to a greater extent than anywhere else in Europe," said a writer from *Golf World* in 1965 after playing it for the first time. "Certainly none that I have seen reminded me so vividly of golf as it is played in the United States. . . . The contour of the greens, the white and gleaming sand traps, the variety of pin positions, and the subtly shaded falls and burrows of the putting surfaces, all quicken memories of golf far away." The "long savage outlines" of the Sierra Blanca mountains "might be those of Nevada," the palm trees (all imported from Valencia) and the artificial lakes, "those of the desert courses in California."

At the same time he was building the championship course at Sotogrande, Jones also put in an accompanying nine-hole short course, also finished in 1965.

He remained immensely proud of everything about Sotogrande for the rest of his life—and equally proud that he "brought American golf to Europe for the first time." Other course designers, even American ones, might have preferred to adjust, or even set aside, their American style in favor of the native culture of Andalusia, but not Trent Jones. His style and spirit was American through and through, and it was those characteristics he wanted to introduce to Europe, because in his mind they *were* modern golf.

Jones was soon at work building other courses in Spain. In Málaga, Jones laid out the Club de Golf Nueva Andalucía, which featured an 18-hole championship course called Las Brisas (6,703 yards, par 72) as well as a nine-hole par-3 course, both completed in 1968. Jones built the course for Don José Banús (whom Trent called "my Spanish Texan"), a local property developer and close friend of Spanish dictator Francisco Franco who would make a fortune by developing Puerto José Banús, a luxury marina and shopping complex that became an elite vacation hangout for international celebrities and other rich and famous people who owned large yachts and drove Ferraris and Lamborghinis. Las Brisas, too, was a very American golf course—that was what Banús wanted, because American-style golf courses, after Sotogrande, were the new status symbol of world golf. Jones had Banús's construction crew create ten artificial lakes fed by two engineered streams. Greens were raised significantly and were well protected with bunkers. Today, even after a great many new golf courses have been built in Spain over the past forty-five years, Las Brisas and Sotogrande are still among the top courses in Spain as well as in Europe.

Trent was really starting to like Europe—partly because his birth roots were there and he was comfortable with European culture and foods—and other courses followed in France, Belgium, Switzerland, Italy, Greece, Germany, even one in England. The prestige of a Trent Jones course was so powerful that the Golf Club de Genève on the south shore of Lac Léman (Lake Geneva) selected him to create a new course for them even though he asked for twice as much money as the other three architects who submitted proposals—a difference of a million Swiss francs. (Jones's two-million-franc fee was for the design and "turnkey" construction of the course. Because of bad weather and heavy soils, Jones's men took three seasons to get it all done. In the end, the fee was not at all excessive.) On Sardinia he built Pevero Golf Club for the Aga Khan (Prince Karim Al Husseini) on a site so forbidding that other architects and agronomists believed the job to be impossible;[‡] Jones's experience at Mauna Kea had taught him that the disintegrated granite on the site could be pulverized and enriched to serve as topsoil. In Castelgandolfo, southeast of Rome, he placed 18 holes within the crater of an extinct volcano, and used the seventeenth-century residence of Cardinal Flavio Chigi as a clubhouse. (The first tee of Country Club Castelgandolfo is set on the rim of the crater, with a panorama of the course spread out below it. In his 2005 book, *1001 Golf Holes You Must Play Before You Die*, author Jeff Barr included the fourth hole at Castelgandolfo.)

One of Trent Jones's more unlikely ventures involved an effort in 1974 to create the first golf course in the Soviet Union. The project took shape at the behest of American industrialist Dr. Armand Hammer, the head of Occidental Petroleum, although its germination actually began a decade earlier.

The original idea seems to have come from Robert F. Dwyer, the owner of huge timber plantations in Oregon and founder of Dwyer Overseas Timber Products Co. In 1962, Dwyer entertained a group of visiting Soviet officials with a visit to a golf course, where they followed a foursome around, learning the game. Two years later, Dwyer, who served as a USGA official on the West Coast, accepted an invitation from his Soviet friends to visit Moscow. In his luggage, Dwyer not only brought his golf clubs (the Russian customs agents thought the bag was filled with submachine guns) but also films of the last world golf championship. At a meeting hosted by the Russian minister of agriculture, Dwyer showed the films in a Kremlin auditorium. At the end of the movie, in front of an audience that "squirmed in their chairs, laughed, and commented on the pictures in excited voices," Dwyer suggested to the minister of agriculture, "Why don't you build a golf course in Russia?"

An article published in the August 1975 issue of *Golf européen* continues the story: "The idea was so incongruous and ill-advised that Dwyer feared he had made an irreparable blunder. But since offense is the best defense, he continued, 'I know I am only a capitalist, but I am just like 250 million American capitalists.' 'You,' he added, pointing to the minister, 'are a communist, like 250 million Russians. You think you are the strongest? Fine! But we think *we* are the

---

‡ For a while, Jones thought it was impossible, too. On his first visit to Sardinia, Trent and Ione rented a car and drove to the site of Aga Khan's golf course. It was dark and the closer they came on winding roads to where he thought he should be going, the worse the landscape became. Huge boxcar-size boulders were everywhere. Apparently lost and discouraged by what he felt was an impossible place to do a golf course, he and Ione returned to a hotel in Olbia.

strongest.' Then, with an inspiration he still can't explain, Dwyer finished by saying, 'With the handicap system, in golf everyone is equal.' He had won. Dwyer could see it in the faces of his listeners. He led them into the Kremlin gardens. There, under the bewildered gaze of the employees, of all the secretaries looking out the windows, unfolded an incredible spectacle: a Russian minister of agriculture, under the eyes of his associates, making his first whiffs on the green (red!) of the Kremlin! Dwyer had done well to bring his bag to Moscow. He left without it, as his new Russian friends had begged him to leave the clubs."

A few years later, in a meeting with Armand Hammer, who had recently completed a multibillion-dollar deal for Occidental Petroleum with the Soviets, Dwyer recounted the story and told Hammer that he should build a golf course in Moscow. He also told him that the architect who should build the course was Robert Trent Jones. (A typescript draft of the story, "The Man Who Sold Golf to the Europeans," was found in Dr. Armand Hammer Files, JP, CUA. In the Jones Papers there is also a letter from Dwyer to RTJ, dated 18 Dec. 1973. In the letter Dwyer explained: "Dr. Hammer has most generously agreed to donate the non-ruble costs of the course to the Russian government. It would behoove us to use all the Soviet equipment and material possible to hold down his costs." In the Jones Papers, there is also a long typescript entitled "Par for the Soviet Course," by Glenn Lewis, which recounts another tale of how the idea for the first course in the Soviet Union originated.)

Hammer, a non-golfer, had the idea to build a hotel, conference center, and office complex near Moscow, and in the spirit of the blossoming détente between the U.S. and the U.S.S.R., he convinced Soviet Premier Leonid Brezhnev that the capital city and the complex Hamner was building for it needed a golf course. It would be the country's first, and would at least serve as recreation for the men who would come to work on Hammer's enormous project, not to mention all the foreign visitors and ambassadors who spent time in Moscow. Asked who should build this golf course, Hammer told Brezhnev that none other than Robert Trent Jones should get the job. Jones had produced many great championship golf courses in North America, Latin America, South America, Europe, Africa, and Asia, Hammer told the Kremlin leader. No other golf architect came close to matching Jones. If Robert Trent Jones produced a golf course for the environs of Moscow, it would instantly be recognized as one of the world's best. After thinking it over, Brezhnev decided to give golf, and "this Jones," a try. He told Hammer to bring Jones for a visit to Russia.

Late in life Trent would recall his Moscow adventure as the major highlight of 1974 for him. "This was the year I was selected to design and build a golf course in Russia," he would say. Dr. Armand Hammer "called me on the phone and set up a meeting in Moscow to discuss building a course for the Russian people." This was "quite an unbelievable request, since Russia had a communistic government and I wondered if golf could ever be introduced to the people there." (Bobby had first visited Moscow in 1961 after graduation from Yale. On a couple of occasions, he met separately with Dr. Hammer as per his request, to discuss the prospects for the first Soviet golf course.)

In June 1974 Trent arrived in Moscow, all expenses paid by Armand Hammer, with Bobby at his side, who had been involved in the deal with Occidental Petroleum from the start. They flew over together in Armand Hammer's private airplane. After a warm reception at Moscow City Hall, where they "met with some of the top leaders at the Kremlin," followed by a comfortable night in The National, one of Moscow's best hotels, their Soviet hosts, led by the deputy minister for foreign affairs, Vladimir Kuznetsov, escorted the Joneses on an inspection tour of two possible sites at Zavidovo and the Moscow River. Twenty miles northwest of Moscow, near the town of Krasnogorsk, they found a wooded tract of land that was part of a forest known as Nakhabino that Trent and Bobby both felt could be made into a fine parkland golf course. The Kremlin appointed a Russian engineer, Ivan Ivanovich Sergeyev, to direct, and the Joneses were ready to go. The "Protocol of Intent" (June 28, 1974) was actually between Occidental Petroleum and the "Chairman of the Executive Committee (*Ispolkom*) of the Moscow City Council (*Mossoviet*)." Hammer's company was picking up most of the expenses for the preliminary visits and early studies of the golf course; after all, he had just concluded a twenty-year deal with the Russians worth a billion dollars a year.

"I designed the layout of the [prospective] course," Trent asserted in *Golf's Magnificent Challenge*. "It was a lovely spot for a golf course." During their visit in 1974, Trent "suggested to the mayor of Moscow (Vladimir Promyslov) that such a course would be an ideal site for golf's World Cup, but the mayor suggested instead to introduce golf into the Olympics, scheduled for Moscow in 1980. It would have taken thirty-two countries participating to get approval for a demonstration sport. Trent told the mayor and other Russian authorities that getting thirty-two countries to compete in an Olympic golf competition was "very possible."

A Russian project engineer was appointed to the construction work, but no construction was done on the golf course until 1989. Trent traveled back to Russia a couple of times, Bobby several more. The idea of the possible creation of a golf course in the Soviet Union of the 1970s—any golf course, but especially an American-style golf course—made international news. Headlines in English-speaking newspapers and magazines read: ROBERT TRENT JONES COMPLETES SUCCESSFUL "LITTLE SUMMIT" IN RUSSIA; IVAN MAY SOON BE CALLING FORE!; RUSSIA IMPORTING U.S. GOLF; IRON CURTAIN GOING UP FOR JERSEY'S JONES; SPECTACULAR GOLF COURSE FOR RUSSIA?; REACH FOR YOUR PUTTER, COMRADE; RUSSIANS REACH FOR THE UNSPEAKABLE—A FIVE IRON; BRINGING RUSSIANS UP TO PAR; GOLF INVADING SOVIET UNION; JUST PUTTING AROUND WITH THE RUSSIANS; THE VOLGA BECOMES A WATER HAZARD; ROYAL AND ANCIENT TOVARICH HILLS; and Trent's personal favorite, FORESKI! But along with such publicity came controversy and political battles inside the Kremlin. The golf course did not get final approval from the government. Perhaps, as Trent thought, it was because the Russians "decided they didn't want to bring in all those countries and finish last" in an Olympic golf competition. Or when the Soviet Union's invasion of Afghanistan happened, the U.S. government cut off participation in their Olympic Games and the building of a golf course was also included in suspension of sports exchanges. Whatever the exact reason, the Moscow golf course project ground to a halt.

Son Bobby never gave up on building the former Soviet Union's first golf course. He served on the U.S. delegation to the Helsinki Accords Review Conference with wife Claiborne, held in Madrid, Spain, after Ronald Reagan was elected president in November 1980. While there, Bobby discussed the project with Soviet officials in attendance, including Andrei Gromyko, minister of foreign affairs. With the thawing of relations between the U.S. and U.S.S.R. in the late 1980s known as *glasnost*, Jones Jr. quickly grasped the chance to renew old Russian friendships and revive the Nakhabino project. According to Bobby, "The revived golf project was proposed by Secretary of State and golfer George Shultz and embraced by Foreign Minister Eduard Shevardnadze as a new symbol of friendly sports competition. The Soviets formally announced the deal at the U.S.-Soviet summit between President Ronald Reagan and General Secretary Mikhail Gorbachev on June 1, 1988. While Reagan and Gorbachev, the two most powerful political leaders in the world, sat in the front room discussing cutting nuclear arsenals, I was in the back room talking about golf balls with members of the Supreme Soviet."

It took until 1994, three years after the demise of the Soviet Union, for Robert Trent Jones II to complete the course, known as the Moscow Country Club (and later Le Méridien Moscow Country Club). To the Russians, it was a Robert Trent Jones design, period. It turned out to be a very fine course. *Golf World* named it one of the top 100 courses in Continental Europe. Playing through forests of birch and evergreens, the 7,015-yard layout featured water on half the holes—a risk/reward design in the tradition of his father's golf courses. As host to the PGA European Tour's Russian Open, the venue put Russia on the world golf map. The club has turned out to be far more successful than Armand Hammer, Leonid Brezhnev, Moscow Mayor Promislov, or the Joneses could have ever imagined, with an active membership fueled by the fact that Russia today is home to some hundred thousand millionaires. In 2008, the Russians awarded Bob Jr. with the honor of "Patron of the Century" (#87) and awarded him a beautiful medal and certificate. Then, together, they planted a tree in Trent's memory.

Interestingly, Trent never included Moscow Country Club on his official list of golf courses.

"The 1970s were turning out to be the most exciting period of my life," Jones said, looking back on his life two decades later. "The golf course business had gone through a slump in the United States in 1973–1974, but more and more projects were developing for me in Europe. I think I spent most of my time on a plane, train, or automobile. I thought nothing could be better. But things did get better."

Trent built a second course at Sotogrande for Joe McMicking, on the other side of the coastal highway. The original golf course west of fashionable Marbella, with its view of Gibraltar, had made Sotogrande "a byword for quality and a fashionable address for the international set." McMicking had parceled out just a few residential lots around the golf course; they were quite large and attracted a very select group of very wealthy buyers. On the next course, he envisioned a number of smaller plots for smaller, less expensive homes, and, beyond that, condominiums, condo-style villas, and even apartment buildings. This was the business plan behind the "Sotogrande New," and Jones and McMicking believed that it would be the first "real estate" golf course in Europe.

"Our original layouts were for 36 holes," Cabell Robinson remembers, "as

Mr. Jones felt certain the site would permit that many and that he could convince McMicking to do so. We staked the 36 holes and on walking and driving the proposed layout Mr. Jones quickly realized what Joe already knew; that 36 was too many. At one point on that same visit Jones remarked to Joe that it was a shame that the course would occupy some of the higher and therefore best real estate. To his inestimable credit, Joe replied to Mr. Jones to lay out the best course that he could and to let them worry about what to do with the real estate. He knew that the course was everything."

Sotogrande New opened in 1974. Somewhat to Jones's surprise, "the Europeans were surprised and delighted with the idea" of buying a condominium on a golf course. The golf course and most of the property around it had been part of the Valderrama *finca,* which McMicking had acquired a short time after his purchase of the Sotogrande and Paniagua properties. Fortunately, McMicking's master plan did, in fact, make it possible for Jones to design Sotogrande New without any intrusion of homes, condos, or roads. Jones was given his choice of the land available (in total, McMicking's Sotogrande covered more than four thousand acres) and a construction budget reportedly of $1.2 million, the equivalent in 2014 dollars of nearly $7 million. It is hard to say whether those numbers are real, however, as both architects and developers tend to exaggerate on the high side once something is done.

Jones made sure that Sotogrande New featured subtle yet distinguishable differences from the Old. The course moved over the same sort of quietly rolling Andalusian terrain but with hills higher than those on the Old, providing better vantage points for glimpses of the Mediterranean and the Rock of Gibraltar. Sotogrande New was more demanding than its older sister but not dramatically so. Tee shots faced the challenge of fairways fringed more tightly by indigenous cork oaks than on the Old Course, but their canopies shaded the ground and extinguished undergrowth, facilitating low escape shots back to the fairway. The New Course was longer than the Old, but water came into play on only two holes, rather than six. Because McMicking wanted Jones to remove as few of the beautiful cork oaks as possible, the resultant fairways were—and still are—fairly narrow. The result was fewer, not more, fairway bunkers than on the old Sotogrande. Many club members felt that the New offered even greater diversity in its routing and individual hole designs, with no two holes alike. Soon after Sotogrande New was opened, the well-known British professional Henry Cotton, a three-time British Open winner ('34, '37, '48), moved from Portugal to take the post as director of golf at the club. The well-heeled culture of Sotogrande and the nearby attractions of the Costa del Sol were perfect fits for the British golf legend; he loved the high life of champagne, caviar, tailored clothes, and traveling in a Rolls-Royce or with his trademark donkey as his "caddy." McMicking wanted Cotton to help with real estate sales, but Cotton didn't sell many properties, and he returned to Portugal. McMicking then gave the job to British and U.S. Open champion Tony Jacklin, who played as a touring professional out of Sotogrande for the next several years.

One of the first people to build a house—in this case, a villa—on the Sotogrande estate in the late 1960s was Jaime Ortiz-Patiño. Born to a Bolivian father in 1930 and raised in Paris, Ortiz-Patiño inherited a fortune from his family's ownership of tin mines back in South America. Although "Jimmy," as his friends called him, had pursued a hectic career in international business in his youth, by this time he was living a more leisurely aristocratic lifestyle. He built a fine-art collection, started philanthropic organizations, presided over the World Bridge Federation, and started playing a lot of golf. Finding himself increasingly attached to life in southern Spain, specifically Andalusia, Ortiz-Patiño hosted neighbors and friends who came to visit him at Sotogrande for polo and tennis as well as golf. As Jones remembered, Ortiz-Patiño "absolutely fell in love with the place."

Life was grand for Ortiz-Patiño at Sotogrande into the 1970s. The volume of play on the Old Course was so light that Jimmy could walk right out of his villa and onto the course whenever he felt like it. One of Patiño's neighbors, Paul Jeanty, was a retired Belgian banker. "We played many enjoyable rounds together on the Old Course," Patiño recalled, "strolling across the lawns of my villa in the early morning straight out onto the fourth tee, long before anyone was about. At the rest hut by the 10th tee we would pause for a breakfast of hard-boiled eggs and vodka and orange juice brought to us by faithful Paco Paco, who would pedal alarmingly along the Paseo del Parque with the goodies balanced on his handlebars. In the early years we would reach the 18th green before there was any real traffic on the first tee and we were able comfortably to play holes 1, 2, and 3, finishing up at my villa."

Seven years after Sotogrande New opened, its name was changed to Las Aves ("The Birds"). Eighty different types of birds inhabited the grounds, among them five species of warbler, four species of owl, three species of wagtail, and two species of woodpecker, lark, swallow, fly, bunting, and tit. Golfers and homeowners at Las Aves could also spot grey heron, white storks, mallards, osprey, booted eagles, red-legged partridge, and red-necked nightjars.

Patiño was not in favor of the type of real estate development that Joe McMicking had in mind for Las Aves. "I realized that smaller plots, apartment buildings, and the influx of many new residents would mean more crowded golf courses and a threat to our peaceful and harmonious lifestyle," Patiño recalled. Sotogrande had been put discreetly on the market, as oil-rich Arabs found the fashionable Costa del Sol attractive, and Jimmy decided to buy the golf course. Interestingly, he put up only 50 percent of the sale price when, with his great wealth, he could have easily afforded the entire sum. When Trent Jones later asked him, "Why only 50 percent, Jimmy?" Patiño explained:

> The purchase of high-profile property by foreigners in any country can be [an emotional] issue—and Andalusians are an especially proud people. They do not accept [newcomers], even from other provinces of Spain, with any ease. In my heart I do not see myself as a foreigner. But my family's ancestral links with Spain are several generations removed. Therefore, I do not want to appear in a dominating role.

The answer was to form a consortium, which Paul Jeanty, his Belgian banker friend and early-morning golf partner, put together. This was comprised by himself, Patiño, and four other Sotogrande homeowners. It was a "seriously serious" group of individuals that included the former chairman of De Beers, the chairman of Crédit Suisse, the chairman of Nestlé, and the former president and CEO of Citibank.

Patiño's goal was to create a golf course for Spain, his adopted country, which would "equal the best in the world" and "be a real service to Spanish golf." Golf was starting to thrive on the Iberian Peninsula, in Portugal as well as Spain. Not only were there new resort developments along the Mediterranean and Atlantic coasts, but Spain's professional golfers, such as Roman Sota and the Miguel brothers, and the great Severiano Ballesteros, whose successes in Europe and America inspired a generation of professional golfers and delighted the Spanish public.

In Patiño's mind, the entire deal hinged on getting Trent Jones on board with his plan. That plan required the repurchase of many lots on the periphery of Las Aves that had already been sold and making that land available for a re-modeling of Trent Jones's original Sotogrande New golf course of 1975. What Jimmy wanted from Jones was not just a minor remodeling of Las Aves. The layout's most notable shortcomings were imposed by the requirements to conform to McMicking's residential plan. Jimmy wanted to remove those constraints and allow Jones to transform Las Aves into his dream course, worthy of a world championship.

Patiño asked Jones a question to which no golf architect in his right mind would have ever answered "no": "Trent, if I can get those plots back, and if I can give you an open-ended budget, will you redesign the course the way you would have originally wanted it?" Jones could not conceal his enthusiasm. "You ask me, Jimmy, if I would accept being put in the favorable position of being able to do the things I wanted to do in the beginning—and do them with an ample budget and with knowledge of how the course has developed its own character since then, in the way good golf courses do. Of course I would! When do we get started?" Never before had a client told Jones "to let his imagination slip the collar of financial restraint and explore the possibilities of an ideal world in which money was a secondary consideration," and it would not happen again. With a smile on his face, Jones assured Ortiz-Patiño that he would do his absolute best not to let him down.

By 1985 Trent Jones had transformed Las Aves into Valderrama Golf Club, a name chosen by Patiño to commemorate the third and final *finca* that Joe McMicking had acquired back in the early '60s. (McMicking told Jimmy years afterward, "Had I been able to buy the Valderrama estate at the start, I would have called the whole shebang Valderrama instead of Sotogrande.") Twelve years later, in 1997, Valderrama captured the attention of the golf world when it hosted the Ryder Cup, the first time the esteemed international competition had been played outside Great Britain and the United States. As for its rankings as a golf course, no course ever designed by Robert Trent Jones Sr. has ranked higher than Valderrama. For many years considered the No. 1 course in Continental Europe, Valderrama today still occupies the top position in some rankings of European golf courses. In terms of lists of the world's top 100 golf courses, Valderrama was from the start, and remains to this day, a fixture. In sum, in the opinion of the world's golf course architects, Valderrama is Robert Trent Jones Sr.'s *very best course*.

What made Valderrama so great?

The first thing to say is that Las Aves itself had been a pretty darn good golf course, as Jones and even Patiño themselves would always say. "Valderrama was already a course of quality, in no way a poor relation to its companion Soto-grande down the hill," Jimmy would say. Tony Jacklin went even further in his 2007 autobiography, saying that Patiño (a man Jacklin described as a "tyrant") "spent millions upgrading Trent Jones's original design, though he really didn't improve it much at all, if you want to know the truth."§ As a member and one-time director of golf at Sotogrande who had played several dozen rounds on the Sotogrande courses, and as someone who loved Spain, especially the Cádiz area, Jacklin's opinion of the character of the Sotogrande courses was credible.

Valderrama turned out so well in part because Jones was already familiar with the site from his experiences building Sotogrande Old and New. He was "able to go straight into my usual design routine," concentrating in particular on identifying ways to improve the green sites and putting surfaces.

The availability of the additional land for golf led Jones and Patiño to con-trive "a brilliant change that cost nothing": They flipped the nines. The switch was inspired by the desire to improve the competitive strengths of the golf course. The old front nine featured "the more testing holes and therefore de-served to form the inward nine." What had been the ninth hole was the best par-4 on the course, "as good a finishing hole as you could possibly wish for." Furthermore, it was also "well suited to the formation of spectator mounds [first invented at Augusta National for the Masters patrons]—far more pleasing to the eye than grandstands, and another reason why it would make an ideal 18th." Patiño and Jones were thinking about Valderrama as a venue for major champi-onships, possibly even for a Ryder Cup. But in switching the nines Trent defi-nitely recalled for Jimmy the example of Green Lakes. In this case, moving from

---

§ To say that Tony Jacklin did not like Jaime Ortiz-Patiño is an understatement. In his autobi-ography, Jacklin wrote: "Patiño turned out to be a bit of a tyrant around Valderrama. It became less and less of a golf club, and more his personal playpen. He was a character, but what a dic-tatorial streak the man had." At one point Patiño banned Jacklin from the course because his two dogs had gotten out of the yard and ran across the lawn of one of Patiño's friends. Eu-ropean Tour player Sam Torrance (himself a Valderrama member) was also banned at one point from the course for "taking an orange off a tree he shouldn't have, or some ridiculous thing like that." Jacklin tells the story of Patiño once seeing a cow on the course, out near one of the greens. "He took a revolver out of his desk drawer, walked outside and shot the animal right in the head. Just dropped it on the spot. He walked back inside and had the course workers haul the carcass away" and barbecue it for Patiño and themselves. See *Jacklin: My Autobiography*, p. 287.

the new ninth green to the 10th tee brought one past the beautiful Andalusian villa-style clubhouse, "obviating the need for a halfway house elsewhere on the course." The change also brought the new first hole nearer the putting green, "allowing those waiting to tee off to practice their putting while keeping the first tee in view."

The extra land for golf enabled Jones to remodel the 11th green as well as the tees on the 12th, 15th, and 16th holes, improving the shot values in each case. It also allowed Jones to turn the par-5 fourth into what came to be regarded as Valderrama's most memorable hole. No single hole in Jones's career was ever so engineered or cost so much. The hole "cost the earth," Patiño would say, meaning it literally and figuratively. Building the 565-yard hole completely anew from tee to green, Jones moved more than ninety thousand cubic yards of earth, more than he had ever moved *for a single hole*. The earthwork on the fourth exceeded the total volume that Jones had moved on most of his golf courses. (By the 1960s, modest cut-and-fill earthmoving plans rarely exceeded 150,000 cubic yards *for the entire course*.) With Patiño at his side—and Jimmy barking out most of the orders—Jones had the construction crew lower hills, fill in ravines, reposition a greenside lake and create an artificial waterfall that cascaded down into it, and move the green farther up a hill. For big hitters it was possible to get home in two shots, particularly if a strong *levante*—an easterly wind that blows in the western Mediterranean—was behind the golfer, but for everyone else it was a solid three-shotter that required a precise approach shot through a narrow entrance to a green well protected by bunkers.

Next to the fourth, the hole that took the most work was the 17th (the old eighth), another par-5, one that offered the golfer something less than championship caliber. British golf writer Peter Dobereiner described the 567-yard hole as "a long, slogging par-5 where the only requirement is to move the ball forward." When it was #8, that didn't matter so much, but for what Jones and Patiño wanted at Valderrama, "its lack of character was all too obvious." So the duo decided to rebuild the hole completely, just as they had the fourth, turning it into a more strategically challenging par-5 that doglegged slightly to the right. "Transforming the hole was a mammoth task," Patiño remembered, "involving changes to the fairway contours, the formation of a lake and stream, the building of a new green and tees, and the extension of the gabion walls [covered with bougainvillea] near the green." The lake wasn't put in until just before the 1997 Ryder Cup. By then Trent was nearly ninety and not physically able to supervise the construction—although he did attend the matches. Patiño offered the job of putting in the lake to Spanish golf hero Seve Ballesteros, who was playing fewer tournaments and was interested in becoming more involved in golf course design. Seve agreed to carry out the assignment. (The rumor has always been that Patiño, in order to eliminate Ballesteros's opposition that the Ryder Cup be played at Valderrama, paid Seve a million dollars and gave him the job of re-doing 17. Initially, Ballesteros had tried desperately to have the Ryder Cup staged at his course south of Seville, and lacking support for that idea he pushed for a new yet-to-be built course of his design outside Madrid. In short, he was competing against Patiño for the tournament.) With that final touch of adding the lake, in Patiño's view, the 17th became "visually more attractive, much more exciting for spectators, and tactically much more demanding on the players. Now the agonizing decision must be made: to lay up short of the water, or go for the carry and the sure reward of a birdie."

The hole was "winning," but not without very strong critics. Jones himself was not in favor of moving the 17th green down from its then naturally elevated position. Nor was he keen on the lake idea. In the end, Patiño won out. He always liked the drama of the 15th hole at Augusta with its water and he wanted to create something similar in the way of a dramatic finish at Valderrama.

What Patiño was not happy with was the new bunkering behind the 17th green that had been created by Ballesteros's design company. To him, it seemed "incongruous," not in keeping with "the authentic Trent Jones look" but rather with tongues of turf and other irregularities in the outlines of the sand traps. Jones was not fond of the bunkers either, but even more he disliked what Ballesteros did with the pond protecting the green. He and everyone else watching live or on TV saw that Ballesteros had gone too far with it in giving the front of the green an even more sharply shaved and precarious slope than the 15th at Augusta. Even well-hit balls could not find any purchase on the front of the green, and a spinning wedge shot was doomed to a "watery grave."

The results of Seve's redesign of Valderrama's 17th hole were nastier than even Jones, "The Devil's Architect," could have imagined. Just two years later, in the 1999 American Express Championship at Valderrama, Europe's David Frost took a 10 after three balls wound up in the water; teammate Thomas Bjorn made a 9. In all, eleven out of sixty-one players made double-bogey or worse on the hole during the tournament. At the time, most of the buzz centered, naturally, on what had happened to Tiger Woods. In the final round, Woods led Spaniard Miguel Ángel Jiménez by four strokes playing the 17th. After a perfect drive and layup to 100 yards from the hole, Woods chose to hit a 9-iron rather than a wedge to protect against backspin. He hit the shot just the way he wanted. The ball bounced once on the green and stopped. Then the ball began to move, and it kept moving until it reached the shaved slope, picked up speed, and plunked into the water. It was a "perfectly struck shot," which Woods felt should have left him with an uphill 8-footer for birdie. Instead, it went in the water. Woods scored a triple-bogey, letting Jiménez back into it. Tiger won the championship on the first hole of a sudden-death playoff. The reactions from the players were sharply critical of the 17th hole's redesign. "Pitiful," America's Hal Sutton said after watching Woods's ball crawl at a snail's pace across the green and down into the watery grave. "That hole needs to be changed," Tom Lehman said. "I hate that hole," agreed Europe's Colin Montgomerie. After the tournament, Patiño invested more money in his beloved golf course, adding four feet of green to eliminate the severity of the front slope.[¶]

Although Las Aves had plenty of trees, Jimmy Patiño wanted a virtual arboretum. At great expense, he arranged to transplant hundreds of mature trees, some brought from as far away as Seville. More than five hundred of them were olive trees, "wonderfully gnarled" by age. Some were more than four hundred years old, and these were placed near the native cork trees. Three hundred additional cork oak trees were brought in—"young" at only sixty years old—to augment the natural forest. Patiño also had more than three thousand *Halepensis* pine trees planted around the perimeter of the property, to shield the course and its golfers from some nearby villas that Jimmy didn't like because they were "built exceedingly close to the golf course."

Money also gave Patiño some of the world's best greens, as good or better—and faster, some said—than Augusta National's. Jimmy wanted nothing less

---

¶ Valderrama's competition for the 1997 Ryder Cup was another Spanish course, Novo Sancti Petri, which Seve Ballesteros had designed. When Jaime Ortiz-Patiño won out with his Valderrama proposal, the offer to let Ballesteros help with the changes to hole number 17 was an effort to salve his bruised ego. Besides the lakeside green, Ballesteros replaced fairway with rough in the long driving area, to force a layup for the longest hitters and effectively lengthen the reachable par-5. The shaved slopes, à la Augusta, seem to have been Patiño's idea. According to Roger Rulewich, Patiño "took childish glee every time a ball trickled into the water. The green was his pet. He had me build new tees, lower and re-bunker the first landing area after the Ryder Cup but the green was his baby." Patiño also rebuilt the lake, no small feat, with its concrete liner, between the 1999 and 2000 World Golf Championships. The green got rebuilt *annually* for the Volvo Championships when it returned to Valderrama in 2001 but always with shaved banks. Even a miss to the right would catch the close-cut swale and end up in the lake!

than an immaculately maintained course, just like Augusta. He wanted absolutely no *Poa annua* (an annual bluegrass) on his course, anywhere. None. *Poa*
was much inferior to creeping bent grass, and not only did *Poa* not provide a
true and uniform putting surface, it made bent-grass greens look splotchy. (The
grass in both the fairways and rough at Valderrama was Bermuda 419.) Patiño
knew that every other course on his side of the Atlantic had some *Poa annua* in
it during certain parts of the year, but he wasn't about to tolerate that at
Valderrama. There would be *no Poa*. Jimmy put himself through "a crash
course" in turfgrass management and allied disciplines, attending courses and
seminars in the United States, and even requiring his club professional, Juan
Zumaquero, to complete the diploma course in turf management at the University of Massachusetts. One of the major elements of the high ranking given
to Valderrama over the years would be that there were no better putting surfaces in Europe at that time—and very few could equal them in the United
States or anywhere else in the world. ("I know of only one course in Spain that
has better greens," Patiño would say with a little wry, impetuous smile. "In 1989
we opened our nine-hole par-3 course, which is integral with the main course
and was also designed by Robert Trent Jones.")[**]

Valderrama proved spectacular both for its beauty and its difficulty. The
first Volvo Masters, the culminating event of the PGA European Tour, was held
there in 1988. The four best players in the world at the time—England's Nick
Faldo and Sandy Lyle, Wales's Ian Woosnam, and Spain's Seve Ballesteros—
finished at the top, with only two of them breaking par—Faldo, the champion,
at -4, and Ballesteros at -2. Jones commented after the event, "As at all great
courses, the cream rises to the top." The Volvo Masters continued to be played at
Valderrama until 1996; it then took a hiatus from Cádiz but returned to the
course from 2002 to 2008. And, of course, the Ryder Cup came to Valderrama
primarily due to Patiño's influence on the European Tour. Captained by Balles-

---

[**] Jones designed the nine-hole par-3 course at Valderrama "for the members who owned
small houses and condominiums surrounding it so they could putt and chip." Trent felt this
"gave them the opportunity to play on a wonderful course especially designed for them, so
they could practice and improve their game" before they attempted to play the two regulation
courses. Some members played the short course all the time, simply to relax and not have to
face the challenge of the larger courses. RTJ, "Just Me, Trent Jones," pp. 91–92. See also Ortiz-
Patiño, *Valderrama: The First Ten Years*, 1985–1995, p.31. Patiño always claimed that Jones
modeled the par-3 course after the one at Augusta National. Neither Rulewich nor either of
Trent's sons believes that is true.

teros, the Europeans won the rain-soaked competition over the Americans with 14½ points against the U.S.A.'s 13½. All of Spain was jubilant.

Having become good friends during what almost amounted to a joint design at Valderrama, Jones and Patiño remained very close for the rest of Trent's life. (Jimmy died on January 3, 2013, at eighty-six.) The two men were born on the same day—June 20—though not in the same year, and whenever they could they celebrated their birthday together. In Europe, there was no place Trent would rather go, and he stayed as a guest in Patiño's villa "many, many times."

Jones regretted that he never got a chance to create a golf course in Scotland. But in the early 1980s he embraced the opportunity to design a second course at Ballybunion, on the west coast of Ireland in County Kerry; Herbert Warren Wind called the original there "nothing less than the finest seaside course I have ever seen."

Jones's "embrace" of the opportunity at Ballybunion had nothing to do with money. It was a very low budget course. The design fee was 50,000 Irish pounds plus travel expenses. That amount wouldn't have been terrible if Jones had only gotten it. "Soon after work began," Cabell Robinson remembers, "it was evident that the club really had very little money to do the job and they certainly weren't paying us. We weren't even being reimbursed for our travel expenses, so Mr. Jones curtailed our visits and eventually stopped them altogether. What would happen was that Mr. Jones would fly into Shannon and be picked up by the club secretary Sean Walsh and driven to the site. There Jones and Eamon Allen, the course superintendent, would make their way around what was very difficult terrain as best they could. In the end we received little if any of our fees. Instead, a number of us, including many who had nothing to do with the project, received life-time memberships and Ballybunion club blazers."

Despite the money problem, Trent persisted in seeing it as "a chance that comes once in a lifetime," the opportunity to build a partner course to a storied links, in a place where golf had been played since 1893. To have the chance not just to add to Ballybunion's legacy but to build a brand-new course on a stunning seaside property—classic linksland, with rolling, tumbling sandhills along the estuary of the River Shannon as it flows into the Atlantic Ocean—was, as Jones knew, an extraordinary opportunity. Naturally, it was Jones's stated ambition to create "the finest links course in the world," even better than Ballybunion's marvelous original.

The "New Course" at Ballybunion would hardly become that. But it certainly became a golf course that, as soon as it opened for play in 1984, stimulated very strong feelings. As Tom Doak has written about New Ballybunion: "Like many new courses, it is one of those you are bound to either love or hate—because that's exactly how it treats your golf shots. If you're not hitting your irons within 25 feet of the hole, through a stiff breeze at that, you'll need strong legs just to finish the round. I don't see how any sane man can rate it superior to its older sister."

The endurance it took to walk up, down, and across the many high dunes of Ballybunion New in all of their grandeur was, indeed, one of its problems. Some of the elevation changes around the layout simply wore the golfer out. To get from some of the greens to the next tee on the course required some awfully long walks—and worse, required, in almost every case, directional signage that proved to golfers "not only a distraction, but a reflection of the confusion of the routing." Jones had laid out very few links-like holes over the course of his career (holes #1 through #5 were certainly exciting links holes), and never on anything resembling this sort of terrain. "It was an extremely difficult piece of dunes topography," Cabell Robinson emphasizes, "and very unusual in the sense that the major dunes ran perpendicular to the sea rather than parallel to it." But rather than pointing at the difficult topography, critics blamed the Jones paradigm of golf design as the reason the course did not turn out as well as everyone had hoped. "Jones was never known for designing links courses," an outspoken critic would remark, "and it shows here." Too many holes were "quirky" or "odd" and "not based in the spirit of links design." Golfers on Ballybunion's "Old Course" were rewarded with just what they expected from links golf: a layout conforming to nature—and seemingly all natural as a landscape—calling for an intuitive approach to play, whereas teeing it up on the New Course confronted them with imposing challenges that were mostly contrived—some said contrived "American style." The greens were guilty of the same artificiality, several of them "poorly and unfairly contoured." That was a crying shame, many felt, because as Jones had noted, the land offered "so many natural sites for the bunkers and greens" that it gave him "every opportunity to use every spot I could to enhance its beauty."

The fundamental rebuke that critics of Ballybunion New directed at Jones was that he fell flat in making truly outstanding use of what Trent himself called "the finest piece of linksland I have ever seen." How and why after so many years of experience had he let this golden opportunity slip away?

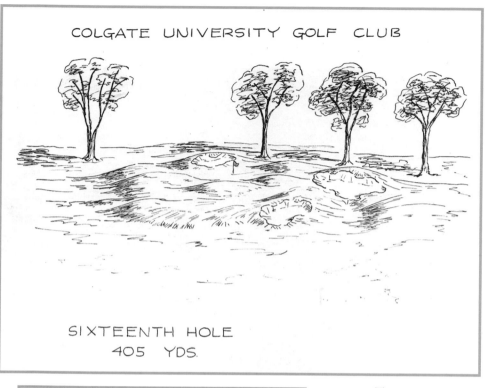

COLGATE UNIVERSITY GOLF CLUB

SIXTEENTH HOLE
405 YDS.

GREEN: AN EXTREMELY LARGE AND TREACHEROUSLY CONTOURED GREEN WHOSE SURFACE IS KEPT VERY FAST SO SHOT DEMANDED IS OF A PITCH AND RUN TYPE   THE HOLE IS MADE DIFFICULT BY SUBTLE GREEN CONTOURS. A DECIDED CONTRAST TO THE PREVIOUS HOLES

TRAPS: THE SMALL POT TRAPS FLANKING THE GREEN ARE ADROITLY PLACED AS ONE WILL SEE IN CHARTING THE ROUTES MAKING THEM PUNISHING INSPITE OF THEIR APPARENTLY INSIGNIFICANT SIZE

THE LONG HITTER (A) MUST TAKE A GAMBLE, HUGGING THE POOL WITH HIS DRIVE FOR POSITION SO THAT THE SECOND SHOT WILL BE EASIER.

THE SHORT PLAYER (B) HAS AMPLE ROOM FROM THE TEE. THE SECOND SHOT WILL BE JUST SHORT OF THE GREEN. THE THIRD A PITCH AND RUN TO THE PIN.

DR: RTJ.

16.

405 YDS.

CREEK

POOL A

B

335

235

200

0 YDS.

The green complex at Colgate University's original 405-yard par-4 sixteenth hole as "designed and sketched by Robert Trent Jones" July 1936. The two nines of the Colgate golf course, known as Seven Oaks, would be built by Jones according to his old designs but not until 1957 and 1965, respectively.

In his plan for the original sixteenth hole at Colgate, Jones describes an "extremely large and treacherously contoured green," small but "punishing" traps, and the need for the long hitter to "take a gamble" by hugging the stream to the left side of the straightaway fairway.

Trent Jones's career benefited enormously from the talent and hard work of his construction superintendents, notably Bill Baldwin (to the far right, in sunglasses), a man who worked for Jones for forty years and who, according to one golf magazine, was "Michelangelo with a bulldozer," for his genius in translating Trent's design ideas into reality on the ground. In this photo from early 1971 on the site of what was to be a 36-hole facility at Point Aquarius in east central Alabama, Baldwin is joined (in order to his right) by Rees Jones; Rees's father, Trent; and John Schmeisser, one of Jones's other construction foremen.

Robert Trent Jones Jr., Laurance Rockefeller, and Trent Jones looking over plans for Mauna Kea Beach Resort Golf Course in 1964

Cabell Robinson, Roger Rulewich, and Rees Jones not long after Cabell and Rees began working for Robert Trent Jones, Inc.

Young Roger Rulewich at work with Trent Jones in 1961. Rulewich would work for Jones for the next thirty-two years.

In 1970 Trent sent Cabell Robinson to Spain to organize a European office for the Jones company. Over the next seventeen years, Robinson handled most of the Jones projects in Europe, North Africa, and Britain. In this photo, Robinson and Jones survey the construction site for the new Valderrama Golf Club in Cádiz, Spain.

VIDAUBAN

ROBERT TRENT JONES

ROBERT TRENT JONES INC
GERARD P. SAUBE

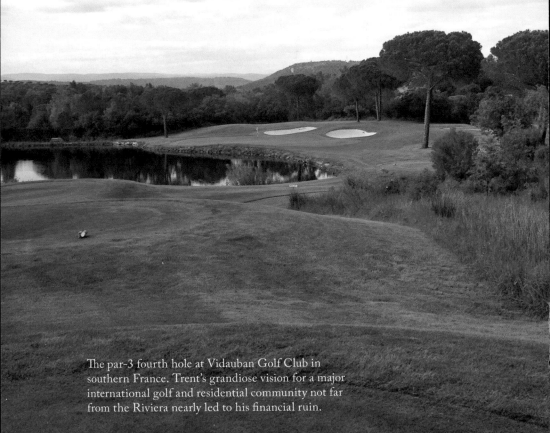

The par-3 fourth hole at Vidauban Golf Club in
southern France. Trent's grandiose vision for a major
international golf and residential community not far
from the Riviera nearly led to his financial ruin.

Bobby and Trent at
Spyglass Hill in 1992

In 1979 the Metropolitan Golf Writers
Association of Greater New York
presented its Golf Family of the Year
Award to the Joneses. Rees stands to
Trent's right; Bobby stands to Ione's left.

In 1992 Trent addressed a meeting of the Virginia State Golf Association in Colonial Williamsburg while son Rees looks on. Trent called the Golden Horseshoe
course, which he completed there in 1963, his "finest design" and "one of the best
examples of traditional golf architecture in the world." Trent regarded the four
par-3s at Golden Horseshoe to be one of the best collections of par-3s in all of golf.
In 1998 Rees completed a major touch-up of the classic golf course.

Robert Trent Jones Sr. at a ceremonial opening of one of the golf courses on Alabama's Robert Trent Jones Golf Trail in 1992

Trent and Ione with their granddaughters, Alden and Amy, daughters of Rees and Susan Jones

A unique view of "the three Trents"—from right to left, Trent Sr., Trent Jr., and Trent III (Bobby's son)—as they prepare to take off from Palo Alto Airport in December 1987, five months after the death of Ione. Their flight took them down to the Monterey Peninsula, where two of Bobby's newest courses had just opened: the Links at Spanish Bay and Poppy Hills Golf Course.

Jones stands between the first tees of the Ridge and Valley courses at Birmingham's Oxmoor Valley on Alabama's Robert Trent Jones Golf Trail in 1992.

Trent sits in a golf cart with SunBelt president Bobby Vaughan, who, along with Dr. David Bronner, the visionary head of the Retirement Systems of Alabama, was responsible for creating Alabama's Robert Trent Jones Trail.

Trent shows that he still has the touch by making a long putt during the ceremonial opening of Huntsville's Hampton Cove on Alabama's Robert Trent Jones Golf Trail.

No one is better able to answer this question than Roger Rulewich, Jones's longtime associate, who staked out the centerline of the New Course during its preliminary design. "Mr. Jones would make visits and go look at the green sites. By that time, a job visit for him on most golf courses was for him to go around looking at the green sites, giving contractors or his own shapers his own hand-drawn sketches and an idea of what he wanted them to do." Doing those sketches, according to Rulewich, had become "his main tool with which he was able to challenge the golfers," given that he had so many different courses underway, and in such far-flung places. Later, when Rulewich returned to Ballybunion to survey how the links was coming along, "I was amazed to see, going over there after he had gotten most of it done, that he had forgotten to follow through with so much. It was missing almost all the things we had on the original plans, even where some of the tees were supposed to be." Roger said to himself, "This is a shame. This is a disappointment." Still devoted to Jones, Roger was nonetheless "so very unhappy" with what resulted at Ballybunion that to this day "I really don't want to be associated with any of the work there, because I don't think he finished the whole golf course there." Why did that happen? The course was difficult to build—"a tremendous challenge," in Jones's own words. It meant working on sand with little irrigation, on terrain where it was very hard to establish turf. "So instead of tackling some of the grading that was needed," Rulewich explains, "Mr. Jones just accepted what was there." One of the holes at Ballybunion New, the original 12th, even had to be abandoned, because the huge sandhills directly in play were far too severe.

The Old Course at Ballybunion "should have been a good model, but Mr. Jones "never spent enough time on it to find out why it was so good."

Although the construction budget was very tight in a then more impoverished Ireland, it is surprising that someone whose architectural roots went back to Stanley Thompson would have neglected the opportunity to study a classic links such as Ballybunion, to learn what qualities made it such a perennial challenge and an enduring favorite among aficionados of links golf. Jones had written all kinds of articles about what made Pine Valley great, what made Pebble Beach great, and what virtues a host of great golf courses possessed. Then to go to a place like Ballybunion and not learn from its merits seems paradoxical. Perhaps Jones, by this time in his career, was so focused on the ideas of his own design that he didn't pay much attention to other architects' great works. Trent thought he knew what to do best, and he didn't have to take many guides or leads from what other people were doing—or had done well, for that matter.

Once he had achieved his ambition by the 1960s of being regarded as the world's greatest golf architect, a degree of hubris and overconfidence settled in over Jones. When that hubris was yoked to so many course projects under way in such widely separated regions, it was impossible for Jones to give even an assignment as desirable and significant as a new course at Ballybunion the attention it deserved. He delegated and occasionally collaborated on some projects. However, according to Rulewich, "It was hard for him to design and be involved with all these golf courses and really be on top of all the details related to grading, building tees, and so forth. He would look at it after it was done, say it was fine or whatever. Somehow he didn't get involved with the whole-cloth of the golf course in many ways. He was amazing in how much he was able to do without help or without his complete and continued attention."

As hard as it is for Rulewich, he says, "I think the lesson I learned from him was a negative lesson. You get into a place with the high hopes of your clients and the promises you made to them. When you don't pay close attention to this, they grow very disappointed and upset. I could see that happen with some clients. Mr. Jones was more interested in the next job than the one in hand. Once secured, his interest waned and other people, Cabell or myself, could fill the void. Ballybunion was different. This was a job for 'Himself,' as they called him there."

Readers should not be left with the idea that the New Course (now known as the Cashen Course) is a bad golf course. Jones made sure that the layout was a combination of long and short holes. He also made it clear that he didn't want to put many bunkers on the course, but insisted that every bunker produce a severe penalty. Jones's great imagination gave life to several of the golf course's best holes and most memorable features. Cabell Robinson recalls how he himself was having difficulty finding a route for the 15th hole, but during one of Jones's visits he saw it immediately. "I took him out to the area," Robinson recalls, "and right away he saw a green site. And it made the hole. That's a gift, perhaps, but it's a gift that comes from knowledge and experience, what you've learned from a lifetime of doing that sort of thing. Mr. Jones had some great imagination." The resulting 15th hole, a par-5 at 487 yards, was spectacular, playing down into a sunken fairway with tall dunes to each side that would bring comparisons to being in the Roman Colosseum and hitting to the elevated green from the lion's den. Among the other truly impressive holes that Jones gave to the course was the 154-yard par-3 third, where golfers played to heights above the Cashen River, whence the course eventually got its name.

Then there was also the extra-special green location for the 389-yard par-4 13th—it was a tiny shelf that turned into a putting surface that Trent called "the best he had ever designed."

The truth is, although Jones could have done better, if his Irish links course had been ten miles down the road rather than right next to Ballybunion's Old Course (rated No. 1 in Ireland and in most top 20s in the world), golfers might have flocked to his course—which, despite all the criticism, is rated by many as one of the ten best in Ireland. Once again quoting one of today's most acute critics of golf architecture, Tom Doak: "In the end, it must be admitted that the New Course is one that gets the pulse going quicker, and the pioneer spirit in me says that is a mark of greatness; it's too bad the recent 'softening' [in the early 1990s, due in part to overwatering and in part to sand collapses on cliffs] has taken some of that grandeur away, since it may have been the only thing the original design got right. But why waste our time arguing a point akin to whether Tommie Aaron was a good ballplayer? (Tommie Aaron was a Major League Baseball player who was the younger brother of Hall of Famer Henry Aaron.) It's another member of the Ballybunion family, which is the reason you must go there."

"Personally, I have always considered Ballybunion to be the last course that Mr. Jones himself did," says Cabell Robinson. "Sadly, I feel it would have been a much better swansong for him had he let Roger or any of us be more involved. It was certainly evident to both of us that, for Mr. Jones, the chase was more enthralling than the capture."

Robert Trent Jones Sr. was a dreamer and a visionary—a man with big ideas. Without those qualities, he could not have survived the Depression as a golf course designer. He might have gone to work for New York Bell where his father-in-law was a vice president, or sold insurance, or scraped out a living as a golf club professional. He would not have become a world-famous, globe-trotting, uniquely accomplished, highly distinguished and somewhat wealthy person.

But Jones's big ideas could—and occasionally did—get him into trouble, financially and otherwise. By the late 1970s he was accustomed to decades of rubbing elbows with some of the world's richest and most influential men—the likes of Lowell Thomas, Laurance Rockefeller, Juan Trippe, Dwight Eisenhower, Joseph McMicking, Aga Khan, Arthur Vining Davis, King Hassan, and Harvey Firestone—and was always looking for ways to leverage his position as the world's leading golf course architect into participation in his clients' land-development plans. Sometimes, as in Eleuthera, he was essentially betting his fee by taking it in shares of the operation. But he got no less ambitious as he got older, and his enthusiasm could run far ahead of his expertise and judgment.

In the south of France, not far from St. Tropez in Provence, Jones's dreams focused on a parcel of land covering nearly three thousand acres in Vidauban. The minimum investment required to develop it in 1974 would have been upward of $20 million—money Jones did not have. But the biggest impediment to executing his grand scheme at Vidauban was not funding, but rather the bureaucratic warren of permits and approvals required to build such a golf fantasy land. The French legal labyrinth led to a discouraging series of dead ends, false starts, and dashed hopes. What happened in the "Vidauban Affair" between 1971, when Jones first moved to acquire the land, and 1991, when a single, private 18-hole golf course—and nothing else—managed to open, is a tale of misplaced aspirations amplified by poor judgment, foolish decisions, and more than a touch of arrogance. No single subject in the Jones Papers at Cornell, recording a business career of more than seventy years, generated as much documentation as Vidauban. Vidauban nearly bankrupted him.

Jones's grandiose master plan for the Vidauban property called for three golf courses, at least two clubhouses, three thousand condominiums, and two large hotels with more than three hundred rooms. Members and guests at Vidauban would also enjoy horseback riding, tennis, swimming, canoeing, and sailing. An early marketing piece articulated Jones's vision:

One course will be designed on the British linksland style of architecture, another following the parkland like Augusta National style, and the third a heroic style similar to Oakland Hills and others. The courses will be the [magnet] to attract the best European and American golfers; an international set of attractive, successful, and affluent people—the business, social, and government leaders of the West. In the fall or spring each year a major tournament would be held (perhaps called the International Open) to attract the best professionals from throughout the world. In time it is intended that the tournament would rival the Masters and the U.S. and British Open [tournaments].

Jones imagined Vidauban, somewhat oxymoronically, as the "largest exclusive" club in the world, with a hand-picked international membership paying premium fees to join. Joe McMicking's plan to turn Sotogrande into an international golf club surrounded by condos and villas strongly influenced Jones's plans for Vidauban—in Jones's grandest vision, he imagined a Sotogrande on steroids. Already considered the world's greatest golf architect, Jones was certain that success at Vidauban would transform him into a leading business tycoon as well.

As with many of Jones's business dealings, the origin of the Vidauban debacle is shrouded in mystery. According to the most reliable account, Paul Rolin, a Belgian baron who partnered with Jones for the 1968 design of the Golf de Bercuit course in Baron Rolin's home country, introduced him to a man named DuBois, owner of a large property along the l'Argens River in southern France that DuBois wanted to sell. By the 1970s, Trent did have a great deal of overseas experience, mostly in Europe, but nothing that would have made him an expert in international business. In fact, the very volume of work in his portfolio stretched his attention across many countries and tested his ability to manage an expanding consulting company. He struggled to keep his clients happy; he never turned down work; and he savored his skills as a salesmen. But only a savvy and experienced developer, assisted by a skillful team of lawyers and business associates, could have carried out the mammoth development that Jones had in mind for Vidauban. Trent Jones had neither.

Cabell Robinson watched the Vidauban affair unfold with a dark foreboding, but he felt helpless to protect his employer from his colossal ambitions. Robinson's recollections provide the most complete and plausible account of the early Vidauban calamity.

"I started visiting Vidauban with Mr. Jones in the early 1970s, when his acquisition of the property was going through the French zoning process," Robinson recalled. "It was coming down to what they were going to grant him in terms of building space. He was waiting for a decision for what the French call a 'ZAC'—a *zone d'aménagement concerté*. According to the ZAC being offered to Jones, he would have had to give up 300–350 hectares of open space at the upper end of the Vidauban property, which was pretty ugly property anyway in terms of development, very rocky. You couldn't do much with it anyway. But Jones was totally angry that he had to give up all this land. I told him, 'Mr. Jones, it doesn't matter. What they're giving you is permission to build many tens of thousands of square meters of construction and whether it's spread out over 1,100 hectares or 790 hectares or whatever the number, it's immaterial, because what you're getting regardless is the amount of square meters.' Well, Mr. Jones could never come to grips with that principle. The fact was, he was granted, preliminarily by the Central Government in Paris, something on the order of 270,000 square meters of construction, which was enormous! Especially in a rural area in France! It was the equivalent, say—take an average home of 330 square meters, which was a fairly decent size—that was a couple thousand of these homes! I mean, it was an unbelievable amount."

Jones invited Charles Fraser, the American developer of Sea Pines Plantation on Hilton Head, to consider investing in Vidauban. Fraser possessed the qualifications Jones lacked: a law degree and experience developing large properties. Sea Pines Plantation was almost twice the size of Vidauban, and according to John McPhee, in a profile of Fraser in *The New Yorker*, featured "ironclad" restrictions on every deed, granting Fraser full control over all of the covenants, conditions, and restrictions throughout the development. The prospect of Fraser agreeing to participate as a passive investor was slim, given his approach to development. Fraser was Jones's opposite in many respects. Where Jones slid into Vidauban on the seat of his pants, Fraser planned his developments in elaborate detail and controlled the careful, deliberate rollout of every phase. Fraser did not invest in Vidauban and later went bankrupt himself.

The demand for golf course design had weakened in the late '70s, Robinson explained, and the firm's revenues were suffering. Jones struggled to keep up with the Vidauban payments. "The ZAC the French had given him really amounted to a quid pro quo," Robinson noted. "They told Jones, 'We're going to give you this amount of building permission and, in return, you better do x, y, and z for us.'" Jones was supposed to buy the township of Vidauban a new fire truck, but couldn't. "So, little by little, the ZAC—the planning permission—was in danger of not being approved."

Robinson believed that Jones "was a lousy businessman—a marketing genius, in many ways, but a lousy businessman." Jones did not commission a marketing study of the property, the first step any experienced developer would take. What's the level of demand? What prices can the real estate expect to achieve? What's the projected velocity of sales? What are the expected rates of return? These are the kinds of questions developers try to answer before they start moving dirt, but Jones insisted to Robinson that Vidauban "will sell itself," and at projected prices that were, in Robinson's words, not "even good educated guesses." Jones believed he would net a pre-tax profit of "$200 or $300 million"— a figure constructed entirely of gossamer.

Robinson, meanwhile, was visiting bankers and potential investors in Geneva, Zurich, and London on Jones's behalf, and all of them asked to see a feasibility study. Some of them, Robinson recalled, "seemed quite interested," but balked when they learned that there was neither a business plan nor any viable financial projections. "I certainly wasn't doing this on my own," Robinson stresses, "and the net result was always the same."

John Laupheimer, Jones's longtime friend, was also his partner during Vidauban's infancy. The principals of the "Jones Laupheimer Joint Venture" asked Charles Gordon, director of the Brighton Marina Company, to join them. Gordon, a major shareholder in Archer Golf and Sports, then the largest golf retailer in Europe, did invest in Vidauban, but regarded his participation as a loan, demanding interest at 22 percent. The partnership also engaged a Polish-born American attorney residing in France (also a Holocaust survivor), Samuel Pisar, to assist in the land purchase and help with the zoning and development certification. The bill for Pisar's legal services soon rocketed to nearly $100,000. Pisar sued Jones for the money in 1979 and charged Jones, in Robinson's recollection, 30 percent interest on his outstanding bills.

Between 1972 and 1981, Jones made sixty-nine trips to Europe, most of which included business matters related to the development of Vidauban. That was how deep into this morass he had gotten.[††]

In yet another example of poor judgment, Jones hired the American wife of an old friend, Alan Hirsch, who owned a winery in France, to lobby for Vidauban. Denise Hirsch was fluent in French, and Jones was convinced that she could help him find investors. Jones's sons believed she was taking their father to the cleaners, running up a big expense account for herself in Paris, on the Riviera, all around. "I know Trent's boys always thought she was ripping their dad off," Robinson explains. "But I have never believed that."

[††] After ten years on the project, Jones's own personal investment in Vidauban totaled more than $3 million in costs for land, permits, lawyers, and zoning. Somehow, though, Trent was still optimistic that major investors would come to his project, even though virtually none had done so in the prior decade. In August 1981, a highly frustrated Paul Colwell, Jones's financial and legal adviser, wrote the following comments on Jones's updated prospectus for Vidauban development: "It epitomizes the insanity of RTJ's thought process and his irrationality. The ship is completely sinking. He has invested and at risk $1.75M. He has no hard offers and he is wanting to settle 50/50 for $25M! This is not to be believed." Next to the paragraph in the prospectus outlining Jones's role in leading the project management company that would oversee the design, construction, and commercialization of the project, Colwell wrote: "RTJ has never managed anything in his life. This is a sad, sick joke."

As with most of Jones's schemes for Vidauban, Denise Hirsch's campaign to find investors produced only bad feelings. "Mr. Jones would never tell people what he was going to do," Robinson recalled, and "when he did tell or promise a person something, he didn't do it. He would make promises and then forget about them. So he may have promised Denise stuff, I don't know."

During the period that Hirsch was combing France for investors, Jones was introduced to an Italian businessman, Georgio Gianola, who offered him $2.5 million for a 50 percent stake in Vidauban. Jones asked Robinson to arrange the details of the deal. Robinson's assessment after almost three decades of reflection is that Gianola and his allies were "much smarter than Mr. Jones." Jones intended to use Gianola's money to pay Vidauban's debts to lawyer Samuel Pisar and Jones's partner, Charles Gordon. But, as Robinson recalled, "Gianola didn't pay Jones all that he was supposed to. There was also a lot of concern about the state of long-term capital gains taxes in France. Potentially each investor needed to pay some pretty high taxes. Gianola eventually sued Jones over the contracts between them; it was a lawsuit that challenged Jones's control of the property, and I thought it was the most egregiously unjustified lawsuit I'd ever heard of. Mr. Jones almost lost it. Gianola was a tough guy. He had a lot of connections in southern France."

In 1989, concerned about the toll that Vidauban was taking on his father both financially and emotionally, elder son Bobby prevailed on his friend and lawyer, Blake Stafford, to help him sort out the tangled mess at Vidauban. Bobby stepped into what Robinson remembers as "an extraordinarily complicated situation, a real mess. Mr. Jones had thirty-six bank accounts, because we were being paid design fees in different currencies throughout Europe. Virtually all of these accounts really had nothing to do with Vidauban per se. I had signature on all of them, and so did Mr. Jones. It is true that I did not know the total balance on hand, but I did know that we had enough to pay all our bills and salaries on time. It is not true that nobody had anything close to a full understanding of how much money or many jobs the company was currently responsible for, but I accept that we had become so busy job-wise that I was losing artistic control of the jobs under construction. I felt that we had too much going on for me to handle. That, and for personal reasons, was why I decided to leave the company. I had loved working for Mr. Jones but I felt that my family took precedence."

It was hardly Robinson's fault but by the late 1980s, Jones's situation in Europe, mostly due to Vidauban, was "approaching financial disaster." That is what Blake Stafford, a partner in a Silicon Valley law firm and a business adviser to Bobby, found when Bobby sent Stafford to France to get his dad out of trouble. "Somehow we had to cut a deal with somebody," Stafford recalls, "and sell the Vidauban property."

Bobby and Blake Stafford brought to Vidauban a French developer named Pierre Schnebelen, known for developing two famous ski resorts, Tignes and Megève. Schnebelen was also developing a project in Idaho called Valbois, a four-season resort about a hundred miles north of Boise. Schnebelen planned a golf course, too, for Valbois, which Bobby later designed.

Schnebelen liked what he saw at Vidauban. And, as Stafford recalled, he "had all sorts of connections. One of his buddies was an Algerian guy named Malik Bencheghib. He was the head of a bank in Paris that had a lot of Russian money in it. We cut a deal with Malik and his partners. We sold him the property for five million, plus Bobby and his father got a contract assuring that they would get to design and build the golf course at Vidauban, for slightly above their regular fees and everything."

But, as always seemed to be the case with Vidauban, this silver lining had summoned a dark cloud. Stafford remembered the denouement of the Vidauban saga as somehow fittingly inconclusive.

"Mr. Jones got the $5 million, but then it was basically levied upon by Michel Benedetti, the head of the construction company that was owed money for already having done a great deal of work at Vidauban." Benedetti, whose independent French construction company was based in Chamonix, had built the Club de Golf de Chamonix for Jones in the early 1980s, and they knew each other pretty well. "The construction contract was with Jones's company but Benedetti was pretty clever, because he was sending the invoices both to Jones's company and to Jones individually. Jones would say to Benedetti, 'Why the hell are you sending these to me?!' So we ended up settling with Benedetti and got rid of his lien on the $5 million worth of proceeds."

News of the cash infusion attracted a new round of claims, with Denise Hirsch first in line.

"She had been what was called the *gérant*," Stafford said, "the manager of Jones's Vidauban company." Hirsch "made a claim that she was owed all this money due to promises made to her by Mr. Jones. She had gotten all her expenses paid, which were pretty extravagant, and she was also supposed to get a salary of something like $300,000 a year, she said, even though as far as we could tell she was doing nothing. Her main business background was as a stewardess for Air France. Part of the problem was that Mr. Jones always liked stewardesses and pretty women in general, and Denise Hirsch was certainly that. She sued Jones for all the money she allegedly was owed, making a claim against the money being held in escrow. We had this big weird trial down in a little town in Provence called Draguignan. After a big go-around, we prevailed. But then Denise appealed the ruling, which took place in a French labor court, which still continued to tie up our monies in the escrow. So we settled with Denise for a couple hundred thousand dollars."

Bobby's intervention with Stafford restored some credibility to the Vidauban project, but it would never come close to realizing Robert Trent Jones's grand vision.

"After settling with Benedetti and with Hirsch," Stafford said, "we ended up having come out of the escrow something north of $3 million. That all went to Trent. But then Trent had to pay back some debts. One of the debts was to Bobby, who had put up a lot of money during the time Trent was really in extremis. So Trent paid back Bobby for the real cash Bobby had put up to keep Trent going, both for legal fees and operating expenses. It was the least we could do, put a penny in to keep the old man from going bankrupt."

The truncated version of Vidauban did produce a golf course, but as with the entire enterprise, it was immediately bogged down in controversy and financial woes. Robinson observed the early clearing stages of the course's construction, but left the firm in 1987 before it was revived and redesigned. Robinson laid out the original routing, but once Bobby took charge of the project, he assigned his associate, Don Knott, who had worked for Senior along with Cabell in the Spanish office in the early 1970s, to oversee the project.

Vidauban, according to Robinson, "was one of the few courses that only had one routing plan, the one we first plotted." However, that plan was significantly rerouted, especially the front nine. The course opened in 1991, but very few people have ever seen it or played it. The course changed its name, after it was purchased by a Norwegian owner, to "Prince de Provence." Until recently, it was still wrapped in controversy, burdened by such environmental issues as water use and storm drainage.

As late as the publication of *Golf's Magnificent Challenge* in 1988, Trent was still singing the praises of Vidauban. It would "rank high among my finest works, from the standpoint of marvelous golf courses" (note the plural, as if the original vision still held) "as well as unparalleled facilities for the combination of golf and business." Trent's book even had a half-page schematic of the route plan for the Vidauban golf course. It showed all 18 holes, the location of the two clubhouses, as well as the footprint for the proposed condos and homes.‡‡ Later, the master plan and layout changed under Schnebelen's management.

At the ceremony that "opened" the course in 1991, Bobby spoke to a small audience, a group that included such dignitaries as Hiroyoshi Aoki, president of the Aoki Corporation, Edouard Brunner, Switzerland's ambassador to the United States and a friend of Bobby's from service on the Helsinki Accords in 1980, and Sir Michael Bonallack, secretary of the Royal & Ancient Golf Club of St. Andrews. At a party a few years later, when the Norwegians took control, Bobby said: "I am delighted that my father found this property and had the vision that we and our team were able to help him to achieve. It is a true masterpiece and one of the few joint ventures in which my father and I have collaborated in his later career. I hope all of you who play it will join me on the course and on the terrace afterwards to recount the many joyful games that we have had and will have on this magnificent golf course. It is strategically bunkered, with lightly contoured greens and with a variety of holes, naturally flowing and following the landscape. It is beautifully maintained by Otto Berg [one of the new Norwegian owners] and his people and is a true tribute to the game itself from its earliest origins in Scotland to its current home."

Given how Trent poured so many of his dreams into Vidauban, however naïvely or blunderingly, the golf course certainly merits inclusion in the legacy of Robert Trent Jones Sr. whatever its quality. Though hardly anyone has gotten to play it, those who have seen it consider it one of Europe's greatest golf courses. The *Peugeot Golf Guide* for many years has ranked it as the No. 1 golf course in France, and one year of Continental Europe as well, giving it 19 out of a total 20 rating points. Travel guides and golf magazines would undoubtedly rate Vidauban even higher if their writers or representatives were ever allowed to play the course. The place is so secretive that sometimes the members blindfold

---

‡‡ The golf course at Vidauban plays to a par 72 and a championship distance of 7,092 yards (3,460 out, 3,632 in). From the regulation men's tees, it plays at 6,683 yards. There are only two holes on which water comes into play: the par-3 fourth and the par-4 seventh. On a few holes, rocky outcroppings, some of them quite sheer, are the main feature of the surrounding landscape, notably at the par-4 second and par-5 eighth. The course is replete with beautiful trees of many varieties. It is a highly manicured course, purposely emulating the elite conditions of Augusta National.

their guests to keep the route to the golf course a secret, adding to the club's mystique. All of the marking signs that had once been posted along the roads to show the way to the golf course have been removed. There are no signposts, no marked gates, certainly no website. Thanks to Google Maps, it can now be found and seen from above in enormous detail. Still, if a group of golfers somehow find their way to the gate and beg to play, or just ask to see the course, they are turned away, just as the gatekeeper would do at Augusta National. Until very recently, this inaccessible golf course, technically, did not even exist, because it had not legally opened. Vidauban is still there today for the serene—and highly private—enjoyment of the very, very few. In 2013, the owners finally resolved all legal impediments and Vidauban now is officially permitted to operate by all relevant French authorities. The new owners are committed to improving course conditions and have shown more openness than ever to receiving special guests of their membership for a round of golf and a "glorious all-round day."

Building his first green complex back at Midvale seven decades earlier, twenty-four-year-old Robert Jones could never have imagined where his love of golf courses would take him. The journey for the immigrant boy from Ellis Island to Genundewah to Oakland Hills to Vidauban was as enigmatic as it was improbable. Jones had achieved all of his dreams, and then some; at least he should have felt that way about it. Vidauban almost proved his undoing. As Ione so accurately described, her husband had always been a "plunger." But Jones somehow always emerged whole.

By the end of the 1980s, he would take delight in the marketing phrase he had borrowed from the British Empire: "The sun never sets on Robert Trent Jones's courses." By then his courses occupied ground on every continent save Australia and Antarctica. But in no way did that slogan signify that Trent, not even as he approached his own ninth decade of life and seventy years of working as a golf architect, was ready to stop traveling the world in his quest to build the next great golf course—or to achieve the stature and prominence he had always envisioned for himself.

CHAPTER THIRTEEN

THE END OF THE TRAIL

To the end, Trent Jones remained optimistic that his two talented sons, both highly distinguished golf architects, would return to his business and work together as part of a Jones team. The formal dedication in 1991 of the Robert Trent Jones Golf Course at Cornell University, a course which Trent had started building at his alma mater in the mid-1930s but did not have the opportunity to finish until 1953, provided one of the rare occasions when Bobby and Rees set aside their differences to honor their father.

J ones's beloved wife and partner, Ione, died in her sleep at home in Montclair on July 7, 1987, after a lengthy fight with lung disease. The cause of death was heart failure.

Obituaries in the local newspapers could not do justice to Ione's brilliance and kindly spirit or to her contributions to communities within and apart from the world of golf:

> Mrs. Jones held executive positions in several family-owned businesses that were based in Montclair and Fort Lauderdale. . . . She had worked as a librarian in the New York Public Library from 1932 to 1935 and in the Glen Ridge Public Library from 1935 to 1936. . . . Outside of golf she was involved in charitable, civic, and historical organizations and her college, Wells, from which she graduated with Phi Beta Kappa honors. . . . She was the major fund-raiser for the Aurora, N.Y., school. In addition, Mrs. Jones was a member of Planned Parenthood of Montclair, a founder of the Montclair Guidance Center, and a member of the Mental Health Association and Retarded Children's Association and the Junior League, all of Montclair. She was a member of the board of managers of the National Society of Colonial Dames of New Jersey and of the New Jersey Historical Society, the Mayflower Society, the Montclair Historical Society, the Montclair Library Association, the Mountainside Hospital Association, and the Metropolitan Museum of Art in New York City. Mrs. Jones was the great-granddaughter of Alfrederick Smith Hatch, a former president of the New York Stock Exchange. She is survived by Trent, two sons, Robert Trent Jr. and Rees Lee; a sister, Mrs. Mary Conger, and four grandchildren.

Her funeral was at St. Luke's Episcopal Church in Montclair, where she had been baptized and where she and Trent were married. Bobby, who had been working on a golf project in Europe, quickly returned to Montclair and was joined there by his wife and children. Following the church service, the immediate family gathered at the gravesite in Mount Hebron Cemetery in Upper Montclair. Ione had insisted on being buried on the third day following her death. An increasingly religious woman who thought about God's love in a very intellectual way, she and her sister Mary had often discussed the importance of the Resurrected spirit, which had interested them deeply since the death of their sister Alma. Accordingly, Rees and his wife, Susan, saw to that instruction, and the burial took place on July 10. Later, in Florida, there was a memorial service for Ione at Christ United Methodist Church in Fort Lauderdale. At both events, attendees were told that, in lieu of flowers, they could make donations in her memory to the Wells College Development Fund. Trent said later, "It was quite a shock to all of us" when Ione died. He was in town when it happened, and called Rees to ask for help with arrangements. Trent later spoke fondly of Ione: "I will always remember what a beautiful and remarkable woman she was. She was my right hand and without her patience and understanding I would never have been able to succeed in the golf course design business or, for that matter, succeed in much of anything at all."

Trent's loving words came in 1998, eleven years after his wife's passing and just two years before his own death in 2000. One hears in them strong echoes of the deep love and affection he felt for his "dear Ione" during their long courtship in the early 1930s.

Unfortunately, the union of Trent and Ione did not end as harmoniously as it began. In the years immediately preceding her death in 1987, they were more upset with one another than at any time during their long marriage. The stress stemmed from tensions over both the business and the boys, the two complicated pillars of the Jones family's emotional life. More and more, Ione had come to regard Trent's schemes as careless and foolhardy, and a good number of his business associates as shady characters and con men capable of improper, perhaps even criminal, behavior.

Jones's financial affairs in the 1980s were nothing like what one would expect from such a famous and successful figure. There are many letters demanding money in the Jones Papers from people and organizations to whom Jones, or one of his many companies, owed money—and, in some cases, a great deal of it. More than her husband ever had, Ione paid attention to the family's finances. She knew the books. She knew budgets. She knew the precarious state of their assets, and the uncertainty of their cash flow, especially with Vidauban, the most grandiose scheme of her husband's entire career, draining away millions of their dollars, all of which might very well be lost. "You are throwing our money away!" she would say to Trent. "But Dad wouldn't listen," Rees remembers. "Maybe he did once, but he didn't anymore." Trent's long absences might not have bothered Ione in prior periods, even when he left messes for her—or Rees and Roger, even Bobby out west—to clean up. But by the 1980s, Ione rarely knew either where Trent was or what he was up to—a distinct difference from earlier in his career, when she knew his every move. In the last years of her life, Ione primarily felt relief when Trent was out on the road. That allowed her to live her own life, be with friends, play bridge, do things for Wells College, participate in her favorite charitable organizations, and be free of the messes that faced her when he was home. She was also free to think—about the past and the future.

What Ione really had on her mind in the last months of her life was embodied, as is often the case for people approaching death, in her last Will and Testament.

No one in the family knew that she was having a new Will drawn up. After all the legally required signatures and formalities, it was finally completed on April 3, 1987, thirteen weeks and four days before her death. The Will that her new one replaced dated back to October 14, 1981, and the lawyer who oversaw the new one was James I. Ridley, a junior partner in the firm of Friedrich, Blackwell, Mikos & Ridley in Fort Lauderdale. Family legend is Ione had never met him before seeking his services. How Ione happened to choose Ridley is unknown. Perhaps he was recommended by a friend, perhaps by someone at Coral Ridge, or possibly he was recommended privately to Ione by the family's regular attorney in South Florida, Louis J. DeReuil. In any case, Ione went to Ridley's office, walked in, and wanted him to redo her Will. Whether the legend is accurate or not, it does seem to convey a basic truth: Ione did not want Trent or anyone else in the family to know about what she had done until after her death.

Ione's Will was destined to upset every member of the family in different ways. In Article Three, she left all of her tangible property "to my spouse, Robert Trent Jones, if he survives me, otherwise to my son Rees Lee Jones, if he survives me." Bobby was not bequeathed any of that property. Article Four specified gifts to a variety of organizations and individuals: Wells College ($100,000), as well as her church ($50,000) and the National Society of Colonial Dames of New Jersey ($10,000) received the largest ones. Among a list of people receiving money from Ione's estate, Bobby was given $10,000, the same amount Ione gave her daughters-in-law. Bequests in the amount of $5,000 were specified for Mary Conger, Ione's surviving sister; for June Benson, Ione's secretary and good friend; and even for Cabell Robinson, whom Ione held in high regard. The explanation for Cabell receiving a monetary gift, while Roger Rulewich did not, was that over the past few years Cabell had not received all of the salary he had coming to him, while Roger had always been paid. Gifts of $2,500, $2,000, $1,500, and $1,000 were made to nine other friends, among them Eileen Vennell, Trent's longtime secretary, and Paul Colwell, who had been the family's trusted business adviser for many years. In all, Ione's monetary gifts added up to $209,000. In the paragraph in which she "devised" the sum of $10,000 to Bobby, the Will read, "This modest devise to my son shall not be taken as an indication of any lack of love or affection that I bear for him. It is my intention to prepare a letter to my son explaining my actions."

Ione's letter to Bobby has remained private. According to Bobby, the modest monetary bequest to him was "carefully phrased to avoid any lack of affection" and was, as unlikely as it seems, "not a personal concern to him." Speculation that Ione sought to use her Will to redress what she perceived as "imbalances" between her two sons—things that over the years had favored Bobby over Rees—has never been clearly resolved. But such speculation is not without foundation, especially given the contents of her Will.

Trent was unhappy generally with the terms of Ione's Will, but was truly hurt by Article Five: her disposition of the family home in Montclair. They had lived there since the 1950s, but title to it stood in Ione's name, a protection that she had insisted upon, and gotten. By the 1980s, it was her financial security blanket, one which her husband's endeavors could not endanger.

In her Will, Ione bequeathed their longtime home not to her husband but to Rees. However, she did qualify that Trent could live there as long as he wished to. Furthermore, if Rees died before Trent, the property would pass in equal shares to Rees's descendants—not to Trent or Bobby, who would inherit only if Rees died and left no descendants.

And another heavy blow for Trent was still to come in Article Six.

Ione presided as an officer and a major shareholder not just in Robert Trent Jones, Inc., but also in many of her husband's shadow companies. Article Six made reference to three of the many corporations in which she held stock: Landlords, Inc.; Coral Ridge Golf Course, Inc.; and American Golfers Club, Inc., All of her shares in these companies were incorporated into a testamentary trust, "for the benefit of my spouse," to be administered so that Trent would receive "quarterly or more frequent installments." Trent would receive a regular allotment from the trust Ione was setting up, but he was not to receive ownership of her shares in those companies. Nor were her boys. Clearly, Ione worried about her husband's habit of throwing big money away on speculative ventures, and, by creating the trust and giving him a regular allowance, she was trying to protect him from himself. What would happen to the trust fund after Trent died? "This Trust shall terminate upon the death of my said spouse and after the payments, the Trustee shall distribute the remaining trust principal to my son, Rees Lee Jones . . ." Again, Bobby would only receive any of the trust if Rees died and had no heirs.

Article Six sounded simple, but it created a *very* serious problem for Trent, Bobby, and Rees alike. In listing the companies in which she was a partner and an officer, Ione's Will failed to mention all the companies that actually existed. Elderly and ill, breathing from an oxygen tank, she seems simply to have forgotten to name them all for her new lawyer. Rees recalls that she had become "very forgetful," still "very bright" but she would have these spells of not remembering. When she gave the lawyer the necessary information, she did not give him complete information. She forgot about a lot of Jones companies. "There were a gazillion," recalls Roger Rulewich. "Mr. Jones, every time he turned around, he was forming another company for some reason."

Ione neglected to name no fewer than six Jones companies in which she held shares, an omission that created an absolute panic when the Will was read. Anything unmentioned in her Will fell into the "residual estate," consisting of all of the assets in Ione's estate remaining after the specific bequests in Article Four were made, and the debts, taxes, administrative fees, court costs, and other expenses were paid. And the Will bequeathed her entire residual estate to Wells College.

The family was certain that was not her intention—and surely it was not: Ione wanted to leave a generous sum of money to Wells, but not all her shares in the family businesses. If that part of her last Will and Testament was enforced, it would be a disaster for the Jones enterprise—a prospect which was one of the very few things about which Trent and both sons agreed. It would not even have been possible to give Wells the $100,000 donation that Ione wanted—or, for that matter, any of the other dollar donations she specified (to her church, to her friends, to Bobby)—without liquidating some of the companies. The assets of the still viable companies were all tied up.

It was difficult and time-consuming to deal with the lawyers and judges, to straighten out the Wells bequest. Wells College had the wisdom not to go to war with the Joneses. The president of the university and the school's trustees—Ione herself had been one—knew that she had not intended to damage her family's companies. Understanding the situation, Wells accepted an offer from the Jones men to substitute their own donations, adding up to the $100,000 that was Ione's intended gift. In March 1989, Bobby wrote a $50,000 check to Wells, and Rees did the same. (They each also wrote $5,000 checks to St. Luke's Church and $500 checks to the National Society of Colonial Dames.) Earlier, Trent had written to the chairman of the board of trustees at Wells "confirming my intent and that of the Jones family to continue as benefactors of Wells College." For his contribution, in lieu of cash, Trent was "to provide a redesign of the existing nine hole golf course at the College and also to design a further nine holes so that the college will eventually have an eighteen hole championship golf course." (Even that offer from Trent led to a round of legal exchanges in which Jones's attorneys clarified that he was only committing to design the golf course free of charge, not to construct it for nothing. It mattered little in the end; the full course was never designed or completed.)

Ione had done her family no favors by writing a Will that was so tilted in favor of Rees. (For example, Article Fourteen appointed Rees as "the Personal Representative of my estate" and as "the Trustee of the Trust described in Article Six.") Even Rees thinks that his mother made a big mistake in many of her bequests, including giving the Montclair home to him rather than to Trent. She most certainly did not help Rees's relationship with his father, and most certainly not with Bobby. As for the Montclair house, Trent kept it running even though he was in Florida 95 percent of the time. Shortly before Trent died, Rees sold the Montclair house. The 1994 tax assessment put the value of the property at $721,000, the land on which the house sat alone was worth $437,000. The sale proceeds went entirely to Rees.

In the wake of the legal overhauling of Ione's estate and the exacerbation of bad feelings between his two sons, Trent tried to make peace with Rees. On June 22, 1992, the week after the U.S. Open at Pebble Beach, Trent wrote his youngest son a rare personal letter:

Dear Rees,

I am glad we met on Thursday during the Open and had a chance to talk. I remain concerned about our talk, however. While I'm proud that you have become an accomplished golf architect and will carry on our name and family tradition, I think your own health of mind needs to correct some mistaken recollections of family relations.

Mother and I always tried to do the best for you boys. You were very close to her since the time you had polio, and she loved and helped you a lot to overcome that health problem for which I know you were naturally very grateful. But, on my part, I earned the money for your and Bobby's educations, and I trained both of you as golf architects.

You were always reluctant to learn from me. You didn't even play golf in high school, preferring basketball and baseball even.

There came a time after [Bobby's infant son] David died to settle the family business matters. Bobby wanted to earn his own reputation and so did you shortly thereafter.

The money and companies in the west were divided among the family. You and mother got your share. You still operate your construction from one of the west's companies, Calgolf. In addition, mother and you arranged for Coral Ridge to pay you a salary for many years because you weren't satisfied.

Unless you deal with the truth about this time [sic] you cannot understand my deep hurt at the way you persuaded mother to leave only you our home in Montclair.

I don't have many Opens to go, and I wish you would cooperate about Coral Ridge and not just complain. I created it for you [sic] and Bobby benefit. If you are grateful for all that has been done for you, please help when asked.

Let's continue to have a good family. We are #1 in the golf world today. Let's keep it that way. We are a talented family. I want all of us to be a loving family too.

Love,
Dad

The letter did no good. Trent's efforts were too little, too late, and he also did not help the situation by criticizing some of Rees's redesign work on Trent's championship layouts. "I was sorry to hear the work you did at Congressional is being criticized," he wrote in February 1994, in advance of the 1995 U.S. Senior Open at Congressional. "If you would work with me instead of remodeling my work at many sites, the members would appreciate the results." Further aggravating the situation, Trent's secretary in Fort Lauderdale, Marge Darwell, sometimes faxed copies of Trent's critical letters to Bobby in California, with a note on the cover sheet reading "Here is a copy of letter we mailed just this morning. FYI." In that way, Bobby learned things about Rees and Rees's relationship with his father that he likely would not have known otherwise.

Trent's reference to Coral Ridge in his June 1992 letter to Rees was not a casual one. Ione's death caused serious issues for the family at the Fort Lauderdale golf course that Trent designed in the mid-1950s, leased for some ten years, and then bought outright with money Trent borrowed from an insurance company. For more than thirty years, Coral Ridge Country Club served as the Jones family's winter haven. For Trent it was like hallowed ground, the only club that he personally owned and operated. In some respects it was the truest—and longest-lasting—"family" business in which all of the Joneses were involved.

From its inception, ownership of Coral Ridge Golf Course, Inc., was divided among the four members of the family, with Bobby and Rees each getting 25.25 percent of the stock and Trent and Ione each holding 24.75 percent. Had Ione's Will been followed precisely after her death, Rees would have controlled exactly half of the Coral Ridge stock. Knowing how upset that would make his father, Rees agreed to hold his mother's 24.75 percent in trust as co-trustee with his father until Trent's death. Trent was president of the company, and each of the boys was a vice president. However, as part-owner and vice president, Rees drew a salary of $25,000 per year. Trent and Bobby received only the perks of due directors of the country club, which, though not insubstantial, were not financial. All family members also benefited otherwise. When visiting Fort Lauderdale, everyone stayed in beachside apartments, or at the Lago Mar, at Coral Ridge's expense, and their travel and daily needs were covered.

Coral Ridge ran very smoothly as long as Ione was alive. When she was in Florida, she oversaw everything from the choice of fabric for the curtains in the clubhouse, to the size of salad portions on the restaurant menu, to the hiring of secretaries, bartenders, and valets. When she was in Montclair, she phoned Coral Ridge every day to see how things were going. She mostly spoke to her right-hand lady, Eileen Kestel-Goodman, who started at the club in the late 1950s and became Ione's good friend, and whose talents and initiative led Ione to promote her from receptionist to assistant manager, and finally to general manager. Rees remembers: "As long as Mother was alive she very much had a finger on what was going on at the club. Every day she was in contact with it. . . . After she passed away, the decisions were really made on a sporadic basis. Dad didn't like formalities. He wanted to keep everything informal and that was okay with us. There were very few official board meetings, even when Mother was alive. We'd get together as a family, usually at Christmastime, and talk everything over. A lot of various small decisions had to be made, primarily about revenues. . . . Prior to Mother's death, she was the one who prepared all of the information and got the family together to agree upon it. After she died, things changed pretty dramatically."

In 1984 Trent had brought a young man named James B. Singerling to Coral Ridge as his club manager. Jones held strong opinions on how golf and country clubs should be run—not by the members but rather by trained club managers. Jones met Singerling when he was paying a visit to Point O' Woods Golf & Country Club, a course he designed in Benton Harbor, Michigan, which was the home of the Western Amateur. Singerling was the club manager. Trent later remembered: "Members told me Jim Singerling was doing a good job. I proposed that he come with me to Florida. I had him down for a trial. He liked it. Rees and Bobby interviewed him. Ione liked him, too. He came down on trial one winter. That's how he got to be manager of Coral Ridge." In fact, Singerling became manager not just of Coral Ridge but also of American Golfers Club, Inc., the public executive golf course and driving range adjoining the back side of Coral Ridge.

Jim Singerling started out as just the type of "trained club manager" Trent Jones wanted. He worked well with Ione and took directions from her promptly and politely as he should have been doing, given that "Mrs. Jones" was not just one of the club's owners, she had personal knowledge of the club's daily operations and the tastes and interests of the entire Coral Ridge membership. Trent took a great personal liking to Jim: "We talked a lot," he recalled. "I had total confidence in him, total. I took him everywhere. I introduced him to the biggest people in America, the top people in America. I took him to the Masters with me because he wanted to go with me, paying all the expenses. I took him to U.S. Opens. . . . When I was lame, when I had a bad back, he stayed in the next room.

When I got in the shower, he'd see that I wouldn't fall. He didn't dress me totally. He'd help me put on my shoes, my pants, maybe. I really liked the guy. I felt like he was like a son. That's how I treated him, like a son, not like an employee. . . . He did a lot of things on his own that I had no objection to. I thought he was trying to do the best interests of the club."

Ione's death in the summer of 1987 created a management vacuum. Bobby lived in California and rarely visited. Rees came to South Florida sometimes, but not often. Trent spent much of the winter in Fort Lauderdale but was rarely there in the summertime. Trent acknowledged, "I was a pretty soft employer. I wasn't tough. I gave the manager pretty much the right to run it. But not totally." Singerling was not empowered to make decisions about money and employees, or exercise any of the power specifically reserved by the board, which consisted of Trent, as president, and Rees and Bobby as vice presidents. Nor was he to make any changes to the golf course, make any sort of lump-sum cash payments, or allow any personal borrowing from club accounts. In any case, by 1990, all three Jones men thought Singerling was in gross violation of the terms of his employment agreement. Additionally, Rees and Bobby feared that Singerling (as well as a lawyer, Russell E. Carlisle, who was supposed to be representing Trent's interests but was viewed as working in concert with Singerling) was taking advantage of their aging and increasingly forgetful father. So the Joneses fired him, with Bobby assuming the task of telling Singerling.

Within weeks of his termination, Singerling filed suit against the Joneses, who countersued. They also sued the attorney Carlisle for malpractice. Singerling claimed that he had never done anything that he was not authorized to do by Trent Jones, the president of the Coral Ridge corporation. Authority, therefore, became the problem: at age eighty-four in 1990, and in declining health, Trent was not always sure what documents he had signed, or what exactly he was agreeing to, when Singerling asked for something. According to Trent and his two sons, Singerling had, after Ione's death, taken more and more actions on his own initiative, such as promoting a club bartender to the post of assistant manager. The worst abuse alleged by the Joneses was that Singerling had manipulated Trent into appointing him as an officer to some of Trent's other companies. One of those was Florida Golf Corp., a golf course construction company created to build the Flamingo Island Club in Naples, on the Gulf Coast, a layout that opened in 1990. According to Trent, "I made a construction company to build the golf course down in Naples. I was head of the company. Next thing I knew I was the chairman of the board and Jim Singerling was the president. I have no recollection of ever approving that. Under no circumstances would I have made him president because he had no ability whatsoever to be president of a construction company." Trent was also terribly upset to discover that Singerling had made himself the president of Robert Trent Jones International, Inc., the company that Jones had created to handle a number of his jobs in Europe. In both cases, Singerling allegedly told Jones's comptrollers at Coral Ridge and in Europe to cut checks for him to use for various purposes—in the process making the comptrollers think that Mr. Jones had approved the payments. The Joneses accused Singerling of having a $50,000 check written to him personally from the account of Florida Golf. Singerling testified in his defense that Mr. Jones had, in fact, approved all these activities, and that he therefore could not be blamed if Mr. Jones could not remember what he had in fact done. Singerling cited, as a defense, his 1984 employment agreement that read: "Duties shall be assigned to employee by Robert Trent Jones, Sr., from time to time with Coral Ridge Golf Course, Inc., its related corporations, or Robert Trent Jones, Inc., its related corporations as appropriate." Trent replied that it was preposterous to imagine that he would have ever agreed to make Singerling president of any of his companies: "Jim didn't do any design work. He created nothing. He wasn't capable of creating anything in the design of a golf course. He had never been on construction. He couldn't help on that score. He had no ability to help other than try to administer. . . . For years, I trusted him implicitly, and it was a shock to find out that my trust had been a big mistake. . . . He made a number of trips to Europe, sometimes with me, sometimes on his own volition. Once he took his daughters there on a vacation. Coral Ridge ended up paying for everything. . . . Jim is not a golf architect or golf construction man. He is a club manager. He had no authority or no right to do what he was doing."

Under questioning by Singerling's attorney, however, Trent's deposition contains this interesting passage:

Q: Do you recall anyone advising you that it was not to your advantage to be president of both the design corporations, which would be Robert Trent Jones, Inc., and Robert Trent Jones, Florida, and as well the construction company, which would be Florida Golf Corp.?

Jones: I'm trying to think. I don't think—No, I don't think so. There was at one time where I was told they might be in conflict with one another, and that's when we dropped it.

Q: When you say that's when you dropped it, what do you mean by that?

Jones: Well, we separated the corporations from construction. I didn't want to have them in conflict with one another.

Q: And as a result of that, do you recall getting advice that you should not be president of both the design corporations and the construction corporations?

Jones: I don't remember that.

Q: Do you recall that being the reason that you requested that Mr. Singerling be made a president of Florida Golf Corp.?

Jones: No.

Clearly, Singerling's attorneys were suggesting that Jones had made him president of Florida Golf Corp. to avoid the appearance of a conflict of interest—an issue Jones was very aware of over the course of his long career. If such a shadow company needed a shadow head, it was not illogical for Trent to turn to a man he considered to be "like a son."

The case was settled out of court shortly after Rees's deposition on January 23, 1991. Singerling received a small amount of money, and the Joneses agreed not to say anything about the case or the circumstances of Singerling's termination. By that time he had become an executive vice president with the Club Managers Association of America, and eventually became its CEO. The success of Singerling's subsequent 20-year-plus career with the CMAA suggests that Trent Jones's original assessment of Singerling's abilities were well founded, even if the Coral Ridge episode raised serious questions.

Coral Ridge remained a haven for Trent. As Rees would say at his father's funeral in 2000, "Coral Ridge was the place my father was happiest." By the early 1990s, Trent was staying in Fort Lauderdale almost year-round, living in the ocean-side high-rise apartment paid for by Coral Ridge. "I'm quite busy in the morning," Trent would explain. "I work out of my apartment and take a lot of business calls, then go to the club at noon." After eating lunch, always at his favorite table, and flirting with some of the waitresses, he would take a golf cart over to a building off the ninth fairway, where he had an office. A new club manager was hired, with much clearer instructions about what he could and could not do without approval from Rees and Bobby. The brothers started paying closer attention to the operation of the club, which invariably led to more disagreements. In November 2004, "with their rift leading to member complaints" about the deterioration of both Coral Ridge and American Golf, the brothers agreed to sell the club to local auto dealer Phil Smith and his partners. "We were absentee owners," Rees explained at the time. "It's a lot easier for the local people to run it." Rees later regained some financial interest in the club.

The five years following Ione's death were the low point of Trent Jones's life, much worse for him personally than the darkest years of the Great Depression, when his ambition had fueled the hearty optimism that would propel him from obscurity to universal recognition as "the world's greatest golf architect." "It turned out that 1987 became a very busy year for my company," Jones would later recall, "and the traveling I had to do helped in a small way to occupy my mind enough to ease my grief somewhat." Most of that travel was to Europe, and, while extensive, little of it paid off for him financially.

Most of his projects in the late 1980s were located in France: "I designed and built about eleven courses in France, and I believe I spent more time in France than any other country in Europe during the time I was building courses over there." Unfortunately, very few of his French golf courses made much money for him, especially the ones he built from 1986 on; they may have even cost him more money than he earned from them. This was partly attributable to the fact that Jones's construction company did not do the work, which instead was mostly performed by Benedetti SA, an independent French-based golf construction firm founded by Michel Benedetti.

But Jones didn't blame Benedetti for his problems in Europe. Instead, he pointed the finger at the lawyers representing him. When asked in his September 1990 deposition in the Singerling case about the success of Robert Trent Jones International, Inc., Jones said: "It's a corporation that builds courses in Europe, and it's been losing money like Grant took Richmond. . . . We've done about eight jobs in the past five years. They have all been not very effective financially. . . . They weren't run properly. I didn't have the control over them that I should have had and it was just a bad deal. . . . If you want the names of all the people involved, I'll get them for you. I can tell you one thing. All of them were losing propositions. . . . I was one of the shareholders, of course. They periodically have changed. Cabell Robinson was one. We had an Englishman once, I forget his name. I'll try to remember. [It was a man by the name of Peter Charles.] There's been two or three different chairmen. . . . A friend of mine who was a lawyer went over and started giving orders. . . . He was making decisions that were not his and shouldn't have been, and we were losing money all over the place. I don't think he was a good lawyer. . . . He was taking authority with contracts, with personnel, with construction companies, the works. He wasn't supposed to be, but he took that authority. I knew about it and called him on it and he said, 'I'll take care of this,' and went on. Okay, you are hitting me on a very low point of my life because it was a disaster. . . . The corporation is no longer active. We've finally eliminated it. . . . We still owe money to a lot of companies in Europe. . . . I wasn't getting anything on what was going on and whether we were getting paid. It's been a disaster. Most of my companies over there are now in bankruptcy."

Trent should have been blaming himself. By the late 1980s, he was in his eighties. Ione was gone. His own health was failing. His memory was growing worse. More and more he had come to rely on others to take care not only of his business operations but also his personal needs—his health, his traveling, his meals, his bathing, his general welfare. It is surprising, in retrospect, that Trent, after six decades in business, could be so naïve and foolish about so many things related to his money and other people's motives. The elderly man of the late 1980s and 1990s, however sharp of mind he remained in certain respects, was by then only a shell of Robert Trent Jones in his prime. He was still the dreamer, the eternal schemer, and a charming leprechaun when he wished—or needed— to be, but the international business world, into which he had expanded so extensively, overwhelmed him. He no longer possessed the savvy to warn him of the dangers inherent in his persistent ambition. Ione was no longer nearby to act as his rudder—the cautious, shrewd intelligence always standing behind him, propping him up, looking after him, was no longer around to harness his indiscriminate vitality. Even when he had been in his prime, Ione had not always been able to save him from himself.

Is it your normal business practice in over fifty years of business to ever sign anything without reading it or having your attorney read it? Jones was asked in his deposition for the Singerling case. "I don't say it's my normal . . ." Jones answered. "I think in my younger days, I probably read everything very thoroughly and checked it with a lawyer. I have signed some things recently that I didn't read."

Did different lawyers that were working for you bring you documents to sign almost on a daily basis? "Yes, a lawyer would say sign it here, sign it there, and I did. I figured the guy was my attorney and he was protecting me. . . . I signed a lot of things without reading them. . . . Jim Singerling would also routinely present me with stacks of documents for my signature, and based on the trust and confidence I had in him I routinely signed them without reading them. I'd give him twenty signatures at a time and I'd get writer's cramp, and I didn't read them all. I signed them because I thought they were verified and true."

And is it similarly your style to leave the business details for the management of your corporations and other business ventures to the professionals you've hired to oversee them? "Well, I don't make all the decisions and they don't make all the decisions. We confer and we do what's in our best judgment."

You were asked many questions about the many corporations that you own. Do you feel that you're able to recall and keep track of all those corporations and their function? "No, because over forty years, I've had so many corporations. You see, when we go into a state or a country, we usually have to make a new corporation to operate there, and so we've had maybe a hundred corporations. We're trying to weed them out right now, and we're making a list and all the places we have done work in to cut them down."

The octogenarian Robert Trent Jones was spending more time talking to lawyers and dealing with lawsuits than sketching golf holes. First came what seemed like an endless series of estate proceedings related to the divisive terms of Ione's Will. Then the worst years of the Vidauban debacle ensued, with lawsuits from Denise Hirsch, Michel Benedetti, and others. He hadn't paid all his employees—and certainly not all his lawyers—what they were due. The Singerling case, though it didn't cost Jones much money, took a lot out of him. The malpractice suit against attorney Russell Carlisle had also dragged on and on, but was eventually resolved with a nice settlement in Jones's favor, but only after many stressful months had passed. He also started working on a new Will, intending to divide everything equally between his two sons. It took his lawyers more than a year to finish.

Trent's troubles kept snowballing. His longtime secretary, Eileen Vennell, grew upset with him for not living up to some of the promises that both he and Ione had made to her. Although she had worked for the Joneses since 1952, she had no pension or other retirement benefits, nor did she have ongoing health insurance, which was a problem because her health was suffering. By late 1990 she was all but begging for help. Unfortunately for Vennell, when making her case to Jones she solicited the help of Jim Singerling and Russell Carlisle. Jones agreed for a few years to give her an annual stipend [a little more than $6,000 a year] but when asked about a renewal by his chief business adviser, Jones's response was "Is she still alive?" He refused to continue the payments. At that point, Vennell brought suit against him. It was yet another matter that was eventually settled out of court (when Bobby offered to pay her "a little something").

Another lawsuit involved Ipswich (Mass.) Country Club and the company that developed its golf course and surrounding residential lots. Jones had joined with a pair of developers named Austin C. Eaton Jr., and Edward S. Keating to "organize, develop, market, and sell real estate as part of a country club and residential development in Ipswich, Massachusetts, including subdivision of the property, planning and building of roads, a common sewer-treatment facility, a Robert Trent Jones golf course, tennis courts, a swimming pool, a clubhouse and other utilities and common amenities, supervision of [the] organization of a homeowners association and in general to undertake any and all activities related to such development."

As with many such properties in the early 1980s, things went smoothly at first. But then came "Black Monday," October 19, 1987, when the stock market crashed and the Dow Jones Industrial Average fell by nearly 23 percent. Wall Street recovered, but the savings and loan industry was on the verge of collapse. Housing values fell precipitously, and many houses and lots were being sold at a fraction of their initial cost. Eaton and Keating (and Jones, too, through the Massachusetts business trust they had formed) were the holders of a large bank note that stipulated that for each $100,000 borrowed, they were stuck personally for $80,000. The developers assured the Ipswich club members, "Don't worry, we'd never stick you for the shortfall." But the recession hit Eaton and Keating so hard that they had no choice but to sell off their notes from club members to a major Massachusetts banking institution in order to get some cash out of the deal. The bank was not bound by the developers' reassurances to the club members, and therefore stopped paying on their notes.

The bank decided to foreclose and came after Eaton, Keating, and Jones for the shortfall. The people who had bought lots from Ipswich Club Development Company were not happy, and they brought action against all three trustees.

The tenets of a Massachusetts Business Trust made Jones a liable party, even though his involvement had been limited to providing the land and designing the golf course.

The jury hearing the case could rightfully have imposed triple damages, but only awarded the individuals single damages of $150,000. But Eaton and Keating had both filed personal bankruptcy, having put everything in their wives' names, so Jones had to pay the entire amount, plus attorneys' fees for his side and the plaintiffs as well.

Being in business with partners whom one doesn't know very well can be treacherous. Deceit and betrayal inflected Jones's business deals on a number of occasions, especially in the closing era of his long career. In the 1980s, Jones got entangled in yet another potentially very large mess, due to the irresponsible behavior of someone with whom he had acquired a parcel of land some thirty years earlier.

In the federal district court in Charlotte, North Carolina, the case was known as *United States v. Taylor*. It involved an EPA "Superfund" pesticide cleanup on a 580-acre tract of land just south of Pinehurst, in Aberdeen. Jones and a man named J. D. Farrell had purchased it together in 1965 with the idea of creating a golf and residential development. Previously, the land had belonged to the Taylor Chemical Company, primarily a manufacturer of pesticides.

Part of the property, it turned out, had been a major chemical dump site. In the late 1960s, Farrell spent some $20,000 burying more than 25,000 tons of DDT that had been dumped by Taylor Chemical on the site. DDT, short for dichlorodiphenyltrichloroethane, was a colorless, nearly odorless, and spectacularly successful insecticide; first made available commercially in the late 1940s, DDT was better than the coming of sliced bread, at least as far as many American farmers were concerned. But the use of DDT was full of hazards. The initial outcry against the pesticide came in 1962, when American biologist Rachel Carson published *Silent Spring*, a powerful attack not only against DDT but the entire idea of releasing large amounts of chemicals into the environment without fully understanding their effects on ecology or human health. Carson's book helped give birth to a widespread environmental movement in America by the late 1960s. DDT was banned in 1972 by the newly created Environmental Protection Agency. Until it was banned by law, DDT was widely used on golf courses in the United States and around the world. Instead of calling in the authorities about the DDT problem on the property, Farrell buried hundreds of bags of the toxic chemical in a series of huge pits and had them covered. One of the pits was actually a trench with a volume in excess of 500,000 cubic yards.

In 1971, Farrell and Jones divided up their land. In terms of creating a golf course, Trent did no more than devise a simple routing, but he was confident that a great golf course could be built there; bordering his property to the north was the Country Club of North Carolina, one of the top courses in the state, which had opened in 1963.

Whether the partition of the land between Farrell and Jones occurred because Jones had found out about the burying of the DDT isn't certain. Whatever Jones knew (his sons say he knew nothing about it), Farrell's half included the acreage where the pesticide was buried. No one seems to have known about the chemical dump on the Aberdeen property other than Farrell—at least not until 1984, when he sold part of his acreage for the construction of a golf course that became known, ironically, as "The Pit." During the construction of the 18-hole Dan F. Maples design, the State of North Carolina learned that DDT was buried under portions of the site. After Maples made some changes to his route plan, the course opened in 1985; at the same time the EPA designated the polluted sections of Farrell's property as a National Priorities List (NPL) site, which meant that it required a major environmental cleanup. (One of the polluted sections lay in what would have been the golf course's sixth fairway.)

In 1989 the EPA filed suit against the Taylor Chemical Company, but it soon went out of business. In 1991 the EPA filed an amended suit that went after Taylor's corporate customers: Union Carbide, Growers Chemical Corp., Shell Oil Co., Kaiser Aluminum, DuPont, and a handful of others. Because these were powerful transnational corporations, the companies in the EPA's sights turned around and filed "third-party complaints" against everyone who was in the chain of title to the polluted Aberdeen property. That brought Farrell and Jones into the case, and not only them: to "muck up the situation" and give the government "some big heartburn," the lawyers for the big chemical companies also filed complaints against neighboring landowners, claiming they should have been aware of the dumping by noticing plumes of chemical residue. Most of these landowners were African-American subsistence farmers who owned small parcels of land in the Aberdeen area, where for years they had scratched out a living growing tobacco.

The litigation crept along for a couple of years. Farrell died. Jones claimed that he was totally innocent; in his deposition, Jones explained that he and

Farrell had split up the property back in 1971, and that his land was clean, "the only dumping being household garbage." The problem for Jones was that Farrell had sent him letters telling him about the chemical pits on Farrell's part of the property, and thus he arguably had a duty to report the facts. Trent's lawyers worked hard to exonerate him, but when it came to Superfund lawsuits, the EPA was very reluctant to make any deals even based on a "small-landowner ex-emption." The EPA also resisted out-of-court settlements, because it might ap-pear as if the Agency was essentially accepting bribes. The lawyers for Jones did everything they could to reach a settlement, including talking to congressmen in California, Florida, and New Jersey, but even political connections could not help. The case trundled along, and Jones's legal bills kept stacking up because the lawyers representing Jones had to stay on top of everything that was hap-pening and be aware of all the court dates and deadlines, some of which were sudden. "If you don't do X, Y, or Z before the deadline comes," one of Jones's attorneys remembers, "then, it's like a statute of limitations. You lose your right to make that kind of maneuver, to make certain kinds of motions. We would have been putting Jones in extreme peril if we had not been tending this case as closely as we did."

Finally, in late 1991, the case was settled. The penalty imposed on the defen-dants totaled $90 million. Jones personally had to pay $100,000. But he also had to pay all his legal fees, which added up to nearly another $100,000. In the early 1990s, that was a tremendous amount of money for a man who was facing many different troubles. His legal bills for the year 1994 alone totaled $290,553.46, with bills from thirteen different law firms. Fenwick & West, the Palo Alto firm that Bobby principally used, and the one Bobby brought in to help his father clean up various messes, notably Vidauban, was owed over $160,000 for legal work. (Blake Stafford, Bobby's lawyer, was an associate of Fenwick & West.)

Trent Jones was no "environmentalist." Into the 1990s, very few golf architects were. For the most part, Jones saw environmentalists as anti-developer ex-tremists and left-wing nimbys, and he regarded environmental issues as some-thing to ignore or overcome. "Once the architect signs a contract to build a course, whether public or private, the real problems begin," Jones wrote in *Golf's Magnificent Challenge* in 1988. "The major hurdle to be leaped before anything can begin is consideration of the environment. It has become a primary issue in almost anything, particularly a golf course. With everything that man is doing these days to really rape the land, environmental protection has become a cause célèbre and the environmentalists have become, in some circles, national heroes. This is all well and good, because the environment must be protected. But it does create a great deal of difficulty for people trying to build golf courses."

One place where Trent did overcome potentially serious environmental issues was in Prince William County, Virginia, near the town of Manassas, where in the 1970s and 1980s Jones sought to develop a private golf club with a prestigious international membership. It was to be his American version of Vidauban—all the more remarkable since both of those grandiose, multimillion-dollar facilities were being developed simultaneously. Unfortunately, the development of what became the "Robert Trent Jones Golf Club" shared some of Vidauban's unfortunate storylines, including another near financial disaster for Jones.

According to one version of the story, Trent first saw the property in 1973 as he was flying over Prince William County, just west of Washington, D.C, to survey a tract of land that had been suggested to him as a fine spot for a golf course. On the way to that destination he spotted an irregularly shaped 800-acre lake bordered by beautiful wooded land. The site turned out to be Lake Manassas, a public reservoir that had been created in the 1960s, to provide potable water for three hundred thousand area residents. Jones knew immediately that he wanted to buy the surrounding property. It was 1973. Economic recession would not hit until the following year, and Jones, as ever, was a "landaholic," as Ione called him. He found a pair of partners to go in on the land deal with him, a deal that initially included big plans for residential real estate. Jones and his two partners—Tom Ryan, a New Jersey banker whom Trent knew from an earlier golf course project, and Jay Saunders, a Montclair-based real estate developer—formed "RTJ International Partnership," borrowed money, took out a mortgage and, after overcoming several legal difficulties pertaining to the properties, bought enough land along the long stretches of the lake for three golf courses, fulfilling the first stage of Jones's original intent. Trent later recalled his enthusiasm for the Lake Manassas property: "The day I found the site I marveled at its beauty. It was too beautiful to describe with words. The terrain was aesthetically perfect. I don't think we could have done anything better anywhere. My dream became to build a golf-only club like Augusta, Pine Valley, and Cypress Point, where members can experience playing golf in a natural setting without interference of housing developments and condominiums that encircle most courses.

There are islands and trees and everything else. It is 1,100 acres. We are going to have three 18-hole golf courses and a nine-hole short course in there. It will be one of the great tests of golf, hole by hole, in the world." An early marketing brochure described plans for "A luxurious 1,100-acre retreat," which will bring "a new level of hospitality to the Washington metropolitan area;" it was to include not only 63 holes of championship golf but also a "first-class 500-room international hotel and conference center, deluxe commercial park and shopping plaza, and exquisite residential community to open in 1987." With the exception of one 18-hole golf course, none of Trent's visions would come to pass.

By the mid-1980s it became clear that Trent had once again bitten off more than he could chew at Lake Manassas. While Ione smoked more cigarettes, drank extra coffee, and shuffled due bills that could not be paid on time, Trent went out with his characteristic optimism looking for financial help. John Laupheimer, who was involved with Trent in the purchase of Vidauban, invested some money in the Manassas project. So, too, did Jimmy Patiño. One of the most significant business connections that Trent made for the project was with Bobby P. Russell, chairman of Crum & Forster Inc., an insurance holding company based in New Jersey. Trent knew Russell from his many years as president of Baltusrol Golf Club, and from his chairmanship of the USGA's nationwide capital campaign, "Golf Keeps America Beautiful." After seeing the Lake Manassas property, Russell told Trent, "This course is destined to host major championships." The insurance man even suggested to Trent that the USGA might want to turn the golf course into a permanent site for U.S. Opens; besides being so close to the nation's capital, the tract of land was so spacious that it could provide ample parking as well as all the other amenities for spectators that a major championship needs. Having a permanent home for the Open near Washington D.C., Russell felt, would also "ease the difficulty of the USGA going around from place to place." Failing that (the idea went nowhere), Russell proposed to name the golf course "Robert Trent Jones International," the centerpiece of a golf-only club whose membership would likely include not only many of Washington, D.C.'s golf-playing dignitaries but also many foreign ambassadors and diplomats.

The real financial godsend for the Lake Manassas project was W. Clay Hamner, a North Carolina real estate developer who was the managing director and CEO of the Montrose Capital Corporation. Based in Durham, Hamner's company owned or held majority interest in more than forty businesses.

Hamner happened to be a friend of Dave Thomas, founder of Wendy's International, having met him when both men were teaching courses at Duke University. Dave Thomas and Trent Jones also knew each other well. They were neighbors in Fort Lauderdale; Thomas was a member at Coral Ridge. The two men had worked together in an unsuccessful attempt to buy Firestone Country Club. With the Lake Manassas project needing a big infusion of cash, Thomas approached Hamner, who had access to millions of dollars through his company's association with the Bernice P. Bishop Estate/Kamehameha Schools and Pauahi Management Corporation of Honolulu—better known as the Bishop Estate. Hamner's Montrose Capital served as an asset manager for the Bishop Estate and was indeed interested in the big land deal at Lake Manassas. As Hamner wrote to Trent Jones in December 1990, "The Bishop Estate are our partners in all of our projects and are the people arranging for us to be able to separate the Robert Trent Jones International Course from the real estate development as an independent free standing course in perpetuity subject to paying back the funds advanced."

In August 1986, the "DC Land Group" was formed with Hamner as the managing partner and Jones, Dave Thomas, Jimmy Patiño, and three other men as "general partners." The final general partner was the Bishop Estate itself. The cash infusion from the DC Land Group at the time of its formation was roughly $6.5 million. That same month the Land Group formalized an agreement with Robert Trent Jones, Florida, Inc., "to undertake the design and supervision of construction" of "at least one and up to three golf courses" for the project. If Jones Sr., who was eighty-two years old in 1986, could not fill this role, the agreement provided that Jones's son Rees would take over the design of the golf course.

The story of what ultimately became the Robert Trent Jones Golf Club is almost as convoluted in its financial and legal details as the saga of Vidauban, but Trent's biography requires that we touch on only a few major points about the tale of Manassas, given that its trajectory echoes the path of other torturous Jones projects.

First, by the end of it all, Trent no longer owned a single acre of the Lake Manassas property. It all belonged to his investors, notably the real estate entity that had been created by Clay Hamner, who brought in some $25 million from the Bishop Estate to develop the property.

Not only did Jones not profit from his involvement in the land deal, it seems that he made nothing off his design of the golf course, either; needing to take care of some of the debts he owed to investors, he agreed to lay out the golf course for nothing. His dream of building three 18-hole golf courses collapsed, just as it had at Vidauban. In the end, only one golf course was built. Important parcels of land that would have been needed for the second and third golf courses were sold off by Clay Hamner. Slowly but surely, Hamner's access to capital and his real-estate moxie pushed Jones completely out of the ownership picture and allowed the survivor to break off different pieces of the property and sell them for a tidy profit.

Unlike Vidauban, however, Trent got out of this financial mess without help from Bobby or his lawyers. Avoiding the task of cleaning up his father's affairs had a downside for Bobby, however. Unlike at Vidauban, where his involvement earned him a role in designing the course, Bobby would have no role in designing the Lake Manassas course. There are different versions of whether or not Bobby desired to be involved in the design of the Robert Trent Jones Golf Club. According to Bobby Russell, Bob Jr. tried to convince the directors of the club that he should be the golf course's designer. Russell claims that neither he nor any of the directors wanted that—and reiterates that the original agreement with Trent stipulated that Rees would design the course if his dad could not. Bob Jr. scoffs at Russell's assertions, but does admit some degree of involvement. "Russell was always pushing his own design concepts, and Dad asked me to protect his original ideas and plans, which I tried to do, but only as to remodeling. I was too busy to take on Lake Manassas, and did not try."

Though the details of the course design were placed in the capable hands of Roger Rulewich, Trent Jones did pay a great deal of attention to the golf course—perhaps the last time he did so in his long career. Jones visited the property many times, tweaked the routing, and drew sketches for many of the green complexes. He wanted to use the lake to the full advantage of the golf course. "Wherever it lies," Jones believed, "water lures us to a supreme triumph or a painful death." The architect was intent upon bringing the course as close to the water as possible. The problem was, the City of Manassas owned the lakeshore up to 300 feet above the water level. The dam that the city had originally built brought the water level in the reservoir to 285 feet and "intended eventually to raise the water level to 290 feet." Jones, with the DC Land Group behind him, maneuvered behind the scenes to allow him to use the land down to the 290-foot level "for golf purposes." It cost the Land Group an additional $175,000 in proffers to the city, which later used the money to pay for raising the dam.

Jones wanted even more from that lake. The ninth hole was a par-3 that played downhill to the edge of the lake. Jones wanted to build an artificial peninsula jutting out into Lake Manassas and to put a green surrounded on three sides by water on it. Authorities from the City of Manassas, as well as from Prince William County, were already worried enough about the possibility of the golf course leaching chemicals into their drinking water without having to fret over the impact of a golf green extending out into that lake. A number of holes already bordered it, especially on the back nine. But Jones wouldn't take "no" for an answer. He appeared at a public meeting of the Lake Manassas board, whose approval the developers of the golf course needed to build the ninth green out into the lake. The reputation and charisma of the world's number-one name in golf architecture "bowled them over," and he was granted the approval the course needed that very evening. "Mr. Jones already had a relationship with the local community," Rulewich remembers. "They knew him. He did it more than once. He would come to meetings where there would be environmental issues discussed and he'd walk in and say, 'Well, we're just going to go ahead and do that.' They might not have agreed with him, but they didn't oppose him. When Mr. Jones was at the meeting, it was all easy. He didn't get away with anything per se. It's just that they would tend to let him have his way because of who he was. In every dispute, he won the day every time."

In a draft version of *Golf's Magnificent Challenge*, which was being published just as construction started on the Lake Manassas golf course, Jones described "the impact of the constraints against chemical runoff and soil erosion" on his design:

> The courses are being built on the Manassas Reservoir, which supplies drinking water to the surrounding area. Naturally, officials have been concerned about the impact of our work. We were directed to build dikes, retention ponds and basins all over the property. If they could be placed in the rough or woods and out of the way, there was no problem. But a lot of them cut into fairways with their rigid grades. Sometimes trees had to be cleared to build them, trees that we would have left on the golf course, which is sad. We could soften those harsh lines, blending them into the contours of the course, as long as we didn't destroy their intent. That's where creative design can overcome problems and restore the natural, flowing look of a golf course.

It wasn't up to Jones alone to protect the Lake Manassas environment. A Fairfax, Virginia–based company, Dewberry & Davis, provided the engineering expertise in soil and groundwater contamination, wetlands protection and restoration, water quality, and natural resource conservation that enabled the golf course to be built safely and effectively around the edges of the reservoir. Most of the interactions with the Army Corps of Engineers were handled by Dewberry & Davis. In turn, the contractor laid out the parameters for Jones's own construction company, Florida Golf, to ensure that runoff from the maintained turf did not drain into the lake. Once the course opened, the club directors made sure that their greens superintendent adhered to a tightly controlled turf-grass management program. The water quality in the reservoir was monitored annually by the City of Manassas, and in no year since the monitoring began has there been any evidence of elevated levels of sediments or nutrients in the lake as a result of the golf course.

Jones would have liked to have brought the golf course even closer to the water. He wanted the finishing hole, instead of being a par-4 that played down to an elevated green on the very edge of the lake, to cross the water to a little skid of land, turning the 18th into a par-5 with a virtual island green. But as Rulewich points out, "that did not work out for a lot of legal and technical reasons." Instead of attributing any of his course's architecture to compromises forced by environmental matters, Trent claimed publicly that the layout was all part of his master plan for a visually spectacular championship track. "Lake Manassas is visible from practically every hole. I could have brought the lake into play on many of the holes but I didn't because I didn't want the players to think of it as a hazard and feel they were competing with it." His description was accurate. While most of the holes on the back nine ran adjacent to the lake, only on the par-3 11th (215 yards from the back tee) did a player have to hit across a portion of the lake. The lake was thus much more of a visual centerpiece than a significant factor in playing strategy.

To give golfers and spectators even better views of the lake, Jones cleared out a lot of trees. "Almost every hole is heavily wooded," Jones explained, "but we decided to use the trees as a framework, too, and rely on other design factors to give the course its character and playability." On only one hole did Jones end up using trees—in that case, a single tree—as a key design feature. The tree was the club's lone walnut, and it stood proudly on the 17th hole, a short par-4 that played no more than 380 yards. During construction, there was quite a debate between Jones and Dan Garson, the construction supervisor, about saving that tree, which stands 70 yards from the green on the right side of the fairway and creates an obstacle for approach shots coming in from the right. Roger Rulewich, stuck in the middle between Jones and Garson, recalls that on one occasion Garson literally stood "hugging the tree to make a point about how important it was." In the end, it stayed.

As is often the case, it took longer to acquire and finance the property than it did to build the golf course. Nevertheless, it still took almost three years to finish construction because there were so many issues to overcome, many of them related to the environmental concerns mentioned above. Construction started in 1988, and the golf course formally opened in April 1991. On opening day, it was still called the Robert Trent Jones International Golf Club; it did not become the Robert Trent Jones Golf Club until 1994. Among the founding trustees were Clay Hamner, Bobby Russell (who had gone on to serve as secretary of the USGA), and Ernest L. Ransome III, the longtime president of Pine Valley Golf Club. Trent was in fine form at the ceremonies, telling the members and their guests, "I do believe that this may turn out to be the best course I ever built." He had made such a statement many times before, and it seems that he probably meant it every time.

Jones loved the Robert Trent Jones Golf Club and visited it whenever he was able. He loved the grandiose, over-the-top clubhouse: a 65,000-square-foot Georgian-style mansion with a red brick exterior, stately white columns, and a portico, though he had nothing to do with its design. He was especially honored by the creation of "The Robert Trent Jones Room," which featured some of the architect's most historic and valuable memorabilia. (Here again, there arose another "Jones-Russell" contest: The Jones Papers at Cornell contain letters documenting how difficult it was for Bobby Russell, whose idea it was to create the "Jones Room," to get cooperation from Trent—or from either of his sons [Rees states that he "gave him what he could"]—to provide Russell with what he considered "suitable memorabilia.")

In 1994 the Robert Trent Jones Club hosted the inaugural "Presidents Cup," a set of professional matches fashioned after the Ryder Cup, with the U.S. team opposing an international side made up of players from the rest of the world outside Europe. Trent attended, as did his sons, and he considered the event "a smashing success." "President Clinton hosted a dinner at the White House before the tournament began," Trent would recall, "and it was a very memorable occasion. (Bobby and wife Claiborne attended.) All the players plus a great number of dignitaries were there. During that week I was also invited to the Australian embassy for a reception by Dr. Don Russell, the ambassador of Australia." Trent thought that the golf course (at 7,415 yards, one of the longest he'd ever designed) would become the permanent home for the Presidents Cup; while the biennial event was held there when the U.S. team hosted in 1996, 2000, and 2005, the event moved to Harding Park Golf Club in San Francisco in 2009 and in 2013 to Muirfield Village Golf Club in Dublin, Ohio. The PGA Tour, which sponsors the event, believed it was a good idea to stage the event in different parts of the country.

The Robert Trent Jones Golf Club on Lake Manassas was not the only golf course formally dedicated in honor of Trent Jones in 1991. Cornell University officially renamed the 18-hole course that Jones had designed for its campus (the first nine in 1941, the second in 1954) the "Robert Trent Jones Golf Course at Cornell University." "We're happy to welcome a legend home today," said Frank H. T. Rhodes, the university president and a good friend of Trent's, who spoke at the course's naming ceremony on September 28. Following the dedication, Trent was driven in the personal automobile of Dick Costello, the university golf pro, right onto the first tee, where Costello presented Trent with a beautiful new persimmon-headed driver that had been specially made for the ceremony. Trent did not venture hitting a tee shot, but both of his sons did—first Bobby, then Rees, who remembers that he outdrove his older brother.

Of all the honors that Jones received in his career—and he had already received many by September 1991, including a repeat induction into the World Golf Hall of Fame in 1987—Jones may have appreciated the Cornell honor more than any other. It had been sixty-three years since he first walked on the Ithaca campus as a "special admission" student, and whether or not he would actually have needed the select curriculum of courses he took there between 1928 and 1930 in order to become a golf architect, Trent always considered his years at Cornell to be his springboard, and not just into his professional career, but also into his manhood. Not to mention that Cornell was where he first met Ione Davis. So taken was Jones with the moment at the golf course's dedication that, during his own remarks to the crowd, he personally pledged $100,000 to his alma mater for the purpose of improving the Robert Trent Jones Golf Course. What most likely freed up Trent Jones to promise such a generous donation to Cornell was the lucrative contract his company had secured to design a series of golf courses in Alabama.

Like manna from heaven, the job to create Alabama's Robert Trent Jones Golf Trail fell into Trent Jones's lap just when he needed it the most. Ironically, given how aggressively Jones had pursued golf course projects over the course of his long career, in this case he really did nothing—and *had to do nothing*—to become the designer of the largest golf course project ever attempted anywhere in the world. He had already done all he had to do to get the Trail contract: established his reputation over many decades as the foremost brand name in golf architecture.

The client was the Retirement Systems of Alabama, the entity that managed the pension funds for all public employees in the state. Its driving force was Dr. David G. Bronner, an Iowa native who been educated at Mankato State University in Minnesota, before earning law ('71) and doctoral ('72, in finance) degrees from the University of Alabama. In 1973, at the tender age of twenty-eight, Bronner took over as RSA's chief executive officer. At first he concentrated on traditional investments, but by the mid-1980s, facing the challenges of diversifying a billion-dollar pension fund and bringing more business and industry to an underdeveloped state economy, Bronner began to think more creatively. His passion for golf played a part from the start. Though not a highly skilled golfer, he was tenacious on the course, with an iron will and icy-cold temperament, the best type for a partner in any game. Bronner thought golf could help Alabama. "You didn't really have any decent public courses in the state of Alabama," Bronner would later recount. "There was a little one in Montgomery that's in some magazine's top 100, but it was the only one in the whole state that I would consider to be sharp. We had some state parks that had nice courses, but because of the heavy, heavy play, you would have to say they were just . . . okay." Bronner tried to buy those state park golf courses, promising to put in "a lot of money" for their upgrading. "But I couldn't get them to bite."

Then one day in 1986, Bronner met a young man named J. Robert "Bobby" Vaughan Jr., a former professional golfer who was now in the business of building golf courses. Vaughan was building the Joe Lee–designed Wynlakes Golf & Country Club, a large residential golf course development in the southeastern suburbs of Montgomery, Alabama's capital city and home of the RSA. "The golf course was still in the dirt, and we had just had a rainstorm," Vaughan recalled. "All the work we'd done that day, I saw washing down the river. It's 5:30 in the afternoon and I'm sitting there in a Jeep, covered with mud. I'm drenching wet, and this guy walks up from out of the blue and says, 'How do you build a golf course?' I laughed. But he had a cooler with him and I said, 'You know what? You give me one of those beers and we'll have a talk. Come on. Hop in the Jeep and I'll take you for a tour.' We sloshed around and he got muddy and I got muddier. We had a great conversation. I had some chemistry with this guy."

Three weeks later, Bronner showed up again at Vaughan's golf-course-in-progress. "This went on for several weeks until I finally figured it out," Vaughan remembers. "Oh, my! I didn't understand who this guy was! Now he was my friend." The two men, neither one of them native Alabamians, spent a lot of time together in the coming months, during which Vaughan shared an idea that had been bubbling around in his head for the past several months. Keenly aware of trends in the golf course business during the 1980s, including the PGA Tour's creation of its Tournament Players Club (TPC) courses, Vaughan had been asking himself: "Would it be possible to do upscale, public, championship golf courses at an affordable price for people? Could you do that? That was really a big dream, because there really wasn't any great upscale golf for the public—not that was affordable. People couldn't get it. Where could you get it?" Bronner was very interested in the question. In the meantime, with Wynlakes completed, Vaughan went back to North Carolina and went to work for RJR Nabisco, a major player in the world of American sport, not just through its sponsorship of NASCAR and other motorsports organizations but in professional tournament golf as well. Vaughan's assignment with RJR Nabisco was to direct the construction work involved with remodeling the tournament course at Tanglewood Park in Clemmons, North Carolina, site of the 1974 PGA Championship. It was there during a "complete redo" of the Tanglewood Championship layout for the 1987 Senior PGA Tour's Vantage Championship that Vaughan first met "Mr. Jones." At the same time, he met Roger Rulewich and Niall Fraser, Jones's top shaper with Florida Golf. "We tore the golf course up completely," recalls Vaughan. "We rebuilt the whole thing. It was a model for speed of construction, a model that we emulated and improved when we got to Alabama."

In 1988, RJR Nabisco was acquired by Kohlberg Kravis Roberts & Co. (KKR), a private equity firm that specialized in leveraged buyouts (this one was the largest in American history). Bronner and Vaughan had kept in touch, and when the RSA leader heard about the buyout, he gave his golf friend a call: "The phone rang and it was my old friend from Alabama," Vaughan recalled. "'What does this mean for you?' he asked. 'I'm worried about you. I'm coming up for a visit.'"

Bronner stayed for nearly a week, playing a lot of golf on the renovated course at Tanglewood. One night after dinner, Bronner, a cigar sticking out one side of his mouth, said, "Let's talk about that crazy idea of yours."

"What are you talking about, David?"

"Let's talk about the crazy idea to build public golf courses."

Bronner then asked a breathtakingly naïve question: "How much does it cost to build one of these things?" Anyone who had ever built a golf course knew there were a great many variables in estimating such a thing. It wasn't just about what it cost to build the golf course, it was all the equipment, the clubhouses, grow-in, the start-up, and a whole lot more. Vaughan hesitated to offer an answer, but Bronner kept trying to pin him down, "What's it going to cost me to do one of these crazy things that you want to do?"

"David, my best guess . . . It's probably going to be about $5 million apiece."

In 1988, when this conversation was taking place, there was a recession going on. For many businessmen, not just those in golf, the world was upside down. Nobody had work, not much of it anyway. That was also true for Trent Jones and Roger Rulewich—the Jones company's only new 18-hole course in the United States was Ipswich Country Club, where more lawsuits were flying than golf balls!

Vaughan continued, "David, 78 percent of corporate executives around the world play golf. In Alabama you need to recruit industry. You need couples to retire to your state. Retirees are big business. Retirees play golf. They spend money. The next biggest issue for you is tourism. People don't understand that in forty-two of the fifty states in the U.S., the number-one industry is what? It's tourism. It's big business. In Alabama, tourism isn't big business. You need to make it that. If you did all that you could change the state. It will take about $5 million per course." Bronner was way ahead of him. "I was looking for a stimulating effect for Alabama, which is a big geographical area," Bronner would later explain. "Championship golf courses like Ballybunion and Lahinch provide the entire economic impact for the little Irish towns where they're located, not only for the golf courses, but for the restaurants, gas stations, hotels, the whole works."

Without blinking an eye, Bronner, representing a state whose own government was nearly bankrupt, then uttered what may be the greatest line in the history of golf course development. He said, "Well, can we open with twenty?" Here was a businessman-visionary embodying the sort of aspirations which had fueled the extravagant dreams of Robert Trent Jones. But unlike Jones, Bronner controlled the resources to make his dreams come true. While Bobby Vaughan choked on his drink, Bronner went on: "You have to understand, Bobby, I represent a pension fund that has between $30 and $40 billion. Unless the scale of this thing is big enough, it doesn't make any sense. If I can't make it a hundred, a couple hundred, million dollars, it's not even worth the paperwork for me to mess with it." One can only imagine what Trent Jones would have thought, while still stuck in the middle of the Vidauban fiasco, if he had heard Bronner make that statement. It certainly sobered up Bobby Vaughan quickly.

"Yeah, David, we could do that," Vaughan managed to utter.

"How long is it going to take you to do it?"

Not quite comprehending the full scope and implications of what they were discussing, Vaughan replied, "David, we could do twenty in two years."

Bronner stayed in North Carolina with Vaughan for a few more days. During those days Vaughan did some research, wondering, "What was the largest golf course construction project in the history of the world?" He found that there were a few places where three courses had actually been done at once. In the early 1970s Jones, Inc., had begun 72 holes in Japan at Karuizawa. (Jones would also eventually do 72 holes at Dorado Beach in Puerto Rico.) That was the most Jones had ever done. Bobby Vaughan had told David Bronner he could do twenty courses in two years.

Bronner told Vaughan it was a go. He had just seen the movie *Field of Dreams,* in which a farmer from Iowa builds a baseball field to attract tourism; Bronner was born in Cresco, Iowa, and the inspiration he took away from the movie clinched it for him. Using RSA's millions, he would fund the construction of a series of championship-caliber public golf courses spread strategically throughout the state, from the foothills of the Appalachians in north Alabama to the Gulf of Mexico in the south. The golf courses would be the fulcrum that boosted tourism, attracted retirees, and spurred economic growth. "If you have a group of great golf courses," he figured, "then you can tell tourists that this is a golf mecca. All the courses are within five to fifteen minutes of an interstate. The theory was to have them within an hour and a half of each other. Alabama has always been a pass-through state. But the Florida courses that are the destination of our travelers are costly compared to our projected green fees. [We] can give them the same product, cheaper, [and] the residents can appreciate it and tourists can say, 'Hey, this is something else.'" Tourists could also say that Alabama had more going for it than they ever realized. As Bobby Vaughan laid it out: "We were racist. We were rednecks. We were hillbillies. Just name every negative connotation you could, and it applied to Alabama. The state was forty-eighth, forty-ninth, or fiftieth in every category there was. How crazy was our notion that you could possibly change all that by developing first-class public golf?"

As a state retirement system, the RSA, no matter how much money it had, could not just go out and start a business to build golf courses; a private company had to be formed. In Birmingham, Alabama's largest city, Vaughan formed SunBelt Golf Corporation. Its task, a herculean one, was to oversee the entire operation, from acquisition of the needed land to construction to administration. SunBelt's situation was wholly unique: a private company, with access to pension funds belonging to a public company, with both direct and indirect ties to state government. Depending on what needed to be done, one day SunBelt wore its private hat, the next day its public hat, the day after that its government hat. Having all those hats enabled Vaughan to get things done that he could never have managed to do otherwise. But the enterprise was still very high risk. "When I personally borrowed $100 million," Vaughan recalls, "that was an eye-opener. The first $10 million that I borrowed, let's face it, that's when they take your wife, your kids, your dog, everything you have and you sign them away. I don't think I slept for three weeks. The good news was, [with] all those other tens of millions of dollars, I didn't blink an eye. I figured, what are they going to do? Let you hang longer on the tree?! Eventually they'll cut you down.

"Then you wake up. How in the hell are you going to do this? That's when I went back to Tanglewood and met again with Roger Rulewich and Niall Fraser and started to put a plan together. What do we need to pull this thing off?"

Vaughan wanted the "Robert Trent Jones" brand name for their courses; Bronner wanted that, also. Both men knew that Jones himself would probably not be doing much of the design work. "When I first visited Mr. Jones at Tanglewood, he was eighty," Vaughan remembers. "By the time we started the Trail, he was eighty-three or eighty-four." SunBelt would work with Rulewich. "Roger is the only golf architect in the world without an ego," declares Vaughan. "There is no designer in golf that's had the impact that Roger has had without any fanfare. If you really want to start with what Roger does best, it is that when you look at golf courses, you look at what's important. First and foremost, the important thing is having a great site. The second most important thing is great routing. If you get those two right, it's pretty hard to screw it up. I can promise you from the perspective of routing a golf course, there's not a better guy in the world than Roger Rulewich." Of course, Vaughan's rhetoric excluded "the Master": Trent Jones himself. But Rulewich's modesty and lack of ego made him a great working partner for Vaughan, because Vaughan did have an ego, and he expected to be intimately involved in the design of the Alabama golf courses. Roger accepted Vaughan's participation, but Robert Trent Jones, in his prime, would have resisted it.

Vaughan and Bronner very much wanted Jones Senior to be the figurehead of the Alabama Trail. The Jones name was "the brand and the key to our success for going forward." Trent, of course, saw his role from the start as quite a bit more than that. "This will be one of the thrills of my life," he told reporters. He could not believe what was coming together for him. All the land and the infrastructure for the Trail was *free*. It was all *given* to SunBelt. It had *zero* cost. Jones just shook his head in disbelief, and smiled.

Had he been twenty years younger, Jones would have blown in like a gale to take over the project. But his age now prevented him from doing anything close to fully designing the Trail golf courses, even though he still was at this point relatively okay health-wise. He would visit the sites of as many of the golf courses as he could: ultimately, 22 of the 26, but seldom more than once or twice—and that's counting the golf courses' grand openings. Rulewich and Niall Fraser gave him regular updates on the progress of their work. Throughout the construction they sent him videotapes, which were narrated to describe what he was seeing. Trent watched them in the living room of his Fort Lauderdale apartment, and sometimes reviewed the plans at the desk in his Coral Ridge office. He sent Roger a number of sketches, asking that they be incorporated into the green complexes and bunker arrangements. Roger graciously accepted, but didn't have the heart to tell Jones that, in most cases, the designs of the courses had already been finished and that the sketches would never be used.

The pace of the Trail's construction was so extraordinarily fast that it was hard for Rulewich and Vaughan, let alone Trent Jones, to keep up. SunBelt broke ground on 54 holes in Birmingham in December 1990, then 54 holes in Mobile in January 1991, 54 holes in Opelika in February 1991, and 54 holes in Huntsville in March 1991. SunBelt built those twelve courses while still putting together deals for six more layouts: 36 holes in Greenville, 36 holes in Dothan, and 36 holes in Anniston/Gadsden. The lightning pace required focusing 100 percent of everyone's attention on the Trail. That included all the resources of Trent Jones's operations, both in design and in construction, the latter via Florida Golf. But more important than even Jones's resources were the capabilities of Phillips & Jordan, Inc., a large general construction contractor whose main offices were in Robbinsville, North Carolina, and Knoxville, Tennessee, and whose specialty was large-scale land clearing, earthmoving, underground utilities, erosion control, storm drainage, and debris management. P&J was the second-largest owner of Caterpillar equipment in the world, after Saudi Arabia. Without the complete resources of P&J behind the building of the Trail, there was no way it could have been finished in such a short time. In 1992 the Robert Trent Jones Golf Trail opened to the world for play with four facilities: Grand National in Auburn/Opelika, Hampton Cove in Huntsville, Magnolia Grove in Mobile, and Oxmoor Valley in Birmingham. That was 216 holes of golf. The following year, 1993, three additional locations opened: Highland Oaks in Dothan, Cambrian Ridge in Greenville, and Silver Lakes in Anniston/Gadsden. That was an additional 108 golf holes. In less than three years' time, 324 holes of championship-caliber public golf opened in Alabama, a golf feast that included four 18-hole plus three 9-hole par-3 "short courses."

The first reactions to the Robert Trent Jones Golf Trail were glowing. The courses won accolades and awards from numerous golf and tourism magazines, and quickly transformed Alabama into one of the world's top golf destinations. With green fees initially starting at less than $50 for a round, The Trail, noted *The Wall Street Journal,* "may be the biggest bargain in the country," and *The New York Times* called it "some of the best public golf in the world." Travel magazines named Alabama one of the world's top-10 golf destinations. Golf course raters included The Trail collection among their lists of the best new American courses.

Although Trent had little to do directly with the design of the golf courses, the layouts nonetheless were highly characteristic of the Jones style, which Trent had nurtured over his long career and taught to his successors. Rulewich had worked for Trent for thirty years and his architectural approach followed Trent's templates. Neither Bobby nor Rees had a comparable fidelity to their father's style, although their courses bore the inevitable family resemblance. The Trail courses, in other words, though not directly from the hand of Trent Jones himself, may as well have been. They were virtually indistinguishable from Jones's own work. The courses reflected all of the essential elements of Jones's long-established design philosophy, in which water, strategically located framing bunkers, and contoured fairways with variable-width landing areas, were principal features. The characteristic opportunities for risk-reward and heroic shots, which Trent employed in abundance even in his earliest work of the 1930s, were plentiful on The Trail. The greens on the Trail courses were also in the Jones manner: large (averaging about 7,500 square feet), with significant contouring and multiple hole locations. Pins could be tucked into a well-guarded section of the green, but there would also be a safe route to the green, which would leave a long, sloping putt.

Bobby Vaughan's influence on the Trail courses ensured that they would be longer and more difficult than Roger Rulewich would have preferred. Even if golfers did not play the back tees (and he hoped most would not even try), he wanted the scorecards for all the courses to show formidable length. All of them stretched to more than 7,000 yards; most were well in excess of this figure, and two—the Fighting Joe Course at The Shoals in Muscle Shoals and Ross Bridge in the Birmingham suburb of Hoover—tipped the scales at a gargantuan 8,000-plus. The various courses included par-3s as long as 258, 260, and 275 yards, and par-5s of up to 716 yards. Vaughan believed that visitors would be impressed by the figures and that the media would duly report them, even though the vast majority of players would choose a much shorter set of tees.

Trent himself expressed reservations to David Bronner about the length and difficulty of the courses. Bronner's response was that they needed to make them even harder. "What? We can't do that," said Jones. But Bronner replied, "Trent, I just went out to Pete Dye's TPC Stadium Course in Palm Springs, and all I saw was people with hundreds of dollars in cash trying to hurt themselves on that damn tough golf course." According to Bronner, his mentioning of Pete Dye was enough to convince Jones. "Then go ahead and toughen them up."

Bobby Vaughan remembers receiving a phone call early on in the building process from Ron Whitten, the architecture writer for *Golf Digest*. "Bobby, you told the world you were going to open with twenty golf courses," Whitten said. "How are you going to keep from cookie-cutting? You have the same people doing all the courses, how in the world are they just not all going to look alike?" Whitten's question "struck a chord" with Vaughan, but he replied that the key to having variety in the golf courses lay in the diversity of the sites. Elevation in the state ranged from sea level at Mobile Bay to more than 1,800 feet in the Appalachian Mountains to the northeast. It had an abundance of natural resources. Eighteen percent of all the freshwater in the United States flowed through Alabama. The second-largest river delta in the United States (after the Atchafalaya in Louisiana, where the Atchafalaya River and Gulf of Mexico converge) wasn't the Mississippi, it was Alabama's Mobile-Tensaw River Delta. Throughout the state lay numerous creeks, streams, rivers, and lakes, as well as four national forests. The golf courses of the Alabama Trail would all be different because the sites would be so different, reflecting the geographic diversity of Alabama itself.

In the end, everyone involved with the remarkable achievement that was the Robert Trent Jones Golf Trail came away happy. David Bronner and the people of Alabama certainly were. "When we started The Trail," Bronner said in 2013, "tourism in the state was a $900 million a year industry. Today, tourism in Alabama is an $11 billion industry. The tourism sector is now even bigger than agriculture. The taxpayers in the state get $8 billion more a year, each and every year, because of the Retirement System. The golf industry in Alabama supports more than twenty-one thousand jobs with a wage income of roughly $460 million. It's not just due to The Trail, because the RSA has a lot of ancillary assets, [including] ownership of more than eight dozen newspapers and four dozen television stations, spread all around the country. It's all that media that gives us the ability to get in people's homes—about 14.6 percent of the American population, to be exact. We bring them all the Robert Trent Jones Golf Trail."

Alabama's success inspired imitators. Tennessee created "The Bear Trace," a series of existing courses as well as two original Jack Nicklaus designs. Louisiana established its "Audubon Golf Trail." In recent years, Georgia, Idaho, and Montana have also created golf trails, again not involving any original courses but linking a dozen or more of some of the top golf resorts in their states. But none of them have been nearly as successful as the Robert Trent Jones Golf Trail. Bronner certainly does not see anything coming close to matching Alabama's success. "Nobody's got the guts. They don't have the money. The only state that came close was Tennessee with its Bear Trace, but they did it totally wrong because they put things onto the state parks, which are beautiful, but their courses are not on the interstates, or in or around population centers, with other things to do besides golf, they are in little spots, too remote."

In October 2013, The Trail recorded its ten millionth customer.

The Trail saved Robert Trent Jones from suffering through his last years in financial distress, if not in ruin. However much money made it into Jones's bank accounts because of The Trail, it was enough to pay off most of his out-standing debts, with some left over for himself. It was an undeniable godsend. Exactly how much was left over is uncertain. All that Bobby Vaughan will say about it is, "Probably saved them from closing the company and/or bank-ruptcy. Ultimately, a true 'win-win' for all. And a great story for the history books."

One person who likely knew exactly how much money Trent had coming to him through the contracts for the design and building of the Alabama Trail courses was son Bobby. Following Ione's death, and certainly by the time of the Singerling lawsuit, Bobby had assertively come to assist his father in both his personal and business affairs. Bobby brought his advisers and consultants to the task of reviewing Trent's situation. Some of them were lawyers, like R. Allen Zink, a Harvard Law School graduate who had worked at Palo Alto's Fenwick, Davis & West (later known as Fenwick & West) in the early 1980s before going into private practice in Redwood City, California. By 1990, Zink was spending a great deal of time in Fort Lauderdale at Bobby's behest, looking after and cleaning up different legal affairs for Trent. Along with the lawyers, Bobby also sent Alan Blake Davis to Fort Lauderdale to manage his father's daily business affairs. Davis, an Alabama native, had been managing the golf courses at the Princeville resort on Kauai, which Bobby had completed for Jones, Inc., in 1970. Trent did not always appreciate the help Bobby sent, finding Davis a particu-larly stressful intrusion. On Davis's office door at the "Coral Ridge Corporate Offices," as well as on his business stationery, Davis identified himself as "Chief Operating Officer" of Robert Trent Jones, Florida. When Trent saw that, he became irate and demanded that what he saw as usurpation cease. Trent never liked Davis and wouldn't talk to him. This frustrated Davis, but didn't stop him from doing the job that Bobby had sent him to Fort Lauderdale to do: use the receipts from The Trail and other projects to pay off debts, and then direct the rest of the money to where it needed to go. Where that was exactly is a question that brother Rees has repeatedly asked over the years. Bobby counters: "Rees had been kept informed by Lou DeReuil on every aspect of Dad's finances," to which Rees replies, "DeReuil did not have the financial data himself, let alone be able to pass it to me."

Back in Montclair, in the Gates Avenue house, Roger Rulewich maintained his base of operations for the Jones design company. He was assisted there by a young Michigan State graduate, A. John Harvey, whom Jones had hired in the late 1980s to assist Rulewich as Roger taught him the ropes of designing golf courses. As was the case on the Trail courses, Roger was chiefly responsible for the design of virtually all of Jones's work in North America and the Caribbean, as well as projects in Ireland and Wales, from 1981 to 1994. For all practical purposes, Roger Rulewich had *become* Trent Jones design, not because he had usurped anyone's authority or in any way pushed his mentor—"Mr. Jones," always "Mr. Jones"—out of the way, but simply because he was doing the job Mr. Jones had trained him for and asked him to do.

In late October 1995, Roger was asked to fly down to Florida for meetings with Trent about the permanent closing of the Montclair office. Roger was to bring along John Harvey and Niall Fraser, the chief shaper whom Rulewich had been using not just for the building of the Alabama Trail but for all the other courses Rulewich was then designing for Jones. Trent's personal attorney, Louis J. DeReuil, called the meeting for Trent, and both of them attended it. Neither of Jones's sons was present. The upshot was that the Montclair office would be closed as soon as possible (the date November 10 was given) and that notice be given to all the Montclair employees of the immediate termination of their employment (except for the administrative assistant Marilyn Gallagher, who was to be retained there until the end of the year).

What was the rationale behind the closing of Montclair, and who was behind it? Once again, as so often in Jones matters, there are strongly contrasting versions of the story, depending if one is listening to Bobby, Rees, or, in this case, Roger.

There is a version that Trent wanted the Montclair office closed. In the summer of 1995, Trent was 89 years old and not in good health. He was also increasingly dependent upon around-the-clock health caregivers and could hardly travel anywhere without one. (He did manage to attend the 1999 U.S. Open at Pinehurst, his last tournament ever.) Besides relying upon those who attended him, Trent had become dependent upon others to administer his business operations and personal assets. No longer able to travel to New Jersey without great effort, he was desirous of consolidating his affairs in Fort Lauderdale. He may also still have had hopes of bringing his sons back together in the company's work, and a Florida center could have been such a way. Another possibility that Bobby suggests is that his father may have preferred for Roger to begin operating out of the Florida office, and gave him that choice. However,

Rulewich denies that ever happened, and there is no evidence in the Jones Papers that Trent ever made such an offer.

There is also the version—held by Bobby—that Rees wanted Montclair closed. Rees benefited financially from the sale of Montclair, not just the cash proceeds from the sale of the home, but also from the relief he gained from ownership costs. Rees thus had at least one good reason for wanting the Montclair office closed—or so Bobby asserts. What seriously undermines that assertion is the fact that the house was not sold until well after the office was closed. "Dad then gave me the power of attorney to sell the house," Rees explains. "As a matter of fact, Roger had already settled in Massachusetts by the time I sold the house, and I had all the office furniture shipped up to him there."

Then there is the notion that Roger Rulewich himself wanted it, a version also purported by Bobby. Roger was ready to move on professionally and try his hand at independence, so goes this story. He did not fight the closing of Montclair, even if he did come out of the whole experience with a few scars.

Rees and Roger do not accept any of these versions: They believe that Montclair was closed because Bobby wanted it. Trent was no longer actively designing golf courses. He had been slowing down for some time. As long as Roger Rulewich was still working in Jones's Montclair office, Robert Trent Jones Sr. golf courses were going to be designed by Roger. In sum, Rulewich would execute the work accomplished under the imprimatur of his mentor's brand name. To borrow from the world of fine art, which Trent enjoyed comparing his profession to, Rulewich's work was in the master's workshop—in the "school of." That attribution did not diminish its quality, or its faithfulness to the tenets and practices of the master.

So there was the rub: the Jones brand name.

Son Bobby—"Robert Trent Jones, Jr.," the owner of the design firm "Robert Trent Jones II" in Palo Alto—felt that the brand name "Robert Trent Jones" rightfully belonged to him. "Robert Trent Jones" was his given name. That was a simple fact. To Bobby, the ownership issue connection seemed both logical and legal—and in his favor. Moreover, his father had trained him, too. In the late 1960s and early 1970s Bobby worked on numerous courses with his dad. Since then, he had been out designing golf courses all over the world under the brand name. Roger Rulewich had always worked *for* Jones, but never *as a Jones*. The ambiguity now surfacing was deeply entrenched in the family business. By the late 1980s, clients like David Bronner, Bobby Vaughan, and Bobby Russell not only knew they were getting Roger when they hired Trent, they *wanted* to work with the agreeable Rulewich, who was capable of creating "Robert Trent Jones" golf courses that were indistinguishable from Trent's own work. The client got the "name" it wanted—as Bronner and Vaughan did for the Robert Trent Jones Golf Trail, and Bobby Russell got for the Robert Trent Jones Club—without dealing with Bobby.

In order for Bob Jr. to gather for himself the full power of the RTJ brand, it was arguably essential that he divorce Rulewich from Montclair. That would mean Roger would likely have to find another job, and also another place to live (he and his wife, Sandy, as well as a couple of Roger's shapers, had been living in the house, with Trent's and Rees's permission). But for Trent to acquiesce to such a fate for Roger, it was necessary to insert a degree of alienation between them. The first step came at that late October 1995 meeting in Fort Lauderdale to which Rulewich was summoned.

At that meeting, Trent opened the discussion by expressing "concern that his advice had not been sought nor had he been kept current on the status" of ongoing projects. Rulewich replied that he had communicated with Trent on each of these projects, but had kept his reports brief as that seemed to be all that Trent wanted. According to the minutes of the meeting, which were kept by Lou DeReuil, "Roger then stated that he felt his professional future lay outside the RTJ organization; that, reluctantly, it was time to leave; but that he would not abandon his responsibilities on any current golf course projects should Trent Jones desire that he remain to complete those projects. . . . Trent expressed his appreciation for Roger's services over the past 35/40 years and appears reluctant to see Roger go, although the financial condition of RTJ Florida requires the closure of the Montclair office. Trent, nevertheless, sought to maintain a core team of Roger, perhaps John Harvey and Niall Fraser to pursue future golf projects." To which Roger "repeated his financial need to pursue other projects." As for the Montclair home, DeReuil directed Roger to "leave within a week or two" and that "appropriate termination agreements" with Roger and the other Montclair employees still needed to be addressed. According to Trent's lawyer, "The meeting was conducted in a cordial atmosphere but ended on a somewhat somber note."

Cordiality vanished once Rulewich received the termination agreement draft from Blake Stafford, who was still doing some of Trent's legal work. The very first clause called for a "complete corporate and household inventory" to be conducted by Marilyn Gallagher. The implication was that Roger might take something from the house that didn't belong to him. Deeper in, the document demanded repayment of an old $49,000 debt from Roger to Trent. To that demand, Rulewich replied in writing to Stafford: "Mr. Jones and I always operated on the basis of mutual respect and trust. Thirty-four years does that. When, years ago, I attempted to pay him back the note and Mr. Jones said, 'Forget it. It's a gift,' it meant finished business to him and to me. Obviously, however, not to you. So we have a little problem." The proposed agreement further required the return of a 1991 Buick that Roger had been using as a company car, and contained no severance pay for either him or John Harvey, instead offering "per diem income derived from site visits for current projects," and demanding an extensive list not only of all active projects but all potential leads for new work.

In Rulewich's letter to Stafford, his sense of hurt and betrayal is palpable:

For more than 34 years, virtually all my working life, my relationship with Robert Trent Jones, the man and his companies, has been characterized by deep affection, shared respect, mutual benefit and absolute honesty and trust. . . . I was never unmindful of the privilege of working with Mr. Jones nor did I ever fail to earn and appreciate his generosity. It is my loyalty to Mr. Jones that kept me with him all those years and it is in this spirit and in recognition of obligations he and his companies must fulfill that I have offered, despite my formal separation from the Jones Companies, to make myself available in a design capacity where my specific [presence] is either contractual or where my absence from the job site would be detrimental to Mr. Jones, his companies, or the job itself. . . . I will do this upon request, as my schedule allows; the cost to the Jones Group will be based on the specific work involved and will be quoted by me at a fair price, plus expenses, on a job by job basis. Further, the Jones Group must continue to provide health insurance for me and my wife Sandy, at Jones' expense until 1 March 1996. Finally, because you saw fit to make this a legal matter, you must pay any and all attorney's fees incurred by me in connection with any agreement that results from these discussions. . . . I know I have made myself clear. Don't send me any more Settlement Agreements unless consistent with my expressed positions.

When Rulewich used the word "you" in his letter, he was addressing Blake Stafford, but knew very well that Stafford was an attorney who was being paid to carry out an assignment. In explanation, Roger says that he had no doubt that the "you" behind the proposed agreement, the closure of the Montclair office, and any suspicion that might have infected Trent's thinking about Roger, was Bob Jr.

Rulewich eventually received a letter from Mr. Jones, dated December 14, 1995, and signed by Trent, but it contains two slight insertions that appear to be in someone else's hand. They are shown in italics below:

Dear Roger,

I am writing this letter to you with regard to your departure from my companies. After you came down this fall with others from the Montclair office and indicated that you wished to go your own way, I put forth an offer *through Blake Stafford,* which would have made a smooth transition of the current work in progress which you rejected in your November 17, 1995 letter. In this same letter you made a counter-offer which you stated was non-negotiable. While the substance of *your* letter is not without distortion, it is pointless to debate now. Unfortunately, as you are well aware from Lou DeReuil, we are not in a *financial* position to accept your non-negotiable offer. Therefore, it is with some regret that I must reject it.

With respect to the [$49,000] note you reference in your November 17th letter, it had not been canceled. My associates will be in touch with you to make provisions for its replacement.

I wish you the best of luck in your new endeavors.

Regards,

Trent

Correctly or incorrectly, Roger did not believe the letter came from Trent. To him, it did not read anything at all like a letter Mr. Jones would have written, and certainly not to a man he had often referred to—and treated—as a third son. (Rees, in commenting to the author upon seeing his dad's letter to Rulewich for the first time, declared: "Wow! Dad wouldn't think this way.") Despite his doubts, Rulewich sent a polite reply back to Mr. Jones, thanking him for his many years of kindness and opportunity, and for paying the college tuitions of Roger's children—

Trent knew how important it had been to his own career that his benefactor, James Bashford, had paid his expenses to Cornell—and concluding, "I wish you continued success, the best of health and think of you with great affection. I look forward to hearing from you, and until then, I remain . . . Sincerely, Roger."

Rulewich loyalists may wonder whether Trent himself ever saw the letter, let alone wrote it. Whether he did or not is pure conjecture, but a copy of it was certainly seen in the Fort Lauderdale office, and a missive was immediately sent out from there to the Jones clients:

> Our company is in a transition period. Roger Rulewich recently in- formed us that he no longer wishes to work for the Robert Trent Jones Companies and that he would like to venture out on his own. As a result, we have been attempting to reach an agreement with Roger that would allow him to continue to represent us on [our projects], where he has been the Chief Designer. Unfortunately, despite our best efforts we have been unable to reach any accord with Roger. Therefore, effective immediately, Roger will be succeeded by Don Knott as our Chief De- signer for the remainder of [your project].

The letter was signed by Matthew S. McDonald on behalf of "Robert Trent Jones Companies, International Golf Course Architects, Builders & Consultants," who had replaced Alan Blake Davis for the management of Jones's daily business affairs in his Fort Lauderdale office in 1995.

One client who received and reacted to that letter was Kan Morimoto, the president and chairman of Kajima Associates, Inc., long one of Japan's largest general contractors. Morimoto was developing an upscale golf course project in New York's Westchester County, and he had an excellent relationship with Rulewich. "This course is nearly two thirds completed with Roger's design input," Morimoto wrote to Matthew McDonald on January 4, 1996, "and it would be detrimental to the integrity of the Robert Trent Jones, Sr., design if we change a chief designer at this point. . . . While we are sure that Mr. Don Knott is an experienced and qualified architect, he has not been on Robert Trent Jones, Sr.'s staff." (In fact, Knott had been a Jones employee in the 1970s with Trent's Spanish office and later involved at Vidauban.) Morimoto received no reply for more than a month, which angered him and led to a more pointed letter sent on February 22: "Since our last letter, Kajima International . . . has become quite concerned that your organization has not responded to our demand that Roger Rulewich be reinstated as Chief Designer for our project. The least that your company could do would be to acknowledge that you are working to solve this problem. As we have stated before, there is no substitute for Roger Rulewich as Chief Designer, and again strongly request that your company resolve this problem."

By then, the Jones companies had no choice but to agree to Morimoto's demand, and to do it promptly. Rulewich completed the golf course according to terms negotiated by lawyers representing both sides, and the course, Anglebrook Golf Club, was completed in Somers, New York, in 1996.

Rulewich ultimately started afresh with a company of his own, "The Golf Group, Inc., Golf Course Construction and Remodeling," based in Bernardston, Massachusetts. As directed, he had provided "the name, address, and telephone number" of all leads on course projects while in Jones's employ, as well as "the status of the relationship or opportunity prior to your separation from Jones, and a description of your last contact with each such project." Nonetheless, some carryover from his tenure with Jones was natural. When Bobby Vaughan and SunBelt decided to add two new facilities to the Alabama Trail—Ross Bridge in 2004 and The Shoals in 2004–5—he and David Bronner did not consider any architect other than Roger Rulewich.

As for the $49,000 debt, Roger never repaid it, at least not directly. He had money due him from past jobs as well as from work he agreed to finish after he was no longer a Jones employee. He received payment, and accepted it as final, but his recollection is that he received "much less than what it should have been." From Bobby's point of view, "Perhaps it all came out about even."

Bobby Russell, the autocratic director of the Robert Trent Jones Club, was another figure who resisted written entreaties to sever all of Rulewich's involvement in Jones projects. The RTJ Club was considering some remodeling, and Russell wanted Rulewich to carry it out. On December 19, 1995, a letter went out over Trent's signature to Russell, expressing "my sincere disappointment over the changes to the golf course which you have initiated." The letter detailed the "dramatic changes" that Russell had authorized for the 18th hole in particular, and stated that the alteration "does not invite great shot-making, creates discord with the rest of the course and is particularly inappropriate for a finishing hole." It further went on to say, "When you asked me who I would like to designate to work with me on proposed changes to the golf course, I repeatedly informed you that it was my desire to work with my son, Bobby. As you may be aware, Roger Rulewich no longer works for me and so it troubles me that you have continued to ignore my request that you work with my son rather than Roger. . . . I find it surprising that you consistently refuse to listen to my ideas regarding my design ideas on a club which I chose to bear my name."

Bobby Russell did not answer Trent's letter, because he did not believe it actually was from him. Rather than replying, Russell got on a plane and flew to Fort Lauderdale to talk to Jones about the letter and whether he actually wrote it. The content of that conversation is not known, but the relationship between Bobby Russell and Bob Jones Jr. became more strained, assuring that the two of them would never work together at the Robert Trent Jones Club in Manassas— or anywhere else, for that matter.

Eventually the Lake Manassas course underwent some significant remodeling, but not with Rulewich. The PGA Tour told the club in 2001 that it needed to make some major changes to the last few holes of the course in order to enhance their appearance on television during the Presidents Cup. Instead of Rulewich, the club and the Tour brought in architect Bobby Weed to do the revisions demanded. In Bob Jr.'s view Weed's changes, especially at the 14th hole, would not have been acceptable to his dad. The PGA Tour eventually turned to one of Bob's former employees, forty-three-year-old Kyle Phillips, who had recently gone out on his own, to take over the assignment and complete it. One change that Phillips made that Trent would have liked was to relocate the green on the 18th hole, which Jones had wanted to put out into the lake. Phillips did not take it that far, but he did find a way to move the putting surface back from its elevated perch and down nearer to the water. The result was good, and the change stayed.

Trent's last real work as a golf architect came in association with projects started by his son Bobby. In April 1992, they had entered into a father-son partnership that was called "RTJ Golf Ventures," a joint venture between Robert Trent Jones, Florida, Inc., and Robert Trent Jones II. The name of the new partnership was important in that it symbolized and further strengthened Bobby's claim to ownership of the Robert Trent Jones brand name. As Bobby would note in a memorandum in 1998, "We can't promote and sell the Jones name in the commercial world without having control of the name. Right?" RTJ Golf Ventures was specifically created to design a new golf course for the Disney Development

Company's large-scale, master-planned residential project in Orlando known as "Celebration." The community of Celebration, Florida, was designed with a healthy family life in mind, totally safe and walkable throughout. In keeping with that concept, Disney wanted to build a daily-fee, 27-hole golf facility with a family theme, one nine designed by father Trent, and the other two nines by sons Bobby and Rees (i.e., one nine each). Rees wanted no part of it. For one thing, he had a problem with the very existence of RTJ Golf Ventures; according to Rees, his dad could not recall ever signing any agreement with Bobby regarding the blending of their names.

Trent definitely visited the Celebration site a couple of times with Bobby, and, according to Bobby, "offered some ideas for the golf course." One sunny afternoon visit, "Dad got out of his golf cart, walked near some of the golf course tees, chatted with the course's construction manager and course shapers, and even 'added' a couple of bunkers to the ninth hole through a quick sketch." The course was ready for play in the late spring of 1996, just in time to coincide with the grand opening of the first phase of residential development. After Jones's death in 2000, the golf course began to advertise itself as "the final course designed by the renowned masters, Robert Trent Jones Senior and Junior," and erected a statue of father and son looking out over the 18th green. The course does not publicize that the chief designer of the Celebration golf course was Don Knott, the lead project engineer for Robert Trent Jones II. (In 1999, Knott formed Knott & Linn Golf Design with his RTJ II associate and fellow ASGCA member Gary Linn.) Celebration wanted, paid for, and received the "Robert Trent Jones Sr. and Jr." designation.

It may not be accurate to credit Celebration as the final course designed by Jones Sr. In 1996, RTJ Ventures was also fulfilling a contract with the Southern California Golf Association to renovate the Rancho California Golf Club course in Murrieta, which Jones, Senior and Junior, had designed together in 1970 when Bobby was working for RTJ Inc., (Bruce Charlton of Robert Trent Jones II was the lead designer on the renovation project.) Also in 1996, RTJ Ventures started on the design of what became the Winchester Country Club, in the Sacramento Valley. "Dad came out at Christmas to look over the SCGA project," Bobby told the golf media, "and while he was here I suggested to the developers of the Winchester project [C. C. Myers and rancher Jerry Johnson] that it might be fun to make the grand master a part of it." The SCGA's renovated golf course opened in 1999. Winchester Country Club began play in 2000. Ranked by *Golf Digest* as one of the best new private courses in the United States and by *Golfweek* as a top-100 modern course and top residential course, Winchester Country Club calls itself "one of only seven courses co-designed by Jones Senior and Junior."

Yet another claimant as the site of Trent Jones Sr.'s last golf course design is Southern Highlands Golf Club in Las Vegas, part of a "high end" master-planned residential community located a few miles south of the Strip. (Bruce Charlton was also the lead designer on this project.) On the tee of the par-3 12th, a plaque reads: "Created in cooperation with his son Robert Trent Jones Jr., Southern Highlands proved to be the final golf course in the career of Robert Trent Jones Sr." The club's website goes on to say that Southern Highlands is "one of only *four* [author's emphasis] in the world co-designed by the late Robert Trent Jones Sr. and his son Robert Trent Jones Jr."

Clearly, those various developers regarded it as a great honor to be considered as the last course designed by Trent Jones Sr., and Bobby was amenable to letting them do it. But the truth is, Trent never set foot on Southern Highlands, though Bruce Charlton sent the route plan and photos of the site to Trent in Florida. He didn't even see a map of the property or any photos of it. Bobby tells the story: "Our client for Southern Highlands was Garry V. Goett, the founder and president of Olympia Companies, a pioneering real estate developer very busy with projects in the Desert Southwest. I arranged for Goett to make a visit to Fort Lauderdale to meet Dad and see Coral Ridge. My associate Bruce Charlton and I flew there with him. This was spring 1999. Dad was quiet but bright-eyed. He listened well. When Gary mentioned his Las Vegas property, Dad looked at me quizzically, because he'd never been there. I told Dad about it and suggested he sketch a hole. Gary wanted something 'like #16 at Augusta.' I got Dad a sketch pad. What he drew was something like a mirror image of the 16th at Augusta, placing the water on the right not the left. The sketch was very lightly drawn, but I understood what he wanted. . . . The next month he had a stroke. That was the last sketch or plan he drew. We—Bruce Charlton and I—built the hole as he wanted it, fitting it into land he had never seen. It was an iconic use of water strategically placed in a created desert oasis golf paradise." (Charlton remembers that he and Bobby had drawings of the course laid out on a table at Coral Ridge and "I showed Trent the basic concept for #12, then Gary requested that the hole be "like Augusta.")

So the true story of the last hole that Trent Jones sketched is more poignant and powerful than any claim that could be made on any plaque or website. The hole he sketched was based on the 16th at Augusta National, which in 1948 he re-conceived and designed anew, thereby turning it into one of golf's most alluring and deceptive tests.

Trent's health had, inevitably, been declining over his final decade. His regular physician in Fort Lauderdale, Dr. Arthur Nadell, remembers: "Trent in his later years was focused on one thing and one thing only, medically speaking, and that was that my job as his doctor was to keep him functioning. He wasn't really interested in you relieving his pain and symptoms. He was only coming to see you for something important. All he ever wanted me to do was patch him up so he could go out and do another golf course deal."

Many times Jones did things against his doctor's advice: "One Saturday afternoon he came to see me on an emergency basis because he was having trouble breathing and he was coughing. I examined him and he had a recurrence of bronchitis with a touch of asthma. I told him, 'I can treat this, but you've got to go home and take care of yourself.' He said, 'No, I have to travel. I have to go to England and I'm scheduled on a flight this evening.' He had just three or four hours to get to the plane. 'Trent, this is a very bad move. You're going to be in an airplane where you are going to be very vulnerable. It's going to be nine hours over the water and you're an older person who's having trouble breathing with a touch of asthma and it could get much worse.' He said, 'You don't understand, I'm going to have lunch with the Queen of England tomorrow at twelve o'clock and we're going to discuss a golf course at Balmoral Castle. I'm going with or without your help.' So I did the best I could. I loaded him up with a whole bunch of medicines he could use on the plane. I was scared shitless that he might die on the airplane or at lunch with the Queen! What sort of doctor would let him go like that?! But he went and came back okay a few days later."

"He had high blood pressure," Dr. Nadell recalled, among other ailments. "He had a gastric ulcer. He had a bad prostate. He had lumbar back disease. He had leg cramps. He had lung disease. Trent wasn't a smoker, but Ione had been one all her life. I would try to slow him down, but there was no way to slow him down. He just wanted the best medical care I could give him, but he had his own agenda and no one could influence that agenda. He was always telling me about new clients and new golf courses, even though I knew nothing about golf. Here he had all these health issues ganging up on him, soon to lead to a stroke, and all he's talking to me about is the next golf course he's planning. He was a very channeled, positive thinker.

"Trent always had a kind word to say to any pretty nurse in my office. He would smile, he would chat, he would hold hands with my nurses. So what [that] he was an old man and in failing health? He never lost his appreciation of a beautiful woman. He had no sexual designs or ideas, he just loved the pretty nurses, remembered all their names. Never the ugly ones; to them, he just smiled. He was very cherubic and non-threatening. 'Why don't you come over to the club? You can have a meal there any time.' They really liked seeing him. He was a different kind of personality."

Trent's death was the culmination of many things that often happen to people as they get older. He suffered from hypertension, a disease of the blood vessels that caused a decreased flow of blood to the brain. Little by little the world's most famous golf architect lost some of his ability to think. He gradually deteriorated over his final years and was in and out of the hospital. His mind remained sharp, but movements became more and more limited. One side of his body was later paralyzed by a stroke at age ninety-three. He became much more dependent on the people looking after him.

Around eight o'clock on the evening of June 13, 2000, Dr. Nadell received a phone call from Joe Fitzgerald, Trent's paid companion and caregiver. Fitzgerald was a former Boston policeman, a "real tough cookie," Dr. Nadéll called him, and "very devoted" to Jones. With Trent spending so much of his life in his last few years in a wheelchair, Fitzgerald was indispensable, "lifting him up and around like a loaf of bread" and taking him wherever he was able to go. From the tone in Fitzgerald's voice, Nadell felt sure that Trent's death was imminent; he had made a few house calls to Jones already that week and his condition was quickly deteriorating. Jones had already told Nadell that "we were not going to put him in a hospital and prolong his life as a vegetable. That would be the last thing he wanted to happen to him." The physician phoned Rees and Bobby. They were both in California for the U.S. Open, scheduled to start later that week at Pebble Beach. The news was not unexpected.

The doctor waited until midnight, then went over to take Jones's pulse, which was stilled. Nadell pronounced him dead, the death certificate indicating that he died on Wednesday, June 14, 2000, six days short of his ninety-fourth birthday. "He went to sleep as normal. He just didn't wake up," Bobby would later remark.

The next day, the 100th U.S. Open got under way at Pebble Beach. In the previous sixty years, Trent had missed very few Opens, and his design work had been an element in the ultimate narrative of many of them. Only over the past few years had he grudgingly stayed at home, watching as much of the tournament as he could on TV. (As stated earlier, he did attend the '99 Open at Pinehurst, which Payne Stewart won so memorably.) "He probably planned this," said Rees. "The Open really was his angel." Trent's death was overshadowed during the championship by the ceremonies marking the tragic death of Payne Stewart, in an aviation accident the previous October. But Trent's death, too, was noted by USGA officials and by the NBC broadcast team during the event. Son Bobby told reporters at Pebble Beach, "I figure he and Payne are talking about it right now."

His funeral took place on his birthday, June 20, at All Saints Episcopal Church in Fort Lauderdale, with Bobby making the arrangements. Frank Rhodes, the former president of Cornell University who had become one of Trent's close friends, gave the eulogy. Rees presented some beautiful remarks. Bobby read a poem he had written in his dad's memory. He called his poem "Father's Day," a date that had just passed. The most touching stanzas were those with the clearest references to the lives of his mother and father:

> *He has released his dream,*
> *His progeny and friends celebrate*
> *His caddy to Hall of Fame theme.*
> *But his wife in white gown*
> *Is calling him for their Millennium dance.*
> *They are born again as soul mates*
> *For yet another chance.*

> *You always keep Ithaca of old*
> *In your mind.*
> *Arrival there was your goal.*
> *Ithaca of new gave you a beautiful voyage.*
> *Without her you wouldn't have set out.*

A reception followed at Coral Ridge. The Fort Lauderdale Police Department provided patrol car escort from the church to the country club. The clubhouse was full of people, mostly Coral Ridge members. A few golf architecture writers came, including *Golfweek*'s Bradley Klein and *Golf Digest*'s Ron Whitten. Given that Jones was a founding member, and past president, of the ASGCA, it was perhaps surprising that so few of his fellow architects—only seven or eight with their ASGCA tartan jackets on—had come to pay their respects. Most expressed their condolences with flowers and cards. Of course, he had lived nearly to age ninety-four, many old friends had predeceased him, and most who had known him best were already gone.

Near the entrance to the clubhouse restaurant, the table where Trent regularly sat for lunch was laid out with a black tablecloth. A few days later, Trent was buried next to Ione in Mount Hebron Cemetery. Rees and his wife Susan arranged for a second, well-attended memorial service at Montclair Country Club.

Incidentally, nothing in Trent's last Will and Testament caused anything like the trouble that had resulted from his wife's Will. Despite that blessing, the hard feelings and resentment between Bobby and Rees continued, and grew even sharper. The worst came in the fall of 2006, when, as the Fort Lauderdale *Sun-Sentinel* reported in its story "Jones Sons in Bitter Flap," Rees filed suit against Bobby (literally *Jones v. Jones*), for his unpaid estate fees and for "misappropriating their father's name when he contracted with a clothing firm to create a Robert Trent Jones apparel line." Bobby countersued, claiming that he had every right to use his birth name, and alleging that Rees had misappropriated their father's title of "The Open Doctor." After several months of legal stalemate, the boys settled out of court and without terms being disclosed.

The New York Times published a lengthy obituary of Jones written by Dave Anderson, its Pulitzer Prize–winning sportswriter and columnist. Virtually every golf publication in the world issued tributes to Trent. None captured the essential character or historical significance of Jones's career better than Ron Whitten, the lead architectural writer for *Golf Digest* and the co-author (with Geoffrey Cornish) of the most important book ever written about golf course architecture, the encyclopedic *The Architects of Golf*, first published in 1981.

"The man who started it all is gone now," wrote Whitten. "But the sun never sets on the Robert Trent Jones empire. In a career that stretched from Calvin Coolidge to the Clinton era, Trent Jones encircled the globe with tees, fairways and greens."

Whitten also praised Jones's prescience, noting that as early as the 1940s, when he was shepherding the American Society of Golf Course Architects into existence, Jones already understood how "livelier balls and clubs, improved maintenance practices and more athletic players" would be changing the game dramatically. He began, as Whitten noted, to "design accordingly." Peachtree, at 7,219 yards, opened in 1948. The Dunes Club, with its horseshoe-shaped par-5 13th hole curving gracefully around the edge of a lake toward a green virtually impossible to hit in two—and which Trent, with his gift for the memorable name, christened "Waterloo"—debuted in 1947. In the years ahead, Trent would continue to innovate, as he did in designing the iconic island green at the Golden Horseshoe's Gold Course in 1964 (antedating the TPC at Sawgrass's famous 17th by a decade and a half), as well as in his design of the South Course at Firestone, one of the toughest par-70s ever built, in 1959.

Jones also understood that with the rise of television coverage of golf tournaments, the courses as well as the players would have a starring role. Golf was, after all, a kind of dialogue between the player and the course, with the best championship courses interrogating the professionals with a skilled detective's cunning. No one had more savvy, brilliance, or guile in constructing a championship test than Robert Trent Jones. "He had," as Whitten noted, "a showman's sense of the theater of golf."

Robert Trent Jones's journey from Ellis Island to the Ivy League launched him on the classic narrative arc of the self-made man's triumph. He managed to rise from caddy to railroad car draftsmen to an anonymous do-it-all job as golf pro-greenkeeper-club manager-chief cook and bottle washer at a little 9-hole course on Sodus Bay in rural upstate New York to a position of unrivaled eminence in his profession as the chief author of America's national championship golf courses. He was unquestionably the world's most famous, and most accomplished, golf course architect, and a friend of kings, tycoons, and U.S. presidents. And because his journey was unprecedented, nothing in the history of golf compares with Robert Trent Jones's epic life story. As dramatic and poignant as are the golf-related lives of Francis Ouimet and Walter Hagen, or of Bobby Jones, Sam Snead, and Ben Hogan, or of Arnold Palmer and Jack Nicklaus, or of Tiger Woods, none means more in the history of golf in America and around the world than the saga of Robert Trent Jones Sr. Equally remarkable was Jones's longevity. Not only was his life as dramatic in some respects as those of the great champions, it was coterminous with the growth of American golf over its first century. Jones knew Hagen, a fellow Rochesterian, and Ouimet, who remained an amateur and a fixture in the USGA. Golf's elite were among his clients and friends. Other golf architects achieved contemporary prominence, but they are better known in retrospect than they were in their own days. Before Robert Trent Jones managed to make the golf course's role as prominent in its own way in tournament golf as the efforts of the players competing on it, golf course architects were perceived as useful and necessary, perhaps, but hardly as celebrities. C. B. Macdonald, Donald Ross, George Thomas, A. W. Tillinghast, and Alister MacKenzie were known among a select coterie of golf aficionados, but unknown in their day among the general public. Students of golf design today may read and admire what MacKenzie and Thomas wrote, but when their works were first published, very few copies of their books were sold. Jones paved the way for their resurrection. His fellow architects from the deepest recesses of the past up to the present day owe a debt of gratitude to Robert Trent Jones. He, more than anyone, created the modern profession of golf course architecture, as Cornish and Whitten were the first to point out. The celebrity and respect Jones earned as a designer, entrepreneur, and promoter were beneficial not just to his own firm, but to the profession he was so instrumental in creating. The interest and respect Jones attracted created a retroactive curiosity about the careers of his predecessors, and accrued to the benefit of everyone who followed in his wide and ever-expanding wake.

Despite the business setbacks that troubled him, and before his company's design work for the Alabama Trail allowed him to settle into a relatively comfortable old age, Robert Trent Jones maintained his eminence as the world's best-known, most influential and formidable golf course architect. His colleagues in the American Society of Golf Course Architects certainly understood what he meant to them: Their status as important, knowledgeable, and trustworthy practitioners of an honorable profession, and the prosperity most of them enjoyed until the recession hit in 2008, were rooted in Robert Trent Jones's ability to not simply promote his profession, but to design the sorts of golf courses which achieved his goal of "easy bogey, difficult par." The courses that Trent Jones designed for private clubs have continued to thrive, in part because the half of his design slogan that is perhaps too often forgotten—the "easy bogey" part—meant that higher-handicap players could make their way around a Trent Jones course without succumbing to utter humiliation seasoned with lost balls. Jones reserved that torment, in principle at least, for the touring pros, who were emotionally equipped—mostly—to deal with it. Trent Jones admired the skills of the touring pros, but also understood that unless the courses they played could test the limits of their skills, the game would turn into checkers. Robert Trent Jones made sure that golf at its highest levels was a kind of athletic chess, a game that had to stimulate the mind as well as engage the muscles. At the same time, he understood in the most fundamental way that in order to prosper in the long term as a popular sport, and not just as an arena for elite practitioners, the courses had to be fun for everyone. No one had ever understood the balance required to achieve that blend of complexity on the one hand and simplicity on the other that every enduringly great golf course has until Jones made the connection between them explicit—and made it the wellspring of his design philosophy, too. "Easy bogey, hard par" distills an essential wisdom acquired through a lifetime of contemplation. The constancy of Jones's approach sustained the popularity of his courses among the vast majority of golfers. The name "Robert Trent Jones" is still synonymous with "golf course architecture," and in death as in life, Jones has no rival as the most famous and influential figure in modern golf course design.

Golf was always in Robert Trent Jones's thoughts, even as his health declined. Once, after suffering a stroke, he awoke in a hospital bed with his two sons at his side. That alone must have confused him. "What are you doing here?" he asked. Rees answered, "You had a little setback." "What kind of setback?" Trent responded. Bobby answered, "You had a stroke."

Trent shut his eyes again, then opened them and said, "Do I have to count it?"

Jones retained his uncanny knack for displaying his magic touch on a golf course, reminiscent of the casual ace he made on his renovated par-3 at Baltusrol. In 1992, at the gala opening of the Alabama Trail's Hampton Cove near Huntsville, Dr. David Bronner and Bobby Vaughan made sure that Trent was present to say a few words at the press conference. (Typically, Jones told the reporters that day that "the golf course here may be my best one ever.") After the media had asked all its questions, Vaughan escorted Mr. Jones over to the back of a green on one of the River Course's holes. With reporters looking on, Vaughan handed the old architect a ball and a putter at the back of the green and told him to have a go at a downhill hole position thirty feet away. Naturally, Jones sank it. When asked for this book if Vaughan remembered what Jones said after sinking that monster putt, the head of SunBelt Golf recalled, "I think he announced that the green was 'eminently fair.'"

So the legend of Robert Trent Jones Sr. grows.

Many times during his career, and especially in its closing years, a person would ask Mr. Jones, "Of all the golf courses you have designed, which one is your favorite?" Peachtree? Dunes Club? Firestone? Mauna Kea? Bellerive? Spyglass? Valderrama? The people asking the question delighted in showing off their knowledge of the names of his great courses. They tried to guess which one he would designate as his favorite, or perhaps was most proud of designing. Would he answer, as other architects had, that "just as a parent must be with his children, I like them all equally"? But that was never his answer. The answer he gave was truer to his character, his ambitions, and his lifelong dreams:

"The next one."

ACKNOWLEDGMENTS

I designed my first, and last, golf course when I was eleven years old. My layout was in back of our house, on the large playground of Maplewood Elementary School, located in a suburb of Fort Wayne, Indiana, known as Waynedale. The first tee I placed to the side of the doghouse of our family pet, Laddie, a collie that could have doubled for TV's Lassie. My target for the first hole was the metal-fence backstop for one of the schoolyard's two baseball diamonds, about 140 yards away. I played with just a couple clubs, and no putter. To "hole out," all I had to do was bounce or fly my golf ball into the middle section of the fence directly behind home plate. If I hit it too far, I came at my target from behind, still shooting for the middle section of the fence. Hole #1 played as a par-3. In my back pocket was a homemade scorecard on which I kept tabs on my round.

My golf course meandered back, forth, and across the big schoolyard for a full nine holes. Besides the two baseball backstops, my targets were a swing set, two tetherball courts, a drainage cistern, and a small tree planted to the far northwestern side of the playground just across a sidewalk leading away from the school. I had some double greens just like St. Andrews. The target for the finishing hole was Laddie's doghouse. I tried hard never to hit him, and I don't think I ever did. But a couple of times on holes #2 and #6 I hit the school building (thankfully never breaking a window) and came close more than once to smacking a kid or an accompanying adult, who for some reason thought that the schoolyard was no place to be firing five-irons, even when I was yelling "Fore!" I regret now that I played "winter rules," which I justified on the basis that the schoolyard was full of bare spots and the grass grew in patches.

Golf had become very important to me by age eleven. Two years earlier, my father had died of a heart attack at age 46 while our family was vacationing with relatives in South Dakota. Following the funeral, my uncle flew out from Indiana to drive the family back home, because my mother had no license and, in fact, had never driven a car. That was soon to change. Following a second funeral and my dad's burial in a Waynedale cemetery, Mom took driving lessons—my 13-year-old brother Larry taught her mainly—and quickly got her license. She also had to go to work outside the home for the first time since she had married in 1946, right after Dad came home from the war. During the summers Mom wanted me, the youngest of three siblings (besides Larry, I had a sister Carol), to be occupied with something. Both Larry and I were avid Little League baseball players (darn good ones, on championship teams, I must say), but our games were played in the early evenings. One day the same summer that Dad died, I rode my Schwinn bike with some friends who were older than me a few miles out to a farm field that bordered Orchard Ridge Country Club, where we looked for golf balls. The contrast between the browns of the farm field and the verdant green of the golf course made an indelible aesthetic impression on me. Even today I can remember the moment I marveled at the beauty of that golf course. My passion for golf courses started right there, now over a half century ago.

The following summer my mother got me a membership at Fairview Golf Course, a public facility with a ramshackle clubhouse and a reputation for being one of the worst-conditioned courses in town. The owners of the golf course, Woody Voight and Chick Monroe, kept "The View," as I came to know and love it, running on a shoestring. There was no fairway irrigation system; in the middle of the summer, puffs of "smoke" accompanied nearly every shot one hit. It was not a bad golf course. The original nine, built back in 1927, was a routing that Donald Ross had "mailed in" for a local contractor to build. The back nine, built in the early 1960s, across Calhoun Street, was nothing like the Ross design. It was quite a bit harder, with longer holes, six of which crossed over the same creek. But the low quality of the course had a lot to do with my becoming a Fairview regular. The price for my summer membership—from the course's opening in late March to its closing in early November—was a whopping $30. For that fee, I was entitled to play as much golf as I wanted, except for Saturday and Sunday mornings when kids couldn't play unless they were with a parent (almost always a father back then) or on weekdays between four and six P.M. when industrial leagues from companies like Magnavox and Bowmar occupied the course. I kept getting memberships at Fairview until I was an early teenager, when I started working at the course, mostly mowing grass, then getting to play for free. I worked at the course every summer until I got married in 1976, when my wife Peggy and I moved to Columbus, Ohio, where I was working on my

Ph.D. I did some caddying at Jack Nicklaus's Muirfield Village course in nearby Dublin, Ohio; carrying two bags, which wasn't easy for my 140-pound frame, earned me $50, including the tips. We needed the money.

Looking back, it was at Fairview that I developed my love for history and storytelling. Many rounds of golf I played with retired gentlemen, with me carrying my little canvas bag on my shoulder and them pulling a golf cart. I can remember playing only once or twice in an electric cart, and then as a birthday treat after I got a "learner's permit" to drive a car, which Woody and Chick required to drive a cart. It didn't matter to me. Golf was about walking, and talking.

Having lost my dad, playing golf with these older men, many of whom had fought in World War II as my dad had, was a formative experience. I asked them a lot of questions, about the war, about the Great Depression, about the jobs they had held, about how and why they had come to play golf. No question about it, I was already conducting oral history interviews, learning things about the lives of these men in a way that I would never know about my father. Golf for me was about much more than golf. It was about life, and death, and all the experiences in between.

Growing up at "The View" was the most important away-from-home experience of my youth. It was where I made my closest and most enduring friendships. I remember everyone who was part of my life on that golf course. It gives me great pleasure to remember my time with them, especially with Dick and Jim ("Bear") Bradow, Jeff Nowak, Dave Foreman, Phil Erli, and Tom Ormsby.

Without the help of a great number of people, I could never have written this book. It was vitally important to have the assistance of Robert Trent Jones Sr.'s two sons, Robert Trent Jones Jr. and Rees L. Jones, as well as that of Roger G. Rulewich and Cabell B. Robinson. To John Strawn, I owe a special debt of gratitude for the very thorough edits he voluntarily made to all of my chapters. I am also deeply indebted to Warner "Butch" Berry for his editorial help, guidance, and encouragement.

I wish to thank Claiborne Jones, Bobby's wife, and Susan Jones, Rees's wife, for all the help they gave me throughout my project. Sandra Rulewich has also been a great friend of my efforts to write this book.

I give my heartfelt thanks to the staff members of both Robert Trent Jones II, LLC, and Rees Jones, Inc., who helped in securing research materials and photographs for me.

A number of people agreed to be interviewed for the book. Some of these conversations took place face-to-face, some occurred over the phone, and some involved e-mail exchanges. To all of my interviewees, I give my sincere thanks.

A number of golf architects were also generous with their time and patience with my inquiries about golf course design, particularly Columbus, Ohio's Dr. Michael J. Hurdzan; Traverse City, Michigan's Tom Doak; and Lakeland, Florida's Steve Smyers.

I have a special place in my heart for architect Geoffrey S. Cornish. Before he became ill and succumbed in 2012, Mr. Cornish wrote me two letters and during one lengthy phone conversation educated and entertained me with stories about Trent Jones, Stanley Thompson, and his own long and distinguished career in golf course design. The consummate gentlemen, he could not have been kinder or more supportive of my writing the Jones biography.

The officers and members of the Robert Trent Jones Society—organized in 2004—have also aided me greatly. I offer my sincere thanks to Jack Borchelt (Pauma Valley), Bob Kummer (Birnam Woods), Jerry Freeland (Old Warson), Heyward Sullivan (Chanticleer), John Kluga (Spyglass Hill), and Ron Fox (Point O' Woods) for their help in getting photographs and additional information about their RTJ courses. Equally helpful have been members of Canada's Stanley Thompson Society—founded in 1998—especially James Harris, James Fraser, and Bill Newton (deceased).

There are many questions still to answer about Trent Jones's work at Sodus Bay Heights Golf Club on Lake Ontario during the late 1920s and I have enjoyed cooperating with Sodus's head golf professional David Jones (no relation) and club member John Wildhack in the attempt to answer them.

Staff members at USGA headquarters in Far Hills, New Jersey, also assisted me by answering questions about their championships and linking me to photographs associated with Trent Jones and with U.S. Opens. Dr. Rand Jerris, the USGA Museum Director and Director of the USGA Communications Department, has always been extremely helpful in reply to any request for information.

So, too, have Dr. David Bronner, head of the Retirement Systems of Alabama; Robert "Bobby" Vaughan, founder of the SunBelt Golf Corporation that built Alabama's Robert Trent Jones Trail; and John Cannon, current SunBelt president.

All of the photos used in the book have their credit lines. I want to thank all the individuals and organizations that provided pictures for the book.

In 2011 I began teaching a Seminar in the History of Golf Course Architecture for the Honors College at Auburn University. One of my first students, Justin Melnick, became so engrossed in golf course design that he sought, successfully, one of Auburn's prestigious Undergraduate Research Fellowships, for which I served as his mentor. The subject I put him on was the history of Trent Jones's Vidauban project in southern France. I want to thank Justin for all the help he gave me about Vidauban.

I owe a special debt of gratitude to Dr. Bradley S. Klein, distinguished golf writer and architecture editor for *Golfweek* magazine. Brad and I have been friends since the late 1990s, when I joined his panel of *Golfweek* course raters and he gave me all the freelance writing assignments I could manage for the *Golfweek* publication he was then editing, *Superintendent News*. Brad has forgotten more golf course history than I will ever know.

As mentioned in my "Note on Sources," my original draft of this book was extremely long and overwritten. I want to thank Jeff Neuman, the co-author of *A Disorderly Compendium of Golf* (with Lorne Rubenstein) and *Just Hit It* (with former USGA technology expert Frank Thomas), for helping me to cut the book down to size.

Jeff Neuman's work made the task of my editor at Gotham Penguin, Charles Conrad, a great deal easier. Still, Charlie's keen eye, editorial acumen, and knowledge of golf history did additional marvelous things for the book. The work of his editorial assistant, Leslie Hansen (no relation!), was also outstanding and very supportive of an anxious author still facing a lot of external challenges.

My literary agent, Laurie Fox, and Linda Chester, head of the Linda Chester Agency, have been enthusiastic cheerleaders for my work ever since I came to them with my proposal for the Neil Armstrong biography more than a decade ago.

My immediate family lives the writing of my books almost as much as I do. I am extremely fortunate that my children, Dr. Nathaniel Hansen, Jennifer Hansen Gray, son-in-law Cole Gray, and new daughter-in-law Jessica Phillips Hansen are so interested in what I do. The same goes for my sister Carol Busse and brother Larry. My wife Peggy is the one who really has to put up with my long stories, late-night hours, cluttered desks and tables, and near-constant obsessive thinking about my books. I want to thank my family for its love and support.

My final thanks go to you, the reader, for investing your time in reading my book. For you, for posterity, and for Mr. Jones, I gave it my best.

—James R. Hansen
Auburn, AL
January 2014

APPENDIX A

CHRONOLOGICAL LISTING OF GOLF COURSES DESIGNED, CO-DESIGNED, AND REMODELED BY ROBERT TRENT JONES SR. WHILE WORKING WITH STANLEY THOMPSON, ROBERT TRENT JONES, INC., AND HIS SONS

Creating a comprehensive list of the golf courses designed by Robert Trent Jones Sr. may seem like a straightforward assignment, but in fact it is a challenging task to establish a set of clear, logical, and historically valid criteria for including any given course on Robert Trent Jones's list.

Courses designed when Trent Jones was a single practitioner pose no difficulty, but how should courses designed by his company once he had taken on design associates, who in many cases were responsible for the day-to-day oversight of the projects, be treated? Should the person (or persons) who actually did the "design" work receive credit for their contributions? (The same issue exists for "redesign" and "remodeling" projects.) Often there was a team of designers within an architectural firm that did the work together, in which cases it is nearly impossible to distinguish who did what. Early in his career, for example, Robert Trent Jones was part of a design partnership with Canadian architect Stanley Thompson. At the height of his career, from the mid-1960s to mid-1970s, Trent Jones was designing courses with the help of his two sons, Robert Trent Jones Jr. and Rees L. Jones. For several of those courses, Bobby and Rees spent more time on-site than their father did. From the early 1960s to the mid-1990s, Roger Rulewich worked for Jones, and as had often been the case with Bobby and Rees, Rulewich would come to do more of the detailed design work than Trent. But the *nature* of the documentation available in the archive reveals little about who did what in terms of designing specific elements of a golf course. Most historians of golf design would regard the route plan as the single most important component of any design, but even here, little in the record indicates whose hand was heaviest on a particular route plan. The inevitable "field adjustments" might not have been recorded at all. Oral history—interviewing the designers—can help discover the "facts" of the design, but not only do memories fade with time, the designers being interviewed may take more or less credit than they deserve.

The ramifications of this issue have embroiled the members of the American Society of Golf Course Architects for decades. As the demand for golf design services exploded after 1970, more and more designers working for big-name firms struck out on their own. Naturally, they wanted to claim credit for the work performed on behalf of their former employers. The standard established under the American Society of Golf Course Architects' ethical guidelines allows a designer to claim that he or she worked on a course design "as designer for X" or "on behalf of architect Y," their previous employer. In practice, the boundaries blur, but the general practice in attribution is to credit the firm with whom the client signed a contract as the designer of record, no matter who did what. Especially after 1980, clients sought the benefit of the "brand name" of the architect, and no one had contributed more to the creation of this "big name designer" trend than Trent Jones. Clients hired Trent Jones because his name helped sell club memberships and real estate.

The list of Robert Trent Jones Sr. golf courses that follows, then, does *not* use as its criterion, "On a given project, who was the 'lead' or 'primary' architect?" Without question, Trent Jones was the lead architect on most of the courses appearing on this list, especially in the first three decades of his career. But, increasingly after 1960, as Jones's business boomed and expanded around the nation and the world, more and more of his company's design work was undertaken with significant input from his associates: for a while from Bobby and Rees, for thirty-plus years from Roger Rulewich, for twenty years (mostly in Europe and North Africa) from Cabell B. Robinson, and for shorter periods from such protégés as Frank Duane, Donald J. Knott, Jay Morrish, Les Furber, and Ronald Kirby. So complicated and impractical is it to sort out the "provenance" of the designs that, as a criterion for determining a meaningful list of Trent Jones courses, the notion of "lead architect" or "primary designer" should be set aside in favor of something more reliable and "depersonalized."

The criterion that has been used to create the following list is simple, straightforward, and inarguable: "Was the design (redesign or remodeling) of the golf course done under contract to a company headed by Robert Trent Jones Sr.?" If it was, it belongs on the list, no matter whether Trent himself did

100 percent of the design, 50 percent of the design, 25 percent of the design, or 0 percent of the design. The course is still a Robert Trent Jones Sr. golf course. Architecturally, each golf course on the list is, at the very least, "in the School of Robert Trent Jones Sr." just as an art historian might call a painting "in the School of" a Raphael, Michelangelo, Titian, or Rembrandt.

In adopting this criterion, I am following the practice employed over many decades in the offices of Robert Trent Jones Sr.—first by Red Hoffman, the RTJ Inc. publicist, and subsequently by Roger Rulewich, custodian of a list that he maintains to this day. Clearly, it was the type of list that Senior endorsed, as he would have seen updated versions of the list often. It is also the list that has been adopted by the Robert Trent Jones Society and, as such, appears on the society's website at http://www.roberttrentjonessociety.com/society-members /course-list.

On the website of Rees Jones, Inc., one can find a listing of golf courses "designed by Rees Jones or his collaborative team while a principal in Robert Trent Jones, Inc.": http://www.reesjonesinc.com/robert-trent-jones-courses.php. The website of Robert Trent Jones II does not include such a list: http://www.rtj2 .com/. However, in his 1993 book *Golf by Design* (Boston and New York: Little, Brown and Co.), there is an appendix (pp. 274–75) in which Jones Jr. lists all of the golf courses he has designed and that identifies those projects "with Robert Trent Jones Sr. collaborating." On the website of Rulewich & Fleury Golf Design, there is a list of "Courses Designed by Roger Rulewich," http://www.rulewich .com/projectList.html., which does not identify any courses on which Jones Sr. collaborated.

Surveying these lists—and others like it—one will find courses claimed and listed by more than one golf course architect. This practice is appropriate, ethical, and historically valid because, in a multitude of instances, more than one architect was heavily involved in the design of the golf course. For example, Robert Trent Jones Jr. lists Princeville Golf Club in Hawaii as a golf course "designed by Robert Trent Jones Jr." The facts are that Bobby *did* design the Princeville golf course and with virtually no assistance from his father. On the other hand, the Princeville Golf Club was designed under contract to Robert Trent Jones, Inc. In such instances, it is totally legitimate for the golf course to be listed by *both* architects. It is then up to the golf course historian to distinguish, and explain, who did what, for those interested in the details of the provenance.

R	Indicates Remodeled
NLE	Indicates Course No Longer Exists
NC	Indicates Started but Not Completed
T&J	Indicates Course Designed under Contract to Thompson and Jones
RTJII	Indicates Input to Robert Trent Jones II Design
QP	Indicates Questionable Provenance

COURSE NAME	CITY & STATE	HOLES
1931		
Locust Hill Country Club	Rochester, New York	R
Midvale Golf & Country Club (T&J)	Penfield, New York	18
Stafford Country Club (T&J)	Stafford, New York	R
1932		
Banff Springs Hotel Golf Course	Banff, Alberta	R
Carleton Island Country Club (T&J, 14 holes)	Carleton Island, New York	NC
1934		
Durand Eastman Park Golf Course (T&J)	Rochester, New York	18
1935		
Gavea Golf and Country Club (T&J)	Rio de Janeiro, Brazil	R
Green Lakes State Park Golf Course (T&J)	Fayetteville, New York	18
Itanhangá Golf Club (T&J)	Rio de Janeiro, Brazil	18
Montclair Golf Club	Montclair, New Jersey	R ('59)
São Paulo Golf Club (T&J)	São Paulo, Brazil	R
Teresópolis Golf Club (T&J)	Rio de Janeiro, Brazil	18
1936		
Battle Island State Park Golf Course	Fulton, New York	R
Bonnie Briar Country Club (T&J)	Larchmont, New York	R
1937		
Capilano Golf & Country Club (T&J)	West Vancouver, British Columbia	18
Garden City Country Club	Garden City, New York	R ('58)
St. Charles Country Club	St. Charles, Illinois	R

1938

Amsterdam Municipal Golf Course (T&J)	Amsterdam, New York	18
Niagara Falls Country Club	Lewiston, New York	R
Vestal Hills Country Club (NLE)	Binghamton, New York	R

1939

Country Club of Ithaca	Ithaca, New York	R
Norris Estate Golf Course (NLE)	St. Charles, Illinois	9
Pottawatomie Park Golf Course	St. Charles, Illinois	9

1940

Duke Farms Golf Club (NLE)	Somerville, New Jersey	18
Fairfax Country Club (now known as Army Navy Club Fairfax)	Fairfax, Virginia	9

1941

Cornell University Golf Course (first of 18)	Ithaca, New York	9
Florida Caverns Golf Course (QP)	Marianna, Florida	9
Quaker Hill Country Club	Pawling, New York	9
Valley View Golf Course	Utica, New York	R

1945

Halloran General Hospital Golf Course	Staten Island, New York	9
IBM Country Club (Casperkill Golf Club)	Poughkeepsie, New York	18 (R '85)

1946

Augusta National Golf Club	Augusta, Georgia	R ('50)
Patterson Club, The	Fairfield, Connecticut	18
Fairfax Country Club (now known as Army Navy Club Fairfax)	Fairfax, Virginia	9

1947

Coakley-Russo Memorial Golf Course	Lyons, New Jersey	9
Hancock Municipal Golf Course (NLE)	Hancock, New York	9
Tamiment-in-the-Poconos	Tamiment, Pennsylvania	18
Tuxedo Club, The	Tuxedo Park, New York	R

1948

Chevy Chase Country Club	Chevy Chase, Maryland	R
Green Brook Country Club	North Caldwell, New Jersey	R
James Baird State Park Golf Course	Pleasant Valley, New York	18
National Golf Links of America	Southampton, New York	R ('69)
Peachtree Golf Club (Collab. with "Bobby" Jones)	Atlanta, Georgia	18
Winged Foot Golf Club, West Course	Mamaroneck, New York	R

1949

Dunes Golf and Beach Club, The	Myrtle Beach, South Carolina	18 (R '79, '93)
Fort Belvoir Golf Course	Fort Belvoir, Virginia	9
Galloping Hill Golf Course	Kenilworth, New Jersey	R
Glen Ridge Country Club	Glen Ridge, New Jersey	R ('78)
Lakewood Golf Club, Dogwood Course, Grand Hotel	Point Clear, Alabama	R
Rockrimmon Country Club	Stamford, Connecticut	9
Sea Island Golf Club	St. Simons Island, Georgia	R
Suburban Club, The	Pikesville, Maryland	R
Sunset Hills Country Club	Carrollton, Georgia	9
West Point Golf Club, USMA	West Point, New York	12

1950

Detroit, Country Club of	Grosse Pointe Farms, Michigan	R ('70)
Eisenhower Park Golf Course, White Course	East Meadow, New York	18
Fort Benning Golf Club, Bradley Course	Fort Benning, Georgia	9
Oakland Hills Country Club, South Course	Birmingham, Michigan	R ('72, '78, '84)
Portland Golf Club	Portland, Oregon	R

1951

Belle Meade Country Club	Nashville, Tennessee	R
Eisenhower Park Golf Course, Blue Course	East Meadow, New York	18
Portland Country Club	Falmouth, Maine	R
Standard Club, The (NLE)	Atlanta, Georgia	18
Wayne Country Club (NLE)	Wayne Township, New Jersey	18

1952

Baltusrol Golf Club	Springfield, New Jersey	R
Country Club of Fairfax	Fairfax, Virginia	9
Pittsburgh Field Club	Pittsburgh, Pennsylvania	R
Raymond Memorial Golf Course	Columbus, Ohio	18
Round Hill Club	Greenwich, Connecticut	R ('70)
St. Louis Country Club	Clayton, Missouri	R

1953

Birmingham Country Club	Birmingham, Michigan	R
Detroit Golf Club, North & South Courses	Detroit, Michigan	R
La Gorce Country Club	Miami, Florida	R
Mid Ocean Club, The	Tucker's Town, Bermuda	R
Powelton Club, The	Newburgh, New York	R
Siwanoy Country Club	Bronxville, New York	R
Woodmere Club, The	Woodmere, New York	R

1954

Broadmoor Golf Club, East Course	Colorado Springs, Colorado	9 (R '60)
Buffalo, Country Club of	Williamsville, New York	R
Camp David Golf Course	Camp David, Maryland	3
Cornell University Golf Course (second of 18)	Ithaca, New York	9
IBM Country Club	Sands Point, New York	R
Olympic Club, The, Lakeside Course	San Francisco, California	R
Ponte Vedra Inn & Club, Ocean Course	Ponte Vedra Beach, Florida	R

1955

Beauclerc Country Club	Jacksonville, Florida	9
Link Hills Country Club	Greeneville, Tennessee	18
MacDonald Estate Golf Course	Bal Harbour, Florida	2
Old Warson Country Club	Ladue, Missouri	18
Wiltwyck Golf Club	Kingston, New York	18

1956

Coral Ridge Country Club	Fort Lauderdale, Florida	18
Dellwood Country Club	New City, New York	R

Elkridge Club, The	Baltimore, Maryland	R
Lido Golf Club	Lido Beach, New York	18
Oak Hill Country Club, East Course	Pittsford, New York	R ('67)
Upper Montclair Country Club	Clifton, New Jersey	27

1957

Congressional Country Club, Blue Course	Bethesda, Maryland	9
Duke University Golf Course	Durham, North Carolina	18
Houston Country Club	Houston, Texas	18
Portsmouth Country Club	Greenland, New Hampshire	18
Scarsdale Golf Club	Hartsdale, New York	R ('61)
Scona Lodge Golf Course	Alcoa, Tennessee	9
Seven Oaks Golf Club, Colgate University (first of 18)	Hamilton, New York	9
Southern Hills Country Club	Tulsa, Oklahoma	R
Tanglewood Golf Club, West Course	Clemmons, North Carolina	18 (R '73, '89)
Tuxedo Club, The	Tuxedo Park, New York	18

1958

American Golfers Club (Executive)	Fort Lauderdale, Florida	18
Dorado Beach Hotel Golf Course, first & second nines	Dorado Beach, Puerto Rico	18
Green Spring Valley Hunt Club	Owings Mills, Maryland	R
Green Spring Valley Hunt Club	Owings Mills, Maryland	9
Itanhangá Golf Club	Rio de Janeiro, Brazil	R
Point O' Woods Golf & Country Club	Benton Harbor, Michigan	18 (R '87)
Stumpy Lake Golf Course	Virginia Beach, Virginia	18
Westmoreland Country Club	Export, Pennsylvania	R

1959

Birmingham, Country Club of, West Course	Birmingham, Alabama	R
Century Country Club	Purchase, New York	R
Chattahoochee Country Club	Gainesville, Georgia	18
Cotton Bay Club	Eleuthera, Bahamas	18
Eisenhower Golf Course, Blue Course, USAFA	Colorado Springs, Colorado	18
Firestone Country Club, South Course	Akron, Ohio	R

Moon Brook Country Club	Jamestown, New York	R
Orlando, Country Club of	Orlando, Florida	R
Otter Creek Golf Club	Columbus, Indiana	18 (R '82)
Ridgewood Country Club	Danbury, Connecticut	R
Rochester, Country Club of	Rochester, New York	R
Shady Oaks Country Club	Fort Worth, Texas	18 (R '82)
Tavistock Country Club	Haddonfield, New Jersey	R
Timberlane Country Club	Gretna, Louisiana	18
Yellowstone Country Club	Billings, Montana	18

1960

Arcola Country Club	Paramus, New Jersey	R ('93)
Bartlett Country Club	Olean, New York	R
Bellerive Country Club	Creve Coeur, Missouri	18 (R '89)
Colonial Country Club	Fort Worth, Texas	R
Custer Hill Golf Course	Fort Riley, Kansas	9
Essex County Country Club	West Orange, New Jersey	R
Hawaii Kai (Executive)	Honolulu, Hawaii	18
Huntington Country Club	Huntington, New York	R
Innis Arden Golf Club	Greenwich, Connecticut	R
New Canaan, Country Club of	New Canaan, Connecticut	R
New York Hospital Golf Course	White Plains, New York	R
North Hempstead Country Club	Port Washington, New York	R
Pauma Valley Country Club	Pauma Valley, California	18
Pines Hotel Golf Course	South Fallsburg, New York	9
Royal Palm Yacht & Country Club	Boca Raton, Florida	18
Wilmington Country Club, South Course	Wilmington, Delaware	18

1961

Half Moon Golf Club	Montego Bay, Jamaica	18
Lower Cascades Golf Course, Homestead Hotel	Hot Springs, Virginia	18
Milwaukee Country Club	River Hills, Wisconsin	R ('76, '82, '92)
North Hills Country Club	Manhasset, New York	18
Patrick Air Force Base	Cocoa Beach, Florida	9
Sands Point Golf Club	Port Washington, New York	R
Upper Cascades Golf Course, Homestead Hotel	Hot Springs, Virginia	R

1962

Apollo Beach Golf Club	Apollo Beach, Florida	9
Charlotte Country Club	Charlotte, North Carolina	R ('84)
Cherry Valley Club	Garden City, New York	R
Congressional Country Club, Blue Course	Bethesda, Maryland	R ('69)
El Rincón de Cajicá	Bogotá, Colombia	18
Fallsview Hotel Golf Course	Ellenville, New York	9
Hazeltine National Golf Club	Chaska, Minnesota	18 (R '82)
Interlachen Country Club	Minneapolis, Minnesota	R
London Hunt & Country Club	London, Ontario	18
Miami, Country Club of, East Course	Hialeah, Florida	18
Miami, Country Club of, North Course (Par 3, NLE)	Hialeah, Florida	18
Miami, Country Club of, West Course	Hialeah, Florida	18
Ponte Vedra Inn & Club, Lagoon Course	Ponte Vedra Beach, Florida	9
Quaker Ridge Golf Club	Scarsdale, New York	R
Royal Ka'anapali Golf Course	Lahaina, Maui, Hawaii	18
Tammy Brook Country Club	Cresskill, New Jersey	18

1963

Albany Country Club	Voorheesville, New York	18
Boca Raton Hotel & Club	Boca Raton, Florida	R
Burning Tree Club	Bethesda, Maryland	R ('77)
Dorado Beach Hotel Golf Course (third of 36)	Dorado Beach, Puerto Rico	9
Frear Park Golf Course	Troy, New York	9
Greenwich Country Club	Greenwich, Connecticut	R
Sunset Dunes Golf Club (Par 3)	Colton, California	18
Woodstock Country Club	Woodstock, Vermont	18 (R '69, '75, '87)

1964

All American Golf Course (Executive)	Titusville, Florida	18
El Caballero Country Club	Tarzana, California	R
El Dorado Hills Golf Club (Executive)	Sacramento, California	18
Golden Horseshoe Golf Club, Gold Course	Williamsburg, Virginia	18
Incline Village Golf Course	Lake Tahoe, Nevada	18
Marine Park Golf Course	Brooklyn, New York	27

Oakmont Country Club	Oakmont, Pennsylvania	R ('89)
Rockleigh Golf Course	Rockleigh, New Jersey	R
Tecolote Canyon Golf Course (Executive)	San Diego, California	27
Turtle Point Yacht & Country Club	Killen, Alabama	18
Willow Lakes Golf Course, Offutt Air Force Base	Bellevue, Nebraska	18

1965

Bellport Country Club	Bellport, New York	R
Broadmoor Golf Club, West Course	Colorado Springs, Colorado	9 (R '65)
Calabasas Park Country Club	Calabasas, California	18
Corpus Christi Country Club	Corpus Christi, Texas	18
Eugene Country Club	Eugene, Oregon	18 (R '92)
Hominy Hill Golf Course	Colts Neck, New Jersey	18
Linville Golf Club	Linville, North Carolina	R
Madeline Island Golf Club	La Pointe, Wisconsin	18
Seven Oaks Golf Club, Colgate University (second of 18)	Hamilton, New York	9
Sotogrande, Real Club de Golf	Sotogrande, Cádiz, Spain	18
Sotogrande, Real Club de Golf (Par 3)	Sotogrande, Cádiz, Spain	9
Spotswood Golf Course (Executive)	Williamsburg, Virginia	9
Sugarbush Golf Club	Warren, Vermont	18
Tanglewood Golf Club, East Course (first of 18)	Clemmons, North Carolina	9
Valencia Country Club	Valencia, California	18
Wigwam, The, Blue Course	Litchfield Park, Arizona	18
Wigwam, The, Gold Course	Litchfield Park, Arizona	18

1966

Bruce Memorial Golf Course	Greenwich, Connecticut	18
Dorado Beach Hotel Golf Course, West Nine (fourth of 36)	Dorado Beach, Puerto Rico	9
Fox Hill Golf & Country Club	Calverton, New York	18
Gulph Mills Golf Club	King of Prussia, Pennsylvania	R
Hartford Golf Club	West Hartford, Connecticut	R
Mauna Kea Beach Hotel Golf Course	Kamuela, Hawaii	18
Melreese Golf Course	Miami, Florida	R
Mission Viejo Country Club	San Juan Capistrano, California	18

Rancocas Golf Club	Willingboro, New Jersey	18
Sleepy Hollow Country Club	Scarborough, New York	R
Spyglass Hill Golf Club	Pebble Beach, California	18

1967

Atlanta Athletic Club, Highlands Course	Duluth, Georgia	9
Atlanta Athletic Club, Riverside Course	Duluth, Georgia	18
Bel Meadow Golf Club	Mt. Clare, West Virginia	18
Black Hall Club	Old Lyme, Connecticut	18 (R '87)
Bondues, Golf de, Blue Course	Lille, France	9
Carambola Beach Golf Course	St. Croix, Virgin Islands	18
Centre Hills Country Club	State College, Pennsylvania	9
Jackson Hole Golf & Country Club	Jackson, Wyoming	R ('69)
Oakcreek Country Club (first of 18)	Sedona, Arizona	9
Silverado Country Club, North Course	Napa, California	R
Silverado Country Club, South Course	Napa, California	18

1968

Birnam Wood Golf Club	Santa Barbara, California	18
Bloomfield Hills Country Club	Bloomfield Hills, Michigan	R ('78)
Bondues, Golf de, Red Course	Lille, France	R
Boyne Highlands Golf Club, Heather Course	Harbor Springs, Michigan	18
California Golf Club	South San Francisco, California	R
Cold Spring Country Club	Cold Spring Harbor, New York	R
Detroit, Country Club of (Par 3)	Grosse Pointe Farms, Michigan	9
Fairington Golf & Tennis Club	Decatur, Georgia	18
Fairview Country Club	Greenwich, Connecticut	18 (R '94)
Golf du Bercuit	Grez-Doiceau, Belgium	18
Las Brisas Golf Course	Marbella, Málaga, Spain	18
Luisita Golf and Country Club	Tarlac, Philippines	18
Lyman Orchards Golf Course	Middlefield, Connecticut	18
Montauk Downs State Park Golf Course	Montauk, New York	18
Muttontown Golf & Country Club	East Norwich, New York	R
Nueva Andalucía Golf Club (Par 3) (NLE)	Marbella, Málaga, Spain	18
Stanford University Golf Club	Palo Alto, California	R
Stone Mountain Golf Club, Stonemont Course	Stone Mountain, Georgia	18

| Tam O'Shanter Golf Club | Brookville, New York | R |
| University of Georgia Golf Course | Athens, Georgia | 18 |

1969

Campo de Golf Tres Vidas, East Course (NLE)	Acapulco, Mexico	18
Campo de Golf Tres Vidas, West Course (NLE)	Acapulco, Mexico	18
Crestview Country Club, North Course	Wichita, Kansas	18
Crestview Country Club, South Course	Wichita, Kansas	9
Firestone Country Club, North Course	Akron, Ohio	18
Greenville Country Club, Chanticleer Course	Greenville, South Carolina	18
International Golf Club	Bolton, Massachusetts	R
Panther Valley Country Club	Allamuchy Township, New Jersey 18 (R '93)	
Speidel Golf Club, Oglebay Park (first of 18)	Wheeling, West Virginia	9
Walden Golf Club	Crofton, Maryland	9

1970

Annandale Golf Club	Pasadena, California	R
Brasilia Golf Club	Brasilia, Brazil	18
Ferncroft Country Club	Danvers, Massachusetts	18
Glen Oak Golf Course	East Amherst, New York	18
Glendora Country Club	Glendora, California	R
Inverrary Country Club, East Course	Lauderhill, Florida	18
Inverrary Country Club (Executive) (NLE)	Lauderhill, Florida	18
Laguna Seca Golf Ranch	Monterey, California	18
Lakeridge Golf Course	Reno, Nevada	18
Menlo Country Club	Woodside, California	R
Moor Allerton Golf Club	Leeds, Yorkshire, England	27
Palmetto Dunes Golf Club, RTJ Course	Hilton Head Island, South Carolina	18
Port Royal Golf Course	Southampton, Bermuda	18 (R '95)
Princeville Golf Club	Hanalei, Kauai, Hawaii	27
Rail Golf Course, The (first of 18)	Springfield, Illinois	9
Rancho California Golf Club	Murrieta, California	18
Royal Golf Dar Es Salaam, Red Course	Rabat, Morocco	18
Sugar Creek Country Club (18 of 27)	Sugar Land, Texas	18
Waikoloa Village Golf Course	Waikoloa, Hawaii	18

1971

Carolina Trace Country Club, Lake Course	Sanford, North Carolina	18
Crag Burn Club	East Aurora, New York	18
Grenelefe Golf Resort, South Course (Routing)	Haines City, Florida	18
Hacienda Golf Club	La Habra Heights, California	R
Heron Lakes Golf Club	Portland, Oregon	36
Incline Green Golf Course (Executive)	Lake Tahoe, Nevada	18
Inverrary Country Club, West Course	Lauderhill, Florida	18
Oakland Hills Country Club, North Course	Birmingham, Michigan	R
Rio Rico Golf Course	Rio Rico, Arizona	18
Sobhu Country Club	Chiba, Japan	R
Spring Valley Lake Golf Course	Victorville, California	18
Springs Course, House on the Rock Resort	Spring Green, Wisconsin	18
Turnberry Isle Yacht & Country Club, South Course	Miami, Florida	18

1972

Alpine Bay Country Club, East Course	Alpine, Alabama	18
Cerromar Beach Hotel Golf Course, North Course	Dorado Beach, Puerto Rico	18
Cerromar Beach Hotel Golf Course, South Course	Dorado Beach, Puerto Rico	18
Eagleglen Golf Course, Elmendorf Air Force Base	Anchorage, Alaska	18
Golf 72, Higashi Course	Karuizawa, Japan	18
Golf 72, Kita Course	Karuizawa, Japan	18
Golf 72, Minami Course	Karuizawa, Japan	18
Golf 72, Nishi Course	Karuizawa, Japan	18
Hilldale Village Golf Course	Hoffman Estates, Illinois	18
Kings Point Golf Course (Executive)	Delray Beach, Florida	18
Lake Shastina Golf Course	Weed, California	18
Lake Shastina Golf Course (Par 3)	Weed, California	9
Navatanee Golf Course	Bangkok, Thailand	18
Ocean Pines Country Club	Ocean Pines, Maryland	18
Pevero Golf Club	Costa Smeralda, Sardinia	18

San Gabriel Country Club	San Gabriel, California	R
Speidel Golf Club, Oglebay Park (second of 18)	Wheeling, West Virginia	9
Tanglewood Golf Club, East Course (second of 18)	Clemmons, North Carolina	9
Turnberry Isle Yacht & Country Club, North Course	Miami, Florida	18

1973

Alpine Bay Country Club, West Course	Alpine, Alabama	18
Canoe Brook Country Club, North Course	Summit, New Jersey	R
Geneva Golf Club	Geneva, Switzerland	18
Horseshoe Bay Country Club, Slick Rock Course	Marble Falls, Texas	18
Kings Point Golf Course (Par 3)	Delray Beach, Florida	18
Rayburn Golf & Country Club, Blue Nine	Jasper, Texas	9

1974

Arcadian Shores Golf Club	Myrtle Beach, South Carolina	18
Bel-Air Country Club	Los Angeles, California	R
Bodega Harbour Golf Course	Bodega Bay, California	9
Cacapon Springs Golf Course	Cacapon State Park, West Virginia	18
Forest Meadows Golf Course (Executive)	Murphys, California	18
Four Seasons Golf & Country Club	Lake of the Ozarks, Missouri	18
Hazeltine National Golf Club (Executive)	Chaska, Minnesota	9
Jackson Hole Golf & Country Club	Jackson, Wyoming	R
Kings Point West Golf Course (Executive)	Sun City Center, Florida	18
Pacific Harbour Golf Course	Deuba, Fiji	18
Pinehurst Country Club, Course No. 4	Pinehurst, North Carolina	R
Rail Golf Course, The (second of 18)	Springfield, Illinois	9
Roxborough Park Golf Course	Denver, Colorado	18
Royal Golf Dar Es Salaam, Blue Course	Rabat, Morocco	18
Royal Golf Dar Es Salaam, Green Course	Rabat, Morocco	9

1975

Bristol Harbour Village Golf Club	Canandaigua, New York	18
Cancun Golf Course (first of 18)	Quintana Roo, Mexico	9

Campo de Golf El Bosque	Valencia, Spain	18
Elkhorn Golf Course	Sun Valley, Idaho	18
Evergreen Valley Golf Course (NLE)	East Stoneham, Maine	9
Gordon Lakes Golf Course, Fort Gordon	Augusta, Georgia	18
Oxbow Country Club	Fargo, North Dakota	18
Pinehurst Country Club, Course No. 5	Pinehurst, North Carolina	R
Sugar Creek Country Club (third of 27)	Sugar Land, Texas	9
Valderrama Golf Club	Sotogrande, Cádiz, Spain	18 (R '86)
Waterway Hills Golf Club at Skyway	Myrtle Beach, South Carolina	27

1976

Golf Club I Roveri	Torino, Italy	18
Mijas Golf Club, Los Lagos Course	Mijas, Málaga, Spain	18
Palma Real Golf Course	Zihuatanejo, Guerrero, Mexico	9
Radisson Greens Golf Course	Baldwinsville, New York	18

1977

Cancun Golf Course (second of 18)	Quintana Roo, Mexico	9
Empress Josephine Golf Course	Les Trois-Îlets, Martinique, F.W.I.	18
Las Naranjos Golf Course	Marbella, Spain	18
North Carolina, Country Club of, Dogwood Course	Pinehurst, North Carolina	R
Oakcreek Country Club (second of 18)	Sedona, Arizona	9

1978

Crestmont Country Club	West Orange, New Jersey	R
Crumpin-Fox Club (first of 18)	Bernardston, Massachusetts	9
Golf Int'l de St.-François	Saint-François, Guadeloupe, F.W.I.	18
Hamburg-Ahrensburg Golf Club	Hamburg, Germany	R
Mazatlan Golf Course	Mazatlan, Sinaloa, Mexico	18
Valley Brook Country Club	McMurray, Pennsylvania	R

1979

Carolina Trace Golf & Country Club, Creek Course	Sanford, North Carolina	9
Glyfada Golf Club	Athens, Greece	R
North Hills Country Club	North Little Rock, Arkansas	R

North Jersey Country Club	Wayne, New Jersey	R
Paducah, Country Club of	Paducah, Kentucky	18 (R '94)
Playa Dorada Golf Course	Puerto Plata, Dominican Republic	18
Troia Golf Club	Setubal, Portugal	18

1980

Country Club of North Carolina, Cardinal	Pinehurst, North Carolina	9 (R '80)

1981

Town of Colonie Golf Course	Schenectady, New York	9
Crooked Oaks Golf Course	Seabrook Island, South Carolina	18
Horseshoe Bay Country Club, Ram Rock Course	Marble Falls, Texas	18
Rivershore Golf & Country Club	Kamloops, B.C., Canada	18

1982

Ash Brook Golf Course	Scotch Plains, New Jersey	R
Brookside Country Club	Canton, Ohio	R
Pierre Marques Golf Club	Acapulco, Mexico	R

1983

Club de Golf de Chamonix	Chamonix-Mt. Blanc, France	18
Kananaskis Country Golf Course, Mt. Kidd Course	Kananaskis, Alberta, Canada	18
Kananaskis Country Golf Course, Mt. Lorette Course	Kananaskis, Alberta, Canada	18

1984

Ballybunion Golf Club, New Course	Ballybunion, Ireland	18
Mijas Golf Club, Los Olivos Course	Mijas, Málaga, Spain	18
Quinta da Marinha Golf Club	Cascais, Portugal	18

1985

Horseshoe Bay Country Club, Apple Rock Course	Marble Falls, Texas	18
St. George's Golf Course	St. George's, Bermuda	18

1986

Carolina Trace Golf & Country Club, Creek Course	Sanford, North Carolina	9
Golf de la Grande Motte (practice)	Montpellier, France	6
Golf de Moliets (first of 27)	Moliets, France	9

1987

Bodensee Golf Club	Lindau, Germany	18
Country Club Castelgandolfo (first of 18)	Rome, Italy	9
Golf Club Castelconturbia	Agrate Conturbia, Italy	27
Golf de la Grande Motte, Long Course	Montpellier, France	18
Golf de Moliets (second of 27)	Moliets, France	9
Golf La Duquesa	Manilva, Málaga, Spain	18
Malone Golf Club	Malone, New York	18
Metedeconk National Golf Club	Jackson Township, New Jersey	18
MetroWest Country Club	Orlando, Florida	18
Royal Golf d'Agadir	Palais Royal, Agadir, Morocco	18
Santa Maria Golf Course	Baton Rouge, Louisiana	18
Treetops at Sylvan Resort	Gaylord, Michigan	18

1988

Country Club Castelgandolfo (second of 18)	Rome, Italy	9
Golf de la Grande Motte, Short Course	Montpellier, France	18
Golf de Moliets (third of 27)	Moliets, France	9
Ipswich Country Club	Ipswich, Massachusetts	18
Minerals Golf Club (Executive)	McAfee, New Jersey	9

1989

Aronimink Golf Club	Newtown Square, Pennsylvania	R
Crumpin-Fox Club (second of 18)	Bernardston, Massachusetts	9
Legends, The Country Club at the	Eureka, Missouri	18
Valderrama Golf Club (Par 3)	Sotogrande, Cádiz, Spain	9

1990

Flamingo Island Club	Naples, Florida	18
Golf de Sperone	Bonifacio, France	18

Marbella Golf Country Club	Marbella, Málaga, Spain	18
Robert Trent Jones Golf Club	Gainesville, Virginia	18

1991

Golf de la Palmeraie	Marrakesh, Morocco	18
Riviera Golf de Barbossi	Mandelieu-la-Napoule, France	18
La Cañada Golf Course	Guadiaro San Roque, Málaga, Spain	9
Medinah Country Club (Course No. 1)	Medinah, Illinois	R
Vidauban Golf Club (aka Prince de Provence—RTJII)	Vidauban, France	18

1992

Golf de l'Estérel	St.-Raphaël, France	18
Grand National, Lake Course	Auburn-Opelika, Alabama	18
Hampton Cove, Highlands Course	Huntsville, Alabama	18
Hampton Cove, Short Course	Huntsville, Alabama	18
Magnolia Grove, Crossings Course	Mobile, Alabama	18
Magnolia Grove, Falls Course	Mobile, Alabama	18
Magnolia Grove, Short Course	Mobile, Alabama	18
Oxmoor Valley, Ridge Course	Birmingham, Alabama	18
Oxmoor Valley, Valley Course	Birmingham, Alabama	18
Oxmoor Valley, Short Course	Birmingham, Alabama	18

1993

Cambrian Ridge—RTJ Golf Trail	Greenville, Alabama	27
Cambrian Ridge (Short)—RTJ Golf Trail	Greenville, Alabama	9
Grand National (Links)—RTJ Golf Trail	Auburn-Opelika, Alabama	18
Grand National (Short)—RTJ Golf Trail	Auburn-Opelika, Alabama	18
Hampton Cove (River)—RTJ Golf Trail	Huntsville, Alabama	18
Highland Oaks—RTJ Golf Trail	Dothan, Alabama	27
Highland Oaks (Short)—RTJ Golf Trail	Dothan, Alabama	9
Silver Lakes—RTJ Golf Trail	Anniston/Gadsden, Alabama	27
Silver Lakes (Short)—RTJ Golf	Anniston/Gadsden, Alabama	9

1994

Celtic Manor Resort, Roman Road Course	Newport, Wales	18
Edina Country Club	Edina, Minnesota	R

Fox Hollow Golf Club   New Port Richey, Florida   18

Medinah Country Club (Course No. 3)   Medinah, Illinois   R

1995

Adare Manor Golf Club   Adare, Ireland   18

Celtic Manor Resort, Coldra Woods   Newport, Wales   18
    Course (Exec., NLE)

Grandee Nasu Shirakawa Golf Club   Fukushima, Japan   36

Playa Grande Golf Course   Rio San Juan, Dominican Republic   18

1996

Anglebrook Golf Club   Lincolndale, New York   18

Celebration Golf Club (RTJII)   Celebration, Florida   18

1999

Southern Highlands Golf Club (RTJII)   Las Vegas, Nevada   18

Winchester Country Club (RTJII)   Meadow Vista, California   18

APPENDIX B

MAJOR AWARDS, HONORS, AND DISTINCTIONS PRESENTED TO ROBERT TRENT JONES SR.

1967

Distinguished Achievement Award, Sales and Marketing Executives of Philadelphia, Philadelphia, Pennsylvania

1971

When astronaut Alan Shepard hit his famous shot on the Moon on February 5, 1971, during the mission of Apollo 14, CBS anchorman Walter Cronkite declared on air, "Soon, we'll have a Robert Trent Jones golf course on the Moon for Al to play." Cronkite's remark came after Shepard hit the first of two golf balls on the lunar surface with a makeshift club (a 6-iron) he had brought from Earth. Trent Jones would comment on Cronkite's remark: "I later told President Nixon that, if he ever wanted a golf course on the Moon, I would build it!"

1972

Golden Plate Award, American Academy of Achievement

1976

Distinguished Service Award, Metropolitan Golf Writers and Golf Casters Association

Donald Ross Award (inaugural recipient), American Society of Golf Course Architects

1979

Golf Family of the Year, Metropolitan Golf Writers Association, New York, New York

1980

Distinguished Alumni Award, Cornell University

1981

William D. Richardson Award, Golf Writers Association of America

Distinguished Service Award, New York Metropolitan Golf Association

"Robert Trent Jones Day," June 22, 1981, proclaimed by James Rhodes, Governor of Ohio

1982

Outstanding Alumni Award, New York State College of Agriculture and Life Sciences, Cornell University

Distinguished Service Award for Development of Public Golf Courses, State of New York

1983

Induction into Cornell University's Athletic Hall of Fame.

1985

Fellow, American Society of Landscape Architects

1987

Induction into the World Golf Hall of Fame (only the second golf course architect [Donald Ross preceded] and the first living inductee)

Old Tom Morris Award, Golf Course Superintendents Association of America

1988

Honorary Doctorate of Humanities, Green Mountain College in Poultney, Vermont

Named one of Golf Magazine's "100 Heroes of Golf Over the Last Century"

1989

Tree bearing Jones's name on a bronze plaque planted on the "Hill of Fame" at Oak Hill Country Club in Pittsford, New York, during the 89th U.S. Open

Rock behind the 18th green dedicated in honor of Jones, Midvale Golf and Country Club, Penfield, New York

"Robert Trent Jones Day," April 3, 1989, proclaimed by Robert O. Cox, Mayor of Fort Lauderdale, Florida

1991

Inducted into Hall of Fame, California Golf Writers Association

Re-induction into the World Golf Hall of Fame, World Golf Village, St. Augustine, Florida (World Golf Hall of Fame reopened after moving from site in Pinehurst, North Carolina)

1992

Don A. Rossi Humanitarian Award, Golf Course Builders Association of America

Byron Nelson Award, National Intercollegiate Golf and Tennis Awards Group, Dallas, Texas

Golfweek's 11th Annual "Father of the Year Award"

1995

Lifetime Achievement Award, South Florida Tri-County Golf Challenge (presented during Doral-Ryder Open in March 1995)

NOTE: Following in the footsteps of his father, Rees L. Jones would also receive the three major awards given by the leading golf industry organizations: Don A. Rossi Award, Golf Course Builders Association of America (2014); Donald Ross Award, American Society of Golf Course Architects (2013); and Old Tom Morris Award, Golf Course Superintendents Association of America (2004). Like his father, Rees also received the Metropolitan Golf Writers Association Distinguished Service Award. Robert Trent Jones Jr. has received numerous awards nationally and worldwide for his outstanding course designs.

In the archives of Cornell University in Ithaca, New York, rest 418 cubic feet—the equivalent of some 280 office filing-cabinet drawers—stuffed full of the business and personal papers of Robert Trent Jones Sr.

The "Robert Trent Jones Collection," as it is known, is practically a complete reproduction of Jones's own massive office records—hundreds of thousands of documents dating back to the early 1930s when Jones set out unsteadily from a small office in Rochester, New York, to grow a business in golf course design and construction that ultimately came to dominate the American—nay, the global—golf market. The many mountains of paperwork that went along with Jones's self-defined quest to become "the world's greatest golf architect"—legal documents, letters, contracts, business and financial records, account files, drawings, freehand sketches, "blueprints," pictures, slides, printed material, and more, spanning the extraordinary seventy-year career of the man who became arguably the most important golf course architect of the twentieth century—rest now in the Division of Rare and Manuscript Collections within the Carl A. Kroch Library at Cornell University, where some of the nation's most expert and well-trained archivists are setting about to maintain it for posterity. More than that, scattered within the files of the Robert Trent Jones Collection at Cornell is a treasure trove of personal letters in which Jones corresponded not just with the likes of Donald Ross, Alister MacKenzie, and other ingenious and influential golf architects, but also with many of America's most noteworthy early golf writers and golf magazine publishers, such as the Graffis brothers, Grantland Rice, and Herbert Warren Wind, as well as with such golf legends as Francis Ouimet, Gene Sarazen, Bobby Jones, Sam Snead, and Ben Hogan.

Within the Jones Collection, there is also extensive correspondence with captains of industry, business leaders, and politicians who either had Jones build golf courses for them or were interested in having him do so. Among the notables on this list of correspondents and clients are Robert Moses, the "master builder" of the twentieth-century Greater New York City area, who helped Jones get his first profitable jobs building parkland golf courses for the State of New York during the Depression; Lowell Thomas, the famous CBS Radio broadcaster, for whom Jones built a course on his private estate just prior to World War II; Thomas J. Watson, president of IBM, for whom Jones built a company course in Poughkeepsie, New York, in the late 1930s; Chase Manhattan's Laurance Rockefeller, venture capitalist and fourth child of John D. Rockefeller Jr., for whom Jones built the Mauna Kea resort course on the black lava rocks of the Kohala Coast in Hawaii; U.S. President Dwight D. Eisenhower, for whom he built a single golf hole with multiple tees at Camp David; King Hassan of Morocco, for whom in the late 1960s he built the 45-hole Royal Dar Es Salaam Golf Club at Rabat; Aga Khan IV, for whom he built the fabulous Pevero Golf Club on the coast of Sardinia for opening in 1972; and Dave Thomas, the founder of Wendy's, who became Jones's great personal friend and golf buddy late in life. In the Jones Papers there is also correspondence with R. J. Reynolds of Reynolds Tobacco, Arthur Vining Davis of Alcoa, Juan Trippe of Pan Am, and Harvey Firestone, for all of whom he built courses.

In terms of the printed material within the Jones Collection, much of it is comprised of newspaper clippings and magazine articles that Jones and his staff collected and preserved for their office files. Thus, for the most part, I did not need to go hunting through the archives of *Golfdom*, *Golf Digest*, *USGA Golf Journal*, *Golf Magazine*, *Golfweek*, or *Sports Illustrated*, nor through the archives of innumerable city newspapers, to find a virtually complete set of published stories and news items about, or relevant to, Trent Jones.

Another critically important source for writing this biography, which again lay mostly within the Jones Collection at Cornell, was Trent Jones's own substantial set of writings about golf course design. Starting in the early 1930s Jones began writing regular columns on golf course design for different newspapers and for magazine publications; these were very hard times, and Jones needed the extra dollars that his writings brought in. Throughout his career, Jones took every opportunity to reflect on what made a golf course great, and this resulted in a number of articles, both published and unpublished. The closest thing to an autobiography that Jones ever produced was 1988's *Golf's Magnificent Challenge*, a book co-written by golf writer Larry Dennis. Most everything about the preparation and publication of this book can be found in files within the Jones Collection at Cornell.

One cannot overestimate the uniqueness and historical value of the Jones Collection. In sum, this voluminous material—the full and exact contents of his ongoing business operation over seven decades, from his first little office in Rochester to office locations (and home offices) in New York City; Montclair, New Jersey; and Fort Lauderdale—captures the near-totality of Robert Trent Jones's professional life in golf design, from its faltering beginning in the midst of the Great Depression to the year 2000, when he died. There is simply nothing to compare with it in all of golf. No single archive offers what the Jones Collection offers—not even the records of the United States Golf Association, Royal & Ancient, or American Society of Golf Course Architects offer anything close to what the Jones Collection can provide when it comes to pulling back the drapes and illuminating the evolution of golf course architecture, both in terms of design history and business and professional history.

Full access to the Jones Collection is what made the writing of *A Difficult Par* possible. Only by sampling large chunks of the 418 cubic feet of records— and delving deeply into many of them—was it possible to relate Jones's remarkable life story with so much thoroughness and detail.

For nearly a decade following Trent Jones's death in June 2000, not a single document in the Jones Collection was accessible, certainly not for any sort of research. Boxed up as they were from his office at Coral Ridge Country Club in Fort Lauderdale, and from materials he had kept in his nearby residential apartment, what amounts to the single most important archival collection related to the history of golf course architecture existing anywhere in the world sat locked up in dusty, insect-ridden, non-climate-controlled commercial storage units in different facilities around the Fort Lauderdale area. Fortunately, in April 2009, the heirs to the collection, Robert Trent Jones Jr., of Palo Alto, California, and his younger brother, Rees L. Jones, of Montclair, New Jersey, reached an agreement to donate their father's papers to precisely the place he would have wanted them to go: Cornell University, where Jones as a twenty-two-year-old had received special permission from the faculty to fashion a personalized course of study, one that to this day stands for anyone going into the field of golf course architecture—with courses in agronomy, landscaping, horticulture, surveying, and public speaking. Jones dearly loved his alma mater. He built a golf course there that would come to bear his name. He enjoyed a close friendship over many years with the gentleman serving as Cornell's president, Frank Rhodes. In return, Cornell loved Trent Jones and his beloved connection to the Ithaca campus and its golf course. It was delighted in 2009 when word came from Jones's sons (both Yale graduates) that the entirety of their father's surviving papers was heading to the university archives.

On a personal note, I had been trying to research a book on the life of Robert Trent Jones Sr. since the mid-1990s. While researching in the Jones Collection at Cornell, I found, in fact, the letter I had written to Mr. Jones in 1995, advising him of my interest in writing his biography and asking for permission to come visit with him. I thought, perhaps, that the fact I lived in Alabama, home of then brand-new Robert Trent Jones Golf Trail, and taught at Auburn University, might appeal to him. Unfortunately, my plan did not work out; I'm not sure why. All of my books had centered on the history of aeronautics or the history of space exploration; there was no reason whatsoever that Mr. Jones would know my name, or any of my work. If he were to sanction someone to write his full life story (something more like a biography than what had been done for his 1988 book, *Golf's Magnificent Challenge*, co-authored by Larry Dennis), Mr. Jones had a great many friends and contacts among veteran golf writers. He didn't need some university professor he had never heard of who specialized in aerospace history taking over the writing of his life story.

A few weeks later, I received a letter from Mr. Jones's lawyer, Louis J. DeReuil. It notified me that Mr. Jones intended to write his own autobiography and that it would not be possible for him to assist me in any way with my project. Lacking access to Mr. Jones, I shelved my idea, but I did not forget about it. In the meantime, I turned my attention to writing the life story of another important figure of the twentieth century, Neil Armstrong, the first man on the Moon. So much about life seems to be about compromise and making the best of the situation one finds himself in. Mr. Jones turned me down, but as a consequence I was able to carry out the writing of *First Man: The Life of Neil A. Armstrong*, which was published in 2005. Getting Neil to allow me to write his biography had been no easy task; it had taken nearly three years, but I finally, somehow, wore him down. Writing that book turned into my own "Moon landing," of a sort, and I certainly do not regret the turn of events that put me in a place to write *First Man*, even though it meant that I never got to meet Mr. Jones. I am not sure how *A Difficult Par* would be different if Mr. Jones had agreed to my project, but I suspect it would be different in some significant ways. With Neil, I have nearly sixty hours of tape-recorded interviews, just he and I sitting in the study of his home, talking. I would have loved to have been able to do that with Mr. Jones; although he was interviewed several times late in his life about his historic career (and I sought to find recordings or transcripts of all his interviews), I am sure I would have asked him at least a number of questions that were different and unique to my own sense of history and his life's flow. On the other hand, if Mr. Jones had agreed to a series of interviews with me for my proposed biography of him back in 1995, I seriously doubt that he would have given me free and complete access to his personal and business files. In fact, he—or his lawyers—might not have allowed me any access to them at all . . . and Mr. Jones's sons, Bobby and Rees, might not have wanted me doing my project, either.

Thanks to Mr. Jones (or was it just his lawyer, Louis J. DeReuil?) telling me "no" in 1995, I not only wrote the life story of Neil Armstrong, but when I turned back to the topic of a Robert Trent Jones biography, I ultimately benefited enormously by getting complete access to what became the Robert Trent Jones Collection at Cornell. It is my belief, then, that the book you have in your hands is far superior to what I could have ever written if Mr. Jones had given me his permission to go ahead in 1995. Such are the ironies of our lives.

The key to my seeing Mr. Jones's papers in all their bounty lay entirely with his two sons. As hard as it was for me to convince Neil Armstrong that he should allow me to write his biography, it was at least ten times harder to convince Bobby and Rees, *both* of them, that I should be the one that should tell their dad's life story.

My break came with Bobby, a little over a year after my Armstrong biography came out. The break came thanks to John Strawn, who, after working for a period with Toledo, Ohio–based architect Arthur Hills, went to work for eight years with Bobby in California.

I forget how I made my first contact with John Strawn; I believe it was at the annual meeting of the Golf Course Superintendents Association, held in Las Vegas in 1997, when John was still working for Hills. I was at the GCSAA meeting to attend some seminars and to continue looking into the subject of the environmental impact of golf courses, about which I had given some talks and written some papers. (I had been fortunate to be a neutral third-party participant in the "Golf and Environment" initiative of the early 1990s, which, beginning at a meeting at Pebble Beach, brought representatives of the golf industry—USGA, GCSAA, ASGCA, Royal Canadian Golf Association, *Golf Digest,* and others—and the environmental community—the Sierra Club, Audubon International, Friends of the Earth, and the EPA—together, with the

Colorado-based Center for Resource Management serving to bridge the two sides as mediator. In 1996 this initiative culminated with the publication of *Environmental Principles for Golf Courses in the United States,* a document that set forth a voluntary program of guidelines to which both sides agreed.) Before the GCSAA meeting in Las Vegas, I had written Strawn asking for a chance to meet and talk with him. I was a great admirer of his 1991 book *Driving the Green: The Making of a Golf Course* (New York: HarperCollins): a totally fascinating firsthand account of the many intertwined technological, economic, political, and environmental complexities associated with the building of an Arthur Hills golf course in West Palm Beach called Ironhorse. In John Strawn, I found a kindred spirit. He himself had done doctoral work in history, back in the early 1970s at the University of Wisconsin–Madison. In our conversation I mentioned to John that I had written to Trent Jones asking to write his biography and that it had not worked out. He encouraged me to keep trying—or failing that to write the environmental history of American golf course development, with which I had already grown relatively familiar.

Fast forward eight years, to 2005, the year my Armstrong biography was published. John Strawn had gone to work for Jones Jr. in Palo Alto, and the two of us had stayed in contact with an occasional e-mail or letter. Sometime shortly after the appearance of *First Man* (I believe I sent a copy to John, as he had autographed a copy of his book for me in Las Vegas in 1997: "To Jim Hansen— Looking forward to your contributions to golf lit! Warmest Regards, John Strawn, Las Vegas, 97"), John mentioned me to Bob Jones. Finished as I was with my Armstrong book (which spent three weeks on the *New York Times* Bestseller list), it was the perfect time for John to tell Bobby about me and my interest in writing his dad's biography, which he did. Again, I forget exactly who did what first, but the upshot of Strawn's recommendation was that Bobby and I started talking. Long story short, Bobby embraced my ambition to write a book about his father.

But two major problems, directly related to one another, had to be solved. First, all of Jones Sr.'s papers were locked up in commercial storage units in South Florida. Both Bobby and his brother Rees were heirs to their dad's papers, and neither of them had the right to do anything with them without the other's approval. At least that was my understanding. Until there was an agreement about what to do with all of their dad's filing cabinets, boxes of stored materials, and hundreds of cardboard tubes filled with years and years of golf course plans, I was not seeing anything, nor was anyone else.

I could write a book about the writing of the book. Anyone who knows about the bitter feelings between the two brothers—which have lasted for veritably their entire lives but which only got nasty when both went to work for their dad in the 1960s and then independently split from the parent company in the 1970s—can imagine the challenges I faced in writing a book about Trent Jones Sr. that his two sons, *both* of them, would support, which is what I needed if my book could ever be a success and what I wanted it to be . . . what I knew it *could* be. I had Bob's support. That was great. Without it, my book plan could go nowhere. But, *because* I had Bob's support, Rees, for at least three years, wanted nothing to do with my project. He figured that Bobby had me in his back pocket and that my book would turn into whatever Bobby wanted it to be.

In April 2009, as stated above, somehow, some way, Bobby and Rees agreed to donate their dad's papers to Cornell. Bobby set it up with the Cornell archives so that I, and I alone, could get into the papers, even before the Cornell archivists started processing them. I did not need Rees's approval. As a lawyer later explained it to me, it was like the Jones brothers owned a cow. Either brother was free to milk the cow whenever he wanted, but neither of them could sell or butcher the cow unless the other approved. So for three straight summers, I spent intense weeks, working from open to close, deep in the bowels of the Carl A. Croch Library, where Dr. Elaine Engst, Director of Rare and Manuscript Collections and University Archivist, and Dr. Lee Cartmill, Associate University Librarian, not only received me warmly but did everything they could to help me make sense of and use the more than 350 boxes of materials—still in boxes!—that had only recently been trucked up from Fort Lauderdale. I had worked in NASA, government, university, and corporate archives for more than thirty years by this time, and never had I faced such a challenge. But it was wonderful! Essentially, Mr. Jones's entire office filing system, with files in alphabetical order by subject, lay at my feet! There was absolutely nothing about Jones's seventy years as a golf course architect—truly, nothing, or very close to it: tax forms, bank accounts, court depositions, and equally sensitive materials—that couldn't be found, if I could get the archivists to help me get my hands on the right boxes.

I had neither the time nor the energy to see everything. I would still be at it, if it took that to write this book. What I did was sample as much of the material as I could, based on my understanding of what seemed most important, most typical, most illuminating, most extraordinary, most telling. I took hardly any notes (except for a digest of what I was seeing), but rather used a camera to take digital images. I snapped and snapped pictures of any and all the documents that even looked as though they might be significant, several hundred of them per day. When I returned to my office in Alabama, I printed a copy of every single image. Then I put them all in chronological order in large three-ring binders, many of them so stuffed with pages that one binder held only one year, such as 1931. Other binders held three to four years of material. One can imagine the shelf space needed to hold what ended up being (I have never counted) approximately forty binders, all full of copies of material from the Jones Collection.

I now had more than enough to write the book. But documents—even a collection of thousands—never tell the whole story. As much value, even enjoyment, as I can get out of archival research, what's also important, and far more enjoyable, is conducting oral history interviews with people who have firsthand knowledge of the historical experience and the actors that were part of it—in this case, the life and times and associations of Jones Senior.

Some of the oral history was easy to arrange. Bobby was very welcoming and invited me to Palo Alto for long conversations not just with him but with people who had known his father in one way or another and whom Bob had encouraged to come over to talk with me. That included his wife, Claiborne, and his partner in golf architecture Bruce Charlton, the attorney Blake Stafford, who had done a great deal of work for Trent at Bobby's behest over the last decade and a half of his life, and a number of others. I learned a lot about Mr. Jones through these interviews.

But I knew I could not talk to just one brother. Somehow I had to connect with Rees and persuade him to talk to me, that I was not under Bobby's control and was, in fact, doing my best to write a scholarly biography of his father that was independent of such influence and truly my own.

Enter kindred spirit number two, in the person of Roger Rulewich.

Because I wanted to meet and talk with some of the men who had worked for Jones Senior over the years, I had started to attend annual meetings of the American Society of Golf Course Architects. I was not invited to attend, of course, and I never stayed in the same hotel in which the ASGCA meeting was being held, but I managed to conduct a handful of in-the-lobby interviews with individuals, such as Ron Kirby and Don Knott, who had worked for Mr. Jones. Most importantly, I had a couple of brief conversations with Rulewich, who had worked for Mr. Jones for more than thirty years. I could sense that Rulewich was a little uncertain about talking to me at first, and what we talked about was mostly superficial to the Jones story. But I knew Roger had much more to say that he was holding back.

The second key moment came when Roger invited me to visit with him in Bernardston, Massachusetts, where he had moved his design office to the edge of the Crumpin-Fox Club, an 18-hole course that Roger had helped Jones finish in 1989, and had built a home for himself and his wife, Sandy, on a beautiful hilltop nearby, following his leaving the Jones company in 1996. During one of my summer research visits to Cornell, I drove over to Bernardston from Ithaca for a weekend. For two days I asked questions of Roger with my tape recorder running. Not only did I hear the complete story of Roger's time with Mr. Jones, but Roger came to appreciate all the efforts I was making to write a genuinely scholarly biography of Robert Trent Jones Sr., which inevitably also had to deal with the relationship of Trent's two sons to the family business and to their own significant careers as golf architects.

Less than a week after visiting with Roger, I received a phone call from Rees Jones. He was ready to talk to me about his father. Although Rees did not say so, Rulewich had clearly told Rees about my visit with him and shared his opinion that I was honestly trying to write a biography independent of his brother Bobby's control. Rees and I started to talk. In September 2012, I spent three days in Montclair interviewing Rees about his father. I met his wife, Susan, who also shared memories of her father-in-law.

One night after dinner with Susan and Rees, I was invited back to their home. I was taken up to the attic, where Susan opened a chest and picked up a big handful of letters. "I am not sure if these will help you any," she said to me, "but these are love letters that Trent wrote to Ione back in the early 1930s before they got married." It turned out that there were more than four hundred love letters in that chest. We opened one of them and I knew immediately that the chances for my biography becoming something special had just shot up a thousand percent.

The letters, which were written between 1930 and 1934 by Trent Jones to his eventual wife, New York City debutante Ione Tefft Davis, during what turned out to be their long and torturous four-year engagement during the depths of the Great Depression, came to provide vivid and moving three-dimensional insights into Jones's driving ambition and dogged willfulness, as well as his financially miserable and spiritually exasperating early years as a fledgling golf course designer. Even more significantly from the point of view of the history of golf course architecture, the letters, which Jones wrote while working on his earliest golf course designs (many of the courses built with New Deal money and WPA labor), shed broad beacons of light on the nature of building golf courses during the classic era of golf course construction and, before the bull-dozer, when simple farm machine technologies and hand labor created golf courses. The content of many of the letters also helped answer many important questions about Jones's earliest golf course work and its connections to Canada's most famous golf course designer, Stanley Thompson, with whom the young Jones had entered into a formal partnership in 1930, one that lasted late into that decade.

In addition to these remarkable letters, I was also given access to a large collection of letters that Ione penned while attending Wells College in the late 1920s, the last years of which involved correspondence with her father, mother, sisters, cousins, and friends about her developing romantic involvement with Robert Jones, as well as some letters from Ione written to her handsome beau "Bobby."

Unfortunately, the letters that Ione wrote back to Robert during their four-year engagement of the early 1930s were not kept by him. It would have been great to have seen them, too, although the gist of what Ione was writing to her future husband is usually quite apparent from the contents of the letter that Robert wrote back to her.

For the duration of my project, Rees (and Susan) helped me in every way I asked: additional interview time, answering questions by e-mail, and pro-viding additional documentation and photographs. I continued to receive the full assistance of Bobby (and Claiborne and son Trent) as well. In sum, both brothers and their families gave me extremely generous assistance. In return, I lived up to the promise I made to both Bobby and Rees—that I would show them the completed draft of my manuscript and would "engage" every comment they offered, as best as I could, "consistent with my own voice and professional judgment as a historian and biographer."

The Cornell University Archives were not the only archives I visited. To answer just this group of questions, my research did not stop with what I found in the Jones Papers at Cornell, notwithstanding their voluminous nature. I also conducted a thorough review of the Stanley Thompson Papers located at the University of Guelph in Guelph, Ontario. The documents in this collection are actually quite sparse. Following my visit, I strongly suggested to officers of the

Stanley Thompson Society, the driving force behind the Guelph collection, that there were hundreds more documents about Thompson in the Jones Collection at Cornell than what existed in the Thompson Collection at Guelph. My suggestion was that the Society dispatch a researcher to the Cornell archives to make copies of all the Thompson documents therein, and add them to the archival collection at Guelph.

Nor were Bobby, Rees, and Roger Rulewich the only individuals with whom I conducted lengthy interviews. I conducted lengthy interviews with Cabell B. Robinson, who handled most of Mr. Jones's work in Britain, Europe, and North Africa from 1970 to 1987, and Tony Jacklin, champion of the 1970 Open at Hazeltine National Golf Club in Minnesota, which at the time was one of Jones's most controversial courses, much criticized by the tournament players (but not by Jacklin).

A significant number of people turned down my request to be interviewed for the book. That included a number of people who had worked for Mr. Jones or for the Jones family. It also included a number of fellow architects. I can only hope, now that they see this book, that they conclude that they made the wrong decision, and that they should contribute what they know to the story. If they have changed their minds, I want them to know that I would still be very interested in hearing what they have to say, so that I might someday include it in a revised version of the book.

As this is a "Note on Sources," I would like to notify the reader of the existence of additional information about the life of Robert Trent Jones Sr. that I have made available on a website designed to supplement the precise contents of the book and to include a complete rendering of my source notes. Although *A Difficult Par* is a long book, it was much longer in manuscript form. Some 100,000 words have been cut. On the website, a great deal of what has been cut is reproduced in short feature stories. Accounts of a number of Jones's golf course projects which did not make it to the book, for example, appear on the website. Thus, if a reader is disappointed not to see anything in my book about their home course or favorite Jones golf course, they may very well find it on the website. Also on the site are all of the source notes for the book, the book's bibliography, and additional pictures. There is also a place for reader comments, which will hopefully engender a constructive, ongoing, online discussion of the golf course architecture of Robert Trent Jones Sr. The address for this site: www .adifficultpar.com.

A final word about the Jones Collection at Cornell—officially labeled as Collection No. 6855. The process of organizing, cataloging, and preserving the equivalent of 280 office filing-cabinet drawers, more than four hundred blueprint plans for golf courses, and assorted memorabilia is no easy task and takes a great deal of time. Trying to re-create the original order of the materials is vitally important to a collection like Jones's, and it is impossible to work with such a large number of boxes without carefully categorizing them. As Dr. Elaine Engst, the head of the archives has said, "It's a big jigsaw puzzle." Currently, the Jones Collection is closed until processing is complete. The Cornell library is seeking funding to have professional archivists and student assistants go through all of the materials, work that will probably take up to two years to complete. In the meantime, Dr. Engst's staff is carrying out a basic survey of the collection to identify categories to "get the materials into some kind of reasonable order." "Even how to store them properly is an interesting question."

I would strongly encourage the admirers of Robert Trent Jones Sr. and the lovers of golf course architecture and its history to make generous donations to the Cornell library for this purpose.

Someday, hopefully not too far in the future, I hope to return to Ithaca and see the Jones Papers in their final resting place, all organized and ready for the projects of other researchers who love the history of golf course architecture as much as I do.

INDEX

PHOTO AND ILLUSTRATION CREDITS

Colgate University Golf Course

Courtesy of Rees L. Jones

Interior Photographs

Courtesy of Rees L. Jones: Frontis 2; Chapter 1, 2, 3, 5, and 6.

Courtesy of Robert Trent Jones Jr. (© Robert Trent Jones Licensing, Palo Alto, CA/www .roberttrentjonesjr.com): Chapter 11 and 13; Cauldron hole (page 47).

Spyglass Hill Golf Course and its distinctive images are trademarks, service marks and trade dress of Pebble Beach Company. Used by Permission. © Joann Dost: Title page.

Courtesy of Valderrama Golf Club: Chapter 12.

Black-and-White Insert

Courtesy of *Golf Course Architecture*: Durand Eastman golf course (page 4; page 5, top).

Courtesy of Rees L. Jones: Basketball team (page 1); Cornell men (page 2, top), Jones (page 2, bottom); Jones and Ione (page 3, bottom); Wedding reception (page 5, bottom); Lowell Thomas course sketch (page 6, top); Cornell course blueprint (page 6, bottom); William Rees Jones with grandsons (page 7, top); Rees, Bobby, and Ione (page 8, top).

Courtesy of Robert Trent Jones Jr. (© Robert Trent Jones Licensing, Palo Alto, CA/www .roberttrentjonesjr.com): Midvale course map (page 3, top).

Color Insert

Courtesy of Bill Mark: Jones family with award (page 5, top left).

Courtesy of Rees L. Jones: Colgate University course sketches (page 1); Rees, Rulewich, Baldwin, and Schmeisser (page 2, top); Rulewich and Jones at table (page 3, top left); Robinson, Rulewich, and Jones (page 3, top right); Jones addressing Virginia State Golf Association (page 5, bottom); Jones and Ione with grandchildren (page 6, top left).

Courtesy of Robert Trent Jones Jr. (© Robert Trent Jones Licensing, Palo Alto, CA/www .roberttrentjonesjr.com): Bobby, Rockefeller, and Jones in Hawaii (page 2, bottom).

Courtesy of Robert Vaughan: Jones at opening of RTJ trail (page 6, top right); Jones at Oxmoor Valley (page 7, top); Jones in golf cart (page 7, bottom); Jones on green at Hampton Cove (page 8).

Courtesy of Tony Roberts (© Tony Roberts): Jones and sons in airplane (page 6, bottom).

Courtesy of Valderrama Golf Club: Jones and Robinson at Valderrama (page 3, bottom).

Courtesy of Vidauban Golf Club: Course map and 4th hole (page 4).